2009 LECTURES

PROCEEDINGS OF THE BRITISH ACADEMY · 167

2009 LECTURES

Published for THE BRITISH ACADEMY
by OXFORD UNIVERSITY PRESS

Oxford University Press, Great Clarendon Street, Oxford OX2 6DP

Oxford New York
Auckland Bangkok Bogotá Buenos Aires Cape Town Chennai
Dar es Salaam Delhi Hong Kong Istanbul Karachi Kolkata
Kuala Lumpur Madrid Melbourne Mexico City Mumbai Nairobi
São Paulo Shanghai Singapore Taipei Tokyo Toronto

British Library Cataloguing in Publication Data
Data available
978–0–19–726477–5
ISSN 0068–1202

Typeset in Times
by New Leaf Design, Scarborough, North Yorkshire
Printed in Great Britain
on acid-free paper by
Antony Rowe Limited,
Chippenham, Wiltshire

The Academy is grateful to Professor Ron Johnston, FBA
for his editorial work on this volume

Contents

The History of Romantic Love in Sub-Saharan Africa: between Interest and Emotion

MEGAN VAUGHAN
Fellow of the Academy

IN 1937 THE BRITISH SOCIAL ANTHROPOLOGIST, Godfrey Wilson, was writing to his wife Monica (also an anthropologist) from his field site in south-west Tanganyika, where he was studying ritual amongst a group of people who had come to be known as the Nyakyusa.[1] The subject of Wilson's letter was intimacy. Over the previous year or so, Wilson had become particularly close to a man named Kasitile, a local ritual expert with whom he had discussed, again and again, the complex symbolism of Nyakyusa ritual and religion. Sexual symbolism was a central feature of many Nyakyusa rituals, including mortuary ritual. Sex, it appeared, was far from a private matter, even outside the ritual context. Wilson had already gathered from Kasitile that marital sexual intercourse never took place without a third party being present—that third party being the ancestral spirits. Excited by this discovery, Wilson wrote to his wife:

Read at the Academy, 26 February 2009.

[1] Godfrey Wilson died before most of his work came to publication. His widow, Monica Wilson (née Hunter), incorporated the results of his extensive research into a series of books: Monica Wilson, *Rituals of Kinship among the Nyakyusa* (London, 1957); Monica Wilson, *Good Company: a Study of Nyakyusa Age-Villages* (London, 1951); Monica Wilson, *Communal Rituals of the Nyakyusa* (London, 1959); Monica Wilson, *For Men and Elders: Change in the Relationships of Generations and of Men and Women among the Nyakyusa-Ngonde, 1875–1971* (London, 1977).

Proceedings of the British Academy, **167**, 1–23. © The British Academy 2010.

> I am pretty sure that the spirits come into the body at *every* sexual intercourse,
> cause the penis to erect and the loins of the woman to get hot, and that the
> man's ejaculation drives them away again . . . The Freudian I fear will have a
> romp with all of this![2]

Wilson felt an intimacy with Kasitile. He thought that they had broken
through the 'crust of culture' as he put it, and had become real friends.
Sex began to enter their conversations in a rather different way. Spirits or
no spirits, Wilson's model of male friendship included the man-to-man
exchange of sexual experiences. They talked about the desirability of sexual partners reaching orgasm together, and Wilson tried to convert
Kasitile to the practice of kissing. Kissing during intercourse was, according to Kasitile, unknown in his part of the world. In fact, he said, 'we look
away from one another'. Undeterred, Wilson tried to convince Kasitile
that his wife, Jane, would be delighted by this innovation: '. . . the lips are
the tenderness', Wilson told Kasitile, 'the loins are the strength of love,
the lips are for Jane only!' Kasitile went away to try it out, 'positively
trembling with the excitement of a new delight . . .'. But, wrote Wilson
regretfully to his own wife, there was no escaping the fact that Kasitile's
relationship with Jane lacked something which they, as a couple, took for
granted as desirable: '. . . I don't know, there is less tenderness between
them than us, he told me that if Jane refused him one night, and said she
was tired, "then there is war until dawn, I beat her, and after intercourse
we don't speak to each other".'

Wilson seemed to be confusing sex with intimacy, and both of these
with something called 'love'. It seems that Kasitile did not completely
share Wilson's Christian ideal of a companionate marriage in which love,
sexual satisfaction and intimacy would congeal in the course of a lifetime's
cohabitation. Romantic love, companionate marriage and sex as a heightened form of intimacy appear to have been concepts which, if Kasitile was
familiar with them at all, he was unlikely to put together in the way that
Wilson did. That was Wilson's own peculiar cultural baggage.

But things were changing, as Wilson's wife, Monica, was documenting
in her study of the small but growing community of Nyakyusa Christians.
Here, as elsewhere in Africa, the economic, social and political changes of
the colonial period seemed, for some at least and for the moment, to be
accompanied by changes of heart. It reads like the classic tale of modern-

---

[2] Godfrey Wilson to Monica Wilson, 8–10 May, 1937, file B2 in Monica and Godfrey Wilson
Papers, BC880, University of Cape Town Libraries, Manuscripts and Archives Department
(hereafter Wilson Papers, UCT).

isation, and the rise of what Lawrence Stone called 'affective individual-ism' transposed to Africa with a bit of an imperialist twist.[3] Colonialism and capitalism would combine to create a new more autonomous subject, one who would assert his or her 'right' to chose the partner of their choice—to marry out of *love*, not out of obedience to parents or out of economic obligation. Even in the Nyakyusa area, which had been rela-tively remote from such influences, significant changes could be docu-mented. Young men, benefiting from the new cash economy, were less dependent on their male elders to determine who they would marry and when. They began marrying earlier, choosing their own brides. Women did not experience any such economic empowerment, but if they came under the influence of Christian missionaries they were encouraged to refuse early betrothals, polygamous marriages and the practice of widow inheri-tance—and some, at least, did. Even if they were not Christians, with increased movement and migration, and creeping literacy, both men and women became aware that there was an alternative version of married life out there, of men and women in monogamous marriages, apparently freely entered into.[4]

Despite the powerful interventions of historians of premodern periods, the theory that romantic love is closely tied with processes of 'moderni-sation' is a remarkably durable one.[5] And despite a fair amount of cross-cultural research, the master narrative linking love and modernisation is the European one. Elite courtly love traditions (so the story goes) were incorporated into bourgeois culture of the late eighteenth century, but really flourished in the nineteenth century as a result of the alienation of the individual attendant on processes of industrialisation and urbanisa-tion, and the spread of literacy producing a new kind of reflexivity.[6] In this account romantic love is both the symptom and the solution to the

---

[3] Lawrence Stone, *Family, Sex and Marriage in England, 1500–1800* (London, 1977).

[4] Wilson, *For Men and Elders.* Such marriages and households were in a very small minority in this rural area, but those of the Wilsons' research assistants were among them and these are described vividly in the Wilsons' fieldnotes: Wilson Papers, UCT, file D4.2, Christian Amusements.

[5] See for example, Anthony Giddens, *The Transformation of Intimacy: Sexuality, Love and Eroticism in Modern Societies* (Cambridge, 1992). The argument has Durkheimian roots: Emile Durkheim, *The Division of Labour in Society* (New York, 1933).

[6] Giddens, *Transformation of Intimacy*, p. 40. On literacy and romantic love cross-culturally see Jack Goody, *Food and Love: a Cultural History of East and West* (London, 1998). David Lipset presents a very insightful critique of the association between romantic love and modern individ-ualism in David Lipset, 'Modernity without romance? Masculinity and desire in courtship stories told by young Papuan New Guinean men', *American Ethnologist*, 31 (2004), 205–24.

problems of identity created by modern life. The atomised individual longs to be reunited with something. In place of kin or community or religious experience he or she falls in love in a bolt from the blue—a quasi-religious experience radically at odds (for men at least) with day-to-day life in which this same person must be fully in control and autonomous— and having fallen in love she or he exalts this experience. Love is a transformative thing and the relationship which (ideally) should follow from falling in love defines the adult self.[7] Other relationships fade in romantic love's shadow. Marriage without love is not only undesirable, it is also faintly immoral and suspect, implying as it does some rational calculation of *interest* at the expense of *emotion.*[8] The romantic love discourse is contradictory then, implying both individual choice (marrying the one you love not someone chosen for you), but doing so on the basis of a process beyond your control.

Elizabeth Povinelli takes a hefty swipe at this tradition in her powerful book *Empire of Love*, in which she argues that liberalism, in its expansionist imperialist mode, relies heavily on the extension of this very particular and exclusivist notion of love and intimacy.[9] She argues that love, as an apparently self-evident good, is central to the liberal discourses and practices of modern empires, and that the liberal discourse of love *opposes* itself to all other modes of organising and experiencing intimacy. Love between two people, love freely chosen without the constraints of societal norms or external considerations, this kind of love is the higher civilisational form. True love is a 'socially exfoliating love', as she puts it, a love that knows no bounds, no religious restrictions, no interfering elders and (presumably) no vengeful or inquisitive ancestral spirits. In making romantic love and the 'intimate couple' into an attribute of higher civilisation, western empires simultaneously defined as inferior the indigenous peoples they encountered who apparently did not share this ideal.

Though I disagree with Povinelli's over-simplistic narrative of the 'empire of love', it certainly finds resonances in parts of contemporary

[7] Eva Illouz, *Consuming the Romantic Utopia: Love and the Cultural Contradictions of Capitalism* (Berkeley, CA, 1997); Ulrich Beck and Elizabeth Beck-Gernsheim, *The Normal Chaos of Love* (Cambridge, 1995).
[8] The assumed opposition between 'interest' and 'emotion' was challenged in the 1980s by historians of early modern Europe: Hans Medick and David Warren Sabean (eds.), *Interest and Emotion: Essays on the Study of Family and Kinship* (Cambridge, 1984).
[9] Elizabeth A. Povinelli, *The Empire of Love: Toward a Theory of Intimacy, Genealogy and Carnality* (Durham, NC, and London, 2006).

Africa, as anyone who reads the continent's newspapers and blogs will know. In parts of the continent affected by the HIV/AIDS epidemic there is a debate on the utility, desirability, or possible dangers associated with health education messages which stress the importance of life-long, monogamous, 'love'-based relationships.[10] In Botswana a wave of so-called 'passion killings' (in which young men, jilted by their girlfriends, kill them and then sometimes kill themselves) has given rise to public discussion on the politics of emotion.[11] Gay and lesbian activists on the continent, as elsewhere, campaign not only for their sexual rights but also for the recognition of their closest emotional attachments and are accused of having been colonised by a non-African perversion.[12] There *is* an unmistakably post-colonial feel to some of this—whether people are asserting that romantic love is an alien import which is at odds with African 'tradition', or whether they are arguing that Africa also has its romantic traditions, its love stories, its princesses in castles, ignored and sidelined like so much of African cultural tradition by western preconceptions, and particularly by western obsessions with African sexuality at the expense of 'feelings'.[13]

Valentine's Day is celebrated all over Africa (though frowned upon in Muslim countries) and it is an occasion which gives rise to debates on the nature of romantic love in modern Africa. In the lead up to Valentine's Day 2009 in Nigeria, one woman newspaper columnist berated her female friends for allowing their minds to be 'mentally and emotionally colonised' by feminist anti-Valentine's Day propaganda coming from outside the country. Let the Londoners do what they like, she wrote, 'We

---

[10] Daniel Jordan Smith, 'Romance, parenthood and gender in a modern African society', *Ethnology*, 40 (2001), 129–51; Daniel Jordan Smith, 'Love and the risk of HIV: courtship, marriage and infidelity in southeastern Nigeria', in Jennifer S. Hirsch and Holly Wardlow (eds.), *Modern Loves: the Anthropology of Romantic Courtship and Companionate Marriage* (Ann Arbor, MI, 2006), pp. 135–57.

[11] Dr Maude Dikobe, 'Report on the "National Conference on Crimes of Passion among Youth of Botswana', held in October 2008, *The Courier*, December/January/February 2009: <www.acp-eucourier.info/PASSION-KILLINGS-A-Fest.605.0.html> (accessed 31 March 2009); Dr Tsayang, Prof. Sheldon Weeks, Mrs Nonofho Mathibidi Ndobochani, 'Passion Killings: a Botswana Society Report', <www.botssoc.org.bw/reports/passion-killings.htm> (accessed 31 March 2009); Luca Letlhogile, 'Botswana floored by passion killings', BBC website, 2 Feb. 2006: <http://news.bbc.co.uk/1/hi/world/Africa/4685216.stm> (accessed 31 March 2009).

[12] Chris Dunton and Mai Palmberg, *Human Rights and Homosexuality in Southern Africa* (Uppsala, 1996); Neville Hoad, *African Intimacies: Race, Homosexuality and Globalization* (Minneapolis, MN, 2007).

[13] Ama Ata Aidoo, 'Introduction', *African Love Stories: an Anthology* (Banbury, 2006), pp. vii–xiv.

Nigerians express love with price-tags, public displays and matching outfits.' [14] But it was precisely this attitude which was worrying another columnist: the growing obsession with Valentine's Day in Nigeria, he wrote, served to demonstrate 'the emptiness of our passions … our expression of love is libidinal, selfish and alimentary'.[15]

The nature of romantic love is then the subject of much contemporary debate in Africa, but is it correct to assume that romantic love is a recent import to the continent and a consequence of 'globalisation'?

Comparative history and history of the emotions

In setting out to explore the history of romantic love in societies of sub-Saharan Africa one is already located at the intersection of two different (but related) kinds of historical exercise. One is comparative history; the other the history of the emotions. Whilst the best of work in the history of the emotions follows the best social anthropological scholarship in this area and sets out to reconstruct the emotional lexicons, discourses and emotional communities of the past at least partially in their own terms, the comparative studies, particularly of love, often fall into that trap of citing non-European experiences merely in order to establish a European-type ideal.[16] When 'Africa' is incorporated into comparative history it frequently suffers in just this way—comparing 'Africa' as an entity to other regions of the world has the drawback of obscuring what might be much more useful comparisons, for example, between *particular* societies of sub-Saharan Africa.

This is an area of inquiry in which anthropology and history intersect fruitfully, but on occasions social anthropologists and historians have been guilty of caricaturing each others' work to serve their own purposes. When Lawrence Stone produced his seminal work on *The Family, Sex and Marriage in England, 1500–1800*, he was taken to task, not only for his selective reading of the English historical record, but also for his misuse of anthropological examples to bolster his argument for the absence of

---

[14] 'Valentine's Day—a golden opportunity!', *Next*, 13 Feb. 2009: <www.234next.com/csp/cms/sites/Next/Home/3448954-146/Valentine's_Day/> (accessed 13 Feb. 2009).
[15] Reuben Abati, 'Ah, God, what's wrong with Valentine?', *Guardian* (Nigeria), 13 Feb. 2009: <www.ngrguardiannews.com/editorial_opinion/article02/indexn2_html?pdate=13> (accessed 13 Feb. 2009).
[16] Heinz-Gerhard Haupt, 'Comparative history: a contested method', *Historisk Tidskrift*, 127 (2007), 697–716.

romantic love in premodern societies.[17] Meanwhile, those anthropologists who work within a comparative approach have a tendency to represent 'western' emotional regimes as unproblematic and uncontested in their 'home' contexts.[18] In the case of romantic love, this frequently involves a slippage between the ideals of romantic love and the institution of companionate marriage with which it is associated and between the ideal of romantic love and the reality of peoples' emotional lives.[19] A recent volume on the globalisation of love recognises this problem, yet some of the essays in this same volume seem unable to resist pointing out that there are non-Western communities in which people *profess* a belief in romantic love whilst organising their love lives according to quite other principles—economic needs, for example.[20] But of course this is also a feature of the heartlands of 'romantic love', perhaps more so now than ever. Eva Illouz, for one, believes that in the developed world we are living in an era of 'Cold Intimacies'—while economic relations have become deeply emotional, our closest intimate relationships have become infected by economic models of bargaining, exchange and equity, manifest, for example, in the technology and languages of internet dating.[21]

So when Elizabeth Povinelli characterises love as hegemonic within post-Enlightenment western societies, she ignores a large body of scholarship which problematises this. The discourse of love may indeed have a magically appealing quality which survives on (maybe even thrives on) the contradictions of everyday life, but those contradictions within the heartlands of romantic love are still worth mentioning. In the United States in the twentieth century, for example, the 'intimate couple' was not always viewed benignly by governments worried about their populations getting romantically over-excited at the expense of marital and social stability.[22]

[17] Alan Macfarlane, review in *History and Theory, Studies in the Philosophy of History*, xviii (1979), 103–26.
[18] For example, William Jankowiak (ed.), *Romantic Passion: a Universal Experience?* (New York, 1995).
[19] Jennifer S. Hirsch and Holly Wardlow, 'Introduction', in Jennifer S. Hirsch and Holly Wardlow (eds.), *Modern Loves: the Anthropology of Romantic Love and Companionate Marriage* (Ann Arbor, MI, 2006), pp. 1–34.
[20] Mark B. Padilla, Jennifer S. Hirsch, Miguel Munoz-Laboy, Robert E. Sember and Richard G. Parker, 'Introduction: cross-cultural reflections on an intimate intersection', in *Love and Globalization: Transformations of Intimacy in the Contemporary World* (Nashville, TN, 2007), pp. ix–xxxi; L. A. Rebhun, 'The strange marriage of love and interest: economic change and emotional intimacy in Northeast Brazil, private and public', in Mark B. Padilla *et al.* (eds.), *Love and Globalization*, p. 111.
[21] Eva Illouz, *Cold Intimacies: the Making of Emotional Capitalism* (Cambridge, 2007).
[22] Jennifer S. Hirsch and Holly Wardlow, 'Introduction'; Illouz, *Consuming the Romantic Utopia*; Ann Swidler, *Talk of Love: How Culture Matters* (Chicago, IL, 2001).

Rising divorce rates, juvenile 'delinquency' and the social cost of housing single people moving from one big love affair to another are regarded by governments of the developed world as the unfortunate consequences of the apparent dominance of the 'intimate couple' idea and they are constantly devising social policies which attempt to temper its effects.

Though the development of industrial capitalism and of liberal thinking may have played an important part in the rise of the romantic love ideal, nowhere has this followed a simple linear trajectory and, as historians of premodern periods complain, the modernising narrative frequently relies on a misrepresentation of earlier periods.[23] In addition, as both Barbara Rosenwein and William Reddy have argued, different 'emotional regimes' and 'emotional communities' can co-exist in societies, though at any given time one might dominate others and, depending on the nature of the dominant regime, individuals might find 'emotional refuge' in a range of situations.[24] All emotional regimes demand emotional effort on the part of individual members of society, though some are more demanding than others. Love, argued Laura Kipnis in her polemic 'Against Love', is just another mode of production, and an onerous one at that.[25] No emotional regime is without its contradictions. In contemporary Britain 'chick lit' is full of angst expressed by women who want to 'have too much': children, a family, money, an emotionally satisfying job, romantic love, security and an exciting sex life.[26] Despite the evidence provided by contemporary neuroscience for the biological basis of love, it appears that we seem often to get our neural pathways crossed.[27] 'Chick-lit' heroine Bridget Jones and her contemporaries constantly worry about whether they are in lust or love, and why they fall in love with people who are clearly so unsuitable as long-term partners. Confusion reigns in the heartlands of the romantic love ideal.

Although the comparative study of the emotions is fraught with problems, fortunately there is some insightful recent work in the *history* of the

---

[23] Barbara H. Rosenwein, 'Worrying about emotions in history', *American Historical Review*, 107 (2002), 921–45.

[24] Barbara H. Rosenwein, *Emotional Communities in the Early Middle Ages* (Ithaca, NY, and London, 2007); William M. Reddy, *The Navigation of Feeling: a Framework for the History of the Emotions* (Cambridge, 2001).

[25] Laura Kipnis, *Against Love: a Polemic* (New York, 2003).

[26] Suzanne Ferris and Mallory Young (eds.), *Chick Lit: the New Women's Fiction* (New York and London, 2006).

[27] Larry J. Young, 'Being human: love: neuroscience reveals all', *Nature*, 457, 148 (Jan. 2009): <www.nature.com/nature/journal/v457/n7226/full/457148a.html> (accessed 9 Nov. 2009); Helen Fischer, *Why We Love: the Nature and Chemistry of Romantic Love* (New York, 2004).

emotions which points the way forward: most notably Barbara Rosenwein's study of *Emotional Communities in the Early Middle Ages*, and William Reddy's work, *The Navigation of Feeling*, on which she draws.[28] In the Introduction to her book Rosenwein deftly and elegantly deals with the major theoretical and methodological issues raised by the very idea of writing a history of the emotions. Rosenwein is clear, for example, that there can never be any way of directly accessing the emotions in history; that emotions are always 'delivered secondhand', as she puts it, and that yes, of course, there were and are prevailing emotional norms, and *genres* which 'shaped emotional expression even as they themselves were used and bent so as to be emotionally expressive'. Rosenwein makes strategic use of a capacious category she calls 'the emotions' as a starting point from which to analyse specific historical understandings of a range of feelings, affects, sentiments and passions in early mediaeval Europe. She acknowledges in the process that the meaning of the word 'emotions' is far from self-evident. Indeed, as Thomas Dixon's important work has shown, the category of the emotions in European thought is a recent one (nineteenth century) and there are problems with the over-inclusiveness of this modern-day term.[29] Furthermore, there is a distinct Anglophone bias to this category.

Social anthropologists have explored many of the same issues, simultaneously describing and questioning 'emotional' phenomena cross-culturally.[30] While some of his colleagues asserted that the expressions of the emotions *were* the emotions and describing this expression was as far as one could go, social anthropologist John Leavitt argued that emotions had a bridging character which made them peculiarly susceptible to cross-cultural analysis.[31] Emotion terms and concepts, he wrote, refer to experiences that inherently involve *both* meaning and feeling; they are both individual *and* social in nature, learned and expressed in social interactions. Because they are socially and symbolically produced and felt this makes them not only observable but also available to translation and interpretation across societies (and, I would add, historically).

---

[28] Rosenwein, *Emotional Communities*; Reddy, *Navigation of Feeling*.

[29] Thomas Dixon, *From Passions to Emotions: the Creation of a Secular Psychological Category* (Cambridge, 2003).

[30] The social anthropological literature on this subject is very large and has been usefully summarised in Reddy, *Navigation of Feeling*, and William M. Reddy, 'Against constructionism: the historical ethnography of emotions', *Current Anthropology*, 38 (1997), 327–51.

[31] John Leavitt, 'Meaning and feeling in the anthropology of emotions', *American Ethnologist*, 23 (1996), 514–39.

Drawing on the theoretical and methodological insights of both Rosenwein and Leavitt I hope, in the larger work of which this lecture is part, to be able to convince my readers that a study centred on the history of emotions in African societies is not only feasible but also illuminating of a range of concerns as diverse as the history of African capitalism and the nature of political authority. I remain, however, acutely aware of the complications entailed in attempting a study of emotion which is not only historical *and* cross-cultural but is also further complicated by colonialism.

Romantic love in sub-Saharan Africa

There must be two interrelated strands to any history of romantic love in African communities. Firstly we can attempt to reconstruct emotional regimes and genres over time and look for different configurations of love under changing economic and political conditions. Secondly, we can trace the history of what Povinelli calls the 'empire of love', that is, the particular version (or versions) of love which travelled with colonialism and has since gained ground with recent globalisation. The justification for this latter exercise is (as David Lipset argues in his work on Papua New Guinea) that many people in the post-colonial world do themselves perceive romantic love as a distinctively modern and imported discourse *particularly* when it is viewed as the exclusive motivational basis for marriage.[32] We may want to contest the neat association between romantic love and 'modernity', but the fact is that many contemporary African discourses make this association very powerfully themselves.

Colonial anthropologists, if they mentioned love at all, generally argued that romantic love was an alien concept in Africa, but there is some evidence for questioning the generalisation.[33] There are of course

---

[32] Lipset, 'Modernity without romance?', p. 208.

[33] Evans-Pritchard wrote that '. . . while there may be plenty of love-making, there is seldom anything corresponding to what we mean by romantic love . . . The primitive girl, though naturally she has her preferences, would find it difficult to understand either sentimental love, or what it has to do with marriage.' E. Evans-Pritchard, *The Position of Women in Primitive Societies and Other Essays in Social Anthropology* (London, 1965), p. 47. See the useful discussion of love in social anthropological literature by William J. Goode, 'The theoretical importance of love', in Marcia E. Lasswell and Thomas E. Lasswell (eds.), *Love, Marriage and Family: a Developmental Approach* (Glenview, IL, 1973), pp. 162–9. The scholarship on love in Africa is also discussed in an important forthcoming volume co-edited by an historian and an anthropologist: Lynn M. Thomas and Jennifer Cole, 'Thinking through love in Africa', in Jennifer Cole and Lynn M. Thomas (eds.), *Love in Africa* (Chicago, 2009), pp. 1–30. See also the very illumin-

vast differences in political systems, cultural and religious traditions and economic circumstances on the continent at any one time. In addition some parts of Africa had been receptive to 'external' cultural influences long before the imposition of European colonial rule (I am thinking espe- cially of those parts of the continent which had for centuries been absorb- ing and indigenising Islam). To assume that anything at all is inherently 'African' must be mistaken. My own discussion, which follows, focuses on the Anglophone parts of central Africa, though I also draw on insights from scholars working in other regions of Africa.

Dating historical linguistic material is difficult, but there is certainly evidence that some precolonial African societies had rich vocabularies for the feelings and emotions which 'western' traditions would associate with passionate desire and with love, and that some, at least, had vocabularies that signalled the existence of the *idealisation* of the object of desire. It is this idealisation of the experience of love which is usually seen as defini- tive of 'romantic love'. The expression of this feeling, when we have evidence for it, is superficially at least strikingly familiar to that of a European romantic tradition. Hearts, in particular, seem to ache across cultures.[34] Jim Bell's discussion of the love vocabulary of the Taita of Kenya includes words for lust, for infatuation (interpreted as irrespon- sible feelings of longing felt by the young for each other) and something he reads as 'romantic love' (combining passion with enduring affection).[35] But the value attached to the 'idealisation of the object of desire' varied widely from one African society to another, which is hardly surprising given the size and diversity of the continent.

A wave of social anthropological work in the 1960s and 1970s, whilst focused on 'modernisation' and marriage, revealed love discourses in a number of societies from western to southern Africa, some of which pre- dated colonial rule. Amongst others Victor Uchendu in 1965 examined passionate love in the context of concubinage in Southern Nigeria; Paul Riesman wrote on 'Love Fulani Style', and Christine Oppong on love and

---

ating work of Mark Hunter on ideas and practices around love in Kwazulu-Natal: Mark Hunter, 'Courting desire?: love and intimacy in late 19th and early 20th century Kwazulu-Natal', *Passages*, 2 (2005), <http://hdl.handle.net/2027/spo.4761530.0010.016> (accessed 9 Nov. 2009).

[34] See for example, Rosemary M. F. Joseph, 'Zulu women's bow songs: ruminations on love', *Bulletin of the School of Oriental and African Studies, University of London*, 50 (1987), 90–119. There is scope for a great more historical linguistic work on lexicons of love in African languages.

[35] Jim Bell, 'Notions of love and romance among the Taita of Kenya', in Jankowiak, *Romantic Passion*, pp. 152–65.

marriage in Ghana.[36] Indeed, Oppong attempted to turn the dominant
analysis of the relationship between romantic love and modernisation on
its head by arguing that love in marriage *decreased* with modernisation.
Ethnomusicologists collected traditional African love songs which are
full of loss and longing, and of unrequited love, particularly (and not surprisingly) where there are clear institutional obstacles to the fulfilment of
individual desires.[37] Traditional Swahili love songs meanwhile form a
remarkable corpus of passionate love poetry.[38]

Some communities then had long been singing about true love, the
pain of love, the confusion of love and the obstacles placed in the way of
love. But this was extremely variable: other emotional and political communities existed where such feelings and obstacles were apparently not
considered worthy of much comment. For example, in 1933 the anthropologist Audrey Richards, working in Northern Rhodesia, wrote in a
footnote to a paper on marriage that she had once recounted an 'English
folk tale' to a group of elderly people. It was about the difficulties experienced by a prince in winning the hand of his bride: 'glassy mountains,
chasms, dragons, giants and the like. The old chief present was genuinely
astonished. Why not take another girl? he said.'[39]

What is clear from this material is that whilst many 'traditional'
African societies had a vocabulary of passionate love which was at least
to some extent distinct from that for sexual desire and sometimes
included a degree of idealisation, most utilised these feelings by setting
them up in opposition to the centrally important institution of social
reproduction—marriage. Marriage, as Kasitile had reminded Wilson,
involved others (alive, dead and yet to be born) and was too important to
be left to individual passion.

Many societies associated passionate love (both heterosexual and
homosexual) with the emotions of youth. To a greater or lesser degree

[36] Victor U. Uchendu, 'Concubinage among Ngwa Igbo of Southern Nigeria', *Africa*, 35 (1965),
187–97; Paul Riesman, 'Love Fulani style', *Society*, 10 (1973), 27–35; Christine Oppong, 'From
love to institution: indications of change in Akan marriage', *Journal of Family History*, 5 (1980),
197–209.
[37] Joseph, 'Zulu women's bow songs'; Hugh Tracey, *Catalogue of the Sound of Africa Series: 210
Long Playing Records of Music and Songs from Central, Eastern and Southern Africa*, vol. 11
(Roodeport, South Africa, International Library of African Music, 1973).
[38] Jan Knappert (ed.), *A Choice of Flowers: Swahili Songs of Love and Passion* (London, 1972);
Said A. M. Khamis, 'Images of love in the Swahili Taarab lyric: local aspects and global influence',
Nordic Journal of African Studies, 13 (2004), 30–64.
[39] Audrey Richards, 'Bemba marriage and present economic conditions', *Rhodes–Livingstone
Paper No. 4* (Livingstone, Rhodes–Livingstone Institute, 1940), p. 22, fn. 1.

they indulged those feelings but they also made a clear distinction between youthful passion and the emotional tenor thought appropriate to the marital relationship, and this is an issue to which I will return. In Gouin communities in Burkina Faso, for example, feelings of love, particularly those expressed by women, were regarded as a potential threat to social order and marriage, as elsewhere, was carefully controlled by the elders. Until the 1960s young men struggled to achieve the economic standing required of a bridegroom and marriages were consequently delayed. While they waited to marry spouses chosen by their elders young Gouin men and women were allowed to have unions with lovers of their choice, sometimes producing children. But once the bridegroom was ready to marry, the parents brought an abrupt end to these love relationships and the rupture was marked by the circumcision of the young woman. She was now ready to marry, relations with her former lover were forbidden and any children she had had by him were now formally the children of her husband. By the 1960s some Gouin women were expressing the view that they wanted to love their future spouses before marrying them. The elders were baffled: marry first and then you will love, was their answer.[40]

In some societies, where betrothal took place at an early age, young men and women had very limited influence over the choice of their future spouse, but where divorce rates and death rates were high the probability of remarriage was also and sometimes this also implied a greater degree of individual choice over second and subsequent marriages. When an elderly Hausa woman, Baba of Karo, recounted her life history in the 1940s, she recalled being betrothed at the age of 14 years to her cousin, against her wishes. Hausa girls were expected to weep profusely at their weddings, and she found no difficulty in doing this. She was distraught at having to leave her family *and* she was in love with someone else. After a few years of marriage to her cousin (during which, crucially, no child was born) Baba initiated and secured a divorce. She then married the man she loved and stayed with him for fifteen years. But still there was no child. Once again the family asserted itself. Blaming her husband for her childlessness, they forced her, against her wishes, to divorce again. Years later Baba told her interviewer 'Even now I love him and he loves me', but fertility concerns were considered more important than her feelings of love for a man.[41]

---

[40] Michele Dacher, 'Les difficiles conditions de l'amour en pays gouin (Burkina Faso)', *L'Autre: Revue Transculturelle*, 4 (2003), 183–97.

[41] Mary F. Smith, *Baba of Karo: a Woman of the Muslim Hausa* (New Haven, CT, and London, 1981 [1954]), p. 159. See also Odile Journet-Diallo, 'Sur les traces d'un objet insaisissable', *L'Autre: Revue Transculturelle*, 4 (2003), 211–25.

When Godfrey Wilson talked of marriage in terms of intimacy and saw the practice of kissing as representative of this—Kasitile spoke of the presence of the ancestral spirits at every act of marital intercourse. Passionate love and marriage did not always go together, not only because marriage was an important social and political institution which could not be left to individual passion, but (in the case of the Nyakyusa at least) because the marital relationship had a distinct and important *mystical* element. Marital sexual relations, in particular, involved an intimacy which included a powerful element of danger, and any inappropriate conduct had potentially disastrous consequences on the health, not only of the two spouses, but on their families and communities.[42] It follows that the set of emotions associated with marriage was often focused on something which can be glossed as 'respect', but which is much more powerful and complex than is implied by the English term. Respect was not simply a value—it was a value to which were attached strong feelings. It was, if you like, an *emotion* but only if we understand that term to include a strong sense of moral responsibility.[43]

Colonialism and affective regimes

Emotional regimes were not left untouched by the economic, social and legal changes which accompanied colonial rule, but these changes were often contradictory and non-linear. Creeping colonial capitalism had important effects on social relations of course, but this is not a simple tale of the triumph of economic or affective individualism. The spread of rural capitalism and the development of urbanisation and industrialisation were not linear processes, they proceeded in fits and starts and, as much important work in the economic anthropology of African societies has shown, both surviving and succeeding in the capitalist economy have

---

[42] Megan Vaughan, 'Divine kings, sex, death and anthropology in interwar East/Central Africa', *Journal of African History*, 49 (2008), 383–401. On the construction of intimacy see Lauren Berlant (ed.), *Intimacy* (Chicago, IL, 2000); Povinelli, *Empire of Love*.

[43] The importance of respect in marriage emerges strongly from a variety of colonial anthropological accounts from central and southern Africa. See for example, A. L. Epstein, *Scenes From African Urban Life: Collected Copperbelt Papers* (Edinburgh, 1992), p. 159; A. L. Epstein, *Urbanisation and Kinship: the Domestic Domain on the Copperbelt of Zambia, 1950–1956* (London, 1981); Elizabeth Colson, *Marriage and the Family among the Plateau Tonga of Northern Rhodesia* (Manchester, 1958). Colonial anthropologists also noted that affection between spouses often grew (and its expression became more socially acceptable) over time: Isaac Schapera, *Married Life in an African Tribe* (London, 1939), p. 276; Richards, 'Bemba marriage'.

often necessitated a continued attention to and investment in a wide network of kin and community.[44]

Meanwhile, colonial rulers were torn between advancing the cause of 'civilisation' and its implied liberation of the individual African subject from the repressive control of 'primitive' political regimes, and, on the other hand, reinforcing the traditional order and keeping all those potentially explosive emotions under control. Their legal regimes had an impact, certainly, on the regulation of gender and generational relations and, crucially, on marriage.[45] New languages to describe close relationships were evolving partly in the court room but, in British colonial central and eastern Africa at least (the region from which most of my material is drawn), the job of the colonial courts by the interwar period was primarily to uphold 'tradition', with varying degrees of success.[46]

Colonial courts were flooded with marriage cases, or 'girl' cases as they were sometimes tellingly called, and historians of colonial Africa have used this material to explore conflicts in generational and gender relations.[47] Women took advantage of the colonial courts to try and escape

---

[44] Jane I. Guyer (ed.), *Money Matters: Instability, Values and Social Payments in the Modern History of West African Communities* (Portsmouth, NH, 2000); Sara Berry, *No Condition is Permanent: the Social Dynamics of Agrarian Change in Sub-Saharan Africa* (Madison, WI, 1993); Parker Shipton, *The Nature of Entrustment: Intimacy, Exchange and the Sacred in Africa* (New Haven, CT, and London, 2007).

[45] There is now a large literature on the history of marriage and gender relations in colonial Africa, and specifically the impact of colonial legal systems: Martin Chanock, *Law, Custom and Social Order: the Colonial Experience in Malawi and Zambia* (Cambridge, 1985); Richard Roberts, *Litigants and Households: African Disputes and Colonial Courts in the French Soudan, 1895–1912* (Portsmouth, NH, 2005); Dorothy Hodgson and Sheryl McCurdy (eds.), *'Wicked' Women and the Reconstruction of Gender in Africa* (Portsmouth, NH, 2001); Diana Jeater, *Marriage, Perversion and Power: the Construction of a Moral Discourse in Southern Rhodesia, 1894–1930* (Oxford, 1993); Sean Hawkins, '"The woman in question": marriage and identity in the colonial courts of Northern Ghana, 1907–1954', in Jean Allman, Susan Geiger and Nakanyike Musisi (eds.), *Women in Colonial African Histories* (Bloomington, IN, 2002), pp. 116–44; Victoria B. Tashjian and Jean Allman, 'Marrying and marriage on a shifting terrain: reconfigurations of power and authority in early colonial Asante', in Allman *et al.* (eds.), *Women in Colonial Africa*, pp. 237–60; Derek R. Peterson, 'Morality plays: marriage, church courts, and colonial agency in central Tanganyika, ca.1876–1928', *American Historical Review*, 111 (2006), 983–1010.

[46] Chanock, *Law, Custom and Social Order*.

[47] Margaret Jean Hay and Marcia Wright (eds.), *African Women and the Law: Historical Perspectives* (Boston, MA, 1982); Marjorie Mbilinyi, 'Runaway wives in colonial Tanganyika: forced labour and forced marriage in Rungwe District, 1919–1961', *International Journal of the Sociology of Law*, 16 (1988), 1–29; Elizabeth Schmidt, 'Negotiated spaces and contested terrain: men, women and the law in colonial Zimbabwe, 1890–1939', *Journal of Southern African Studies*, 16 (1990), 622–48; Brett. L. Shadle, 'Bridewealth and female consent: marriage disputes in african courts, Gusiiland, Kenya', *Journal of African History*, 44 (2003), 241–62.

forced marriages, violent husbands, and sometimes polygamy. Young people eloped, either because they were tired of waiting for protracted marriage arrangements to be concluded by their parents or because they wanted to marry partners of their own choice. If this is evidence of love, then there was quite a bit of it around and it was being used powerfully by rebellious adolescents against controlling parents. In some places elopement created serious moral concerns which combined with economic considerations, as Kenda Mutongi showed in her study of widows in Western Kenya in the 1940s.[48] Girls in patrilineal societies who eloped deprived their parents of bridewealth, a major form of family capital, and in the process made it more difficult for their brothers to marry. In some places parents recouped this loss by going to court and claiming damages from their daughter's lover. British colonial officials sometimes suspected collusion and worried that by awarding damages they were themselves implicated in a moral decline.[49] In the interwar period especially they shared, with African elders, a sense that things were falling apart and that uncontrolled female desire was to blame. Sex dominated colonial thinking on these matters. No one (except perhaps a few of the more sentimental missionaries) appears to have viewed these developments in the interwar period as evidence of the arrival of romantic love or 'affective individualism', though that would certainly be a plausible interpretation.

Inconsistency is a critical component of this story. Anyone entering a colonial courtroom had to be armed with more than one set of legal arguments and be adept at the strategic use of apparently conflicting languages on questions revolving around the nature of personal autonomy, values, responsibilities and emotion. In the urban courts of the Copperbelt of Northern Rhodesia in the 1940s and 1950s African court elders usually adopted a traditionalist approach to the marriage cases before them, instructing people to remember their tribal traditions, women to obey their husbands, men to obey their fathers and so on. Occasionally, though, they took another tack, urging partners to adopt a more 'modern' approach to marriage, as in the following case recorded by the anthropologist A. L. Epstein:

> Elders: Do you love one another?
> Husband: Yes.

---

[48] Kenda Mutongi, *Worries of the Heart: Widows, Family and Community in Kenya* (Chicago, IL, 2007).
[49] Bonnie B. Keller, 'Marriage by elopement', *African Social Research*, 27 (1979), 565–85.

Wife: I love him, but my sister-in-law does not like me.
Elder: No, no. A marriage is between the woman and the man. If a couple love one another, then the marriage can stand. If not, then the relatives themselves cannot support the marriage. Now, my question to you is—'Do you love your husband?'
Wife: Yes.[50]

Not only were colonial laws and institutions often internally inconsistent and at odds with prevailing social and economic circumstances (in this case the consequences of labour migration), but Christianity was also a powerful force in the affective lives of many communities in colonial Africa and Christians shared a new language of love. True Christian love could not be coerced, it had to be freely given. Missionaries translated Christian love into African languages, along with brotherly love, conjugal love and lust. African lexicons of passion and love were consequently revised, producing new languages of the passions. Christian missionaries did not usually actively promote the idea of romantic love amongst their converts—they shared with African societies the idea of the centrality of marriage as the foundation of reproduction—but they did promote the ideal of companionate marriage and the individual choice of spouses (within reason).[51] They also insisted on monogamy. Male converts were required to give up (that is, divorce) all but one of their wives. From the point of view of some African traditionalists the result was decline in moral standards. Men would now take lovers rather than additional wives, and these relationships were not subject to the oversight of family elders. Undoubtedly some women did welcome the refuge from forced marriages offered by Christian missions, and missionaries often prided themselves on their support of female freedom of choice. But, there is more than one story to be told here. As Mark Hunter shows in his study of courtship in late nineteenth- and early twentieth-century Natal,

[50] Epstein, *Urbanisation and Kinship*, p. 287; James M. Ault, 'Making "modern" marriage "traditional": state power and the regulation of marriage in colonial Zambia', *Theory and Society*, 12 (1983), 181–210. On women in Copperbelt communities in this period see also Jane Parpart, 'Sexuality and power on the Zambian Copperbelt, 1926–1954', in Sharon B. Stichter and Jane L. Parpart (eds.), *Patriarchy and Class: African Women in the Home and the Workplace* (Boulder, CO, 1988), pp. 141–60; Jane L. Parpart, '"Wicked women" and respectable ladies: reconfiguring gender on the Zambian Copperbelt', in Hodgson and McCurdy (eds.), *Reconfiguring Gender*, pp. 274–92; Jane L. Parpart, '"Where is your mother?": gender, urban marriage and colonial discourse on the Zambian Copperbelt, 1924–1945', *International Journal of African Historical Studies*, 27 (1994), 241–71.
[51] Peterson, 'Morality plays'; Parpart, '"Where is your mother?"'.

Christianity could also merge with a form of neo-traditionalism to restrict young women's love lives.[52]

By the 1940s in many urban areas of Africa there was more than one version of 'modern' love around in addition to any pre-existing ones. On the Copperbelt of Northern Rhodesia, for example, while missionary societies promoted the idea of companionate marriage and respectability, and cultivated the arts of female domesticity, urban residents were also watching Hollywood films in which women were dangling cigarettes from their mouths and falling passionately and helplessly in love with unsuitable objects of desire. The anthropologists watching Copperbelt residents watching films (microphones suspended over their heads) noted that one of their most frequent reactions was that of shock and moral outrage. The public display of intimacy between men and women, and kissing in particular, gave rise to the view that Europeans were 'basically immoral'.[53] The long-standing colonial suspicion of Africans 'aping' Europeans in their clothing and gestures was supplemented by an internal critique, directed mostly at those women whose version of the modern was less Christian housewife and more Hollywood movie-star. Popular songs on the Copperbelt mocked the lipsticked woman, 'tottering' along the road in her 'European' sandals, but they also celebrated romantic love.[54] The hugely popular singer, Alick Nkhata, performed on the radio, singing of love in a number of languages and drawing on a number of musical traditions.[55]

'Love' was undoubtedly sometimes part of a performance of a certain kind of modernity, and one whose stage instructions one had to learn. But was it less 'emotional' for having to be learned? Northern Rhodesia did not have the equivalent of the extraordinary output of 'pamphlet literature' on love which was produced in Nigeria around the same time, with titles like 'The School of Love and How to Attend it', 'How to Play Love', 'How to Make Love' and 'How to Get a Lady in Love', but it did

[52] Mark Hunter, 'Courting desire?'; Mark Hunter, 'Masculinities, multiple sexual-partners, and AIDS: the making and unmaking of Isoka in KwaZulu-Natal', *Transformation*, 54 (2004), 123–53.
[53] Hortense Powdermaker, *Copper Town: Changing Africa: the Human Situation on the Rhodesian Copperbelt* (New York, 1962), p. 166.
[54] Both attitudes are evident in the songs collected by ethnomusicologist, Hugh Tracey, on the Copperbelt in the 1950s: Tracey, *Catalogue*. Some of Tracey's original Copperbelt recordings are available on compact disc: *From the Copperbelt . . . Zambian Miners' Songs, 1957* (International Library of African Music and Original Music OMCD 004, 1989).
[55] A selection of Alick Nkhata's songs is available on compact disc: *Alick Nkhata: Shalapo and other love songs: original Zambian hits from the 1950s* (RetroAfrica, RETRO4CD, 1991).

(like South Africa) have agony columns in the newspapers where young people (mostly men, reflecting their higher literacy rates) sought advice on the interpretation of their emotional states and the confusing choices that faced them in their love lives.[56] Sometimes these questions referred to traditional obstacles in the way of desires: my parents won't let me marry the girl I love, what shall I do? Sometimes the letter-writers asked for confirmation that the symptoms they were experiencing were, indeed, those of love. Sometimes they reflected confusion over powerful feelings felt for a person of the same sex.[57] More frequently they sought counsel on pragmatic questions of choice of marriage partner, for example in weighing up the advantages and disadvantages of marrying a 'village girl' over a more sophisticated but possibly more independent 'town' woman.

The comparative historical literature places considerable emphasis on literacy as a technology with the capacity to produce a new self-reflexive subject, and a new private sphere of the emotions.[58] Literary scholars and historians of Africa, whilst acknowledging the great importance of the written word, have produced an important powerful critique of the more simplistic versions of this idea.[59] Literacy, as it spread in Africa, was a technology which was adapted to local circumstances. Love letters were, it seems, a blossoming literary form amongst the emerging middle classes and the labour migrants of the 1950s and 1960s, but they were often composed collectively and read aloud.[60] As Stephanie Newell and others have shown, there is no escaping the theme of romantic love in African popular literature from the 1940s onwards, and it is a theme which ranges in

---

[56] Donatus Nwoga, 'Onitsha market literature', in Stephanie Newell (ed.), *Readings in African Popular Fiction* (Bloomington, IN, 2002), pp. 37–44; Kenda Mutongi, '"Dear Dolly's" advice: representations of youth, courtship, and sexualities in Africa, 1960–1980', *International Journal of African Historical Studies*, 33 (2000), 1–23; Gustav Jahoda, 'Love, marriage and social change: letters to the advice column of a West African newspaper', *Africa*, 29 (1959), 177–90; Barbara Hall (ed.), *Tell Me Josephine* (New York, 1964); J. H. Chaplin, 'Wiving and thriving in Northern Rhodesia', *Africa*, 32 (1962), 111–22; Powdermaker, *Coppertown*.

[57] Chaplin, 'Wiving and thriving', p. 115. This issue is also evident in the letters to the South African Drum magazine discussed by Mutongi, '"Dear Dolly's" advice'.

[58] Goody, *Food and Love*; Stone, *Family*; Charles Taylor, *Sources of the Self: the Making of Modern Identity* (Cambridge, MA, 1989).

[59] Karin Barber, 'Introduction: hidden innovators in Africa', in Karin Barber (ed.), *Africa's Hidden Histories: Everyday Literacy and Making the Self* (Bloomington, IN, 2006), pp. 1–25; Thomas and Cole, 'Thinking through love'.

[60] Keith Breckenridge, 'Love letters and amanuenses: beginning the cultural history of the working class private sphere in Southern Africa, 1900–1933', *Journal of Southern African Studies*, 26 (2000), 337–48; Lynn M. Thomas, 'Schoolgirl pregnancies, letter-writing and "modern" persons in late colonial East Africa', in Barber (ed.), *Africa's Hidden Histories*, pp. 180–207.

tone from frank sentimentalism to brutal realism.[61] Sometimes it promotes the mystical version of love which triumphs over 'backward' traditions and oppressive parents, and is closely tied to middle class identity and new forms of consumption. Sometimes it pitches romantic love against new forms of consumerism. Shakespeare's 'Romeo and Juliet' was widely performed in African boarding schools, and, thinly disguised, continues to be performed in numerous African TV soap operas. Unsurprisingly, where love across racial divisions was frowned upon (or, in the case of South Africa, legally prohibited), interracial relationships come to represent the highest romantic love ideals. But often African cultural productions around love reflect a realistic version of the love story, a more socially embedded love and one in which economics and emotion are closely related.

Love, sex and economics in everyday life

Late colonial central Africa had its love stories and love letters and agony columns, but there is little evidence for romantic love triumphing over other ways of understanding and ordering intimate relationships, particularly those associated with marriage.

In the 1950s when the anthropologist A. L. Epstein was conducting research on urban politics and kinship in the towns of the Copperbelt, the classic circulatory male migrant system was slowly giving way to the creation of a more settled urban population, now including many more women, though still with a highly skewed sex ratio. Epstein's imaginative and practical research strategy was not only to employ African research assistants to interview, listen into and record the daily lives of urban residents, but also to employ their wives and girlfriends to write (or if they were illiterate) record daily diaries.[62] These are of course problematic texts, written and recorded for 'Mr Epstein' (whose precise instructions to his informants I have so far not been able to locate) but the records and transcripts of these diaries give us the possibility of some insight into the lives of a working class elite of urban women, and the shifting emotional

[61] Newell (ed.), *African Popular Fiction*; Aidoo, *African Love Stories*; T. Odhiambo, 'Troubled love and marriage as work in Kenyan popular fiction', *Social Identities*, 9 (2003), 423–36. There is nothing peculiarly 'African' about this, of course: Swidler, *Talk of Love*.
[62] On the methods of colonial anthropologists, including Epstein, see Lynn Schumacher, *Africanizing Anthropology: Fieldwork, Networks and the Making of Cultural Knowledge in Central Africa* (Durham, NC, 2001).

communities in which they lived.[63] The following extract gives some sense of the tone and content of these diaries.

> (12 December 1955)
> This afternoon at round about 4 o'clock bana Mambwe came to our house. She first knocked at the door by saying Odi. I then answered and allowed her to come in. 'Have you got a piece of washing soap to give me please?' she asked me. 'I have a very small piece', I replied. Then I went in the kitchen and but [sic] a piece of soap and gave her. She thanked for that. 'Bana Mambwe are you just thanking for such a piece of soap?' I asked her. 'I should do so' she replied 'because I am leading such a boring life'. 'Why are you suffering so much?' I asked. 'I have failed to get a proper husband', she replied. 'You are just worrying yourself bana Mambwe, you will soon get married', I added. 'I know you are mocking me' she said. 'It is a very long time since I asked you to give me some love medicine to make my husband love me but you did not give me' she said. 'I have no idea of such things' I concluded. Shortly I heard her friends call her. And so she walked off and said, we shall talk over this matter about love medicines next time, 'cheerio'. She went away.[64]

Epstein's diary-makers were married women. If notions of romantic love had informed their marriage choices at all, they were apparently little evident after marriage. Against the background of the regular rhythm of everyday life, the endless housework and attention to detail which marked respectable from unrespectable, and the daily work of lighting fires and heating water and procuring food for dinner, what emerges from these diaries are personal lives dominated by economic insecurities, the desire for children and anxiety about pregnancies and miscarriages and infertility. Marriage was central to life but women's dependence on male incomes produced powerful feelings of insecurity, hence the need for 'love medicines' mentioned in this excerpt. In the crowded conditions of the Copperbelt it was sometimes difficult if not impossible to maintain the spatial configuration of conjugal life which in the village had had strong spiritual overtones. Husbands and wives on the Copperbelt argued about household economics and sex, but they also argued and worried about 'respect'. Even those who were committed to a Christian-style companionate marriage worried at times of crisis (especially when experiencing infertility or child deaths) that modern urban marriage was endangering their wellbeing and that of their children. Practising

---

[63] A. L. Epstein's fieldnotes and other papers are held at the University of California, San Diego: Arnold Leonard and Trude Scarlett Epstein Papers, 1949–1995, MS 0022, Mandeville Special Collection Library, Giesel Library, University of California, San Diego.
[64] Epstein Papers, MS 0022, Series 2 (Field Notes, A. L. Epstein), Box 11/f/3, Kabushi interviews, Mrs Nyirenda, 12.12.55.

'affective individualism' was a dangerous business if this entailed neglect-
ing the interests and wishes of a wider set of relations among the living
and dead.

Colonial anthropologists of central Africa were accused of painting a
bleak picture of marital relationships, and no doubt there were many
happy loving marriages amidst all the difficulties. However, it is not surprising in the circumstances that marital relations were often fraught, with
men and women attempting to bend different available emotional languages for their own purposes. Economics and emotion were closely
bound up in matters of 'love' and of course there is nothing specifically
'African' about any of this.[65] Urban women, though they did their best to
make an independent living in the interstices of the male mining economy,
were still economically dependent on their husbands and vulnerable to
being either neglected or sent home to rural areas. Some found themselves
caught up in circumstances which amounted to a new and unwelcome
emotional regime. Living independently of a man on the Copperbelt was
extremely difficult, not least because access to housing for women
depended on their 'marriage', formal or informal, to a male wage-earner.
If your husband did not provide for you, you had either to return to a rural
area or find a lover. Women's complaints about marriage largely revolved
around the lack of generosity of their husbands in sharing their wages
with them. 'Love' for them meant being cared for and provided for materi-
ally, shown respect and being endowed with children. When asked what
defined a good husband women used a word (*uwatekanya*) which Epstein
translated as 'patient, good-hearted and attentive'.[66]

Many of these issues have surfaced again in the literature on the gendered experience of both poverty and HIV/AIDS in Africa. Taking lovers
or engaging in transactional sex is a necessity for many women and girls,
and their economic realism in this context leads to male accusations that
they are (variously) 'gold-diggers' or 'razor blades' or 'blood suckers'.
Women's necessary realism about the economics of relationships with
men lives alongside *both* the apparently growing attraction of the language of romantic love and sexual fidelity *and* the continuing importance
of marriage as an institution involving a wider set of relations and still (in
some places at least) concerns over fertility. Daniel Jordan Smith's study
of love and marriage in Southern Nigeria, for example, shows that modern
courtship practices (for both men and women, and in both urban and

---

[65] Illouz, *Cold Intimacies.*
[66] Epstein, *Urbanisation and Kinship*, p. 118.

rural areas) are imbued with the ideals of romantic love, but once married, couples are subject to the expectations of a wider set of kin, as well as their own concerns over achieving an ideal of parenthood. Married men typically take additional lovers while married women hold on for longer to the discourse of romantic love and fidelity in their attempts to maintain the attentions, both affectionate and economic, of their husbands.[67] The language of romantic love in this context looks very much like a weapon of the weak—but it also seems to be a rather weak weapon.

Love, as the evidence of African societies reminds us, and as Godfrey Wilson learned, takes forms that are far richer and more diverse than can be allowed for by the restrictive ideals of romantic love. While Kasitile had challenged Wilson's views of the centrality of love to both sex and marriage by referring to the role of ancestral spirits in the marital bed, this did not exhaust his views on love and intimacy. Wilson wrote to his wife Monica that at the end of one long day Kasitile had turned to him and said, 'I have exhausted all the thoughts of my heart to you, I have told you everything I know.' But then he added 'If I were a woman I would go to bed with you, so that you might know the very body of the Black People', a statement which I read as both a lesson in the multiple forms of love and of the politics of knowledge of which this lecture is inescapably a part. [68]

Note.   My thanks go to the archivists and librarians at the University of Cape Town Libraries (Manuscripts and Archives Department) and at the Giesel Library, University of California at San Diego, for their assistance. I owe particular thanks to Professor Francis Wilson for generously allowing me to consult private correspondence between Godfrey and Monica Wilson. I am also grateful to Lynn Thomas and Jennifer Cole for giving me access to their book on *Love in Africa*, which is in press as I write, and to Tiffany Sithampwi, Professor Mwelwa Musambachime, Dr Walima Kalusa and to the anonymous reviewer for their insights. My research on the history of the emotions in Africa has been generously funded by the Leverhulme Trust through a Major Research Fellowship. I am deeply indebted to the Leverhulme Trust for their support.

[67] Daniel Jordan Smith, 'Romance, parenthood, and gender in a modern African society', *Ethnology*, 40 (2001), 129–51; Hunter, 'Masculinities'; Andrea Cornwell, 'Spending Power: love, money and the reconfiguration of gender relations in Ado-Odo, Southwest Nigeria', *American Ethnologist*, 29 (2002), 963–80.
[68] Wilson Papers, UCT, B2, Folder 4, Letter from Godfrey Wilson to Monica Wilson, 21 Feb. 1937.

Leon Battista Alberti and the Redirection of Renaissance Humanism

MARTIN McLAUGHLIN
University of Oxford

IN 1916 MRS ANGELA MOND provided funds for 'a lecture series on subjects relating to Italian literature, history, art, history of Italian science,
Italy's part in the Renaissance, Italian influences on other countries, or any
other theme which the Council may consider as coming within the scope of
such a Lecture'. While the subjects of previous British Academy lectures
will have been relevant to one or two of the above fields, Leon Battista
Alberti (1404–72) is perhaps unique in being relevant to all of them.
Despite that, he has only been the subject of one lecture in recent times,
Cecil Grayson's 1963 lecture to the Academy on Alberti's *Grammatica* of
the Italian vernacular.[1] For that reason alone Battista Alberti would be an
appropriate subject for this year's lecture: but in fact this fifteenth-century
polymath is highly relevant to our own times since we live in an age in which
the humanities are increasingly taking on interdisciplinary perspectives and
are currently much concerned with innovation, both key components of
Alberti's intellectual make-up.

   Yet modern scholars face two main problems in dealing with Alberti.
The first is that trying to establish what the humanist was really trying to
do is like restoring a work of art: we have to remove the accretions and
misguided restorations that have taken place over the centuries to return
to the original painting, sculpture or building. One of the most influential

Read at the Academy, 26 March 2009.
[1] Cecil Grayson, 'Leon Battista Alberti and the beginnings of Italian grammar', *Proceedings of
the British Academy*, 49 (1964), 291–316.

Proceedings of the British Academy, **167**, 25–59. © The British Academy 2010.

portraits of the artist was that provided by Jacob Burckhardt in 1860 which was largely modelled on the humanist's Latin autobiography, but carefully rewritten by the Swiss historian in order to accentuate the positive, sunny aspects of his multitalented personality, and to elide the darker, melancholic notes of the authentic source.[2] Burckhardt's picture of what he called a 'Renaissance or universal man' also tended to emphasise Battista's practical talents and physical prowess rather more than his intellectual achievements. It was only in the second half of the twentieth century that scholars such as Cecil Grayson and Eugenio Garin began to restore the darker, pessimistic side of Alberti's make-up, particularly the melancholic dimension that emerged from Latin works such as the *Intercenales*, a new manuscript of which was discovered in the early 1960s.[3] Joan Kelly Gadol's 1969 volume emphasised the artistic rather than the literary side of the man, but after her monograph there was a striking lull of three decades before Anthony Grafton's book at the end of the last century.[4] This volume and Grafton's other studies have refocused our attention on Alberti's scholarly credentials.[5] Now in the last decade, and especially since the sixth centenary of the author's birth in 2004, the bibliography on the humanist has increased exponentially: at least six major conferences and four exhibitions, as well as new editions of works, have led to the publication of almost twenty substantial volumes.[6] Thus more has been written on Alberti in the last ten years than in

---

[2] Jacob Burckhardt, *The Civilization of the Renaissance in Italy*, trans. S. G. C. Middlemore, new intro. by P. Burke, notes by P. Murray (Harmondsworth, 1990), esp. pp. 102–4.

[3] The manuscript containing many new *Intercenales* was published by Eugenio Garin: Leon Battista Alberti, *Intercenali inedite*, ed. Eugenio Garin, *Rinascimento*, 4 (1964), 125–258; for a more balanced view of both the 'sunny' and 'dark' sides of Alberti see also Garin's 'Il pensiero di Leon Battista Alberti: caratteri e contrasti', *Rinascimento*, 12 (1972), 3–20; for Grayson's work, see now the collection of his articles in Cecil Grayson, *Studi su Leon Battista Alberti*, a cura di P. Claut (Florence, 1998).

[4] Joan Gadol, *Leon Battista Alberti. Universal Man of the Early Renaissance* (Chicago and London, 1969).

[5] Anthony Grafton, 'Leon Battista Alberti: the writer as reader', in his *Commerce with the Classics. Ancient Books and Renaissance Readers* (Ann Arbor, MI, 1997), pp. 53–92; id., *Leon Battista Alberti. Master Builder of the Italian Renaissance* (Harmondsworth, 2000).

[6] Amongst the conference proceedings, see *Leon Battista Alberti. Architettura e cultura. Atti del Convegno internazionale, Mantova, 16–19 novembre 1994* (Florence, 1999); *Leon Battista Alberti: Actes du congrès international de Paris (10–15 avril 1995)*, ed. Francesco Furlan et al., 2 vols. (Paris and Turin, 2000); *Leon Battista Alberti e il Quattrocento. Studi in onore di Cecil Grayson e Ernst Gombrich. Atti del Convegno internazionale, Mantova, 29–31 ottobre 1998*, ed. L. Chiavoni, G. Ferlisi, M. V. Grassi (Florence, 2001); *Leon Battista Alberti teorico delle arti e gli impegni civili del 'De Re Aedificatoria'*, ed. A. Calzona, F. P. Fiore, A. Tenenti, C. Vasoli, 2 vols. (Florence, 2007); *La vita e il mondo di Leon Battista Alberti. Atti dei Convegni internazionali del Comitato*

the previous half-millennium.[7] Two main aims of this lecture, then, are to suggest a way of returning to the essence of Alberti's humanism while at the same time bearing in mind the most recent scholarship.

The second problem facing today's Albertian scholars stems from the increasing specialisation of scholarship: this means that conferences on this multifaceted writer, theorist and architect are still split into different areas of expertise, broadly speaking the literary and the artistic or practical sides of the humanist's output. Grayson pointed out at the start of his British Academy lecture the risk that Alberti might seem broad but not deep in his interests, since he was a wide-ranging writer who might have been accused of being an amateur, but he added: 'though his range was broad, covering both literary and scientific subjects, his learning and understanding were no less profound'.[8] Battista cultivated an unparalleled range of literary and other genres in both Latin and the Tuscan vernacular, but today it is just the tip of the Alberti iceberg that is studied and taught: in UK Italian and history departments we study mostly *De familia*, art historians read *De pictura*, architectural historians research *De re aedificatoria*. These are the only three works that are studied in our undergraduate courses. How many Italianists can say they have read not just all the Latin works, but even the other three vernacular dialogues? Perhaps it is for this reason that conferences have proliferated, and the interdisciplinary nature of such gatherings means that conference proceedings are perhaps a better way of approaching this 'chameleon-like'

Nazionale VI centenario della nascita di Leon Battista Alberti (Genova, 19–21 febbraio 2004), 2 vols. (Florence, 2008); *Leon Battista Alberti e la tradizione. Per lo 'smontaggio' dei mosaici albertiani. Atti dei Convegni internazionali del Comitato Nazionale VI centenario della nascita di Leon Battista Alberti (Arezzo, 23–24–25 settembre 2004)*, ed. Roberto Cardini, Mariangela Regoliosi, 2 vols. (Florence, 2008); *Alberti e la cultura del Quattrocento. Atti dei Convegni internazionali del Comitato Nazionale VI centenario della nascita di Leon Battista Alberti (Firenze, 16–17–18 dicembre 2004)*, ed. Roberto Cardini, Mariangela Regoliosi, 2 vols. (Florence, 2008); *Leon Battista Alberti umanista e scrittore. Filologia, esegesi, tradizione. Atti dei Convegni internazionali del Comitato Nazionale VI centenario della nascita di Leon Battista Alberti (Arezzo, 24–25–26 giugno 2004)*, ed. Roberto Cardini, Mariangela Regoliosi, 2 vols. (Florence, 2008). Amongst the exhibition catalogues, see *La Roma di Leon Battista Alberti. Umanisti, architetti e artisti alla scoperta dell'antico nella città del Quattrocento*, ed. Francesco Paolo Fiore with Arnold Nesselrath (Milan, 2005); *Leon Battista Alberti. La biblioteca di un umanista*, ed. Roberto Cardini with L. Bertolini, M. Regoliosi (Florence, 2005); *Leon Battista Alberti e l'architettura*, ed. Massimo Bulgarelli, Arturo Calzona, Matteo Ceriana, Francesco Paolo Fiore (Milan, 2006); *L'uomo del Rinascimento. Leon Battista Alberti e le arti a Firenze tra ragione e bellezza*, ed. Cristina Acidini, Gabriele Morolli (Florence, 2006).

[7] Roberto Cardini, 'Alberti scrittore e umanista', in *La vita e il mondo di Leon Battista Alberti*, I, 23–40 (24).

[8] Grayson, 'Leon Battista Alberti and the beginnings of Italian grammar', p. 291.

writer.[9] Nevertheless, the best scholarship ought to take account of both the intellectual and the practical Alberti, the writer of literary and technical works, the Latin and vernacular author. My own approach follows Grafton's to a certain extent, in stressing the highly refined literary author, a humanist steeped in an almost unparalleled range of classical texts, but whereas Grafton's methodology has its centre of gravity in the history of ideas, my aim here is more literary, paying close attention to Alberti's sources, for as a genuine humanist he was an avid reader of classical literature and, as in Petrarch and other exponents of Renaissance humanism, what Alberti read explains what he wrote.

I want to begin by looking at the very different ways in which Alberti develops humanism in the century after Petrarch. In order to do so we should first remind ourselves of what Renaissance humanism consisted in. There is a helpful recent definition of it provided by Nicholas Mann: 'Humanism [. . .] involves above all the rediscovery and study of ancient Greek and Roman texts, the restoration and interpretation of them and the assimilation of the ideas and values they contain.'[10] In this definition there are three sequential elements: first, the (re-)discovery and restoration of classical texts; second, their study or interpretation; and thirdly, the assimilation of their ideas and values. In what follows I want to consider to what extent Alberti embraced Petrarch's enthusiasm for these three elements, the recovery and analysis of classical texts, as well as the emulation of their values; what will emerge, I think, is that his interests were focused less on the first element, philological restoration of texts, and more on the other two, analysis and assimilation of their content and values, but in addition we will see that he moved outwards towards a much wider range of disciplines than his predecessor. This enlargement of his interests had important consequences, resulting in attitudes that distanced him substantially from Petrarch. But let us start by simply comparing their lives and literary works.

---

[9] Cristoforo Landino was one of the first to apply the image to Alberti: 'come nuovo camaleonta sempre quello colore piglia il quale è nella cosa della quale scrive'—see Cristoforo Landino, *Scritti critici e teorici*, ed. Roberto Cardini, 2 vols. (Rome, 1974), I, 120. On this topos in Alberti criticism, see now Gabriella Albanese's fine survey, 'Leon Battista Alberti nella storiografia letteraria e artistica dell'Umanesimo e del Rinascimento', *Rinascimento*, 47 (2007), 49–91.

[10] Nicholas Mann, 'The origins of humanism', in J. Kraye (ed.), *The Cambridge Companion to Renaissance Humanism* (Cambridge, 1996), pp. 1–19 (2).

Petrarch and Alberti

There are striking similarities between Alberti and Petrarch. David Marsh in a 1985 article pointed out many of them.[11] Born in the fourth year of their respective centuries, of Florentine fathers in exile, both men died in the eighth decade of the Tre and Quattrocento. Each studied law at Bologna, took minor orders, and enjoyed the income from ecclesiastical benefices throughout their life. Both were creatively inspired by the sight of the ruins of ancient Rome, travelled widely within Italy, and found patronage in the Northern Italian courts. The first work by each was a Latin comedy in which characters had names that were personifications of abstract qualities. Both wrote works complaining about the mercantile, anti-literary culture that surrounded them. And while Petrarch received a laurel crown in Rome in 1341, exactly a hundred years later, in 1441, Alberti organised a literary competition in Florence where the prize was a silver laurel wreath for the best vernacular work on the theme of friendship.

Nevertheless, the differences between the two humanists are more illuminating than their points of convergence. The condition of being born in exile appears to have weighed more heavily on Alberti than on Petrarch: in the former's case the condition of exile was further exacerbated by being born illegitimate, and Alberti stresses on several occasions, especially in the dialogue *De familia*, the travails brought upon his family by their exile. The Albertis were exiled from Florence in 1401 and only allowed to return in 1428, a period corresponding to Battista's early life up to his twenty-fourth year.[12] Another difference in outlook is their attitude to the canon of classical authors to be studied. Alberti's more open attitude particularly to 'scientific' writers derives from the breadth of his education: he tells us in his Latin autobiography that when he became ill through excessive study of literature and law, he turned to physics or philosophy and mathematics. There is a dispute as to whether the abbreviated form 'pham' found in the best manuscript of the *Vita* stands for 'ph[ysic]am' or 'ph[ilosophi]am', though most scholars now opt for the latter, which probably meant 'natural philosophy' (i.e. studying Aristotle's *Physica*, *De coelo*, *De*

[11] David Marsh, 'Petrarch and Alberti', in *Renaissance Studies in Honor of Craig Hugh Smyth*, ed. A. Morrogh *et al.*, 2 vols. (Florence, 1985), I, 363–75.
[12] On the Alberti family exile, see the first chapter of Girolamo Mancini, *Vita di Leon Battista Alberti* (Florence, 1882), pp. 1–20, later revised in the 2nd edn. (Rome, 1911), pp. 1–16; more recently see the first chapter of Luca Boschetto, *Leon Battista Alberti e Firenze. Biografia, storia, letteratura* (Florence, 2000), pp. 3–67.

anima).[13] In a sense the reading does not matter, since for Aristotelians physics and natural philosophy are the same thing, and either of them would imply a substantial broadening of his education away from strictly literary and legal disciplines—indeed we shall see when we look at his own works that what counted was the second term, 'mathematicas artes'. It is this 'mathematical turn' in Alberti that makes him so different from the founder of humanism. In fact Battista's capacity to 'turn', especially in pursuit of innovative fields of enquiry, is a key characteristic of his intellectual temperament. Petrarch on the other hand hardly ever mentions mathematics as a subject and his aversion to the natural sciences is well known: in a famous passage of his invective *De sui ipsius et aliorum ignorantia* (*c*.1371) he argues that it is misguided to know how many hairs a lion has in its mane, how many feathers a hawk has in its tail, how elephants mate and so on, all details found in Pliny's *Natural History* and medieval encyclopedias.[14] For Alberti, on the other hand, Pliny will be one of his most quoted authors, and the humanist's treatise on horses, *De equo animante* (*c*.1444), deals with precisely the kind of topic from natural science and uses exactly the scholastic sources that Petrarch abhorred. Similarly in Petrarch's *Invective against a Detractor of Italy* (1373) he attacks his Aristotelian opponent for asking why Cicero had not written a *Physics* or Varro a *Metaphysics*, claiming that this detractor is only happy when he is spouting Greek titles.[15] This dismissal of certain aspects of Greek culture opens up another difference between the two humanists. In short, as I have suggested elsewhere, Alberti's canon of authors differs from that of Petrarch and other humanist predecessors in four main areas: his interests in 'scientific' texts; his knowledge of Greek literature; his insistence on the humorous component in many of his writings; and his stylistically anti-Ciceronian Latin.[16]

---

[13] For the text of the *Vita*, see Riccardo Fubini and A. Menci Gallorini (eds.), 'L'autobiografia di Leon Battista Alberti. Studio e edizione', *Rinascimento*, 12 (1972), 21–78 (70). The interpretation 'philosophy' is maintained by Lucia Cesarini Martinelli, in her edition of the *Philodoxeos Fabula*, *Rinascimento*, 17 (1977), 111–234 (112–13, n. 2), by Luca Boschetto, *Leon Battista Alberti e Firenze*, p. 72, n. 4, and by David Lines, 'Leon Battista Alberti e lo studio di Bologna negli anni venti', in *La vita e il mondo di Leon Battista Alberti*, cit., II, 387; in addition Alberti himself uses the abbreviation 'phum' to mean 'philosophum' in his autograph letter to the philosopher Crates: see *Leon Battista Alberti. La biblioteca di un umanista*, p. 208, Tavola 32.

[14] Francesco Petrarca, *Invectives*, ed. and trans. David Marsh (Cambridge, MA, 2003), p. 238.

[15] Petrarca, *Invectives*, cit., pp. 450, 454.

[16] Martin McLaughlin, 'Alberti and the classical canon', in Carlo Caruso and Andrew Laird (eds.), *Italy and the Classical Tradition. Language, Thought and Poetry 1300–1600* (London, 2009), pp. 73–100.

Apart from these questions of their education and their attitude to the canon, another fundamental difference between the two men is that Petrarch's synthesis of humanism and Christianity finds very little echo in the later humanist: it is true that Battista does write in Latin the *Vita Sancti Potiti* (*c*.1433) and a dialogue on the duties of a bishop (*Pontifex*, *c*.1437),[17] but these are brief, early works whose Christian tone is totally absent in Alberti's major outputs. The difference emerges most strikingly in the two writers' autobiographies: Petrarch's *Letter to Posterity* (*c*.1350, revised 1370) is structured around an Augustinian model of sin and repentance, and indeed opens with a list of the subject's differing levels of propensity to the seven deadly sins; Alberti's *Vita* (*c*.1438), on the other hand, is totally secular, there is no mention of God or sin, and the major underlying model is a classical one, Diogenes Laertius' *Lives of the Philosophers* (it even ends, like many of Diogenes' lives, with a list of the subject's famous sayings): it is a portrait of the artist not as an Augustine-like repentant but as a Stoic philosopher. Other fundamental differences emerge simply by looking at the prolific output of both men.

If we just examine the list of works by both writers, what instantly stands out is that while Alberti did not write any poetry in Latin himself, he adapts several Latin poetic genres that Petrarch had embraced and transfers them to the *volgare*: in his few vernacular poems we see that where Petrarch had revived classical pastoral poetry with his *Bucolicum Carmen*, Alberti wrote the first vernacular eclogues;[18] Petrarch wrote Latin elegiac verse and Battista wrote the first elegies in *terza rima*;[19] and if Petrarch had written a number of poems in Latin hexameters, Alberti was the first to accommodate Italian vernacular poetry to the classical hexameter rhythm.[20]

The same tendency to 'transfer' is found in his prose works. Petrarch first, and humanists such as Leonardo Bruni later, had revived the

[17] See the recent edition: Leon Battista Alberti, *Pontifex*, ed. A. Piccardi (Florence, 2007).

[18] 'Corimbus' and 'Tirsis', in Leon Battista Alberti, *Opere volgari*, ed. Cecil Grayson, 3 vols. (Bari, 1960–73), II, 22–7 (henceforth *OV*, with volume and page number). See also C. Grayson, 'Alberti and the vernacular eclogue in the Quattrocento', *Italian Studies*, 11 (1956), 16–29, now in C. Grayson, *Studi su Leon Battista Alberti*, pp. 103–18.

[19] 'Mirzia' and 'Agilitta', in *OV*, II, 11–21. In fact Petrarch's metrical epistles, the *Metrice*, may have inspired Alberti to write vernacular verse epistles, though only one couplet of them survives, cited by Vasari: see Giorgio Vasari, 'Leonbatista Alberti, Architetto fiorentino', in *Le vite de' più eccellenti architetti, pittori, et scultori italiani, da Cimabue, insino a' giorni nostri. Nell'edizione per i tipi di Lorenzo Torrentino*, Firenze 1550, ed. L. Bellosi, A. Rossi, 2 vols. (Turin, 1986), I, 354–58 (356).

[20] Alberti's poem 'De amicitia', written for the Certame, is in *OV*, II, 45.

Ciceronian dialogue in Latin, indeed it had become the prestige genre of
Latin humanists in the first half of the Quattrocento.[21] However, Alberti
wrote just one brief dialogue in Latin (*Pontifex*), but went on to write the
first ever ethical dialogues in the Italian vernacular, four of them altogether. His first substantial work was the *De familia* (1433–7), a
Ciceronian dialogue in Tuscan, an extraordinary novelty at the time, and
it is interesting to note that the one explicit model that Alberti names as
inspiring one of the four books is not Cicero (which might have invited
invidious comparisons), but the Greek writer Xenophon, and the adjec-
tives used to describe him ('nudo, simplice . . . dolcissimo e suavissimo')
show that Alberti is aiming not at the highest but at a middle rhetorical
style.[22] This was a completely original initiative, especially as vernacular
prose up until that point had only been used for urban chronicles or *nov-
elle*, not works of high literature. He also wrote his first technical work,
De pictura (1435–6), in Italian, consciously providing a treatise on painting for the first time in the new language to match the lost works by
ancient artists and writers such as Apelles and others.[23] In addition, as
Grayson showed us, his *Grammatichetta* did for the Tuscan *volgare* what
Priscian had done for Latin. This systematic transferral of genres from
the learned language to the vernacular accounts for Cristoforo Landino's
praise of Alberti as the writer who had expanded the popular language
by 'transferring' all sorts of elegance and dignity from Latin texts to the
volgare.[24]

In his Latin works we find many short pieces: *brevitas* was one of his
favourite stylistic ideals. Thus, despite the fame of Petrarch's *Africa* and
Trionfi, Alberti has no time for epic poetry in either language. However,
after about 1442 there appears to be a shift from short narrative texts
towards more technical works, such as the *Descriptio urbis Romae* (1446–7),
De statua (1450), and *De componendis cyfris* (1466). His mathematical

---

[21] David Marsh, *The Quattrocento Dialogue. Classical Tradition and Humanist Innovation*
(Cambridge, MA, 1980).
[22] Martin L. McLaughlin, *Literary Imitation in the Italian Renaissance. The Theory and Practice
of Literary Imitation in Italy from Dante to Bembo* (Oxford, 1995), pp. 160–1.
[23] '[W]e are not writing a history of painting like Pliny, but treating of the art in an entirely new
way. On this subject there exist today none of the writings of the ancients [. . .]': Leon Battista
Alberti, *On Painting*, trans. Cecil Grayson, with an Introduction by Martin Kemp
(Harmondsworth, 1991), pp. 61–2. For the Italian original of book 2.26, see *OV*, II, 46–8.
[24] 'Ma uomo che più industria abbi messo in ampliare questa lingua che Batista Alberti certo
credo che nessuno si truovi. Legete, priego, e' libri suoi e molti e di varie cose composti, atten-
dete con quanta industria ogni eleganza, composizione e dignità che appresso a' Latini si truova
si sia ingegnato a noi transferire' (Landino, *Scritti critici e teorici*, I, 35–6).

interests and use of measuring instruments are well to the fore in all three works, though they were also evident in the first book of *De pictura*. His three most ambitious compositions in Latin, however, are the ten books of short Lucianic 'dinner-pieces' known as the *Intercenales* (*c.*1432–40), the four-book satirical 'novel' *Momus* (1443–53) and the ten-book architecture treatise, *De re aedificatoria* (1443–52). As in the vernacular works, here too he is motivated by the pursuit of originality: if the *Intercenales* are modelled on Lucian, a 'new' author at the time, and represent a genre that was up till then totally lacking in Latin literature, and the architectural treatise was inspired by Vitruvius' *De architectura*, *Momus* is possibly the most original work of all, and certainly the first modern 'novel' in Latin. These are three substantial works that give an idea of the importance of those two major strands in Alberti: the humorous work, and the technical treatise. In the latter genre he eventually wrote a total of eight treatises on quite original topics (on painting (two), sculpture, architecture, the buildings of Rome, horses, mathematics and cryptography). Thus if in the vernacular the dominant note of his major works, the dialogues, is ethical, in Latin the two main strands of his output are the humorous and the technical. While he shares with Petrarch a concern for the ethical dimension, his cult of humorous and technical works is far removed from the interests of his great predecessor and most of his humanist contemporaries. Alberti clearly changes the direction of humanism: he extends the confines of the two languages, vertically elevating the vernacular by writing in it philosophical dialogues, and horizontally broadening Latin by expanding it to include humorous and technical subjects.

Recovery of ancient texts

I want now to look in more depth at Petrarch's and Alberti's attitudes to the main concepts of Renaissance humanism, as outlined above. Perhaps the most important aspect here is what was called the recovery and restoration of classical texts, either the discovery of works that were wholly or partially unknown to the middle ages, or the restoration of more accurate manuscripts of works that were already known. Here Petrarch, as is well known, played a prime role. By 1330 he had put together in Avignon the most complete and accurate text of the three decades of Livy's *History of Rome* that had survived; in Liège in 1333 he discovered Cicero's speech *Pro Archia*, a speech that was fundamental for the concept of the '*studia humanitatis*' or humanism; and in 1345 he discovered Cicero's *Letters to*

Atticus in the Capitular library at Verona, a discovery that would inspire Petrarch to collect his own letters to his friends. Petrarch's discoveries would inspire the great manuscript hunters of the fifteenth century: the period from 1416 to 1429, while Alberti was studying first with Gasparino Barzizza at Padua and later at Bologna university, has been called the 'heroic age' of humanist recovery of the classical heritage, for it was then that many new texts came to light.[25] In 1416–17 the complete texts of Quintilian, Lucretius, Manilius, Columella and Silius Italicus were discovered or recovered, thanks largely to the researches of Poggio Bracciolini.[26] In 1421 Gherardo Landriani unearthed at Lodi the important Cicero manuscript containing the complete texts of *De Oratore* and *Orator*, as well as the *Brutus*, a work entirely unknown to the middle ages.[27] It was Alberti's teacher, Barzizza, along with Flavio Biondo, who helped disseminate these new rhetorical works of Cicero to other Italian humanists in the 1420s.[28] Lastly in 1429 the manuscript containing twelve new comedies by Plautus arrived in Italy.[29]

What was Alberti's attitude to this key feature of humanism, the recovery of ancient texts? Unlike Petrarch, he did not actually discover any manuscripts but he clearly digested the import of recent discoveries: Cicero's *Brutus* was perhaps the most influential Ciceronian text for Alberti's thought, Quintilian's treatise on the orator clearly shaped *De pictura*, Plautus was a major source for the comic writings, while Pliny and Vitruvius inspired his technical works. Other 'new' texts, such as Lucretius, Manilius, Silius Italicus, Martial and even Tacitus, quickly find their way even into his vernacular dialogues.[30] Similarly with Greek literature, he clearly read some works in the Greek original: he quoted, for instance, from Herodotus in his very first vernacular dialogue, *De familia*, and since the first Latin translation of Herodotus was completed by Lorenza Valla only in 1452, it is certain that Alberti had read it in the original Greek. The fact that he quoted from Herodotus' *Histories* in a work written in the vernacular shows Alberti once more 'transferring' the

---

[25] See L. D. Reynolds, N. G. Wilson, *Scribes and Scholars*, 3rd edn. (Oxford, 1991), p. 139.

[26] L. D. Reynolds, *Texts and Transmission: a Survey of the Latin Classics* (Oxford, 1986), pp. 146–7 (Columella), 221 (Lucretius), 235 (Manilius), 333 (Quintilian), and 389 (Silius Italicus).

[27] See R. Sabbadini, *Le scoperte dei codici latini e greci ne' secoli XIV e XV*, 2 vols. (Florence, 1905), I, 100–1; Reynolds, *Texts and Transmission*, pp. 102, 107–8.

[28] R. G. G. Mercer, *The Teachings of Gasparino Barzizza. With Special Reference to his Place in Paduan Humanism* (London, 1979), pp. 74–5, 132.

[29] Reynolds, *Texts and Transmission*, p. 304.

[30] See McLaughlin, 'Alberti and the classical canon', cit., p. 87

riches of the ancient world to the modern one. Later dialogues would continue to borrow as much (if not more) from Greek authors as from Latin, such as Xenophon, Plato, Plutarch and even Hippocrates.

Although he was no discoverer of new manuscripts, then, his early education had been at the Paduan school of Barzizza, the foremost Cicero scholar of the day. Barzizza had helped to decipher and disseminate the *Brutus* in the early 1420s, and Alberti's own copy of it is in the Marciana library in Venice.[31] This Ciceronian dialogue was of crucial importance in a number of ways: first, it shed light on the history and development of Latin oratory from the earliest times to Cicero's own day; second, it provided the techniques and technical terms for humanists wanting to write literary criticism in Latin.[32] So Battista had his own copy of this 'new' text, and, as has been shown, he studied it thoroughly and highlighted in his works key concepts from Cicero's dialogue.[33] The main lessons he learnt from it were: the cult of a constant work-ethic, attributed to both Hortensius and Cicero in the dialogue; his interest in the education of the writer, painter or architect; the idea that all arts progress and develop over time, that nothing is born already perfect (*'Et nescio an reliquis in rebus omnibus idem eveniat: nihil est enim simul et inventum et perfectum'*, *Brutus* 71; echoed at the end of *De pictura*: *'Simul enim ortum atque perfectum nihil esse aiunt'*, *OV*, III, 106–7), hence the phrase 'in dies' ('day after day') which recurs so often in his works; the notion that not just oratory as a whole has a diachronic development but also that within the one orator or writer there is a development and variety of style; and the view that both the populace and the experts share the same aesthetic sense about what good oratory is. Alberti digested the main lessons of this 'new' text and returned to them throughout his life. In fact it is clear that he remained extremely au fait with all the classical textual discoveries being made in his lifetime, and he was keen to introduce such texts into his works, both vernacular and Latin, thus ensuring a dissemination of the latest humanist discoveries amongst humanist and non-humanist readers.[34]

---

[31] For a description of MS Marciana, Lat.XI.67 (3859), see Maria Luisa Tanganelli, 'Scheda 62', *Leon Battista Alberti. La biblioteca di un umanista*, cit., pp. 404–5.

[32] See the introduction to Pauli Cortesii, *De hominibus doctis*, ed. G. Ferraù (Messina: Centro di Studi Umanistici, Università di Messina, 1979), pp. 5–55.

[33] On the significance of Cicero for Alberti, see Martin McLaughlin, 'Alberti e le opere retoriche di Cicerone', in *Leon Battista Alberti e la tradizione*, pp. 181–210.

[34] See M. Regoliosi, 'Per un catalogo degli *auctores* latini dell'Alberti', in *Leon Battista Alberti. La biblioteca di un umanista*, cit., pp. 105–13: 'Si può dire che non ci sia recente scoperta che non sia stata da lui "annusata" e riutilizzata. [. . .] anche la lettura dei latini risulta aggiornatissima'

Recent scholarship has provided an edition of a letter from the humanist Enoch of Ascoli to Alberti in 1451 sending him an epistle by the late antique writer Sidonius Apollinaris (*Letters* 2.2) which he had found in Röskilde, in Denmark.[35] The date fits with the time when the *De re aedificatoria* was being written, and Sidonius's missive is a detailed description in technical Latin of his villa and baths near Lac Aydat in the Auvergne, even though it is not clear that the letter influenced the architectural treatise in any way. Still Alberti would have appreciated Sidonius's technical language, and he may also have been inspired by the description of Sidonius' villa and its baths to draw up the plan for a baths complex, possibly for the palace at Urbino, another recent discovery in Alberti studies.[36] So Battista was not a discoverer of texts but he was close to those who were, like Poggio and Enoch, and he quickly brought them to the attention of his readers.

In addition, although he made no new manuscript discoveries, Alberti was driven in many of his works by the desire to write modern versions of ancient texts, either of ones that he had read—thus his early reading of Cicero's *De amicitia* lies behind the subject matter of *De familia* book 4, while the *Theogenius* is a vernacular version of *De senectute*—or of works that had been lost, such as the treatises on painting attributed to ancient writers and artists. In fact in some places he uses the language and metaphors of the great manuscript-hunters: his early comedy, *Philodoxus* (1424, revised 1436–7), he passed off as being written by a classical writer and transcribed from an ancient manuscript and 'recovered from exile';[37] and at the end of book 2 of *De pictura* he exploits first the metaphor of exhumation, then the Platonic notion of deriving ideas from the heavens: 'However, whether, if it was once written about by others, we have rediscovered this art of painting and restored it to light from the dead, or whether, if it was never treated before, we have brought it down from

---

(p. 107 'one can say there is hardly any recent discovery he did not "sample" subsequently and re-employ. [. . .] His reading of the Latin authors too is utterly up-to-date'); Martin McLaughlin, 'Alberti and the classical canon', cit.

[35] For the text of the letter see Ida Mastrorosa's edition and translation of 'Enochi Asculani Epistula Baptistae de Albertis, Rome', *Albertiana*, 5 (2002), 191–236.

[36] For an image and description of the architectural drawing, discovered by Howard Burns, see Lucia Bertolini, 'Scheda 51', in *Leon Battista Alberti. La biblioteca di un umanista*, cit., pp. 367–8, and relative bibliography; also Robert Tavernor, *On Alberti and the Art of Building* (New Haven, CT, 1998), pp. 194–200.

[37] See Alberti's introduction to his revised redaction of the comedy in *Humanist Comedies*, ed. and transl. Gary R. Grund (Cambridge, MA, 2005), pp. 70–82 (76–8).

heaven, let us go on [. . .].'[38] An analogous motivation lies behind his *De re aedificatoria*: he clearly did not discover the manuscript of Vitruvius— it was also known to Petrarch[39]—but for Alberti the text might as well not have existed, so corrupt and unintelligible was it.[40] He tried therefore to make sense of it and critically reinterpret it in writing his own modern version of an architectural treatise. Here one can make a direct comparison with Petrarch since we have his annotations on *De architectura*: whereas the latter deal mostly with textual readings, historical cross-references and moralising comments, Alberti absorbs Vitruvius' ideas on ancient architecture but strongly criticises the author for not being intelligible (*'facilis'* was one of Alberti's consistent stylistic ideals). In addition to intelligibility, Alberti also pursued something more physical than texts, namely the precise measurements of ancient buildings and monuments, from which he could learn as much if not more than from any text (e.g. II, 4, p. 111; III, 16, p. 257). In this practical side of his character Battista is more an antiquarian than a philologist, a discoverer of antique remains rather than ancient texts.[41]

Study and analysis of texts

How did Alberti read? Anthony Grafton's fine essay on Battista's reading habits[42] redressed the imbalance conveyed by Burckhardt in his nineteenth-century picture of Alberti, which had emphasised the non-bookish side of his personality.[43] The historian showed him to be every bit as meticulous a reader as his humanist contemporaries, and correctly noted Battista's sensitivity to Latin lexis in his own works: 'It has become clear that

---

[38] Leon Battista Alberti, *On Painting*, cit., 85. 'Noi vero, i quali, se mai da altri fu scritta, abbiamo cavato quest'arte di sotterra, o se non mai fu scritta, l'abbiamo tratta di cielo'; in the Latin version he adds to the first metaphor the notion of searching and returning something from the underworld into the light: 'Nos autem qui hanc picturae artem seu ab aliis olim descriptam ab inferis repetitam in lucem restituimus, sive numquam a quoquam tractatam a superis deduximus' (emphasis mine: *OV*, III, 86–7).

[39] See Pierre De Nolhac, *Pétrarque et l'humanisme*, 2 vols. (Paris, 1907), II, 105, 240, and Lucia A. Ciapponi, 'Il *De architectura* di Vitruvio nel primo Rinascimento', *Italia Medioevale e Umanistica*, 3 (1960), 59–99.

[40] Leon Battista Alberti, *L'architettura [De re aedificatoria]*, a cura di G. Orlandi, P. Portoghesi, 2 vols. (Milan, 1966), book VI, 1 (p. 441).

[41] Roberto Weiss, *The Renaissance Discovery of Classical Antiquity* (2nd edn., Oxford, 1988).

[42] Anthony Grafton, 'Leon Battista Alberti: the writer as reader', cit.

[43] Especially Grafton, pp. 53–5.

Alberti picked his Latin words and phrases with a watchmaker's delicate precision from a wide range of sources, some of them newly discovered.'[44] But how did this process work? Alberti was clearly not as concerned with the philological restoration of texts as Petrarch, even though at an early stage of his life there is some evidence of such interests.[45] Moreover, the few classical manuscripts that have survived from Battista's library are not covered with cross-references as Petrarch's are. There are very few annotations, and the few there are initially seem rather obvious: at *De amicitia* 19–22, where Cicero notes that friendship is intimately connected with virtue, Battista notes in the margin '*laus amicitie*', and in the *Brutus* he writes in the margin '*laus oratoris*', at the point where the virtues of Licinius Crassus' oratory are being extolled (*Brutus* 143–4). These seem insignificant, but on closer examination of these highlighted passages we will see they held a particular resonance for Alberti.

The passage in praise of friendship begins with the phrase 'Let us then discuss these things in a rough and ready way (*Agamus igitur pingui ut aiunt Minerva*).' Cicero's phrase '*pingui Minerva*' (literally 'fat wisdom') meant a practical, rough and ready approach to a subject, as opposed to that of the Stoic philosophers who had been mentioned in the previous sentence (*De amicitia*, 18) as quibbling in an over-subtle ('*subtilius*', literally 'rather thin') manner. Petrarch too had noticed this phrase in that fundamental Cicero text, but predictably he viewed the practical manner as a negative method: thus in his *Invective against a Physician* (1355) he says to his opponent that he will deal with the subject in a rough and ready way, but only because that is what his opponent's crude intelligence demands.[46] For Alberti, on the other hand, the phrase epitomises his poetics, his deliberately undetailed philosophising, his 'ragionare domestico' in the vernacular dialogues, and indeed he uses Cicero's very phrase at the start of *De pictura* (*OV*, III, 10–11). There he states that he will write as a painter rather than a mathematician, since the latter deals with the measurements of things in the mind, whereas 'we, on the other hand, who wish to talk about things that are visible will express ourselves in

[44] Grafton, p. 58.

[45] See his comments about the unreliability of sources for his *Vita Sancti Potiti*, in *Opuscoli inediti di Leon Battista Alberti. 'Musca', 'Vita S. Potiti'*, ed. Cecil Grayson (Florence, 1954), pp. 86–7.

[46] 'So let us proceed "with a slow-witted Minerva", as the ancient proverb says: for that is what your slow wit requires (*Agamus itaque iuxta vetus proverbium: "Pingui Minerva"; sic enim pingue tuum poscit ingenium*)' (Petrarca, *Invectives*, cit., pp. 78–9).

cruder terms (*pinguiore Minerva*)'.[47] Throughout all his writings Alberti adopts this poetics of practical communication as opposed to writing in the highest style (hence his emphasis on communicability and his criticism of Vitruvius).

In fact, this humanist uncharacteristically valued the sheer content of many writers over and above their literary style. Hence his praise, in the first book of *De familia*, of 'scientific' writers even if they did not write the best Latin: pupils should read them for the 'sciences' they profess.[48] This also explains his cultivation of a familiar style in all his dialogues, a 'ragionare domestico', which is defined in book 2 of *De familia* as being 'without any exquisite or excessively polished way of speaking, since what we need is good advice rather than elegance of speech'.[49] He makes the same point about content in other literary works, as well as in his technical treatises.[50] In the dedicatory letter accompanying *De equo animante* (*c.*1444), he provides a lengthy list of his Greek and Latin sources, from Xenophon to Hippocrates and from Cato to scholastic authors such as Albertus Magnus, and then adds that he has also consulted some French and Tuscan writers 'who may be less noble but are useful and expert in the subject', and he also draws 'from the best medical writers the information that seemed to be relevant'.[51] Similarly at the start of book 3 of the treatise, he states that writers such as Albertus Magnus have written

---

[47] *On Painting*, cit., p. 37. The original Italian and Latin phrases were 'useremo quanto dicono piú grassa Minerva'; 'pinguiore idcirco, ut aiunt, Minerva scribendo utemur' (*OV*, III, 10–11).

[48] 'Cerchisi la lingua latina in quelli e' quali l'ebbono netta e perfettissima; negli altri togliànci l'altre scienze delle quali e' fanno professione' (*OV*, I, 71).

[49] 'ragioneremo quanto potremo aperto e domestico, senza alcuna esquisita e troppo elimata ragione di dire, perché tra noi mi pare si richiegga buone sentenze che leggiadria di parlare' (*OV*, I, 105).

[50] In the Vita it is stated that 'he [so] appreciated the exposition of a notion in any discipline that he asserted that even bad writers were worthy of praise (et in quavis re expositam historiam <tanti> faciebat, ut etiam malos scriptores dignos laude asseveraret)': see Fubini and Menci Gallorini, 'L'autobiografia', p. 77. Similarly in the Proem to book 7 of the *Intercenales*, after admitting that very few ancient writers managed to write like Cicero, he notes that 'all of them are still constantly read and appreciated', which is why he himself 'thinks highly of those who make any contribution to knowledge that delights us in whatever style it is written (tamen omnes lectitantur et in delitiis habentur. Ea de re illos ego hac etate haudquaquam esse aspernendos reor, qui aliquid in medium, qualecumque illud sit, afferant, quod quota ex parte nos delectet)': see Leon Battista Alberti, *Intercenali inedite*, p. 180.

[51] 'Hi fuere auctores, qui quidem ad manus nostras pervenere: Graeci Xenophon, Absyrtus, Chiron, Hippocrates et Pelagonius; Latini Cato, Varro, Virgilius, Plinius, Columella, Vegetius, Palladius, Calaber, Crescentius, Albertus, Abbas; Gallici praeterea, et Etrusci complurimi, ignobiles quidem, verum utiles atque experti. Quin et ex optimis medicorum ea deduxi, quae quidem ad rem ipsam facere viderentur': see Leo Baptista Alberti, *De equo animante*, edizione bilingue a cura di Antonio Videtta, con una presentazione di Charles B. Schmitt (Naples, 1991), pp. 92–4.

'learnedly and elegantly (*docte et eleganter*)' on the subject of horses' ill-nesses.[52] Petrarch would never have dealt with this subject let alone quote positively from medical authors or praise scholastic writers for having written elegantly. Even at the end of *De re aedificatoria*, he claims that the ideal architect should imitate the practice of literary scholars who do not count themselves proficient 'unless they have read and become familiar with all authors even those who are not good but who have at least writ-ten something on the discipline they profess'.[53] From the outset of his career to the end, Alberti appreciated the contribution of all writers, tech-nical and scientific as well as purely literary. All of this is in stark contrast to Petrarch who felt that even his lowest Latin prose style was far above anything that could be written either by members of the Papal Curia or by lawyers (*Familiares* 13. 5; 14.2).

The '*laus oratoris*' passage in the *Brutus* also has an abiding signifi-cance for Alberti. There Cicero is describing the rhetorical qualities of Licinius Crassus, saying that he possessed 'the maximum gravitas, but this was coupled with a rhetorical not vulgar sense of humour, full of wit and urbanity, as well as an accurate elegance in his use of Latin, and a wonder-ful way of explaining matters' ('*Erat summa gravitas, erat cum gravitate iunctus facetiarum et urbanitatis oratorius, non scurrilis lepos, Latine loquendi accurate et sine molestia diligens elegantia, in disserendo mira explicatio*', *Brutus* 143). This passage chimes with other lengthy sequences in Cicero on the crucial importance of humour and wit in oratory (*Orator* 87–90; *De oratore* 2. 216–90), passages whose significance was first appre-ciated by Alberti almost a century before Castiglione seized on their importance for the courtier. So the cult of a humorous strain in his Latin works stems as much from this Ciceronian approval of wit as from the dia-logues of Lucian. The annotations 'laus amicitie' and 'laus oratoris' may seem obvious but they point to two key elements of Battista's poetics: a communicative style, and the importance of humour.

---

[52] 'Institueram et de cura aegrotantium equorum aliquid conscribere, sed cum tam multos auc-tores, tamque optimos: Absyrtum, Chironem, Pelagonium, Catonem, Columellam, Vegetium; tum et novissimos bonos utilesque hac in re scriptores: Palladium, Calabrum, Albertum, Ruffum, Crescentium, Abbatem et eiusmodi, docte et eleganter scripsisse animadverterem, decrevi non meas esse partes in ea re operas perdere, quandoquidem neque aliter scribere atque a veteribus scriptum est, servata dignitate, neque ita scribere uti a veteribus scriptum est, furti calumnia evitata, posse me intelligam' (Alberti, *De equo animante*, cit., pp. 166–70).

[53] 'Nemo enim se satis dedisse operam litteris putabit, ni auctores omnes etiam non bonos legerit atque cognorit, qui quidem in ea facultate aliquid scripserit, quam sectentur' (*De re aedificatoria*, IX, 10; pp. 855–7).

Alberti may not have been concerned with the philological restoration of texts, but he was practically concerned with measuring other physical remains of the ancient world, and this highlights another crucial difference with Petrarch. The latter's famous 1337 letter to Giovanni Colonna describing the ruins of Rome is cited by historians as a passage that is prophetic of Gibbon's aesthetic appreciation of the ruins of Rome, and also as the moment when the continuum of history from antiquity to the middle ages is first interrupted and the difference between ancient and medieval history is first posited, as Petrarch tells his correspondent that the ruins of the city inspired their discussions on Roman history: 'And as we wandered round the broken walls of the city or sat there, the fragments of the ruins were before our eyes. What happened? We would talk a lot about history, which we seemed to divide up in this way: you seemed better in recent, and I in ancient history, and by ancient I mean whatever preceded the celebration and veneration of Christ's name by the Roman Emperor, and by modern everything from then to our own times' (*Familiares* 6.2.15–16). It is for passages such as this that historians claim that 'the Renaissance sense of history begins with Petrarch'.[54] Alberti too became deeply familiar with the ruins of Rome, but his reaction was not to meditate on the course of history but more practically to measure the ruins and then record them in such a way that scholars could produce from his *Descriptio urbis Rome* (1446–7) a map of the ancient city's walls, temples and gates. Apart from this short work, his measurement of the ancient buildings also led to the composition of his major technical treatise on architecture, *De re aedificatoria* (*c*.1452), transmitting their proportions in his treatises so they could become models for contemporary architects. Alberti, like all humanists, was interested in the recovery and analysis of ancient remains, textual or otherwise, but he consistently transmitted his findings also to those who were outside the close circle of humanist philologists.

Assimilation, imitation and originality

The third major feature of humanism we mentioned was the assimilation of classical ideas and values, which is clearly in evidence in all Alberti's works, perhaps most obviously in the ethical vernacular dialogues which

---

[54] See Peter Burke, *The Renaissance Sense of the Past* (London, 1969), p. 20.

brought classical—especially Stoic—ideas, to a new public. The other obvious area to exhibit classical ideals was in the major question of literary imitation and originality. The attitude of both Petrarch and Alberti to this key process is broadly similar. Petrarch discussed *imitatio* in three major letters (*Familiares* 1.8; 22.2; 23.19). In all of them he recognised the need to imitate classical authors and genres, but he forbade pedestrian and especially verbatim imitation of an ancient model, insisting always that the modern writer produce something distinctively his own, different yet unified, even though based on a number of sources: '*similitudo*' not '*identitas*', as he put it (*Familiares* 22.2). Closely connected with the idea of *imitatio* is the question of originality. Petrarch's notion of the distinctive element that each writer must preserve even while imitating classical models implies that the writer must retain some originality as well. The clearest articulation of this question in Petrarch is in his late letter to Boccaccio (*Seniles* 5.2, *c*.1364), where he states that since ancient writers had set matchless standards in their writing of both Latin prose and verse, there was nothing left for the modern writer to do in order to be original except to write in the new vernacular. This was one of the motives that had inspired the poet to write a major work in the *volgare* (probably the *Trionfi*);[55] but he abandoned the project when he realised how his vernacular works would be subject to distortion in the mouths of the ignorant public. The letter then goes on to denounce the age in which he lives as hopelessly inferior to antiquity in every respect, from literary culture to military and political matters: Petrarch's attack on the present age finds many parallels in his work, but it is only in this late text that he saw resorting to the vernacular as a way out of the impasse of writing something original when classical writers had said everything, and even then he does so only to dismiss the idea, stating that he then went back to writing in Latin.

In Alberti, however, the motif of originality is sounded time and time again, usually with a very different perspective on the modern age. It is first heard in his early treatise *De commodis* (*c*.1430). In the introduction, the young author complains that he cannot think of writing anything that

---

[55] See Francesco Petrarca, *Senile V 2*, ed. Monica Berté (Florence, 1998), p. 79: 'totum huic vulgari studio tempus dare, quod uterque stilus altior latinus eo usque priscis ingeniis cultus esset ut pene iam nichil nostra ope vel cuiuslibet addi posset, at hic, modo inventus, adhuc recens, vastatoribus crebris ac raro squalidus colono, magni se vel ornamenti capacem ostenderet vel augmenti. Quid vis? Hac spe tractus simulque stimulis actus adolescentie magnum eo in genere opus inceperam [. . .].' For the various interpretations of which 'magnum opus' Petrarch is referring to, see ibid., p. 17.

has not already been covered by classical authors, both in serious and comic genres, so posterity is left only with the option of reading and admiring the ancient writers.[56] His older humanist contemporaries had already seized the few areas not dealt with in classical texts, and had written historical works and dealt with the behaviour of princes:[57] Alberti was probably thinking here of Petrarch's and Bruni's historical works as well as the former's letter-treatise on the ideal prince written in 1373 (*Seniles* 14.1). So he and other young writers could only try to compose something new and original ('*Nos vero iuniores modo aliquid novi proferamus*'), without concern for the harsh criticism of those humanists who only want 'passively to learn and not to write'.[58] This pursuit of originality at all costs recurs throughout many other works such as *De pictura* (at strategic points in both the Latin and vernacular versions),[59] the *De equo animante*,[60] in *Profugiorum ab erumna libri*,[61] and in *Momus*.[62] It is worth returning to

---

[56] *De commodis litterarum atque incommodis*, ed. Laura Goggi Carotti (Florence, 1976), p. 39: 'Ita et seria omnia et iocosa veteres ipsi complexi sunt. Nobis tantum legendi atque admirandi sui facultatem et necessitatem dimiserunt.'

[57] *De commodis*, p. 41: 'Condant illi quidem historiam, tractent mores principum ac gesta rerum publicarum eventusque bellorum.'

[58] *De commodis*, p. 41: 'Nos vero iuniores modo aliquid novi proferamus, non vereamur severissima [. . .] iudicia illorum, qui cum ipsi infantes et elingues sint, tantum aures ad cognoscendum nimium delitiosas porrigunt.' Alberti probably had in mind humanists such as Niccolò Niccoli, who had the finest humanist library of the time but notoriously never wrote anything.

[59] The Latin dedication to Giovan Francesco Gonzaga mentions the work's originality ('rei novitate') as making it suitable for princely ears (*OV*, III, 9). But the the work's novelty is insisted on at strategic points throughout, at the beginning and end of book I: 'in questa certo difficile e da niuno altro che io sappi descritta matera'; 'in hac plane difficile e a nemine quod viderim alio tradita litteris materia' (III, 10–11); 'novità della matera'; 'ob materiae novitatem' (III, 40–1); at the beginning and end of book II: 'poi che non come Plinio recitiamo storie, ma di nuovo fabrichiamo un'arte di pittura, della quale in questa età, quale io vegga, nulla si truova scritto'; 'quando quidem non historiam picturae ut Plinius, sed artem novissime recenseamus, de qua hac aetate nulla scriptorium veterum monumenta quae ipse viderim extant' (III, 46–7); 'Noi vero, i quali, se mai da altri fu scritta, abbiamo cavato questa'arte di sotterra, o se non mai fu scritta, l'abbiamo tratta di cielo'; 'Nos autem qui hanc picturae artem seu ab aliis olim descriptam ab inferis repetitam in lucem restituimus, sive numquam a quoquam tractatam a superis deduximus' (III, 86–7); and at the end of book III: 'Noi però ci reputeremo a voluttà primi aver presa questa palma d'avere ardito commendare alle lettere questa arte sottilissima e nobilissima'; 'Nos tamen hanc palmam praeripuisse ad voluptatem ducimus, quandoquidem primi fuerimus qui hanc artem subtilissimam litteris mandaverimus' (III, 106–7).

[60] 'It seemed appropriate at this point to expound some advice which is very apt and useful for the care of horses and which has never been written down by the ancients themselves (Nonnullas tamen commonefactiones, quae sint ad equorum curam accomodatae atque utilissimae, ab ipsis veteribus non perscriptas hoc loco exposuisse condecet)': Alberti, *De equo animante*, p. 170.

[61] *OV*, II, 161.

[62] Leon Battista Alberti, *Momus*, trans. Sarah Knight, Latin text ed. Virginia Brown, Sarah Knight (Cambridge, MA, 2003), pp. 2–4.

one well-known passage in order to highlight crucial differences between Alberti's humanism and Petrarch's.

The famous prologue to the vernacular version of *Della pittura*, dedicated to Filippo Brunelleschi, architect of the recently built dome of Florence Cathedral, begins with a humanist lament on the decline of those arts and sciences that had been cultivated in antiquity.[63] This opening sequence could have been penned by Petrarch himself:

> I used both to marvel and regret that so many excellent and divine arts and sciences, which we know from their works and from historical accounts were possessed in great abundance by the talented men of antiquity, have now disappeared and are almost entirely lost. Painters, sculptors, architects, musicians, geometers, rhetoricians, augurs and suchlike distinguished and remarkable intellects, are very rarely to be found these days, and are of little merit. Consequently I believed what I heard many say that Nature, mistress of all things, had grown old and weary, and was no longer producing intellects any more than giants on a vast and wonderful scale such as she did in what one might call her youthful and glorious days.[64]

Indeed Alberti's use of the topos of the world grown old, which derived ultimately from either Columella (*De re rustica*, 1 Pref. 2) or the younger Pliny (*Epistles* 6. 21), may suggest he had Petrarch himself in mind since in his *Invective Against a Physician* (1355) the earlier humanist had denounced the contemporary age as having almost no men of genius ('*raros ingeniosos*') compared with antiquity, and this may have been caused by the fact that 'the world has grown old and totters towards its end; sluggish and cold, like an aging person, it slows in its activity'.[65]

The opening of Alberti's dedicatory letter to Brunelleschi is also typically humanist in another way, in that once more it shows how Battista exploited the classical texts he read when he came to write. I have argued elsewhere that the strange presence of augurs in this list of great arts in decline was not due either to the fact that augury was considered a liberal art like rhetoric, or because architects and engineers were modern versions of augurs, who in their role as military advisers had to use astrology to work out when was the best time to attack the enemy.[66]

---

[63] On the idea that the dedicatory letter was written to coincide with the inauguration of the new dome on 17 July 1436, see Lucia Bertolini, 'Nouvelles perspectives sur le *De pictura* et sa réception', in Françoise Choay, Michel Paoli (eds.), *Alberti, humaniste, architecte* (Paris, 2006), pp. 33–45 (34).

[64] Alberti, *OV*, III, 7; Alberti, *On Painting*, cit., p. 34.

[65] Francesco Petrarca, *Invectives*, cit., p. 59.

[66] See Martin McLaughlin, 'Alberti e le opere retoriche di Cicerone', cit., pp. 199–200. Amongst earlier interpretations, Christine Smith argued that the augurs were included along with the

Instead their presence seems to stem from Alberti's deep reading of key Ciceronian texts we know he possessed such as the *Brutus*, the *De amicitia* and the *De senectute*. For a start the fact that augurs are mentioned in this list immediately after rhetoricians suggests a link between the two categories, and this is confirmed by many texts. Cicero's *Brutus* itself begins with the death of Hortensius, the great augur and orator, 'I grieved that the standing of our college [of augurs] had been diminished by the death of such an augur'; and throughout the rest of the dialogue there are several other mentions of great rhetoricians who had been augurs as well, so the link between the augurs' college and rhetoric is well established in this text alone.[67] The opening words of *De amicitia* give similar prominence to an augur: 'Q. Mucius the augur used to tell many memorable and pleasant anecdotes about his father-in-law C. Laelius' (*De amicitia*, 1.1), while in the *De senectute* Cato the Elder praises the rhetorical skills in the augur Q. Fabius Maximus' funeral oration for his son (*De senectute* 12). Here it is worth adding that in the final Cicero text that we know Alberti possessed, the *De legibus*, there is further discussion of augurs. In book 2 Cicero points out that the augurs' capacity to foretell the future was no longer their prime function since already in his time this art had clearly declined through old age and neglect ('et vetustate et neglegentia', *De legibus*, 2. 33). So Alberti's lament for the death of augury in its literal sense of divining was nothing new; but in these fundamental texts, for all of which Alberti possessed his own copy, [68] augurs are consistently linked with orators and lawyers as well with state religion; the augurs' college produced some of the best orators of ancient Rome, Cicero and Hortensius among them, and it is for their link with rhetoricians rather

---

musicians, geometers, and rhetoricians as 'representatives of the liberal arts': see Christine Smith, 'Originality and cultural progress in the Quattrocento: Brunelleschi's dome and a letter by Alberti', *Rinascimento*, 28 (1988), 291–318 (here 292–3); and Grafton claimed that 'engineers, in short, were augurs as well as mathematicians and artists' (*Leon Battista Alberti. Master Builder of the Italian Renaissance*, p. 80).

[67] Mentions of other augurs are in *Brutus* 101 (C. Fannius), 102 (Mucius), 117 (Tubero), 212 (Scaevola, an expert in law), 267 (Appius Claudius, also expert in law).

[68] For his MS containing *De senectute*, *De amicitia*, and *Paradoxa Stoicorum*, Marciana Lat. VI. 205 (386), see Francesca Mazzanti, 'Scheda 61', in *Leon Battista Alberti. La biblioteca di un umanista*, cit., pp. 402–3; for the MS of *De legibus*, Florence Biblioteca Nazionale Centrale, Conv. Soppress. I. 9. 3, see Maria Luisa Tanganelli, 'Scheda 60', *Leon Battista Alberti. La biblioteca di un umanista*, cit., p. 396. See also the wide-ranging article by Cardini, which picks up other echoes of the Cicero text in Alberti: Roberto Cardini, 'Biografia, leggi, e astrologia in un nuovo reperto albertiano', in *Leon Battista Alberti umanista e scrittore. Filologia, esegesi, tradizione*, pp. 21–189 (esp. pp. 28–100).

than their capacity to predict the future that Alberti includes them in this famous list.

Returning to the prologue, if its opening gambit shows Alberti the humanist repeating a Petrarchan lament for the past, and recycling concepts from his reading of Cicero, in what he says next he differs totally from Petrarch: his first contact with Florence after the family's exile makes him realise that the arts practised by Brunelleschi, Donatello, Ghiberti, Masaccio and Luca della Robbia are such that these men 'are in no way inferior to any of the ancients'. In fact, he states that this superiority is as much due to such men's industry and diligence as to Nature or the age they live in, and concludes this section by proclaiming the artistic superiority of the present age over antiquity: since in the past there were plenty of models for the ancients to learn from, therefore 'it follows that our fame should be all the greater if without preceptors and without any model to imitate we discover arts and sciences hitherto unheard of and unseen'.[69] Alberti is interested in the arts *and* sciences, as he says here, and for him Brunelleschi's dome even outdoes the achievements of ancient architecture, a concept unthinkable in Petrarch and other humanists. And that this sense of modern superiority is not simply a rhetorical topos appropriate to introductory letters or prologues is confirmed by the fact that in the treatise itself he states that ancient painting and sculpture show no grasp of perspective (*OV*, III, 40–1), while throughout the *De re aedificatoria* Vitruvius is regularly criticised.[70]

The literary public

One of the major consequences of their different attitudes to Latin and the vernacular was that Petrarch and Alberti held highly differing views on the literary public that the intellectual should be writing for. It is well known that Petrarch despised what he called the 'vulgus', and felt that the serious writer should only be writing for an intellectual elite, the small minority that could read Latin. Both in his late letter to Boccaccio

---

[69] Alberti, *OV*, III, 7; Alberti, *On Painting*, pp. 34–5.

[70] At the end of Book 9 Alberti rejects the idea expressed at the beginning of Vitruvius that the architect must have studied all other disciplines: literature, draughtsmanship, geometry, history, philosophy, music, medicine, jurisprudence, and astrology (Vitruvius, *De architectura*, 1.1.3); instead, for Alberti, the architect must only know those subjects that are linked in some way with architecture, for example painting and mathematics, but not law, astronomy, music and rhetoric (IX, 10; p. 861).

(*Seniles* 5.2) and in his Letter to Posterity he proclaimed that he only wrote vernacular trifles in his youth, but changed to serious works in Latin once he reached maturity. However, it is also well documented that despite many official pronouncements to this effect, the great humanist continued to revise his vernacular poetry, both the lyric poems of the *Canzoniere* and the epic vision-poem, the *Trionfi*, to within months of his death at the age of 70.[71] Nevertheless, what influenced his disciples was not the reality of his revising his vernacular poems until very late on in life, but rather his official pronouncements on the subject. So powerful was Petrarch's message about the inferior status of the *volgare* that his example rerouted the path of the Italian vernacular for about a century: after Petrarch's death in 1374 serious vernacular poetry went underground as Italian writers opted to perfect Latin not the *volgare*, and it was only in the 1470s, in the age of Lorenzo de' Medici, that vernacular poetry starts to revive. One passage in particular is representative of all such statements. In a letter to the friend whom he called Socrates, Petrarch states categorically:

> I prefer to be understood and appreciated by the few rather than be understood by everyone and appreciated by nobody. For the learned are always few in number and in our day very few. [. . .] As long therefore as they remain few in number I do not mind being judged by them; but the judgment of the many, that is of the ordinary people ('*vulgus*'), has always been of such little importance to me that I prefer not to be understood by them than to be praised by them.[72]

By contrast, Alberti composed many works in the vernacular, and the early part of his life saw him mount a series of campaigns on behalf of the new language. Not only did he write the first serious moral dialogues in the *volgare*, but he also inaugurated, as we saw, a series of other genres in the language. In addition to this practical demonstration of his cult of the vernacular, he wrote a Grammar of Tuscan, to show that it was every bit as 'regular' a language as Latin, and in the wake of the famous humanist language debate of 1435, he argued correctly that the language spoken in antiquity was just one language, Latin, and that the vernacular did not exist in Roman times but came into existence only after the barbarian invasions. It was thanks to his reading of Cicero's *Brutus* that he was able to see that Latin too had once been a new language, it had a

---

[71] Francesco Petrarca, *Trionfi, Rime estravaganti, Codice degli abbozzi*, ed. Vinicio Pacca, Laura Paolino (Milan, 1996), p. 889.
[72] *Familiares*, 14.2.6–7. Petrarch's 'Socrates' was Ludwig van Kempen, a Flemish chanter whom he met in Avignon.

diachronic development, and only reached its peak in the time of Cicero and Virgil thanks to the fact that so many writers wrote in the language. In the same way, he argued, the new Tuscan language would only be able to acquire the dignity of Latin if intellectuals are willing to write in it. This is the point he makes in the Proem to the third book of *De familia*, probably written around 1437, in words that seem to echo and rebut Petrarch's position in *Familiares* 14.2:

> But perhaps the prudent will rather praise me if I, by writing in such a way as to be understood by everyone, aim first at benefiting the many instead of pleasing the few, for you know how few are those who know Latin these days. [. . .] And if I do not shy away from being both understood and judged by all our citizens, then let those who blame me either put aside their envy or find some more useful subject matter in which to show how eloquent they are.[73]

This view of the literary public and the promotion of the new language are unthinkable in Petrarch. Battista's campaign on behalf of the vernacular continued a few years later, in 1441, when he organised the Certame Coronario, or Crown Contest, a literary competition for a vernacular poem on 'amicitia', sponsored by Piero de' Medici, with major humanists such as Leonardo Bruni on the jury. Both the original idea and Alberti's protest when the humanist judges failed to award the prize stemmed from his understanding of the development of Latin literature, an understanding acquired through a reading of Quintilian and Cicero's *Brutus*.[74]

No doubt Alberti's more practical pursuits also made him appreciate, in a way that Petrarch could never do, those who were not intellectuals. This emerges particularly in their attitudes to art. Petrarch famously claimed in his will that the beauty of Giotto's painting of the Virgin, which he possessed, was a source of amazement to the experts but could not be appreciated by the ignorant.[75] On this subject Alberti's views were completely opposed: he believed that it was precisely in painting, and the

---

[73] 'Più tosto forse e' prudenti mi loderanno s'io, scrivendo in modo che ciascuno m'intenda, prima cerco giovare a molti che piacere a pochi, ché sai quanto siano pochissimi a questi dí e' literati. [. . .] E se io non fuggo essere come inteso così giudicato da tutti e' nostri cittadini, piaccia quando che sia a chi mi biasima o deponer l'invidia, o pigliar più utile materia in qual sé demonstrino eloquenti' (Alberti, *De familia*, III, Proemio, *OV*, I, 155–6).

[74] For the echoes of Quintilian, see McLaughlin, 'Alberti e le opere retoriche di Cicerone', cit., pp. 191–2.

[75] '[T]abulam meam sive iconam beate Virginis Marie, operam Iotti pictoris egregii, [. . .] cuius pulchritudinem ignorantes non intelligunt, magistri autem artis stupent' ('my panel or icon of the blessed Virgin Mary, a work of the eminent painter Giotto [. . .]. The ignorant do not understand the beauty of this panel but the masters of the art are stunned by it'). See *Petrarch's Testament*, ed. and trans. Theodore E. Mommsen (Ithaca, NY, 1957), pp. 78–81.

fine arts in general, that the views of the masses and those of intellectuals coincided, another idea gleaned from a major passage in Cicero's *Brutus* (183–200) which had made the same point about oratory, and it is reiterated on several occasions in the treatise on painting (three times in book 2. 28).

All this suggests that the paragraph in his autobiography about meeting and questioning artisans, despite it being partly a literary topos modelled on Socrates' behaviour, also reflects what Alberti believed:

> He would enquire of artisans, architects, ship-builders and even from shoemakers and tailors, whether there was perhaps some technique in their craft which was unusual and recherché and which they carefully preserved as something peculiar to their art [. . .].[76]

Such a statement is impossible in Petrarch. Indeed it seems that the categories specified here—artisans, architects, ship-builders, shoemakers and tailors—are precisely those attacked by his great predecessor in his late letters and invectives, as well as by other humanists of Alberti's generation.[77] In book 2 of *De familia* he even lists as the first examples of those who work with their intellect architects, shipbuilders and doctors ('argonauta, architetto, medico e simili, da' quali in prima si richiede giudicio e opera d'animo', *OV*, I, 145), occupations that would never have been so classified by Petrarch. This was all part of Alberti's wider revolution of status which elevated painting, sculpture and architecture from mechanical to liberal arts.[78] In the general humanist context of contempt for manual work, Battista's open esteem for artisans, cobblers and tailors seems to acquire a new significance. Clearly he is going against the humanist grain in showing interest in these tradesmen's arts, and yet there are classical justifications for such a stance. Just as his defence of the *volgare* was carried out in humanist terms, by writing a grammar of the language, as Priscian had done for the Latin language, and also by organising the 1441 literary competition, as had happened in antiquity to promote Latin literature, so here his positive appreciation of shoemakers once more stems also from his reading of ancient texts.

---

[76] Fubini and Menci-Gallorini, 'L'autobiografia', p. 72.

[77] Martin McLaughlin, 'Literature and Science in Leon Battista Alberti's De re aedificatoria', in P. Antonello and S. Gilson (eds.), *Literature and Science in Italian Culture from Dante to Calvino. A Festschrift for Patrick Boyde* (Oxford, 2004), pp. 94–114 (esp. pp. 104–5).

[78] See Jean-Marc Mandosio, 'La classification des sciences et des arts chez Alberti', *Leon Battista Alberti: Actes du congrès international de Paris (10–15 avril 1995)*, ed. Francesco Furlan *et al.*, II, 643–704.

There were two specific classical traditions associated with cobblers. The first of these is the well-known anecdote about the Greek painter Apelles who was fond of hiding behind his paintings to hear any criticisms made by the people. One painting was criticised by a passing cobbler, because on the subject's sandals Apelles had painted one loop fewer than there should be (Pliny, *Natural History*, 35.85); Apelles immediately altered the sandal, but the next day the same cobbler was so pleased to see that the great painter had adjusted this fault in the light of his criticism, that he began to criticise the leg in the painting: it was at that point that Apelles leapt out from behind the painting to warn the cobbler to stick to criticising sandals. Now this anecdote clearly has two stages, one in which the shoemaker's views triumph as they are taken into account by the artist; but in the sequel, when the cobbler criticises things outside his expertise, his opinion is rejected, giving rise to the proverb, 'Cobbler, stick to thy last.' Both Petrarch and Alberti cite the anecdote, but the difference is that Petrarch, in his *Invective against a Physician*, predictably dwells on the second episode, when he urges his opponent to stick to medicine and remember what Apelles said to the cobbler who was stepping outside his area of expertise.[79] Alberti, on the other hand, cites approvingly only the first part of the anecdote in his final piece of advice at the end of *Della pittura*, urging the painter to listen to criticism from friends, chance spectators and the public in general.[80]

The other ancient discipline that enhanced the status of shoemakers was philosophy. Plato wrote many philosophical dialogues where Socrates pretends to be ignorant and asks craftsmen about their skills, as well as using analogies from the practices of artisans in his arguments. That Alberti was aware of this Socratic tradition is confirmed by the fact that the final sentences of this paragraph from his autobiography, which are not quoted by Burckhardt, show a clear attempt by the author to portray himself as a second Socrates: 'and he immediately communicated these same things [artisans' skills] to his eager fellow citizens. He pretended he was ignorant in many matters so that he could question the genius, character and expertise of other people' (*Vita*, p. 72). This portrayal of a

---

[79] 'Prosequere igitur ludum tuum; ita, tamen, ut deinceps ethicam non molestes, sed memineris quid sutori terminos suos excedenti respondit pictorum famosissimus Apelles' (in Francesco Petrarca, *Invectives*, cit., p. 126).

[80] See Alberti, *On Painting* (III, 62), cit., p. 95; (*OV*, III, 104–6). On Alberti's openness to collaboration with others in all his works, see Anthony Grafton, 'Un passe-partout ai segreti di una vita: Alberti e la scrittura cifrata', in *La vita e il mondo di Leon Battista Alberti*, cit., I, 3–21 (13–15).

Socratic philosopher amongst craftsmen also derived from the *Lives of the Philosophers*, Diogenes Laertius' series of biographies of the great philosophers (one of which was actually the life of a philosophical cobbler, *The Life of Simon*). That Alberti knew these two classical traditions regarding shoemakers, the Apellean and the Socratic, is clear from the many references to Apelles in his aesthetic treatises, and in the allusions to Socrates conversing with shoemakers in *Momus*.[81]

In the century that elapsed between Petrarch's world and Alberti's many things had changed under the sun, even inside the humanist movement itself. One of these major shifts was the knowledge of Greek. Battista goes to meet artisans not just because he has a more open outlook, but also because the ancient texts he read, both Greek and Latin, taught him the value of listening to the opinions of such men. He portrays himself, then, not only as someone who is inquisitive about other arts, from architecture to shoemaking, but also as someone who is steeped in classical lore about the model artist and model philosopher.

Quid tum?

One final demonstration of the importance of studying the texts Alberti himself read relates to one of the most enduring enigmas surrounding him: the meaning of his emblem, the winged eye, and its motto '*Quid tum?*' The image of the eye with wings appears on its own next to Alberti's head in the so-called self-portrait, the bronze plaquette in Washington, dating from around 1435 (Fig. 1). The eye is found encircled by a laurel wreath, possibly in the author's own hand, on an MS containing *De pictura* in the vernacular (BNC, Florence, II. IV. 38, f.119v), as well as on the reverse of the medal containing the portrait of Alberti by Matteo de' Pasti, dated to 1453–5 (Figs. 2 and 3).[82] There have been many suggestions regarding the meaning of the emblem and its motto. Edgar Wind suggested that the eye expressed the *terribilità* of the divine eye, and that the combination of eye and wings hinted at a common point of reference in the eagle, which famously could stare directly into the sun. For Wind, the emblem thus signified 'the union of supreme insight and supreme

---

[81] Alberti, *Momus*, cit., pp. 252–4.
[82] For illustrations of these items see Alberto G. Cassani, '*Explicanda sunt mysteria*: l'enigma albertiano dell'occhio alato', in *Leon Battista Alberti: Actes du Congrès International de Paris*, I, 245–304 (256–7).

Figure 1.   Alberti, *Self-portrait*, *c*.1435, bronze, 201 × 136 mm; Samuel H. Kress Collection,
National Gallery of Art, Washington.

power', evoking the ubiquity of the omniscient God.[83] As for '*Quid tum?*',
even though Cicero simply used the phrase as an expression of rhetorical
suspense, Wind interpreted the motto as having a fearful, eschatological
meaning, since the phrase referred, he thought, to the approach of the

[83] Edgar Wind, 'The Concealed God', in *Pagan Mysteries in the Renaissance* (rev. edn.;
Harmondsworth, 1967), pp. 218–35 (232).

Figure 2. Matteo de' Pasti, *Medal of Leo Baptista Albertus*, obverse, c.1453–5, bronze; Paris, Bibliothèque Nationale, Méd. ital. 580.

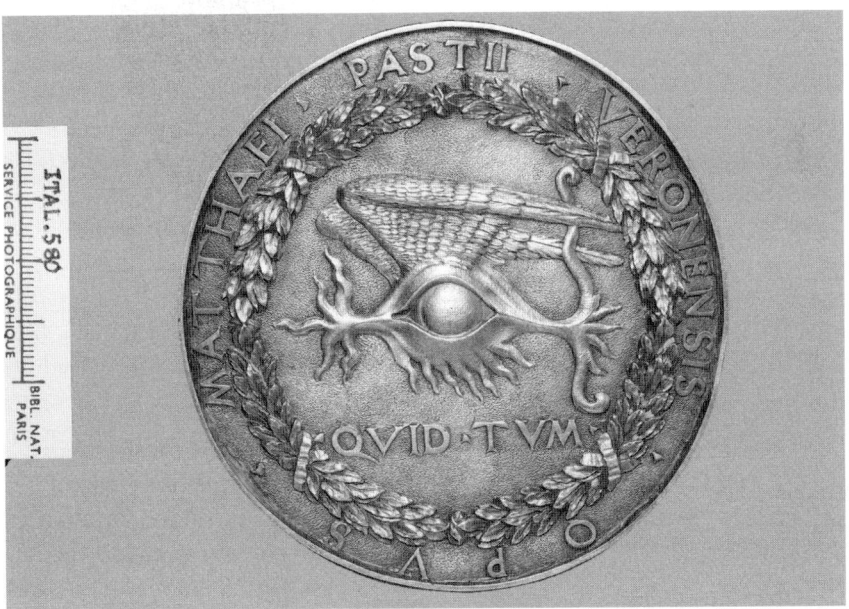

Figure 3. Matteo de' Pasti, *Medal of Leo Baptista Albertus*, reverse, c.1453–5, bronze; Paris, Bibliothèque Nationale, Méd. ital. 580.

God and thus 'the classical phrase of expectation expands into a threatening sense of the *Dies Irae*' (p. 233).

A full survey of interpretations was recently provided by Alberto Cassani. Cassani sees the eye here as symbolising both the human and the divine eye, and notes the author's penchant for riddles, brief enigmatic sayings and hidden codes (including the *De componendis cyfris*); in fact in the architecture treatise Alberti states that the eye in Egyptian hieroglyphs symbolised the deity (*De re* VIII. 4, p. 697). As for the motto, '*Quid tum?*', Cassani suggests that this simple question, exemplifying Alberti's favourite device of *brevitas* but still full of mystery, might stand for the ultimate question, 'What then does it mean to live?' Indeed the fact that the phrase was also much used by Plautus and Terence suggests that the question can be ironic or ridiculous as well as serious. David Marsh has shown that Alberti had read and imitated Lucian's dialogues in several of the *Intercenales*;[84] and Cassani, like Marsh, does not exclude a Lucianic source either, since in Lucian's *Icaromenippus* the protagonist Menippus cuts off the right wing of an eagle and the left wing of a vulture for his flight up to heaven, thus becoming Icaromenippus.[85] From there he looks down on the cosmos, flapping the eagle's wing in order to sharpen his eye-sight to see the earth. At a certain point Menippus says, 'What is it then?'—a Greek phrase equivalent to '*Quid tum?*'—enquiring about the link between a wing and an eye, and he is told that the link is the eagle which can gaze into the sun. Thus the eye and the wing give 'regal', almost 'divine' sight to Menippus, and Cassani concludes 'L'emblema di Battista sembra trovare in questo passo di Luciano la sua fonte letteraria piú evidente.'[86]

However, restricting ourselves to a consideration of the verbal motto, the link posited by Wind between Cicero's phrase '*Quid tum?*' and escha-tology is quite tenuous and it is possible that another more relevant inter-pretation might come, once more, from examining the classical context in which the rhetorical interjection is originally used. It is much used by Plautus and Terence, as Cassani showed, and it may well be that Alberti simply derived it from these favourite comic texts of his to suggest an ironic 'What does it matter?' approach.[87] However, another more obvious

---

[84] David Marsh, *Lucian and the Latins. Humor and Humanism in the Early Italian Renaissance* (Ann Arbor, MI, 1998), pp. 83–92.

[85] Cassani, '*Explicanda sunt mysteria*', p. 275.

[86] Cassani, '*Explicanda sunt mysteria*', pp. 276–7.

[87] See, for instance, Plautus, *Asinaria*, 335, 346, 350; *Curculio*, 726; *Poenulus*, 730; Terence, *Heautontimoroumenos*, 602, 605, 718, 801, 847; *Eunuchus*, 339, 370, 604, 637, 793 etc.; though

source that we know Alberti read might once more offer a clue, namely Cicero's *Tusculan Disputations*. Recent studies by Lucia Bertolini and others have shown how Alberti drew on this dialogue on several occasions in his works.[88] Now in the *Tusculans* '*Quid tum?*' occurs just twice. On the first occasion, the phrase seems a genuine question: when the unnamed protagonist asks 'Do you see that I have plenty of leisure?' the interlocutor replies 'And so? (*Quid tum*)?'; at which the protagonist explains that in his leisure he translated many Greek poets for use in his speeches (*Tusculans*, 2. 26).

But it is the second occurrence of the phrase which may offer us a more relevant clue to its significance for Alberti. Towards the end of the last book the protagonist is discussing the self-sufficiency of virtue, a theme close to Battista's heart. Talking of the fickleness of popular acclaim, he says it is natural for many peoples to hate those with superior virtue, hence Aristides was actually banished for being too just (*Tusculans*, 5. 105), and this example leads into a discussion of exile and how the wise man can rise above it, especially as in exile he can have the leisure to read and write literature. The principal speaker observes that although exile is considered the greatest evil because it separates us from our country (5. 106), yet the various provinces are full of men in exile who never return home. At this point the interlocutor objects: 'But exiles are deprived of their possessions ("*At multantur bonis exules*"),' and that is when the protagonist replies '"*Quid tum?*"' (So what?), and he goes on: 'Have we not said a lot already about how to put up with poverty? In fact if we inquire into the real nature of exile, not the ignominy of its name, how different is it in the end from perpetual wandering? The noblest philosophers have lived like this' (5.107). Here he names men such as Aristotle, Chrysippus and others (many of whom are cited in Alberti's works). Thus exile is not incompatible with the virtuous life. The importance of this passage cannot be overestimated, dealing as it does with exile, one of the major factors that conditioned Battista's life. And although Alberti returned to his native city once the exile ban was lifted, the condition of the intellectual exile continues to

---

Gorni derives it from Virgil's *Eclogues* 10.38–9: 'Quid tum si fuscus Amyntas? | Et nigrae violae sunt et vaccinia nigra': Guglielmo Gorni, 'Storia del Certame Coronario', *Rinascimento*, 12 (1972), 135–81 (139–40, n. 2).

[88] See Lucia Bertolini, *Grecus sapor. Tramiti di presenze greche in Leon Battista Alberti* (Rome, 1998), p. 107, for a list of passages; the *Profugiorum ab erumna libri* were also inspired by Cicero's *Tusculan Disputations*, according to Luca Boschetto, *Leon Battista Aberti e Firenze*, p. 139. See now also Roberto Cardini, *Ortografia e consolazione in un* corpus *allestito da L. B. Alberti. Il codice Moreni 2 della Biblioteca Moreniana de Firenze* (Florence, 2008), pp. LXVII–LXVIII.

haunt the autobiographical characters also of later works such as
Theogenius (*c*.1440) and *Profugiorum* (1441–2). The phrase '*Quid tum?*'
signals the moment in Cicero's discussion when the wise man copes with
the worst evil that can befall him, banishment and loss of belongings, so
the phrase is a shorthand cipher for Alberti's Stoic capacity to rise above
his earthly problems.

Remarkably the section immediately following this passage in Cicero
deals with the eyes. The discussion considers the question whether the
man without sight can be happy: the protagonist argues that unlike the
other senses, pleasure does not reside in the eye itself, as it does with taste,
smell and touch, but in what the soul perceives through sight: 'It is the
soul which receives the objects we see. [. . .] And the thought of the wise
man rarely calls on the eyes for his investigations.' (*Tusculans*, 5. 111). The
fact is that the soul can experience pleasure in many ways without the use
of sight (we remember that the soul was often symbolised by wings, from
Plato's *Phaedrus* onwards, a work Alberti knew well), for the wise man life
involves thinking, and he does not need his physical eyes to carry out
investigations. In this one section, then, at the conclusion of a major
Ciceronian dialogue, and one we know Alberti read, we find the phrase
'*Quid tum?*' signalling a rising above the misfortune of exile and leading
into a discussion about the superiority of mental insight over physical
eyesight. Here, surely, we find at least another likely source and interpretation of Alberti's enigmatic emblem of the winged eye and its motto.[89]

Conclusion

And so (*Quid tum?*)? One point that emerges from all this is that although
Alberti is steeped in ancient texts every bit as much as Petrarch, he inaug-
urates a real change in the direction of humanism. We see him beginning
with traditional humanist genres such as a Latin comedy, a treatise/invec-

---

[89] Luca Boschetto, 'Tra biografia e autobiografia. Le prospettive e i problemi della ricerca
intorno alla vita di L. B. Alberti', *La vita e il mondo di Leon Battista Alberti*, cit., I, 85–116, suggests as another possible source a Seneca passage which uses the phrase 'Quid enim?' as a Stoic
equivalent of 'Quid tum?': Seneca, *De constantia sapientis* (*Dialogi*, 2.1.1–2). For Alberti's
approval of similar brief maxims in temples, see *De re aedificatoria*: 'In temple walls and floors
I want nothing that does not smack of pure philosophy. [. . .] It is right to place there those bits
of advice which make us more just, modest and frugal, more adorned with virtue and pleasing
to the gods above, for instance "be such as you would wish to appear"; "love and be loved"; and
so on' (VII, 10; p. 611).

tive, an early biography, but then comes the revolutionary idea of writing an ethical dialogue in the vernacular, quickly followed by the composition of the first technical treatise in the *volgare, De pictura*. Two other changes of direction come in his Latin works: first he systematically cultivates a humorous strain in works from the early *Intercenales* through the *Apologi* and the mock encomia (*Canis, Musca*) of the 1430s to the major novel *Momus*; secondly after 1443, probably after his departure from Florence, he becomes more interested in technical treatises, mostly short pieces apart from the major treatise on architecture. These shifts towards the vernacular, the humorous and the technical all stem from Alberti himself, and represent an inflection of humanism that would have been unthinkable in Petrarch, but what inspired Battista to do so? To take the first element, his interest in Tuscan began with his return to his ancestors' city of Florence in 1434, became sharpened by the humanist polemic of 1435 about whether a vernacular existed in ancient Rome, and culminated in the many writings and initiatives he undertook to promote the language. If Cicero's *Pro Archia* had inspired Petrarch to inaugurate the humanist movement, it was the new text of Alberti's age, Cicero's *Brutus*, that taught him that even Latin had started from humble beginnings and that the vernacular could therefore develop in the same way: the idea of gradual artistic progress was fundamental to Alberti, and it meant he could champion the vernacular on humanist grounds without having to invoke Dante, Petrarch and Boccaccio, whom he never names.

As for the humorous emphasis, this surfaced already in his early comedy, and was enhanced by his reading of Cicero's rhetorical works, as well as by his interest in Greek literature, in particular the reading of Aesop and Lucian, the latter's influence being particularly strong even in the late work *Momus*.

Thirdly, the contact with Florence, as Grayson suggested long ago, the city of Brunelleschi, Donatello, Masaccio and Ghiberti, also stimulated his interest in the arts and led first to the treatise on painting and later to those on sculpture and architecture. There appears to be a logic also in the other technical works: *De pictura* made him think about the component parts of the art, just as the work on Tuscan grammar broke the language down into its basic elements, and this procedure holds true for the other treatises, as he analyses the constituent parts of painting, grammar, horses, city measurements, mathematical problems, sculpture, architecture and ciphers.

At first sight the *De re aedificatoria* appears to be Alberti's swansong to the written word, as the theoretical treatise gives way in the 1450s to two decades of architectural work: his designs for S. Francesco in Rimini, then the Rucellai commissions in Florence, followed by the works carried out for the Gonzaga in Mantua. Yet two of his late literary works show that he never abandoned literature: the treatise on ciphers illustrated his fascination with letters which was already evident in the *Vita*, in the vernacular grammar, and in the inscriptions on his facades; and his final Tuscan dialogue on leadership, *De iciarchia* (1468), marked a return to the genre which he had himself inaugurated, the vernacular dialogue, and to a topic which brought him back full circle to his first dialogue on the family. The only difference is that by now, in the late 1460s, Battista Alberti the outsider, the illegitimate son of Lorenzo di Benedetto, was a major name in the city both in literary and architectural terms, and owned a share of the family palazzo in Florence that had belonged to his grandfather Benedetto Alberti.

Of course, Alberti was never as influential as Petrarch: there was no movement called Albertism to match Petrarchism. But in many ways he was ahead of his time, and his influence, though less immediate and widespread, did make an impact. He refounded Italian prose as a vehicle for dealing with serious ethical subjects, and this would be taken up later by Lorenzo de' Medici and Castiglione amongst others. His revival of the vernacular eclogue would lead to the vogue for the pastoral half a century or more later, culminating in Sannazaro's *Arcadia*, while many of the poems in the Certame Coronario found their way into the Raccolta Aragonese and thus helped shape the revival of Tuscan lyric in the age of Lorenzo de' Medici. His interest in Greek authors anticipated the Greek revival under Lorenzo at the end of the century, not to mention the Lucianic dimensions of such writers as Erasmus and Ariosto. His mathematical concerns would resurface in the works of his younger friend Luca Pacioli, and fellow theorist Piero della Francesca, while the architectural treatise would influence first Filarete, then Palladio and others. But most of all Alberti would have an impact on that other 'Renaissance man', Leonardo da Vinci: he was the most often cited modern author by Leonardo, and his *Apologhi* would inspire Leonardo's own fables.[90] In general terms, by writing his technical treatises in Latin he was respons-

---

[90] For his influence on Leonardo, see Marcello Ciccuto, 'Alberti verso le città ideali. La sua riflessione sul concetto di figura', in *Leon Battista Alberti: Actes du Congrès International de Paris*, I, 235–44; for the influence on Leonardo's fables, see Pierre Laurens, 'Le retour de l'Alberti Latin (*Apologues, Propos de table, Momus*): une poétique de l'allegorie', in Françoise Choay, Michel Paoli (eds.), *Alberti, humaniste, architecte*, pp. 111–27 (117); see also, Francesco P. Di Teodoro, 'L'influence de l'Alberti sur Raphael, Bramante et Léonard', ibid., pp. 47–61.

ible for raising the status of the painter, the sculptor and the architect in Renaissance Italy, and paving the way for the esteem that would be enjoyed by other writer–artists. Alberti was the first writer–artist of the Italian Renaissance, and provided a model for those who came after: Leonardo, Michelangelo, Vasari, Cellini.

Perhaps it is best to end with Alberti's own image of the humanities. In 'Picturae', one of the *Intercenales*, he describes a temple of Fortune which had ten images of good and evil forces painted on the walls. Amongst the good icons is of course 'Humanitas', and the ekphrasis of this painting is as follows:

> In the first space [on the right wall] an extraordinary image of a woman was painted, who had many different faces sitting on top of her one neck: old, young, sad, merry, serious, witty and so on. In addition she had many hands emerging from her shoulders, one of which held pens, another a lyre, another a beautiful highly wrought gem, another a painted or sculpted emblem, another various mathematical instruments, while another held books. There was a name written above this image: Mother Humanitas.[91]

Once again Alberti's notion of the humanities is emphatically varied and pluralistic, both serious and witty, and it embraces not just literature but the fine arts and mathematics as well. Perhaps if Alberti had been even more influential, the gap between 'the two cultures' would have been less wide, and this Italian lecture would take place not in the home of the humanities and social sciences but in a unified British Academy of Humanities, Mathematics and Sciences.

[91] 'Namque loco primo mira imago adest picte mulieris, cui plurimi variique unam in cervicem vultus conveniunt: seniles, iuveniles, tristes, iocosi, graves, faceti et eiusmodi. ‖ Complurimas item manus ex iisdem habet humeris fluentes, ex quibus quidem alie calamos, alie lyram, alie laboratam concinnamque gemmam, alie pictum excultumque insigne, alie mathematicorum varia instrumenta, alie libros tractant. Huic superadscriptum nomen: Humanitas mater' (Alberti, *Intercenali inedite*, p. 131).

Shakespeare, Oaths and Vows

JOHN KERRIGAN

University of Cambridge

ENTER HECTOR AND ANDROMACHE. He is armed for battle; she, troubled by dreams, urges him not to fight. 'You traine me to offend you', he declares, then swears a mighty oath: 'By all the euerlasting gods, Ile goe.'[1] Oaths, according to early modern commentators, resolve disputed matter. For Shakespeare, however, their decisiveness is frequently deceptive; sworn over points of doubt, they are hedged, conflicted, and unravel. Certainly, when Cassandra enters, she is not satisfied with Hector's insistence that 'the gods haue heard me sweare'. 'The gods are deafe', she replies, 'to hot and peeuish vowes.' At this point, the early texts of *Troylus and Cressida* diverge. In the Folio, which gives us a better, and perhaps a later, version of the exchange, Andromache employs an elaborate, tangential analogy, between Hector's sworn commitment and robbery with violence under-taken for the sake of charity, to persuade her husband not to 'hurt by being iust'. Cassandra then concludes, as Andromache does in the quarto: 'It is the purpose that makes strong the vowe; | But vowes to euery purpose must not hold' (3214–23).

Rereading this passage a few months ago, I realised that, as so often, the familiarity of the dialogue was hiding my ignorance from me. Is F Andromache's ingenuity desperate, or is she justifiably reminding Hector that oaths are not free-standing commitments but caught up in moral

Read at the Academy 23 April 2009.

[1] Folio *Troylus and Cressida*, V.iii; 3201–2, inserting 'all' from the 1609 quarto. Unless otherwise indicated, Shakespeare quotations are taken from *The Norton Facsimile: The First Folio of Shakespeare*, ed. Charlton Hinman (London, 1968), giving act and scene, followed by through-line numbers.

Proceedings of the British Academy, **167**, 61–89. © The British Academy 2010.

reasoning? And how convincing is Cassandra, with her subtle, loaded shift between 'purpose' as intention and 'purpose' as plan of action? For a late-Elizabethan audience, was Hector's oath binding? When I turned to recent editions, the only guidance I could find was a quotation from Dr Johnson, buried in Arden 3: 'The mad Prophetess speaks here with all the coolness and judgment of a skilful casuist.'[2] It is easy to see why Arden has preserved this. Johnson's magisterial disparagement, both of Cassandra's character and of Shakespeare's ability to present it consistently, is obtuse but thought-provoking, and he is also historically perceptive, because he accurately identifies the context of Andromache's ingenuity and concedes that what an eighteenth-century reader will deprecate as casuistry in Cassandra does show skill and judgement. Though he is alive to the issues, however, Johnson barely scratches the surface of a topic that is complicated beyond the dreams of scholarship, and dramaturgically vital—not just in *Troylus*, as I'll demonstrate most immediately, but right across the plays of Shakespeare.

Cassandra's position is orthodox. The homily 'Against Swearyng and Periury', read in churches during Shakespeare's lifetime, insists, against radical Protestants, on the legitimacy of oaths and vows.[3] Through marriage, oaths of office, and sworn testimony in court, they knit together the commonwealth. 'Thou shalte dreade thy Lorde God', the homily quotes from Deuteronomy, 'and shalt sweare by hys name.' Abraham, David, and other Godly men swore, as did Christ himself, though mildly, saying 'verely, verely'. Oaths, however, are sacred and should not be sworn either casually or 'rasshely and vnaduisedly'. This is where Cassandra comes in. Shakespeare's audience would know from the homily, and from the widely acknowledged points of difficulty that were sifted in the casuistical literature, that to keep 'a rash oath, adds sin unto sin'.[4] Just how peevish Hector is being when he swears by all the gods is ultimately up to the actor, but he is resisting a troublesome wife, not exercising deliberation. Does the element of rashness discharge him, though, from an obligation to keep his word? Not straightforwardly, it seems. Once uttered, his oath is not disabled by the conditions set out in the homily, because what he swears to do is neither 'against the lawe of almightie God' nor beyond 'his power to performe'. He will not, like Jephthah sacrificing his daughter,

[2] *Troilus and Cressida*, ed. David Bevington (London, 1998), p. 328, quoting here uncut from *The Plays of William Shakespeare*, ed. Samuel Johnson, 8 vols. (London, 1765), VII. 532.
[3] *Certayne Sermons, Or Homilies Appoynted by the Kynges Maiestie* (London, 1547), L3v–M3v.
[4] Christopher White, *Of Oathes: Their Obiect, Forme, and Bond* (London, 1627), p. 23.

'double' his 'offence' if he keeps his word and goes out to fight, though he does risk weakening Troy.

All, however, is not lost for Cassandra and Andromache. Most members of Shakespeare's audience would agree with Robert Sanderson, whose treatise *De Juramento* is a *summa* of mainstream casuistry on oaths, that binding words need only be kept if they are not overruled by a higher power—such as a father overruling a son, or a king a subject—and 'if things remain in the same state'.[5] I shall get to the latter condition, often crucial in Shakespeare, in a moment. But it should already be clear why, once Cassandra has been rebuffed, she leaves Hector to be harassed by Troilus (who wants his brother to go out and kill Greeks) and re-enters with his king and father. As the Trojan royal family gather and group against him on stage, it becomes even harder for Hector to draw back from his oath. In deference to Priam's authority, however, he does justify his inflexibility by telling him, what the audience already knows, that he 'stand[s] engag'd to many Greekes, | Euen in the faith of valour, to appeare | This morning to them' (3276–8).

Were the faiths exchanged on Hector's visit to the Greek camp, when he fought with Ajax, anything more than pleasantries? Oaths and vows can be dramatically productive because they are uttered in one context but still make claims on fidelity when the setting changes. Once fired off, like rockets, they cannot be recalled. They can, of course, be 'unsworn' (that is, 'denied'), which everyone agreed to be contemptible, or they can be more boldly 'forsworn', but the contradictoriness of that word, which could mean 'sworn against' as well as 'broken', and sometimes, as in *Loues Labour's Lost*,[6] both at once, is telling. The readiest way to adapt an oath or vow is to counter it with another, which is one reason why, once admitted, they become so plentiful, and layered, in Shakespeare. Behind his oath to Andromache, Hector chose not to tell Cassandra, was his light-sounding engagement to many Greeks. What is layered in, behind what he now tells Priam? Audiences will not forget an earlier scene with his greatest rival-in-arms Achilles when they plighted their troth like lovers:

> [ACHILLES]   Dost thou intreat me *Hector*?
> To morrow do I meete thee, fell as death,
> To night, all Friends.
> HECTOR   Thy hand vpon that match.   (IV.v; 2842–4)

---

[5] Robert Sanderson, *De Juramento: Seven Lectures Concerning the Obligation of Promissory Oathes* (London, 1655), II.x–xi.
[6] e.g. IV.iii; 1670.

This is the tryst that matters. Hector's subsequent faiths and oaths start to look like a pretext for ensuring that this fight will happen.

Because scholars have not explored the binding language in this play they have had no reason to explicate what is arguably the biggest change made by Shakespeare to the story of Troy as he found it. In Caxton and Lydgate, Achilles does not see and fall in love with Polyxena until the anniversary of Hector's death. To win her, he then takes a vow that he will not fight alongside the Greeks. In Shakespeare, by contrast—although Ulysses chooses to conceal this, for resentful reasons of his own—he is lurking in his tent from the outset because of that vow. Conceivably he forgets it in the intensity of his tryst with Hector. Even before he goes into his tent to drink with his enemy, however, he announces to Patroclus:

> Heere is a Letter from Queene *Hecuba*,
> A token from her daughter, my fair Loue,
> Both taxing me, and gaging me to keepe
> An Oath that I haue sworn. I will not breake it,
> Fall Greekes, faile Fame, Honor or go, or stay,
> My maior vow lyes heere; this Ile obay: . . .   (V.i; 2906–11)

Here is the language of casuistry filtered through chivalric romance. And it casts an ironic light on Hector's exchange with Cassandra, because he insists on keeping a faith which Achilles has already dismissed as bendable and expendable.

This is not the full chain of Achilles' oaths and vows. The prologue says of the Greek generals, '*their vow is made | To ransacke Troy*'. Again, this is not in Caxton and it marks a promise made before the expedition that Achilles breaks when he lolls in his tent. The play begins as it goes on, shot through with verbal bonds, formal, slackly profane, immediate or peculiarly displaced.[7] It is a drama of high-flown vows, but also of what Thersites calls 'craftie swearing rascals' (V.iv; 3341). Is Achilles above such shifts? Having resolved to keep his major vow, he later abandons it to revenge the death of Patroclus. Does he finally step aside, though, and leave the Myrmidons to kill the unarmed Hector because he is cowardly, or unfit for combat, as critics usually argue, or vindictively determined to degrade his enemy? Or is he casuistically keeping that major vow?

Somewhere near the heart of the play is the uncertain scene of troth-plighting between Troilus and Cressida. Here, as blocking can bring out, is a parallel with the sequence in which Hector and Achilles eye each

---

[7] As when Pandarus says to Troilus, the tongue-tied wooer of Cressida, 'sweare the oathes now to her, that you haue sworne to me' (III.ii; 1674–5).

other up and clasp hands to seal their faith. But it is also, by virtue of Shakespeare's bold treatment of his sources, counterpointed by the attenuated love-plot which ties Achilles to Polyxena. Three word-bound relationships cut across by war. Perhaps we should say four. Because when Cressida submits to Diomedes, she is caught up with a man who is, according to Thersites, a notorious vow-breaker (V.i; 2962–71). Is Cressida just as bad? Troilus assumes so, but her oaths and vows are inextricable from her predicament. We should remember at this point the principle of defeasibility. Cressida has been forced into an unprotected position by Troilus' choice or inability to look after her. Once she goes to the Greek camp, things do not (in Sanderson's words) 'remain in the same state'.

We should also notice that, like Achilles, she now has conflicting vows. 'In faith I cannot', she tells Diomedes, with Troilus and Ulysses looking on, and Thersites throwing in his barbs; but this is just a tactical piece of mild swearing, with a stronger oath in the background:

> DIOMEDES What did you sweare you would bestow on me?
> CRESSIDA I prethee do not hold me to mine oath,
> Bid me doe any thing but that sweete Greeke.[8]

To the eyes and ears of Troilus, that she has sworn this oath, given this promise of sexual access, proves her false already. But the oath may have been thrown, like the flirty-defensive 'In faith', to hold Diomed off with a promise when she could frankly have been forced. And it was of course a rich point of dispute among early modern philosophers and casuists whether coerced promises should be kept.

One of the dramatic attractions of formally constructed oaths and vows is that they can be used to challenge the audience to make a judgement about motives and intentions. They put us close to the onstage witnesses or promisees. Yet Cressida's words to Diomedes we cannot finally judge. Her related use of letters and tokens also appears the more ambiguous because of their contrast with those in the love-plot between Achilles and Polyxena. At this point, most dramatists would succumb to audience-pleasing clarification. In his adaption of the play, Dryden has Cressida kill herself to prove to Troilus, and to us, the depth of her fidelity. Shakespeare, as rather often, uses binding language to create uncertainty, between shifting motives shown and withheld.

Meanwhile, and climactically, Troilus's desire to hang on to a Cressida who is faithful both to him and to her word scours him into declaring

---

[8] V.ii; 2999–3003. F reads (with a Freudian touch) 'Bid me doe not any thing . . .'.

'This is, and is not *Cressid*' (V.ii; 3143). Early modern commentators on promissory oaths and vows, from the homilist to Sanderson, wrote of their 'double' nature. They must be true in the moment of swearing, but also (yet defeasibly) true at the point of redemption.[9] The doubleness of Cressida in Troilus' intense, almost philosophical account is compounded of many factors, including, I do not doubt, the polarising tendency of male projections of good/bad femininity, but it springs from the splitting effect of the then/now doubleness of sworn vows. This is why, for Troilus, who is at least as inflexible as his heroic–foolish brother, Hector, her apparent infidelity takes truth down with her troth. When he says that 'The bonds of heauen are slipt, dissolu'd and loos'd' (3153), he does not just mean, eloquently but flatly, that Cressida has broken her word, but that the breaking of her word has torn apart the structures of reality. It is an effect that, as we shall see, would come to matter greatly in Shakespeare.

* * *

Clearly, it would be possible to lecture just on oaths and vows in *Troylus*. You could do the same, however, for quite a few of the plays, without recycling existing scholarship. There is a large gap in Shakespeare studies which it seems right to do something about. Certainly, the issues that I started with go back to the earliest plays. 'Vn-heedfull vowes may heedfully be broken' says Proteus, in *The Two Gentlemen of Verona*. Whether it is Salisbury declaring 'It is great sinne, to swear vnto a sinne: | But greater sinne to keepe a sinfull oath', or Clarence citing Jephthah, when he returns to the Yorkist faction, the flexibility of the orthodoxy set out in the homily is exploited in the first tetralogy. From *Errors* to *A Midsommer Nights Dreame*, oaths and vows are used, sometimes rather externally, to mark changes in motive and attachment, as when Hortensio and Tranio in the *Shrew* resolve to give up Bianca. Oaths can be offensive weapons — Petruccio uses them to browbeat Kate — or trip-wire indicators of confidence, as when Gremio offers, then refuses, to swear that Vincentio is the right Vincentio.[10]

---

[9] Homily 'Against Swearyng', M3r (the 'double offence' of Jephthah); *De Juramento*, VII.i ('in the promissory a double truth is required, . . . having sworn, it may come many wayes to passe, that he may *not be bound for the future*, to fulfill that afterwards which he formerly promised').
[10] *Two Gentlemen*, II.vi; 940, *2 Henry the Sixt*, V.i; 3182–3, V.i; 2772–4, *Shrew*, IV.ii; 1870–91, IV.iii; 1988 and V.i; 1710, V.i; 2476–84.

The story that I want to tell is not a simple one, of authorial development. Nonetheless, by the mid-1590s Shakespeare was even more involved with the ethical weight and airiness of oaths. *Loues Labour's Lost* is about little else, starting, as it does, from Navarre and his lords' oath to study for three years, a promise which, with typical unstraightforwardness, is shedding its terms and conditions even before Berowne subscribes, and going on to vows comically sworn to the wrong ladies. Pandulph in *King John* is the sort of equivocating papist whose slippery handling of sacred vows gives casuistry a bad name.[11] And Bolingbroke's oath at Doncaster not to unthrone Richard II is repeatedly invoked by the rebels in *1 and 2 Henry the Fourth*. They are finally, ironically, defeated when Prince John sticks so precisely to the terms of the oath that he shares with them that he can send them to execution.[12] This is just one of many points in the plays where oaths and vows prove to be not the opposite of lying but a means of deception.

It is an issue in the Sonnets also. Although I want to focus on oaths and vows in performance, it is important to notice their valency in the non-dramatic poetry, if only as a way of signalling that what went on in the theatre was connected with practices that informed a broad range of texts. Venus prettily swears, 'by her faire immortall hand'—the very hand that is doing the grasping—that she will not detach herself from Adonis' bosom until she is given a kiss.[13] Oppressed by her attentions, he tells her to 'Dismisse your vows', those marks of deceiving love (D1v). In the Dedication to *Venus and Adonis*, Shakespeare himself makes a 'vow' to honour the Earl of Southampton 'with some grauer labour'.[14] In *Lucrece*, the fruit of that promise, the heroine is tormented by the fear that she has broken her marriage vows by being raped.[15] The poem climaxes in Brutus' deep, shared vow to act against the Tarquins. The sonnets to the so-called dark lady are full of false oaths and bed-vows. Where empty deception is by mutual consent, as in 138,[16] swearing and forswearing become perverted, obsessive activities, bonding where no trust exists. When I edited

---

[11] See esp. *King John*, III.i; 1155–1228. On confessional differences, similarities, and controversy see e.g. Johann Sommerville, 'The "New Art of Lying": equivocation, mental reservation, and casuistry', in Edmund Leites (ed.), *Conscience and Casuistry in Early Modern Europe* (Cambridge, 1988), pp. 159–86.

[12] *2 Henry the Fourth*, IV.ii; 2100–2234.

[13] *Venus and Adonis* (London, 1593), B2v.

[14] A2r.

[15] *Lucrece* (London, 1594), H2r.

[16] 'When my loue sweares that she is made of truth, | I do beleeue her though I know she lyes . . .', in *Shakespeares Sonnets* (London, 1609).

the Sonnets myself, and sought to link them with *A Louers Complaint*,[17] I failed to notice how such texts as 152,[18] which concludes the dark-lady group, share the longer poem's preoccupation with vows, consecrations, and strong-bonded oaths, all unhinged by desire.

Most oaths in Shakespeare are not self-consciously framed. They are casual, everyday profanities, circulating in conversation, more inter-personal than individual. Robert Boyle, in the mid-seventeenth century, compared swearing to yawning.[19] We pick up and echo oaths without notic-ing what we are doing. In such late-1590s plays as *Much Adoe*, fashionable, light profanity sets a social tone; yet these oaths can suddenly escalate, convincing the Prince and Claudio that Hero is unfaithful and binding Benedick to kill his friend. *Othello*, *All's Well*, and other plays about sexual betrayal from the same middle period as *Troylus* similarly show oaths and vows shifting from casual interjection to intensity. This is one of the ways in which female characters are disadvantaged. Desdemona would bewhore herself if she swore her truth with Othello's vehemence. Hotspur mocks Lady Percy for swearing 'in good sooth' because, he says, as a noblewoman, she is entitled to 'A good mouth-filling Oath.' But all the women in Shakespeare, except allegedly the whores in *Timon*, are constrained. Even when disguised as a boy, Rosalind playfully swears 'by all pretty oathes that are not dangerous'.[20]

This system shifted after 1606, when Godly opposition to profanity, already evident in the homily, issued in an Act of Parliament which made it a fineable offence 'in any Stage play . . . Maygame, or Pageant jestingly or prophanely [to] speake or use the holy name of God or of Christ Jesus, or of the Holy Ghoste or of the Trinitie'.[21] Scholars have long recognised that the Act to Restrain Abuses created textual problems. The expurga-tion of prompt-books led to the excision or softening of oaths in a number of the earlier plays published in the 1623 Folio, damage which cannot (in F-only texts) be put right with any confidence.[22] It may be that the Act

---

[17] *Shakespeare's Sonnets and A Lover's Complaint* (Harmondsworth, 1986).

[18] 'In louing thee thou know'st I am forsworne, | But thou art twice forsworne to me loue swearing . . .'.

[19] Robert Boyle, *A Free Discourse against Customary Swearing* (London, 1695), pp. 110–11. The publisher's preface dates this posthumously printed work to the late 1640s or early 1650s.

[20] *2 Henry the Fourth*, III.i; 1792–1800, *Timon*, IV.iii; 1750–4, *As You Like It*, IV.i; 2095–6.

[21] 'To Restraine Abuses of Players', quoted in Andrew Gurr, *The Shakespearean Stage 1574–1642*, 3rd edn. (Cambridge, 1992), p. 76.

[22] See, most ambitiously, Gary Taylor, ''Swounds revisited: theatrical, editorial, and literary expurgation', in Gary Taylor and John Jowett, *Shakespeare Reshaped 1606–1623* (Oxford, 1993), pp. 51–106.

played a part in edging Shakespeare away from contemporary subject matter into classical plays and romances where characters could swear 'by Castor'. One point that I want to stress, however, is that oaths and vows remained a potent resource. At the end of this lecture, I'll show, through a discussion of *The Winters Tale*, how the Act encouraged Shakespeare to reflect creatively on the outlawed practices, and how he displayed his usual ability to turn difficulties into opportunities.

Before going any further, I should explain how oaths and vows were constituted, and justify my title. The word *oath*, which has Germanic roots, has been part of the English language since the Anglo-Saxon period. During Shakespeare's lifetime, assertory and promissory oaths were sworn *by* God or one of his creatures. Because they invoke the Divine, oaths have an affinity with prayer, and they can imply the sort of conditional self-curse that is often explicit in the Old Testament. In the early modern period, *oath* could also be used to describe everyday effing and blinding. What you casually swear can rebound on you, and solemn oaths are caught up in a blasphemous counter-life, the surging, phatic noise of the collectively profane. As when the priest asks Petruccio 'if *Katherine* should be his wife, | I, by goggs woones quoth he, and swore so loud, | That all amaz'd the Priest let fall the booke'.[23]

In response to this question, a tractable groom would have taken his marriage vows. *Vow* comes into English, out of French, in the late thirteenth century. We vow not *by* but *to* God, or, during Shakespeare's lifetime (and the *Oxford English Dictionary* credits him, suggestively though questionably, with initiating this change), we vow fidelity to another person.[24] Classically, vowing is involved with presenting votive gifts and doing a deal with the Divine. Hence Cassandra's comparison of 'hot and peeuish vowes', in the exchange that I began with, to 'polluted offrings, more abhord | Then spotted Liuers in the sacrifice' (V.iii; 3215–17). These religious associations persisted: think of the vows taken by the nuns in *Measure for Measure*, and of the Duke's deceptive oath 'By the vow of mine Order.'[25] *Vow* was attractive to Shakespeare because, unlike *oath*, it was lexically well connected (*devotion*, *devout*, and so on) and quick to

---

[23] *Shrew*, III.ii; 1543–5.

[24] *OED* 3, citing '*Mids. N.*, I. i. 175 By all the vowes that euer men haue broke, (In number more then euer women spoke).' For an earlier instance see e.g. the Elizabethan marriage service, where there is formally no vow *to* God, and the plighting of troth between bride and groom is called 'the vow and couenaunte betwixt them made' (*The Booke of Common Praier* [London, 1559], O6r–v).

[25] I.v; 349–63, IV.ii; 2034.

coin new forms—terms like *votary* and *votaress*.[26] It was close, moreover, to 'avow' (which could be 'vow', in its aphetic form), and thus to 'avouch' and 'vouch', words that must have encouraged Shakespeare's use—again, according to the *OED*, for the first time—of *vow* to mean 'A solemn . . . asseveration.'[27] *Vow* in this sense is almost an assertory oath, rather as a promissory oath can do the work of a vow.

More should be said about that overlap. When Hector swears by all the gods, that is an oath, yet Cassandra calls it a 'vowe'. Within a couple of lines Achilles calls his 'maior vow' an 'Oath'. Shakespeare often uses these terms almost interchangeably, and they are only the commonest, decisive practices in an array of binding language that includes *protesting, abjuration, plighting, engagement*, or just giving your *word*. A full account would have to make distinctions. This, though, can be said at once, that, whereas such terms as *perjury* and *expurgation* are associated with a specific domain—in their case legal—*oath* and *vow* are viable in so many contexts that they allow the dramatist to mark parallels and ironic contrasts between situations and plot-lines.

It would, then, have been incoherent, though superficially tidier, to have called this lecture 'Shakespeare's Oaths' or 'Shakespeare's Vows'. Nor, come to that, would 'Shakespeare's Oaths and Vows' have done, because almost all the oaths and vows in Shakespeare are not *his* but have a life and history beyond the plays. They are highly developed instances of the iterability of language. When Hector swears 'by all the euerlasting gods' it is the received nature of the formula that gives his promise weight. The 'vntraded Oath' that he swears to Menelaus, taunting him 'by *Mars* his gauntlet', is, by contrast, a mockery (IV.v; 2745–6). When an oath or vow is fresh it is as likely to seem suspect as it is to be sincere. That Romeo swears to Juliet, 'by yonder blessed Moone . . . | That tips with siluer all these Fruite tree tops' is inventive and exquisite.[28] In performance it is charged with his yearning up to her balcony, his stretching finger-tips. But she is also right to doubt him.[29] His tongue is tipped with silver, and unconstant to Rosaline.

---

[26] For their late-sixteenth-century emergence, see Literature Online <http://lion.chadwyck.co.uk/>.

[27] *OED* 5, citing '2 *Hen. VI*, III.ii.159 A dreadfull Oath, sworne with a solemn tongue: What instance giues Lord Warwicke for his vow.'

[28] *Romeo and Juliet*, II.ii; 905–9, inserting 'blessed' from the quarto of 1597.

[29] Cf. David Schalkwyk, *Speech and Performance in Shakespeare's Sonnets and Plays* (Cambridge, 2002), pp. 70–1.

You will not be surprised to learn that *oath*, *vow*, their cognates, and, it would seem, the associated practices, are more densely represented in Shakespeare than in the work of such contemporaries as Jonson and Middleton. The responsiveness of early audiences to this can be inferred not just circularly from the plays themselves but from the fullest set of annotations that we have in an early edition. The seventeenth-century reader of the First Folio now held at Meisei University picked out vows, oaths, and accounts of swearing with special assiduity. He notes and underlines morals ('mens vowes are womens traitors'), flags up points of advice ('oathes confirmers of false recknings'), and marks the verbal bonds that articulate plot, especially in the histories.[30] He is attracted to the sorts of dilemma that preoccupy early modern casuists, such as whether we should trust the word of someone who swears by a god that he knows we do not believe in (Aaron trusting Lucius at the end of *Titus*). Of the Hector, Cassandra and Andromache exchange, he diligently notes: 'In what sort vowes are laufull and bind honor more deere to man then life.'

All this makes the indifference of scholars the more regrettable. Frances A. Shirley's *Swearing and Perjury in Shakespeare's Plays* (1979) gives a useful account of early modern attitudes. Critically, however, as her title reveals, she has a true-or-false mindset that best fits the early plays. After about 1597, *perjury* fades out of Shakespeare's vocabulary, as he becomes more interested in riddling, paradoxical, and pliable asseverations and promises. Shirley's true/false approach can lead her badly astray, as when she says of the Cressida–Diomed scene, 'There is no doubt about the reaction we are supposed to have as Cressida's lust overcomes any prior commitments.'[31] That we now know more about Cressida's 'prior commitments' is in large part due to the excellent work done over the last couple of decades on marriage contracts and early modern drama.[32] The troth–plight scene between the lovers, with Pandarus acting as a witness, never mentions marriage, but it deliberately, confusingly resembles an Elizabethan hand-fasting. The research into spousals, however, has underinvestigated binding language.

---

[30] *The First Folio of Shakespeare: a Transcript of Contemporary Marginalia*, ed. Akihiro Yamada (Tokyo, 1998), p. 290 (*Cymbeline*), p. 64 (*As You Like It*).

[31] Frances A. Shirley, *Swearing and Perjury in Shakespeare's Plays* (London, 1979), p. 90.

[32] See e.g. Ann Jennalie Cook, *Making a Match: Courtship in Shakespeare and his Society* (Princeton, NJ, 1991), chs. 7–8; B. J. Sokol and Mary Sokol, *Shakespeare, Law, and Marriage* (Cambridge, 2003), chs. 1, 5–6; Subha Mukherji, *Law and Representation in Early Modern Drama* (Cambridge, 2006), ch. 1.

The early plays are also the natural stamping-ground for Tom McAlindon, who believes that, for Shakespeare, 'the oath or vow—the word as bond—is language in its most urgent and solemn form, a symbol almost of human connectedness and interdependence'.[33] Such a view is even more conservative, and more to the point less worldly, than that of the Tudor homily. It gives McAlindon selective access to the *Henry the Fourth* plays (which are his mainstay), but it reduces the King and Prince John to reprehensible eroders of trust. We can learn more about the second tetralogy from the work of Lorna Hutson and others on late-Elizabethan hostility to expurgation (swearing your innocence) in the ecclesiastical courts, and the common-law belief that promises were secured not by oaths or vows but by consideration, by goods or services handed over.[34] Questions can be asked about the extent to which legal culture impacted on early modern drama. But it is clearly worth knowing about these contexts when we try to gauge the reaction of what was most likely an Inns of Court audience[35] to Hector's vow to fight the Greek leaders. For Elizabethan common lawyers, as for Hobbes a few decades later, and the legal philosopher P. S. Atiyah today, Hector's obligation would slip towards the minimal, given that the Greeks' only loss if he unarmed would be a disappointed expectation.[36]

The other book-length study I must cite is by my namesake, William Kerrigan. *Shakespeare's Promises* (1999) gives a bold, under-historicised account of vows in *Othello* and bonds in *The Merchant of Venice*. Its readings are distorted, however, by the unsustainable thesis that the plays are drawn back to the Christian belief that those who break their word will be punished.[37] Such plays as *All's Well* do show, at what can be for modern audiences excessive and obvious length, the social price paid by

---

[33] Tom McAlindon, *Shakespeare's Tudor History: a Study of Henry IV, Parts 1 and 2* (Aldershot, 2001), p. 93. Cf. variously his *Shakespeare and Decorum* (London, 1973) and 'Swearing and forswearing in Shakespeare's histories: the playwright as contra-Machiavel', *Review of English Studies*, 5 (2000), 208–29.

[34] Luke Wilson, *Theaters of Intention: Drama and the Law in Early Modern England* (Stanford, CA, 2000); Lorna Hutson, 'Not the King's two bodies: reading the "Body Politic" in Shakespeare's *Henry IV*, Parts I and II'; David Harris Sacks, 'The promise and the contract in Early Modern England: Slade's case in perspective', in Lorna Hutson and Victoria Kahn (eds.), *Rhetoric and Law in Early Modern Europe* (New Haven, CT, 2001), pp. 166–98, 28–53.

[35] The majority view, that *Troylus* was written for performance at the Inns of Court, was first set out by Peter Alexander, '*Troilus and Cressida*, 1609', *The Library*, 4th ser. 9 (1928–9), 267–86. For doubts, see *Troilus and Cressida*, ed. Bevington, pp. 88–9.

[36] Hobbes, *Leviathan* (London, 1651), ch. 14; P. S. Atiyah, *Promises, Morals, and Law* (Oxford, 1981).

[37] *Shakespeare's Promises* (Baltimore, MD, 1999), pp. 90–1, 198–206.

characters like Parolles who abuse the oaths and vows that were so important in binding together early modern society. But to look for meta-physical payback is to find Falstaff sighing, in *The Merry Wiues*, 'I neuer prosper'd, since I forswore myself at *Primero*' (IV.v; 2316–17). Hector keeps his oath and is slaughtered; Achilles breaks one vow to keep another, then does the opposite, and triumphs. This is not to say that the religious aspect of oaths that we encountered in the homily had no effect. As Brian Cummings has shown, in a fine essay on More and Shakespeare, connections can be made between the trial and burning of heretics in the early sixteenth century and the heated, improperly conducted processes of inquisition in *Othello*, where boundaries between private conscience and public oath-taking are violated.[38]

The neglect of a big topic is a sufficient justification for addressing it. There are reasons, however, for thinking that this is a good time to take up my theme. First, new work by historians has probed swearing as a social practice. Previously, too much reliance was placed on the line of treatises that runs from Becon's *Inuectyue agenst Swearing* (1543) to Edmund Calamy's *Practical Discourse Concerning Vows* (1697). Armed with this material, and limited data from social history, Christopher Hill and others argued for a declining belief in the potency of oaths due to their over-imposition by kings and parliaments, desacralisation, and a new emphasis on interest and contract.[39]

It is likely that such changes occurred. But when Defoe argued against the use of oaths on grounds of reason and politeness, he was responding to deeper shifts in conduct and morality, caught up in evolving attitudes to virtuous respectability. Appropriately, given our venue, he made his case in an *Essay Upon Projects* (1697) which advocated the creation of a national Academy—a body of learned men, who would occupy them-selves, as we are occupied this evening, with making and mulling over crit-ical observations about playscripts, and who would worry (as he does at length) about the rationality of swearing.[40] Around the time Defoe was writing, scatology and sexuality were becoming the primary locus of 'bad language'.[41] A late seventeenth-century watershed separates us from the period in which Shakespearean drama took shape, and we need to be

---

[38] 'Swearing in public: More and Shakespeare', *English Literary Renaissance*, 27 (1997), 197–232.
[39] Christopher Hill, *Society and Puritanism in Pre-Revolutionary England* (London, 1964), ch. 11.
[40] Defoe, *An Essay upon Projects* (London, 1697), pp. 227–51, esp. 238–50.
[41] See e.g. Melissa Mohr, 'Defining dirt: three early modern views of obscenity', *Textual Practice*, 17 (2003), 253–75; Tony McEnery, *Swearing in English: Bad Language, Purity and Power from 1586 to the Present* (London, 2006), chs. 3–4.

aware that some words which now strike us as quaint, such as Othello's and Iago's 'zounds', were shocking during Shakespeare's lifetime, while others, such as 'marry', were not. There is a fluctuating, lost hierarchy to recover.

But there are also contexts to consider, because particular oaths and vows can be frivolous in one setting yet solemn in another. And this is where, as I say, the historians are proving helpful. Thanks to David Martin Jones and Edward Vallance, we now know a great deal more about oaths of allegiance and supremacy, bonds of association and national covenants—relevant to such Reformation-based plays as *Sir Thomas Moore* and *Henry the Eight*, not to mention, as we shall see, *The Winters Tale*, but also to the schedule subscribed at the start of *Loues Labour's Lost*.[42] Oaths of office have been analysed by Conal Condren.[43] Laura Gowing has given us insights into the gendered aspects of oath-taking.[44] And John Spurr has shown, in a number of rich essays, how context-dependent swearing was. Marriage vows were one thing, dicers' oaths another.[45] Any attempt to trace a decline or desacralisation must acknowledge the energy of oaths and vows in specific contexts right through the seventeenth century.

The second reason for feeling timely is that moral philosophy has reacted against Kantian, deontological thinking when it comes to oaths and vows, and it now connects more clarifyingly with a period in which face-to-face relationships and defeasibility were key. God is far more important in the casuistical literature than in *How to Do Things with Words*. But there are still reasons for believing that shared thoughts and values connect Shakespeare's binding language with the arguments between J. L. Austin, John Searle, Jacques Derrida and Judith Butler on speech acts and social performance. When Sanderson starts *De Juramento*

---

[42] David Martin Jones, *Conscience and Allegiance in Seventeenth Century England: the Political Significance of Oaths and Engagements* (Rochester, NY, 1999); Edward Vallance, *Revolutionary England and the National Covenant: State Oaths, Protestantism, and the Political Nation, 1553–1682* (Woodbridge, 2005).

[43] See his *Argument and Authority in Early Modern England: the Presupposition of Oaths and Offices* (Cambridge, 2006). For a compendium see *The Book of Oaths* (London, 1649).

[44] See her *Domestic Dangers: Women, Words, and Sex in Early Modern London* (Oxford, 1996), esp. pp. 50–1.

[45] John Spurr, 'Perjury, profanity and politics', *The Seventeenth Century*, 8 (1993), 29–50; id., 'A profane history of early modern oaths', *Transactions of the Royal Historical Society*, 6th ser., 11 (2001), 37–63; id., '"The Strongest Bond of Conscience": oaths and the limits of tolerance in Early Modern England', in Harald E. Braun and Edward Vallance (eds.), *Contexts of Conscience in Early Modern Europe, 1500–1700* (Basingstoke, 2004), pp. 151–65.

by declaring that an oath is 'a religious act', he is explicitly modifying Cicero's 'An Oath . . . is a religious affirmation' (I.ii). Like Austin, he is wary of imputing intention[46] and believes, almost always, that the speech-act binds, regardless.[47] Both are ordinary language philosophers who give the benefit of the doubt to usage. Sanderson acutely considers whether Cressida's phrase 'in faith' is an oath, since it should formally be 'by my faith', and why 'in faith' should be customarily so taken when 'in truth' is regarded as an asseveration. In each case, he concludes, how formulae are understood in use is decisive (V.vi, viii).

A third reason for feeling timely has to do with our willingness to acknowledge the inextricability of social performatives and speech acts scripted for performance. It is a token of this that Sanderson's doubts about 'in faith' applied equally in the theatre. When Charles I overruled the Master of the Revels', Sir Henry Herbert's, expurgation of Davenant's *The Witts* (1634), Sir Henry put it on record that 'The king is pleasd to take *faith*, *death*, *slight* for asseverations, . . . but, under favour, [I] conceive them to be oaths.'[48] Theatre studies are now, with some loss as well as gain, shifting the focus away from what happens in the playhouse into performativity more largely. Oaths and vows are prime instances of performatives that are also performed. The desire to keep these phenomena separate may be understandable in speech act philosophers. It is there in Austin's insistence that performatives uttered on stage are '*parasitic* upon . . . normal use'.[49] This was a false dichotomy ripe for Derrida to deconstruct, and for Judith Butler and Eve Sedgwick to think with and against in their performative accounts of identity.[50] Relatedly, sociolinguistics has drawn out what Austin, too often, occludes, that performatives are more often acts of persuasion than they are solo, self-binding utterances. We

---

[46] Some, more recent philosophers would agree with Cassandra that the purpose makes strong the vow. See e.g. Michael H. Robins, *Promising, Intending, and Moral Autonomy* (Cambridge, 1984); Michael E. Bratman, *Intention, Plans, and Practical Reason* (Cambridge, MA, 1987), and his *Faces of Intention: Selected Essays on Intention and Agency* (Cambridge, 1999).

[47] e.g. *De Juramento*, I.xiii, J. L. Austin, *How to Do Things with Words*, 2nd edn., ed. J. O. Urmson and Marina Sbisà (Oxford, 1975), pp. 10–11. In both, more intentionally couched formulations can be found.

[48] Gurr, *Shakespearean Stage*, p. 76.

[49] *How to Do Things with Words*, p. 22.

[50] Jacques Derrida, *Limited Inc* (Evanston, IL, 1988), pp. 16–19, 67–72, 88–107 (cf. Stanley Cavell, *A Pitch of Philosophy: Autobiographical Exercises* (Cambridge, MA, 1994), ch. 2); Judith Butler, *Excitable Speech: a Politics of the Performative* (New York, 1997); Andrew Parker and Eve Kosofsky Sedgwick, 'Introduction', in Parker and Sedgwick (eds.), *Performativity and Performance* (New York, 1995), pp. 1–18.

should remember the tacit contribution to the speech act of the addressee of an oath ('I swear to *you*, by God') or the promisee of a vow. Oaths and vows are usually 'joint actions'.[51]

To think about origins and contexts is to return to social performatives scripted for the stage. Where did Shakespeare learn about oaths and vows? The earliest life record we have concerns his baptism, when, as required by the Book of Common Prayer, his godparents took vows on his behalf. One of the latest, in 1612, finds him giving sworn, duly cautious, evidence in a breach of promise case.[52] Shakespeare learned, then, from the church and the law courts, from the street and the tavern, but also (as *Troylus* shows) from the classics: Cicero, Seneca, Plutarch, Ovid. From Quintilian, if not from Aristotle, he would have learned about the tactical advantages of taking an oath in court.[53] The Tudor rhetoricians are, by comparison, disinclined to discuss oaths, vows and their uses. That they are on a spectrum with profanity, and more immediately a topic for moralists than those offering models of good discourse, must be one reason for this. Even so, Henry Peacham gives a full account of the make-up of oaths and vows in the 1593 *Garden of Eloquence*.[54] When reading *The Boke Named the Gouernour*, Shakespeare must have digested Sir Thomas Elyot's influential discussion of how foul-mouthed 'Children . . . do play with the armes and bones of Christe, as they were chery stones', while witnesses and juries perjure themselves.[55] Holinshed, Machiavelli, Montaigne. All these, no doubt, informed him. But he must also have learned about oaths and vows, perhaps supremely, in the playhouse.

The anti-theatrical writers, from Gosson to Prynne, encourage us to recognise, whatever we make of their antipathy, that the playhouse was not just a place where young gentlemen, card players and drinkers went to mill about and utter profanities: on stage, swearing by the heathen gods and taking the Lord's name in vain set a bad example.[56] In his *Anatomie of Abuses* (1583), Stubbes says you should go to the theatre 'if you will

---

[51] See e.g. Herbert H. Clark, *Using Language* (Cambridge, 1996), pp. 136–41.

[52] The Belott–Mountjoy papers, now an appendix to Charles Nicholl's absorbing study, *The Lodger: Shakespeare on Silver Street* (2007; London, 2008), show Shakespeare telling Daniel Nicholas that Charles Mountjoy promised 'about the some of ffyftye pound*es*' to his daughter and Stephen Belott on their marriage, but in court, under oath, he deposed 'what c*er*tayne por*ci*on he Rememb*er*ithe not./ nor when to be payed' (p. 289, cf. p. 293; 290).

[53] Aristotle, *Rhetoric*, I.xv; Quintilian, *Institutio Oratoria*, V.vi.

[54] Henry Peacham, *The Garden of Eloquence*, rev. edn. (London, 1593), pp. 67–8, 75–6.

[55] *The Boke Named the Gouernour* (London, 1531), 193r–195r.

[56] See e.g. William Prynne, *Histrio-Mastix: the Players Scourge, or, Actors Tragaedie* (London, 1633), **3v, pp. 81–8, 520 (citing Gosson), p. 930.

learn to playe the vice, to swear, teare, and blaspheme, both Heauen and Earth'.[57] Friends of the playhouse predictably reversed this libel. Plays, according to the Water Poet, show 'stabbing, drabbing, dicing, drinking' and, at the end of the line, 'swearing' in their true, instructive horror.[58] He could point to the tipsy Cassio in *Othello*, quarrelsome and 'high in oath', then bitterly rebuking himself.[59] But no one will seriously believe that Shakespeare was drawn to swearing because he wanted to be didactic. More relevant is Nashe's defence of the stage, where he celebrates a scene in *The Famous Victories*, a play well known to Shakespeare, in which the King of France and the Dauphin take an oath on Henry V's sword: 'what a glorious thing it is to haue *Henrie* the fifth represented on the Stage leading the French King prisoner, and forcing both him and the Dolphin to sweare fealty'.[60] It is a vivid reminder of the theatrical, even the histrionic power of oaths and vows, to which I now want to turn.

* * *

Shakespeare was not often drawn to the oath as primary utterance, to the moment, so important to moralists, when an isolated character gives his word under the eye of God. He was more interested in joint actions, where speech act and doubt go together. Admittedly, there is Hamlet, alone after seeing the ghost, declaring, 'now to my word; | It is; Adue, Adue, Remember me: I haue sworn't' (I.v; 795–6). It is typical of Shakespeare, however, to destabilise the situation by having Hamlet rebut while echoing the ghost, who wants to be revenged. And the prince's words are further confounded because this initiates a long, stagey sequence that parodies the sort of swearing presented by *The Famous Victories*, as Horatio and Marcellus are required to swear on Hamlet's sword that they will keep the secret of the ghost.

The connection between Hamlet's swearing and the repeated injunctions by prince and ghost which push the scene into fearful comedy are often reinforced in performance by having him swear on his own sword. This impulse to externalise and take hold of something solid goes with the performativity of oaths and vows even outside the theatre. Early modern commentators were struck by the scriptural, classical and anthropological

---

[57] Philip Stubbes, *Anatomie of Abuses* (London, 1583), L8v.
[58] John Taylor, 'To my Approued Good Friend M. Thomas Heywood', one of the prefatory poems in Thomas Heywood, *Apology for Actors* (London, 1612).
[59] II.iii; 1176–1459 (1356).
[60] *Pierce Penilesse his Supplication to the Diuell* (London, 1592), F3v.

evidence of swearers touching Abraham's thigh, holding up their hands, or casting away a stone.[61] In origin these gestures were mnemonic. They made the speech acts easier to recall, in primarily oral societies.[62] But they readily elided with the sacred as people swore on missals or altars. Traditionally, Hamlet swears not just on his sword but the cross of its hilt. He is giddily beside himself and needs to grip his weapon because his distrust of Claudius has been vindicated but also, more obscurely, because we are not quite ourselves when we asseverate or promise. We are trying to manifest a truth, or lean into the future self that will deliver on the vow. We utter 'by Heaven' differently from saying by and Heaven, as though making it citational. But whatever the aspiration the voice cannot be a binding block. The speech-act, so complete for Austin, is dramatically potent because insufficient.

An oath is framed by a formula which gives the language of the speech act something of the firmness of the God or the honour which is called upon to secure it. The mnemonic, ritual context is brought into the utterance. That the form of an oath or vow is given makes it already external enough to be uttered as a thing. This is why I can give you my word. At the end of *Measure* and *All's Well*, Shakespeare brings out the quasi-magical aspects of these formulae,[63] which spring not just from an affinity with incantation but because they jump the gap between doubt and truth and promise to deliver the future. Yet the quality of the performance affects the quality of the performative. I can say 'by Heaven' with a frivolous as well as a solemn air, or impetuously like Hamlet to his friends. This makes oaths and vows an acutely sensitive resource for judgements of intention by audiences, and a subtle opportunity for the actor, who can qualify the absoluteness of asseveration or promise enshrined in the speech act.

So when Hamlet calls upon Horatio and the soldier to swear, the situation oscillates unstably. They do swear, by custom at least, 'in faith', to keep what they have seen secret, but are then asked to swear on his sword. As men of honour, they are mildly insulted. Does Hamlet, like Sanderson, doubt that 'in faith' is binding? If so, it quickly gets out of hand as the prince discovers that repetition and emphasis will not secure

[61] White, *Of Oathes*, pp. 2–3, 14–15; John Bulwer, *Chirologia: Or, The Natural Language of the Hand* (London, 1644), pp. 50–4, 102–5; Sanderson, *De Juramento*, V.iii, xi.

[62] See e.g. Richard Firth Green, *A Crisis of Truth: Literature and Law in Ricardian England* (Philadelphia, PA, 1999), ch. 2.

[63] *Measure for Measure*, V.i; 2391–5, 2579–85, *All's Well*, V.iii; 2890–6, 3022–7.

an oath. As it happens, in all three early texts of the play, Horatio and Marcellus are not given 'I swear', or anything like it, to say. Every time the ghost bellows 'Sweare', there is a flurry of bewildered reaction, yet no word, it seems, is uttered. Casuists did allow that, when you could not speak to swear, you could nod or raise your hand.[64] Perhaps we might take, then, the laying of their hands on the sword as an oath. There are word and deed quibbles in Hamlet's instruction, 'Indeed, vpon my sword, Indeed' (*sword*, *word* and *sworn* were close in Elizabethan pronunciation).[65] As Pistol, in another play, declares: 'Sword is an Oath, & Oaths must haue their course.'[66] But if the actors do opt for the gesture, the rest of their body language can hardly be affirmative. Their posture is going to qualify any utterance in word or deed. Austin regards the body as effectively a cipher, included in or cohering with the speech act rather than seething away around it in an interpretatively dissonant, theatrically involving, way. Judith Butler more accurately observes that 'the body rhetorically exceeds the speech act it also performs'.[67]

The mobility of this scene, as the actors range about, makes palpable for the audience how uncontaining oaths can be. The prince is playing catch-up with a speech act while his friends run away from the ghost. It is not just the taking but the keeping. As the action spins about, Hamlet—who will soon enough break his vows to Ophelia, and probably his word to the ghost—anticipates the temptations. He starts to sound like Polonius as he spells out all the ways in which his associates should not betray their word. They must swear not even to hint at what drives his antic disposition, he says, putting on a mad little pageant,

> With Armes encombred thus, or thus, head-shake;
> Or by pronouncing of some doubtful Phrase;
> As well, we know, or we could and if we would, . . . (870–2)

The sworn word is meant to be brief and sufficient. As Sanderson puts it, '*Simplicity above all things becometh an Oath*' (II.ii). In practice—better say 'in performance'—though, it summons up a mass of supplementary

---

[64] e.g. Sanderson, *De Juramento*, V.i.

[65] See the evidence from rhyming and homophone lists in E. J. Dobson, *English Pronunciation 1500–1700*, 2nd edn. (Oxford, 1968), Fausto Cercignani, *Shakespeare's Works and Elizabethan Pronunciation* (Oxford, 1981).

[66] *Hamlet*, I.v; 844, *Henry the Fift*, II.i; 601. Pistol quibbles on, or garblingly misconstrues, ''s word' ('By God's word').

[67] *Excitable Speech*, p. 155. Behind Butler's thought here is Shoshana Felman, *The Literary Speech Act: Don Juan with J. L. Austin, or Seduction in Two Languages*, tr. Catherine Porter (Ithaca, NY, 1983).

glossing to cover the eventualities. We could be historical and notice how oaths of allegiance and obedience became increasingly elaborate, to guard against equivocation and mental reservation.[68] But the drive to qualification goes deeper. The binding word is a pellet of language which, because of psychological and communicative ambiguities, becomes a machine for generating verbiage.

Loues Labour's Lost is the classic case. Charged with courting Jacquenetta, in the King of Navarre's park, when 'It was proclaimed a yeeres impriso[n]ment to bee taken with a Wench', the clever yokel Costard says he was taken with a damsel (also proclaimed), virgin (ditto) and maid (who will not serve his turn). The proclamation of the oath must have been a copious document. Meanwhile, the sworn word dissolves back into the ordinary language that gives it grammar and purpose. If we did not say by and Heaven we could not swear 'by Heaven'. So when Armado tells the page boy Moth that he has sworn to study with the King for three years, the tender juvenile can reply: 'how easie it is to put yeres to the word three, and study three yeeres in two words, the dancing horse will tell you'. The lords go further down the same path, once they have fallen in love with the ladies. '*Vowes are but breath, and breath a vapour is,*' Longaville declares in his sonnet.[69]

We are getting into a nest of paradoxes congenial to a dramatist who was drawn to plurality and interpenetrating ambiguities. The word that cannot be fixed is subverted by its performance and needs massive supplements to explicate. It is a forceful commitment of the self couched in public, derivative language. Oaths and vows can reinforce the very doubt they are meant to allay—which is why Juliet urges Romeo not to swear, but to say, that he loves her (II.ii; 888–940). (After the Act to Restrain Abuses, as we shall see in a moment, the relationship between swearing and saying would be weighted in new ways.) Oaths and vows tend to be powerful when power is coming into question, as when Lear disowns Cordelia 'by the sacred radience of the Sunne' (I.i; 115). They gain you credit, but put you into debt. They are sociable, joint actions which it can be narcissistic to follow through (as with Hector). They are brittle in their decisiveness because the act of asseveration can make characters aware that we only think what we know, and, when they are promissory, because of what Andrew Lang noted, 'Shakespeare's way of placing a man of

[68] Condren, *Argument and Authority*, pp. 249–50.
[69] *Loues Labour's Lost*, I.i; 283–93, I.ii; 358–60, IV.iii; 1401.

nature more or less noble, but irresolute, in a crisis which demands decision'[70]—that is, they can be stand-ins for decision.

To rely too much on vowing is, we might say, *young*. It represents a development which, for the psychoanalytically minded, is regressive because it undoes the hard-earned distinction between word and deed. It falls back on 'magical thinking', and substitutes a binding word for the moral judgements of maturity.[71] Oaths make claims on truth which expose you to being false, or claims on a future which 'reckening Time, whose milliond accidents | Creep in twixt vows, and change decrees of Kings' is likely to prove hubristic.[72] When, as in *Troylus*, what's past and what's to come are strewn with husks and formless ruin, and faith and troth are only of the moment,[73] vows and promissory oaths have no purchase. Time does not connect. The play unfolds in what is virtually a space of interruption,[74] where oaths and vows contribute to the sense of events suspended, hung up between declaration and act.

Promissory oaths and vows are close to creativity because they conjure into language matters not yet known or done. Yet there is dead weight in there too. When we promise we put the present, as it becomes the past, onto the neck of the future. (No wonder Nietzsche was uneasy, finding an ominous link between promising and punishment.[75]) Yet what, in Shakespeare, is static? The meaning of what we vow is mutable because relative. When I promise you *x* it is not *x* but the prospect of what *x* will be. Then when I perform *x* (if I do) it will have absorbed the value of my fidelity and it will also have shifted in meaning because much else in life will have changed. This Troilus forgets. Swearing is the honourable man's privilege and mark of status. He lives a life of risk and purpose in which the stake is himself, his standing. Yet not if he vows by proxy, or fulfils his oath by proxy, as Henry V does to Williams through Fluellen. Then it gets interestingly problematic because this displays in acute form the always discernible fact that the oath or vow is independent of those involved in the joint action. As Nerissa says to Gratiano, though not for her, yet for

---

[70] Andrew Lang, *History of English Literature: from 'Beowulf' to Swinburne*, 3rd edn. (London, 1913), p. 229. This talk was repeated as an Andrew Lang Lecture at the University of St Andrews on 7 May 2009.

[71] Herbert J. Schlesinger, *Promises, Oaths, and Vows: on the Psychology of Promising* (New York, 2008), pp. 20–2, 50–8, 83–8.

[72] Sonnet 115.

[73] IV.v; 2732–8.

[74] On 'the promise of future action' as 'an interrupted act', see Schlesinger, *Promises, Oaths, and Vows*, pp. 41–6, 89.

[75] *On the Genealogy of Morals*, II.4–6.

his oaths, he should not have given away her ring.[76] This does not mean, of course, that there is no way out of oaths and vows; they can be ways out in themselves, ways of *avoiding* responsibility, of saying that you are bound by a promise to God or your past self to act in a certain way. The binding word simplifies life by removing deliberation. Othello's oaths to punish Desdemona are only the most conspicuous case.

Those are impassioned utterances. Oaths and vows can be outbursts, excesses of agitation, as Thomas Wright and Robert Burton notice in their lively accounts of gamesters,[77] yet they spring from our need for security, the drive to know and plan. Along with prophecies and curses, they consequently feed into Shakespeare's characteristic preference (as Coleridge put it) for expectation over surprise.[78] It would be a mistake to imagine, however, that time under a vow is the same as time without one. Promised things are more exciting than gifts because anticipation is a nervous pleasure. Then postponement stales and the arrival of the promised thing will be an anticlimax. This is very Troilus. So to think of vows as bringing something forward is only part of the story. Anticipation and delay are not neutral in their effects. Is there even an element of threat? Of time suspended to try us. Troilus warns Diomedes that, 'by the dreadfull *Pluto*', if he doesn't use Cressida well, he will cut his throat (IV.iv; 2515–23). But Cressida is under threat too, if she doesn't stay true to Troilus. She is constructed by the rhetoric of their troth-plight into a default position of dishonesty, which is not quite what the play shows us. John Searle wants to believe that a promise only has force if the promisee wants what is promised.[79] But this is not how it feels, at least for those in a society in which oaths and vows have their own potency.

* * *

That characters swear more mildly after the Act of 1606 is not in itself that interesting. Nor is it surprising that, as compared with earlier plays, they more often say they will swear and then do not, and that mere asseverations are retrospectively described as oaths. There are situations in which we expect oaths, such as Caliban kneeling to swear fealty to

<hr>

[76] *The Merchant of Venice*, V.i; 2577–8.
[77] Thomas Wright, *The Passions of the Minde in Generall* (London, 1604), pp. 125–6; Robert Burton, *The Anatomy of Melancholy* (Oxford, 1621), p. 160.
[78] S. T. Coleridge, *Shakespearean Criticism*, ed. Thomas Middleton Raysor, 2nd edn., 2 vols. (London, 1960), I. 199.
[79] John R. Searle, *Speech Acts: an Essay in the Philosophy of Language* (Cambridge, 1969), p. 58.

Stephano, and glugging out of his bottle, without uttering an oath,[80] and stock types of swearing who are said to be, but who are not, profane (the boatswain in *The Tempest*, for instance).[81] Even Cloten, who makes much of his right as a gentleman to swear and give offence, and who is reportedly foul-mouthed in scenes we are not shown,[82] keeps to the letter of the Act onstage. For all that, oaths and vows remain important. Coriolanus swears to ally himself with the Volscians, then dooms yet redeems himself by 'Breaking his Oath and Resolution, like | A twist of rotten Silke'. There is Iachimo, in *Cymbeline*, convincing Posthumous that Imogen has been false with a judiciously placed 'By Iupiter'. The Surveyor, in *Henry the Eight*, testifying that Buckingham swore he would dispose of the king. There is even, in *The Two Noble Kinsmen*, a scene from Fletcher's hand, modelled on Hector's exchanges with Andromache and Cassandra, in which Theseus is urged by Hippolyta and Emilia to retract his 'oth' and 'vow' to have Pirithous and Arcite executed.[83]

What is newer is how oaths are avoided. There had been refusers before 1606, but they tend, like Richard III, to be worse than those who swear, or, like Brutus in *Julius Caesar*, to be too complacent about honour to believe that oaths can bind. Pericles and Marina not only refuse to swear but, in the shadow of the Act, draw on lines of argument that go back to the Tudor homily. 'Ile take thy word, for faith', Pericles tells Helicanus, 'not aske thine oath, | Who shuns not to breake one, will cracke both.'[84] In this play, those who swear are likely not just to be bad but to use oaths to spur their badness. Thus Thaliard, who has sworn to kill Pericles, shuffles off any blame: 'for if a king bidde a man bee a villaine, hee's bound by the indenture of his oath to bee one' (B3r).[85] Pericles does take a vow by Diana. But Marina is impeccable,[86] almost an exemplar of the reaction against profanity that was not just sweeping the stage but would lead, in 1623, the year of the Folio, to a law imposing fines on those who swore offstage as well as on. 'Faith', says Boult, mildly, 'I must rauish her, or shee'le . . . make our swearers priests' (G3v).

---

[80] *The Tempest*, II.ii; 1159–1232.

[81] *The Tempest*, I.i; 11–61, V.i; 2202–6.

[82] *Cymbeline*, II.i; 840–50, 864–8, IV.ii; 2396, V.v; 3571–96.

[83] *Coriolanus*, V.vi; 3763–4, *Cymbeline*, II.iv; 1295–6, *Henry the Eight*, I.ii; 472–568, *The Two Noble Kinsmen* (London, 1634), pp. 52–7.

[84] *Pericles* (London, 1609), B2v.

[85] Cf. Leonine, who, having sworn to Dionyza, pursues without mercy his vow to kill Marina.

[86] Cf. Elena Glazov-Corrigan, 'The new function of language in Shakespeare's *Pericles*: oath versus "Holy Word"', *Shakespeare Survey*, 43 (1991), pp. 131–40, esp. 133, 136–8.

Shirley, the only critic who has investigated swearing across the late plays, has little to say about them. Her basic, limiting conclusion is that, after 1606, there was 'a full-blown compliance with the regulations'.[87] But the effects of the Act went deep. I want to end with *The Winters Tale* because it shows with particular clarity both the continued structural use to which Shakespeare put oaths and vows and the impact of the Act on the ethos of asseveration. For swearing in this play is not just made to accord with the classical romance setting. There is a formative, problematic thrust to its characteristic oathlets, 'in sooth', 'in truth' and 'verely'— which has twelve out of its fourteen Shakespearean uses after 1606, seven of them in *The Winters Tale*. In the late plays, after all, verity is in strong suspicion, either because the story is like an old tale or because, in *All is True*, realism proves inscrutable.

Let me plunge into the exchange which precipitates the main action (I.ii; 50–121). Making an appeal to verity which turns out to be untrue, Polixenes has told Leontes that he will leave the Sicilian court, 'Very sooth, to morrow.' Called upon to make him stay, Hermione exploits the fact that, after 1606, only flaccid oaths can be spoken:

> POLIXENES I may not verely.
> HERMIONE Verely?
> You put me off with limber Vowes: . . .

She also, more ingeniously, takes advantage of the limitation set by the Act to gender dominance. Polixenes must now draw his sooths from the same box as Lady Percy:

>   but I,
> Though you would seek t'vnsphere the Stars with Oaths,
> Should yet say, Sir, no going: Verely
> You shall not goe; a Ladyes Verely' is
> As potent as a Lords.

So will you be our guest or our prisoner, she jests: 'by your dread Verely, | One of them you shall be.' And of course he agrees to stay. 'Sooth' and 'verely', it seems, are little more than charms against the fragility of asseveration, called upon when most in doubt.

There has been much speculation about the sudden outbreak of Leontes' jealousy. It does not seem to have been noticed that it happens when this oathful exchange is correlated with his betrothal vows. As he closely observes Polixenes and his wife, like Troilus watching Cressida and

---

[87] *Swearing and Perjury*, p. 152.

Diomed, sparring and flirting with their oaths, he splits Hermione between the woman who once gave him her hand and her word with delaying modesty (or was it, he now wonders, reluctance) and the sexy immediacy of the onstage handfast:

> HERMIONE What? haue I twice said well? . . .
> LEONTES   Why, that was when
> Three crabbed Moneths had sowr'd themselues to death,
> Ere I could make thee open thy white Hand:
> A[nd] clap thy selfe my Loue; then didst thou vtter,
> I am yours for euer.
> HERMIONE   'Tis Grace indeed.
> Why lo-you now; I have spoke to th'purpose twice:
> The one, for euer earn'd a Royall Husband;
> Th'other, for some while a Friend.
> [*She gives her hand to Polixenes*]
> LEONTES [*aside*]   Too hot, too hot:
> To mingle friendship farre, is mingling bloods. . . .
> But to be padling Palmes, and pinching Fingers,
> As now they are . . .   (I.ii; 160–89)

It is not just the excluding, physical contact which tips Leontes into derangement, nor the suggestive ambiguity of 'Friend',[88] but the implication that Hermione's espousal, her handfast, is being reprised, one vow overlaying another.

What does Diana mean in *All's Well* when she tells Bertram, ''Tis not the many oathes that makes the truth, | But the plaine single vow, that is vow'd true' (IV.ii; 2045–6)? However 'makes' is taken, it must include 'constructs, creates'. You do not have to be a postmodernist to believe that oaths and vows configure truth. You might instead be Shakespeare. But *The Winters Tale* brings together a sceptical, relativistic awareness that truths are sanctioned troths, which can be informed by an almost religious 'faith', with a sense that they reach for 'belief' in the particular, modern sense of 'acceptance of a proposition . . . as true, on the ground of . . . evidence' (*OED* 2) that has been used against those 'that delight in Giddinesse; And count it a Bondage to fix a Beleefe' all the way from Bacon's essay 'Of Truth'—which I have just quoted—to Bernard Williams's *On Truth and Truthfulness*. 'It is not onely,' Bacon goes on, 'the Difficultie, and Labour, which Men take in finding out of *Truth* . . . that doth bring *Lies* in fauour: But a naturall, though corrupt Loue, of the *Lie*

---

[88] *OED* 4, 'A lover or paramour, of either sex' (from 1490, and citing *Loues Labour's Lost*).

it selfe.'[89] The giddy, paranoid ethos of Sicily partly springs from Leontes' jealousy. But when oaths can make the truth, jealousy itself seems the product of deeper epistemological difficulty.

Such oaths may be vowed true, as when, later in the play, Antigonus swears on the king's sword that he will expose the infant Perdita. Something less manageable wells up, however, from this intense, verbal making, when Camillo tells Polixenes that the verity of Hermione's innocence hangs on Bohemia's word against Leontes', who 'thinkes, nay . . . he sweares, . . . that you haue toucht his Queene | Forbiddenly' (I.ii; 527–30). Polixenes' appalled rebuttal, 'Oh then, my best blood turne | To an infected Gelly', and so on, has more than a passing resemblance, in its post-1606, profanity-avoiding way, to the conditional self-curse that was, as we have seen, traditionally embedded in an oath. Denial is of no avail, however, because, as Camillo puts it, in a troubling passage, to swear against Leontes' oath-bound thought, to seek to overturn his thought with an oath, would be to swear over—to validate by overlaying—what is resisted:

> Sweare his thought ouer
> By each particular Starre in Heauen, and
> By all their Influences; you may as well
> Forbid the Sea for to obey the Moone,
> As (or by Oath) remoue, or (Counsaile) shake
> The Fabrick of his Folly, whose foundation
> Is pyl'd vpon his Faith, and will continue
> The standing of his Body.   (I.ii; 527–46)

The fabric of Leontes' universe, the bonds of heaven (Troilus' phrase) for him, are piled upon 'his Faith'—a belief unsecured by evidence that is also his giving of an oath.

When Hermione is confronted with Leontes' sworn, distorting 'Faith', the post-1606 promotion of saying over swearing does not work in her favour. In front of her ladies and his lords, the king declares

> 'tis *Polixenes*
> Ha's made thee swell thus.
> HERMIONE   But I'ld say he had not;
> And Ile be sworne you would beleeue my saying,
> How e're you leane to th'Nay-ward.   (II.i; 661–5)

Taken aback, embarrassed and sensing that she should not lend credibility to the accusation by countering it too strongly (swearing it over), which

---

[89] Francis Bacon, *The Essayes or Counsels, Ciuill and Morall*, rev. edn. (London, 1625), pp. 1–2.

would leave the king no way back, Hermione is also too confident that her truth is self-evident. Like Desdemona, who is slow to swear her honesty, she does not yet understand how deluded her husband is. As she refuses to swear, to perform a performative, before the court, a Jacobean audience must have been conscious on some level that she is subjected to constraints that are an issue for the play as a whole. Limited by her sex, but also by the Act, she cannot vehemently invoke the Divine.

The consequences of this are dire, especially because, in her reluctance, Hermione makes play with the post-1606 limitations, and declares that she will not say, as she 'would', but 'will' swear, which she hardly can. 'But Il'd say he had not; | And Ile be sworne you would beleeue my saying.' The substitution of (not) saying for swearing makes her sound evasive, too clever for the matter in hand, while her sophisticated phrasing awkwardly manages to imply that she will not swear to her truth but only to Leontes' willingness to believe her, and so, from his point of view, to his credulity, which fans his mistrust. Not surprisingly, the king reacts by declaring her 'without-dore-Forme' the cover of 'an Adultresse' (666–80). There is no way back from this, within the resources of saying and swearing, even when, in the arraignment of III.ii, Hermione lucidly protests against the charge not only of adultery but of helping Polixenes and Camillo escape '*contrary to the Faith and Allegeance of a true Subiect*'— against the terms of those oaths of loyalty and obedience that went back to the middle ages, that had been widely imposed in Tudor England, and that, after 1606, subjects could once again be required to swear to their king (1192–3).[90]

What of the question of structure? In the scenes set in Bohemia, Autolycus is a crucial figure. For he is not just, as in Ovid, a duplicitous thief, but a rogue who, like Autolykos in *The Odyssey*, specifically deceives through oaths.[91] The ballads in his pack parody Leontes' faith in the power of oaths to verify, such as the one sung by a fish about the hardness of maidens' hearts on the fourscore of April. 'Is it true too, thinke you,' asks Dorcas. 'Fiue Iustices hands at it, and witnesses more then my packe will hold.'[92] As with testimony, so with promises. The song in Autolycus' pack that Mopsa, Dorcas and the Clown sing together while

---

[90] The same month (May 1606) that saw the passage of the Act to Restrain Abuses also saw king and parliament, in the wake of the Gunpowder Plot, imposing an Oath of Allegiance to identify uncompromising Roman Catholics (3 and 4 James I c. 4).

[91] *The Odyssey*, XIX.395.

[92] IV.iv; 2081–2106.

vows are being exchanged in the handfast between Florizel and Perdita[93] offers new angles on the rivalries of Leontes, Hermione and Polixenes. '*It becomes thy oath full well*', sings Mopsa, who is competing with Dorcas for the Clown, '*Thou to me thy secrets tell.*' But, replies Dorcas, '*Thou hast sworne my Loue to be.*'[94]

It would labour the point to crawl through the fifth act of this play setting out in detail what criticism has overlooked: the mosaic of oaths, vows, and reflections on swearing. Leontes formally swears never to marry without Paulina's permission; she is married to Camillo on the basis of a similar vow.[95] Can the news be true, that Perdita is a princess, asks the Second Gentleman. 'Most true', the Third replies, 'That which you heare, you'le sweare you see' (V.ii; 3040–2). The Clown promises to 'sweare to the Prince' that Autolycus is 'as honest a true Fellow as any is in *Bohemia*'. The Shepherd, as though familiar with the Act, observes 'You may say it, but not sweare it', but the Clown knows his rights: 'Not sweare it, now I am a Gentleman?' What makes the exchange so integral is the Shepherd's persistent worry 'How if it be false (Sonne?)' and the Clown's recklessness with truth (think of Leontes on the queen's adultery): 'If it be ne're so false, a true Gentleman may sweare it' (V.ii; 3164–76).

There is matter in this swearing all the way down to the language used when the statue of Hermione comes to life: 'Would you not deeme it breath'd? and that those veines did *verily* beare blood?', wonders Leontes, to which Paulina adds, 'It is requir'd | You doe awake your *Faith.*'[96] These ripples of swearing through statement would be insignificant details without the pattern to which they belong, and without their ultimate relationship with the oath which makes the breathing of the statue seem like a miracle. For the audience, like characters in the play, have been deceived by an oath—or, rather, by the promise of an oath, which, post-1606, is the more potent for not even being uttered. I mean that the redemptive energy of the scene depends on our having been misled by Paulina's declaration after the trial scene: 'I say she's dead: Ile swear't. If word, nor oath | Preuaile not, go and see' (III.ii; 1391–2).

---

[93] Florizel's commitment to his vow, once Polixenes forbids his marriage, sweeps him into declarations about 'my faith', his 'affection', and 'earth'-shattering claims regarding the potency of his oath, that recall those used of and by Leontes in the first half of the play (IV.iv; 2328–58).

[94] Note Mopsa's insistent response, setting oath against oath, '*Thou hast sworne it more to mee. | Then whether goest? Say whether?*' (IV.iv; 2110–32).

[95] V.i; 2810–26, V.iii; 3349–52.

[96] My italics (V.iii; 3261–2, 3300–1).

As those examples begin to suggest, Shakespeare's binding language is not finally, that easily, delimited. It is not just that oaths and vows overlap with such related practices as *testifying, covenanting, gaging* and, as is now apparent, indicatively, *saying*, but that they draw on performative conventions that are broadly and deeply established in language as a connective medium. A socially articulated, inward medium that was, for Shakespeare, always betrayable and potentially betraying. To pursue that train of thought, however, would require another lecture, when one might just as validly think comparatively about play-texts. Much can be learned, for instance, by noticing how oaths in *The Famous Victories* are redeployed in *Henry the Fift*, or by comparing the group swearing scene in *Hamlet* with the simpler, derivative situation in *The Reuengers Tragaedie*. Work remains to be done. But I hope that I have given you a sense of what a rich and underexplored subject this is, and of how distinctively Shakespearean are its complications in the plays.

Our Unwritten Constitution

JOHN BAKER

Fellow of the Academy

I THINK IT PROBABLE that when I was invited, several years ago, to give this lecture, it was expected that I should speak about more remote legal history.[1] If so, I can only apologise. In my defence I could cite good precedents for legal historians complaining about constitutional dangers, most notably John Selden, whose name would need no commendation to the founders of this Lecture. But he lived in an age when history provided live ammunition in defence of the liberty of the subject and constitutional monarchy. That kind of legal history is no longer of any forensic value in this country. My concerns today are rooted in very recent history, and came into focus after the inept announcement by Mr Blair on 12 June 2003 that he had abolished the office of Lord Chancellor, apparently without consulting anyone outside his own circle.[2] I am going to confine

---

Read at the Academy 24 November 2009.

[1] I am grateful for the many helpful comments which I have received and taken into account. I must in particular thank Dr M. C. Elliott and Professor G. W. Jones.

[2] Since the lecture was given, the circumstances have been the subject of investigation by the House of Lords Select Committee on the Constitution: *The Cabinet Office and the Centre of Government*, 4th Report of Session 2009–10 (HL 30), published in January 2010, at paras 188–217. It was perfectly obvious at the time that the decision had been taken without professional advice or proper circumspection: see, e.g., Lord Woolf, 'The Rule of Law and a change in the constitution', *Cambridge Law Journal*, 63 (2004), 317–30, at 320. The Cabinet Office declined to produce any papers to the Select Committee but claimed it had given advice and (by implication) that the Prime Minister had ignored it. Mr Blair admitted in evidence to the Committee that he had taken the decision on the spur of the moment and that the process was faulty (paras 201–2). The Committee concluded (para. 214) that 'the Cabinet Office was unable to ensure compliance with proper constitutional norms in the adoption of a change of such significance. It is particularly disturbing that these failures occurred without there being any external crisis which might explain, far less justify, such failures.'

Proceedings of the British Academy, **167**, 91–117. © The British Academy 2010.

my remarks to the brief period since then, although there is a good case for regarding the progressive surrender of autonomy to the European Union, and the various experiments with inland devolution and local government, as beginning a major constitutional revolution well before 2003 and as raising concerns at least as troubling as those on which I shall be concentrating.[3]

When I delivered a public lecture in 2004 on 'The Constitutional Revolution',[4] one of my chief complaints was that grave changes were occurring almost daily without much public notice being taken. Five years on, I can hardly complain of a complete lack of publicity—at least for those sufficiently well-informed, and with sufficient leisure, to search the internet regularly for the appropriate keywords. But I have come to the conclusion that the problems which I tried to identify in 2004 have deepened, and that the 'revolution' which I then addressed in somewhat pejorative terms is still underway. It is not, however, to be identified with the 'constitutional renewal' which the government has proudly announced. In fact, there is such a gulf between the public statements of the government and its actions that one might be forgiven for thinking that the language of 'renewal' is more rhetoric than reality, another exercise in 'spin'.[5]

It is admittedly difficult to separate constitutional matters from matters of political judgement. I am not sure that ministerial incompetence, arrogance, inefficiency, excessive centralisation, or over-regulation, can properly be regarded as unconstitutional, except in the sense that it is generally beyond the power of the people to do much about them. They are certainly not wholly new. Nor am I suggesting that the problems with our unwritten constitution all began under Mr Blair; some of them have a

---

[3] For the broader picture see V. Bogdanor, *The New British Constitution* (Oxford, 2009); and for the pre-2004 reforms see L. Dingle and B. Miller, 'United Kingdom constitutional reform' (2004), accessible at <www.llrx.com/features/ukconstitution.htm>. The Human Rights Act 1998 is also a landmark, though in a different way. Britain was bound by the European Convention on Human Rights long before 1998 and that regime still takes priority. The Luxembourg Court, indeed, regards domestic declarations of incompatibility under the Act as legally ineffective. The Act has nevertheless begun to alter the judicial culture in Britain and may have paved the way for judicial review of legislation at some time in the future.

[4] Available at <www.law.cam.ac.uk/faculty-resources/summary/the-constitutional-revolution/1587>.

[5] The present administration has achieved a particular reputation for pursuing hidden policies which differ markedly from those announced in public. The most recent example to be uncovered is the policy of unrestricted mass immigration, which was revealed by a former government adviser at the end of October: see the article by M. Marrin, *The Sunday Times*, 1 Nov. 2009, p. 20.

longer history. But the problems have come to the fore in the last few years chiefly because of widely perceived changes in the style of government.[6]

First there is the concentration of power in the prime minister and his special advisers at the expense of the Cabinet and a professional Civil Service. It has become fashionable to speak of an increasingly presidential style of government. But this does not, of course, mean a constitutional presidency: rather, a novel kind of monarchy. The chief difference from classical monarchy is that our quasi-monarch is indirectly elected—very indirectly, in the case of Mr Brown—but, once in power, he is an absolute monarch for a term of years and rules without the partnership of others.[7] The prime minister would only have to persuade Parliament to suspend the quinquennial system of election and he would really be an absolute monarch. I hope that is still unthinkable; but I am less sure than I was ten years ago. Although the House of Lords retains the power to veto such a measure,[8] with a reconstituted House of Lords, supinely following the party whip, it would only require a supposed national emergency as a pretext; and we have seen that the government is willing to play that card on occasion.

There is nothing new in the notion that we have an 'elective dictator-ship'. I remember Lord Hailsham coining the term in a lecture in 1976.[9] But it has become a more common figure of speech, as evidenced by over 9,000 hits on Google—nine times, incidentally, the number I counted in 2004. Without any opportunity for electoral approval or dissent, we have acquired a form of government which appears to operate without refer-ence to traditional advisory mechanisms or public opinion. Proposals of a fundamental nature often come as a surprise to the outside world, because there has been no preceding clamour for them; and I am not sure the Civil Service or even the Cabinet are always made privy either. There has been some show of a return to public 'consultation' since Mr Blair's departure; but the practice of announcing novelties as decided govern-ment policy still has the practical effect of making the subsequent process

---

[6] This was a matter of comment before 2004: see, e.g., the prophetic assessment by D. Oliver, *Constitutional Reform in the United Kingdom* (Oxford, 2003), pp. 390–1.

[7] See G. Allen, *The Last Prime Minister: Being Honest about the UK Presidency* (2nd edn., Thorverton, 2003), at p. 3: 'The UK Presidency remains unchecked, and it has shown no willing-ness to seek partnership with the legislature, or the wider nation, even when such a partnership would clearly assist its objectives.'

[8] Parliament Act 1911, 1 & 2 Geo. V, c. 13, s. 2(1); *Jackson* v. *Att.-Gen.* [2006] 1 AC 262.

[9] 'Elective Dictatorship', Richard Dimbleby Lecture, published in *The Listener*, 21 Oct. 1976, pp. 496–500. He was, however, more concerned at the use of this 'dictatorship' by governments with a small majority than by those with a large one.

of consultation a meaningless charade. No doubt it makes life easier for a prime minister if he can just turn to his chosen advisers on the sofa for guidance.[10] And, since his party commands a majority in the Commons, it must be an irritation to have to bother about consultation, precedents, or even Parliament. But there is reason to doubt whether the presidential model is working well even in terms of managerial efficiency, since it places a heavy emotional and physical strain on the prime minister if he is to be responsible for every detail in person while trying to appear infallible in public.[11] There is now widespread dissatisfaction with the growing phalanx of special advisers and policy units, and the replacement of old-style Civil Service mandarins with managers appointed, not to advise impartially, but to deliver at all costs. There is also growing popular despair at the processes of government. This can be associated with the emergence of a political class, disconnected from the rest of society, and with no experience of other ways of life, which is motivated principally by the pursuit of power and the perquisites of power.[12] When members of this class find themselves in government, they assume a strident and unmerited self-confidence about their natural superiority to other institutions and professions and their mission to control them. Not the least troubling manifestation of this trend is the seeming indifference to independent legal advice, an observable consequence of which has been regular confrontation with the courts.[13] Another is the indifference to truth: it has been very harmful to popular confidence in government that the public has been routinely misled or kept in the dark about important facts. Freedom of information is a worthwhile objective so long as the information is correct and reliable, and so long as it does not drive real decision-making into informal privacy or encourage disinformation. It is a sad reflection on the government which prides itself on the Freedom of

---

[10] Mr Blair's style of government is now known as 'sofa government', a term popularised by the report of the Butler Inquiry. Mr Straw has distanced himself from 'so-called sofa government': *Hansard*, 24 Feb. 2009, col. 160.

[11] This is no new observation. Sir Robert Peel suffered a breakdown in 1846 after shouldering the responsibility for every department of state in person, and it is thought that the failure of the Duke of Wellington's administration in 1830 was in part a result of his trying to do the same. Cf. Allen, *The Last Prime Minister*, p. 7: 'Exhaustion, defeat, humiliation are the only possible endings to a political career in a unitary system.'

[12] See the perceptive and disturbing study by P. Oborne, *The Triumph of the Political Class* (London, 2003).

[13] See Sir Stephen Sedley's comments in Lord Nolan and S. Sedley, *The Making and Remaking of the British Constitution* (London, 1997), pp. 22–3.

Information Act that it has done as much harm as good by developing the culture of 'spin' and promoting 'sofa government'.

A different problem is that ministers have come to evaluate their performance by legislative hyperactivity rather than effective results. Success is measured in terms of news headlines, most easily captured by announcing something ostensibly new: new targets, new directives, new quangos, new regulations and new statutes. There are around 15,000 pages of new legislation every year, and the present government is famously credited with the creation of some 3,000 new criminal offences. The steady increase in volume has resulted in a corresponding deterioration in the quality of legislation. It is now standard practice to lay bills before Parliament which are little better than outline plans, to be somehow refined as they are pushed through, or (all too often) after they have been passed. Often the main provisions are tucked away in schedules rather than in the body of the statute, rendering them almost unintelligible. In their rush to notch up their contributions to the statute-book, ministers jostle each other for time in the Commons. Why, we might ask, in the 2009 Constitutional Reform and Governance Bill is the Civil Service dealt with in the same measure as bits of the royal prerogative, public order, and amendments to the system for appointing judges? Apparently the government could not spare sufficient parliamentary time to take them separately. That time is allocated by the government, whose stranglehold over Commons business is routinely used to stifle proper debate upon the torrent of legislation which it generates. There has also been a worrying increase in the fast-tracking of legislation so as to preclude scrutiny almost completely,[14] and in the introduction of substantive late amendments to ill-prepared bills, which has the same effect.[15] It is particularly troubling when this careless, helter-skelter approach to lawmaking does not spare even constitutional changes.

And this brings us to the far greater problem, that we have no proper mechanism for constitutional change. The Secretary of State for Justice,

---

[14] See the valuable report and warnings from the House of Lords Select Committee on the Constitution, *Fast-Track Legislation: Constitutional Implications and Safeguards*, vol. I, 15th Report of Session 2008–9 (HL 116–I). There have been perhaps as many as 500 instances in the last twenty years: ibid., para. 21. The usual pretext is that the government wishes to be seen to be acting speedily in response to recent crises, such as threats from terrorists, pit-bull terriers (the Dangerous Dogs Act 1991) or troublesome judges. The consequence is not merely a lack of time for debate in Parliament, but the lack of scrutiny by Select Committees and the prevention of comment by interested parties outside Parliament.

[15] *Fast-Track Legislation*, paras. 98–106.

Mr Jack Straw, said in a lecture in February 2008 that the constitution exists in hearts and minds and habits.[16] It would have been more accurate to use the past tense. But what he did not say, of course, is that it cannot be appropriate for the settled assumptions, which have worked for so long by consent, to be changed unilaterally by the government whose power they are designed to limit, particularly by the very government responsible for some of the most serious challenges to the Rule of Law in recent history. Even among supporters of the government, there seems to be no fear that some future administration—perhaps formed by a party reflecting popular frustration with the present political class—might abuse the newly increased powers which it will inherit. Short-termists do not comprehend the notion of bad precedents.

The creation of a Department of Constitutional Affairs on 12 June 2003 was even more shocking than the bungled abolition of the Lord Chancellor. Although it has now been renamed the Ministry of Justice, the original name let the cat out of the bag. Mr Blair had simply commandeered the constitution and put it on a par with immigration, defence procurement, or the health service, to be managed on a routine basis as an act of governmental power. That is still the current policy, despite the misleading change of title. In fact the offence has been compounded by the establishment in June 2009 of a Democratic Renewal Council—a surprising name, since its last recorded use was by a military junta.[17] The effect was to transfer responsibility for changing the constitution from a ministerial department (which was bad enough) to a secret cabinet committee. Yet how many people have heard of this arrangement? The press and public seem to have become utterly indifferent to these goings on.

What, then, is the government up to? There is now some evidence of a government plan—though it is not the one the government has announced. According to its own Green and White Papers, the guiding objective is to 'rebalance power between Parliament and government', to give Parliament a greater ability to hold government to account, and to surrender or limit powers which in a democracy should not be exercised

---

[16] 'Modernising the Magna Carta', lecture at George Washington University, 13 Feb. 2008, published on the Ministry of Justice website.
[17] The Prime Minister announced in the House of Commons on 10 June that it had held its first meeting the previous day. The Minister of Justice stated shortly afterwards that he was still taking the lead: House of Commons Justice Committee, 11th Report, Session 2008–9 (HC 923), Evidence, q. 2. (The Thai military junta in 2006 called itself the Council for Democratic Reform.)

exclusively by the executive.[18] No one would quarrel with that. In fact, it is exactly what we need. But in practice it is not happening. The Bill which resulted from the proposals relates chiefly to war-making and treaty powers, and to the management of the Civil Service. Those are steps in the right direction, but they fall far short of the announced objectives. The treaty provisions are too late to save us from Lisbon. The problem of special advisers is not to be tackled, and the government has even rejected the advice of Lord Wilson that they should be forbidden to recruit, manage or direct regular civil servants.[19] As to prerogative powers, it was already unlikely that a government would embark on major armed conflict without some form of parliamentary approval. The Iraq war actually gave rise to a proper seventeenth-century-style debate in the Commons; the problem was misinformation rather than the absence of debate. More significant are the prerogative powers which are still not subject to any scrutiny at all.[20] A good example is the power to restructure government itself by abolishing ministries and setting up others—something the government does without any public explanation or costing, let alone discussion.[21] This power is chiefly used, not to increase efficiency, but to favour or remove individuals or to secure votes in the Commons—there are now 120 ministers, and 40 per cent of Labour MPs are on the government payroll. And it is exercised with such dizzying frequency that few ordinary people know what departments are called or what they do.[22]

If we try to discern a guiding strategy from the government's statements, we might conclude that it was the Separation of Powers. This is a

[18] Ministry of Justice, *The Governance of Britain* (July 2007), Cm 7170; *The Governance of Britain: Constitutional Renewal* (March 2008), Cm 7342. Rather oddly, the first item addressed in the White Paper is the control of public protest near Parliament.

[19] Joint Committee on the Constitutional Renewal Bill, 31 July 2008, Report, para. 294. Cl. 8 of the Bill requires the Minister for the Civil Service to publish a special advisers' code, but by cl. 7(5) it need not require special advisers to carry out their activities with objectivity or impartiality.

[20] It has been suggested that all prerogative powers should be abolished: e.g. A. Tomkins, *Our Republican Constitution* (Oxford, 2005), p. 134. Forty years ago, Diplock LJ remarked that they were a continuing residue of absolute power: *R. v. Criminal Injuries Compensation Board*, ex p. *Lain* [1967] 2 QB 864 at 886.

[21] This prerogative is not among those which the government listed for consideration in *Governance of Britain*.

[22] Besides the Lord Chancellor's Department, remodelled as the Department for Constitutional Affairs (2003) and then the Ministry of Justice (2007), we might instance the Department of Trade and Industry (1970), which after various splits and mergers became the Department of Business Enterprise and Regulatory Reform (2007) and then the Department of Business, Innovation and Skills (2009) after merging with the Department of Innovation, Universities and Skills (2007). Education seems recently to have disappeared by that name.

new-found religion, not much revealed in government scripture before 2003. But it provided a convenient excuse for the bungled attempt to abolish the office of Lord Chancellor, and it has borne fruit in the removal of the ultimate appellate jurisdiction from the House of Lords to the Supreme Court. Yet, whatever the merits of rehousing the highest court, no one could seriously suppose that this elaborate and expensive gesture—which was not properly planned[23]—has the slightest practical effect in relation to the Separation of Powers. Indeed, the first members of the new court are to retain their peerages, so that the theoretical (though largely illusory) conflict of interest will continue unaltered. As a piece of ill-conceived symbolism it is far outweighed by the reality of the less trumpeted changes which have placed the Courts' budget under the control of an ordinary government department, subject to competition with prisons, the probation service, tribunals, constitutional reform, and anything else which might be transferred to it in the future,[24] a department which will often be appearing as a party before the courts which it runs.[25] Unconscious of the incongruity, the government announced that this reform would 'strengthen further the already strong judicial-executive links'.[26] We might well conclude that the Supreme Court was an expensive diversionary tactic, drawing attention away from a deliberate and substantial shift in the contrary direction.

Real judicial independence is, of course, crucial; but here also the government is pulling in the wrong direction. It would have been far better if the final decision on appointments had remained in the hands of an old-style Lord High Chancellor rather than a minister in the centre of the political arena, advised by a body which he appoints himself. The woolly

---

[23] Lord Neuberger MR said on the wireless (Radio 4) on 7 Sept. 2009 that it was settled over a glass of whisky and that no thought had been given to the possible constitutional consequences. The presenter of the programme, Joshua Rozenberg, estimated the cost to be at least £80 million. It is true that there was a consultation paper, *Constitutional Reform: a Supreme Court for the United Kingdom* (July 2003), CP 11/03, but the 'consultation' followed rather than preceded the government's decision and views were not sought on whether such a court was necessary or desirable.

[24] Postscript: in March 2010 responsibility for legal aid was transferred to the department, so that the government may impose direct control on access to justice.

[25] It is an open secret that, for this reason, the reform was strongly opposed by the senior judiciary. At the Lord Mayor's dinner to the judges in July 2009, the Lord Chief Justice complained that the decision was announced informally by a minister writing in a Sunday newspaper.

[26] Announcement on the Cabinet Office website. Cf. Lord Woolf, 'The Rule of Law and a change in the constitution', at 323, who made the further point (in relation to the Department of Constitutional Affairs) that 'the Department could give directions to the Court Service staff which result in the courts becoming a tool of Government policy'.

language of section 3 of the Constitutional Reform Act 2005, which commendably purports to preserve judicial independence, does not apply to the appointment process and is not enforceable in the courts. All this matters, because the government is far from neutral. A thread running through their proposals has been the desire to decrease emphasis on experience and achievement and to increase 'diversity'. The Constitutional Reform Bill originally sought to give the government power to redefine 'merit' for the purpose of judicial appointments, a proposal Lord Falconer was reluctant to give up. They now want to achieve a similar end by setting targets for the Appointments Commission, perhaps even quotas. This might make sense for lay magistrates; but if superior judges were chosen in order to fill quotas or represent sectional interests it would not only be patronising and insulting to minorities but, more importantly, it would destroy confidence in the judiciary. A superior judgeship is more than a mere job-opportunity. If it is seen as a mere job, political appointments will be easier to make. And political appointments will soon be on the agenda. Ministers have from time to time indicated a desire to have confirmation hearings, in which politicians can veto candidates; and the impetus for political control of this kind will only increase if judges are given more constitutional powers.[27]

But the chief respect in which the government does not really believe in a separation of powers is the relationship between the government and Parliament. As Lord Scarman said in 1989, 'We have achieved the total union of executive and legislative power which Blackstone foresaw would be productive of tyranny.'[28] Four years later, the Appeal Committee of the House of Lords actually equated the intention of government spokesmen

---

[27] On the potential politicisation of the judiciary see Bogdanor, *The New British Constitution*, pp. 65–8. Professor Bogdanor concluded, rather optimistically, that the appointments procedure has been isolated from political interference. In his view, this would make it safe for judges to become more answerable to Parliament and its Select Committees with respect to their general approach: ibid., pp. 85–6.

[28] Lord Scarman, *"The Shape of Things to Come": the Shape and Future Law and Constitution of the United Kingdom* (Warwick, University of Warwick, 1989), p. 12. See W. Blackstone, *Commentaries on the Laws of England*, vol. 1 (Oxford, 1765), p. 142: 'In all tyrannical governments the supreme magistracy, or the right both of making and of enforcing the laws, is vested in one and the same man, or one and the same body of men; and wherever these two powers are united together, there can be no public liberty. The magistrate [legislator *later eds.*] may enact tyrannical laws, and execute them in a tyrannical manner, since he is possessed . . . with all the power which he as legislator thinks proper to give himself. But, where the legislative and executive authority are in distinct hands, the former will take care not to entrust the latter with so large a power, as may tend to the subversion of its own independence, and therewith of the liberty of the subject.' Cf. ibid., pp. 51, 154, on the same theme.

in the Commons with the intention of Parliament.[29] It was a natural mistake, given that Parliament is widely seen as merely applying its rubber-stamp to government bills. Not that the lack of separation is in itself tyrannical. It has been an accepted feature of our constitution for at least a century that the government may pass any legislation it wishes, provided it is not too shocking. Unfortunately, the broad principle operates whether or not the legislation is properly thought out, whether or not it rides roughshod over minorities, or over long-acknowledged principles such as the rule of law, whether or not it has undesirable side-effects, whether or not there is adequate time for scrutiny or consultation, and whether or not it is generally acceptable to the public or even to their elected representatives on the back benches. The inability of the House of Commons to hold the government to account was actually recognised as a problem in the *Governance of Britain* White Paper, but not surprisingly the government has shown little practical interest in finding a remedy.

The principal check is the House of Lords, to which I shall return. The House of Commons is almost completely ineffective. It is sometimes said that a back-bench member of Parliament has fulfilled his main function on the day he is elected, the purpose of the election being to determine the party which will form the government rather than to impose any check on it once formed.[30] Some apologists have argued for an invisible effectiveness, in that back-benchers are more inclined to revolt than they were fifty years ago.[31] That is debatable, since it is known that former administrations took soundings before decisions were made, to avoid the potential embarrassment of open opposition to positions already taken. At any rate, there has been little sign of restraining influence in the constitutional sphere. Strong contrary evidence is provided by the infamous story of clause 11 (later clause 14) of the Asylum and Immigration Bill

---

[29] *Pepper* v. *Hart* [1993] AC 593; see J. H. Baker, 'Statutory interpretation and parliamentary intention', *Cambridge Law Journal*, 52 (1993), 353–7. It was dissented from by the serving Lord Chancellor, Lord Mackay of Clashfern, albeit on pragmatic rather than constitutional grounds. There is now reason to hope that the aberration will not be followed: A. Kavanagh, '*Pepper* v. *Hart* and matters of constitutional principle', *Law Quarterly Review*, 121 (2005), 98–122.

[30] This is particularly true of back-benchers on the government side. It is widely rumoured that Mr Blair, emboldened by a large majority, once ordered Labour members to spend less time in the Commons, where their presence was not needed, and devote their time to spreading the government word out in the country. See R. J. Johnston, P. Cowley, C. J. Pattie and M. Stuart, 'Voting in the House or wooing the voters at home: Labour MPs and the 2001 general election campaign', *Journal of Legislative Studies*, 8 (2002), 9–22.

[31] Professor Bogdanor has gone so far as to say that we should no longer speak of an elective dictatorship: *The New British Constitution*, pp. 288–9.

2003. This provided that there should be no appeal or judicial review in respect of decisions by the new Asylum and Immigration Tribunal, whether for want of jurisdiction, error of law, or breach of natural justice. This clause was opposed by Lord Irvine when Lord Chancellor because it was contrary to the tradition of the rule of law; and some suspect that his removal from office was related to this disagreement. It was the subject of strong attack by Professor Bogdanor, who said it was a 'constitutional outrage, and almost unprecedented in peacetime . . .'.[32] It was attacked publicly by the then Lord Chief Justice, Lord Woolf, in a lecture at Cambridge, after he and 'other members of the judiciary' had advised that the clause was 'fundamentally in conflict with the rule of law',[33] and also by another former Lord Chancellor, Lord Mackay, who said it was 'obnoxious'.[34] It was condemned by the Constitutional Affairs Committee of the House of Commons as unprecedented; they said it was contrary to constitutional principle to remove judicial oversight of lower tribunals and executive decisions when life and liberty were at stake.[35] Alarmingly, and this is my point—none of this had any effect. The Bill passed the Commons, after a spirited debate in which no one but a junior minister spoke in favour and thirty-five Labour MPs voted against. It was only the threat by Lord Irvine himself to speak against it in the House of Lords which forced his successor to back down. I should make it clear that the controversy was not about asylum or immigration policy: it is perfectly legitimate to argue that the policy should be more ferocious, or even made to work, and the vast funds spent on immigration judges diverted to public welfare.[36] The dispute was about the Rule of Law.

The immediate outcome was satisfactory; but it was only a temporary respite. There have been several attempts in the last few years to confer arbitrary power on the government, not only in emergencies but in everyday situations. We have rightly criticised the Bush administration over Guantánamo Bay, and yet the United States Supreme Court—fortified by English precedents of the kind Selden used—was at least able to override the government and declare *habeas corpus* inviolate and available to

---

[32] *The Guardian*, 11 Feb. 2004.

[33] *The Independent*, 4 March 2004; Lord Woolf, 'The Rule of Law and a change in the constitution', at 327 (adding: 'and should not be contemplated by any government if it had any respect for the rule of law').

[34] *The Times*, 27 Feb. 2004.

[35] House of Commons Constitutional Affairs Committee, 2nd Report, Session 2003–4.

[36] It is not clear now what the true government policy has been: see above, n. 5.

aliens.[37] It is ironic to reflect that those precedents count for nothing here, since in England it is the convention that common law cannot override a statute.[38] We now have several Terrorism Acts,[39] which have caused considerable tension with the Rule of Law as we know it,[40] and even tougher measures may be in train. Traditional modes of trial are in danger; and the more serious the charge, the lower (some say) should be the standard of proof. But the problems caused by terrorism have at least received a good deal of public and judicial scrutiny, and I will not pursue them now.

Not limited to terrorism, however, was the Civil Contingencies Act 2004 (c. 36), a project modelled on the the wartime Defence of the Realm Acts[41] but of almost unprecedented scope in peacetime.[42] Amongst other things, the Bill would have empowered a secretary of state to take emergency powers to do *anything that could be done by Act of Parliament*, including the requisitioning and destruction of property without compensation, and the

---

[37] *Rasul* v. *Bush*, 542 US 466 (2004). An *amicus curiae* brief was submitted by legal historians. A similar brief was submitted in *Boumediene* v. *Bush*, 476 F. 3d 981 (2008), in which the Supreme Court made only a passing reference to history.

[38] According to some commentators, the Anti-terrorism Act of 2001 was the first time since the seventeenth century that *habeas corpus* had been withdrawn. That is not quite right, since it happened for brief periods in 1745, 1791 and 1817; but it is still a rare event.

[39] For the passage of the Anti-terrorism, Crime and Security Act 2001 (passed in the wake of 9/11), and the incidental derogation from the Human Rights legislation—the United Kingdom being the only country in Europe to think this necessary—see A. Tomkins, 'Legislating against terror: the Anti-terrorism, Crime and Security Act 2001', [2002] *Public Law*, 205–20; *A.* v. *Home Secretary* [2005] 2 AC 68 (Belmarsh Prison case).

[40] See, e.g., the five House of Lords decisions in *A. (No. 1)* v. *Home Secretary* [2005] 2 AC 68 (the Belmarsh decision); *A. (No. 2)* v. *Home Secretary* [2006] 2 AC 221; *Home Secretary* v. *J. J.* [2008] 1 AC 385; *Home Secretary* v. *M.*, ibid. 440; *Home Secretary* v. *E.*, ibid. 499.

[41] Note, however, the Emergency Powers Act 1920, 10 & 11 Geo. V, c. 55. This was passed during the miners' strike of Oct. 1920, reviving some of the temporary powers which had been introduced during the Great War. The powers were not invoked until the miners were locked out in March 1921 for refusing to accept cuts in pay; the situation then was considered so grave that troops were placed on alert, and steps were taken to raise a national volunteer force (numbering some 70,000 when it was stood down in April). The original typed warrant dated 31 March 1921 for the proclamation declaring the state of emergency, with the sign manual of King George V, is in the writer's collection (MS 336).

[42] There was once more caution even in war-time. It is noteworthy that when in 1940 the Security Executive—worried about communist revolutionaries—proposed a new defence regulation making it an offence to attempt to subvert duly constituted authority, the Permanent Under-Secretary at the Home Office (Sir Alexander Maxwell) advised that: 'Our tradition is that . . . every civilian is at liberty to show, if he can, that . . . the duly constituted authorities are composed of fools and rogues . . . This doctrine gives, of course, great and indeed dangerous liberty to persons who desire revolution . . . but the readiness to take this risk is the cardinal distinction between democracy and totalitarianism.' What is even more remarkable is that the war-time government accepted his advice: H. Hinsley and A. Simkins, *British Intelligence in the Second World War*, vol. 4 (London, 1990), pp. 57–8.

prohibition of 'movement' and assemblies; to create an offence of failing to comply with his regulations; and to establish an ad hoc criminal tribunal to try offenders. There were several provisions for ministers to 'disapply' sections of the Act itself.[43] Much of this was watered down before it became law—but it was a serious warning of what powers the government would like to possess. The government declined a request to insert a sunset clause: emergency is no longer a finite event.[44] And it declined to exempt legislation of major constitutional importance from the disapplication clause.

I am quite prepared to accept that extreme measures would be needed to cope with, say, a nuclear attack on London. But neither the Bill nor the Act as passed was confined to nuclear attacks, or air-raids on the Palace of Westminster. The Act, as passed, applies to any 'emergency'—defined as an event or situation which threatens serious damage to human welfare, the environment, or national security; and the government clearly believes that such emergency measures apply to economic emergencies such as bank failures.[45] It is not confined to terrorist acts, but includes any loss of life, illness, homelessness, damage to property or human welfare, and disruption of communications and transport. As if this definition was not wide enough, the Bill would have enabled a minister to extend it—that is, extend the scope of the statute itself—by Statutory Instrument.

It has become fashionable to speak of clauses such as the power-to-rewrite clause in the 2004 Bill as Henry VIII clauses, though in fact they have little or nothing to do with the Tudor period.[46] The first example of

---

[43] This euphemism was unknown to the law a generation ago, though it appears in several recent statutes: e.g. Representation of the People Act 2000, s. 11. It may have originated with delegated legislation, on the footing that it is inappropriate for a delegated authority to 'repeal' its parent authority. It was used for a similar reason by the Divisional Court in 1989, when it allowed EU law to override a parliamentary statute: *R. v. Secretary of State for Transport*, ex parte *Factortame* [1991] 1 AC 603.

[44] It has recently been urged by a House of Lords Select Commitee that there should be a presumption in favour of inserting a sunset clause into all legislation passed with unusual haste: *Fast-Track Legislation*, para. 198.

[45] The Landsbanki Freezing Order 2008 (SI No. 2668), freezing the assets of the Icelandic Bank, was expressly made under the 2001 Act.

[46] According to the Parliament website, the name alludes to the Statute of Proclamations 1539, which gave the king power to legislate by proclamation. This is very misleading. The 1539 statute certainly empowered the king to issue proclamations with the advice of his Council, and enacted that such proclamations should be 'obeyed, observed, and kept, as though they were made by act of Parliament'. But this raised fears at the time, which were long debated in Parliament, and in the event the Commons were unwilling to change the constitution by giving the king an unbridled unilateral power to legislate. The statute made it clear that it did not authorise proclamations to be made to the prejudice of any person's life, liberty, or property, or in breach of any

a Henry VIII clause occurs in the Local Government Act 1888,[47] and such clauses were still sufficiently uncommon in 1929 to provoke the then Lord Chief Justice to warn of the New Despotism which they threatened.[48] It is only in very recent times that they have been widened to empower ministers to rewrite parliamentary legislation as they think fit.

A disturbing example occurred in 2006, when the government attempted in the Legislative and Regulatory Reform Bill to sideline Parliament quite independently of any 'emergency'. The government sought to give its ministers the power to amend, repeal or replace any Act of Parliament simply by making an Order.[49] This was said to be potentially helpful in reducing red tape. That sounded wonderful: we all want to reduce red tape. The press and the opposition were taken in and did not notice the small print, and the government almost got away with it. The sheer enormity of the proposition was drawn to public attention by a letter written to *The Times* on 16 February 2006 by six Cambridge Law professors.[50] Some of its defenders thought the offending clause was just a result of over-zealous draftsmanship, that it really was primarily intended to reduce red tape. It was nothing of the kind. If it had been, the government would have accepted amendments. Instead, they fought hard to defend the indefensible and even refused to insert safeguards for fundamental liberties. The letter-writers had the honour of being denounced by Lord Lipsey in the House of Lords as six silly professors who were not living in the real world.[51] Yet this was not even a Henry VIII clause, as understood in 1929; it was more like the Enabling Law of 1933. The

laws or customs currently in force. It was repealed in 1547. See J. H. Baker, *Oxford History of the Laws of England*, 6 (Oxford, 2003), p. 64. The Act concerning Peter-Pence 1533 (25 Hen. VIII, c. 21) gave the king power to abrogate the parent Act by letters patent; but the power was limited to that statute, which conferred on the king ecclesiastical powers which he was seen as having the right to decline.

[47] Lord Rippon, 'Henry VIII Clauses', *Statute Law Review*, 10 (1989), 205–7.

[48] Lord Hewart, *The New Despotism* (London, 1929). This led to the report of the Donoughmore Committee, which seems now to be completely ignored.

[49] Legislative and Regulatory Reform Bill 2006, cl. 2. This was an inordinate extension of the power contained in the Regulatory Reform Act 2001 (c. 6), s. 1. Among earlier vague but more circumscribed precedents was the Local Government Act 2000 (c. 22), s. 6, which empowered the Secretary of State to amend, repeal, revoke or disapply any enactment which obstructs local authorities from taking steps to promote the well-being of their communities.

[50] There were more signatories, but only six names were published. See also J. H. Baker, 'A Charter for Despots' (the editor's title), *Parliamentary Brief*, 10 (2006), no. 5, pp. 7–9; J. R. Spencer, 'Contempt of Parliament', ibid. 5–6.

[51] Speech of 13 June 2006. It was the same Lord Lipsey of Tooting who wrote approvingly in a book review two years earlier of 'a new philosophy for Labour capable of turning into reality Blair's dream of eternal power': *The New Statesman*, 21 June 2004.

House of Lords Constitution Committee woke up to what was happening, and said the Bill would markedly alter the respective roles of minister and Parliament.[52] Even then, the government was minded to push ahead, offering the assurance that it would not abuse the new power. That, of course, is the moment to worry—when a government says, 'Trust us, we don't need a constitution any more: we are so righteous that we will never do anything wrong.' That was exactly how the Enabling Law was presented to the Reichstag on 23 March 1933:[53] 'The Government will use these powers only in so far as they are essential for carrying out vitally necessary measures. The number of cases in which a necessity exists for having recourse to such a law is very limited.' I do not suggest that constitutions can prevent tyranny; they can, however, facilitate it.[54]

In 2006, fortunately, we were saved—saved by the threat that the House of Lords would scupper the Bill. Notably it was the Lords and not the Commons which served to protect Parliament. And that, I suppose, was another nail in their coffin. The underlying lesson was not absorbed in the corridors of power, and things have not changed under Mr Brown and Mr Straw. For example, clause 55 of the present Constitutional Reform and Governance Bill[55] provides that a minister may by statutory instrument make any provision that he considers 'appropriate' in consequence of the Act, and that such an order may 'amend, repeal or revoke any provision made by or under an Act'—that is, any other Act. So ministers now seek the power even to rewrite constitutional statutes. These clauses are now installed in government computers, and they are given a little stretch each time they are dropped into place.[56] There are also more

[52] 'Letter from the Chairman to the Lord Chancellor', 23 Jan. 2006, printed in House of Lords Constitution Committee, 11th Report of Session 2005–6 (HL Paper 194), p. 24, appendix I.

[53] N. H. Baynes (ed.), *The Speeches of Adolf Hitler*, 1 (London, 1942), pp. 246, 420; A. Bullock, *Hitler: a Study in Tyranny* (London, revised edn., 1964), p. 269. The initial pretext was the Reichstag Fire, presented as an act of terrorism. Six days earlier, the Reichstag Fire Decree had suspended the German equivalent of *habeas corpus*, curtailed freedom of speech and assembly, and authorised telephone tapping.

[54] The Law of 1933 has been described as 'a vital step towards consolidating [Hitler's] dictatorship': I. Kershaw, *Hitler 1889–1936: Hubris* (London, 1998), p. 468. Hitler took the trouble to have it renewed twice when it expired.

[55] The Bill was introduced by Mr Straw in July 2009, overtaking the Constitutional Renewal Bill introduced in March. A similar provision (cl. 57) in the earlier Bill was criticised by the Joint Committee on that Bill on 31 July 2008, HL 166–1, paras. 361–2.

[56] Clause 75 of the Banking Bill introduced on 7 Oct. 2008 gave the Treasury what is expressly called a 'Power to change law', a power by Order to amend any statute or rule of common law 'for the purpose of enabling the powers under [Part I] of the Act to be used effectively'; and it provided that such an Order might make provision with retrospective effect 'in so far as the

concealed varieties, such as that under which the Home Secretary recently sought to confer sweeping new powers on local authorities under the Proceeds of Crime Act.[57] At best, these clauses acknowledge that statutes prepared with haste need constant rewriting; but it is a high price to pay for sloppiness, since it prevents proper scrutiny and avoids professional draftsmanship.[58] Even where powers are subjected to the affirmative resolution procedure, there is no possibility of amendment and the time for debate is minimal. Nor is the availability of judicial review a satisfactory solution,[59] since only those who can afford litigation in the High Court will be able to find out which orders are valid and which not. At any rate, we now know what the Goverment means by 'rebalancing power' between the executive and Parliament. There is enough similar-fact evidence to prove a deliberate programme of shifting power *towards* the executive.

Some of these problems have no legal solution under our present constitution. They were avoided in the past by those conventions which existed in hearts and minds and habits. Since these no longer count for anything, we have all been reflecting on the desirability of a written constitution. The government is against this, so there has been another diversionary tactic in the form of proposals for a new Bill of Rights. The first proposal concerned a range of 'Civil and Political Rights', few if any of which are inherently controversial. But the effect of putting them into a new statute would be to create a parallel and possibly conflicting human-rights regime with no obvious purpose—unless, of course, the United Kingdom can be somehow disconnected from Europe. It is then pro-

---

Treasury consider it necessary or desirable for giving effect to the particular exercise of a power under this Act'. The clause was criticised by the Select Committee on the Constitution, because of its retrospective application: HL Constitution Committee, 3rd Report, 21 Jan. 2009 (HL 19); 11th Report, 18 May 2009 (HL 97). The words 'or desirable' surpass even the Enabling Law of 1933, which in its terms was limited to necessity. In November 2008, the government introduced a Planning Bill, clause 118(5) of which would have empowered *commissioners* to modify or repeal statutes relating to any matter in respect of which they might make an order. This seems to be the first attempt to confer legislative powers on a body, as opposed to a minister.

[57] This at least caused an outcry in the newspapers: see, e.g., *The Times*, 28 Oct. 2009, pp. 2, 18–19. (Again, it was the House of Lords which saved the day: *Hansard*, 7 Dec. 2009, col. 896.)

[58] See Lord Oliver, 'A judicial view of modern legislation', *Statute Law Review*, 14 (1993), 1–11, at 3 (referring to Henry VIII clauses): 'It is unfair to the citizen, who is entitled in a democratic society to have the rules by which his life is regulated properly debated and scrutinized by his elected representatives. And, by removing the legislation from the competent hands of the parliamentary draftsmen into those of departmental civil servants, it frequently results in drafting disasters.'

[59] The courts are now prepared to review orders even where the parent statute gives the minister power in subjective language, e.g. to act as he 'thinks necessary'. For an early example of this approach see *Commissions of Customs and Excise v. Cure and Deeley Ltd* [1962] 1 QB 340.

posed to insert 'Responsibilities' as well; but, since these are already part of the law, their inclusion in a separate document, in different language, has no obvious constitutional significance and could only cause legal confusion.[60] More than confusion is threatened by threats to add a new range of 'Economic and Social Rights'. These are found in some other constitutions, but they are not so much legal rights as political aspirations. Fundamental rights are those which no government can lawfully take away. These new 'rights' are not yet in existence but are goals which the government hopes to reach some day, when it can afford to. Now, there is no harm in announcing political goals, especially when they are essentially laudable; but it has nothing to do with constitutional change. It belongs to the same category of law reform as the Fiscal Responsibility Bill, which would halve the national deficit by legislative magic,[61] just as one might reduce the crime rate by abolishing crimes. Misusing the language of rights, however, is potentially dangerous nonsense on stilts—on skates. Even though the rights would not be directly justiciable, judges would be able to take account of them in assessing 'the reasonableness of the measures taken to achieve their progressive realisation'.[62] This would introduce a new kind of law, empowering the judges to exercise an essentially non-legal function of unknown scope. If they are to be given such a broad role, then it needs much more public debate. It ought not to slip into being unnoticed beneath the cloak of vague aspirational rights to which, as abstract propositions, most people would happily subscribe.

The principal question is not whether we should have another Bill of Rights, let alone a Bill of Hopes and Duties, but whether we should have a true written constitution with judicial review of legislation to ensure compliance. It is perhaps a purely academic question in Britain, since no government is likely to agree to confer such a power on judges, and the

---

[60] See *Rights and Responsibilities: Developing our Constitutional Framework* (March 2009), Cm 7577, which is a Green Paper concerning a Bill of Rights. Mr Straw admitted in the Commons that the proposed responsibilities were already law, but 'scattered across myriad legal texts'. The answer given to the charge that this renders their declaration purposeless is that, even if they would not be legally enforceable by virtue of their restatement, there would be some psychological value in declaring them in abstract terms: see the debate in the House of Commons, *Hansard*, 23 March 2009, col. 37.

[61] The Queen's Speech, 17 Nov. 2009: 'Legislation will be brought forward to halve the deficit.' The title of the Bill, which has not yet been published, seems to have been borrowed from Nigeria.

[62] Parliamentary Committee on Human Rights, *A Bill of Rights for the United Kingdom?*, 29th Report for the Session 2007–8 (HL 165–1, HC 150–1), published 10 Aug. 2008.

present prime minister has ruled it out as undemocratic.[63] But there is another way in which it could happen. Lord Millett argued on the wireless in April 2004 that introducing a separation of powers would inevitably, if unintentionally, hasten the end of parliamentary sovereignty; and similar ideas have been mooted by other senior judges.[64] If the government can abandon the conventions of an unwritten constitution, so (in a suitable case) might the judges. Sovereignty of Parliament, it is argued, is no more than a convention. And did not judicial review in the United States of America come about through judicial decision?[65] That could be the next stage in our creeping revolution, 400 years after *Dr Bonham's Case*.[66] But it would be a desperate and unwelcome last resort rather than a satisfactory solution, since the judges would be enforcing an unwritten constitution of uncertain scope.

Until the last few years, I was myself wholly averse to the idea of a written constitution, with a supreme court having the power of judicial review, because it would turn unelected judges into legislators. Written constitutions have a mythical quality about them, and it is surprising how many people assume they are much clearer than unwritten constitutions.[67] In practice the true function of a written constitution is not so much to improve the clarity of the rules as to empower the highest court to strike down legislation according to its own interpretation of the words. The question is therefore whether the time has come to transfer more power to the judges, on the footing that the political constitution has broken down beyond repair. This is far from straightforward, since we cannot assume that the traditional juristic standards of the judiciary will be maintained once they have a political role. The problem is not merely

---

[63] House of Commons Justice Committee (chaired by Sir Alan Beith), 11th Report of Session 2008–9, HC 923, paras. 61–2. Likewise Mr Straw: ibid., Evidence, q. 62.

[64] See the cautious remarks in *Jackson* v. *Att.-Gen.* [2006] 1 AC 262 at 302 (Lord Steyn), 318 (Baroness Hale), 323 (Lord Carswell), 327 (Lord Brown). Lord Steyn hinted (at p. 302) that 'strict legalism' might have to give way in an extreme case to 'constitutional principle'. There was a suggestion at the time of the ill-fated ouster clause in the Asylum and Immigration Bill 2003, above (p. 100), that the judges might find a way of striking down such a clause if it became law.

[65] *Marbury* v. *Madison*, 5 US 137 (1803). (The power was used very sparingly in the nineteenth century.) The Australian High Court has achieved the same power by judicial decision.

[66] *Bonham* v. *Atkins et al.* (1610) 8 Co. Rep. 107, 114; J. H. Baker, *Introduction to English Legal History*, 4th edn. (London, 2002), pp. 210–11.

[67] Not everyone. Napoleon is often credited with saying that a constitution ought to be brief and obscure. In fact the aphorism is attributable to Talleyrand, who on being advised in 1802 that a constitution ought to be 'brief and . . . [clear]', interrupted with 'and obscure': 'Relations particulières avec le Premier Consul' in *Oeuvres du Comte P. L. Roederer*, ed. A. M. Roederer (1854), iii. 428 (translated).

that judges are unelected—and introducing elected judges is not a recommended solution to that problem—but that the judicial role is different from that of the policy-maker responsible for raising and spending revenue. The case for increasing the power of the judges is that they have tenure, which gives them independence, and that they are trained to pick apart arguments in an informed and dispassionate way. But courts are not best suited to decide on the allocation of finite public resources, especially in the context of disputes *inter partes* in which other claims on those resources are not represented. Judges think in absolute terms, they are not apprised of the whole economic picture, and they are not politically answerable for the consquences of their decisions.[68]

Despite these misgivings, we have to face the question, now that our unwritten constitution has been unravelled, whether judicial review might not be the lesser of two evils. We would not have to follow the American model, on which no one is very keen. There is much to be said for a weaker model, such as the Canadian, under which the highest court can annul legislation but subject to a power (little or never used in reality) for the legislature to reinstate it *non obstante* for a limited period. We have an even weaker model ourselves under the Human Rights Act, under which the judges can declare legislation incompatible with the code without invalidating it. I would suggest that the key to any acceptable model is that it ought not to empower or allow judges to second-guess the legislature on issues of policy requiring taxation or coercion. Judicial review of legislation should ideally operate more like judicial review of administrative action: that is, it should enquire whether the legislature has acted consistently and fairly, and *intra vires*, has taken proper account of relevant factors, and has not taken improper account of irrelevant factors; but it should not substitute the judges' decision on the merits for that of the decision-maker. Nowadays there is a wide perception, right or wrong, that the courts are inclined to over-use their powers under the Human Rights Act and to take the political decisions themselves. That has been a failing of the European Court in Strasbourg, and there is no guarantee that our new Supreme Court will not be tempted to move further in the same direction. We therefore need more reflection on how to define the proper judicial function, how to draw the line between fundamental law and politics. It is far from easy or obvious. To whom, for instance, does it

---

[68] Cf. *R.* v. *Cambridge Health Authority*, ex parte *B.* [1995] 1 WLR 898 at p. 906, per Bingham MR ('Difficult and agonising judgments have to be made as to how a limited budget is best allocated . . . That is not a judgment which the court can make').

belong to define life and death, or marriage, or a person's gender? A constitutional 'right to life' might seem to empower judges to decide when life
begins and ends. But, if in a plural society we no longer defer to Christian
Canon Law, it ceases to be clear whether such a question is soluble purely
by legal reasoning. The same is true of many other issues seen as fundamental. We should therefore think very carefully before rushing ahead
with a codified written constitution. Without first achieving some kind of
consensus on the range of matters on which we would be content for
judges to override Parliament, perhaps against the wishes of most of our
fellow citizens, it would be premature to lock ourselves into a system of
judicial review.

It may in any case be questioned whether a written constitution is the
best way in practice to solve the kind of constitutional problems which I
have outlined. Human rights are comparatively easy. We already have a
written code of human rights, though it is not entrenched and already
there are moves to amend it. Some think it is better that way. Fundamental
laws are admirable in the abstract. The problem with them is that when
codified they become absolutes, and absolute law without exceptions for
common sense, equity, local conditions, or changed circumstances is
often bad law. We have learned that from the Strasbourg experience.
Fundamental rights should be kept to a minimum rather than constantly
enlarged, and should be open to reinterpretation. The principal case for
entrenching them, or some of them, is that it might make it possible for
the Supreme Court to reject European legislation which contravened
British principles of justice.[69] Universal human rights were, of course,
invented in England,[70] but they mean different things to different people,
and it would not be easy to entrench other English common-law rights,
which the European powers would take away, without unduly hampering
future parliaments from making minor adjustments.[71]

---

[69] Cf. A. Senior in *The Times*, 6 Nov. 2009, p. 37: 'Our country is being reborn as a satellite of
Europe yet, as the revolution is a bloodless one, it passes without protest. We are alone among
the member states in not having a written constitution. This makes us vulnerable to European
creep, and the dribbling away of civil liberties.'

[70] See J. H. Baker, 'Human rights and the rule of law in renaissance England', *Northwestern
University Journal of International Human Rights*, 2 (2004), 24–40; A. W. B. Simpson, *Human
Rights and the End of Empire: Britain and the Genesis of the European Convention* (Oxford, 2001).

[71] e.g. the right to rescind a contract for breach of condition. The proposal by the European
Commission to abolish this right (draft Consumer Rights Directive 2008, art. 26) has been criticised by the Law Commission and by the European Union Committee of the House of Lords
(18th Report, 7 July 2009). If a party is held to be obliged to perform a contract which was only
made on condition, after the condition has been broken (and not waived), he is being held to a
contract which he did not make.

Enshrining the structure and mechanics of government in a written document would raise problems of a different kind. It would be virtually impossible to codify all the present conventions of the British constitution, especially those which relate to political parties, or the Cabinet, even if it could be decided which of them still exist or ought to be revived.[72] This is partly because they operate more like equity, or fictions, than rules of law. For instance, the mind boggles at any attempt to codify the present procedures for producing a prime minister, covering every eventuality.[73] Entrenched legislation could perhaps solve some of the specific problems I have mentioned.[74] But to that end there would be no necessity to set the whole constitution in stone, an exercise which might result in too much rigidity and prolixity. A line would have to be drawn between form and substance: would the electoral system, for instance, or the size of the two houses of Parliament, have to be enshrined in the constitution?[75] And there might have to be different degrees of entrenchment for different levels of constitutional provision, so that special procedures of different kinds would have to be followed for changing them. In choosing between models, we are brought back to the absence of any proper machinery for going about it. It certainly cannot safely be left to the Democratic Renewal Council.

A better place to start a true constitutional renewal would be the House of Commons itself, since prevention is better than cure. This is now widely accepted by everyone except the government,[76] which has

[72] Cf. G. Marshall, *Constitutional Conventions* (Oxford, 1984), p. 54: 'It is the fitting in of the exception clauses that makes the drafting of a written constitution for the United Kingdom such a hopeless, Utopian enterprise.' By 1984, the convention of collective responsibility (for example) seemed completely dead: ibid., pp. 55 et seq. See now the full discussion in Bogdanor, *The New British Constitution*, pp. 221–8.

[73] A complete written constitution would therefore require some simplifications—perhaps, for example, providing that a prime minister should be recommended to the Queen by a majority vote of the House of Commons. For this and other possible solutions see Institute for Public Policy Research, *A Written Constitution for the United Kingdom* (London, 1991). This showed that it could not be done succinctly: the draft occupies 126 pages. It is worth remembering, nevertheless, that in the 1950s law professors felt it possible to write constitutions for newly independent Commonwealth countries.

[74] e.g. a law that no department of state should be created, abolished or merged without an Act of Parliament, or that no parliamentary statute should be amended or repealed without some special scrutiny procedure.

[75] See Bogdanor, *The New British Constitution*, p. 220.

[76] See *Shifting the Balance: Select Committees and the Executive* (2000), House of Commons Liaison Committee, 1st Report; Hansard Society, *The Challenge of Parliament: Making Government Accountable* (London, 2001); and, only a few days ago, the welcome first report of the Reform of the House of Commons Select Committee, *Rebuilding the House* (HC 1117), published on 12 Nov. 2009.

repeatedly shelved the issue. The use of Select Committees has proved one of the most fruitful reforms of the last thirty years, and it is a shame that the wisdom produced by the committees is so difficult for outsiders to access. Their proper role is not to challenge or seek to change policy, but to scrutinise, warn and criticise. In performing those vital roles, they need to be given more clout, with chairmen elected by secret ballot and with independence from the whips; and perhaps we can learn from Scotland, where they are said to be more effective. Another desirable change which seems to be generally agreed is that the government should lose its absolute control over the management of business in the Commons.[77] The Commons ought also to take back its audit functions, by discussing estimates and controlling supply. And no doubt there are other procedural measures which will occur to those who know the ways of the House. Some way of capping the volume of legislation is desperately needed, helped perhaps by a more liberal use of the 'sunset clause'[78]—a true Henry VIII clause, much used in his time—or by requiring a periodic review of the effectiveness of new measures.[79] None of this forms part of the government's 'renewal' policy; but it is much to be hoped that the present atmosphere of popular disillusionment with the functioning of Parliament will force some improvement in the near future.

For the present, the most effective check on legislation is the House of Lords—effective because its members have tenure and are free to ignore the party whip. Although Labour peers now constitute the largest party in the House, peers have on several hundred occasions in the past decade followed their consciences, or their good sense, to thwart the Labour government in a way that members of the Commons would consider politically or financially risky. There is therefore a true separation of

---

[77] At present this is guaranteed by Standing Order 14(1) of the House of Commons, which itself cannot be altered without government cooperation: 'Save as provided by this order, government business shall have priority at every sitting.' The Select Committee on Reform of the House of Commons, while acknowledging that the government is entitled to have its own business considered at a time of its own choosing, has proposed the establishment of a Backbench Business Committee.

[78] A provision that a statute will expire on a given date unless steps are taken to renew it. It is important to note that such provisions can only work if there is adequate time and information available for Parliament to debate the renewal when the time comes: see the comments in *Fast-Track Legislation*, para. 70.

[79] For some possible solutions to the growing problem of excessive and ill-prepared legislation see *Post-Legislative Scrutiny*, Law Com. No. 302 (2006), Cm 6945. The need for post-legislative scrutiny of all legislation was advocated recently by the House of Lords Select Committee on the Constitution: *Fast-Track Legislation*, para. 208.

powers here, even if the powers were severely reduced in 1911. By a curious reversal of history, the House of Lords has become the principal defender of constitutional liberties, and arguably the more significant legislative chamber, albeit at the cost of endangering its own existence. Having been made more politically correct by the removal of most of the hereditary element in 1999, it has gained confidence; but the sorry consequence is that, in government thinking, it must be made less politically effective. The future of the Lords is, in my submission, the paramount constitutional concern today. Without an effective, independent upper chamber, the entire High Court of Parliament is in danger of becoming fossilised, a magnificent heritage site with no function.

On 7 March 2007 the Commons voted to ignore the conclusions of the Royal Commission of 2000 on the House of Lords and press for an elected (or at least 80 per cent elected) house of senators, composed chiefly of full-time politicians with limited tenure; a few days later the Lords voted (by 361 to 121) in favour of a 100 per cent appointed chamber. Mr Straw subsequently announced his determination to push through the wishes of the Commons, apparently in the (seriously mistaken) belief that this is the course required in a democracy.[80] Even if such a course is not actually illegal,[81] this is another disturbing example of the government's inability or unwillingness to understand what a constitution is for. How can it be the business of the Commons to tamper with the only effective control on their power? It would never happen in a country with a written constitution—that is, most other countries—but, alas, our constitution provides no specific guidance to those who choose to distort it.

The merits were fully considered by the Royal Commission ten years ago and seemed then to fall on the side of an appointed or largely appointed House. Those of us outside the political class can see that popular elections for the entire House of Lords, even if not tied to general elections for the Commons, are likely to give both houses a similar political constitution and almost certain to make the Lords a clone of the Commons in a more insidious way.[82] The conditions of appointment

---

[80] See, e.g., the government's White Paper of 14 July 2008, Cm 7438. The opposition parties have, most regrettably, failed to provide any opposition to this.

[81] It remains to be seen whether the new Supreme Court will agree with the Court of Appeal in *Jackson v. Att.-Gen.* [2005] QB 579 as to the limits of the Parliament Act in the constitutional sphere. Although the House of Lords reversed the Court of Appeal in relation to the Hunting Act, and did not accept a distinction between constitutional and other enactments, several members of the Judicial Committee reserved their position as to whether there might be limits.

[82] Cf. Oliver, *Constitutional Reform*, pp. 200–1.

would only attract those who are already politicians—many of whom would doubtless find a salaried seat in the Lords more congenial than the tedious constituency work which now falls to a member of the lower house. The important element of membership with experience of the real world would be squeezed out,[83] as would the present social diversity of peers. The House would be enslaved by party politics and its valuable function of taking the wider view endangered. Why is this thought necessary or desirable? There is no democratic reason why all the Lords should be elected. Granted that an elected government is entitled to have its policies passed into legislation, it does not follow that the product should be rough or unworkable or unconstitutional; and it is in everyone's interest that problems be ironed out before a bill is passed rather than pursued in the courts afterwards. Unquestionably, there are grave objections to the present process of nomination to the Lords, which has all too often been used to ennoble second-rate or unseated politicians: the kind of people who might pay for peerages or take cash for questions, or even a Speaker who has been effectively ejected from office. Setting up an independent appointments commission would not be without difficulty,[84] though there is an informal model already in place; whatever the difficulties, any sensible system of appointment would seem preferable to general election.[85]

I have only been able to touch on a few of the myriad questions which have been stirred by the constitutional turmoil of the last seven years, and in a very superficial way. But a general observation I should like to underline before I end is that they are interrelated. Most important of all, the question whether we need a written constitution, and more power vested in judges, is directly and necessarily connected with what happens to the House of Lords and the political constitution.[86] There is little indication

---

[83] An extensive survey of other legislatures concluded that 'None of the overseas second chambers studied here achieve the same reputation for expert membership as the House of Lords': M. Russell, *Reforming the House of Lords: Lessons from Overseas* (Oxford, 2000), p. 306.

[84] There are no overseas precedents to guide us: ibid., p. 328.

[85] Cf. Bogdanor, *The New British Constitution*, ch. 6, where it is assumed that a reformed Lords must have democratic legitimacy conferred by election. Professor Bogdanor nevertheless sets out cogent reasons why an elected Lords would be less effective than the present House. The same premises have led Lord Bingham to suggest that the House of Lords should be abolished, and the function of scrutinising legislation transferred to a Council of State, of similar size to the present House of Lords but without any legislative function: 'The House of Lords: Its Future?', Jan Grodecki Annual Law Lecture, University of Leicester, 22 Oct. 2009.

[86] Cf. Oliver, *Constitutional Reform*, p. 384: 'The political constitution depends heavily upon a culture of self-restraint on the part of constitutional actors. If that culture should disintegrate, then the remaining advantages of the arrangements would disappear and the case for a law-based constitution with more judicialism would become the stronger.'

in the government's approach of any coherent strategic vision, and perhaps that is an inevitable result of our constitutional arrangements. Yet much of the recent activity seems to have been a result of short-term expediency: abolish the office of Lord Chancellor as a clever way of removing Lord Irvine; weaken and politicise the House of Lords because it has proved vexatious; scatter 'power to change law' clauses in bills to save the bother of careful draftsmanship. Typical of this approach was the Parliamentary Standards Bill, rushed through Parliament in July 2009 to appease journalists on the expenses front, with no awareness of the wider constitutional implications which were only pointed out in the nick of time.[87]

If there is to be constitutional reform, there ought to be some new mechanism, independent of government, and of the House of Commons, to consider it as a connected whole. The House of Commons Justice Committee, in its report of 21 July 2009, proposed a constitutional convention;[88] and that might well be the best solution, however problematic its own constitution and authority might be.[89] But it should not be expected to deliver results within a short timetable.[90] The mad rush of the last seven years has proved to be the wrong approach.[91] Constitutions must rest on a broad consensus, and we are some way from having any kind of consensus as to what is required. No independent convention will reach agreement at its first meetings. Indeed, it might be advisable to begin with a Royal Commission to prepare the ground and frame the questions.[92] A convention should also resist the temptation to redesign the constitution from scratch, in minute detail. Since the reality is that whatever is proposed would need government support, the effect would be to offer dozens of proposals from which ministers could choose the

---

[87] House of Commons Justice Committee, 11th Report of Session 2008–9, paras. 38–9. The Lord Chief Justice pointed out in a speech at the Mansion House in July that introducing judicial review of parliamentary affairs threatened to bring the judiciary into direct conflict with Parliament.

[88] Ibid., paras. 90–2. Cf. V. Bogdanor, 'We need a new Constitution for Britain', *The Times*, 1 June 2009: 'Important constitutional reform should not be a knee-jerk reaction to crisis, but the result of popular reflection. To be effective, it needs to be a product of popular wishes, not something implemented from on high. All that a government can do is to initiate a debate.'

[89] This is helpfully discussed in Bogdanor, *The New British Constitution*, pp. 228–30.

[90] Justice Committee, 11th Report (see above, n. 63), para. 88 (pointing out that the government's present timetable is over-optimistic).

[91] Even Mr Straw now admits that 'Constitutional change should be approached with caution': *Rights and Responsibilities*, 7. He has expressed the view that a written constitution is twenty years away: 'Modernising the Magna Carta', see above, n. 16.

[92] This is Professor Bogdanor's suggestion: *The New British Constitution*, p. 229.

easy ones while shelving the important ones. And it should be borne in mind that unduly radical changes would divide moderate opinion so as to prevent acceptance. The best way ahead is to seek a broad consensus on the big questions.

In connection with consensus, I would end with the observation that no sensible progress can be made without a greater public awareness of constitutional matters and involvement in the debate.[93] The hearts and minds must be re-engaged. Politicians no doubt suspect that there is not much door-step interest in questions which may seem abstract or academic, and no political profit to be gained from pursuing them.[94] Mr Blair famously tried to put down Mr Hague in the House of Commons in 2000 by saying: 'I don't know whether people in his pubs and clubs are talking about pre-legislative scrutiny, but they are not in mine. These are good issues for academics and constitutional experts, but they are not the big issues that Parliament should debate.'[95] This absence of basic awareness has suited the government well and has been reflected in the press, which—despite the acuity of many individual journalists—feeds the public appetite for personal scandals and no longer seriously reports parliamentary debates, let alone Select Committee reports. When a lord chancellor's wallpaper can attract as much media attention as the abolition of his office, it is hardly surprising that the sordid but titillating business of outrageous expenses claims should fill more column-inches than the far more important constitutional questions currently hanging over us. Yet busy citizens, such as lawyers, have no time to delve into the recesses of the internet on a regular basis to find out what is going on, and so the response to White Papers has been quantitatively thin. It is not that intelligent people are not interested; I have found from giving public lectures on the subject that there is actually great interest and concern amongst lawyers and the lay public alike. But most people simply do not know enough, in detail, about what is happening, and it is all happening too fast. The lack of awareness is also the fault of our educational system. What can the long struggle between Crown and the Commons, the Petition of Right, *habeas corpus*, and all those things which were in the

---

[93] Cf. *The Governance of Britain* Green Paper of 3 July 2007, which Mr Straw announced as 'the first step in a national conversation'.

[94] Professor Bogdanor notes that during the 1997 election campaign the respondents to a poll put constitutional issues lowest among their priorities (14th out of 14): *The New British Constitution*, p. 6. He attributes this, at least in part, to the absence of a written constitution: ibid., p. 10. There is certainly far more interest in constitutional issues in the United States.

[95] *Hansard*, 13 July 2000, col. 1097.

blood-stream of Selden's contemporaries, mean to a generation which has studied no history before 1914 or to lawyers who have studied no constitutional history before 1972?

It may be too late to reverse the present revolution, which has happened so fast that we have all been left gawping. Optimists may be pleased by that; there are always those who enjoy seeing inveterate institutions 'shaken up' and who prefer rapid change (whatever it is) to slow evolution. Some of the reforms have indeed been desirable. My own chief concern is not with change as such, but with the dismal reflection that we no longer have a constitution, in the sense of a set of conventions which set the bounds of executive power and keep the government within those bounds, conventions which—though unwritten and flexible—can be abandoned only by general consensus and after careful thought. The consensus of the last century or more has ended, and the government has stormed into the void, constantly tinkering with constitutional arrangements as a routine exercise of power and without much regard to the consequences. I expect some people will think me a silly professor, an alarmist, to voice such a complaint.[96] Life still goes on more or less as normal. You and I are still free to air our views in public, and we do not have friends who have been incarcerated for expressing their opinions (as Selden was), let alone eliminated. But constitutional slippage is highly dangerous; for when power is allowed to become unlimited and unbalanced, the lessons of history are, I would suggest, alarming.

[96] Cf. Lord Carswell in *Jackson* v. *Att.-Gen.* [2006] 1 AC 262 at 323: 'An unwritten constitution, even more than a written one, is a living organism and develops with changing times, but it is still a delicate plant and is capable of being damaged by over-rigorous treatment, which may have incalculable results.'

Many Legal Orders, One Law

FRANCIS G. JACOBS
King's College London

I. Introduction

IT IS A GREAT PRIVILEGE, and a great challenge, to give the British Academy lecture on law, which complements the older Maccabaean lecture on jurisprudence.[1] I have to confess first of all that I am not sure how far the distinction between law and jurisprudence can be sustained. Leaving aside the point that 'jurisprudence' has several meanings, and confining it to 'legal theory' or legal philosophy, I note that some of the Maccabaean lectures have been as much on the nuts and bolts of law as on legal philosophy; and it might seem that some of the law lectures will embody legal philosophy. Indeed it might be thought that, by analogy with Molière's Monsieur Jourdain speaking prose without realising it, so the best lawyers when discussing law may, not always consciously, speak jurisprudence.

My bold suggestion is that, for that and other reasons, the distinction between law and jurisprudence is, or at least ought to be, of diminishing significance. Good law embodies jurisprudence. Good jurisprudence is essential for good law.

But I must have regard to the rubric of this lecture:

BRITISH ACADEMY LAW LECTURE

The British Academy established a Lecture in Law to be given biennially from 2004 onwards in alternation with the Maccabaean Lecture. It may be upon any legal subject other than jurisprudence.

So perhaps some parts of this lecture must be disregarded.

Read at the Academy 2 December 2008.
[1] The lecture was delivered on 2 Dec. 2008 but has been updated to take account of the entry into force of the Lisbon Treaty on 1 Dec. 2009.

Proceedings of the British Academy, **167**, 119–154. © The British Academy 2010.

Law and values

My next proposition is that law is not, and cannot be, value-free in the way which is sometimes suggested. On the contrary, a legal system today, and the approach of the higher courts to the governing principles, necessarily embodies a system of values. Although the schools of jurisprudence, especially those termed 'positivist', have sometimes sought to suggest the opposite, my proposition, I venture to suggest, hardly needs to be demonstrated today, as might have been necessary in a different age. In any event, it is a theme which runs through, is illustrated by, and if needs be I hope is demonstrated by, the entire lecture. So here again law and jurisprudence are perhaps fused.

In England there has been a tendency for law and jurisprudence, for the academic and the practitioner, to be separate and for interaction to be limited. Happily, in my view, fashions are beginning to change. We now have some judges who were in their previous careers primarily academics. We have perhaps not gone far enough down that route. It has been pointed out for example that the judicial House of Lords might have benefited from the presence of an outstanding scholar, to provide academic expertise in such fields as public law and in criminal law. Indeed English law might in that event have been saved from going down some false tracks.

In other parts of Europe the pattern is different. Continental courts at the highest level are often staffed by judges who have both academic and practical experience. The European Courts—the European Court of Human Rights (ECtHR) and the European Court of Justice (ECJ)—are similarly constituted.

In the ECJ the Advocate General will sometimes infuse his or her Opinion, not with doctrinal niceties but with a principled analysis which will guide the Opinion, and sometimes then the judgment, towards a satisfactory practical outcome. It is then academic in what may be one of the best senses. That is one advantage of the single voice of the Advocate General, as distinct from the collective judgment of the Court, the requirement of a single judgment still being justified for practical reasons.

The approach

Although this lecture is for the British Academy, my aim is that it should not be unduly academic. Indeed a part of the specification, part of my brief, was that it should be accessible to the non-lawyer. It will no doubt be regarded by the stricter academic as too generalised, and insufficiently rigorous. But that may be a price worth paying, if some broader lessons can be found from this essay.

Equally, there is a part of academe today which aims not to be prescriptive, and even to be value-free. Here too I must part company. Having spent so great a part of my time at the coal-face, I confess to feeling slightly frustrated if a scholarly venture leads to no practical outcome.

This goes even for some of the theories of the greatest jurists: Austin, Kelsen, Hart. Austin's theory of law as the command of a sovereign had however a continuing appeal. It reflected a common perception of law as an emanation of the State, and of an authority wielding sovereign power over a defined territory.

To look at the real world, let us start at home, with the English common law. It was not made by a sovereign; it was not derived from a Kelsenite *Grundnorm*. It was developed by the judges. Some parts of it remained rather undeveloped; other parts became a highly sophisticated system. Commercial law in particular proved remarkably successful, partly no doubt because there were judges who understood the needs of commerce.

Yet the common law seems to present a series of paradoxes. First, the law itself is a remarkable construct, but the court system still leaves much to be desired: occasionally, Bleak House almost seems to return from the Dickensian age to haunt us. Something of those anomalies prevails today. You are offered what used to be called a Rolls-Royce system when you may want only to take a bus down the road. As Mr Justice Sullivan (now Lord Justice Sullivan) has recently said, English procedures appear to meet international standards: 'But [as he among others has plaintively enquired] who, apart from the very rich and the very poor, can afford to use them?'[2] In that respect, the system may even raise an issue of compliance with international standards, which may be said to include an effective, rather than illusory, right of access to the courts as a fundamental right.

Second, it is no exaggeration to say that the common law is part of the national culture. Yet it has proved a good export, to the Commonwealth, to some extent to the USA, even to other countries. Third, it is multinational; yet it can also be parochial. It has not been, in the past,

---

[2] In his 2008 report on *Ensuring Access to Environmental Justice in England and Wales* (<http://www.lawcentres.org.uk/uploads/Access_to_Environmental_Justice.pdf> accessed 7 April 2010). It might be added that the ability of the very poor to use the procedures is rapidly diminishing with the erosion of the legal aid budget.

particularly receptive of international law. Yet international law plays an ever-increasing part in the settlement of disputes.

Nowadays different legal systems are increasingly operating side by side in the same legal space. This was illustrated, in the past, by domestic law and international law, as conflicts arose between the different systems which could not be resolved. The difficulties have grown as the reach of international law has hugely extended in recent years. Moreover new legal orders have developed in Europe: notably the European Convention on Human Rights (ECHR) and the European Union (EU). There can thus be serious conflicts between different legal orders, with no clear way of resolving them. This poses novel and difficult problems for the courts. How can these conflicts be avoided or resolved?

The answer may impose new methods on the courts. It may also require a new concept of law. And the journey requires us to look, however inadequately, at the role of the courts, at the position of judges in a democracy, at the issue of sovereignty, at the need to strike a balance between conflicting fundamental interests; all in a manner which has some semblance of academic respectability while not addressed to the specialist. A challenge indeed.

II. International law

International law provides the archetype of the potential conflict between different legal orders. Judges and jurists have wrestled with the relationship of international law, as essentially the law governing the relations between States, and municipal law, as the domestic, internal law of the State.

On the international level, States have traditionally been seen in roles which are apparently contradictory: as the subjects of international law, having rights and obligations towards other States, yet at the same time as sovereign, the doctrine of State sovereignty being a traditional cornerstone of international law. The State's internal affairs were not traditionally the concern of international law.

Jurisprudence, focusing understandably on domestic law, again has found it difficult to resolve these issues. Austin, Kelsen and Hart each had different responses on the relationship between municipal and international law, but all of them were rather rapidly shown to be unsatisfactory.

Analysts classified municipal legal systems as 'monist' or 'dualist', depending on whether they were inclusive of international law: a single system or a dual system. In the case of treaties, for example, a monist system would recognise the internal effect of a treaty to which the State was a party, while a dualist system would not recognise the effect of a treaty, subject only to limited exceptions, unless the treaty had been transposed into domestic law, for example in the UK by Act of Parliament. English law was firmly dualist, indeed it sometimes seemed almost 'duellist'—the duel being between municipal and international law, and a strict dividing-line being drawn between them. But in practice monist systems often proved no more successful in giving effect to international law. Neither monist nor dualist systems had a satisfactory response to the relationship between international and domestic law.

For our purposes, it is necessary to outline the main sources of international law, namely custom and treaties, and to suggest briefly ways in which potential conflicts between international law and municipal law might be avoided or resolved. The subject is also a necessary background to our later discussion of the European systems, namely the European Convention on Human Rights and the European Union, both of which systems are founded on treaties—if treaties of an unusual character.

Customary international law

Custom is probably the origin of law in general, and customary law was historically the most important source of law in most societies. The essential idea is perhaps that what is customarily done becomes, over time, socially required, and comes to be accepted as even legally binding.

So custom is an important base of municipal law, as in England it is the base of the common law, which might be regarded as fundamentally a system of custom developed by the courts into a case-law system. But customary law has been especially significant in international law, if only because international law lacks a legislature and, for the most part, a system of courts which can develop a body of case-law.

In international law, customary law develops from the constant practice of States. The standard example is the traditional grant of immunity to the representatives of foreign States. It is easy to see that such diplomatic immunity is reciprocally beneficial, or even essential if any form of discourse between States is to be achieved. More recent examples of rules of international law evolving from State practice include the recognition of an exclusive economic zone extending beyond the territorial waters of maritime States.

Article 38(1) of the Statute of the International Court of Justice, which is widely regarded as specifying the source of international law, directs that Court to apply, inter alia: 'international custom, as evidence of a general practice accepted as law'. The Statute also refers to 'the general principles of law recognized by civilised nations' thus linking custom to State practice.

Treaties

Treaties are—apart from certain basic principles recognised as customary international law—the main source of international law. The Statute of the International Court of Justice, in specifying what the Court shall apply, refers first to 'international conventions, whether general or particular, establishing rules expressly recognized by the contesting states'.

But treaties—as international conventions and agreements are now collectively called—are traditionally an object of suspicion in domestic courts—unless they have been given explicit effect in domestic law by legislation. And even then, it is the legislative act which is likely to be enforced.

Treaties are essentially agreements between States (but international organisations are now often parties), setting out their respective rights and obligations in a particular field. Nowadays they are sometimes multi-lateral agreements open to many or all States: such treaties usually have special functions, seeking to codify the rules of international law in a particular sector, or setting up an international organisation which may have law-making powers. Most characteristically, however, treaties are bilateral agreements between States, defining the rights and obligations of the parties. Treaties can be compared in this respect to agreements, or contracts, concluded between companies or individuals in the private sphere.

But domestic legal systems have had difficulties in coping with the evolving nature of treaties. The continuing problems were vividly brought home to me when, in preparing this lecture, I went back to a comparative study which I had the privilege of leading some years ago. The study (partly financed by the British Academy) was published as a book under the title *The Effect of Treaties in Domestic Law* (London, 1987).

If I may paraphrase the opening of my introduction to the book:

> Everyday transactions of ordinary life, as well as commercial and financial transactions, international trade, transport and communications, and many other aspects of modern society, are increasingly regulated by treaties. However,

treaties give rise to unique legal difficulties which often arise in seeking to enforce treaty provisions in the courts. The most glaring example of this may be the case where a party to a transaction, intending that the transaction should be governed by a particular treaty, takes care to ensure that the treaty has been ratified by the State of the other party, but finds when a dispute occurs that the treaty does not form part of that State's domestic law and will not be applied by that State's courts. Yet, by a strange legal anachronism, many States still seem to consider that treaties are a matter for governments alone, and fail to take measures to implement even those treaties which are of their very nature appropriate for enforcement in the courts.

The problems are not confined, however, to those States which have no constitutional principle giving automatic legal effect to treaties binding on the State under international law. To give a striking illustration, let me cite a perhaps surprising source. When looking for an authoritative statement of the law, I often look at Professor H. W. R. Wade's classic textbook *Administrative Law*, even on a topic outside the field of administrative law. On treaties, I find this remarkable statement (admittedly I take the passage somewhat out of context):

> No English court will enforce a treaty, that is to say an agreement made between states rather than between individuals.

There follows a quotation from an authority of 1859:

> The transactions of independent states between each other are governed by other laws than those which municipal courts administer.[3]

Many of the English cases of that period reflected the position of the East India Company at a time when it governed much of India and was acting in effect as a sovereign power. The English courts were very ready to disclaim jurisdiction over transactions between the Company and the native rulers of India. That historical context may have coloured the approach of the English courts to treaties generally. And other systems have other constraints. A prevailing difficulty is the understandable tendency of national courts to interpret terms used in treaties in accordance with their own national law.

But the character of treaties has, as I have suggested, evolved, and the subject of the effect of treaties in domestic law should have moved on correspondingly. It can hardly be right to say today that no domestic court will enforce a treaty. My suggestion is that the traditional approach of domestic law to treaties cannot survive the recent transformation of

---

[3] H. W. R. Wade and C. F. Forsyth, *Administrative Law*, 10th edn. (Oxford, 2009), p. 717.

international law. International law was historically concerned with relations between States: it had no application to individuals. The exceptional cases where, even in my recollection as a student, international law was concerned with individuals were, broadly speaking, those cases where individuals could be described as 'objects' of international law, rather than its subjects; the classical examples being pirates and slaves—both categories now once again in the news. Slaves, of course, were simply objects of commerce. Pirates could be captured, even on the high seas.

How different is international law today? Many transnational transactions between individuals or corporations are directly regulated by international law. Often there are specific legal regimes, frequently established by multilateral treaties. There may be more or less sophisticated systems of judicial settlement of international arbitration. Whole branches and systems of international law have developed: we have International Economic Law, International Environmental Law, International Human Rights Law, International Criminal Law, and so on.

The International Court of Justice, in a landmark recent decision, has accepted that a treaty can confer rights on individuals.[4] Yet the difficulties remain; and the difficulties remain essentially the same. National courts often remain reluctant to give full effect to treaties, and where they do give effect to them, they often remain reluctant to interpret them in accordance with their aim and intention.

Let me focus here on interpretation, which goes to the root of the problem of developing a single law. Domestic courts sometimes remain impervious to the need for a single interpretation of a disputed text, even where an authoritative interpretation has been adopted by a qualified international body. Indeed the same difficulties arise even in the case of treaties whose very object is to unify aspects of domestic law. One of the most favoured methods of attaining a single law has been by way of treaty. Both on the universal level, and at the level of regional organisations such as the Council of Europe, many treaties have been drawn up whose very aim is to unify the domestic law in particular fields. The international organisation UNIDROIT, the International Institute for the Unification of Private Law, which exists for that very purpose, has drawn up many conventions and other legal instruments to that end. Yet the domestic courts have found difficulties in interpreting even those instru-

---

[4] Case *LaGrand* (*Germany v. USA*), 27 June 2001, ICJ Reports 2001, p. 466.

ments in a uniform way.[5] As Shakespeare put it, 'men may construe things after their own fashion, clean from the purpose of the things themselves'.[6]

What I would suggest is that many of the profound difficulties in reconciling treaties with domestic law, still widely seen as separate systems, but now manifestly operating in the same space, could be overcome. They could be overcome by what is no more than an appropriate approach to treaty interpretation on the one hand and to the interpretation of the domestic legislation on the other. The treaty is not to be rejected where it appears on its face inconsistent with domestic legislation. On the widely prevailing view, the domestic legislation must be interpreted in the traditional way: rather literally on the traditional English approach to the interpretation of statutes. Only where that interpretation of the legislation leads to a genuine ambiguity—which the legislative draftsman will have taken the greatest pains to avoid—can the treaty be let in by the back door, so to speak.

I would suggest that, on the contrary, the courts have an overriding duty to interpret their legislation, where possible, so as to be consistent with the treaty—a treaty which may not have been expressly incorporated by legislation but which in any event and regardless of that omission is, if duly ratified by the State organs, binding on their State under international law. And one can speak here of a 'duty' precisely because there is a fundamental duty under international law to observe treaty obligations: one of the most fundamental principles of international law—a principle of customary law—is *pacta sunt servanda*, treaties are to be observed. And such fundamental principles of international law, at least, are to be respected by all organs of the States, including their municipal courts. Indeed the duty should extend to all duties arising under international law—including, for example, the duty to respect judgments of international courts giving rise to obligations for the State concerned.

In sum, the correct approach to the treaty is not to be found by starting from domestic law and then considering whether the treaty is compatible with that law. Rather it is to be found by starting from the proper interpretation of the treaty in accordance with the now well-recognised principles of treaty interpretation, themselves the product of customary law as codified by the 1969 Vienna Convention on the Law of Treaties; and where appropriate by looking at the interpretation of the treaty by

---

[5] M. J. Stanford, 'Unidroit', in Francis G. Jacobs and Shelley Roberts (eds.), *The Effect of Treaties in Domestic Law* (London, 1987), p. 253.

[6] *Julius Caesar*, I. iii. 34, cited by M. J. Stanford, 'Unidroit', p. 253.

the courts of other systems. And the domestic courts then have the duty to interpret their own domestic legislation, where possible, in a manner consistent with the proper interpretation of the treaty.

The principle of 'consistent' interpretation, that is, an interpretation consistent with the treaty, and therefore consistent with the State's treaty obligations, is recognised in many jurisdictions, including the USA— where it is charmingly referred to, after a case name, as the *Charming Betsy* principle.[7] But what does consistent interpretation mean in practice? Does it go far enough, where there is superficially a conflict with domestic legislation?

A particularly strong form of the principle of consistent interpretation has been explicitly recognised in the UK by Act of Parliament in relation to the European Convention on Human Rights. There the courts are required by the Human Rights Act to interpret all legislation in a way which is compatible with Convention rights 'so far as it is possible to do so'. It thus adopts a strong form of the principle of consistent interpretation. I will return to this in the context of the Human Rights Act.

But it seems clear today that a strong version of the principle of consistent interpretation should be recognised more generally by the State and by its courts in relation to all treaties in force which the State has ratified and by which it has thereby agreed to be bound. There should be, at the least, a strong presumption that the domestic legislation was intended to be consistent with the international obligations of the State. That would help substantially to give proper effect to the principle *pacta sunt servanda.* There should be recognition of the effect of treaties not only where they have been formally incorporated into domestic law, but also where they have been ratified by the State. And, indeed, even in the absence of ratification, when it can be established that they give treaty recognition to established principles of international law.

Treaties and democracy: the United Kingdom

According to constitutional practice in the United Kingdom, Parliament has no formal role in treaty-making, as the power to conclude treaties is vested in the executive, acting on behalf of the Crown. Where a treaty requires a change in UK legislation or the grant of public money, Parliament may vote in the normal way to make or deny the required pro-

---

[7] *Murray v. Charming Betsy*, 6. U.S. 64 (1804).

vision; in other circumstances it can overcome the will of the executive to conclude a particular treaty only by using political pressure to change the mind of ministers, or, in the extreme case, by withdrawing its confidence from them.

The lack of formal parliamentary involvement in treaty-making differentiates the British Parliament from most other national legislatures. With few exceptions, most written constitutions stipulate that parliamentary approval of treaties is required before ratification for at least some categories of treaty. The difference between the UK and practice elsewhere is less than it appears, especially since there are several conventions which ensure the prior scrutiny of certain types of treaties by Parliament.

Nevertheless the fact that treaties are generally concluded by the executive without full Parliamentary participation has had the unfortunate consequence that the courts will not normally recognise the effects of an untransposed treaty on the ground that to do so would violate democratic principles. The risk then is that instead of a single law, internal and international, there will be a conflict between the United Kingdom's internal law and its international obligations. A solution would be to involve Parliament more closely in the treaty-making process, as indeed is the case for the European Parliament in the conclusion of treaties by the European Union. Such treaties can take effect in EU law without further legislative procedures.

Treaties and democracy: the United States

The United States Constitution gives the power to make treaties to the executive, in the person of the President, but only with the advice and consent of the Senate, representing in effect the fifty-one States. Two-thirds of the Senators present must concur. The House of Representatives has no formal role. Yet Article VI, clause 2 of the Constitution declares that treaties, together with the Constitution and the laws of the United States, are the supreme law of the land. That contrasts with the situation in the UK, where as we have seen treaties are regarded as international obligations without effect as domestic law until Parliament passes the necessary legislation. Treaties in the USA may therefore be regarded as having legal effect, and where appropriate as being 'self-executing'—a concept similar to that of 'direct effect' in EU law.

However a constitutional practice has developed in the USA of 'Congressional–Executive Agreements' made by President and Congress (comprising the Senate and the House of Representatives) together. Such

Congressional–Executive Agreements have certain advantages. They permit approval in both Houses of Congress by simple majority, eliminating the need for a two-thirds majority in the Senate. They give an equal role to the House of Representatives, refuting the charge of 'undemocratic anachronism' which had excluded it from the treaty-making process. And where the implementation of the treaty requires legislation, it improves the prospect of passage of such legislation through Congress.

Fidelity to international law

So far I have addressed treaty obligations in relation to domestic legislation. But there are of course far broader issues of compliance with international law that fall outside the scope of this lecture which is concerned with the interaction of different legal orders. Beyond that, we have broader issues of respect for international law, where politics is often the paramount consideration. States, it may reasonably be thought, will comply with general international law, except where they consider that their interests are excessively affected; and even then, they seek to argue that they are complying with international law. Recent events suggest that in weighing those interests in the political scale, they may seriously miscalculate. The assessments made by the USA, the UK, and some of their allies in relation to the war in Iraq illustrate that only too well.

Given the vast importance of international law today, a new approach is needed: an approach which shows regard for, and fidelity to, international law, including due respect for the decisions of international courts and tribunals.

III. The European Convention on Human Rights

To explore what lessons can be learned from the European legal orders, I turn next to European treaties, and in particular the European Convention on Human Rights, which illustrate, perhaps better than any other, the issues of separate systems operating within the same space. And indeed, as we shall see, there are even issues of the interaction of the European treaties (the ECHR and the EU Treaties) with each other, and with general international law; so that occasionally our domestic courts may be faced with several legal orders, all potentially applicable to the same dispute yet potentially in conflict. But, as we shall also see, the legislature and the courts have found ways of reconciling these distinct systems, in the direction of a single law.

Although the European Convention on Human Rights is a treaty concluded among States, and is subject to the usual rules of treaty interpretation—although see below for a qualification of this view—it obviously has a special character which goes beyond merely setting out the rights and obligations of the Contracting States towards one another. It is expressed as obliging the States parties to recognise and protect the rights of individuals. It is therefore one of the first treaties to recognise that individuals have rights under international law. Moreover the Convention is intended to penetrate the national legal orders by requiring the States to behave in particular ways towards their own nationals and indeed to all within their jurisdiction. In addition, it explicitly requires States to provide remedies within their domestic systems for all violations of the Convention which they may commit. And the Convention has been transposed into domestic law in many of the States parties to it, and has in certain States, notably Austria, been given constitutional status, thereby prevailing, in the event of conflict, over ordinary national legislation.

Moreover the European Convention on Human Rights is exceptional in setting up a transnational court, the European Court of Human Rights, to adjudicate on claims against States, and to do so at the suit of individuals—actions by individuals before international courts still being a novelty in international law. As well as hearing applications brought by States, the Court under Article 34 of the Convention may receive applications from any person, non-governmental organisation or group of individuals claiming to be the victim of a violation, by a State party, of the Convention rights. The potential range of applicants is thus very wide: the categories are sufficiently broad to cover every individual, corporate body, or association, and it is sufficient, in order to have standing, to *claim* to be the victim of a violation, as a result of any measure of any kind on the part of the respondent State. Indeed it can be said that the European Court of Human Rights is the most open court of any—more open, in some respects, than even national courts—to individual claimants.

Thus what was previously treated by international law as matters exclusively within the domestic jurisdiction of States—their treatment of their own nationals—is, under the European Convention on Human Rights, brought within an international system of protection and enforcement.

Approaches to interpretation

There are significantly different approaches to *interpretation* of constitutional and other fundamental texts. Perhaps the main contrast is between a *historical* interpretation, which looks back to the adoption of the text and may seek to ascertain the intentions of the authors; and what might be termed an *evolutionary* interpretation, which regards the text as capable of development in the light of changing circumstances. A leading instance of the historical approach is the view of those who seek the 'original intent' of the US Constitution. The European Courts (ECtHR and ECJ) have generally adopted an evolutionary approach: thus the European Convention on Human Rights is, according to the ECtHR, 'a living instrument'.

It can be argued that the approach to interpretation may legitimately take account of the difficulty of amending the text. Thus both in the case of treaties, and in the case of constitutions and similar texts, it may be very difficult in practice to amend the text. The courts may therefore need a certain licence to, in effect, update the text; on the other hand, they may be criticised for going too far, where the effect of their decisions cannot be reversed.

The US Constitution, which can claim to be both the first modern constitution and the oldest surviving constitution in the world, provides an example. It can be amended only by a cumbersome procedure, requiring the assent not only of Congress but also of three-quarters of the States. In more than 200 years, apart from those constituting the Bill of Rights, there have been only seventeen amendments. Consequently it may prove necessary to reinterpret the Constitution, and to depart from what may have been the original intent; indeed there have been many striking examples of reinterpretation of the US Constitution.

In the case of treaties, especially multilateral treaties, the amendment procedure is also difficult, since it will normally require agreement by all the States parties.

The European Convention on Human Rights can be amended only by Protocols which must be ratified by all States parties (currently forty-seven). Most of the Protocols do not in fact amend the text of the Convention, but make additional provision, for example by recognising additional rights. Adaptation of the core substantive rights of the Convention, the text of which has remained unchanged since 1950, has been largely achieved by the evolving case-law of the Court (and before 1998 the case-law of the European Commission of Human Rights also).

It seems clear that social changes and evolving values require an evolutionary interpretation of the Convention. The text is often sufficiently broad and 'open-textured' to allow this. It cannot be objected that that evolutionary approach extends the obligations of the States beyond the undertakings which they accepted when they ratified the Convention. On the contrary, such an approach is necessary, if effect is to be given to their intentions, in a more general sense. It should be presumed that the States did not intend solely to protect the individual against the threats to human rights which were prevalent when the Convention was drawn up, with the result that, as the nature of the threats changed, the protection gradually fell away. Their intention was to protect the individual against the threats of the future, as well as the threats of the past.[8] Thus the Strasbourg Court has rightly described the Convention as 'a living instrument'.

But evolutionary interpretation has its limits: 'It is true that the Convention and the Protocols must be interpreted in the light of present-day conditions. However, the Court cannot, by means of an evolutive interpretation, derive from these instruments a right which was not included therein at the outset.'[9]

The European Union Treaties, which we discuss shortly, have also proved difficult to amend. Again, ratification by all Member States (currently twenty-seven) is required. The founding Treaties of the 1950s were relatively unchanged until the 1980s: the amendments in those decades concerned relatively minor budgetary and institutional provisions. More recently there were more ambitious changes, with the Single European Act, the Maastricht Treaty, the Amsterdam Treaty, and the Nice Treaty. The Constitutional Treaty was rejected by referendum, and the Lisbon Treaty has had a difficult path. But even where there were substantial amendments, they have rarely changed the main provisions of the founding Treaties. They have added new tasks, and introduced new principles (often foreshadowed by the case-law).

Again, therefore, the main task of keeping the EU Treaties up-to-date has fallen to the European Court of Justice, which has performed it remarkably: many examples could be given, such as developments in the principles of equal treatment, fundamental rights, external relations, protection of the environment, and other fields.

---

[8] See C. Ovey and R. White, *The European Convention on Human Rights*, 4th edn. (Oxford, 2006), chap. 3.
[9] *Johnston v. Ireland*, 18 Dec. 1986, § 53, Series A no. 112.

Some fundamental features of the European Convention on Human Rights should be noticed here, as it both reflects, and contributes to, the development of a shared system of values among the States members of the Council of Europe.

Although some fundamental values are at one level unchanging—as witnessed by the terms of the Convention itself—their understanding may evolve—thus requiring an evolving interpretation of the Convention's provisions. And if it is asked how that is possible, where some rather fundamental differences remain among European societies, the answer is at least partly to be found in the approach of the European Court of Human Rights, which respects a degree of diversity; which recognises pluralism as part of the foundations of modern society; which accepts, at the margins of the Convention rights, a measure of discretion for the national authorities with which it will not interfere; and which is prepared to engage in a continuing dialogue with the national courts—a dialogue of which the English courts provide excellent illustrations since the entry into force in 2000 of the relevant provisions of the UK's Human Rights Act of 1998.

English law and the European Convention on Human Rights

It is just ten years since the passage of the Human Rights Act, and eight years since the 'Convention rights', as they are termed in the Act, became enforceable in the UK Courts.

Before the Act there was the spectacle, sometimes frankly unedifying, of English courts trying with little success to reconcile English law with the Convention. The United Kingdom had long been bound under international law by the Convention (indeed the UK was the first state to ratify it as long ago as 1951) but had not incorporated it into UK law by Act of Parliament. The Convention thus had a perilous status before the courts, and a person claiming Convention rights had regularly to seek a remedy in Strasbourg. Yet the litigant was required, as the Convention reasonably insisted, to exhaust all possible recourse in the domestic system before applying to Strasbourg. There was thus much uncertainty and unnecessary delay and costs. But this was perhaps part of a wider problem: the reluctance on the part of the courts to take a more constructive approach to treaties. The courts could certainly have adopted a more positive line.[10]

[10] For instructive discussion see (before the Act) M. Hunt, *Using Human Rights Law in English Courts* (Oxford, 1997); and for a comparison of the courts' approaches before and after the Act

The situation has changed radically since the entry into force of the Human Rights Act. I will focus here on three aspects—those most relevant to my theme. These are, first, the development of a new relationship between the domestic courts and Parliament; second, a new relationship between domestic courts and the Strasbourg Court; and third, some issues of shared and divergent cultures and values.

Constitutionally the most significant feature is the new relationship between courts and Parliament. As already mentioned, the Act requires the courts to interpret all legislation in a way which is compatible with Convention rights 'so far as it is possible to do so'. It thus adopts a strong form of the principle of consistent interpretation.

The Act also requires the courts to take account of the case-law of the European Court of Human Rights—although that case-law is not made binding on the UK Courts (in contrast to the case-law of the European Court of Justice). The Act thus recognises that conflicts between competing values are justiciable issues, and are indeed well suited for resolution by the courts.

In formal terms, too, there is a new relationship between the courts and Parliament. The Act does not give the courts the power, available under national constitutions in some other jurisdictions, to strike down legislation held to infringe fundamental rights (how could it have done so, given Parliamentary sovereignty?) but instead it gives the higher courts the power to issue a declaration of incompatibility. Where such a declaration is made, the offending legislation may be amended, if the government so chooses, not by the more cumbersome method of a new Act of Parliament but by way of an order adopted by a simplified procedure: but the 'remedial order', as it is termed, must be approved by resolution of each House of Parliament. It is apparent that this mechanism changes the relationship between Parliament, the Government and the Courts. In effect, it empowers the Executive, at the instigation of the Courts, to pass amending legislation without the full panoply of Parliamentary procedures. Several such orders have been adopted.

Indeed the power to issue declarations of incompatibility has been used sensibly, yet perhaps surprisingly frequently: in nine years, there have been about twenty-five declarations, most of which survived on appeal, and several of which led promptly to amending legislation.

---

see R. Clayton and H. Tomlinson (eds.), *The Law of Human Rights*, 2nd edn. (Oxford, 2009) and compare with the first edition.

Thus, insofar as there is a conflict between Convention rights and Acts of Parliament, the Human Rights Act gives a powerful role to the courts, yet leaves the last word with the legislature. Indeed the technique of the declaration of incompatibility seems exceptionally well designed: while formally consistent with Parliamentary sovereignty, such a declaration may be even more effective for the protection of human rights than a strike-down power, which might, as the experience of other jurisdictions suggests, be used less frequently. The Act has thus led to a wholly new relationship between the English courts and the Strasbourg Court.

Since the entry into force of the Human Rights Act, and despite the different techniques required to interpret and apply the Convention compared with UK legislation, the courts have proved equal to the task. They have adopted a faithful but not uncritical approach to the Strasbourg case-law, and where there is no such case-law directly in point, they have generally sought to follow the methodology of the Strasbourg Court. As a result, a substantial body of Convention case-law has been developed: in many areas of civil liberties, the law is now clearer, more coherent and more effective. Incidentally the feared abuse of the Act by 'vexatious litigants' or for trivial purposes has not materialised, except in the view of sections of the tabloid press and some political commentators, but not I think in the view of the judges themselves.

Cases involving human rights are now resolved on a principled and systematic basis, as is particularly appropriate to the protection of fundamental rights, rather than on the earlier somewhat haphazard approach based on a patchwork of legislation and common law. At the same time, the courts have become somewhat bolder, but not immoderately so. Judicial review has become significantly less deferential: in sum, it can be said that the courts generally, and properly, exercise a rather more intense and certainly more principled scrutiny of the exercise of public powers.

Moreover, the new case-law of the English courts has become influential. English judgments applying Convention rights are regularly cited both in other jurisdictions and, perhaps more significantly, in Strasbourg by the European Court of Human Rights itself. Frequently they have a persuasive effect on that Court, as indeed was one of the purposes properly pursued by the Human Rights Act.

Indeed it is striking to note that in several significant cases, considered judgments by English courts have persuaded the European Court of Human Rights to revise its own case-law to take account of the concerns advanced by the English judgments.

As the United Kingdom's new Supreme Court has recently put it, normally the requirement in the Human Rights Act that the courts should take account of the case-law of the Strasbourg Court would result in the domestic court applying principles clearly established by the Strasbourg Court. But on rare occasions there might be concerns whether the Strasbourg Court's decision sufficiently appreciated or accommodated the domestic process. The domestic court could then decline to follow the Strasbourg decision, giving reasons for doing so. That would give the Strasbourg Court the opportunity to reconsider so that there took place what might prove to be a valuable dialogue between the domestic and Strasbourg courts.[11]

There are also doubtless very many cases where the availability of Convention rights in the UK courts has made it unnecessary to resort to Strasbourg at all. English courts have had the opportunity in these ways to contribute to the shaping of the Convention system. In particular, they have the opportunity to address the value system which the Convention involves.

Judgments on human rights by English courts under the Human Rights Act have been cited not only in Europe but also outside Europe, notably by courts in Commonwealth jurisdictions and in the USA; many of those jurisdictions have Bills of Rights similar to the provisions of the European Convention on Human Rights. In the case of some Commonwealth countries, their independence Constitutions, drawn up with the assistance of British Governments, included Bills of Rights historically based on the Convention, which was regarded by the UK as a good 'export model'. Some of these Commonwealth courts may find some guidance in the interpretation by the English courts of the European Convention on Human Rights—perhaps more so nowadays than in the more insular English law of civil liberties.

The introduction of the Human Rights Act has also led to the development of a human rights culture—not in the bad sense but in the better sense of a new approach by public authorities which is well documented.

Issues of democracy once again

A major concern is that the courts are taking over a role which at least in the British tradition is a role for parliament: the democratic concern.

---

[11] *R v. Horncastle and others* [2009] UKSC 14, 9 Dec. 2009.

There are two different issues here: first, the effect of treaties which have not been incorporated into UK law by Act of Parliament—as was the case with the European Convention on Human Rights before the Human Rights Act; second, even where duly incorporated, treaties which are regarded as requiring courts to take decisions which it is thought should be taken by Parliament rather than the courts.

The issues here are too wide-ranging to be addressed in detail but three points should be made. First, we are looking at competing values in specific contexts: that is a task for the courts, as the Human Rights Act in effect acknowledges, rather than for the legislature. The legislature simply cannot draw the line and take over the role of adjudicating between competing interests. Moreover, the specific context is all-important: the balancing of interests must take account of the context, and that will often require anxious consideration of all the circumstances of the particular case. Second, insofar as there is a conflict between Convention rights and legislation, the Act, as we have seen, leaves the last word with the legislature. Third, the Act does not normally interfere with what are truly general policy matters: for example the allocation of finite—currently, very finite—economic resources of the State; these remain a matter for government and parliament.

It has not of course been possible to review all the issues raised. But we can at least see in outline the effect of the Convention as a valuable model for the interaction of interlocking yet independent legal systems.

The ECHR and uniform law

How far then does the ECHR, as interpreted by the Strasbourg Court, lead to uniform law across the forty-seven Contracting States? Once again, the answer is qualified. The answer must take account both of the approach of the Strasbourg Court and of the approach of the domestic courts. As we have seen, the Convention is not intended to establish a complete code of uniform law: rather, it seeks to lay down, in many areas, a minimum standard: the States remain free to go further in their protection of human rights.

The overall picture is not, however, straightforward, and further analysis would be helpful. For our purposes, it may be useful to distinguish three basic categories.

- First, in some cases there may be, in effect, a uniform standard: as where there is an absolute prohibition—for example, a prohibition of the death penalty, in the thirteenth protocol. Or, to take a less obvious example, a prohibition on criminalising sexual relations between consenting adults, by interpretation of Article 8 of the Convention. In such a case, the Court may take account of the fact that such a prohibition is not found necessary in other States: how then can it be justified where it does exist?

- Second, in other areas, however, the Court expressly allows for a varying standard by leaving the State a 'margin of appreciation'. This doctrine applies particularly where the Convention accepts that the rights guaranteed may be limited on specified grounds. Here, in contrast to the first case, there may also be specific reasons for accepting wider restrictions for reasons specific to a particular State. For example, greater restrictions on free expression might be justified where there are special threats to public order or national security.

- Third, there may be a need for special tolerance where there is a potential conflict between two fundamental rights: for example, between freedom of expression and the protection of privacy.

In such cases, it is unhelpful to think of higher levels of protection, because that would imply giving priority to one fundamental right over another.

IV. EU law

While the relationship of the ECHR and English law is now relatively clear, in other cases potential conflicts between different legal orders remain indefinitely unresolved. Possibly the best example is again to be found in European law, and again in relation to a Treaty: here, not in the ECHR but the EU Treaties, and in the relationship between EU law and national law. Under EU law, that law takes precedence over the laws of the Member States. That precedence was not explicitly laid down by the Treaties establishing the European Communities,[12] or in subsequent treaties (except in the failed Constitutional Treaty), but could rightly be regarded as inherent in their very nature: how could a single market function, how could

---

[12] The States of Europe were not content to establish a European Community; they established three Communities: the European Coal and Steel Community (Treaty of Paris, 1951), the European Economic Community and the European Atomic Energy Community (Treaties of Rome, 1957).

the Union operate at all if each Member State remained free to override Union law?

Thus the precedence of EU law is not necessarily a consequence of any political or other hierarchy, or of a federal or quasi-federal relationship between the Union and its Member States, but is inevitably a consequence of that feature which is the theme of this study: the theme of a unified law. It can indeed be contended that the need for a unified body of law was sufficient to justify the precedence of that law. The concern of the Treaties for such uniformity was apparent from the outset in the jurisdiction assigned to the ECJ to rule, on a reference from a national court or tribunal, on the interpretation both of the Treaty itself and of EU legislation. It is clear that the purpose of the procedure is to ensure the uniform application of the Treaties and of legislation in all Member States.

The system of references for preliminary rulings has proved a very effective means of unifying the law. It seems clear from the system itself, although again the Treaty is not explicit on the point, that a ruling of the ECJ is binding not only on the national court which referred the question, but also on all courts in the EU confronted with the same question, although a national court in a subsequent case may refer the question anew, if it considers that there are reasons why the ECJ might now give a different answer.

Now it may be thought that EU law, in contrast to the European Convention on Human Rights, is concerned to establish in all cases a single law, uniformly applying across the EU. But just as with the ECHR, the picture is rather more complex. Many of the provisions of the EU Treaties and of EU legislation are indeed to be interpreted and applied uniformly. But in some areas a different approach is accepted.

Let me mention briefly some examples. EU legislation consists primarily of regulations and directives. Whereas regulations are binding in their entirety and directly applicable in all Member States, directives are expressed to be binding only as to the result to be achieved, and leave to the national authorities the choice of form and methods. Yet, although regulations are normally given a uniform interpretation, they may in some circumstances properly be interpreted differently in different parts of the EU, or even within Member States. Moreover directives, which leave Member States the choice of form and methods, are often given by the Court of Justice a binding uniform interpretation. And even the Treaty provisions may be interpreted with different effects for different

Member States: we shall see an example when we look at relations between EU law and the European Convention on Human Rights.

For our purposes however we should perhaps focus on a more fundamental issue affecting the development of a single law within the EU: this is the issue of potential constitutional clashes between national law and EU law. For it is only EU law which raises that problem in a truly fundamental way. Let us return then to the precedence of EU law. That precedence of EU (or Community) law was inevitably deduced by the ECJ some years before the UK joined the Community, was well known and was broadly accepted—even though the British Government's notorious White Paper at the time of accession suggested something different.

The equally inevitable consequence is that from the point of view of EU law national courts, faced with a conflict between EU law and national law, must apply EU law. (According to the ECJ, they are not required to treat national law as invalid, but are required to 'set aside', that is, simply not to apply ('disapply'), the conflicting provisions of national law. That is significant not least because the same provisions might remain applicable in situations where they did not conflict with EU law: for example, a national statute constituting a trade barrier might be inapplicable in the context of trade between Member States, while the same provision might remain applicable in trade with third States.) Thus, although the EU is premised on the primacy of EU law, that primacy is not made explicit in any text other than court decisions—the decisions of the ECJ and of some national courts, including in the UK the House of Lords.

In my view, however, it might have made little difference if precedence had explicitly been laid down in the EC Treaties, or even perhaps if it had explicitly been laid down by UK legislation on accession. That may seem surprising; but the fact is that there is simply no straightforward solution to the problem of resolving the relationship and settling conflicts between what remain separate and autonomous legal orders. What is essential, I suggest, in order to avoid conflicts is a constructive approach by the courts—an approach which reflects the true intentions, and the true interests, of the States. In the absence of such constructive approaches by the courts concerned, the problems seem insoluble.

In view of the general approach taken hitherto by the Member States, whose acceptance of the primacy of Union law is apparent—not least from the fact that they collectively included an explicit primacy clause in the European Constitution, and by the general approach of their supreme and constitutional courts, which have in general entered only somewhat hypothetical reservations to the primacy of EU law—perhaps the most correct approach is that the fundamental rule in the national laws of the EU Member States recognises the primacy of EU law, although such recognition may not, at least for the time being, be altogether unqualified. At the same time, the prospect of such qualification seems rather remote. It would be most likely, on the indications given by national courts to date, if the EU were to act either wholly outside its competence or in clear violation of fundamental rights.

The first course seems unlikely, since there are multiple checks. The ECJ can hold that measures envisaged would be outside the EU's competence (and as such unlawful and invalid), as the Court has done, for example, on several occasions in relation to the EU's international competence (e.g. the European Economic Area Agreement, the World Trade Organisation Agreement, the ECHR). And it can quash a measure as being outside the EU's legislative competence (as it did in the tobacco advertising case). Moreover any formal extension of the EU's competence requires the agreement of all the Member States: that can be done only by Treaty amendment, which necessitates action by all Member States in accordance with their own constitutional requirements. Otherwise, if the EU wishes to act and the Treaty does not provide the necessary powers, action again requires the agreement of all Member States: such action can be taken, under Article 352(1) of the Treaty on the Functioning of the European Union, only by unanimous decision of the European Council.

It seems unlikely also that the EU would act in clear violation of fundamental rights to such an extent as to compel one or more Member States or their courts to refuse to recognise the act as lawful. That prospect may be even more unlikely after the entry into force of the Lisbon Treaty, not only because that renders legally binding the EU Charter of Fundamental Rights and allows—indeed requires—the EU to accede to the ECHR, but also because the jurisdiction of the ECJ is extended. Among other reforms introduced by the Lisbon Treaty to improve judicial protection, one is particularly noteworthy: in the more sensitive areas of EU action, notably in relation to Freedom, Security and Justice, the necessary jurisdiction for the protection of individual rights is conferred on the ECJ.

So far we have considered possible qualifications of the primacy of EU law in particular instances. A more general revocation by a Member State or its courts of such primacy seems unlikely except in the event of withdrawal of a Member State from the EU. As mentioned above, the Lisbon Treaty makes express provision for withdrawal from the Union. It requires, however, agreement of all the Member States. A general revocation of primacy without such procedures would probably be regarded as tantamount to a *de facto* (and illegal) withdrawal.

The United Kingdom presents a traditional obstacle to the primacy of EU law, as indeed of law from any other source: the obstacle of the sovereignty of Parliament. As discussed, the effect seems to be that Parliament *cannot* secure the primacy of EU law. By whatever means, and by whatever form of words, Parliament endeavours to secure the primacy of EU law, a subsequent Act of Parliament must, on the accepted doctrine, be given precedence. The sovereignty of Parliament itself entails that the later Act always prevails.

The European Communities Act 1972, drafted by a brilliant lawyer, Fiennes, sought, by an ingenious form of words, to give effect, obliquely, to the primacy of EC law. But was not that formally and technically impossible? Whatever form of words was chosen, would it not be overridden, if only impliedly, by a later Act which conflicted with EU law? What may well seem extraordinary is that, after more than thirty-five years of UK membership, it cannot be maintained that that central issue has been resolved. But it may seem less extraordinary if it is realised that there is simply no clear solution to that issue. Again the problem is that of two autonomous legal systems coexisting in the same space.

The *Factortame* litigation was at one time thought to have resolved the issue definitively—so far as a court decision can do so, it may be said: but my thesis is that it is only court decisions which can resolve such issues, as when the House of Lords (as the final court of appeal) seemed explicitly to accept that EC law prevailed over Acts of Parliament.[13] Lord Bridge in particular made it clear that that was so, and had been the intended result of the 1972 Act.

Remarkably, however, it is still widely considered today that, in terms of Parliamentary sovereignty, nothing has changed. European law is given primacy over an Act of Parliament, it is said, only because Parliament itself had so ordained.[14] Moreover, that result was reached by

---

[13] *R. v. Secretary of State for Transport (No. 2)* [1991] 1 AC 603.

[14] See Lord Bingham of Cornhill, 'The rule of law and the sovereignty of Parliament', *King's Law Journal*, 19–2 (2008), 223–34 at 223. Recognising that the courts have declined to apply Acts of Parliament, subsequent to the European Communities Act, which conflict with EU law, Lord Bingham adds (at p. 230): 'But the courts act in that way only because Parliament, exercising its legislative authority, has told them to.' However, on the orthodox and hitherto universally accepted doctrine of Parliamentary sovereignty, Parliament cannot bind a future Parliament, and the later Act always prevails.

the courts, it is said, not on the heretical basis that Parliament had succeeded in the EC Act in binding its successors, but rather because the Act included an interpretation clause which requires all statutes to be interpreted as being without prejudice to directly enforceable Community rights. Equally it is said that, since the courts apply EC law only because Parliament requires them to do so, it follows that such observance depends entirely on the will of Parliament, which could, by a new exercise of the legislative power, be reversed.

Is this view, although apparently accepted by many senior judges and some leading academics, not a trifle disingenuous? Does it not disguise (whether or not by intent) the true constitutional position? EU law does of course owe its status in the UK, as a matter of UK constitutional law, to the statutory effect given to it by the 1972 European Communities Act. By the same token, as a matter of UK constitutional law, the 1972 Act could be repealed, and the courts could then be instructed no longer to apply EC law. But until such repeal, the UK courts are declining to apply subsequent Acts of Parliament which conflict with EU law: a clear departure from the traditional doctrine of Parliamentary sovereignty.

In the event of repeal of the European Communities Act, it might be necessary to consider whether such a measure would be lawful under EU law—and which law would prevail in which courts. The logical consequence in the event of repeal of the 1972 Act or its central provisions would be withdrawal from the European Union. Until now, the Treaties contain no provision for withdrawal from the European Union. The failed Constitutional Treaty did contain such provision, and those provisions are maintained by the Lisbon Treaty. So in the future, withdrawal might be facilitated. If Parliament, in a new legislative measure clearly conflicting with EC law, specifically purports to override the provisions of the European Communities Act, that might be regarded as incompatible with continuing membership of the EU.

But this is all a matter of speculation. What is the law at present? It seems to me that, so long as the UK courts are required to apply EU law, it is no mere rule of statutory interpretation—that is, interpretation of Acts of Parliament—which applies. Where there is no scope for consistent interpretation of the UK legislation—that is, in the event of a straightforward clash between an Act of Parliament and EU law—the UK Courts can and must—and indeed they do—apply EU law. It would involve setting aside, as they are required to do, the offending provisions of the Act of Parliament—even one that is subsequent to the European

Communities Act—and thus, in effect, allowing the EC Act of 1972 to prevail over both prior and subsequent Acts of Parliament.

Nor is this a peculiarity of the United Kingdom constitution, even if the reason for it—Parliamentary sovereignty—is peculiar to it. There are certainly similar constitutional conundrums in other Member States, and probably in many of them. Nor—and this is the most striking feature— is it easy, or perhaps even possible, to see how the conflicting constitutional positions could be reconciled. If we take again the example of the United Kingdom, there seems hardly to be even a theoretical solution.

But wait, I hear you cry: did not the failed 'Constitutional Treaty' make express provision for the primacy of EU law? If that Treaty had not been voted down in referendums in France and the Netherlands, and had been duly ratified and transposed into law in all the Member States, would not that have put an end to all uncertainty about the primacy of EU law? Certainly, the now defunct Constitutional Treaty (the Treaty establishing a Constitution for Europe) boldly spelt out, for the first time in a Community text, the primacy of EU law: it would have provided (in Article I-6):

> The Constitution and law adopted by the institutions of the Union in exercising competences conferred on it shall have primacy over the law of the Member States.

The Lisbon Treaty, which replaced the Constitutional Treaty, and which generally is very similar in content though not in form, contains no such provision. Instead, there is a tame statement in a mere 'Declaration concerning primacy' appended to the Treaty, Declaration No. 17. In that declaration 'The Conference recalls that, in accordance with well settled case law of the Court of Justice of the European Union, the Treaties and the law adopted by the Union on the basis of the Treaties have primacy over the law of Member States, under the conditions laid down by the said case law.' The Declaration also refers to an opinion of the Council Legal Service according to which 'The fact that the principle of primacy will not be included in the future treaty shall not in any way change the existence of the principle and the existing case-law of the Court of Justice.'

However, even in the event of express treaty provisions on primacy, the position is less clear than it may appear at first sight. Let us take first the case of the UK. Even if the Constitutional Treaty had been ratified and given effect in the UK—how else than by Act of Parliament?—the problem would not have been resolved. Parliament would have provided that the Constitutional Treaty would have the force of law in the UK. Conceivably, it might even have on this occasion explicitly enacted, by separate and express provision, the primacy of EU law. But could Parliament have thereby bound its successors? Not according to the conventional view of the fundamental norm—not to say the *Grundnorm*—of the UK constitution.

Indeed it is not clear whether any solution could be found to the conflicts of separate legal orders, other than by a wholly new constitutional settlement, perhaps with a new written constitution, adopted or given effect by some even more solemn method than a traditional Act of Parliament.

Let it be noted that problems of this kind are not unique to the peculiarities of the UK Constitution, but are found in other systems even where there is a full constitutional text. A particularly illuminating example is the case of the Federal Republic of Germany. Here the traditional, if largely hypothetical, question of possible conflict between EC law and the fundamental rights protected by the German Basic Law (its constitutional text) would not, as it seems to me, be resolved even by incorporation into the German Constitution of a clause providing for the primacy of EU law. That is because the Constitution itself, in the interest of giving fundamental rights the most secure anchorage, also provides that its provisions on fundamental rights are not amendable. So even an amendment to the German Constitution, purporting to give precedence to EU law, would not succeed in resolving the problem. Alleged infringements of those rights by EU provisions would still fall to be considered by the German Constitutional Court, notwithstanding a constitutional guarantee of the primacy of EU law.

German constitutional law in its approach to EU law raises two main issues: apart from the fundamental rights issue, there is the issue of what competences have been transferred to the EU. This issue, described as the issue of *Kompetenz-Kompetenz* (who has the final say as to the demarcation between the competence of the EU and the competence of the Member States), may also—like the fundamental rights issue—be invoked to challenge the validity of EU measures. But here the challenge would be on the ground that the EU has acted outside the competences transferred to it by the Federal Republic. Just as the Constitutional Court claims the final say on fundamental rights, so it claims to decide on the scope of the EU's competences. That claim does however seem contestable: again, it is difficult to see how the Union could function if each Member State could decide for itself what was the scope of the Union's competence. Moreover the scope of the Union's competence is clearly assigned to the jurisdiction of the ECJ under the Union Treaties: 'lack of competence' has from the outset been the first ground on which the Court may quash an EU measure.

In relation to the issue of fundamental rights, however, a certain accommodation has been established between the ECJ and the Federal Constitutional Court—and indeed, as we have seen, the European Court of Human Rights. The approach of the ECJ has been outlined above. The Federal Constitutional Court, for its part, has developed the *solange* doctrine, which seems to preserve a degree of harmony between the *Grundgesetz* and EU law. According to this doctrine, developed by the German Constitutional Court, *solange* (so long as) EU measures might not be subject, within the EU, to the same standard of review as prevailed under the German Basic Law, such measures could be controlled by the German Constitutional Court.

The concerns of the German Constitutional Court first surfaced in 1974, where it introduced the *solange* doctrine. In understandable reaction to the atrocities of the Nazi era, the German Constitution (the *Grundgesetz* or 'Basic Law'), the German Federal Constitutional Court and German scholars generally attach greater significance to fundamental rights issues than is the case in most other States.

In the context of EU law, such rights have often been invoked in a commercial context, by traders in a challenge to Community legislation, just as they were accustomed to challenging domestic legislation as infringing such rights. The first leading case in Germany on Community legislation was *Internationale Handelsgesellschaft*, decided by the Constitutional Court in 1974. A trader challenged certain EU regulations as infringing its fundamental rights. When the case reached the Constitutional Court, it first considered the relationship between German constitutional law and EU law. It took the view that EU law 'is neither a component part of the national legal system nor international law, but forms an independent system of law flowing from an autonomous legal source'.[15] The Court went on to hold that, so long as EU law did not contain provisions on fundamental rights measuring up to those in the German Basic Law, it would be competent to review EU measures for compliance with fundamental rights: not with a view to ruling on the validity of an EU measure, but possibly that such a measure could not be applied in Germany. The *solange* doctrine was refined in later cases (*Solange II* and *III*).[16]

---

[15] Case 11/70 *Internationale Handelsgesellschaft* [1970] ECR 1125.
[16] See *Solange I* (BVerfGE 37, 271), *Solange II* (BVerfGE, 73, 339), and *Solange III* (BVerfG, 2 BvL 1/97).

Difficulties of a similar kind have surfaced from time to time in the Constitutional Courts or Supreme Courts of other Member States. Such courts may take what can be described as a dogmatic view of the relation between their own Constitution and their own law on the one hand, and EU law on the other hand. I do not use the term 'dogmatic' here in a pejorative sense; rather, it reflects an adherence to a particular doctrine to which the courts, and many jurists, may be understandably wedded, but which is increasingly difficult to reconcile with the changing character of law and the emergence of what may be described as multipolar systems. Indeed in some instances the doctrine seems to go back as far as the Westphalian system, and the traditional model of the sovereign State.

The conclusion which seems to follow is that there is no formal, even theoretical, solution to the interaction of different legal orders; such solutions can and must be found, pragmatically, by the courts. I would suggest that, faced with apparently conflicting obligations, the courts have some form of obligation to find a constructive resolution of these conflicts. It would not be an obligation of domestic law, nor of international law, but one which might be described as a meta-legal obligation.

The recent approach of the French courts has been elegantly synthesised by Jean-Marc Sauvé, who presides over the French Conseil d'État:

> This new approach helps us greatly to open the way to a system aimed at *combining* instead of *opposing* European law on the one hand, constitutional rights and liberties on the other hand. This seems consistent with the fact that, when it comes to implementing European law, you simply no longer have the domestic judge on the one hand, the ECJ and the European Court of Human Rights on the other hand. The domestic judge is himself a European judge. . . . The way we look at EU law has . . . changed greatly over the past 10 or 20 years. We no longer look at EU law as an *external* source of law; it is simply part of the legal norms that we must implement daily in our courts . . .[17]

Those views were held in the past by some European law scholars as a statement of aspiration. Today such views are increasingly expressed by senior judges themselves.[18]

The courts, since they have ultimately to resolve conflicting obligations, thereby necessarily have a choice. The reality is that they may adopt

---

[17] Jean-Marc Sauvé, 'Judging the administration in France', in M. Andenas and D. Fairgrieve (eds.), *Tom Bingham and the Transformation of the Law* (Oxford, 2009), p. 327. Jean-Marc Sauvé is Vice-President of the Conseil d'État but effectively its president, the titular president being the President of the Republic.

[18] For the views of English judges, see my paper 'European law and the English judge', in Andenas and Fairgrieve (eds.), *Tom Bingham and the Transformation of the Law*, pp. 419–38.

an interpretation of their basic constitutional texts which enables those to coexist with their treaty obligations—as the House of Lords did in *Factortame*, and as other supreme and constitutional courts have done. Or they may consider themselves free to ignore that obligation: put on their internal constitutional spectacles and refuse to look beyond the confines of their own system as traditionally conceived and interpreted. But if they do that, then they will succeed only in generating conflicts between different legal systems: conflicts which will generate profound legal confusion, which run deeply counter to legal clarity and legal certainty, and for which there is no resolution.

The conclusion I reach is that, just as treaties can find no complete solution to the relation between treaty and domestic law, so domestic law too can find no complete solution. The courts are under an obligation to find a solution to what in formal terms may be irreconcilable conflict. To a great extent, in the context of EU law, they have succeeded in doing so.

V. EU law and ECHR: Strasbourg–Luxembourg

There are as we have seen not one but two separate systems of transnational European law: European Union law, overseen by the European Court of Justice, and the European Convention on Human Rights, overseen by the European Court of Human Rights. Although the two systems, and the two Courts, emerged independently, the overall pattern, while it did not result by design, seems rather appropriate. The jurisdiction of the two Courts is wholly distinct, since the function of the ECtHR is essentially to receive applications alleging breach of the ECHR after all domestic remedies have been exhausted, while the ECJ has no specific human rights jurisdiction but may apply principles of respect for fundamental rights in the context of its various heads of jurisdiction, notably on references from national courts and tribunals.

Moreover the Courts themselves are entirely separate and independent, and the organisations within which they operate are different and have different membership. Each organisation has grown remarkably in coverage of European States: the EU from six to twenty-seven Member States; the Council of Europe has no fewer than forty-seven members (including some mini-States).

Nonetheless the resulting structure can be seen as rather appropriate to the developing European legal family. Indeed both the separate development of each organisation and their mutual relations may suggest a form of organic development or evolution: organisations, no less than individuals, may respond to the pressures and needs to which they are subject, and the European Union and the Council of Europe may reflect those processes.

Yet difficulties might have been anticipated where these separate systems of law, operating under the aegis of independent courts, have jurisdiction over the same territories and the same legal space. The ECJ and the ECtHR are independent and there is no formal provision for their interaction. The EU is not, as yet, subject to the ECHR although the EU Member States are all parties to the Convention; the Council of Europe, within which the ECtHR operates, is an organisation entirely separate from the EU. In practice, such difficulties have largely been avoided: partly at least by the Courts listening and responding: by processes of judicial dialogue.

In the result, the scene has changed dramatically. In outline, since the original Treaties contained no provisions on human rights, the ECJ initially rejected attempts to challenge EU measures as contrary to the fundamental rights protected by the constitutions of the then Member States. The ECJ apparently feared that challenges based on national law would threaten the primacy of EU law and so endanger the whole system. But when national courts suggested that they could not apply EU measures contrary to fundamental rights, the ECJ changed tack, partly perhaps again to avoid threats to the primacy of EU law; the ECJ now stated that there was 'an analogous guarantee inherent in Community law'. In a judgment delivered in 1970 the Court first restated its original approach as follows:

> Recourse to the legal rules or concepts of *national* law in order to judge the validity of *Community* measures would have an adverse effect on the uniformity and efficacy of Community law. The validity of such measures can only be judged in the light of Community law. Therefore the validity of a Community measure or its effect within a Member State cannot be affected by allegations that it runs counter to fundamental rights as formulated by the Constitution of that State[19].

'However', the Court now added by way of an important qualification, 'an examination should be made as to whether . . . any analogous guarantee inherent in Community law has been disregarded.' And here, the Court produced a new principle: 'In fact, respect for fundamental rights forms an integral part of the general principles of law protected by the

---

[19] Case 11/70 *Internationale Handelsgesellschaft*, para. 3.

Court . . .' So, a remarkable innovation. But there was a caveat; it would be for the Court to determine the scope of such protection: 'The protection of such rights, whilst inspired by the constitutional traditions common to the Member States, must be ensured within the framework of the structure and objectives of the Community.'[20] So it was ultimately for the ECJ to strike the balance.

From the point of view of our theme, that turning-point in the case-law of the ECJ was a significant development in the direction of a single body of law, both in relation to the ECHR and in relation to the constitutional principles of the Member States.

However, the early case-law following that judgment showed rather little propensity for rigorous scrutiny of Community measures and was even considered by some critics as paying only lip-service to the protection of fundamental rights. Gradually the case-law developed, and the Court took the ECHR as the prime point of reference, increasingly referring also to the case-law of the Strasbourg Court. A practice of dialogue, formal and informal, developed between the European Courts in Strasbourg and Luxembourg. The Strasbourg Court, in a remarkable judgment in the *Bosphorus* case, accepted that the review by the ECJ of compliance with fundamental rights made it unnecessary for the Strasbourg Court to conduct its own scrutiny.

The European Court of Justice, for its part, has developed an approach which seems in harmony with that of the Strasbourg Court. A striking example of the new approach of the ECJ is the *Omega Spielhallen* case.[21] Here the German authorities had banned a game played in a laserdrome operated by the applicant company, which involved the simulated killing of humans using laser guns. The company, Omega, challenged the ban as contrary to the freedom to provide services, since the equipment and technology were supplied by a British company.

The case again raised the issue of a conflict between fundamental economic freedoms under the Treaty and fundamental human rights, since the German courts upheld the ban on the ground that the commercial exploitation of a game involving simulated homicide was an affront to human dignity protected by the German Basic Law. The ECJ customarily applied a rigorous scrutiny to restrictions on freedom to supply goods and services—the core of the internal market—requiring the most compelling justification and insisting on the need for uniformity.

---

[20] Case 11/70 *Internationale Handelsgesellschaft*, para. 4.
[21] Case C-36/02 *Omega Spielhallen* [2004] ECR I-9609.

In *Omega*, however, on a reference from the German court, the European Court of Justice accepted that the restrictions on the freedom to provide services satisfied the principle of proportionality: they did not go beyond what was necessary to protect the values in question. Moreover the Court expressly accepted—and here the ruling perhaps goes further than the previous case-law—that the outcome did not depend upon all Member States having a shared conception of the scope of the fundamental rights to be protected. The Court here recognises the possibility—or even perhaps the merit—of value diversity.

(But it is not only a two-way dialogue: there is a triangular dialogue, involving the national Court as well as the two European Courts. As one might say, a *ménage à trois*?)

So the first part of the solution is judicial dialogue. But there is also the substantive question: how—in which direction—are the different systems to be reconciled? As we have seen, even identical provisions can be interpreted in different ways, perhaps especially where courts are required to balance competing interests. Here we are driven to consider the basic values which do—and should—drive the solutions. Where these values are shared, common solutions can be found. And perhaps shared values can increasingly be found today.

This may be true to some extent even on the broadest global level. The developing principle of respect for human rights, despite gross and spectacular failures, provides an illustration. The basic notion is not seriously contested: a minimum level of treatment must be guaranteed to all individuals, by virtue of the fact that they are humans. Of course standards vary around the world—sometimes unforgivably, but sometimes understandably. To take one of the less controversial examples, free speech is more strongly protected in the US under the First Amendment than it generally is in Europe. In Europe, privacy is more protected, at least until recent tolerance, at least by the executive, of increasing incursions into private life in the interest of 'security'.

Bills of rights, or statements of fundamental human rights, present one of the best illustrations of the point that it is the way the courts interpret what may be a very similar wording which ultimately counts, and that that interpretation may reflect the political and social values of the jurisdiction concerned. But in Europe, at least, there seems increasingly to be common ground, and so a single law.

VI. Concluding remarks

In conclusion, I turn to the story by Antoine de Saint-Exupéry, *Le petit prince*, a fable especially relevant to our time. The prince, rather bored by being alone on his own small planet, and curious to see more, decides to visit other planets. But he finds his curiosity is not shared. To his surprise and disappointment, the inhabitants of these planets are wholly absorbed in their domestic affairs, with no wish to look beyond their limited horizons.

On Earth, there are different approaches in different courts, and even by different judges in the same court. Notoriously a battle has raged in the US Supreme Court between those who are ready to look at other systems, and those who refuse to do so. Refreshingly, the Chief Justice of the Court, John Roberts, very recently stated (extra-judicially) that this was a false debate: it was obvious that the courts must look at other systems.[22] In England, the courts have more generally been ready to follow the little prince, and to accept, as Shakespeare's *Coriolanus* puts it, that 'There is a world elsewhere.'[23]

Today, it is no longer a matter of chance, or even discretion: the supreme courts, at least, of all our countries have a duty to look beyond their immediate horizons. Even if that duty cannot be characterised as a legal duty, explicitly imposed on the courts by their own domestic legal systems, it does seem some form of prudential duty.

But we must draw a distinction between two very different situations. In one, the courts may be encouraged to look at other systems, at their discretion, so as to learn from their experience, and perhaps to avoid unnecessary divergences. But in another situation, where two independent systems, both applicable in the same legal space, may conflict, it seems to me that there is a clear duty on the courts to seek to avoid such a conflict. Any other solution is likely to put States, or indeed those subject to the legal systems in question, under irreconcilable obligations.

I would suggest that there may be a new role both for judges and for academics. The role of judges is changing: they are also more conscious of their role, more conscious of making choices, and of the need to make

---

[22] Statement at the public session of the Judicial and Academic Conference on the role of Supreme Courts, held at King's College London, July 2009.

[23] The title of Tom Bingham's F. A. Mann lecture of 1991, in which he expressed one of his own outstanding qualities: his openness to new ideas from other quarters and other sources. See T. Bingham, *The Business of Judging* (Oxford, 2000), p. 87.

informed choices. They are also increasingly ready to discuss their tasks: to engage in discussion with judges from other jurisdictions, and with academics.

The role of academics, in some ways, is what it has always been: it includes understanding, explaining, guiding. But now, perhaps more specifically, further functions can be identified:

1. since different models are now more readily available, to evaluate them and draw attention to those which might be useful;
2. to criticise: an important resource for the judges, and perhaps also a restraint for them, to meet the risk that, in their new, less restrained, functions, they may go too far—or perhaps not far enough; and
3. to explain, if I am right, what may be needed: no less than a new conception of law itself. But that might be to embark on the prohibited territory of jurisprudence.

I will only say this by way of general conclusion. International law and European law are increasingly invoked in our courts. But possible conflicts between different legal systems can be resolved in part by new techniques: courts in different systems are increasingly listening to one another, as if working together. This 'judicial dialogue' is necessary where there is no formal means of resolving conflicts. Moreover the courts, especially in Europe, are able to rely increasingly on shared values, and indeed are contributing to the development of these values. The English courts are playing an especially important role under the Human Rights Act; in other fields, they are able to use valuable inputs from other European systems. They are able to take advantage of the experience of other systems, to see how defects in their own might be cured. Thus although the legal scene is now more complex, with the courts having to consider the impact of international law and European law, there are also advantages for the mutual benefit of the different systems. And increasingly, in Europe at least, the different legal systems are moving, as the need arises, towards a single law.

Buddhist Archaeology
in Republican China:
a New Relationship to the Past

SARAH E. FRASER

Northwestern University

ARCHAEOLOGY STARTED rather late in China. The first large-scale state-sponsored excavation directed by indigenous scholars began in December 1928 when Fu Sinian 傅斯年 (1896–1950), the director of the new Institute of History and Philology, charged China's first Anthropology Ph.D., Li Ji 李濟 (1896–1979), to establish an office near Anyang in Henan Province (Fig. 1).[1] In the late Qing dynasty, accidental finds of oracle bones and bronzes gave some indication of the region's extensive deposits in Bronze Age materials. Late nineteenth-century looting of bronze artefacts and tomb goods propelled a thriving Tianjin art market.[2] These amateur, unofficial excavations produced finds that entered the market without provenance. But as soon as government fieldwork and excavations began systematically, the Anyang area did indeed prove to contain the remnants of the last Shang (*c*.1150–1050 BCE) capital and its royal cemetery. Quite

---

Read at the Academy 28 October 2008.

[1] Trigger (2006), p. 265. Fu Sinian Library (FSN) 元25-3, 20 Dec. 1928. Actual excavations at Yinxu began in February 1929. Dong Zuobin conducted preliminary excavations earlier in 1928, FSN 元23-1, Institute of History and Philology (IHP). Li Ji worked with the Freer Gallery, Smithsonian and Tsinghua University on other excavations in Shaanxi 1926, but these were not wholly Chinese-government sponsored digs, Zang Zhenhua 藏振華 (2008); Li Ji (1926). The efforts of the Swedish archaeologist J. Gunnar Andersson (1874–1960), sometimes working in collaboration with China's National Geological Survey, excavated Yangshao culture sites in 1921–3 and the Paleolithic site in Zhoukoudian, near Beijing beginning in 1921 preceded the Anyang digs.

[2] Brown (2008).

Proceedings of the British Academy, **167**, 155–198. © The British Academy 2010.

Figure 1.   From left front, Liu Yuxia, Shi Zhangru, Wang Xiang, Wu Jinding, Dong Zuobing, Ma Feibai, and Li Guangyu each stand at the position of a foundation stone, Shang palace ruins, sixth campaign, east of A4, pit E53, Xiaotun. 4 April 1932. © Institute of History and Philology, Academia Sinica, Republic of China.

dramatically, in just one year, the nascent field of Chinese archaeology went from being a small enterprise of a few test pits to being the locus of spectacular bronze and jade discoveries dating to the end of the first dynastic period (Fig. 2). The excavation photographs suggest the potential drama in the archaeological work process at this time. Shi Zhangru 石璋如 (1902–2004) and others establish a measured work grid with rope and stakes along the stone foundation of a Shang palace in a reclaimed field. In the massive pit of the later excavation photograph, a Shang necropolis extends forty feet below ground. Spectacular finds in fifteen campaigns continued unabated until the summer of 1937 when the Japanese invasion forced an exodus of the Chinese government into the interior. Archaeology in Bronze Age sites came to a halt as precipitously as it began. These rather dramatic historic circumstances pressed researchers to develop new research sites away from the war zone (Fig. 3). The capital was moved to Chongqing and scholars relocated all their field specimens, notes, libraries, and archaeological finds, in addition to the entire collection of the former

Figure 2. Xibeigang site, royal tomb 1001. 28 May 1935. Shi Zhangru, Head of the Yinxu Excavations for the IHP, photographer. © Institute of History and Philology, Academia Sinica, Republic of China.

Figure 3. The Republican Government's Northwest History and Geography Research Group 西北史地考察團 on their way from Lanzhou to Dunhuang, *c*.1942–4.

imperial palace, to the interior. Over 16,700 crates weighing thousands of
tons were sent to Guizhou, Sichuan and Yunnan from the coast.[3] The
north-west and south-west became the new base for Republican research
and intellectual efforts for the next eight years.

The shift to a new geographical home base changed the landscape of
archaeology. It also changed the kinds of questions that researchers were
able to ask and the type of objects they would investigate. In nine short
years from the inception of the Anyang digs to the 1937 exodus, the history of early China had been rewritten. But then, due to the war, scholars
had to rise quickly to the challenge of investigating new terrain. The rate
of academic inquiry and discoveries during this time was fast-paced; these
were exciting times. In addition to formal, state-sponsored archaeological
projects, many artists and small teams of researchers emulated the spirit
of the Anyang inquiry, striking out on their own and in small government
teams, to create a new history of Chinese art and culture based on concrete specimens, excavated evidence, and direct observation.[4] Artists, in
particular, developed a new approach to studying objects; *meishu kaogu*—
an archaeology of art—drew on a German style of art history transformed by excavated objects from extensive campaigns in Greece and
Turkey. Archaeology of art was established as a new methodology to
formulate an understanding of stylistic chronology and material culture
(Fig. 4).[5] In wartime China, the land-locked interior became the focus of
these efforts and the frontier of Inner Asia became the new intellectual
centre during the Sino-Japanese conflict.

New research methods to uncover the old

To be sure, scholars had focused on the inner frontier before the 1937
exodus. While excavations took place in the east at Anyang, researchers in

---

[3] 考19-2-8 (d. after 30 Aug. 1938), IHP. Overall, almost 16,700 boxes of relics and research
materials, including archaeological finds, were transported out of Nanjing at the onset of the
war. On 14 August 1937, 80 boxes of the most important treasures were transferred via Hankou
to Changsha and then moved to Guiyang. Beginning in November 1937, the remaining majority
of relics were transferred in two ways. Just fewer than 9,400 boxes were transferred by boat from
Hankou to Chongqing and 7,300 boxes were transferred by railway via Xian to Baoji, Shaanxi;
they were then trucked to Hanzhong and transferred again by vehicle from Hanzhong to a
Chengdu storehouse.
[4] Chen (1997); Dunhuang Academy (2002); Editorial (1942); Editorial Page (1942); Fa (1944); Fu
(1929–33); Fu (2003); He (1943); Shi (2002); Xia (2002); Wei (1941); Zhu (1942).
[5] Marchand (1996; 2003).

Figure 4.   Wang Ziyun, sculpture of horse at Jianling 建 陵, the necropolis for Suzong 唐肅宗 (711–62), *in situ*, Liquan 醴泉, outside of Xian, 1944. Suzong (Li Xiang 李享) was a son of the Tang Emperor Minghuang. Photo courtesy of Wang Qian.

archaeology's new associated fields of anthropology and ethnography found ready research grounds in the south-west. Li Guangming 黎光明 (1901–46) and Wang Yuanhui 王元輝 (1900–92) completed their survey of Qiang people in Sichuan Province in 1929; Ling Chunsheng 凌純聲 (1902–81) and Rei Yifu 芮逸夫 (1898–1990) conducted a thorough investigation of Miao ethnic linguistics in western Hunan in 1933; and Zhou Zhenhe 周振鶴 researched Qinghai ethnicity and folk customs in the early 1930s.[6] The motivations for such broad and deep considerations of the frontier were connected to the uncertain nature of borderlands in imperial history and their equally imprecise status in modern nation-building. The frontier was an unknown entity—a 'blank ground' 白地; for political and economic purposes it was necessary to determine the boundaries of the new state and identify the population it encompassed.[7] For intellectuals, defining the boundaries of common cultural experience was a question of modern identity and history writing. Li, Wang, Ling, and Rei's studies directly addressed the multi-ethnic nature of the inner frontier. And it was, in part, their focus on ethnicity and the role of the minorities in a modern Han state that would frame the kind of research scholars conducted once the north-west and south-west cultural regions became home during the war. Frontier studies also gave vent to a long-standing preoccupation with ethnicity and Han identity that can even be traced back to the Han dynasty during the second century, particularly focused on the south-west and north-west (Fig. 5).[8] In eighteenth-century paintings of the Miao people in Guizhou Province (located in southern China near the Vietnamese border) and of Tibetans across the empire under Emperor Qianlong (r. 1736–95), court painters satisfied the imperial demand for typing and categorising frontier peoples in an ethnographic paradigm.[9]

Li Ji, considered to be the father of Chinese archaeology, was trained as an anthropologist, demonstrating how close the links were between these new disciplines in the early twentieth century. His Harvard dissertation explored the ethnographic formation of Chinese people. It

---

[6] Li Guangming and Wang Yuanhui 黎光明, 王元輝, ed. Wang Mingke 王明珂編 (2004). Ling Chunsheng and Rui Yifu (1947; 1993); Zhou Zhenhe (1938; 1987).

[7] The photographer Zhuang Xueben was referring to northern Xikang (now northwest Sichuan) and southern Qinghai—both areas are part of Khams, the eastern part of cultural Tibet. Zhuang Xueben 莊 學本 (1937), 1.

[8] Wang Mingke (1997); (2003).

[9] National Palace Museum (2005), pp. 242–3; 252–3. Yang Tingshi 楊庭碩 (2004), vols. 1–2; Rui Yifu (chief ed.) (1973), vols. 1–2.

Figure 5.   Miao Peoples. In *Daily Life Illustrations of Miao and Yao Ethnic Groups* 苗瑤族生活圖,
  c. eighteenth century. ©The East Asian Library and the Gest Collection, Princeton University.

reflected contemporary worldwide racial preoccupations, focusing on
physical traits including a close comparison of forehead, nose and eyes,
and hair.[10] Although he wanted to return to China to conduct skeletal
measurements—the core data for his study—he settled on 110 Chinese
students and 'Chinese laborers' in the Boston area for his control group
and conducted detailed biometrics. While this may have been the only
pool available to him, he also appears to divide them according to class
and intelligence.[11] This legacy of physical anthropology remained with

[10] Li Ji (1923; 1928), pp. 10–28.
[11] Ibid., p. 8.

him through the Anyang digs; using the skeletal remains from Yinxu, Anyang, he proposed a racial interpretation of early China and advanced the claim that the skulls of five different races were present in the excavation pits. (This, of course, proved to be wrong—later scholars argue that the skeletal remains were indicative of regional not racial variation.[12]) Thus, the fields of archaeology and anthropology were intertwined since their inception, placing questions of genetic and physical traits in the foreground. When archaeologists, artists, and researchers were inspired to conduct fieldwork, their studies were shaped by early twentieth-century concerns of physical anthropology. Art discovered *in situ* took on the racial and ethnic qualities of the Han and non-Han framework of intellectual activity during this period. In the case of Buddhist Archaeology, the proximity of artefacts to non-Han ethnic groups in frontier zones proved a ready ground for researchers to explain the links between icon and ethno-history. This essay considers the ways in which ethnographic concerns and finds in frontier zones were central to the new discipline of the archaeology of art (*meishu kaogu*). To establish the framework of discussion, I explore briefly the intellectual stakes of these methods.

Chinese researchers were deeply affected by a range of European theories of culture and research in developing their own brand of archaeology of art. Especially key was the work of the German archae-ologist Adolf Michaelis (1835–1910). Guo Moruo (1892–1978) translated Michaelis' *Die archäologischen Entdeckungen* (Leipzig, 1904), in 1947.[13] Guo started the translation in 1929 when he was in Japan; but it is clear that Michaelis' ideas of 'spade archaeology' as the necessary precursor to writing art history circulated widely well before the publication date. Guo was the editor of the highly respected *Arts and Literature Journal* 文詩雜誌 where influential scholars published opinions on establishing an intellectual roadmap for developing the north-west, problems associated with the Dunhuang site, and other key issues in archaeology. Michaelis' programme to study works of art in their original content (his 'source material' was in Greece and Italy) was consistent with the expansive sense of history that held sway in the circles associated with National Institute of History and

[12] Li Ji (1977); Li Ji's theory of five racial types in Anyang skeletal remains has since been discredited, see Keightley (1978).

[13] Michaelis (1904); Michaelis (1929), trans. Guo Muoruo (1929–48; 1998).

Philology in China. Thus, the attraction of the archaeology of art as a theoretical and practical exercise as espoused by Michaelis was that it echoed the ideology of Republican scholars in China.

Meishu kaogu solved looming problems with the study of art, according to Ruan Rongchun; scholars had relied on subjectively formed opinions about the history of art based on objects in connoisseurs' collections (to which access was extremely limited and based on personal relationships) rather than a systematic engagement with art broadly.[14] Three main factors explain why in the face of art-historical archaeology older connoisseurship techniques were considered inadequate, according to Ruan.[15] Traditional collecting practices stopped at acquisition; only a simple apparatus was in place to note differences between the collector's own objects, but no adequate methods were available to categorise larger groups of material. Second, relics in a single collection did not come from known places. Encounters with objects were accidental and random, occurring either at the market or at fellow collectors' homes; there was no academic interface. Before the late Qing there was no concept of field research, either. Third, categorisation schemas were not based on scientific or objective criteria; instead typologies were subjective (and not widely held or agreed upon among a number of scholars). The discipline of art-historical archaeology solved these problems and filled a void.

Both Buddhist archaeologists and *Meishu kaogu* artists were committed to a new approach to gathering information about art, conducting extensive reviews of objects out in the field. While much of Buddhist material was above ground, and therefore particularly suited to the artists and their informal understanding of archaeology, early archaeologists also engaged in excavation. This movement, while not under the auspices of any one entity, was made up of professionals, para-professionals with expertise in adjacent fields such as epigraphy and geography, and amateurs who learned on the job. During the period from 1928 to 1937 archaeology became a well-honed set of practices during the Anyang years; at the start of the war we enter a new phase of para-archaeology, which did not always build on the expertise of earlier skills and successes.

---

[14] '中国美术考古学的历史, 理论与实践 [The History, Theory and Practice of Chinese Archaeology of Art],' pp. 91–4, chap. in Ruan Rongchun 阮榮春, *et al.* (2004).
[15] Ibid; Yang (1997).

Buddhist archaeology and the archaeology of art: some beginnings

In the frontier areas and border zones opportunities for striking new finds were plentiful and field-changing. Two artists, Zhang Daqian 張大千 (1899–1983) and Wang Ziyun 王子雲 (1897–1990), were each committed in their own distinct ways to creating a systematic index to long-forgotten artisanal arts associated with tomb and temple painting (Fig. 6). While not self-proclaimed *meishu kaogu* practitioners, their field research can be productively understood in this context. They were interested in capturing pictorially the history of China's art in Buddhist and mortuary ruins by cataloguing chronological development and style (Figs. 7 and 8). For Wang Ziyun this included reproducing the designs on Neolithic pots, Buddhist icons, stone engravings, tomb figurines, and Buddhist murals. In this view of his research workroom at Northwest University, Xian, one sees a display of articles gathered during his tenure as director of the Education Ministry's Northwest Art and Relics Team 教育部藝術文物考察團, in the 1940s. Wang's copy of a mural's large donor figure, Cao Yuanzhong, who ruled (944/945–974 CE) the small but independent Dunhuang-area kingdom during the third quarter of the tenth century, is mounted on the back wall; rubbings from Han tombs appear on the upper walls. It is the display of these together as much as it is the actual objects themselves that is important to Wang. Central to the methodology of *meishu kaogu* is the placing of like objects together comparatively to construct a larger continuum in the history of art.

Zhang's capture of Buddhist wall painting involved a different type of collecting; primarily interested in painting, he recorded hundreds of Buddhist mural compositions on canvas. In a photograph taken in spring 1942, his Tibetan painting assistants copy a mural of Manjusri on his lion vehicle in cave 159 (Fig. 9) in faithful detail, first tracing the contour lines of the original on a blank canvas and then adding details and colour directly in front of the wall painting during their sixteen-month stay in Gansu copying Yulin and Mogao murals. Zhang relied on a wide range of artists, family members, students, and friends—sometimes approaching twenty in number. In another photograph, taken a year later, he and his entourage assemble in the Gobi desert, including his five Qinghai painting assistants, his third wife, and the photographer James Lo and his wife, Lucy (Fig. 10).

Zhang and Wang's commitment to collecting specimens and bringing them back to the studio has its roots in larger trends in historical studies;

Figure 6.   Zhang Daqian and two Qinghai painting assistants, Yulin Caves, May 1943. Photo courtesy of The Lo Archives.

high value was placed on fieldwork and verifiable evidence in all sectors of the humanities during the Republican period. In addition to Zhang's independent (personal) trip and Wang's Education Ministry expedition, the National Museum, the Geography Institute and the Academia

Figure 7. Wang Ziyun's research work room and exhibition space displaying samples, drawings and recreations of Neolithic pots, Han tomb figures, tomb relief rubbings, and tenth-century Dunhuang wall paintings, Northwest University, Xian, *c*.1944–5. Photo courtesy of Wang Qian.

Figure 8. Wang Ziyun measuring excavated Northern Dynasties (datable to the fifth to sixth centuries) Buddhist sculpture, from the ruins of the Zhongsheng Temple 崇聖寺 in the western suburbs of Xian, February 1941. Photo courtesy of Wang Qian.

Figure 9.   Three Qinghai painters, including the most prominent member of the group, An Ji (far right), hired as assistants by Zhang Daqian for the Dunhuang project, in cave 159 copying the ninth-century, west wall composition, the *Debate between Manjusri and Vimalakiriti*, spring 1942. © Institute of History and Philology, Academia Sinica, Republic of China.

Sinica—a science and humanities research arm of the Republican government—sponsored three expeditions in 1942 and 1944 to obtain scientific data on the Dunhuang caves, nearby Buddhist ruins, and Silk Road tombs of the north-west. Shi Zhangru, who played a critical role in the Anyang digs during the previous decade as lead measuring specialist and then headed for the Bronze Age excavations at Yinxu, travelled throughout the north-west with Lao Gan 勞榦; in addition to documenting the Buddhist caves at Dunhuang and Yulin they also surveyed the Han watchtowers and Heicheng, the Tangut site near the Gansu-Ningxia

Figure 10. Zhang Daqian (eighth figure from left), with Qinghai painting assistants (centre), army guards (right), James and Lucy Lo (fourth and fifth figures from left) and his nephew (far left), Dunhuang area, spring 1943. Photo courtesy of The Lo Archives.

border in 1942–3.[16] Xiang Da 向達 (1900–66), the eminent historian from Peking University based with other national university faculty in Lizhuang, Sichuan for the duration of the war, led the Northwest Scientific Research Team 西北科學考察團 collaborating with Xia Nai 夏鼐 (1910–85) and Yan Wenru 閻文儒 (1912–94), Xiang's student.[17] In a series of two on-and-off-again campaigns, they conducted excavations from Lanzhou out to Dunhuang exploring remnants of the Great Wall, Toba Wei tombs and other Northern Dynasty remains that represent the cultural remains of ethnic minorities from the medieval period. Together with Shi and Lao, their efforts constitute the origins of Buddhist archaeology in the first half of the 1940s. The multicultural objects and traditions they documented encouraged an ethnographic impulse in their fieldwork. Due to the fact that many Silk Road objects were the product of Tibetan, Tangut, Turkic, Sogdian, and Khotanese cultural traditions and these objects were often connected to the Buddhist temple, the study of Buddhism during the Republican period became inextricably linked with frontier minority cultures.

One of Xiang Da's missions was to buy loose, individually circulating manuscripts in Dunhuang and neighbouring communities. In correspondence back to the director of the Institute of History and Philology, Xia Nai recounts the possibility of buying Tangut manuscripts (written in a dead language none of the researchers were trained to read); in others Xia describes how Xiang barters with a miller to trade grain for medieval Dunhuang texts.[18] Clearly Chinese archaeologists and Buddhist historians were conducting a salvage project in Silk Road sites in the aftermath of the British and French removal of much of Dunhuang's manuscript treasures. What was left of portable materials in the area circulated in the hands of private individuals. The caves themselves, containing thousands of square metres of murals dating to the fifth–thirteenth centuries, were largely intact, but unprotected (the exterior antechambers had collapsed

[16] Shi Zhangru 石璋如 (1996).

[17] The earlier History and Geography team, funded by the Boxer Indemnity Foundation, was co-administered by the Institute of History and Philology, Academia Sinica, the Central Museum and Geography Research Institute; the 1944 expedition was organised by the Institute of History and Philology.

[18] The details of Tangut manuscripts unearthed in Ningxia, and their possible acquisition, are described in Xia Nai's letter to Fu Sinian, 李38-5-17, 26 March 1945; a fragment of *Lotus Sutra*, one of sixty Northern Dynasties-period texts supposedly found August 1944 inside a late Qing sculpture, is explained in a letter from Xia Nai to Fu Sinian, 李38-5-5, 25 Nov. 1944. In other correspondence to Fu Sinian, Xia discusses Tibetan manuscripts (from the Dunhuang caves) in the possession of the Education Ministry 李38-4-11, 31 July 1944, IHP.

over the centuries) and the wall paintings were exposed to the elements. Xiang Da's main mission was to gather what was left of the transitive archaeological remains and to establish proper administration of the exposed cave shrines.

Purity

The frontier was a place to recapture the multicultural dimensions of Buddhism and its relationship to an imperial Han-centric history, and as such it was also a site of purity and cultural simplicity. These cultural concerns of tradition propelled anthropological work as well as archaeology in the Republican period. Scholars and painters were interested in shapes and forms that evoked an early period, which had become unavailable during the later dynastic period and were preserved in an unadulterated state deep in the interior away from modernisation or the taint of foreign cultures. As it became increasingly clear to Chinese scholars by the early 1940s, the caves at Dunhuang still contained *c.*25,000 square metres of wall painting dug into the living rock. And its stylistic diversity spanning eight centuries in dark caves suggested a preserved treasure of fixed cultural experience untouched by the modern world. The influx of foreign cultures during the late Qing, when China's semi-colonial ports on the coast were occupied by European, American, and Japanese officials and merchants, was culturally problematic for many modern Chinese intellectuals.[19] The West was admired for its scientific achievements—and in post-4 May China (the 4 May movement was from 1915 to 1921), science was a tool to overcome the limitations of premodern culture. But the subjugation of China under a modern system of unequal treaties as a result of the Opium and Arrow Wars (1839–40; 1856–60) also meant that Western forces devalued China's cultural relevance, particularly the significance of its modern experience. Despite the technological progress and commercial infrastructure of the International Concessions, these spaces were understood as zones of Chinese inadequacy. The interior was uncomplicated by the contingencies of semi-colonial modernity. The pace of change along China's coast was peripatetic; but due to geography and economics, the north- and south-west remained largely closed, involved in little exchange with outside communities. And in the north-west, the locus of Buddhist remains, the extreme desert terrain added to its isolation.

[19] Barlow (1997).

Consequently, art in this interior was of immense interest and provided an outlet for a nationalism fueled by the Japanese invasion. In a general way, artistic archaeology (*meishu kaogu*) and Buddhist archaeology—neither of which required (but did not exclude) digging and were suited to the diminished resources of wartime circumstances—were efforts to locate a primitive cultural tradition in the north- and south-west beyond the pressures of the war and a Western-style modernity.

Early anthropologists and ethnographers articulate clearly that the inner frontier was the essence of this purity that they craved. In the early 1940s, Hu Qingchun 胡慶鈞 (1918–), an ethnographer of the Institute of History and Philology, explained to Fu Sinian—the director of the Institute—how the words of Confucius a millennium earlier echoed his recent findings on the frontier:

> I've noticed the 'sinicization' problem in Miao area specifically, and found one interesting example. As a result of Western invasion of China in the past century, the progressive (or avant-garde) thrust of the Han people is 'Westernization,' or so called 'Modernization'; but the Miao's progressive (avant-garde) force is Sinicization, not Modernization. Therefore, Confucius' famous quote 'Our lost ritual or propriety can be found with the Barbarians,' is well applicable; and the slang that I have heard from the Shanghai-Nanjing area 'country girls always imitate the Shanghai style, but they're not similar; when they are finally similar to Shanghai, Shanghai has already developed a new style,' also seems to be applicable here.[20]

Hu's point describes how the most essential elements of pure Han culture would be best preserved by the ethnographic primitive—by peoples out of touch with recent technological advances and culturally inferior, or less civilised, than the mainstream Han population (largely on the coast). It is an odd argument to make—that the core of a culture's traditions are best preserved by an inferior sector—but it also makes sense if one considers the thrust of the argument in terms of political conditions. That is, in the worst of times, because earlier, out-of-date trends trickled to backward places and trends are slow to change there, a dominant culture can go back to the frontier or the primitive stronghold to rediscover itself. This is essentially what happens in the Republican period in the north- and south-west frontier; archaeology reclaims unadulterated cultural 'essence' in the face of Western colonial culture and the fear of the extinction of Chinese traditions under the Japanese.

---

[20] Hu (1941).

Dunhuang: loss and memory

The two artists, Zhang Daqian and Wang Ziyuan, were drawn to caves, tombs and ruins beyond the reach of average travellers. Both spent considerable time at Dunhuang in 1941–3, the Buddhist cave-shrine site that British audiences had become well acquainted with decades earlier. In 1906 Sir Aurel Stein had purchased portable treasures from its hidden library discovered in 1900; his camel caravan is shown loaded with treasure (Fig. 11). Stein's finds were deposited in London in the British Library and British Museum; later a portion was eventually sent back to India (post-independence) due to financial support his expeditions received from the colonial British government in India. Stein's documents were and still are the most important extant medieval documents of the Silk Road. In China there was an acute awareness of how much a loss these manuscripts were to modern Chinese scholarship. Much of popular opinion was focused on what was gone, not what remained. By 1910 four-fifths of the cache of portable documents were in Europe. Although all of the wall painting and 2,500 sculptures remained *in situ*, there was little awareness nationally of this remaining storehouse of medieval painting and three-dimensional art. But with the move to the interior during the war years, remote sites on the Silk Road became accessible and popular.

Archaeology of the Shang royal sites in 1928 was new and exciting for a nascent Republican China, but the Dunhuang material perhaps struck even a deeper cord on many complex levels. The sheer vastness of the Dunhuang site and the 'finds' that were spirited away from China to Europe drew on nationalism during the war; the site became a symbol of national essence. Also, the fact that its Buddhist wall paintings represented a pure, untouched cultural record uncontaminated by modernisation was one of the primary factors behind the site's popularity. By reclaiming the site through copies, research artists elevated a golden age no longer in the modern Chinese imagination; their work restored the historical memory of China's reach westward into Central Asia during the Han-Tang dynasties—the halcyon years of Chinese rule into this region. While a significant number of the population of the vast lands of the west and south were ethnic minorities, the preponderance of Chinese language material in Dunhuang's manuscripts and in wall inscriptions made it easy to set aside its multi-ethnic dimensions and claim a Han dominance in an open empire with a long history. A site like this established the groundwork for territorial claims for the country's boundaries in the modern period. Zhang memorialised the rediscovery of this forgotten past in a seal he

Figure 11. Aurel Stein's caravan laden with Silk Road treasures from Dunhuang, marching over high dunes of the Taklamakan Desert, south of the Tarim River. Xinjiang. Team includes, Hassan Akhun, Turdi, and Naik Ram Singh. Photographer: M. Aurel Stein, 1906–8. © The British Library.

applied to the surface of his copies, that read 'laoqi dunhuang' (老棄敦煌 long forgotten Dunhuang). He applied this seal to many of his Dunhuang copies, including on the lower left corner of the bodhisattva reproduction (Fig. 12).

The layers of loss and recuperation were manifold. In making the case for the nationalisation of the site and moving it into government hands Xiang Da, the scholar of Buddhist culture and Tang history and leader of the history expedition sent by the national research institute, described the loss of the site as datable in the first instance to the late tenth century when the region 'fell to the barbarians'.[21] The Tang style of the seventh to ninth centuries established the Silk Road link to the Imperial capital, Chang'an. But it was a widely held belief that the aesthetic value of the site drops precipitously after the period of Tibetan control from 781–848, and then later when the Tanguts establish a presence in the region in 1035. Xiang Da writes that the site had been forgotten because after this takeover by ethnic minorities of the north-west, no (Han) men of letters visited or wrote about it; it is only when Qianlong establishes control in his military campaign of 'Pacification of the Tribes of the northwest' in the mid-eighteenth century that visitors begin to stop at the site (again). Dunhuang then re-enters the humanistic map. As with Zhuang Xueben's notion of the Tibetan-Yi Minority (*zangyi* 臧彝) corridor (Qinghai and north-west Sichuan) being a 'blank ground' or void, the Northwest Corridor from Shaanxi to Xinjiang had been erased from Han consciousness for 800 years, Xiang asserts. Thus the modern effort to recuperate control over the Silk Road reached back to the medieval period when first the Tibetans (in the eighth century) and then the Uighurs (tenth century) limited contact of metropolitan China to points west.

The inscriptions and manuscripts at Dunhuang, largely in Chinese, constituted evidence of how this zone once belonged to a larger empire from at least the Han Dynasty to the early Song (second century BCE to eleventh century CE). Evidence can be read in many different ways. And artistic remains served as tactile proof of Han Chinese cultural domin-ance (real or imagined). Zhang Daqian's copies of the Dunhuang murals, such as a painting of a bodhisattva holding a scroll, typically depicted to the left of Sakyamuni preaching, evoked the frontier and the close connec-tion between Han imperial interests and Buddhist monuments that spread along the Silk Road (Fig. 12). Zhang's paintings often contained copies of

---

[21] Fang Hui (Xiang Da) 方回 (向達) (1942); reprinted (1944): 44–7.

Figure 12. Zhang Daqian (1899–1983) and Shawo Tsering (Ch. Xiawu Cairang 夏吾才讓) (1922–2004). Copy of a bodhisattva (possibly Ananda) from Yulin cave 8 (DRA YL14), 1942. © National Palace Museum, Taiwan.

figures and motifs from the kingdoms of these frontier groups and he brought to life that history through Sinicised copies.

Xiang Da and other scholars, such as Chen Yin'ge 陳寅恪 (1890–1969) and Chen Yuan 陳垣 (1880–1971), wanted to recuperate a Chinese cultural presence in the north-west, revitalise a Han-Tang identity, and take back the intellectual momentum in Buddhist studies enjoyed by foreign institutions and affiliated scholars, who possessed the bulk of the manuscripts.[22] Xiang and Yu Youren 于右任 (1879–1964), the Director of Control Yuan (the ministry responsible for censure and audit 監察院), who visited Dunhuang in 1943, also, ironically, wanted to save the site from its most celebrated resident, Zhang Daqian.[23] Zhang had been living at Dunhuang on and off since May 1941 and by the time that both Xiang Da and Yu Youren arrived the following year Zhang had already been tearing off systematically the outermost layers of the wall paintings dating to the Tangut (1035–1227 CE) and the later Guiyijun (914–1006 CE) periods—searching for earlier layers that were 'more Chinese' buried underneath the later rededications by 'minority' patrons. Zhang highly valued the murals of the earlier periods, such as the N. Wei (386–539), Sui (581–618), and early-high Tang (618–766). In addition to the political associations of a Tang Central Asia when the imperial court exerted a strong presence along Silk Road communities, from an aesthetic perspective Zhang viewed Wei-Tang brushwork as simultaneously achieving the qualities of spontaneity and realism. Zhang and the larger scholarly community rejected the sophisticated precision of the later paintings as formulaic and rote; there was little patience for eleventh- and twelfth-century overdrawing, executed by Tibetan, Tangut, and Mongolian painters.

In December 1942, Fu Sinian and Li Ji, the director of the government-supported Institute of History and Philology and the director of its Archaeology Division, wrote to Yu Youren, Chief Control Yuan, exposing Zhang's ruinous treatment of the Dunhuang murals.[24]

> We received a letter from the Sichuan Museum's Director Feng Hanji 馮漢驥 and Huaxi University 華西大學's Museum Director Zheng Desheng 鄭德坤, . . .

[22] 陳寅恪 Chen Yin'ge, 序 [Preface] in Chen Yuan 陳垣 (1931), pp. 1–3.
[23] Yu Youren 于右任 (1942).
[24] Fu and Li (1942).

Dunhuang's Caves of the Thousand Buddhas still have N. Wei, Sui, Tang, Song, Yuan, and Ming-Qing wall painting. Zhang Daqian has cut into the walls of the caves copying the wall painting of each period. But not all of these [period wall paintings] are on one surface. The earlier layers are in the interior or innermost sections. People of later periods covered the outer layers with mud and made new paintings [on top].

Mr. Zhang wants to know every layer of the traces of artists from every dynasty. First Zhang paints [copies] the outer layer, then he peels off the outer layer, and then after he copies that layer, he peels and paints the next layer. He wants to capture the painting style [method] of each dynasty.

. . . [Y]ou cannot do this well. After you take off the layer, you ruin the layer. So Mr. Zhang has made great benefit and progress in art. However, regarding the issue of culture, it is a kind of irretrievable loss.

They then explain how they were hesitant to send Yu third-hand information about this destruction, but recently an eyewitness confirmed the rumours.

This year (1942) the Northwest History and Geography Investigative Team [hired some additional participants]. . . . Xiang Da [was one] and he is a professor of the four United Universities that moved [to Sichuan] and we invited him to participate. Mr. Xiang is an authority in Dunhuang studies. He is recognized nationally and internationally as an expert.

During September [1942], the History and Geography Team went west to Dunhuang, and [we] received information about what was going on with our own eyes at Qianfodong. Mr. Zhang has hired four lamas as assistants all day, and they are a big help in the caves.

Mr. Zhang likes the N. Wei, Sui, and Tang a lot. But when he sees Song-Yuan-Xi Xia (paintings) on top of N. Wei, Sui, and Tang, he does exactly what he wants. He takes the outer layer and crudely chops and splits it to expose the lower layer. Usually, the outer layer is destroyed. The upper layer is totally destroyed and the lower layer is also destroyed because of his peeling [of mural layers].

The number of caves and compositions are both numerous. And the composition subjects are still recognizable. Also among these are Zhang Daqian's personal marks [directly on the wall]. This is proof of Mr. Zhang's squandering behavior. Where he is doing copying work, without respect he casually marks the contour lines, takes instruments and equipment and puts them against the wall. He does not care whether or not these hurt the wall painting surface.

Mr. Xiang thinks that if this kind of behavior continues, after two to three years Qianfodong wall painting will be totally destroyed. Because the article [written by Xiang Da] . . . was mailed to Chongqing's *Public Record* 大公報, and [also] published in the *Yunnan Daily* 雲南日報, hopefully this will catch the public's attention and correct it.

In (Xiang Da's) article Zhang Daqian is not mentioned by name. His contribution to Dunhuang painting [studies] is vast, ruining wall painting is also enormous. When we blame him for his terrible behavior we can keep in mind his contribution. . . .

Mr. Zhang's ability in art and his dedication to ancient drawing and scholastic depth are of great depth. There has to be a way to benefit our national cultural activity. But Dunhuang's Qianfodong is our country's incomparable national treasure. And it is known all over the world. In matters like this, we cannot just let one or two people's interests ruin it.

. . . I dare to beg you to send a telegraph, and state that Zhang's peeling of the wall painting's layers, casually tracing the contour lines, and leaning equipment against the wall, must stop. I have high expectations as Mr. Xiang has already said that Qianfodong should be transformed into a national property and someone sent to administer and control [the site]. Let us preserve the things that have been ruined. Mr. Xiang's suggestion, is not yet executed, so I hope, dear Sir, you will do something to conserve the treasure of our nation so that it can be preserved permanently. . . .

I, Fu Sinian, would be the gracious recipient if you can do this.

In another version of the same letter, transcribed by the Institute's secretary, one passage clearly indicates the core of the problem.[25]

> Although Mr. Daqian's painting is a highly exalted treasure by the artist, however, from the point of view of preserving archaeological things, we do not yet know how to permanently preserve peeled layers. So when Mr. Zhang copies the wall painting, the layer is ruined when he peels it. This is very beneficial for Mr. Zhang's progress in his artistic development, but from the point of view of culture, it is an incomparable loss. You ruin an antique because you love it.

This letter did have an impact on the government officials; in six months, Zhang was gone from Dunhuang. And as he passed through Lanzhou his luggage was inspected to make sure he was not bringing out any relics from the site. But somehow this behaviour did not diminish his reputation; he goes on to be heralded as one of the most important painters of the twentieth century.

While it is hard to find a plausible explanation for his destroying murals at a site widely recognised as national property and one of the world's most spectacular collections of medieval murals, we can view his actions in a broader Republican context as a search for the primitive. As he 'excavated' down to find a more natural painting state, he attempted to uncover art that had been lost from Chinese history to the modern sensibility. The outer layers hid the true early drawing, much like Hu Qingchun's analogy (cited above) about the fashion of frontier girls preserving the earlier styles of cosmopolitan culture which had since been replaced. That is, for many

---

[25] Fu and Li (1942).

Republican intellectuals and artists, the pure essence of the centre's flourishing culture was best preserved in the margins. The caves could not have been a more apt metaphor for the cultural primitive hidden away for rediscovery by the centre after frontier treasures had been erased from cultural memory. Buddhist archaeology, and specifically the study of monuments in which artists such as Zhang and Wang identified important period styles and designs, was bound with a sense of recovery of a lost and valuable past so that his contemporaries still recognised his contributions (despite real damage caused by the artist himself).

The interest in recovering lost artistic styles was ultimately connected to the actual French, British, Japanese, American, and Russian removal of Dunhuang objects from the 42,000-manuscript library, as established scholars were very aware of the disappearance of materials by looting and purchase during the semi-colonial period through to the end of dynastic China in 1911. Republican intellectuals were determined to undo as many of the mistakes and lack of oversight during the late Qing government that lead to vulnerability of historical monuments all over China. So Zhang's efforts to locate primitive forms of artistic expression were imbricated in larger academic initiatives to transform the wrongs during this pre-imperial period and celebrate past cultural achievements.

The attraction of archaeology and the allure of the field were linked to a preference in modern Chinese historical studies, as we have established, for actual objects and substantiated evidence gathered in the field. Gu Jiegang 顧頡剛 (1893–1980), the leader of the *yigupai*, 'doubting the old' school represented a larger intellectual trend, rejected Pre-Shang history as being the stuff of folklore including the largely mythical 'three sovereigns' and 'five emperors'.[26] The interest of discovering history in tactile, physical terms was echoed in Fu Sinian's positivistic and proscientific framework for research. In his inaugural speech as the first director of the Institute of History and Philology in May 1928, Fu urged scholars to get out of the libraries and into the field.[27] Fu's perspective, located somewhere between Ranke and Qing old-text *kaozheng* research methods, according to Wang Fansen (the current director of the IHP), opposed theory and interpretation in order that 'the facts would be naturally revealed' through concrete data.[28] Fu's paradigm reflects both the iconoclasm and nationalism typical of May Fourth intellectuals. In aligning himself with Gu Jiegang

---

[26] Ruan (2004), *et al.*, p. 93; Gu (1926–41; 1931); Wu and Zhao (2003).
[27] Fu (1928): 1.
[28] Schneider (2001): 1040–1; Wang (2000), p. 78.

and emphasising science and reform, it is indeed ironic that, contrary to expectations, the finds from the Anyang excavations proved consistent with traditional book-based accounts of early history, particularly the late Shang.[29]

Zhang Daqian's copying project at Dunhuang

The notion that the field held the clues to a long history of art is the basis of the artistic archaeological work of Zhang Daqian's project at Dunhuang. Despite his blatant destruction of cultural property, Zhang saw the value of investigating paintings on cave walls because they provided raw data for his larger project of creating a pictorial canon of period painting styles. Wang Ziyun, who obtained two degrees in sculpture in France, where he studied from 1931 to 1937, was interested in the history of design, decorative motifs and sculpture (Fig. 13).[30] In both cases, the larger trend to contextualise objects in a spatial and temporal continuum and to recuperate gaps of knowledge about early art based on first-hand knowledge was critical in terms of shaping approaches to the study of Dunhuang.

As established, Zhang Daqian arrived with a small entourage in May 1941 at the desert oasis of Dunhuang; its wall was the most complete collection of painting from the fifth to thirteenth centuries anywhere in China. Yulin, a sister site, had paintings dated to the early ninth to the twelfth century. During his two years based at Dunhuang, Zhang made additional copying trips to two other smaller cave sites in the region (the Eastern and Western Caves of the Thousand Buddhas); his coverage in his copies of the range of styles and subject matter in these four cave sites was fairly thorough. Despite his interest in early murals below the later paintings, he did make copies of the outer layers before destroying them. When he first arrived, he expended his first efforts in removing sand from the mouths of lower caves and assigning numbers for organisational purposes (which he noted directly on the murals themselves). This tendency to write freely on the walls and touch the murals were what would bring him censure and cause his departure.

---

[29] Trigger (2006), pp. 265–6. There were, of course, many periods that were still not resolved such as the existence of Xia dynasty and the specific start and end dates of the first three dynasties. The recent Xia-Shang-Zhou Chronology Project, 1996–2000, was organised to settle those outstanding questions of dynastic time Li (2002).
[30] Wang Qian (1995).

Figure 13.   Wang Ziyun (1897–1990), second front left, front row, in graduation photo with classmates and teachers, École nationale supérieure des arts décoratifs de Paris. Advanced Sculpture degree awarded 15 February 1937 (undergraduate degree studied 1931–5).

Writing later in 1947, when he published the plates of his Dunhuang copies, Zhang describes how the known historical record of pictorial tradition had no real traces of the Six Dynasties, Sui and Tang (fourth to eighth centuries). He began marketing his extended exposure to this site as unique, establishing himself as a special interpreter of the past. He rhapsodises that before he came to Dunhuang he could only dream of finding the treasure trove of painting that he saw upon arrival.[31] Zhang describes early primitive painting as if it were part of a dream—equating his unconscious with forgotten memories of a collective artistic past.

Zhang came to the site in June 1941, but by the late fall he sent his son back to Xining to establish a liaison with officials at Ta'ersi (Kumbum), the large Gelukpa monastery that was the primary regional temple for the (current) fourteenth Dalai Lama, and, as a result, received sustained patronage that supported extensive building projects.[32] Zhang had met five monk painters at Kumbum in spring 1941 before he first went west; their mastery over icon, complex Buddhist narrative, and especially colour impressed him. After spending a summer at the site, he realised their expertise was essential and hired them for the remainder of his sojourn. When he returned to the site in March 1942, these five painters from Qinghai accompanied him. Although they were based at Ta'ersi on a long-term project their home was Wutun—an important cluster of villages to the south of Xining famous for the great skill of its artists identified as the Rebgong style or school.

The expertise of these first-rate painters in fine-line drawing, colouring, and Buddhist compositions transformed Zhang's attempts and brought them to a professional level. Zhang is conscious of their contributions and notes the names of individual painters in the copies' inscriptions; Shawo Tsering's co-authorship is noted in the rendering of a bodhisattva from Yulin cave 14 (Fig. 12). Zhang's other painting assistants, such as his nephew Zhang Xinde 張心德 (1922–53) and students such as Xie Zhiliu 謝稚柳 (1910–97), had no experience with complex Buddhist narrative depictions; collaborating with regional artists, who regularly executed complex Buddhist compositions for high-level patrons in one of China and Tibet's largest temples, enabled the team to capture the complexity of Dunhuang's wall painting.

Zhang and his assistants experimented with ways to convey the antiquity of the murals, including the use of diffuse brushwork and few

---

[31] Zhang Daqian [1947].
[32] Fraser (2010); Hu Suxin (Fraser) (2009).

contour lines; some sections are intentionally unfinished. For example, he depicts facial features in the copy of the Vessantara jataka tale 悉達太子施捨白象本生故事, but they are only faintly rendered. In this Buddhist story the householder gives away all his possessions and brings his family to live a life of poverty in the forest to gain good merit (Fig. 14). Fine boundary lines shape the multicoloured landscape, but few interior contour lines or texture strokes define the mountains. On one level the pictorial reticence echoes the partially damaged state of the painting—much of the surface definition typically provided by the overdrawing is gone—but Zhang rarely shies away from providing full surface details even when the original is unclear. Therefore, one could argue that Zhang used this fainter brushwork to suggest the antiquity of the tale's setting occurring during one of the Buddha's previous lives. What is clear is that, by emphasising the ruinous and ancient quality of the wall paintings, Zhang emphasises that the wall paintings sit within a deep past slightly obscured, rather than being wholly visible; this coheres with the sense of loss and ruin associated with the north-west. The response from the wartime Nationalist audience to Zhang's copies was extremely favourable; Zhang's representation of ancient ruins and the way they evoked the lost empire of the Silk Road brought him acclaim in painting circles and among the public. His first public forum for the Dunhuang copies was opened on 14 August 1943 in an exhibition in Lanzhou, and then later in two 1944 exhibitions in Chongqing and Chengdu; he continued to gain critical acclaim precisely for this ability to evoke the past in a modern idiom.

Zhang repackaged the paintings to appeal to the mainstream, but ironically only with help from the cultural 'margins'. In fact, Zhang was well suited to 'translate' the interior for a nationalist audience. Nanjing officials and their families moved inland, but their knowledge of the multi-ethnic population and cultures in the region was minimal; coastal officials would not have been savvy about minority arts. Zhang, born in a Han-majority part of Sichuan but acculturated to the diverse social fabric of the province and the Tibetan frontier, was able to work between Tibetan and Han traditions. Nonetheless, he displayed a total disregard for them, destroying what he perceived to be an early minority culture, literally hacking through it.

The key to understanding Zhang's approach to documenting frontier ruins is that he wanted to restore the murals to their original brilliance in his own reproductions. Every artist who arrives at an archaeological site with the hope of copying and transmitting its art has to grapple with

Figure 14. Zhang Daqian. Vessantara Jataka, 悉達太子施捨白象本生故事. Copy of east wall, Cave 428, Dunhuang, 1942–3. © National Palace Museum, Taiwan.

developing principles for addressing damage, decay, and colour change. In the case of Dunhuang, the fading and colour changes in the murals added special challenges to the documentation process. Zhang took a bold approach—one that would not be followed by subsequent artists who were more interested in capturing the current state of the paintings. He imagined the original colours and lines; in the process he created a new compositional cohesion that knits a damaged composition together. Zhang inserts himself into the logic of the old painting to create a new idiom. Guan Youhui 關友惠 (1932–), the retired head of the Dunhuang Academy art department, studied with Wang Ziyun at Xian Art Academy and frequently went to Dunhuang on copying expeditions with his teacher before joining the Institute in the 1950s.[33] Guan describes four style types that artists used in state-supported copying work at the site.

1 The first is the objective style 客觀臨摹, 'like a photograph', Guan states. Damaged sections of the mural are depicted as carefully as undamaged parts of the painting. The rationale is that the artist is to record the current state of the painting, regardless of what it may have looked like originally.

2 The second type is 'retain old colours, [but] complete lines', 舊色完整. In this style, the artist also reproduces the palette at face value—the current appearance of the colours is retained. But the artist connects original contour lines and reinstates the compositional coherence of the original where possible.

3 The third type of copying is to 'restore the original appearance', 復原 (*fuyuan*). The rationale for this type is to account for dramatic changes in the original, particularly in palette. By researching other paintings dating to the same period, and noting standard conventions across many examples, it is possible to make an educated guess about the 'original appearance' of forms.

4 The fourth type, according to Guan Youhui, is the 'inspired copy' 仿, used to make new creative works of art based on old traditions. Guan believes that modern society needs new paintings based closely on the old; new works touch the past, but the modern artist's interpretive spirit is the primary subject or focus of the work.[34]

---

[33] S. E. Fraser, 1999 interviews with Guan Youhui: <http://buddhist-art.arthistory.northwestern. edu/buddhistweb/index.html>.
[34] See Appendix I.

Zhang's three paintings of Dunhuang copies reproduced here conform to the third style of copying—*fuyuan*. Even in his copy of the *Vessantara Jataka*, in which he intentionally omits details to indicate an affinity with the ancient, Zhang presents a definitive compositional outline (Fig. 14). In all three paintings, he removes any trace of damage and disrepair, and depicts each hue at its most saturated intensity—an idealised representation of the medieval colour palette. The figures of the bodhisattva and the offering attendant paintings are described with fine line and colours (Figs. 12 and 15). The precision of the drawing suggests a new pious work of art. No suggestion of the age of the original works appears in the copies. Instead, the colours are brought to their full (imagined) saturation and brilliance. While it is not possible to judge the original appearance of many of the figures, Zhang confidently fills in the missing contours of the composition. In the bodhisattva, Zhang adds additional flowers that are not part of the original, but on the whole the figures in these direct copies are proportionally correct and bear a strong relationship to the pictorial structure of the eighth- and ninth-century murals which they reference. One reason for this fidelity is that Zhang's assistants were instructed to trace the original compositions on the wall; these contour lines serve as the foundation of the copies. But Zhang's *fuyuan* 'restore to the original' style goes beyond what other artists such as Guan Youhui subsequently used, particularly in the coloration. Guan's rationale for the third style is that oxidisation and other dramatic colour changes create misinterpretation. For example, facial contour lines in N. Wei paintings were originally flesh tone but had turned black, producing a strange, angular edge to the figures. The amber-hued faces of early Tang bodhisattvas took on a dark maroon patina over the centuries; initially twentieth-century Gansu artists did not entirely understand the skin tone conventions in Buddhist paintings developed in Indian Buddhist workshops. After careful study of damaged and undamaged portions of the caves, they were able to present their 'corrections' to a larger public through corrected copies. Zhang's hue corrections and contour transformations go beyond this modest approach; they are aggressive and interventionist. The structure of the paintings is accurate, but in the application of colours such as the browns, greens, deep reds and blues, Zhang suggests definition and palette that are not visible in the extant works.

Figure 15. Zhang Daqian (1899–1983). Copy of Heavenly Attendant, Dunhuang cave 155 (DRA 9). 1942–3. © National Palace Museum, Taiwan.

Differing styles and practices of *Meishu kaogu*

The precision of Zhang's figural structures (if not his coloration) is what sets him apart from Wang Ziyun's mural copies. Wang and his wife, He Zhenghuang 何正璜 (1914–94), painted in a watercolour-like style that approximates the contours of figures in early wall paintings thus rendering an impression, but not a precise record, of medieval forms. Compare, for example, Wang and He's *apsara* to Zhang Daqian's heavenly attendant, both after Tang dynasty figures (*c.* eighth to ninth centuries) (Figs. 15 and 16).[35] The flying *apsara* playing a flute is a quick rendition of a figure glimpsed in a cave; it captures the spontaneous energy of Tang heavenly attendants. The addition of light brown, blue, and black small clouds adds to the sense of movement. But Wang Ziyun, trained as a sculptor and interested in writing comprehensive overviews of sculptural history and design, never produced second and third renditions of Dunhuang wall painting figures as Zhang did (Fig. 13).[36] Zhang's Tang figure is reproduced on silk, repainted based on sketches and tracings made in the cave, but produced at a later date in the quiet stability of the studio. Care is given to convey three-dimensionality and rotundity even against the blank ground—typical features of Tang figure painting. Zhang has applied the details to make the painting a work of fine art, smoothing out the edges in precise iron-wire line evoking the sweetness of the attendant. Wang's painting is a quick watercolour sketch that records the general subject matter; he aims to make a record of, but not to embody, the original figure in a new form. Zhang is interested in restoring the figures to their original appearance; Wang aims to merely capture their existence. The opacity of the hue in Zhang's copies leaves an indelible image in the viewer's mind. We sense the hand of a painter who carefully adheres to pictorial historicity of the original work, adding line where appropriate to make a complete interpretation of the original, adhering to the boundaries. He is often inaccurate or too aggressive in his application of colour, but Zhang compels the viewer to register antiquity in a modern frame.

Each artist follows a different path in his pursuit of *meishu kaogu* (archaeology of art). Zhang's work rests solely in painting. His

---

[35] He Zhenghuang's signature is on the verso of the Apsara scroll, but the style is completely consistent with all of Wang Ziyun's other Dunhuang mural copies and other members of his team; e.g., Wang's 1942 version of 'Zhang Yichao's Army Conquering the Tibetans and Retaking Dunhuang' (from cave 156), his depiction of the Dunhuang environs, and rendering of other cave sites such as Qizil he investigated in 1953. Wang Huangsheng (2005).

[36] Wang Ziyun (1955); (2005*b*).

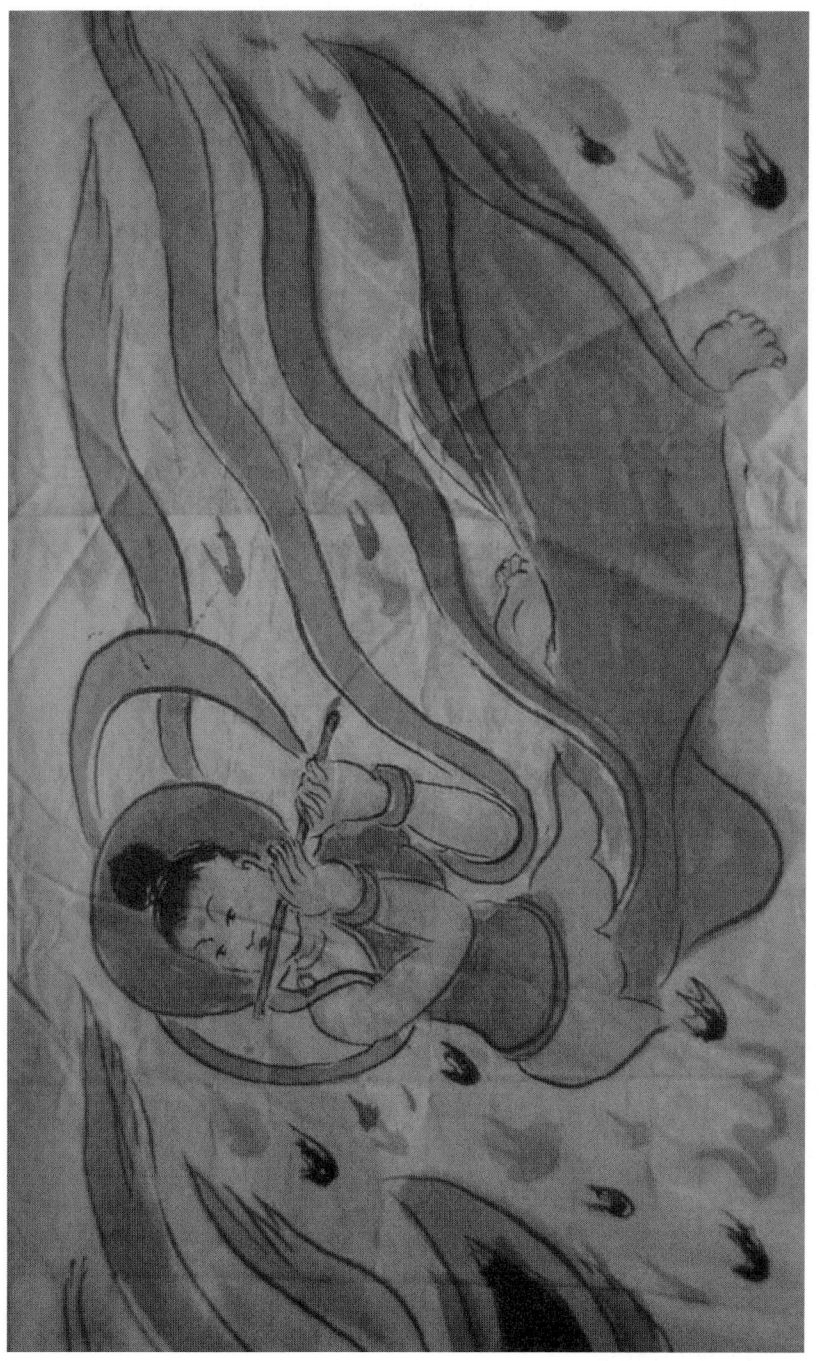

Figure 16. He Zhenghuang 何正璜 (1914–94) with Wang Ziyun, Copy of *Apsara* 飛天 in Tang Cave. Dunhuang, 1941–2. Photo courtesy of Wang Qiang.

documentation lies in the copies themselves. He and his collaborators carefully recorded pictorial details, such as the raised toe in the heavenly attendant. Zhang's team takes care to capture the echoing circles in the scarves trailing the attendant's body; these impart a sense of the figure's movement and forward motion. The arms and shoulders, balanced in relation to the feet, reach to offer the tray laden with coral and semi-precious jewels. Zhang's efforts are devoted to capturing a period style within the brushwork itself, believing that little details convey dynastic style. Wang Ziyun's *meishu kaogu* efforts were spread across a range of media. He made sketches of murals, watercolour panoramas of caves, and thousands of photographs of sculpture, returning home to the studio to display these in an academic setting (Fig. 7). In his Xian studio (and in his January 1943 exhibition at the National Library in Chongqing—eight months before Zhang Daqian's first show of Dunhuang copies) it is evident that Wang was largely interested in an historical documentation of a range of objects from many different sites—incorporating Dunhuang art into a framework that would become the basis of a larger comprehensive study he completed over the next decade, culminating in *The History of Chinese Artistic Sculpture* 中國雕塑藝術史.[37] In some ways Wang treats the wall painting in the same way that he paints scenic views of the north-west. His image of a pack of camels grazing in Jiuchuan near the Gobi desert during his October 1942 sojourn, for example, has the look and feel of his copy of the *apsara* wall painting.[38] Both are quick sketches to convey an impression of landscape and icons; he used the same format to paint studies of ethnographic groups in the region, too.

Wang also wrote comparative histories of sculpture and design, incorporating his photographs to create a survey of design motifs for each dynastic period.[39] In his two-volume *Pictorial Overview of Chinese Applied Arts Throughout the Ages*, Wang places six small photographs of Tang floral designs in comparative display; typically these designs would appear behind Buddhist sculptures as painted aureoles and in the well (apex) of a temple ceiling (Fig. 17). Each figure is numbered and is placed in a larger design history documenting hundreds of types and variations from a range of sites. Zhang, too, was interested in creating a dynastic framework for explaining pictorial development, but in regards to Buddhist material

[37] Later, reprinted Wang (2005*b*); Editorial Pages (1943*a*, 1943*b*).
[38] Wang painted the Silk Road scene when he was in Jiuchuan, east of Dunhuang, Wang Huangsheng (2005), 3–22; sketches from his research trip are collected in Wang Ziyun (2005*a*).
[39] Wang Ziyun (1955); (2007).

he limited himself to Dunhuang only, publishing a guide to the caves organised by grotto number (not by style, theme, or period).[40] Many artists painted interpretations of the Dunhuang wall paintings in the 1940s when artists, government officials, and teams of researchers descended on the site and its environs; in subsequent decades there has been no shortage of new copies as painters have fervently continued the practice. A recent exhibition at the National Fine Arts Museum in Beijing brought together hundreds of examples executed from 1942 to 2005 under official auspices; although Zhang's work was absent from the show, the enormous collection on display made clear that Zhang established the conditions and methods through which all subsequent artists would approach the site, despite his aggressive pictorial invention.[41] His work at Dunhuang was a watershed event; graduates of the National Fine Arts Academy and other top art scholars were all sent to Dunhuang to make copies, beginning in the 1950s; it was a rite of passage that put young, talented artists on site with the largest gallery of early painting within China. But Zhang's copying style will always stand out from the other early prominent artists who dedicated themselves to documenting the site. Chang Suhong 常書鴻 (1904–94), the first director of the Dunhuang Art Academy, and Duan Wenjie 段文杰, Chang's successor, attempted to capture the antiquity of the wall paintings, but in order to do this they chose to document the murals in their current damaged state. They noted in paint all the imperfections, such as cracks, areas of peeled paint exposing dirt walls, and the present state of colours, which had changed over the centuries. While their works could be considered a more accurate register of the art historical record, it could be argued that Zhang Daqian's freer interpretations, based on both a fidelity to the originals and his own strategic changes that resonated with the present, were more dynamic and effective.

The paintings of other artists represented in the 2008 exhibition, such as Wu Zuoren (吳作人) and Guan Shanyue (關山月), demonstrate what can be done working in the spirit of Dunhuang (Guan's fourth style of copying). Yet, in this mode as well, Zhang excelled at incorporating a Dunhuang style into new paintings (a consideration of which is beyond the scope of this essay).

Zhang Daqian's fame rests in part on his path-breaking interpretations of the Dunhuang murals. He was able to reintroduce long forgotten brushwork and subject matter to the repertoire of early painters. His

[40] Zhang (1985).
[41] Fan and Fan (2008).

Figure 17. Wang Ziyun, Six Buddhist Floral Designs. From Wang Ziyun, 中國歷代應用藝術圖綱 [Pictorial Overview of Chinese Applied Arts Throughout the Ages], c.1955, Xian; reprinted 2007.

copies called attention to elaborate Buddhist narrative; vignettes executed with excitement and spontaneity; donor portraits of Silk Road officials possessing great historical value; and complete icon installations preserved untouched since the Tang—these are just a few of the features that Zhang brought to a larger, nationalist audience. Zhang Daqian copies captured for a wartime audience the spirit of the old while putting the past in the context of the modern (era). Zhang's post-antiquarian sensibilities were especially popular in Shanghai, where the local media covered Zhang's comings and goings in and out of the city with great enthusiasm.[42] It is often said that Zhang's genius lay in his ability to isolate the essential features of any period or style and capture them in poignant brushwork. In the Dunhuang case, Zhang immediately recognised what was special about Dunhuang: it preserved aspects of the painterly tradition that had been long out of circulation.

The frontier for Zhang and other art-historical archaeologists was an outlet for an anxious modernity. Their copies, especially Zhang's successful adaptations done with Tibetan painters, transported the viewer to a previous moment in history, erasing years of lost territory to northern nomadic tribes and reclaiming cultural authority from foreign explorers who plundered the site. Dunhuang was the perfect cipher for recuperating these losses and recapturing cultural dominance and pride.

The question remains, why are Zhang and Wang's paintings examples of archaeology of art (*meishu kaogu*) and not art? That is, what makes this material archaeological? How is it different from art? One could argue that Zhang's paintings approach art in their creative spirit, but we also must remember that these works by both Zhang and Wang were first and foremost copies. Their primary function was to record an historical progression of styles and artistic production in China over the millennium and then to inspire other artists to make new works. These paintings will never be admired as independent works of art, at least in Europe and the United States; one will always refer back to the originals to ascertain their importance and meaning. But they do reflect a critical transition in the study of art and archaeology in China; they point to a period when scholars and artists realised the value of archaeological material and methods for the study of art.

---

[42] Zhang is discussed in ten articles in *Shenbao* from March to Sept. 1948, Yan (ed.) (2006), pp. 453–64; the 1947 yearbook of artists describes his post-Dunhuang genius, Wang Yichang (ed.) (1948), p. 70; earlier press stresses Zhang's collaborations with his brother, for example the photo spread in *Arts-Life* (1936).

Appendix

Sarah E. Fraser interview (June 1999) with Guan Youhui (1932–) 關友惠 retired Director, Art Department, Dunhuang Research Academy

Full interview available online:
<http://buddhist-art.arthistory.northwestern.edu/buddhistweb/index.html>.

I. Guan Youhui on four kinds of copying:

1. objective style (*keguan* 客觀), like a photograph; damaged sections of the mural are depicted as carefully as parts of the painting that are still intact;
2. the second type is (*jiuse wanzheng* 舊色完整)—'retain old colours, [but] complete lines', the current appearance of the colours is retained, but the artist connects faded contour lines; and
3. type three is 'restore to the original' (*fuyuan* 復原) appearance, relevant especially in cases of dramatic palette change or damage;
4. inspired copying (*fang* 仿)—see Part II below.

過去我們敦煌研究院這個臨摹，有3種方法．哎，有三種方法．一種就是我們說的，我們叫它客觀臨摹，就是照原本原樣，它殘破的像這樣子處理哦，　像這個就是基本上，照原本的樣子臨摹．這是最主要的，殘破的就沒有，就像這樣殘破，就是殘破的，不給它完整，這是一種方法，而且是我們主要的方法．另外一種方法，是叫舊色完整，這個色彩是舊的，色彩完全是舊的．但是如果這個手的這條線從這兒斷了，我們可以把它連接起來．這是有把握的，不是隨便接的，我們把它完整起來．這叫舊色完整，這樣對觀眾比較好理解，因為太破舊的時候有些不容易理解．這是一種方法．還有一種叫復原，就比如說這個黑色，敦煌畫裡面大部分這個黑色都是變的，都是變色．因為它這個都是一種暖色，偏紅的一種顏色變的．那麼這個變色以後呢，這個人就變成黑的了．所以有些觀眾不知道就提出問題，說你們畫的這些佛、菩薩是不是都從印度來的．因為佛教是從印度來的，這人、菩薩都是黑的，是不是從印度來的，這是一種誤解．所以我們就搞一部分復原，黑的就把它畫成白的．當然這是屬於研究工作的一種，這種量呢是比較少的，因為這也是比較難做的．

II. On question of new Buddhist art and '*fang* 仿' (not *linmo* 臨摹, but new creative works based on the old):

社會它需要新的美術創作，它不僅需要新的佛教美術創作，也需要新的風景畫創作，也需要新的人物畫創造．那麼作為敦煌研究院的新美術創作，我認為它應該逐漸探索一條具有一些敦煌佛教藝術傳統的一些特色（的路）．如果說照這個原作原樣，它的大小、它的色彩完全一樣，像照相一樣，像照相技術，這是比喻的意思，這我們認為應該是臨摹．但中國過去還有一種叫'仿'，'摹仿'的'仿'．這在過去一些前人的畫畫呢，他提款呢也是說'仿某某人'．這個'仿'和臨摹是不一樣的，應該是有差別的．仿呢就是比較接近大意，基本仿他的風格，仿他自己的基本筆法，這是一種仿，臨摹必須要和那個完全一樣．

References

Arts-Life 美術生活. 'Zhang Shanzi, Zhang Daqian 張善孖，張大千'. Vol. 28 (Aug. 1936).

Barlow, Tani E. (ed.) (1997), *Formations of Colonial Modernity in East Asia*. (Durham, NC).

Brown, Clayton D. (2008), 'Li Ji: the father of Chinese Archaeology'. *Orientations*, 39/3: 61–6.

Chen Kong 塵空 (1944), '民國佛教年紀 [The Annual Records of Buddhism during the Republican Era]'. 文史雜誌 *Wenshi zazhi*, vol. 4, 9/10 (Dec. 1944): 37–66.

Chen Xingcan 陳星灿 (1997), 中國史前考古學史研究 [Research on the History of Chinese Pre-Historical Archeology]. (Beijing: Sanlian).

Chen Yuan 陳垣. (1931), 敦煌劫餘錄 [An Analytical List of the Dunhuang Manuscripts (in the National Library)]. (Beiping: National Institute of History and Philology).

Dunhuang Academy (ed.), 敦煌研究院編 (2000), 敦煌研究院 [Dunhuang Academy]. (Shanghai: Shanghai Guji Publishers).

Editorial, [Anon.]. '認識西北與建設西北 [Understanding the North-west and North-west Development]'. 文史雜誌 *Wenshi zazhi*, vol. 2/2 (Feb. 1942): 1–3.

Editorial Page (1942), '西北考察團抵新疆後開始參觀 [The Northwest Investigation Group started their visit after arriving in Xinjiang]'. 大公報 *Dagongbao*, 29 Dec. 1942.

Editorial Page (1943*a*), '敦煌藝術展覽今起在中央圖書館開幕 [The Dunhuang Art Exhibition opens today at Central Library]'. 大公報 *Dagongbao*, 16 Jan. 1943.

Editorial Page (1943*b*), '敦煌藝展，昨日開幕，觀者踴躍 [The Dunhuang Art Exhibition opened yesterday, crowds gathered enthusiastically]'. 中央日報 *Central Daily News*, 17 Jan. 1943.

Fa Zun 法尊 (1944), '元明間與中國有關之西域佛教 [China Connected Western Region Buddhism during the Yuan and Ming Dynasties]'. 文史雜誌 *Wenshi zazhi*, vol. 4, 9/10 (Dec. 1944): 30–6.

Fan Jinshi 樊錦詩 and Fan Di'an 范迪安 (2008), 盛世和光: 敦煌藝術大展 [The Lights of Dunhuang: the Great Exhibition of Dunhuang Art]. (Renmin jiaoyu Publishers).

Fang Hui (Xiang Da) 方回（向達）(1942), '論敦煌千佛洞的管理研究以及其他連帶的幾個問題 [On the Management and Research of Dunhuang Thousand Buddha Caves and other Correlated Questions]'. 大公報 *Dagongbao*, no. 3: parts I–III, Dec. 27–30, 1942.

Fang Hui (Xiang Da) 方回（向達）(1944), '論敦煌千佛洞的管理研究以及其他連帶的幾個問題 [On the Management and Research of Dunhuang Thousand Buddha Caves and other Correlated Questions]'. 文史雜誌 *Wenshi zazhi*, vol. 4, 1/2 (July 1944): 44–54.

Fraser, Sarah E. (2010), 'Shawo Tsering, Zhang Daqian and Sino-Tibetan Cultural Exchange, 1941–42'. In PIATS 2003: *Tibetan Studies: Proceedings of the Tenth Seminar of the International Association for Tibetan Studies* (Oxford, 2003), ed. Erberto Lo Bue, 1–25. (Leiden; Boston: Brill), forthcoming.

Fu Sinian 傅斯年 (1928), '歷史語言研究所工作之旨趣 [The purpose of (Our) Work at the Institute of History and Philology'. Planning Meeting for the Institute of History and Philology, Academic Sinica 中央研究院歷史語言研究所籌備處 (Guangzhou, May *Minguo* 17 [1928]): 1–10.

Fu Sinian 傅斯年 (2003), 傅斯年全集 [Collected Works of Fu Sinian], ed. Ouyang Zhesheng. 欧阳哲生, 7 vols. (Changsha: Hunan Educational Publishers).

Fu Sinian, Li Chi, Shi Zhangru, *et al.* 傅斯年，李濟，石璋如 (1929–33), 安陽發掘報告, 第1-4期 [Excavation Reports from Anyang, v. 1-4]. (Beiping [Beijing]: Academia Sinica, Institute of History and Philology). *Minguo*, 18–22.

Fu Sinian and Li Ji (1942), Letter to Yu Youren 于右任. 5 Dec. [*Minguo*, 31], 1942. Xichuan, Lizhuang 西川李莊. Fu Sinian Archives, I-68; I:71. (IHP, Republic of China).

Gu Jiegang (1931), *The Autobiography of a Chinese Historian, being the Preface to a Symposium on Ancient Chinese History (Ku Shih Pien)*, trans. and annotated by Arthur W. Hummel. (Leiden).

Gu Jiegang 顧頡剛 (1926–41; 1982), 古史辨 [Symposium on Ancient History] (1926–41). (Beijing: Pushe; Shanghai: Guji), 1982.

He Changchun 賀昌群 (1943), '敦煌千佛洞應歸國有贊議 [Support of the Nationalization of Dunhuang's Thousand Buddha Caves]'. 大公報 *Dagongbao*, 7 Jan. 1943.

Hu Qingchun 胡慶鈞 (1941), Letter to Fu Sinian. Fu Sinian Archive III: 266. 11 Jan. [*c.*1941]. (IHP, Republic of China).

Hu Suxin (Sarah E. Fraser) (2009), '夏吾才让、张大千和汉藏文化交流，1941–1943：界定中古和现代安多地区画坊生产的研究方法 [Shaowo Tsering, Zhang Daqian and Sino-Tibetan Cultural Exchange, 1940–1943: Researching the Boundaries of Ancient China and the Artistic Production of Amdo]'. *Sino-Tibetan Art Studies*, Proceedings of Third Tibetan Archaeology and Art International Conference, 485–98, ed. Xie Jisheng, *et al.* (Shanghai: Millennium Publishers) (*in Chinese*).

Keightley, David N. (1978), 'Review of Li Chi, *Anyang*', *Journal of Asian Studies*, 38 (1): 171–3.

Li Chi (Li Ji). (1977), *Anyang*. (Seattle, WA).

Li Chi (1923; 1928), 'The Formation of the Chinese People', Ph.D. Dissertation, Harvard University, 1923. (Cambridge, MA: Harvard University Press), 1928.

Li Chi (1926), 'Archaeological survey of the Fen River Valley, Southern Shansi, China', in the *Smithsonian Miscellaneous Collections,* 78(7): 123–37.

Li Guangming and Wang Yuanhui 黎光明, 王元輝 (2004), 川西民俗調查記錄, 1929 [Records of Investigations of Folk Customs in Western Sichuan, 1929], 王明珂編, ed. Wang Mingke. (Taipei: Academia Sinica, Institute of History and Philology).

Li Xueqin 李學勤 (2002), 'The Xia-Shang-Zhou Chronology Project: methodology and results', trans. Sarah Allan. *Journal of East Asian Archaeology*, 4: 321–33.

Li Zhuchen 李燭塵 (1943), '開發西北管見 [Humble Opinions on the Development of Northwest]'. 大公報 *Dagongbao*, 6 March 1943.

Lin Jiyong 林繼庸 (1943) '西北工業考察歸來的感想 [Reflections after the Investigation of the North-west Industrial Prospects]'. 大公報 *Dagongbao*, 28 Feb. 1943.

Ling Chunsheng 凌純聲 and Rui Yifu 芮逸夫 (1947; 1993), 湘西苗族調查報告 [The Miao Tribe of Western Hunan]. (The Institute of History and Philology, Academia Sinica. Shanghai: Shangwu Publishers; Taipei: Changda).

Lo Wei 羅偉 (1941), '組織西北文化協會的緣起 [The Origin of North-west Cultural Association's Establishment].' 中央日報. *Central Daily News*, 9 Jan. 1941.

Marchand, Suzanne L. (1996, 2003), *Down from Olympus: Archaeology and Philhellenism in Germany, 1750–1970*. (Princeton, NJ).

Miao Fenglin 繆鳳林 (1942), '西北問題一夕談 [One Night's Discussion on the North-west Problems]'. 文史雜誌 *Wenshi zazhi*, vol. 2, 2–3 (Feb. & Mar. 1942): 43–59, 52–67.

Michaelis, Adolf (1904), *Die archäologische Entdeckungen des nuenzehnten Jahrhunderts* [Archaeological Discoveries of the Nineteenth Century]. (Leipzig).

Michaelis, A. [Mihai lisi 米海里司] (1904–8; 1929), *Die archäologische Entdeckungen des nuenzehnten Jahrhunderts* [第十九世紀考古學的發現 *Archaeological Discoveries of the 19th c.*). Guo Muoruo, trans. and modified, 郭沫若. 美術考古一世紀 [A Century of Artistic Archaeology], 1947. (Shanghai: Shanghai Bookstore), 1998.

National Palace Museum 故宮博物院 (2005), ed. 盛世文治， 清宮典籍文化 [Flourishing Age of Humanistic Society: The Culture of Qing Court Classical Books]. (Beijing: Forbidden City Publishers), 2005.

Ruan Rongchun 阮榮春, Zhang Tongbiao 张同标 and Liu Hui 刘慧 (2004), 中國美術考古學史綱 [Outline of the Chinese Fine Art Archaeology History]. (Tianjin: Tianjin renmin meishu Publishers).

Rui Yifu 芮逸夫 (chief ed.) (1973), 苗蠻圖冊 [Eighty-two aboriginal peoples of Guizhou province in pictures], vols. 1–2. (Taipei: Institute of History and Philology), 1973.

Schneider, Axel (2001), 'Review of Wang Fan-sen, *Fu Ssu-nien, A Life in Chinese Politics*', *The China Quarterly*, 168: 1040–1.

Shi Zhangru 石璋如 (1996), 莫高窟形 [Dunhuang Cave (Structural) Designs], 3 vols. (Taipei: Institute of History and Philology, Academia Sinica).

Shi Zhangru, Chen Cunru, *et al.*, (ed.) 石璋如. 陳存恭. 陳仲玉. 任育德編 (2002), 石璋如先生訪問紀錄 [Records of Interviews with Shi Zhangru]. (Taipei: Institute of Modern History, Academia Sinica).

Trigger, Bruce G. (2006), *A History of Archaeological Thought*, 2nd edn. (Cambridge).

Wang Fan-sen (2000), *Fu Ssu-nien, A Life in Chinese Politics*. (London: Cambridge University Press).

Wang Huangsheng 王璜生 (ed.) (2005), 抗戰中的文化責任：西北藝術文物考察團六十周年紀念圖集 [Cultural Responsibilities during the Sino-Japanese War: Pictorial Collection Commemorating the Sixtieth Anniversary of The North-west Art and Cultural Relics Expedition]. (Guangdong Art Museum. Guangzhou: Lingnan Arts Publishers).

Wang Mingke 王明珂 (1997), 華夏邊緣：歷史記憶與族群認同 [On Chinese Borderlands: Historical Memory and Ethnic Identity]. (Taipei: Chongnong wenhua).

Wang Mingke 王明珂 (2003), 羌在漢藏之間：一個華夏邊緣的歷史人類學研究 [The Qiang, between the Han and the Tibetans: a Historical Anthropological study of Chinese Borders]. (Taipei: Lianjing Publishers).

Wang Qian 王蒨 (1995), '王子云年表 [Wang Ziyun, Biographical chronology]'. 西北美术 *Northwest Art*, 4.

Wang Yichang, 王辰昌 (chief ed.) (1948), 中國美術年鑑, 中華民國 三十六年, 上海市文化運動委員會 [Chinese Art Yearbook, 1947, Committee on the Shanghai Municipal Cultural Project]. (Shanghai: Zhongguo tushu zazhi gongsi) [*Minguo*, 37].

Wang Ziyun (ed.) 王子雲編 (1955), 唐代彫塑選集 [Collected Works of Tang Dynasty Sculpture]. (Beijing: Chaohua Fine Art Publishers; Xinhua).

Wang Ziyun (ed.) (2005*a*), 王子云西北写生选, 1940–1945 [A Selection of Wang Ziyun's Painting Sketches in the North-west, 1940–1945]. (Changsha: yuelu shushe).

Wang Ziyun (ed.) (2005*b*), 中國雕塑藝術史 [History of Chinese Artistic Sculpture], 3 vols., repr., 1988. (Changsha: Yuejian shushe Publishers).

Wang Ziyun (ed.) (2007), 中國歷代應用藝術圖綱 [Pictorial Overview of Chinese Applied Arts Throughout the Ages], n.d.; repr., Wang Qiang 王薔 (ed.), (Xi'an: Taibai wenyi Publishers).

Wei Juxian 衛聚賢 (1941), '古物展覽會的意義 [The Importance of the Cultural Relics Exhibition]'. 中央日報 *Central Daily News*, 13 Feb. 1941.

Wu Shaoming and Zhao Jinzhao (eds.) 吳少珉. 趙金昭 (2003), 二十世紀疑古思潮 [The Trend Towards Skepticism of Antiquity during the 20th Century]. (Beijing: Xueyuan Publishers).

Xia Nai 夏鼐 (2002), 敦煌考古漫記 [Random Notes on the Archaeology of Dunhuang]. Wang Shimin and Lin Xiuzhen (eds.) 王世民、林秀貞編. (Tianjin: Baihua wenyi Publishers).

Yan Zhuanying (ed.) (2006), 上海美術風雲, 1872–1949 申報藝術資料條目索引 [Trends in Shanghai Arts: Index to Art Materials and Subjects in *Shenbao* 1872–1949]. (Taipei: Institute of History and Philology).

Yang Hong 楊泓 (1997), 美術考古半世紀, 中國美術考古發現史. [A Half Century of Artistic Archaeology, A History of the Discovery of Artistic Archaeology]. (Beijing: Wenwu).

Yang Tingshi 楊庭碩 (2004), 百苗圖抄本 [Pictures of Aboriginal Peoples of Guizhou Province], vols. 1–2. (Guiyang: Guizhou renmin Publishers).

Yin Jiawu 岑家梧 (1945), '中國民俗藝術概說 [Overview of Chinese Folk Arts]'. 文史雜誌 *Wenshi zazhi*, vol. 5, 9/10 (May 1945): 19–28.

Yu Youren 于右任 (1942), '建議成立敦煌藝術學院 [The Suggestion on the Establishment of Dunhuang Institute],' 文史雜誌 *Wenshi zazhi*, vol. 2/2 (Feb. 1942): 42.

Zang Zhenhua 臧振華 (2008), '李濟與殷墟發掘：一個學術史的透視與省思 [Li Ji and the Yinxu Excavation: A Perspective and Introspective Look on Academic History]'. (Institute of History and Philology, Academia Sinica).

Zhang Daqian 張大千, [1947] 張大千臨撫燉煌辟画 [Zhang Daqian's Copies of Dunhuang Wall Paintings]. ([Taipei?] : Dafeng Studio.

Zhang Daqian 張大千 (1985), 張大千居士遺著漠高窟記 [Records Left by the Scholar Zhang Daqian on the Mogao Caves]. (Editorial Committee of the National Palace Museum. Taipei: National Palace Museum).

Zhou Zhenhe 周振鶴 (1938; 1987), 青海 [Qinghai]. (Changsha: Shangwu xinshua; Taipei: Nantian).

Zhuang Xueben 莊學本 (1937), 羌戎考察記. (Shanghai: Liangyou tushu yinshua gongsi).

Zhu Jiahua 朱家驊 (1942), '西北建設問題與科學化運動 [The Problem of North-west Construction and the Scientific Movement]'. 文史雜誌 *Wenshi zazhi*, vol. 2/2 (Feb. 1942), 60.

The British Industrial Revolution in Global Perspective

ROBERT C. ALLEN

Fellow of the Academy

THE INDUSTRIAL REVOLUTION was a turning point in the history of the world and inaugurated two centuries of economic growth that have resulted in the high incomes enjoyed in developed countries today.[1] Technological progress is the motor of economic growth, and the Industrial Revolution is defined by famous technological breakthroughs: machinery to spin and weave cotton, the use of coal to smelt and refine iron, and the steam engine.[2] In the words of the schoolboy made famous by T. S. Ashton: 'About 1760 a wave of gadgets swept over England' (Ashton 1955: 42). The questions for today's lecture are: How can we explain the technological breakthroughs of the Industrial Revolution? And, why did the Industrial Revolution happen in Britain, rather than France, the Netherlands, or China?

These questions will be answered by developing these themes: in comparison with other countries, Britain had an unusual structure of wages and prices in the eighteenth century, and this structure of wages and prices was a major factor in explaining why the revolution happened in Britain. In addition Britain had an effective 'innovation system' based on a high

---

Read at the Academy 29 October 2009.

[1] The issues in this lecture are treated at greater length and with fuller referencing in Allen (2009a).
[2] There has been a debate about the breadth of technological progress during the industrial revolution with Crafts (1985), and Crafts and Harley (1992, 2000) arguing that productivity growth was confined to the famous, revolutionised industries in the period 1801–31, while Temin (1997) has argued that many more industries experienced productivity growth. Whatever one believes about 1801–31, it is clear that many non-revolutionised industries experienced productivity growth between 1500 and 1850. The incentives to invent discussed in this paper applied to all industries, not just the famous ones I discuss here.

level of human capital, the appropriate engineering capability, and a few scientific breakthroughs. These features of the British economy, which distinguish it from other countries in the world at that time, were consequences of Britain's superior trade performance and success in the European and global economies in the seventeenth and eighteenth centuries.

My interpretation is opposed to a common view that goes like this: because the inventions of the Industrial Revolution had momentous consequences, they must have been the result of momentous ideas. On the contrary, I contend that the explanation of the inventions should not be sought in great leaps of the imagination. Instead, the inventions can be better understood in terms of the hard work of research and development that was required to turn what were often banal ideas into effective technology. Hence, I take very seriously Edison's quip that invention is '1 per cent inspiration and 99 per cent perspiration'. The Industrial Revolution was primarily an engineering challenge rather than a scientific challenge.

Because so much of invention was the hard work of perfecting machinery and new products, it was an economic activity. Consequently, economic incentives were critical in explaining why that work was done and, hence, why inventions took place. Research and development became a more common business activity in the eighteenth century than it had been previously.

Many other explanations have been offered for the Industrial Revolution. Geographical dichotomies (tropics versus temperate, rain-fed versus irrigated agriculture, resource-abundant versus resource-scarce, etc.) have been invoked but face formidable counter-examples as well as the difficulty that the purpose of much technology is to overcome the burdens of nature. Culture has often been invoked (Landes 1969, Clark 2007). Europeans have usually fancied themselves more rational and hard working than the natives, and social scientists like Max Weber (1904–5) have given these views some respectability. The agricultural history of the tropics calls these thoughts into question, however, by showing that African and Asian farmers responded to economic and environmental considerations in their choice of crops and farming practices (Hopkins 1973). Less grandly, it has been claimed that cultural developments like the Scientific Revolution of the seventeenth century are responsible for the Industrial Revolution of the eighteenth. I will take up this view later.

Among economists today, 'better institutions' is the most common explanation for economic development.[3] In the case of Britain, the case

---

[3] Proponents of this view include North and Weingast (1989), De Long and Schleifer (1993), LaPorta, Lopez-de-Silanes, Schleifer, Vishny (1998), Acemoglu, Johnson, and Robinson (2005).

rests on the Glorious Revolution of 1688, which assured parliamentary ascendancy, limited the power of crown, guaranteed private property, and prevented arbitrary taxation. Another line of argument is that English common law was better than French law. These explanations, of course, are restatements of eighteenth century liberal views.

If we consider the role of institutions and culture in a broader intellectual perspective, however, we notice an odd disjunction. As economists have been deciding that institutions explain everything, historians have been coming to the opposite conclusion. They have been re-evaluating many of the despotic regimes disparaged by the liberals in the eighteenth century and discovering that they functioned quite well. France, for instance, looks much better now than it did 250 years ago. Detailed comparisons show that France had lower taxes than England (Mathias and O'Brien 1976, 1978), and that French property was arguably too secure. Socially profitable irrigation projects, for instance, were not undertaken in eighteenth-century Provence because there was no legal mechanism for the compulsory purchase of land. It was only after the revolution and the ascendancy of the *Assemblée nationale* in Paris that these projects were taken forward (Rosenthal 1990). Indeed one could argue that a virtue of the English Constitution was that Parliament overrode private property with enclosure acts, turnpike acts, and canal acts. As one historian of Parliament has remarked, the great achievement of the Glorious Revolution was that the 'despotic power [that] was only available intermittently before 1688 ... was always available thereafter' (Hoppit, 1996: 126). Indeed, we see it in action today.

Empire after empire has been rehabilitated. China has figured prominently in these discussions, and the so-called California School has argued that China's institutions were as good as Europe's in the eighteenth century, and, indeed, its economy was as productive (Wong 1997, Pomeranz 2000). It has also been argued that India had effective enough institutions to sustain a vast intercontinental trading empire, extensive manufacturing, large cities and realise high living standards (Parthasarathai 1998, 2001, Bayly 1989, Chaudhuri 1985). The Roman empire is another example where revisionist historians claim that imperial power created a large free trade area and sustained an extensive division of labour, advanced manufacturing, and high productivity (Bowman and Wilson 2009, Scheidel,

---

For critical or contrary perspectives, see Clark (1996), Epstein (2000), Quinn (2001), Hoffman, Postel-Vinay, Rosenthal (2000), Pomeranz (2000), Mathias and O'Brien (1976, 1978), Hoffman and Norberg (1994), and Bonney (1999).

Morris, and Saller 2007, Ward-Perkins 2005). The revisionists argue that their empire created internal peace, order and good government. When these conditions were established over a wide area, interregional trade expanded and localities exploited their comparative advantage so production became spatially differentiated. The legal systems of these empires, while foreign, turn out to have been adequate to sustain this exchange and production. The result was high incomes.

In view of these findings, I take my cue from Charles Lockyer, who was an officer on the East India Company ship *Streatham*. He went to Asia to make his fortune in private trade. He was a keen student of Asian markets. He remarked:

> Arek, commonly called Bettle-nut from [Burma] would bear all Charges of Freight, Package and China Duties, and fetch fifty per Cent. Profit in Canton on a large Quantity, towards the End of Anno 1704, which is more than any other Commodity within my knowledge would do: But this is not always the same; for the Chinese, who like bees search all the coasts betwixt [India] and their own Country for Profit, have undoubtedly long since brought down the Price [in Canton] by filling their Markets with it.   (Lockyer 1711, p. 72)

If the Chinese merchants were actively arbitraging markets across Asia, it shows that their legal arrangements were sufficient to support extensive trade, and they were evincing a commercial spirit as well. So it is hard to believe that China was really held back by bad institutions or a non-commercial culture. Conversely, if Britain was not blessed with better culture or better institutions, why did it make the Industrial Revolution?

The demand for technology

To make progress on this question we have to focus on the invention and adoption of technology, because technological change is the proximate cause of growth. I use a demand and supply framework. The demand for technology depended on factor prices, market size, and the imitation of novel products. Britain's unusual wage and price structure is a key for understanding the demand for technology there and why it was different to that in other countries. The supply of technology was also important, and it depended on the standard of living and accumulated knowledge, skills and inventive institutions. North-western Europe (including Britain) stands out in these regards by virtue of high levels of literacy and numeracy, but Britain was not ahead of the Netherlands or present-day Belgium. The Scientific Revolution of the seventeenth century also played a role by providing a couple of key ideas, which were the basis of important technology.

I begin with the demand for technology, which was determined by Britain's unique factor prices. In particular, wages were remarkably high in Britain, while coal and energy were cheap. This price structure created a demand for labour-saving, energy-using technology.

British wages were high in four senses. The first is comparison with wages in other countries. These comparisons require exchange rates, and I use the silver value of the currencies since silver coins were the principal medium of exchange. By the eighteenth century, British wages were higher than those almost anywhere else in the world, as Figure 1 shows.[4] This is a

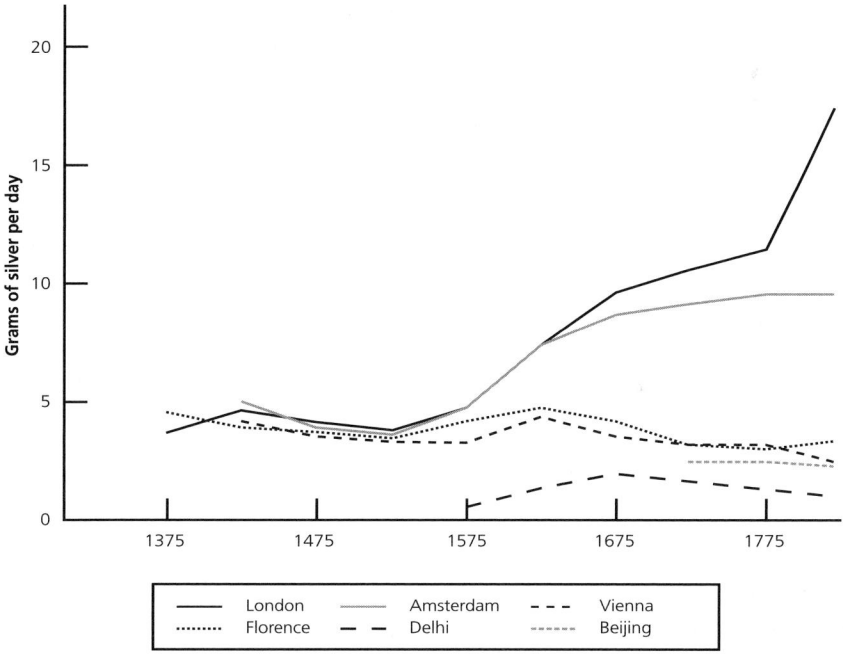

Figure 1.   Labourers' wages around the world.

[4] Figures 1–6 are based on price histories of the cities concerned. With co-authors, I have computerised these and converted the local weights and measures to metric or engineering units and the currencies to grams of silver for these comparisons. As a result, we can now compare wages and prices across Eurasia from the late Middle Ages to the twentieth century. For full sources and discussion, see Allen (2001, 2007, 2009a, 2009b) and Allen, Bassino, Ma, Moll-Murata, and van Zanden (2007).

marked change from the late fifteenth century when the wage of building labourers, for instance, was the same everywhere. Beginning in the sixteenth century, there has been a three-way split. There was little increase in wages in Central or Eastern Europe. In contrast, in Western Europe, wages rose during the price revolution (1560–1620), and they rose particularly in Britain. In the eighteenth century, British wages were higher than Asian wages, which, of course, is one of the reasons Brits went there to shop!

The second sense in which British wages were high is relative to the cost of living. Figure 2 shows the wage rate deflated by an international, intertemporal consumer price index. I will explain in a moment how it was calculated. It is a commonplace today that the standard of living is more or less the same everywhere in Western Europe, so we can ask: when in the past (if ever) was that last true? The answer is the end of the fifteenth century. At that time real wage differences between European cities were small. Since then, they have diverged. Real wages in North-western Europe remained more or less constant from the end of the Middle Ages until the 1870s. (It is remarkable that the Industrial Revolution passes through

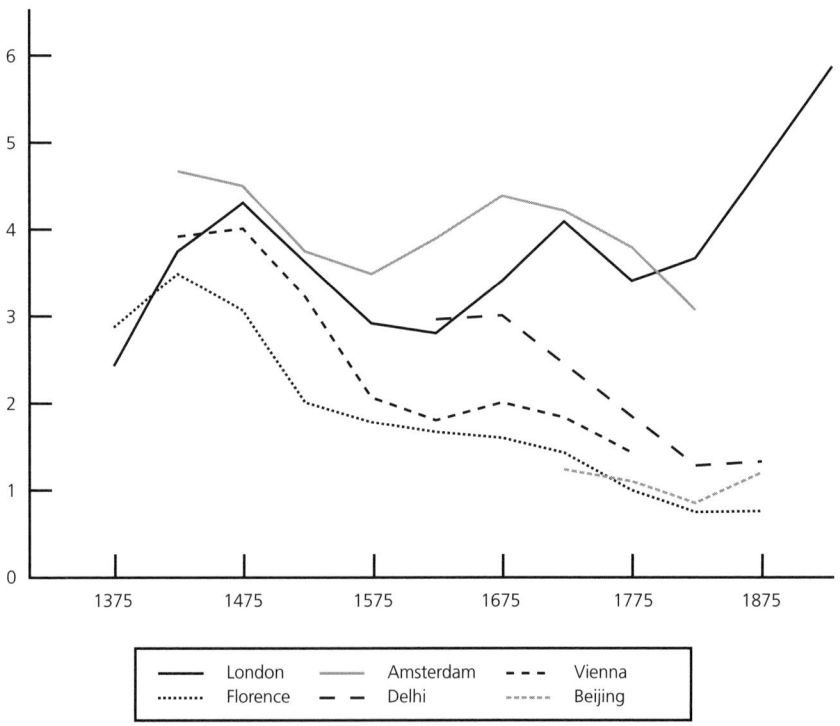

Figure 2. The subsistence ratio for labourers.

these time series without a trace!) The real wage, however, in Central and Southern Europe dropped. As a result, there was a great divergence of living standards within Europe before the Industrial Revolution. Also, living standards in the Asian cities were on a par with those of Southern and Central Europe in the eighteenth century—not with England or the Low Countries. A rich North and a poor South was not a consequence of the Industrial Revolution but preceded it. Indeed, my argument is that the Great Divergence caused the Industrial Revolution.

These figures have a further interpretation because of the way they have been scaled. Most of the Central and Eastern European real wage series as well as the Asian series end up with a value of about one in the eighteenth century. What that means is that a labourer who worked full-year, full-time earned just enough money to support a family at a bare-bones standard of living. This standard was one in which an adult male consumed 1940 calories per day. The calories came mainly from boiled grains and beans. The diet was quasi-vegetarian with very little flesh and some butter or oil. Non-food items included a few candles, soap, and three metres of cloth for clothing. There was a 5 per cent allowance for house rent. Table 1 shows the spending pattern as it was specified for North-western Europe where oatmeal was the cheapest source of calories. The diet was modified for other parts of the world to use the cheapest available carbohydrate, that is polenta in Florence, sorghum in Beijing, millet chipatis in Delhi, rice in Madras, maize in Mexico. This kind of bare-bones diet was common in most of Asia and Southern and Central Europe. It was all that labourers could afford.

Table 1. The annual subsistence spending pattern of a man in North-western Europe

	Quantity per year	Calories per day	Grams of protein per day
Foods			
Oats	155 kilograms	1657	72
Beans	20 kilograms	187	14
Meat	5 kilograms	34	3
Butter	3 kilograms	60	0
Total		1938	89
Non-foods			
Soap	1.3 kilograms		
Cotton	3.0 metres		
Candles	1.3 kilograms		
Lamp oil	1.3 litres		
Fuel	2.0 million BTU		

Source: Allen (2009a, p. 37), which also gives examples of subsistence based on maize, millet, and rice. The basket in the table is the consumption pattern of a man. The annual cost of maintaining a family is taken to be the cost of three of these baskets plus 5% for rent.

As Figure 2 shows, labourers in North-western Europe earned four times bare-bones subsistence in the eighteenth century. They did not eat four times as much oatmeal as shown in Table 1. Instead, they upgraded the quality of their food to bread, beer and beef. They also had a bit of purchasing power left over to buy the Asian commodities like tea and the manufactured goods of the consumer revolution in the eighteenth century. That is why the consumer revolution happened in North-western Europe in the eighteenth century and why it was mainly confined to North-western Europe insofar as it affected the working class.

A third sense in which British wages were high is relative to the cost of capital goods, and this is critical for the choice of technology and the process of invention. Figure 3 shows the builder's wage rate relative to the user cost of capital based on the prices of wood, iron, non-ferrous metal, and bricks and an interest rate and depreciation rate. In Strasbourg, Vienna, and southern England there was not much difference in the ratio of the wage rate to the price of capital early in the seventeenth century, but by the eighteenth century a big differential had emerged. Labour was much more

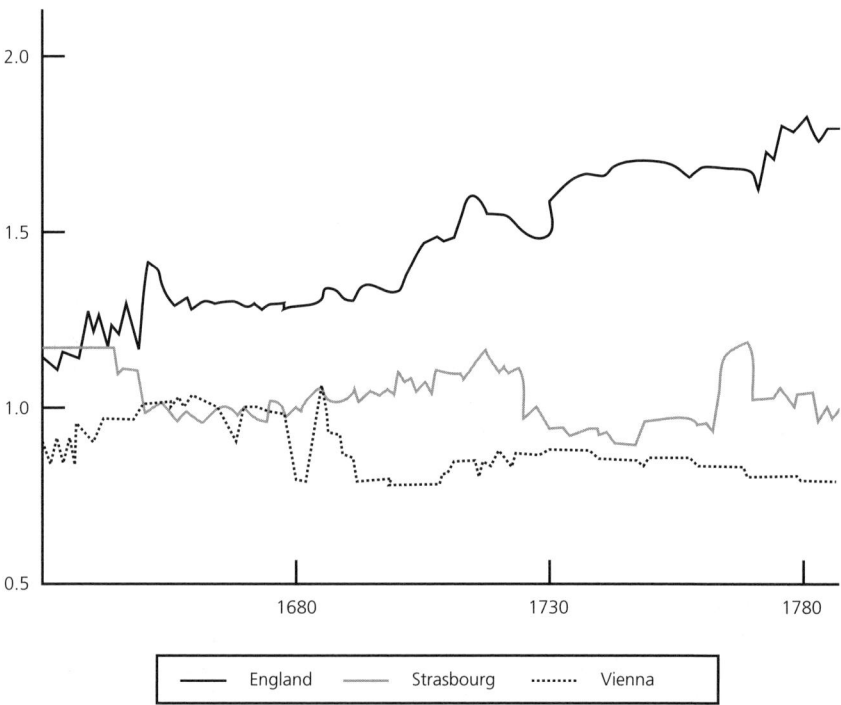

Figure 3.   Wages relative to price of capital.

expensive relative to capital in Britain, and that difference gave British businesses a strong incentive to use capital intensive technologies and British inventors an incentive to invent them.

The fourth sense in which British wages were high was relative to the price of energy. Figure 4 shows energy prices in different cities early in the eighteenth century. In this figure the prices of the various fuels (coal in London, peat in Amsterdam, etc.) are reduced to their energy content measured in British Thermal Units (BTUs). Newcastle had the cheapest energy since coal was mined there. Beijing had the most expensive energy, Paris was almost as expensive, while Amsterdam and London were in the middle. The difference between the price in London and Newcastle reflects the transportation costs incurred in shipping the coal down the coast from Newcastle to London. Coal reached Amsterdam at almost the same price as it was available in London because it was just as cheap—or as expensive—to send a boat from Newcastle to Amsterdam as to London.

The low cost of energy on the British coalfields meant that the wage rate relative to the price of energy was very high in Newcastle (Fig. 5). High British wages also contributed to this result, but cheap coal was the decisive factor.

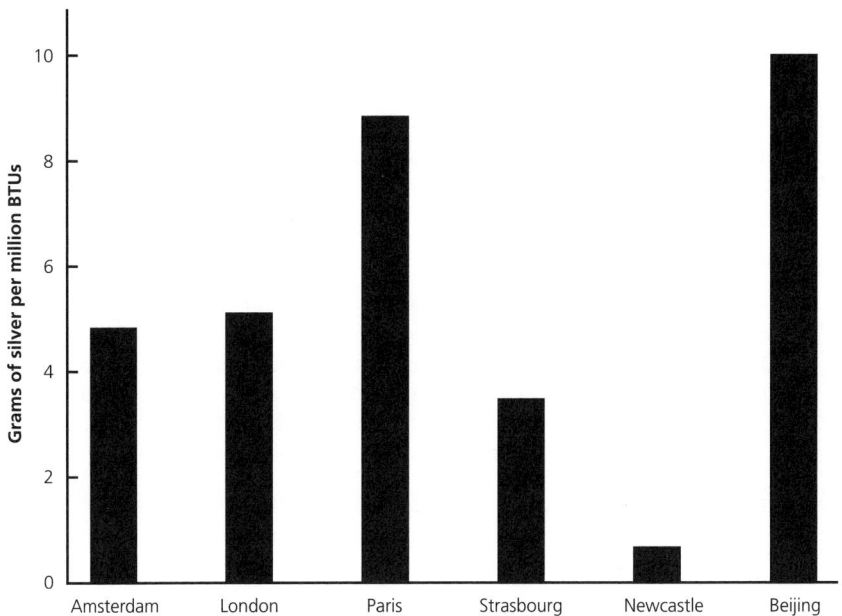

Figure 4.   The price of energy in the early 1700s.

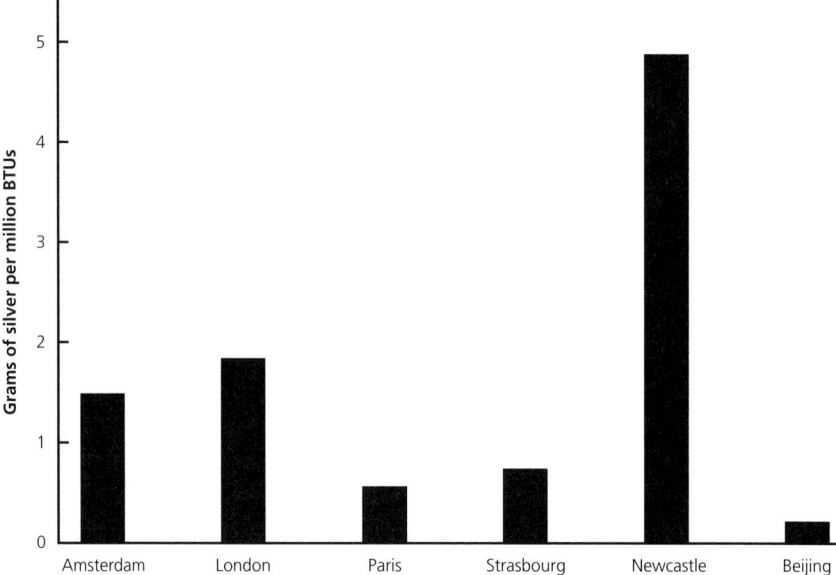

Figure 5.   The price of labour relative to energy, early 1700s.

Contemporaries were aware of these relative prices. An interesting case in point is the production of plate glass, which was an industry in which the French were technological leaders. They had a major production centre at Saint Gobain, and the British imported the French technology to Ravenshead in the late eighteenth century. This was not just theft. There was cooperation with the French works. Delaunay Deslandes, who was the director of Saint Gobain, thought this was a quixotic thing for the British to do because he could not imagine how they could compete against the French. As he said,

> Given the manner in which the English and French lived … they could never make plate [glass] which could enter into competition with ours for the price. Our Frenchmen eat soup with a little butter and vegetables. They scarcely ever eat meat. They sometimes drink a little cider but more commonly water. Your Englishmen eat meat, and a great deal of it, and they drink beer continually in such a fashion that an Englishman spends three times more than a Frenchman.[5]

Deslandes was describing the high cost diet that English workers could afford with their high wages in the eighteenth century. If the British glass works were going to have to pay these high wages how could they compete

---

[5] Quoted by Harris (1975, p. 67, n. 42).

with low-wage French labour? The answer is that English coal cut fuel costs to one-sixth of the French level. Cheap coal sustained the high-wage economy.

High wages and cheap energy were the distinctive features of the British economy during the Industrial Revolution. Where did this price structure come from? It was a result of Britain's foreign trade boom in the seventeenth and eighteenth century (Allen 2003, 2009a, pp. 106–31). The boom began in the seventeenth century with the new draperies and was consolidated with the creation of a world empire in the eighteenth. The trade boom pushed the urbanisation rate from 7 per cent in 1500 to 29 per cent in 1800, which was one of the highest percentages in Europe. The growth of London accounts for much of this urbanisation. Its population rose from about 50,000 in 1500 to 200,000 in 1600, to half a million in 1700, and reached one million in 1800. The growth of the city was driven by the growth in the volume of trade though the port. The resulting tight labour markets were the proximate cause of the high wages. They were sustained eventually by the cheap energy.

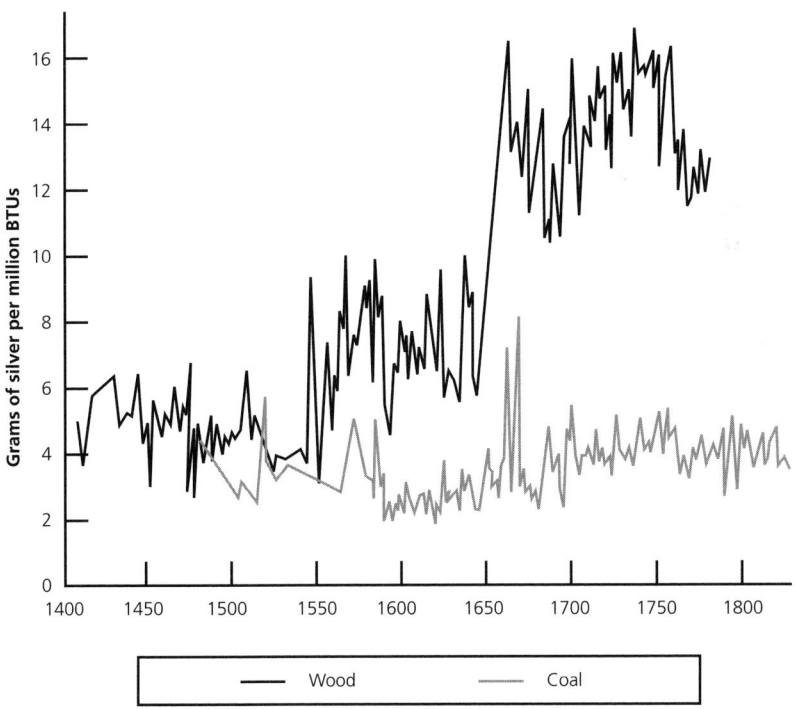

Figure 6.   The real prices of wood and coal in London.

As London grew, the demand for fuel for industrial purposes and domestic heating increased as well. At the outset, most of the fuel was either firewood or charcoal, and this had to be shipped over greater and greater distances at greater and greater cost. Consequently, the price of fuel rose as the city expanded. Eventually, the prices of wood and charcoal rose high enough to make it profitable to use coal. Figure 6 charts this transition. The figure shows the real price of fuel, that is the price per BTU deflated by a consumer price index. At the end of the Middle Ages the prices per BTU of wood fuels and coal were similar. Under those circumstances, coal was only used to burn lime and for blacksmithing, uses in which it was regarded as superior to wood. In all other uses, wood was preferred. For heating, cooking, and most industrial processes, coal was the inferior fuel since it contained sulphur, which burnt with a foul smell and contaminated industrial processes (Nef 1932, Hatcher 1993).

The price of wood and charcoal rose in the sixteenth century and, by 1580, the price of charcoal per unit of energy was twice the price of coal. That differential was large enough to induce people to redesign their technologies, so that they could use the cheaper fuel. Indeed that is when the coal trade took off.

Technology responded to factor prices

High British wages and cheap coal underpinned the Industrial Revolution by creating a demand for technology that substituted capital and energy for labour. In Asia and much of Europe, low wages and dear energy had the opposite effect. Silk weaving is one example. The English industry began when the Lombe brothers built a mill in Derby in 1715–19. It was expensive to erect and was powered by a water wheel, which was a capital-intensive system. What about the situation in Asia? The Tsukiji silk mill was built in Japan *c.*1870. It used European-style machinery, but it was re-engineered to be more labour-intensive in accord with Japanese factor proportions. It did not have a water wheel. Instead it was powered by a man turning a crank—a labour-intensive process, indeed! In England where labour was very expensive and capital was relatively cheap, a capital-intensive method was used, whereas in Japan, where labour was cheap, a labour-intensive method was preferred. Factor prices influenced the choice of technique at the opposite ends of Eurasia.

Figure 7.   An English-style pottery kiln.

Another example that relates to energy is pottery production in China and England. Pottery kilns in England were built to economise on capital and were profligate in their use of energy. Figure 7 shows an English-style kiln. It had a coal fire in the bottom. The heat rose, enveloped the pots, and then vented out of the furnace through the hole in the top. Much of the energy was wasted. The English kiln was cheap to build but not thermally efficient. In contrast, the Chinese kilns used lots of capital and employed lots of labour to preserve energy. Figure 8 shows a fire at the entrance to the lower chamber where the heat was drawn in to bake the pots. The heat was not vented out of a hole in the top in the English manner. Instead, it was forced down through a hole at the bottom into the next chamber. The heat was reused in chamber after chamber, so it was not wasted. This design, of course, equated to more capital. Pottery kilns, therefore, are another example of the way in which technology was designed in response to factor prices. In this case, expensive fuel in China led to the substitution of capital for energy, in contrast to English design.

The same considerations governed invention in Europe. Nail making is a prosaic example. One of the steps in making nails is putting the head

Figure 8. A Chinese-style pottery kiln.

on the nail. In Britain at the end of the seventeenth century a machine was developed to mechanise that process. It was called the oliver. It was a device like a sledgehammer. The shaft was hinged at the base. The head of the 'hammer' had a hole in which a dye was placed to shape the head of the nail. The hammer was raised with a foot pedal and then released so the head would drop on a nail and shape it. In contrast, in French nail shops there was no oliver. Again we have a situation where the low-wage country, France, was using the more labour-intensive process.

The two stages of technological evolution

The history of technology is a two-stage process. So far I have been discussing the first stage. It includes the famous macro-inventions of the Industrial Revolution—the spinning machinery, coke blast furnaces, weaving machines, and steam engines. These involved substantial changes in input proportions. They radically increased the amount of coal that was used, for instance, or increased capital relative to labour. They turn out to have been profitable at British input prices because they used intensively things that were cheap in Britain. At the outset, however, they barely covered costs, even in Britain. Despite the fact that a hundred years later these machines revolutionised the world, in the beginning they just barely paid their way.

The second stage of the history of technology comprises the improvement of the revolutionary machines. This is the phase of micro-inventions. Engineers, owners, and operators studied the machines to improve them. The objective was to reduce costs, and, in the event, all inputs were saved, irrespective of whether they were abundant or scarce. Eventually a tipping point was reached when it became profitable to use these technologies (in their improved form) outside Britain. That is when the Industrial Revolution spread around the world.

We can illustrate the two stages with isoquant diagrams. In the mid-eighteenth century, the only way to make coarse cotton yarn was with a spinning wheel. In Figure 9, this is represented by a single point corresponding to the labour of one woman and the cost of a wheel. Together they produced one pound of yarn per day. Two isocost lines are drawn— one for a high-wage economy and one for a low-wage economy. Both

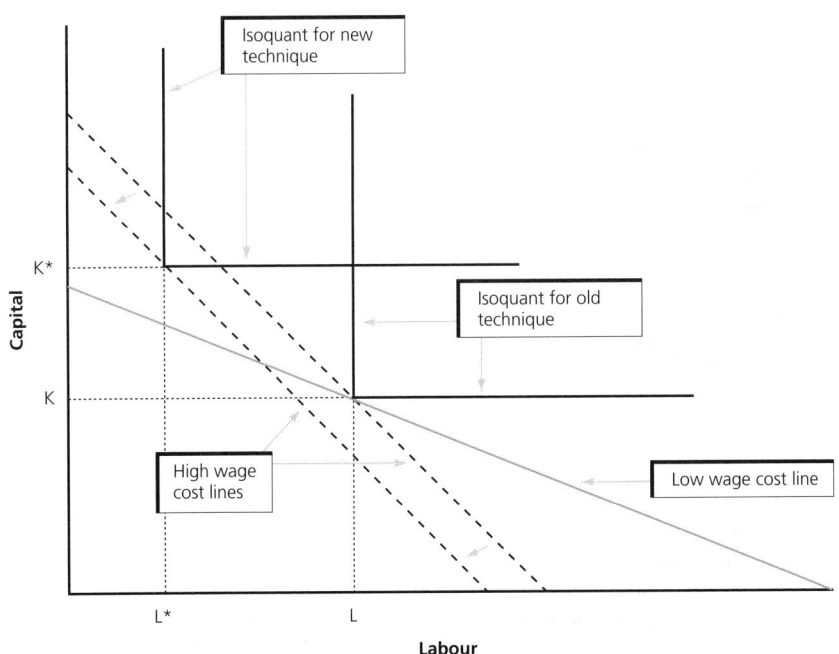

Figure 9.   Isoquants for spinning yarn: mid-eighteenth century.

touch the single point of the isoquant since that represents the only way to make cotton whatever your factor prices.

The spinning jenny is represented on the diagram with another point with more capital and less labour. With a jenny, a woman could spin one pound of coarse yarn in a couple of hours rather than a full day, but the jenny cost considerably more than the wheel. As the points are drawn, it would have been profitable to adopt the jenny in the high-wage economy, but it would have raised costs in the low-wage economy, so it would not have been used there. In 1787, over 20,000 jennies were installed in Britain but only 900 were installed in France in 1790, and most of those were in large state-assisted factories rather than in women's cottages as in England (Aspin and Chapman 1964, p. 49, Wadsworth and Mann 1931, pp. 195–9, 503–4). This diagram illustrates the important point that biased technical changes do not cut costs in the same proportion everywhere. The reduction depends on factor prices, so biased technical change favours some parts of the world over others. The technologies that were invented in Britain raised labour productivity and covered their costs only when they were used under the conditions of Britain in the eighteenth century.

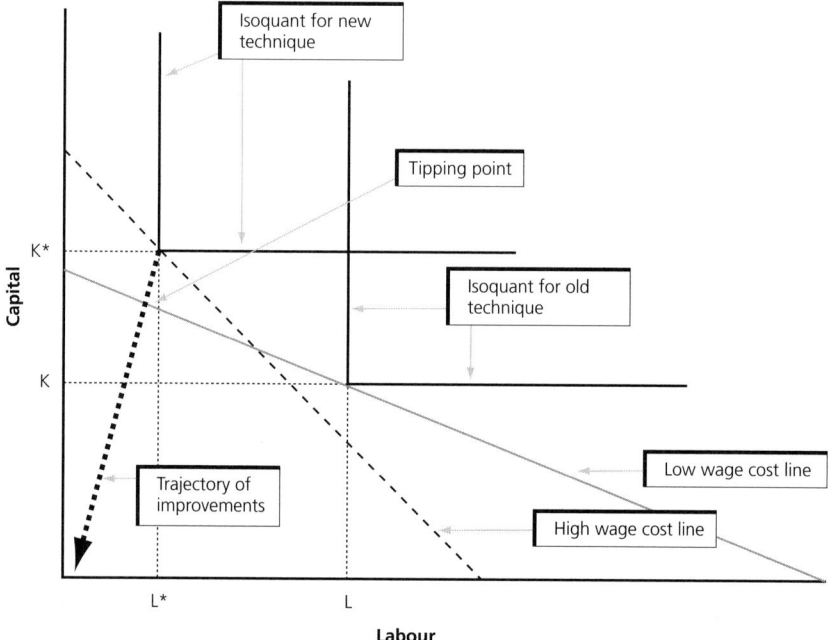

Figure 10.   Isoquants for spinning yarn after technological improvements.

Table 2.   Adult literacy, 1500–1800: percentage of the adult population that could sign its name.

	1500	1800
England	6	53
Netherlands	10	68
Belgium	10	49
Germany	6	35
France	7	37
Austria/Hungary	6	21
Poland	6	21
Italy	9	22
Spain	9	20

Source: Allen (2009a, p. 53).

The second stage of technological development proceeded in this way: British engineers learned how to improve the spinning jenny as they used it and studied it. The mule was one of the first spin-offs, and improved versions of it were used in many countries in the middle of the nineteenth century. This trajectory of improvement is represented by the arrow towards the origin in Figure 10. As the technology was improved, labour and capital were saved. By installing the first cotton spinning machines, Britain became the world's technological leader, and the subsequent improvements extended Britain's lead. Historians as well as contemporaries have debated why France was not keeping up. Was it bad entrepreneurs or an engineering culture that was too theoretical? In fact, it was neither. At the end of the eighteenth century, it did not pay to spin with machines in France. Eventually, however, enough inputs were saved so that the cost of producing cotton with the improved process dropped below the cost of spinning with a wheel *even in the low-wage country*—like France. That juncture was the tipping point when the industrial revolution shifted abroad. Indeed, there was a great leap forward as the foreigners adopted the technology in its most advanced form. That, of course, was the only form that paid, given their lower wages.

The supply of technology

Thus far, my argument has been about the demand for technology. There was also a supply-side story that is prompted by the observation that not all high-wage economies have invented labour-saving machinery. The late Middle Ages had a high-wage economy, but it did not lead to an Industrial

Revolution. Why not? The answer has two parts. First, commerce and urbanisation were more widespread in the eighteenth century than they had been in the Middle Ages, and trade and cities led to high levels of human capital. Second, the Scientific Revolution of the seventeenth century included scientific discoveries that led to two important technologies.

First, with respect to human capital, Table 2 shows estimates of literacy rates in different countries (defined on modern borders) in 1500 and 1800. These estimates are based on the proportions of people who could sign their name. In 1500, literacy was low everywhere. By 1800 it was higher everywhere and especially in North-western Europe. One explanation for the rise in literacy is the Protestant Reformation. This is doubtful, however, since the highly literate parts of Europe in 1800 included Belgium and North-eastern France, which were Catholic countries. The driving force behind literacy was really urbanisation and the expansion of commercial society. Literacy was valuable in trade and cities, and that value led parents to pay for schooling for their children. So far as we can tell from phenomena like age heaping, numeracy also increased in the early modern period in North-western Europe (Thomas 1987, A'Hearn, Baten, and Crayen 2009). Few people studied arithmetic for fun; the acquisition of numerical skill was entirely driven by economic value.

Second, the Scientific Revolution was another important difference between the Middle Ages and the eighteenth century. Some historians have emphasised its impact on the culture at large, but I concentrate on specific connections between scientific discoveries and technological advances. Two discoveries were bases for two General Purpose Technologies (GPTs). The concept of General Purpose Technology was inspired by the computer and refers to technologies that can be adapted to many sectors of the economy. In the Industrial Revolution, the GPTs were steam power and 'clockwork', or gearing. Both had connections to the Scientific Revolution, although in the case of gearing the relationship was a distant one. Both technologies required Research and Development (R&D) projects to make them effective in the various settings. The R&D projects were more profitable in Britain than elsewhere, which is why the Industrial Revolution was invented in Britain, as I will show you.

The steam engine was an important application of knowledge discovered by seventeenth-century scientists.[6] The science began with Galileo,

---

[6] Standard works on the history of the steam engine include Farey (1827), Dickinson (1939, 1958), Forbes (1958), Hills (1970, pp. 134–207, 1989), Nuvolari (2004), and von Tunzelmann (1978).

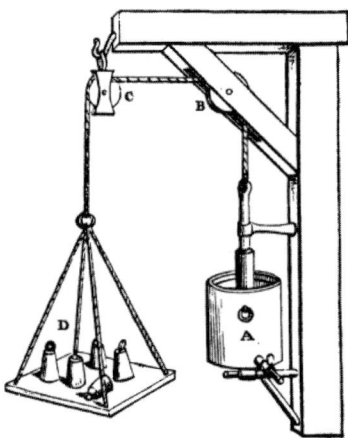

Figure 11.   von Guericke's apparatus.

who was the first to suspect that the atmosphere had weight. The idea occurred to him when he studied the problem of draining mines and noticed that suction pumps would not lift water more than about thirty feet. He put his secretary Evangelista Torricelli to work on this project. Torricelli invented the mercury barometer and weighed the atmosphere. In 1672, von Guericke of Magdebourg designed the apparatus shown in Figure 11, also to weigh the atmosphere. The cylinder, which is labelled A, contained a piston from which ropes went over the pulleys to hold the platform on which he put weights. He found that by pumping the air out of the cylinder the atmosphere pushed the piston down and raised the platform. He could offset that rise and weigh the atmosphere by putting weights on the platform. In 1675 Denis Papin eliminated the vacuum pump by filling the cylinder with steam and then condensing it. Papin had invented a proto-steam engine.

The von Guerick experiment shown in Figure 11 is similar to the first successful steam engine invented by Newcomen in 1712 (Fig. 12). Newcomen's engine has the cylinder on the right (B) with a piston (D) in it. Instead of the pulleys, there is a balance beam (HF) and, instead of the weights on the left, there is a pump (I) for lifting water out of a mine. By filling the cylinder with steam from the boiler (A) and then condensing it with a squirt of cold water (B), the atmosphere would push the piston down and raise the pump. When the vacuum was relieved, the weights (K) above the pump pulled the left end of the beam down, steam was allowed to enter the cylinder, and the cycle was repeated. Newcomen had found

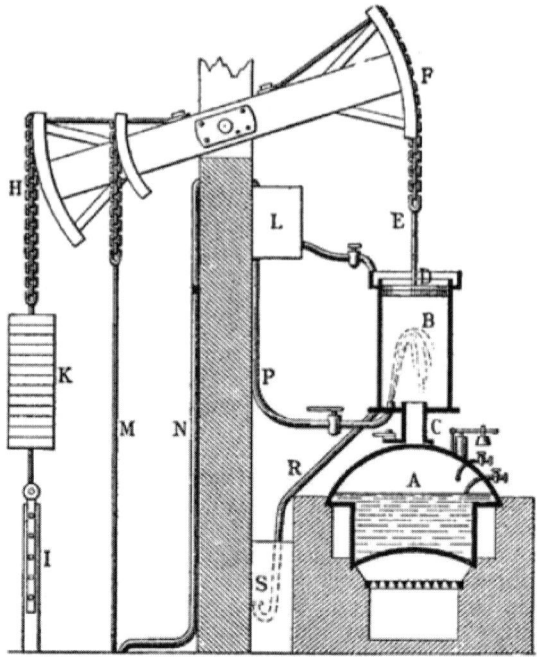

Figure 12.   Newcomen's steam engine.

a way to raise water—and make money—from the weight of the
atmosphere.

The science underlying the steam engine was pan-European (the leading scientists were Italians, Germans, and French), but the R&D was carried out in Britain by an Englishman. The reason is that Britain was the
only place where it was profitable to use the engine on a large scale, for two
reasons. First, the main use of the engine was to drain mines, and Britain
had the largest mining industry in Europe thanks to coal. Second, the
engine used prodigious amounts of fuel, and coal mines offered cheap
fuel. John Theophilus Desaguliers, a leading engineer in the early eighteenth century, observed that 'where there is no water [for power] to be
had, and coals are cheap, the Engine now call'd the Fire Engine, or the
Engine to raise the Water by Fire, is the best and most effectual. But it is
especially of immense service (so as to be now of general use) in the Coal-
Works, where the Power of the Fire is made from the Refuse of the Coals,
which would not otherwise be sold' (Desaguliers 1744, II, pp. 464–5). The
reason it was profitable to develop the Newcomen engine in Britain was
because there were coal mines to be drained.

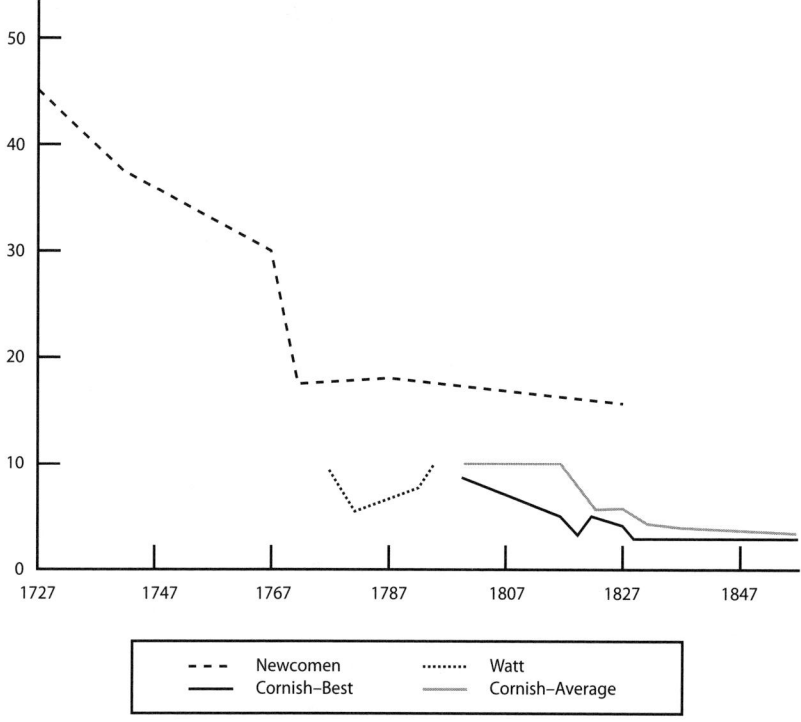

Figure 13.   Coal consumption in pumping engines (lbs per HP-hour).

Newcomen's engine was the macro-invention that marked the first phase of this technological trajectory. The second phase consisted of the perfection of the engine and involved many of the most famous engineers of the Industrial Revolution. This phase involved saving all inputs and, in particular, coal, which was cheap in Britain. Figure 13 shows the evolution of fuel consumption in pumping engines from an early Newcomen engine in 1727 to the highly efficient engines of the mid-nineteenth century. It includes the contributions of John Smeaton, James Watt, Richard Trevithick, Arthur Woolf, and the many engineers who improved Cornish engines. Fuel consumption dropped from 44 pounds of coal per horsepower-hour in 1727 to 3 pounds in 1847. This improvement was a triumph for British engineering, and it also destroyed the country's competitive advantage by turning the steam engine, which had mainly benefited Britain in the early eighteenth century, into a technology that could be used anywhere in the world. Once the coal consumption was reduced to 3 pounds per horsepower-hour, the price of coal became irrelevant to the engine's commercial application.

British engineers had invented the 'appropriate technology' for the rest of the world.

Clockwork was the second General Purpose Technology in the Industrial Revolution.[7] Clockwork refers to the use of gears to control and distribute power in machinery. Gears had been used for a long time. Medieval gears, however, were usually large, wooden, and crude. By the eighteenth century, gears had become small, metallic, and precise. The improvement in gears goes back to the invention of the pendulum clock by Christiaan Huygens in 1656. He was, of course, a world-class scientist and mathematician, and he was working on a world-class scientific problem. This was the measurement of longitude, and it had come to the fore with global navigation. The solution was easy if you knew the time difference between your location and Greenwich, and that was simple if you carried a time piece set to Greenwich Mean Time. The problem was designing an accurate clock or watch. Huygens realised that he could improve the accuracy of a clock by adding a pendulum. The result was a better clock, and the clock industry expanded considerably. However, Huygens' clock was not a satisfactory solution to the longitude problem since a pendulum clock did not keep good time on a ship pitching at sea. Huygens did not give up, however. He applied himself to improving the accuracy of watches and invented the coiled spring. This greatly improved their accuracy, although again not enough to determine longitude with sufficient precision. Nonetheless, the watch industry grew enormously since the more accurate watches were in demand. Attention was directed towards improving the production of gears. In 1656, each gear had to be laid out by hand on a sheet of brass with a protractor. The teeth were marked and then sawn out individually with a file. In the second half of the seventeenth century, machines were developed that did the laying out and cutting automatically with the result that, by the eighteenth century, gears had become not only cheaper but also standardised and more accurate.

Gears had uses besides watches. Early applications included automata—clockwork toys, some of which were very elaborate. One of the most famous was the duck made by the great French engineer Vaucanson. The duck walked across the floor eating and pooping. It was a great hit at Versailles; according to Voltaire, 'Without Vaucanson's duck, you would have nothing to remind you of the glory of France.' Of course, if you could control the movement of a toy duck with gears, perhaps you could do something useful like spin yarn or weave cloth. Edmund Cartwright,

[7] On the history of clocks and watches, see Weiss (1982) and Landes (2000).

the inventor of the power loom, was inspired in part by automata, and the distribution of power to the rollers in Arkwright's water frame was called 'the clock work' since it used gears like a watch or clock. Indeed, Arkwright hired clockmakers over a five-year period to design it.

The possibility of using gears to design machinery was greatest where gears were made. As it happens, Britain had the largest watchmaking industry in the world since the high-wage economy sustained a high demand for watches. While final assembly was done in London, the watch movements themselves were outsourced to southern Lancashire. Preston and Warrington had large industries making gears and supporting industries that made the tooling to make the gears. The watchmakers and the toolmakers provided the 'high tech' inputs to produce textile machinery in the 1780s and 1790s. Britain's success in 'practical skills and engineering', which has often been identified as a cause of her industrial success, was the result of her earlier success in watchmaking.

The economic basis of the Industrial Revolution

Both steam power and clockwork were rooted in scientific discovery; nonetheless, they illustrate the importance of incentives in explaining eighteenth-century inventions. This lecture has advanced an economic explanation of the Industrial Revolution that involves three key ideas relating to incentives:

- Engineering problems were the crux of invention;
- The engineering problems were addressed in response to economic incentives resulting from Britain's high wages and cheap energy; and
- *The famous inventions of the Industrial Revolution were made in Britain because it paid to invent them in Britain, not because the British were more practical, more enterprising, or better governed.*

References

Acemoglu, Daren, Johnson, Simon, and Robinson, James (2005), 'The rise of Europe: Atlantic trade, institutional change and economic growth', *American Economic Review*, 95: 546–79.

A'Hearn, Brian, Baten, Jörg, and Crayen, Dorothee (2009), 'Quantifying quantitative literacy: age heaping and the history of human capital', *Journal of Economic History*, 69: 783–808.

Allen, Robert C. (2001), 'The great divergence in European wages and prices from the Middle Ages to the First World War', *Explorations in Economic History*, 38: 411–47.

Allen, Robert C. (2003), 'Poverty and progress in Early Modern Europe', *Economic History Review*, 56: 403–43.

Allen, Robert C. (2007), 'India in the Great Divergence', in Timothy J. Hatton, Kevin H. O'Rourke, and Alan M. Taylor (eds.), *The New Comparative Economic History: Essays in Honor of Jeffery G. Williamson* (Cambridge, MA), pp. 9–32.

Allen, Robert C. (2009*a*), *The British Industrial Revolution in Global Perspective* (Cambridge).

Allen, Robert C. (2009*b*), 'The Industrial Revolution in miniature: the spinning jenny in Britain, France, and India', *Journal of Economic History*, 69: 901–27.

Allen, Robert C., Bassino, Jean-Paul, Ma, Debin, Moll-Murata, Christine, and van Zanden, Jan Luiten (with Jean-Pascal Bassino, Debin Ma, Christine Moll-Murata, and Jan Luiten van Zanden) (2007), 'Wages, prices, and living standards in China, 1739–1925: in comparison with Europe, Japan, and India' (Oxford, Oxford University, Department of Economics, Working Paper 316, forthcoming in *Economic History Review*).

Ashton, T. S. (1955), *An Economic History of England: the 18th Century* (London).

Aspin, C., and Chapman, S. D. (1964), *James Hargreaves and the Spinning Jenny* (Preston, Helmshore Local History Society).

Bayly, C. A. (1989), *Imperial Meridian: the British Empire and the World, 1780–1830* (London).

Bonney, Richard (1999), *The Rise of the Fiscal State in Europe, c.1200–1815* (Oxford).

Bowman, Alan and Wilson, Andrew (eds.) (2009), *Quantifying the Roman Economy: Methods and Problems* (Oxford).

Chaudhuri, K. N. (1985), *Trade and Civilisation in the Indian Ocean: an Economic History from the Rise of Islam to 1750* (Cambridge).

Clark, Greg (1996), 'The political foundations of modern economic growth: England, 1540–1800', *Journal of Interdisciplinary History*, 26: 563–87.

Clark, Greg (2007), *A Farewell to Alms* (Princeton, NJ).

Crafts, N. F. R. (1985), *British Economic Growth during the Industrial Revolution* (Oxford).

Crafts, N. F. R. and Harley, C. K. (1992), 'Output growth and the British Industrial Revolution: a restatement of the Crafts–Harley view', *Economic History Review*, 2nd series, 45: 703–30.

Crafts, N. F. R. and Harley, C. K. (2000), 'Simulating the two views of the Industrial Revolution', *Journal of Economic History*, 60: 819–41.

De Long, J. Bradford and Schleifer, Andrei (1993), 'Princes and merchants: European city growth before the Industrial Revolution', *Journal of Law and Economics*, 36: 671–702.

Desaguliers, J. T. (1734–44), *A Course of Experimental Philosophy* (London).

Dickinson, H. W. (1939), *A Short History of the Steam Engine* (Cambridge).

Dickinson, H. W. (1958), 'The steam-engine to 1830', in Charles Singer, E. J. Holmyard, A. R. Hall and Trevor I. Williams (eds.), *A History of Technology, Vol. IV, The Industrial Revolution, c.1750– c.1850* (Oxford), pp. 168–98.

Epstein, S. R. (2000), *Freedom and Growth: the rise of States and Markets in Europe, 1300–1750* (London).

Farey, John (1827), *A Treatise on the Steam Engine, Historical, Practical, and Descriptive* (London).

Forbes, R. J. (1958), 'Power to 1850', in Charles Singer, E. J. Holmyard, A. R. Hall and Trevor I. Williams (eds.), *A History of Technology, Vol. IV, The Industrial Revolution, c.1750–c.1850* (Oxford), pp. 148–67.

Harris, J. R. (1975), 'Saint-Gobain and Ravenshead', in Barrie M. Ratcliffe (ed.), *Great Britain and Her World, 1750–1914* (Manchester), pp. 27–70.

Hatcher, J. (1993), *The History of the British Coal Industry, Vol. I, Before 1700: Towards the Age of Coal* (Oxford).

Hills, Richard L. (1970), *Power in the Industrial Revolution* (Manchester).

Hills, Richard L. (1989), *Power from Steam: a History of the Stationary Steam Engine* (Cambridge).

Hoffman, Philip T. and Norberg, Kathryn (1994), *Fiscal Crises, Liberty, and Representative Government, 1450–1789* (Stanford, CA).

Hoffman, Philip T., Postel-Vinay, Gilles, and Rosenthal, Jean-Laurent (2000), *Priceless Markets: the Political Economy of Credit in Paris, 1660–1870* (Chicago, IL).

Hopkins, Anthony G. (1973), *An Economic History of West Africa* (London).

Hoppit, Julian (1996), 'Patterns of Parliamentary legislation, 1600–1800', *The History Journal*, 39: 109–31.

Landes, David S. (1969), *The Unbound Prometheus: Technological Change and Industrial Development in Western Europe from 1750 to the Present* (Cambridge).

Landes, David S. (2000), *Revolution in Time: Clocks and the Making of the Modern World* (revised edition) (London).

LaPorta, R., Lopez-de-Silanes, F., Schleifer, A. and Vishny, R. W. (1998), 'Law and finance', *Journal of Political Economy*, 106: 1113–55.

Lockyer, Charles (1711), *An Account of the Trade in India* (London).

Mathias, P. and O'Brien, P. K. (1976), 'Taxation in England and France, 1715–1810', *Journal of European Economic History*, 5: 601–50.

Mathias, P. and O'Brien, P. K. (1978), 'The incidence of taxes and the burden of proof', *Journal of European Economic History*, 7: 211–13.

Nef, J. U. (1932), *The Rise of the British Coal Industry* (London).

North, D. C. and Weingast, B. R. (1989), 'Constitutions and commitment: evolution of institutions governing public choice in seventeenth-century England', *Journal of Economic History*, 49: 803–32.

Nuvolari, Alessandro (2004a), *The Making of Steam Power Technology: a Study of Technical Change during the Industrial Revolution* (Eindhoven).

Parthasarathi, P. (1998), 'Rethinking wages and competitiveness in the eighteenth century: Britain and South India', *Past & Present*, 158: 79–109.

Parthasarathi, P. (2001), *The Transition to a Colonial Economy. Weavers, Merchants and Kings in South India, 1720–1800* (Cambridge).

Pomeranz, K. (2000), *The Great Divergence: China, Europe, and the Making of the Modern World* (Princeton, NJ).

Quinn, Stephen (2001), 'The Glorious Revolution's effect on English private finance: a microhistory, 1680–1705', *Journal of Economic History*, 61: 593–615.

Rosenthal, J.-L. (1990), 'The development of irrigation in Provence, 1700–1860: the French Revolution and economic growth', *Journal of Economic History*, 50: 615– 38.

Scheidel, Walter, Morris, Ian, and Saller, Richard (2007), *The Cambridge Economic History of the Greco-Roman World* (Cambridge).

Temin, Peter (1997), 'Two views of the British Industrial Revolution', *Journal of Economic History*, 57: 63–82.

Thomas, Keith (1987), 'Numeracy in Early Modern England: the Prothero Lecture', *Transactions of the Royal Historical Society*, 5th series, 37: 103–32.

von Tunzelmann, G. N. (1978), *Steam Power and British Industrialization to 1860* (Oxford).

Wadsworth, Alfred P. and Mann, Julia de Lacy (1931), *The Cotton Trade and Industrial Lancashire, 1600–1780* (Manchester).

Ward-Perkins, Bryan (2005), *The Fall of Rome and the End of Civilization* (Oxford).

Weber, Max (1904–5), *The Protestant Ethic and the Spirit of Capitalism*, translated by Talcott Parsons (London, 1930).

Weiss, Leonard (1982), *Watch-Making in England* (London).

Wong, R. Bin (1997), *China Transformed: Historical Change and the Limits of European Experience* (Ithaca, NY).

Anthropology in the Territory of Rights, Islamic, Human, and Otherwise …

LILA ABU-LUGHOD

Columbia University

IT IS AN HONOUR to deliver the 2009 Radcliffe-Brown Lecture. On such occasions one feels a mixture of awe and discomfort: awe at the prospect of filling the shoes of, or paying tribute to, a major forefather in one's discipline; discomfort at the distance between the kind of world that anthropology was then and what it is now. Colonialism was the enabling backdrop to Radcliffe-Brown's anthropological research and theory-building, which spanned the first half of the twentieth century. The colonial condition was evident in his travels and the remarkable range of ethnographic cases he could marshal for his theories—from Australia, the Andaman Islands, and Native North America to West, South, and East Africa. It also informed, as Adam Kuper (2005)[1] has suggested in his 'alternative histories of British social anthropology', such matters as the problematic of tribes and kinship in African political order, since indirect rule was based on these, even if Radcliffe-Brown and his followers distanced themselves from the messy contact that Malinowski's rival group sought with colonial policy-makers. This larger political condition was only occasionally acknowledged in Radcliffe-Brown's more theoretically oriented investigations of social structure, kinship, law, and religion. In passing, for example, he might mention that his analysis of the role of the mother's brother in South Africa—of interest from the point of view of structural-functionalist theory—supported a decision of the Native

Read at the Academy 17 November 2009.
[1] Adam Kuper (2005) relies on the work of Benoît de L'Estoile (2004).

Proceedings of the British Academy, **167**, 225–262. © The British Academy 2010.

Appeal Court on a matter of rights to bride-wealth cattle (Radcliffe-Brown 1952: 30).

Anthropologists working today find themselves doing ethnography in a world characterised by new forms of empire—some call it liberal—that are intertwined in complex ways with the transnational hegemony of rights discourse, especially human rights. The Universal Declaration of Human Rights was issued at the twilight of Radcliffe-Brown's career and it has taken half a century for it to have become what Wilson (2006: 77) has characterised as 'a political value with global ambitions analogous to political metanarratives such as "liberal democracy" or "socialism"'. If only a few European anthropologists did ethnography of the colonial encounter, even while many worked in various ways either in tension or collaboration with colonial officials and missionaries, many anthropologists today are taking the human rights system as an explicit object of study, even as others work more or less comfortably alongside human rights advocates on behalf of subaltern communities whether in the Amazonian jungle or the Palestinian refugee camp.

I entered this territory of 'rights' not so long ago because of my consternation about the international politics of Muslim women's rights (Abu-Lughod 2002). It was the campaign to treat women's rights as human rights that brought me in contact with debates about human rights. And the advances of feminists into the international institutions and local organisations of transnational governance led me to think about rights activists as not outside power, even if the structures or imaginations of solidarity and common subordination differentiate women's rights work from some other forms of international human rights work.[2]

Perhaps because I was a late-comer and an anthropologist whose ethnographic work over thirty years had not been organised around rights, human or otherwise, I have struggled uncomfortably with the framework.[3] I want to reflect on some problems of fit I experience when I think about 'rights' in light of two kinds of ethnography I have done, one 'thick' and one 'thin'. The thick ethnography is of everyday life in a village in rural Egypt where I have worked for over fifteen years. The thin is some modest research I have done on organisations that promote women's rights in and

---

[2] Mandating women's rights as individual humans, MacKinnon (2006) plaintively charges: 'Are women human?' Yet as Janet Halley *et al.* (2006) have examined, we are witnessing now the emergence of Governance Feminism in international institutions from the UN to the World Court.

[3] I drew some implications of feminist ethnography for debates about rights in the preface to the new edition of my ethnography, *Writing Women's Worlds* (2008).

across the Muslim world. My question is: does anthropology have some-thing particular to contribute to the analysis of the growing hegemony of 'rights' as the means of addressing and redressing suffering and social injustice?

Most of the anthropological literature on rights has been on *human* rights. One could think of these developments as bookended by two strong edited volumes, one published in 2001 by Jane Cowan, Marie-Benedicte Dembour, and Richard Wilson, the other in 2009 by Mark Goodale.[4] Taking the world of rights, both conceptual and practical, as their objects, anthropologists have considered everything from rights as cultural and performative (Slyomovics 2005), through to the ways rights talk is mobi-lised (Hodgson 2002, 2003, forthcoming), the dynamics of transplanta-tion and vernacularisation of 'rights' frames, and the social machinery of the production and reproduction of rights (Merry 2006; Levitt and Merry forthcoming). Others have invoked human rights to find ways to assist indigenous communities (Robbins and Stamatopoulou 2004).

Those more critical of the rights regime and its terms range from political theorists who denounce human rights and humanitarianism as the new colonialism or interrogate the 'paradoxes' of rights at the heart of liberalism (the assertion of rights resting on and therefore ossifying iden-tities based on injury, (Brown 2004))[5] to anthropologists who interrogate the workings of rights claims and practices on the ground. Anthropologists, for example, have been sharply critical of the binds into which aboriginal Australians are placed by the demands of liberal multiculturalism and recognition (Ginsburg 2002; Povinelli 2002); others working in Africa, like Englund (2006) and Jackson (2005), writing on Malawi and Sierra

[4] As Cowan, Dembour, and Wilson (2001) note, anthropology's breakthrough has been to see the pursuit of human rights 'itself as a cultural process which impinges on human subjects and subjectivities'. In the introduction to the latter volume, Goodale (2009: 11) argues that there are three modes of anthropological engagement with human rights: making anthropological knowledge relevant for activists; developing methodologies that could 'reveal the contradictions and unintended consequences in the practice of human rights'; and criticising the misapprehensions of 'culture' in both theory and practice in the rights field. In reflecting on her earlier effort and the current state of the field, Cowan (2009: 325) calls for empirically grounded but theoretically informed studies that can force us to confront 'the messiness, contradiction, ambiguity, impasses, and the unintended consequences' that tidy theory and plans for political reform cannot anticipate.

[5] For the most sophisticated critique of 'human rights' as reducing people of the non-West to wards of a freshly laundered international order whose Western base and civilisational mission is disguised, see Asad (2003). For a classic critique that focuses on whether human rights are doing more harm than good, see Kennedy (2002; 2006 for an update).

Leone respectively, have explored the function of human rights in promoting social distinction, opening career paths, and depoliticising power
in situations where human rights discourse participates in transnational
governance and neoliberal governmentality (see also Ferguson and Gupta
2002). Some have worked on humanitarianism (e.g. Fassin 2005; Feldman
and Ticktin 2010; Redfield 2005; Ticktin 2006) while others have worried
about how human rights claims that depend on naturalised suffering dis-
place other sorts of political claims. As Lori Allen (2009: 163), who worked
with Palestinians, puts it, one problem is that 'appeals to human rights
constitute a particular kind of subject whose rights are seen to arise not
from a political status but from the state of (human) nature'.

Feminist critiques of human rights as/and women's rights have taken
various forms from Ratna Kapur's (2002) biting charge that such discourses
construct women of the so-called Third World as 'victim-subjects' to the
more Foucauldian argument that women's rights partake in a larger complex of human rights which Inderpal Grewal describes as 'a regime of truth
disseminated through transnational connectivities which came to power
as a mode of transnational governmentality producing technologies of
welfare alongside modes of disciplinary and sovereign power' (2005: 125).

Feminist anthropologists have tended instead to observe the workings
of women's rights in particular contexts, whether CEDAW Commission
hearings (Merry 2006) or local women's organisations. The development
of such organisations is often accompanied by tensions between what elite
nationals and transnational feminists, not to mention donor organisations, want and the women's priorities in their communities (Hodgson
forthcoming; Walley n.d.).[6] In an important contribution aptly titled 'Rights
inside out', Riles (2002) has shown the peculiar way women's groups in
Fiji adopted 'women's rights as human rights' as a framework, despite their
own doubts, convinced of the efficacy of a discourse that they imagined
others 'out there' found persuasive.

Despite a history of anthropologists acting as activists and advocates,
Jean-Klein and Riles (2005: 174–5) have made a strong case that anthropologists' role in the rights world should be as ethnographers.[7] They argue

---

[6] Hodgson (forthcoming), for example, gives a wonderful account of the resistance of Maasai
women's groups to pressures to focus on female genital modification; they keep insisting that their
priorities are land, livelihood, and health; they want political and economic empowerment not
the eradication of 'cultural' practices.

[7] They argue that, as anthropologists, our job is neither to denounce human rights regimes and
machineries nor to co-construct them by empathetically amplifying claims made in the name of
rights or working alongside those doing rights work—lawyers and others.

that 'Ethnography, and the commitments it demands, is in fact the only form of engagement that our profession is uniquely qualified to administer.' This is a compelling argument. But I would suggest that doing disciplined ethnography often leads to profound critiques of both the framework and practices of rights. In this lecture, I hope to illustrate this through a look at some new initiatives that are seeking to establish women's rights through Islam, whether through reform of Islamic law, particularly family law, or simply through offering interpretations of the Qur'an not driven by 'patriarchal' thought.

My ambivalence about such activist projects—diverse, innovative, and potentially transformative as they may be—arises from trying to think about them in light of what I know about women's lives in one Egyptian village where I have done ethnography for fifteen years. Such women are the imagined beneficiaries of the new Muslim feminists' efforts to guarantee women's rights through a more indigenous framework and in the spirit of contributing as insiders.[8] If I entered the territory of rights because I was critical of the way outsiders justify military, political, and economic intervention in the name of bringing rights to Muslim women (Abu-Lughod 2002), the question that now troubles me is whether these very different initiatives that are distinct from imperial projects and that distance themselves from more secular traditions of women's rights work in their regions, manage to resolve the problems of power that haunt other rights projects.

There are two parts to my argument. In a sociological vein, I ask whether such initiatives can be understood as outside the frames of global governance that are tied to class privilege and education, even though the participants work with a shared sense of religious community and, in some cases, religious knowledge that is substantial and important. Second, I ask whether any legalistic framework of 'rights', even the alternative one based on Islamic principles, guidelines and aspirations, can do justice to the complexity of women's lives and suffering. A glimpse into the lives of women in one Egyptian village leads me to suggest that there is always a certain incommensurability between everyday lives and the social imagination of rights, whether by outsiders, veterans of women's activism in the region, or these new cosmopolitan Islamic feminists.

---

[8] As Norani Othman (1999: 192), one of the founders of Sisters in Islam, explains, 'The experience of many women's groups operating in Muslim countries these past two decades demonstrates that in their daily battles a great deal more progress is achieved by working with their religious and cultural paradigm.'

I will tell only one story from the village about a case of 'domestic violence'—a classic violation of women's rights in the international language of rights and a focus of at least one of the new Muslim feminist initiatives—to try to articulate my discomfort with the application of a 'rights' frame.[9] My main concern is that, given the current geopolitical distribution of power, the rendering of women's lives in the Muslim world primarily in terms of 'rights' risks reinforcing already existing (and sometimes malicious) simplifications of their complex lives. This is the case even though most of those working to improve women's rights in these communities do not share these negative or simplistic views and even though women across the world now, even in villages such as this one in rural Egypt, use various languages of rights—hybrid and complicated—to assert claims.

I. Women's rights and Islamic reform

Several recent transnational initiatives suggest the emergence of a new social configuration and playing field for advocacy of Muslim women's rights. Building on many local initiatives in Iran, Afghanistan, Turkey, Indonesia, Lebanon, and Egypt, and responding in complex ways to the Islamic revival and the growing appeal of Muslim politics, many educated cosmopolitan Muslim women are no longer defensive about 'faith-based' feminism.[10] I want to describe two such initiatives (distinct from and contrary to the highly publicised and pernicious efforts of some individual women in the West who claim to criticise Islam 'from within') before asking how such initiatives relate to the everyday lives of women in one village.

Musawah

Musawah (equality) is one important new initiative, announced by a brochure in 2008 and then a public launch in Kuala Lumpur in February

---

[9] The focus will be on one of the key 'violations' of women's human rights that has mobilised the transnational community in recent years: domestic violence; see Grewal (2005). For a questioning of the capacity of legal language to capture the experience of violence, see Hastrup (2003).
[10] Those concerned with women's rights realised that for the 'grassroots'—their objects of concern and intended beneficiaries—the moral appeal of fidelity to Islam had never wavered, and in fact has been enhanced in the last few decades with the spread of education, media, and the growing funding of Islamic education and proselytising.

2009.[11] Calling itself 'a global movement for equality and justice in the Muslim family', it was spearheaded by the Malaysian-based feminist organisation, Sisters in Islam.[12] Registered as an NGO in 1993, SIS has been active since the late 1980s in advocacy around Muslim women's rights and discriminatory family law. It is a leading organisation in what some call Islamic feminism.[13] Musawah's goals were formulated, as its brochure states, by 'a planning committee of Muslim activists and academics from 11 countries' that included, very centrally, the prominent British-based Iranian legal anthropologist and filmmaker Ziba Mir Hosseini. The brochure notes that Musawah drew inspiration from Moroccan feminists (a major figure among whom is listed on the planning committee) who are credited with having just successfully campaigned for reform of family law.

I want to note three features of Musawah's mission statement: 'We, as Muslims and as citizens, declare that equality and justice in the family are both necessary and possible. The time for realising these values in our laws and practices is now.' First, note the 'we' as an entitlement to speak from within. Second, note the mixed religious and political identities (as Muslims and citizens) that define the rights claims. Third, consider the hybrid sources of rights they invoke in the two sentences that follow: 'Musawah declares that equality in the family is possible through a framework that is consistent with Islamic teachings, universal human rights principles, fundamental rights guarantees, and the lived realities of women and men.' Musawah's reasoning follows two principles: they prioritise the objectives (maqasid) of Shari'a rather than the legal schools as they have developed historically, and they insist that there must be a fit with the contemporary world: 'Muslim laws and practices must reflect justice, which is the indisputable objective of the Shari'ah. They must also uphold equality, which is an essential part of today's understanding of justice.'[14]

---

[11] Their website went live in conjunction with the public launch: <http://www.musawah.org/.>

[12] SIS was, according to some accounts, catalysed when theologian Dr Amina Wadud, who has since achieved fame through her books like *Inside the Gender Jihad* and through leading a mixed congregation prayer, came to teach in Malaysia (Sunder 2009). See Anwar (2005), Barlas (2005), and Al-Hibri (2000, 2000–1) for other important arguments about achieving women's rights through feminist interpretations of the Qur'an. For an overview of issues, see Badran (2009) on Islamic feminism.

[13] But Basarudin (2009: 14), writing her dissertation about SIS, describes the organisation more neutrally as those 'working from within their religious and cultural frameworks'.

[14] The statement continued, 'Today's Muslim family laws are human interpretations of the Shari'ah, based on juristic theories and assumptions. Therefore, they can change in accordance with the changing realities of time and place and contemporary notions of justice.'

According to one report from the February launch, SIS and Musawah were accused by a Malaysian group of being part of a plot by Western funders to 'liberalise Islam'. What might this mean? And what basis might there be for thinking so? On the one hand, a statement like this must be dismissed as the sort of hysteria that has become a tired feature of polemics and politicking across the Muslim world: discrediting women's rights work as a western plot in order to bolster the legitimacy of Islamist groups, conservative social forces, or states.

On the other hand, without doubting the sincerity of the participants or their seriousness of purpose, one still needs to study the framework and suppositions of the initiative. The UN Special Rapporteur on Violence against Women who gave the keynote speech at the launch used only a rights-based language, reducing religion to an aspect of 'culture'. Her only concession to the conference was to praise Musawah's 'strategy' of using a religious framework for women's rights by noting that she herself always sought to 'identify viable entry points within a given country context where change can be introduced'. What is the significance of choosing as your keynote speaker a Turkish feminist who neither invokes the authority of God nor declares her piety and who instrumentalises the religious grounds for arguing for rights?

Second, it is apparent that the generic models for Musawah are drawn as much from the ideational world of liberal international organisations as Islamic legal or moral discourse. Take its 'Framework for Action'. This is a standard element of UN campaigns. A recent example is the 2008 'Framework for Action of the UN Secretary-General's Campaign to End Violence against Women'.[15] Musawah's 'Framework for Action' is structured along the lines of documents such as the Universal Declaration of Human Rights: it has a preamble that declares principles and states the conditions, followed by a delineation of principles using the form of numbered articles. What distinguishes it from its models and marks it as a hybrid form is its religious opening line: 'We hold the principles of Islam to be a source of justice, equality, fairness and dignity for all human beings.'[16]

The third issue to consider in Musawah's construction of its reform project is its family resemblance to some political efforts from which it

[15] <http://www.un.org/en/women/endviolence/pdf/framework_booklet.pdf> (accessed 26 May 2010). In fact, Ziba Mir Hosseini (e-mail communication, 23 Aug. 2010) says that Musawah deliberately modeled their documents on the VAW campaign and explains that part of their strategy has been to persuade secular feminists to ally with them.
[16] <http://www.musawah.org/framework_action.asp> (accessed 23 May 2010).

would distance itself unequivocally. In her provocative article 'Secularism, hermeneutics, and empire: the politics of Islamic reformation', Saba Mahmood has drawn attention to the awkward relationship between liberalism and US imperial projects directed at the Muslim world (Mahmood 2006). As she notes, somewhat surprisingly for a secular state, 'the United States has embarked upon an ambitious theological campaign aimed at shaping the sensibilities of ordinary Muslims whom the State Department deems to be too dangerously inclined toward fundamentalist interpretations of Islam' (2006: 329). She argues that 'secular normativity' is not, as it avers, about separating church and state or promoting tolerance of differences but about 'remaking religious subjectivities' (p. 328) and that this can be seen in the targets of US fears (the 'traditionalist Muslim'), the goal of their reform efforts (encouraging 'moderate Islam'), and their methods, which are, as she describes them, theological. She notes, for example, that a portion of the $1.3 billion allocated to the Muslim World Outreach initiative has gone into training Islamic preachers, establishing Islamic schools that could counter the 'madrasas', and shaping the content of religious debate in the media. This is perfectly in line with the media efforts of states like Egypt to drive a wedge between a good moderate enlightened Islam and bad and wrong-headed extremism (Abu-Lughod 2005). What Mahmood argues, however, is that the partners these US initiatives have sought to encourage are those who consider themselves moderate Muslim reformers who are distinguished by the fact that they agree with the 'diagnosis that the central problem haunting Muslim societies lies in their inability to achieve critical distance between the divine text and the world'. So it is not just ideology or practice but hermeneutics that distinguishes the reformers to be encouraged from the rest of society that is dangerously literalist, ritual-bound, and in danger of being therefore attracted by the messages of extremists (2006: 330–1).

Although some might (and do) disagree strongly with her reading of the reformers' diagnosis of the problem as hermeneutical, Mahmood draws our attention to a possibly uncomfortable connection between reformist Muslim thinkers and an imperial project. The history of modern Muslim reform is complex, usually traced to the turn of the century Egyptian Muhammad 'Abduh and, in Hallaq's summary, arising from the confrontation with colonialism and the West and branching out in two directions that he characterises as utilitarian and liberal (Hallaq 1997: 207–54). If the utilitarians stripped away the history of jurisprudence and elevated the minor principle of istislah (interest or benefit) to guide legislation for modern problems and social worlds, while not forfeiting the

Qur'an and Sunna, the liberals more properly historicised the Qur'an, separating clearly the truths of religion from human interpretations. Among the latter, Hallaq names Fazlur Rahman, a modernist reformer whose projects and associations Hicks has traced carefully in new research to a Cold War effort, moving through McGill University and Harvard, to cultivate moderate Muslims (Hicks 2010). This suggests an earlier connection between US interests and Muslim reform, even if the local histories and impetuses to religious reform must be taken seriously.

The question that presents itself about the Muslim feminists who have established organisations like Musawah is whether their reformist project shares qualities of thought and argumentation with those Mahmood has described, not to mention their predecessors in North America in the 1950s and 1960s. The explicit focus of Musawah is Muslim family law. It does not engage in debates about how best to interpret the Qur'an; instead it begins with the more modest and sound observation that family laws are man-made, the result of interpretations shaped by the social conditions of the periods in which Islam's sacred texts were turned into law by jurists.[17] However, it also follows the standard modernist reformist arguments of the last century that one must seek an ethical Islam, true to its spirit and guided by the objectives of Shari'a, as noted above, and to thus make Islam appropriate for contemporary realities. The objects of their critiques are the jurists and the claims to expertise and authority of those conservatives who claim to follow them. To support its stance, Musawah reminds people of the importance of diversity of opinion in the Islamic tradition, points to specific verses of the Qur'an that promote equality and thus exposes the corruption of human interpretation (a feminist strategy that has been central in the scholarly world since the 1970s), and highlights concepts within the tradition that could support human rights.[18]

Musawah's form of argumentation is saturated with the vocabulary of democratic liberalism (which Mahmood and others label secular, though many Muslim reformers argue is integral to Islam). A key concept in Zainah Anwar's introduction to the resource book, *Wanted: Equality and Justice in the Muslim Family* (2006), is holism. She notes that women's groups in various Muslim countries 'have begun to explore a broader,

---

[17] Mir Hosseini's (2009) contribution to Musawah's resource book is 'Towards gender equality: Muslim family laws and the *Shari'ah*' but she has published widely on such issues, starting with her excellent piece in Yamani (1996) and extending to her essay in *Critical Inquiry* (2006).

[18] The latter article is by Khaled Abou Fadl, named in Mahmood's article as one of the 'good Muslims', the moderate Muslim thinkers with whom the US government wishes to partner even if they are more or less critical of US policy in the Middle East.

more holistic framework that argues for reform from multiple perspectives—religious, international human rights, constitutional and fundamental rights guarantees, and women's lived realities' (Anwar 2009: 3). One aspect of holism for Anwar is thus limiting the role of religion: she advocates treating religion as only one source for policy and legal reform. She extols pluralism and internal dissent and then goes on to argue that 'the right to define what these religious beliefs are and what role they should play in public law and policy must be open to public debate and pass the test of public reason' (Anwar 2009: 8–9). The concept of public debate and public good are certainly part of the tradition of Muslim argumentation, especially modernist reformist traditions, as noted above, but the use of 'public reason' in this context seems innovative. What concept does this translate and what discursive tradition does it index?[19]

Mahdavi Sunder (2003), a legal scholar, celebrates groups such as SIS, Women Living Under Muslim Law, and now Musawah, as heralding a New Enlightenment in the Muslim world. This suggests that at least some people associate such reform initiatives with the tradition of secular liberalism. The clever title of her blog about the Musawah launch played on, and thus reinforced in a ghostly way, a key literary text in the 'liberal' critique of the oppression of Muslim women that has been promoted so hard by neoconservatives in the US. 'Reading the Quran in Kuala Lumpur' (Sunder 2009) inflects Azar Nafisi's bestselling *Reading Lolita in Tehran* (2003).[20] Thus at least this representation of Muslim women's rights groups like Musawah reproduces the standard liberal views, both within and outside the Muslim world, that contrast religious backwardness and conservatism to enlightened modernism.

Before turning to another initiative and considering the sociology of these new groups (their metropolitan weight, their professional middle class character, and their sources of funding), I want only to point out how Sunder's analysis of what these Muslim women's groups are doing echoes uncannily the self-representations of the likes of Irshad Manji, despite the fact that Sunder and the Islamic feminist initiatives she describes take opposite views on the value of Islam (they value it) and on imperial politics (they are critics). On the Macmillan speaker's bureau website, Irshad Manji, the 'best selling author' of *The Trouble with Islam Today: a Muslim's Call for Reform in Her Faith* (2004) offers a number of

[19] Basarudin (2009) has described the launch and the issues; she notes in the piece that a part of her dissertation will discuss Musawah and Sisters in Islam.
[20] For more on Nafisi, see Alami 2006; Bahramitash 2005; Dabashi 2006; Mahmood 2008.

high fee public lectures. One is titled 'Women as the key to reforming the Muslim world'. Its summary begins: 'Women's rights are human rights. But Muslim women today still suffer profound ill-treatment. Is there something inherent to Islam that opposes women's equality? Or is the issue more cultural than religious? Above all, how can liberating the entrepreneurial talents of women be the key to reforming the Muslim world?'[21]

If Mahmood (2008: 87) is right to suggest that women like Manji 'authenticate and legitimise' anti-Muslim sentiment (the emancipatory models of their autobiographical writing tightly linked to the cultural imagination of democracy, freedom, and secular reform that justifies all forms of intervention and promotes civilisational thinking), the question is whether the more sober, sophisticated, knowledgeable, and committed Muslim feminists involved in genuinely grounded reform organisations like Musawah can keep their distance from, or avoid being appropriated by, those who glorify projects like Manji's that they abhor. As we have seen, they use some of the same available language and have at least one foot in that same international or global public sphere organised in terms of the value of human rights and/as women's rights in which these others' work circulates. This is a public sphere generally considered secular.

Women's Islamic Initiative for Spirituality and Equality

Not as far along in its institutionalisation is another initiative that dovetails with Musawah, treading some of the same pathways and having some overlapping membership. With a very different kind of institutional base and orientation, a more cosmopolitan and deterritorialised outlook, and a more explicitly religio-spiritual cast, the Women's Islamic Initiative in Spirituality and Equality (WISE) had its first public event in 2006 in New York.[22] Out of this conference came the decision to form a global women's Shura Council (consultative body) to address a perceived 'lack of women's participation in the discourses on Islamic law'. WISE is directed by Daisy Khan as part of the American Society of Muslim Advancement (formerly the American Sufi Muslim Association, ASMA, though nowhere in their materials is this acknowledged) that was founded in 1997 in New York by her husband, Imam Feisal Abdel Raouf. ASMA is closely connected to an

[21] <http://www.harrywalker.com/speaker/Irshad-Manji.cfm?Spea_ID=702> (accessed 12 October 2010).
[22] Their sophisticated new website is <http://www.wisemuslimwomen.org/> (accessed 21 May 2010).

initiative he now directs: the Cordoba Initiative dedicated to 'Muslim-West understanding' and 'bringing back the atmosphere of interfaith tolerance and respect that we have longed for since Muslims, Christians and Jews lived together in harmony and prosperity eight hundred years ago'.[23] Moderation, pluralism, toleration—these are the watchwords of liberalism and allegedly crucial in a polarised world.[24]

I was invited to participate in and observe one of WISE's preparatory meetings in 2008. This is the kind of fieldwork that anthropologists of human rights do when they work with lawyers and commissions, or observe the social processes of the bureaucracies that establish and negotiate human rights issues. What struck me most about the daylong delibera-tions was how complex, creative, and unpredictable is the process by which collective decisions are made. No sweeping critiques about rights regimes or humanitarianism as the new colonialism capture this fact. The women who gathered for this meeting brought to the table a cultural imagination formed by modernist liberal Sufi ideals, UN and human and women's rights documents, models of transnational feminist organising and activ-ism, as well as academic conferencing. They brought tools of knowledge drawn from everything from Qur'anic exegesis to feminist historiography and quantitative social science.[25]

Like any emergent organisation, especially one that seeks to be par-ticipatory and collective, WISE is evolving. Even in its short lifespan its mission has shifted as a result of participants' contesting views, constraints and funding opportunities, and the assessment of the realistic prospect of achieving certain goals. For example, although WISE initially planned to create training programmes for women in the Islamic legal traditions, it has prioritised in the short run the issuing of learned statements on women's Islamic rights that could persuade and be useful tools for other Muslim leaders and activists.

In a survey sent out to members in 2008, the steering committee had proposed five potential issues to research and then use as the testing

---

[23] See Cordoba Initiative: <http://www.cordobainitiative.org/> (accessed 21 May 2010). See Hicks (2008, 2010) for more on the cosmopolitan ideology of Sufis in New York and the work of Imam Feisal.

[24] Brown (2006) shows that contemporary liberal tolerance discourse in the US masks some unsavory politics.

[25] Even the visions of femininity were multiple. Some capitalised on the fact that the acronym WISE had a meaning: some of the women present spoke about women's wisdom as a source of authority. Others were uncomfortable with the essentialisation of femininity sometimes invoked.

ground for its first fatwa or statement (as they began to call it more neu-trally, to draw away from the negative cast of fatwa in the West and per-haps not to antagonise official sources of fatwas in different countries). The statement was to constitute the focus of the official launch of the Women's Shura Council in July 2009 in Kuala Lumpur. The membership overwhelmingly voted for two issues: domestic violence (40 per cent) and women's religious authority (31 per cent). Much less popular were the other three candidates on the ballot. These were staples of sensationalised Western media representations of negative practices in the Muslim world: female genital mutilation (FGM), honour killings, and forced marriages.

Yet in the give and take of the meeting, a consensus emerged around a slightly different focus for the Shura Council's first pronouncement. To the initial consternation of the steering committee, who felt committed to the membership they had consulted and who ultimately had responsibility for doing the preparatory work for the conference and wanted a simple and appealing issue, the free flow of discussion took the group away from the survey. A few strong personalities led them to an ambitious project: they would deal with domestic violence and violence against women more broadly, but in tandem with violent extremism. Over the course of the day and with thoughtful objections being raised by different participants to aspects of what was being proposed (for example 'How was extremist vio-lence a gendered issue?', 'Weren't there formidable analytical challenges in linking domestic and military violence?', 'Weren't the religious textual sources that would have to be brought into conversation quite diverse?', and 'Wasn't it dangerous to invoke the term jihad?'), a general enthusiasm developed for 'Jihad against Violence' as the Shura Council's first cam-paign.[26] Although the staff communicated criteria for choosing an issue—its importance to women, its likely support by women, its feasibility in terms of research, its ability to draw media attention, and the level of resistance it might provoke from traditional institutions—the outspoken professional women at this meeting, mostly academics, journalists, and lawyers, went their own way.

My ethnography, thin as it was, reveals that the outcome emerged from a lively social process, not a conspiracy or any sort of engineering. Those with strong convictions, good analyses, and experience shaped the result. Diverse in outlook and background (with family origins in South Asia, the Arab Middle East, Turkey, Iran, and the US), some were experts on

---

[26] See poster on website <http://www.wisemuslimwomen.org/pdfs/jihad-report.pdf> (accessed 21 May 2010).

Islamic law and practice, some were experts on the Qur'an and the history of Islam. Some seemed to use the vocabulary and tools of Islam strategically because of their imagined persuasive power for others; others were secure in and vocal about their conviction that the Qur'an was the word of God. Some were devout followers of Sufi Shaykhs, learned and philosophical students of the faith and veterans of interfaith dialogue. Some covered their hair, some didn't. Notably, some were sharply critical of western imperialism while others were more supportive of the US government's 'war on terror'.[27] The discussion was heated at times, but the participants remained civil and respectful over these divides. The democratic, inclusive, and positive tone set by the director helped the women work hard toward the common goal of figuring out what the Shura Council might best do.

WISE had already achieved a good deal in its two years of existence. It had a structure (diagrammed neatly in its 2008 report), a talented staff, a strategic plan and vision, and a major conference and several planning meetings under its belt. It had hammered out a Compact that, like Musawah's brochure, drew on Shari'a by grounding their commitment to women's rights in 'the six objectives [maqasid] of Shari'a—the protection and preservation of religion (al-din), life (al-nafs), the intellect (al-'aql), the family (al-nasl), property (al-mal), and dignity (al-'ird)'. These, the accompanying letter sent to the membership explained, 'have a long history in the Muslim tradition and are protections that are rooted in the Qur'anic text'.[28]

WISE had also been successful in fundraising. It had just won a €1 million grant from the Dutch Foreign Ministry's MG3 Fund, an initiative related to the third Millenium Development Goal of 'Gender Equality

---

[27] The ideological positioning of one of the most forceful women in the group placed her squarely in that camp that Mahmood called reformist. Her biographical sketch notes that she 'has spent the past decade assisting moderate Muslim communities around the world to resist the ideological onslaught of Islamic extremism. She advises both government and civic leaders on the threat posed by the extremists, as well as on policies to transform stifled Muslim societies into progressive participants of a free society.'

[28] What follows in the Compact is a series of declarations about exactly what, in these six domains, WISE women are dedicated to: in the sphere of protecting religion, for example, the Compact states, 'We are dedicated to advancing Muslim women's positions as religious and spiritual authorities.' In the sphere of the intellect, 'We are dedicated to defending Muslim women's freedom to interpret, think, and express, especially concerning Islam's primary texts.' Under property they support 'Muslim women's financial independence.' And under dignity, 'We are dedicated to empowering Muslim women to make dignified personal, familial, and career choices' <http://www.wisemuslimwomen.org/resources/> (accessed 21 May 2010).

and the Empowerment of Women'.[29] €70million went into grants for NGOs that were working on the ground to help realise this goal.[30] In seeking the grant, ASMA's WISE proposed to 'work with local and national women leaders and the organizations they work in' to provide: 'a) a global infrastructure for shared work among Muslim women's groups, organizations, institutions, and networks, b) religious context for Muslim women's dialogue about, and advocacy for, their rights, c) an institutional voice for gender equality, and d) accessible knowledge about effective ways to promote the equitable ethic of Islam'.[31] As Daisy Khan stressed at the meeting, WISE planned to facilitate and enhance the work of others, not to compete.

The meeting I attended was followed four months later by a two-day retreat at which certain principles were agreed upon. After this retreat, in its usual consultative manner, the WISE steering committee sent out to the membership a summary, built into which were survey questions again. They were to vote on how best to organise the research and disseminate findings, what slogans to use, what mode of representation to use for what was now called 'the report', and to whom the solutions proposed to the problem of violence should be addressed.

Again, there was an unanticipated outcome in terms of content and rhetorical strategy. The major breakthrough of the brainstorming meeting was to have found a way to link domestic and extremist violence.

---

[29] Ironically, at the same time one of the more extraordinary scholarly ventures of the last decade on Islam and the Muslim World lost its funding from another Dutch ministry: The Institute for the Study of Islam in the Modern World (ISIM).

[30] As the publicity for the grant notes, 'Concrete action is called for to achieve equality between women and men. As a result Dutch NGOs, companies and the Ministry of Foreign Affairs have decided to put their back into the fund.' Note the partnership between government and corporations and that PricewaterhouseCoopers and a feminist consulting firm were administering it for the Dutch government. <http://www.minbuza.nl/en/Key_Topics/Millennium_Development_Goals_MDGs/Dutch_aim_for_MDG_3/MDG3_Fund/Parties_involved> (accessed 21 May 2010).

[31] Since the grant had listed twelve countries in which it would work with women leaders and develop training programs, the instructions for drawing case studies to use in the research and statement on domestic/extremist violence for the launch cautioned participants to focus on Afghanistan, Pakistan, and Egypt. Since obtaining the grant, WISE had shifted its goals slightly, or at least made priorities. According to the invitation letter for the Kuala Lumpur 2009 launch, the conference would convene 'the first-of-its kind global Muslim women's Shura Council'; unveil 'a newly created Muslim Women's Fund, to provide funding opportunities for strategic projects'; and create a 'state of the art Muslim women's online portal' to share information. Announcement of the grant can be found at <http://www.minbuza.nl/en/Key_Topics/Millennium_Development_Goals_MDGs/Dutch_aim_for_MDG_3/MDG3_Fund/List_of_45_Projects/American_Society_for_Muslim_Advancement_ASMA> (accessed 21 May 2010).

Drawing on the Islamic tradition, the two would be linked by the question of leadership.[32] The Queen of Sheba story would be used as the organising parable. This creative choice is perhaps significant in that the Queen of Sheba is mentioned in all the Abrahamic traditions, and it is precisely this Abrahamic identity for Islam that ASMA and the Cordoba Initiative, as Hicks has argued, are actively promoting.[33] Indeed, the final digest (WISE 2009: 17–18) of the 'Jihad Against Violence' goes to the Qur'an to find 'different models of behavior in which some characters dictate reality and resort to coercion, while others—those at peace and willing to change themselves—achieve change gently'. They contrast the tyranny of Nimrod and the Pharaoh to the Queen of Sheba who in Surah 27 is powerful but noncoercive.

At this retreat, multiple models and genres of representation and argumentation were brought into play by the worldly participants who shared deep Islamic knowledge and the skills and vision of the cosmopolitan professional women Merry (2006) has described as those who get heard in transnational women's rights initiatives: they are fluent in the languages of English, rights, and bureaucratic UN-speak.[34] The document they produced had a Preamble, for example. The women also used the social science-based instruments of 'democracy'—surveys and polls. Yet at the same time, they made arguments on precisely the same ground as male religious authorities by quoting from and interpreting the Qur'an and hadith. One of the members of the steering committee is the first woman

---

[32] Interestingly, ASMA's other big initiative is to train young leaders.

[33] See Hicks (forthcoming). Daisy Khan deliberately places this initiative in an American setting, as is evident in the 2009 interview she gave to the online magazine, *Sojourners: Faith, Politics, Culture*. She stated:

> Our country was founded as a shining beacon of life, liberty, and the pursuit of happiness. For many Americans, this ideal proved true. Many other Americans, however, only lived in the shadow of this beacon. Religious women courageously stepped into this arena and shook up the status quo. Driven by faith to fight for their freedoms, women such as Harriet Tubman, Susan B. Anthony, and Amelia Boynton Robinson led some of our country's most extraordinary large-scale political and social changes, including the abolitionist, suffrage, and civil rights movements. ... [T]he passionate, courageous, and dynamic Muslim women who have dedicated their lives to the causes of justice and equality, fighting for the rights of Muslim women, are contemporary inheritors of this great American legacy of women's faith-based activism.

[34] Sally Engle Merry has written an ethnography of the transnational feminists who attend the meetings in New York, Geneva, and Beijing where the Commission on the Status of Women holds its hearings on CEDAW and where documents and platforms are tortuously composed to produce consent by delegates from many nations.

to have published an English translation of the Qur'an.[35] Even more prominently than in the case of Musawah, WISE's discourse of religious exegesis and quotation sits side by side with the generic conventions of culturally secular international rights work.

Initiatives like Musawah, WISE, and the Women's Shura Council seem to be the wave of the future. Although they build on a decades-long tradition of Muslim women's activism, some of which has been explicitly grounded in religious identity and conviction, they are finding surprisingly strong support now from western foundations and governments.[36] Their efforts are commendable, particularly in light again of recent Western alarmism about Shari'a and headscarves, represented in the

[35] A follower of the reformist Sufi thinker Seyyed Hossein Nasr, she has come under some fire for being neither an Arabic speaker nor a trained Qur'anic scholar. For more on Nasr's involvement in moderating Islam during the Cold War development of Islamic Studies in North America, see Hicks (2010).

[36] In addition to the major competitive grant from the Dutch Ministry of Foreign Affairs, WISE lists an impressive group of supporters: The United Nations Population Fund; William & Mary Greve Foundation; Rockefeller Brothers Fund; Sister Fund; Ford Foundation; Global Fund for Women; Danny Kaye and Sylvia Fine Kaye Foundation; Graham Charitable Foundation; Deak Family Foundation; Henry Luce Foundation; Elizabeth Foundation; and Ms. Foundation. Although the women participating in its projects are volunteering their time, all having professional positions in universities and elsewhere, they do get compensated for their travel to the conferences and retreats. Sisters in Islam, the Malaysian-based organisation, has also been successful in fundraising, although, again, a good deal of hard volunteer work has gone into it for years. Since 2005, for example, it has been a grantee of the Sigrid Rausing Trust, which claims to fund international human rights work; the current £100,000 sterling grant they have seems to be for establishing Musawah, the organisation discussed above.

An intriguing initiative out of North Africa that has received extensive European government funding has produced something more concrete and defined than the wide-ranging ambitions of these two organisations: a way to try to guarantee women's rights through a legitimate instrument within the Islamic tradition, the prenuptial contract. The Model Marriage Contract, published in 2008, was developed out of coordinated efforts in Morocco, Tunisia and Algeria through partnering with Global Rights, self-described as a thirty-year old international human rights advocacy organisation <http://www.globalrights.org/site/PageServer?pagename=gr_index>. The North African feminists who developed the Model Marriage Contract consulted with a wide range of ordinary women about their experiences and desires in marriage and the published contract is 'intended to guide future spouses as they draft their marriage contract by providing suggestions for topics to discuss as well as examples of clauses to stipulate'. The booklet recognises that contracts must be tailored to individual situations but insists that they should be 'rights protective for women' and should promote 'equality within marriage'. Like so many of the feminist projects of the last decade and a half that work for reform within an Islamic framework, the project found enthusiastic funding from outsiders: the United Kingdom Foreign and Commonwealth Office Global Opportunities Fund, the British Embassy in Rabat, the Norwegian Royal Ministry of Foreign Affairs, and the Norwegian Embassy in Rabat are thanked. In turn, the drafters' expertise was sought by Musawah. <http://www.globalrights.org/site/DocServer/Conditions_not_Conflict_Marriage_Contract.pdf?docID=10183> (accessed 21 May 2010).

British and Canadian outrage at Shari'a family arbitration councils, proposed bans on burqas in France and Belgium and absurd proposals such as the 'Jihad Prevention Act' introduced by a Republican in the United States House of Representatives in 2008 which would require aliens to attest that they will not advocate installing a 'Sharia law system' in the United States as a condition for entry visas and even naturalisation.[37] Moreover, as with the hysteria about NGOs in places like Egypt, where these facts of outside funding could be—and often are—blown out of proportion and used to discredit rights initiatives in the service either of the religious right or states anxious to limit independent political activity (Sakr 2004; Abdelrahman 2004, 2007), one must be cautious about making too much of foreign funding of Muslim projects of internal reform.

However, the new consensus in the international rights community and among many Muslim feminist activists and scholars that Islam and women's human rights must be reconciled and that internal reform is necessary is a phenomenon worth examining more closely. A human rights lawyer and scholar published in 2006 an important article about the crisis facing international nongovernmental organisations like Human Rights Watch and Amnesty International that have been working in the Middle East and Muslim world. Uncomfortable about how the human rights movement's rhetoric 'echoes that of the Bush administration', the dilemma facing the practitioners, she noted, was 'how the human rights movement should deal with Islamic law' (Modirzadeh 2006: 192). Current practice, she argued, was to evade the issue by beginning every report with a caveat that it would take no position on Islamic law (to appear neutral and non-imperialist) but then proceeding in the body of the report to report violations that are linked to 'rules of Islamic law' without admitting it explicitly (Modirzadeh 2006: 207). She offered three ways out of the dilemma. She was surprised, two years later, at the outcome of her assessment of the way International NGOs dealt with or avoided dealing with Shari'a. Human Rights Watch decided to create a position for an in-house Shari'a expert.[38]

---

[37] This act, presented to the Judiciary Committee, would amend the Immigration and Nationality Act by including the following: 'Any alien who fails to attest, in accordance with procedures specified by the Secretary of Homeland Security, that the alien will not advocate installing a Sharia law system in the United States is inadmissible'; 'The visa of any alien advocating the installation of a Sharia law system in the United States shall be revoked'; and the Act would even make advocating Sharia grounds for revoking naturalisation. The bill was proposed by Congressman Tom Tancredo. I thank Mahmood Mamdani for bringing this to my attention.

[38] Modirzadeh's presentation was at the workshop, 'Who's Afraid of Shari'a?' held at the *Center for the Critical Analysis of Social Difference* (co-sponsored by the *Institute for Religion, Culture,*

Twenty years ago, no one would have predicted that Muslim women's rights would be travelling so regularly in and out of Islamic law, Islamist parties, and the discourses and practices of moderation and Islamic reform among an educated and cosmopolitan professional elite.[39] Rather than question the authenticity of such projects, as an ethnographer I have been looking at some of the social, political, and economic circuits in which they participate and the multiple cultural resources they draw on to formulate their quite distinct 'rights' projects.

However, one of the most important questions an anthropologist like me with experience in rural areas and among nonelite women feels compelled to ask is how such organisations, conceived and run by educated urban elites who spend a good deal of energy studying, thinking, drafting position statements, applying for funds, and presenting Islam to the West (and the East) as something not incompatible with gender equality, relate to those in whose name and on whose behalf they work. These are what are often called 'the grassroots'. These new groups working within the framework of Islam hope to ameliorate the lives of women by finding locally and personally meaningful resources. They also hope to avoid accusations that they are importing foreign ideologies, devaluing women's commitments to being good Muslims, or not caring about God, even while most of them argue that religion is a matter of private faith. How do

---

and Public Life) at Columbia University, 3 Oct. 2008. I am grateful to Katherine Franke for bringing this job advertisement to our attention. Posted in 2007, it was for an 'Advisor on Sharia in the Women's Rights Division'. This person was to provide HRW 'with advice on the application of sharia as a legal system, the variations in its employment by states and other agents in different regions of the world, and how it is used to advance or restrict women's human rights, in areas including civil and political rights, family law, and sexuality'. The qualifications included 'deep expertise in Islamic jurisprudence and history' and 'a history of involvement with women's organizations and human rights organizations in Muslim communities'. Also required was an advanced degree, work experience, fluency in English, and advanced Arabic. Described as 'beneficial' were other linguistic talents: 'knowledge of one or more of the languages of countries in Asia, Africa, or the Middle East with substantial Muslim populations' and 'knowledge of international human rights law and experience with field research, report writing, advocacy, and media work'—in other words, the transnational language of rights. A tall order. Three feminist anthropologists I know who work on Islamic law or Muslim societies were rejected for the position; they believed that HRW had a very specific kind of candidate in mind: a more 'authentic' Muslim woman trained in Islamic legal studies, perhaps wearing a hijab. This just might be the kind of woman that the Women's Shura Council has envisioned training and that, as the President of Union Theological Seminary the Reverend Serene Jones would announce at their conference in Kuala Lumpur in 2009, her institution was prepared to help train (Elass 2009).

[39] For various treatments of women in/and Islamist parties, see Deeb (2006), Jad (2005) and Shehabuddin (2008). For more on NGOs and the introduction of debate about Shari'a in Egypt, see Abu-Lughod (2010).

these new reformist projects, with their constructions of women's rights in terms of Islamic law, spirit, and tradition, yet arising from these women's own social locations in global fields of feminist governance in which elites from the South have a very visible and prominent place, sit with or fit with the everyday lives of ordinary Muslim women in particular communities?

II. Incommensurate lives: religion in the everyday and violence in the domestic sphere

No one can pretend to 'represent' ordinary women. But I think it is fair to use some stories from one Upper Egyptian village to clarify the conundrums I face as an anthropologist trying to think about the complex terrain of women's rights in the Muslim world today. Ethnography allows us to reflect on existing frameworks for addressing Muslim women's problems that organise initiatives like WISE or Musawah or, for that matter, other international and local projects of empowerment and rights advocacy. I have found that the incommensurability between the lives of these particular 'grassroots' women and the terms in which they are being imagined in the field of rights, Islamic or otherwise, is profound.

I begin by outlining some of what religiosity or piety means to some women these days in this one Egyptian village in which I have been working for over fifteen years, drawing a picture of the varieties of and tensions among 'everyday forms of the religious life' and the ways these have changed over the past fifty years. This might clarify the particular cast and the class politics—both national and international—of the projects of Islamic reform I have been describing. One question that the juxtaposition of projects and lives raises is how far visions of a modern enlightened interpretation of the Qur'an or legal reforms guided by the 'objectives' of Shar'ia take into account the variety of meanings of Muslim religious experience in this village. A more urgent question is what authority and channels might such projects find in order to compete with existing authorities and institutions on the ground, from Sufi brotherhoods to new Islamic institutes, from teachers in Azhar schools or local kuttabs (Qur'anic schools) to popular televangelical preachers? Then I move on to a single case of 'domestic violence' in the village to ask again whether the framework of rights can begin to capture the complexity of this vexing problem in the lives of women in this village and, by extension, elsewhere.

Islam in village life is evolving and variegated. There are generational differences related to the political, social, economic and cultural transformations in Egypt over the past decades. Older women think of themselves as good Muslims and wear modest wide clothing and cover their hair. The oldest generation also still wears the traditional black wool cloak over their clothes for social visiting but this has been replaced, for the women in their forties, by the more fashionable abaya, or tailored overcoat. Although the national trend to become more strictly observant had already reached the village when I arrived in 1993, older women's regular prayers were not something new.

For the new generation, the key factors have been the simultaneous spread of the influence of education and television and the Islamic revival. They increasingly express their faith in other ways and dress differently. Some young women wear jeans and various forms of long-sleeved fashion tops or tunics. Some wear sweaters and long skirts. These are urban forms of dress that link them to Luxor and Cairo. No one would think of leaving the house without a hijab or headscarf; the more fashionable wear colourful hijabs that change with the current styles. But not all the young women are like this. Those who attend the Azhar schools, a parallel system that follows the national curriculum but includes significant Islamic studies, pull their hijabs more fully over their hair and wear long shapeless dresses (albeit of pretty fabric). These are the girls whose families prefer schooling that is not co-ed, where the fees are lower, and where religious study is more serious. Many appreciate the more plentiful opportunities for higher education because of the lower standards and the greater choices of fields to go into after secondary school.

Multiple religious activities engage girls in the village. Most girls and boys are sent from a young age to the kuttab, to learn Qur'an, as an after-school and summer holiday activity. In fact, most parents swear that the only way their kids learn to read is from the kuttab. Those who have the interest and talent continue; many of these are also in the Azhar schools where religious knowledge is valued. Through the kuttab children gain new opportunities, the most exciting of which are annual competitions held in Cairo for Qur'anic recitation. Smart and studious girls relish the trips to the capital with their group: the nine-hour train journey, the thousands of kids from all over Egypt during the day of the competition, the trips to the Zoo and the Citadel on the second day. In addition to whatever religious reward and social approbation they gain along with certificates and complete sets of the Qur'an recorded on cassette, they have a chance to win prize money. One girl in the community had come first two years in a row—she got 750 L.E. (Egyptian pounds, worth approximately £85) one time, 500 L.E. the other. This is significant for a fourteen year old, given that a local teacher might have a salary of 100 L.E. per month and someone working for the Antiquities Service, the big local employer, gets 80 L.E.

More recently, an Islamic institute for girls has opened in the next village. Young women are eagerly taking up training in religious studies both for its own sake and because it is meant to prepare them to teach in the Azhar schools where there is a shortage of women teachers. For one young woman I knew, working toward the certificate was her salvation from boredom. Having finished her vocational business degree, she had found herself stuck at home. It was hard to go from dressing up and heading off to Luxor every day to study, take exams, mix with other girls, and endure the pleasant annoyance of the boys who hung around the school, to doing housework. An avid soccer fan, she came alive cheering her teams on television. But most of her time was taken up with lonely housework that she did to relieve her mother, who herself was busy with the cows and sheep that helped supplement her husband's income from farming and stonemasonry at a Pharaonic temple. Only a marriage proposal would give her a different life since there is precious little employment in the area, especially for a girl from a poor family with no connections. While she waited for someone to come and ask for her hand—and perhaps mindful of the increasing number of young women in the village who never got asked— the religious institute gave her intellectual challenge, an unimpeachable moral claim to be out and about (after four years in the house), and possibly, later, a respectable way to make some kind of living. She could go for up to eight years; she would get a certificate after two years, then another after two more. She said she liked knowing more about her religion and she loved studying, though she was finding terribly confusing the different interpretations of the four schools of Islamic law.

All those in the Azhar schools, the kuttabs, the university courses in religious studies, and this new kind of institute were becoming knowledgeable about Islam in ways their mothers, and even fathers, were not. They were literate and they studied the Qur'an, Islamic history, exegesis and law. They were empowered by this knowledge: others in the local setting, and even their families, respected them for it. They had confidence and knew more about their rights. They were also empowered in practice as they had good reason to be out and about, independent. But the kind of religious education they were receiving was, by the standards of the US State Department initiative and the modernist reformers discussed above, distinctly traditionalist. Though the students might be equipped to understand the grounds on which arguments by Musawah or the WISE Shura

Council were being made, at least insofar as they draw on Islamic concepts and sources, it is unlikely that they will ever hear such arguments. And the interpretations of women's role in Islamic society they are hearing in such institutes is probably far from egalitarian or revolutionary, even if some key principles, such as the importance of consent to a marriage, have now become widely established among this group of young women.

This new generation is participating in forms of religious life that are in tension with the more 'popular' local traditions of religious experience and practice, some associated with the Sufi brotherhoods, that are still strong in Upper Egypt (Chih 2004). One small indication of this new conception of proper religiosity can be seen in young women's ambivalence about such practices as possession or other popular religious practices of uneducated women of an earlier generation. Funeral lamentation, traditionally an elaborate expressive form in which some women excelled, is now considered religiously wrong (*haram*) and no young women participate (Wickett 2010). Piety is becoming more and more limited to conventional prayer, fasting, and scripture.

It is women and girls like these in one village in Egypt that the cosmopolitan professional women of Musawah and the Shura Council project as the beneficiaries of their efforts to reinterpret Islam and introduce reforms in the laws governing family and marriage. These are the sorts of marginalised women and girls the grant proposals promise to train in their rights. Yet the distance between the reformers and these girls and women embedded in the particular socio-religious institutions of one village in Egypt, and similar ones elsewhere, is vast. What social and political mechanisms might bridge this?

A different gap exists between the framework used by reform organisations and these village women's imaginations of social responsibility and individual desire. To explore this, I want to unpack one case of 'domestic violence' in the village. Domestic violence is a cornerstone of women's rights work in NGOs around the world and in international forums, in recent years the splashiest issue the United Nations Development Fund for Women (UNIFEM) is promoting. It is also, as we will recall, a central element in the WISE Shura Council's first campaign, 'Jihad against Violence', and something that Musawah would treat as a key dysfunction in marriage and family that reform of Islamic family law and education about more just interpretations of Islam must address. For this part of the world, such violence—now labelled a violation of women's human rights—is generally represented as the result of tradition or patriarchal culture. If outsiders blame Islam for this 'culture' (see Abu-Lughod 2011), the Muslim feminists of Musawah or WISE are quick to argue that the fault lies in cultures that, contra the arguments of some Muslim conservatives, are based on insufficient knowledge of, or adherence to, true Islam. Islam, they want to argue, enshrines justice, equality, human dignity, and love and compassion among humans and in the family.

I want to show why village women's lives confound for me this subject of advocacy for women's rights. As an anthropologist familiar with the complicated lives of women in this one village, I stumble when I try to apply the standard feminist framing of and solutions to domestic violence. The standard idea is that patriarchy is the problem and the solutions are shelters, police training, anger management training, media campaigns to increase awareness, the development of women's rights consciousness, holding governments accountable for not protecting women, modernising or, now, increasingly looking for bases in Islam for care, love and peace within families, as the 'Jihad against Violence' campaign and Musawah's appeal to basic principles do.[40]

The case of one young woman whose situation has troubled me ever since I met her more than twelve years ago suggests the inadequacies of these analyses and solutions. I will sketch the contours of Khadija's situation to show why an anthropologist might be reluctant to mediate such an unhappy story through the language of women's rights, Islamic or otherwise.[41] Resisting the women's rights frame and exposing the poverty of the categories set by the Violence Against Women (VAW) discourses, including on 'domestic violence', her domestic life needs to be understood in terms of both global forces and local bonds of attachment and dependency.[42] I also note the special remainder, a personal circumstance that complicates her marriage further, with the goal of suggesting that there

[40] As Merry (2006) notes of successful social work projects against domestic violence in Hawa'ii, anger management for men and police training are among the practices that have been transplanted to that locale that may be helping women develop 'rights consciousness'. (See also Merry 2009.)

[41] For some examples of such projects in Egypt and Palestine, see Abu-Lughod (2010).

[42] I am not arguing with the Egyptian feminist, scholar and would-be parliamentarian Iman Bibars (2001: 170), who anticipates criticisms of her focus on battering in her study of the urban poor by saying, 'I could be accused of applying my Westernized middle-class biases in assessing, interpreting, and analysing the stories of the women interviewed in this study', but the issues came from them. 'Wife-battering is a violent and humiliating experience, as stated by the women themselves in their own words.' Then she quotes one informant who said, 'I felt like dying. I hate him and hated my life.' The question I ask, instead, is how the things these women say about their husbands or brothers or fathers are translated into the language of women's rights through the medium of reports and projects by rights advocates, and how the re-embedding transforms their own readings. I am fully aware that my own intimate rendering of Khadija's situation as an ethnographic case study may make her stories part of the rights discourse (Lazreg 2002).

may always be such particulars that confound easy generalisation. Khadija's life need not be typical to teach us something general about the relationship between everyday life and rights frames (Abu-Lughod 1993).

When I saw her mother in the spring of 2009, I learned that Khadija had just returned to her husband after a month or so living back home. This had become a pattern in her six-year marriage. Khadija was unhappy and her husband was sometimes violent. Khadija's mother was particularly galled that during her daughter's latest crisis, when her hands had been clenched and her body twisted, the husband had taken her to the local hospital and, in front of a group of people who knew them, announced loudly, 'She has the worst kind of illness there is.' I knew that, for her part, Khadija complained that her husband did not like her to leave the house or go to visit her mother. He stayed at home most of the time and would start drinking early in the morning, first coffee (when most villagers drink tea), then beer, then whisky. During this latest escape home Khadija was taken by her brother to Cairo (which neither had ever visited) to consult a psychiatrist recommended to them by a European expatriate neighbour. The doctor, according to Khadija's mother, had talked with her at length and told her there was nothing wrong with her except unhappiness. He advised her to come talk to him every three days. And to leave her husband.

As Khadija's mother explained, neither was possible. There was no way her family could afford to stay in Cairo or pay the psychiatrist's fees. Even the medicine he had prescribed was expensive. They could not afford to refill the prescription. But why couldn't Khadija leave her husband? Her mother put it starkly: she has two children already, and one on the way. Who would support them? How could she bring them with her to stay in their crowded house? Khadija's mother and father were long divorced. Khadija's mother lived with and was supported by her brother, along with her son, her parents, her widowed sister-in-law and her three children. This maternal uncle of Khadija's was the only one in the family with a job, and since it was as a teacher it paid little. Khadija's father had little work and had a new family to support.

The vectors of oppression that consign Khadija to remaining in a conflictual and violent marriage can be traced here not so much to traditional forms of gender inequality but to the poverty that is a result of local family histories and larger political economic transformations that for a century at least have concentrated wealth in the capital and the north of Egypt and that now, thanks to neoliberal reform, organise the distribution of property and welfare in even more unequal ways. Global inequalities that have their own colonial and contemporary histories have positioned places like Egypt in certain ways too, condemned to endemic poverty.

Financial and social pressure had certainly made Khadija feel vulnerable and tense in the months before her wedding. She had confessed to me that she felt so much pressure because they were having trouble getting the bride's family's share of the marital goods purchased. Marriage is notoriously expensive and burdensome across Egypt since the groom's and bride's families must provide everything for the marriage at the beginning.[43] As is customary, she was expected to furnish the kitchen goods while the groom provided the house and furniture, as well as her gift of gold jewellery. If she didn't bring the expected contribution to the marital home, people would gossip, she said bitterly: 'People have nothing else to do here, no work, so all they do is talk about everyone else.'

The global, national, and local dynamics of inequality that have placed the poor under such pressure also have had a peculiar impact on Khadija's marriage because of how they have shaped her husband's life. Why does he drink in a community where most people do not and where religion specifically proscribes it? He and his brothers were among the first men in the village in this region of Egypt where Pharaonic sites have attracted Western tourists and archaeologists for a century to get involved in tourism in the period after feminism, women's employment, and other transformations in Europe and the United States had made independent women active participants in the global tourist industry.[44] As a youth he mixed with tourists, drank with the foreigners, and took up with European women. Like many of the young men in the area who have done this in the last twenty-five years or so, he become involved with an older European divorcee (Mitchell 1995; Van der Spek 2010). These men have found a new way to make a living without migrating. The European and American women build them houses; buy them taxis; partner with them to run hotels; and occasionally take them home with them.

Khadija's husband has had an Austrian 'friend' for twenty years. He goes to visit her in Europe in the summer and she comes to visit in the winter. Sometimes she brings her grown son, which shocks some village women, although everyone these days is having to come to terms with

---

[43] This has led to what is often called a 'marriage crisis' and has delayed marriage for many men and left many women unmarried. Khadija felt rushed into things; her aunt was helping out financially but they were having to buy most things on credit. For more on the marriage crisis, see Singerman (2007), Hasso (2010).

[44] Enloe (1989) has drawn our attention to the shifting gender dynamics produced from mass tourism by European and North American women.

such lucrative transnational arrangements. Like most local men, Khadija's husband had wanted to start a family. When he had saved up enough, he married this local girl. It was not surprising that Khadija's husband had chosen her, much younger, to start his own family. His mother seems to have been involved in arranging the match since she is always the one who intervenes to persuade Khadija to return. He built a house for Khadija in 2001 but didn't tell his Austrian friend. These kinds of situations can be difficult for all concerned. The tricky time for everyone seems to be when she comes to visit. Some people say that at first she didn't know the truth. Now that she knows, others say, she is jealous. Khadija's mother, though, six years into the marriage, insists that the Austrian 'wife' adores his children and walks proudly around the village hand in hand with his little boy. Everyone in the village notes with a certain respect that this woman, unlike many of those duped, had made sure that the house she built was legally in only her own name. Her relative wealth and European status confound norms of gendered power, perhaps compromising his masculine standing. Khadija's husband, everyone comments, is docile around this woman. Might he be compensating in this marriage to the much younger and more vulnerable Khadija? I can only speculate. What is apparent, and significant for my arguments, is that domestic violence in this case is anything but traditional: it is produced in the nexus of the global field of European/ Third World tourism and inequality in which villagers have been involved for a long time, including the alcohol that is so taken for granted in the European circles in which men like Khadija's husband travel.

Intimate knowledge of Khadija's circumstances furthermore reveals that the 'domestic violence' Khadija suffers in her marriage must be understood in terms of something else, beyond the compulsions of poverty and the fallout of global inequalities I have outlined. There is also kinship. Because it turns out that Khadija's husband is a precariously well-off relative whose marriage to a troubled cousin from a broken home may also have been a way to help out these poor relations. Khadija had been engaged briefly to someone outside the extended family but that had fallen through. It could well be that this marriage had been arranged to protect his cousin from spinsterhood and give her a more comfortable life than she otherwise would have. Khadija was attractive, but this marriage may have been something of a protection and a gift—to Khadija and her family.

In this aspect of her life, there seems to be something of a repetition (with a more unfortunate outcome) of Khadija's own grandmother's history. Khadija's grandparents, who were cousins, had married for the same reason—as a way to make sure her grandmother was cared for. She had been possessed by spirits at the age of twelve or thirteen and was a volatile young woman who ran off to saint's tombs and Sufi centres. Although many young men had wanted to marry this beautiful girl, their mothers and family would forbid them, knowing that she ran off to religious sanctuaries and was not normal. So finally her cousin had married her, taking on the life-long responsibility for caring for her. He got her treated at a psychiatric hospital. She got much better (after electric shock therapy) but he was warned that no one should upset her. She was stable for about ten years but then reverted to her religious practices, running off and leaving her family for periods of time. Khadija's father, who was her son, himself has had a history of abusive behaviour, much worse when he was married to Khadija's mother. He was not good to his children from this first marriage, though his second marriage has been smooth and his three children from that marriage are fine. The difference in the two stories is that Khadija's grandfather was kind to his wife and loving to his daughters. Khadija was not so fortunate in her husband but her relationship with him cannot be disentangled from the family bonds of attachment and dependency that help keep her in the marriage.

This story suggests that not only must we see Khadija's difficult marital situation as something that the language of violations of women's rights in traditional patriarchal culture cannot begin to describe, overdetermined as it is by global dynamics and more intimate family dynamics, but also that there might be a further complication—a sort of 'remainder'—outside the social, cultural, or economic. It may be that her husband's violence toward her, or her inability to extricate herself from the marriage, are not the main sources of her wretchedness. Long before she was married, she was subject to crises regularly covered up by her close kin in the face of village gossip, explained in various ways by different people close to her, and leading her to be subjected to various medical interventions, the Cairo psychiatrist being only the latest.

I will never forget the day I stopped in to see her family just a week before the first of what would become several planned wedding dates. I found a terrible situation. Khadija was lying on the couch. Her tongue was swollen and she couldn't speak. She was dazed and in pain. Her mother, worried sick about her again, had this time taken her to an irresponsible specialist, an expensive neurosurgeon who flew in from Cairo once a week. Allegedly, he had talked very briefly with Khadija and then prescribed medicines and administered an injection that knocked her out. Enmeshed, as all Egyptians are now, in a flawed medical system driven by the politics of expertise, profit, and the pharmaceutical industry, this was not the first or last time Khadija would fail to be helped by medical intervention, just as she had not been helped by forms of religious healing her concerned mother had pursued earlier.

What then are we to make of Khadija's problem of 'domestic violence' given the complex bonds of protection and constraint that kinship introduces to her marriage, her husband's oddly international circumstances, the various aspects of globally regulated poverty that foreclose her options, the uneven reach of an inadequate medical system, and the demons she lives with, whether they are the result of childhood trauma, inherited mental illness, or parasites and anaemia, as the various interpretations circulating in and out of the family suggest? Can the framework of rights, even if expressed in the new more 'indigenous' initiatives to reform Muslim family law or to promote and publicise gender egalitarian interpretations of the Qur'an, capture the complexity of her life situation? Does a 'rights-based' approach enable us to disentangle the strands of her suffering or offer a solution to her complicated problems? Does it appreciate the everyday compulsions of 'social forms and moral norms' (Cowan 2009: 312)?

Women in the village used other frameworks for judging and analysing Khadija's unhappy situation. They had a variety of opinions about and levels of empathy with Khadija. When asked why Khadija didn't leave her husband, they might explain that she didn't want to end up like her mother, divorced and raising two kids on her own. Or that she didn't want her children to grow up, as she had, without the love of a father. Others mentioned that she had wanted to marry this particular man, knowing full well his situation and his drinking problem. It was her choice and therefore she had some responsibility to make it work. Some women put some blame on her for being overly sensitive, contrasting Khadija's flighty mother who had provoked violence to Khadija's father's calm second wife who had managed just fine to get along with her husband. Once I asked Khadija's aunt why, if she believed her brother was mentally ill and knew that he could be violent, she hadn't warned this woman's family. She said she had actually gone to see them, fully intending to. But then she saw how happy they were. They were extremely poor and the bride was no longer young; they had despaired of anyone coming to ask for her hand. So she hadn't had the heart to tell them. And everything had turned out fine, she added: he had three lovely children and was not violent with this wife.

The frameworks they used were drawn from local ways of understanding the many sorts of difficult situations in which women find themselves.

Some were religious, having to do with patience and fate. Others were based on intimate knowledge of what women value and a fuller recognition of the messiness of what is possible in life. They were quick to point out to me that Khadija had sought her third pregnancy. Did this suggest to them a comprehensible desire, even will, to stay in the marriage and to have a family life—a value that remains unquestioned in their social world, even if its realisation is so often fraught? Six months after Khadija's crisis and trip to Cairo, in fact she had delivered safely a lovely baby girl. Khadija's mother confided happily that from the moment of the birth of this child, Khadija's husband had stopped drinking completely. He had become pious, observing Ramadan for the first time in decades. Others told me that he had been very ill and the doctor had warned him that if he did not quit drinking, he would have complete liver failure. There was now marital harmony.

III. Conclusion

Through juxtaposing a set of social and moral relations in one Egyptian village to another set of relations that constitute new and interesting forms of rights activism by Muslim women working explicitly within an Islamic framework, I have tried to use ethnography to reveal both the inadequacy of any kind of global rights discourse to assess or judge the lives of those it seeks to redeem and the necessity of being specific about the social and political locations of activists who work in the name of rights. It is not my intention to dismiss or denigrate individual efforts on behalf of women or any of the forms of activism organised in the name of improving women's (human or Islamic) rights. I see these new projects of Islamic feminism, for example, like the more secular women's rights projects before them, as having mobilised concerned, hard-working, creative, committed and in this case learned individuals. And I do not deny that they may indeed contribute to improving lives by making certain critiques of social inequality and social injustice possible—or provide some legal and moral remedies for intractable problems. Elsewhere I have described the ways that some village women now deploy multiple vocabularies of rights—drawn from the national political and legal sphere, from local familial and religious norms and practices, and from knowledge of Islamic law and texts—to make claims when they feel wronged (Abu-Lughod 2010).

However, I insist that in addition to being more attentive to the intersection of rights work with global and class inequalities, and being more realistic about what rights work actually produces in the world (especially for those whose business it becomes) by way of careers, social distinctions, public discourse, new social and financial circuits, documents, legal debates, travel opportunities, intellectual excitement and even hope, we ought to be vigilant about the limits and locations of the vocabularies and hybrid imaginations of 'rights'.

Some have argued that as anthropologists we should take the 'social practice of rights as an object of ethnographic inquiry' (Goodale 2006: 3; Wilson 1997). I have done some of that both in this lecture and elsewhere (Abu-Lughod 2009, 2010). But what I have tried to show in particular here is that anthropology can uncover, especially when it juxtaposes the discourses and social practices organised around rights with the everyday lives of some of the intended objects of rights efforts, the inadequacy of rights as a gloss for the lives of 'others' and the inevitability of its intellectual tools being inextricable from the socially located political projects of the people and groups who deploy them.

For me, as an anthropologist, reducing the poignant and complex lives of women to a question of rights—whether women's or human—is unsatisfying. Partly this is because the lives of the unschooled or the poor or the rural seem to be more regularly rendered legible through the legalistic discourse of rights—or their violation—than the lives of the rest of us. Partly it is because their rights are usually represented as violated because of their cultures. Don't Khadija and others in her village have complex feelings, tangled relations, and dreams even as they manoeuvre within their circumstances and constraints, and explore the creative possibilities open to them in this hamlet in Upper Egypt?[45] Aren't they as much part of a complex modern global economy and culture as we are? Who has the power to reduce them to subjects known only by their deficits in rights, with the answers—in development, empowerment, women's rights, human rights, or Islamic reform, known in advance by others?

---

[45] The short stories of the Canadian writer Alice Munro about the everyday lives of women are a model for me—the opposite of what a rights discourse can do to gloss the lives of women. She captures exquisitely their desperate searches for meaning or happiness in and out of marriage. She writes hauntingly about the compromises they make in life, the ambivalences they can't escape, the desires and dreams that die. She quietly draws out the sudden strength of character or the impulsive transgression, the misunderstandings between those who love, the ties that strangle, the lies that poison, and the judgements and solaces of social convention and religion. As I have argued in *Writing Women's Worlds* (Abu-Lughod 1992/2008) one problem is that we do not balance rights discourse or social science discourse with this humanising discourse when it comes to those who are culturally distant.

What social capital enables such projects of bringing rights to the Third World poor?[46]

This is not a matter for moral judgement but social analysis. Ethnography helps us uncover activities, relationships, cultural imaginations, and social locations in a world riven by patterned difference. I am aware of the ironies of a privileged scholar invoking the lives of poor rural women to comment on the gap between such lives and the visions put forth by other privileged educated cosmopolitans, in this case Muslim women activists who write sophisticated articles, take online surveys, arrange conference dates in New York and Kuala Lumpur on GoogleCalendar, discuss feminist strategies used by activists in Geneva and Iran, quote fluently from the Qur'an, invoke precedents from early Muslim history, seek training in Islamic jurisprudence, propose model marriage contracts and other reforms of personal status codes, and draw on a wide range of experiences of organising for change in their nations of origin and abroad. My excuse is that a devotion to observation rather than intervention in village lives has made me sensitive about the complexity and even the richness of the 'objects' of their concerns, and the global inequalities that make them vulnerable to intervention, imagined or actual.

The world in which I most want to intervene with my scholarship is the world of the privileged in which I participate as an equal. I began this lecture with Jean-Klein and Riles's compelling argument that the role of anthropologists is to do ethnography in the world of rights. They propose, beyond this, that our self-disciplined ethnography should be oriented toward anthropological knowledge production (Jean-Klein and Riles 2005: 174–5).[47] I would not want to forfeit ethnography's wider potential for intervening. But I believe that in light of the hegemony and global reach of rights work and right talk, this intervention should be into the worlds of power that authorise, shape, and naturalise rights work and the understandings of human social life to which it gives rise.

---

[46] I am not the first to suggest the inadequacy of 'women's rights' as a gloss or solution in Egypt. In her study of poor urban women in Cairo, another anthropologist, Heba El Kholy (2002: 25–6), also refuses this concept because of 'the subtle, elusive, overlapping, and diffuse nature of the constraints on women, the intermeshing of exploitation and reciprocity, the fluctuations of their power due to life cycle changes, and the lack of a clear person, group, or class to confront'.

[47] 'What', Jean-Klein and Riles (2005: 174) add, can 'anthropological encounters with human rights contribute to the development of our discipline?'

Note: I am grateful to Havva Guney Ruebenacker, Rosemary Hicks, Daisy Khan, James King, and Ziba Mir Hosseini for insights into Islamic feminist projects; to Jane Cowan, Ayse Parla, and participants in (1) the 'Liberalism and its Others' project of the Center for the Critical Analysis of Social Difference and the Institute for Religion, Culture, and Public Life at Columbia University, (2) the Postcolonial Legal Orders Seminar at Harvard Law School (especially Janet Halley and Duncan Kennedy), (3) my feminist reading group, and (4) the British Academy where I presented an earlier version of this lecture, for helpful comments; to Ali Atef, Amina Ayad, Sara Layton, and Nikolas Sparks for research assistance; and to my friends in the village in Egypt who have shared their lives and thoughts with me and enabled me to think critically about rights. I am grateful to the Carnegie Foundation for enabling this research by naming me a Carnegie Scholar from 2007 to 2009. The views expressed here are solely my own.

References

Abdelrahman, M. (2004), *Civil Society Exposed: the Politics of NGOs in Egypt* (London).

Abdelrahman, M. (2007), 'The nationalisation of the human rights debate in Egypt', *Nations and Nationalism*, 13: 285–300.

Abu-Lughod, L. (1993/2008), *Writing Women's Worlds* (Berkeley, CA).

Abu-Lughod, L. (2002), 'Do Muslim women really need saving? Anthropological reflections on cultural relativism and its others', *American Anthropologist*, 104: 783–90.

Abu-Lughod, L. (2005), *Dramas of Nationhood: the Politics of Television in Egypt* (Chicago, IL).

Abu-Lughod, L. (2008), 'New preface for the twenty-first century', in *Writing Women's Worlds* (Berkeley, CA).

Abu-Lughod, L. (2009), 'Dialects of women's empowerment: the international circuitry of the Arab Human Development Report 2005', *International Journal of Middle East Studies*, 41: 83–103.

Abu-Lughod, L. (2010), 'The active social life of Muslim women's rights: a plea for ethnography, not polemic, with cases from Egypt and Palestine', *Journal of Middle East Women's Studies*, 10: 1–45.

Abu-Lughod, L. (2011), 'Seductions of the "Honor Crime"', *Differences*.

Alami, L. (2006), 'The Missionary Position'. [Online] *The Nation* (published 1 June 2006). Available at: <http://www.thenation.com/doc/20060619/lalami> (accessed 2 September 2009).

Allen, L. (2009), 'Martyr bodies in the media: human rights, aesthetics, and the politics of immediation in the Palestinian intifada', *American Ethnologist*, 36: 161–80.

Anwar, Z. (2005), 'Sisters in Islam and the struggle for women's rights', in F. Nouraie-Simone (ed.), *On Shifting Ground: Muslim Women in the Global Era* (New York), pp. 233–47.

Anwar, Z. (2009), 'Introduction: Why equality and justice now?'. [Online], in Z. Anwar (ed.), *Wanted: Equality and Justice in the Muslim Family*, pp. 1–9. Available at: <http://www.musawah.org/background_papers.asp> (accessed 25 May 2010).

Asad, T. (2003), 'Redeeming the 'human' through human rights', *Formations of the Secular: Christianity, Islam, Modernity* (Stanford, CA), pp. 127–58.

Badran, M. (2009), *Feminism in Islam* (Oxford).

Bahramitash, R. (2005), 'The war on terror, feminist orientalism, and orientalist feminism: case studies of two North American bestsellers', *Critique: Journal of Middle Eastern Studies*, 14: 223–37.

Barlas, A. (2005), 'Globalizing equality: Muslim women, theology, and feminism', in F. Nouraie-Simone (ed.), *On Shifting Ground: Muslim Women in the Global Era* (New York), 91–110.

Basarudin, A. (2009), 'Musawah movement: seeking equality and justice in Muslim family law'. [Online] *CSW Update Newsletter, UCLA.* Available at: <http://repositories.cdlib.org/csw/newsletter/Mar09_Basarudin> (accessed 10 September 2009).

Bibars, I. (2001), *Victims and Heroines: Women, Welfare and the Egyptian State* (London).

Brown, W. (2004), ' "The most we can hope for . . .": human rights and the politics of fatalism', *Southern Atlantic Quarterly*, 103: 451–63.

Brown, W. (2006), *Regulating Aversion* (Princeton, NJ).

Chih, R. (2004), 'The Khalwatiyya Brotherhood in rural Upper Egypt and Cairo', in N. Hopkins and R. Saad (eds.), *Upper Egypt: Identity and Change* (Cairo), pp. 157–68.

Cordoba Initiative (2008), *Our Mission.* [Online] Available at: <http://www.cordobainitiative.org/?q=content/our-mission> (accessed 2 September 2009).

Cowan, J. (2009), 'Culture and rights after *Culture and Rights*', in M. Goodale (ed.), *Human Rights: an Anthropological Reader* (Oxford), pp. 305–31.

Cowan, J., Dembour, M., Wilson, R. (eds.) (2001), *Culture and Rights: Anthropological Perspectives* (Cambridge).

Dabashi, H. (2006), *Native Informers and the Making of Empire.* [Online] Ahram Weekly (published 1–7 June). Available at: <http://weekly.ahram.org.eg/2006/797/special.htm> (accessed 2 September 2009).

Deeb, L. (2006), *An Enchanted Modern* (Princeton, NJ).

Elass, R. (2009), *Conference told of plan for female muftis.* [Online]. Available at: <http://www.wisemuslimwomen.org/images/uploads/2009_WISE_Conference_Report.pdf> (accessed 14 October 2010).

Englund, H. (2006), *Prisoners of Freedom: Human Rights and the African Poor* (Berkeley, CA).

Enloe, C. (1989), *Bananas, Beaches and Bases* (Berkeley, CA).

Fassin, D. (2005), 'Compassion and repression: the moral economy of immigration policies in France', *Cultural Anthropology*, 20: 362–87.

Feldman, I. and Ticktin, M. (eds.) (2010), *In the Name of Humanity: the Government of Threat and Care* (Durham, NC).

Ferguson, J. and Gupta, A. (2002), 'Spatializing states: toward an ethnography of neoliberal governmentality', *American Ethnologist*, 29: 98–110.

Ginsburg, F. (2002), 'Screen memories: resignifying the traditional in indigenous media', in F. Ginsburg, L. Abu-Lughod, and B. Larkin (eds.), *Media Worlds* (Berkeley, CA), pp. 39–57.

Goodale, M. (2006), Introduction to 'Anthropology and human rights in a new key', *American Anthropologist*, 108: 1–8.

Goodale, M. (2009), 'Toward a critical anthropology of human rights', in M. Goodale (ed.), *Human Rights: an Anthropological Reader* (Oxford), 372–94.

Goodale, M. (ed.) (2009), *Human Rights: an Anthropological Reader* (Oxford).

Grewal, I. (2005), '"Women's rights as human rights": the transnational production of global feminist subjects', in I. Grewal, *Transnational America: Feminisms, Diasporas, Neoliberalisms* (Durham, NC), pp. 121–57.

Hallaq, W. (1997), *A History of Islamic Legal Theories* (Cambridge).

Halley, J., Kotiswaran, P., Shamir, H. and Thomas, C. (2006), 'From the international to the local in feminist legal response to rape, prostitution/sex work, and sex trafficking: four studies in contemporary governance feminism', *Harvard School of Law and Gender*, 29: 335–423.

Hasso, F. S. (2010), *Consuming Desires: Family Crisis and the State in the Middle East* (Stanford, CA).

Hastrup, K. (2003), 'Violence, suffering and human rights: anthropological reflections', *Anthropological Theory*, 3: 309–23.

Al-Hibri, A. (2000), 'Deconstructing patriarchal jurisprudence in Islamic law', in A. Davis (ed.), *Global Critical Race Feminism: An International Reader* (New York), pp. 221–30.

Al-Hibri, A. (2000–1), 'Muslim women's rights in the global village', *Journal of Law and Religion*, 37: 37–66.

Hicks, R. (2008), 'Translating culture, transcending difference? Cosmopolitan consciousness and Sufi sensibilities in New York City after 2001', *Journal of Islamic Law and Culture*, 10/3: 281–306.

Hicks, R. (2010), 'Creating an "Abrahamic America" and Moderating Islam: Cold War political economy and cosmopolitan Sufis in New York after 2001', Ph.D. thesis, Columbia University, NY.

Hicks, R. (forthcoming), 'Comparative religion and the cold war transformation of Indo-Persian mysticisms into liberal Islamic modernity', in M. Dressler and A. Mandair (eds.), *The Politics of Religion Making* (New York).

Hodgson, D. (2002), 'Introduction: comparative perspectives on the indigenous rights movement in Africa and the Americas', *American Anthropologist*, 104: 1037–49.

Hodgson, D. (2003), 'Women's rights as human rights: women in law and development in Africa', *Africa Today*, 49(2): 1–26.

Hodgson, D. (forthcoming), '"These are not our priorities": Maasai women, human rights and the problem of culture', in D. Hodgson (ed), *Gender and Culture at the Limit of Rights* (Philadelphia, PA).

Jackson, M. (2005), *Existential Anthropology* (New York).

Jad, I. (2005), 'Between religion and secularism: Islamist women of Hamas', in F. Nouraie-Simone (ed.), *On Shifting Ground* (New York), pp. 172–98.

Jean-Klein, I. and Riles, A. (2005), 'Introducing discipline: anthropology and human rights administrations', *Political and Legal Anthropology Review, 28:* 173–202.

Kapur, R. (2002), 'The tragedy of victimization rhetoric: resurrecting the native subject in international/postcolonial feminist legal politics', *Harvard Human Rights Law Journal*, 15: 1–38.

Kennedy, D. (2002), 'The international human rights movement: part of the problem?', *Harvard Human Rights Journal*, 15: 245–67.

Kennedy, D. (2006), 'Humanities and human rights: critiques, language, politics', *PMLA*, 121: 1656–7.

Khan, D. (Feb. 2009), *Balancing Traditions and Pluralism: An Interview with Muslim Leader Daisy Khan.* [Online] *Sojourners: Faith, Politics, Culture.* Available at: <http://www.sojo.net/index.cfm?action=magazine.article&issue=soj0902&article =balancing-tradition-and-pluralism&cookies_enabled=false> (accessed 10 September 2009).

El-Kholy, H. (2002), *Defiance and Compliance: Negotiating Gender in Low-Income Cairo* (New York).

Kuper, A. (2005), 'Alternative histories of British social anthropology' *Social Anthropology*, 13: 43–76.

Lazreg, M. (2002), 'Development: feminist theory's cul-de-sac', in K. Saunders, *Feminist Post-Development Thought* (London), pp. 123–45.

de L'Estoile, B. (2004), 'L'Afrique comme laboratoire', doctoral thesis, EHESS, Paris.

Levitt, P. and Merry, S. (forthcoming), 'Making women's human rights in the vernacular: navigating the culture/rights divide', in D. Hodgson (ed.), *Gender and Culture at the Limit of Rights* (Philadelphia, PA).

MacKinnon, C. (2006), *Are Women Human?* (Cambridge, MA)

Mahmood, S. (2006), 'Secularism, hermeneutics, and empire: the politics of Islamic reformation', *Public Culture*, 18: 323–47.

Mahmood, S. (2008), 'Feminism, democracy, and empire: Islam and the war of terror', in J. Scott (ed.), *Women's Studies on the Edge* (Durham, NC), pp. 81–114.

Manji, I. (2004), *The Trouble with Islam Today* (New York).

Merry, S. E. (2006), *Human Rights and Gender Violence: Translating International Law into Local Justice* (Chicago, IL).

Merry, S. E. (2009), *Gender Violence: a Cultural Perspective* (Chichester).

Mir Hosseini, Z. (1996), 'Stretching the limits', in M. Yamani (ed.), *Feminism and Islam* (New York), pp. 285–319.

Mir Hosseini, Z. (2006), 'Muslim women's quest for equality: between Islamic law and feminism', *Critical Inquiry*, 32: 629–45.

Mir Hosseini, Z. (2009), 'Towards gender equality: Muslim family laws and the Shari'ah. [Online] in Z. Anwar (ed.), *Wanted: Equality and Justice in the Muslim Family*, 23–63. Available at: <http://www.musawah.org/background_papers.asp> (accessed 25 May 2010).

Mitchell, T. (1995), 'Worlds apart: an Egyptian village and the international tourist industry', *Middle East Report*, 196 (September–October): 8–11, 23.

Modirzadeh, N. (2006), 'Taking Islamic law seriously: INGOs and the battle for Muslim hearts and minds', *Harvard Human Rights Journal*, 19: 191–233.

Modirzadeh, N. (2008), Presentation at the workshop, 'Who's Afraid of Shari'a?', held at *Center for the Critical Analysis of Social Difference*, Columbia University, 3 October 2008.

Nafisi, A. (2003), *Reading Lolita in Tehran* (New York).

Othman, N. (1999), 'Grounding human rights arguments in non-western culture: *shari'a* and the citizenship rights of women in a modern Islamic state', in J. R. Bauer and D. A. Bell (eds.), *The East Asian Challenge for Human Rights* (Cambridge), pp. 169–92.

Povinelli, E. (2002), *The Cunning of Recognition* (Durham, NC).

Radcliffe-Brown, A. R. (1952), *Structure and Function in Primitive Society* (New York).

Redfield, P. (2005), 'Doctors, borders, and life in crisis', *Cultural Anthropology*, 20: 328–61.

Riles, A. (2002), 'Rights inside out: the case of the women's human rights campaign', *Leiden Journal of International Law*, 15: 285–305.

Robbins, B. and Stamatopoulou, E. (2004), 'Reflections on culture and cultural rights', *South Atlantic Quarterly*, 103: 419–34.

Sakr, N. (2004), 'Friends or foe? Dependency theory and women's media activism in the Arab Middle East', *Critique: Critical Middle Eastern Studies*, 13: 153–74.

Shehabuddin, E. (2008), *Reshaping the Holy: Development, Democracy, and Muslim Women in Bangladesh* (New York).

Singerman, D. (2007), 'The economic imperatives of marriage: emerging practices and identities among youth in the Middle East', Middle East Youth Initiative Working Paper (Wolfensohn Center for Development at the Brookings Institution and Dubai School of Government).

Slyomovics, S. (2005), *The Performance of Human Rights in Morocco* (Philadelphia, PA).

Sunder, M. (2003), 'Piercing the veil', *The Yale Law Journal*, 112: 1401–72.

Sunder, M. (2009), *Reading the Quran in Kuala Lumpur*. [Online] University of Chicago Law School. Faculty Blog (published 16 February 2009). Available at: <http://uchicagolaw.typepad.com/faculty/2009/02/reading-the-quran-in-kuala-lumpur.html> (accessed 13 July 2009).

Ticktin, M. (2006), 'Where ethics and politics meet: the violence of humanitarianism in France', *American Ethnologist*, 33: 33–49.

United Nations Development Fund for Women (UNIFEM), *United Nations Secretary-General's Campaign to End Violence Against Women*. [Online] Available at: <http://endviolence.un.org/framework.shtml> (accessed 2 September 2009).

United Nations Development Programme. *Goal 3: Promote Gender Equality and Empower Women*. [Online] Available at <http://www.undp.org/mdg/goal3.shtml> (accessed 2 September 2009).

Van der Spek, K. (2010), *The Modern Neighbors of Tutankhamun—History, Life and Work in the Villages of the Theban West Bank* (Cairo).

Wickett, E. (2010), *For the Living and the Dead: the Funerary Laments of Upper Egypt, Ancient and Modern* (London).

Wilson, R. (ed.) (1997), *Human Rights, Culture and Context: Anthropological Perspectives* (London).

Wilson, R. (2006), 'Afterword to "Anthropology of human rights in a new key: the social life of human rights"', *American Anthropologist*, 108: 77–83.

WISE. WISE Brochure. [Online] Available at: <http://www.asmasociety.org/wise/wise2009-brochure.pdf> (accessed 2 September 2009).

WISE (2009), *Jihad Against Violence: Muslim Women's Struggle for Peace*. [Online] Digest. Available at: <http://www.wisemuslimwomen.org/pdfs/jihad-report.pdf> (accessed 25 May 2010).

Wadud, A. (2006), *Inside the Gender Jihad* (Oxford).

Walley, C. (n.d.), *What We Women Want: an Ethnography of Transnational Feminism*. Unpublished book MS.

Shitao (1642–1707) and the Traditional Chinese Conception of Ruins

WU HUNG

University of Chicago

SHITAO IS ONE OF THE most celebrated painters in Chinese history. Born two years before the fall of the Ming in 1644, his relationship with the bygone dynasty was more spiritual than political, and his identity as a 'leftover subject' (*yimin*) was complicated by his shifting religious affiliation with Buddhism, Daoism, and Confucianism. Except for a short stay in Beijing, he spent most of his life in the lower Yangzi River region, where he travelled to famous mountains and historical sites. His theoretical treatise *Huayulu* articulates his nearly mystical notion of 'one line' (*yi hua*), a state of complete self-immersion with the Dao that transcends any method or style. Whereas the idea of an ecstatic union with nature was not new in traditional Chinese aesthetics, Shitao pursued this elusive goal through vivid, spontaneous visual expressions. As one modern scholar observes: whatever Shitao paints—landscape, figure, or still-life—'his forms and colors are ever fresh, his spirit light, his inventiveness and wit inexhaustible'.[1]

Why do I link Shitao with the conception of ruins—a topic which has not been addressed in the rich scholarship on the artist?[2] Briefly, this

---

Read at the Academy 10 November 2009.

[1] Michael Sullivan, *The Arts of China*, 5th edn. (Berkeley, CA, 2008), p. 269. For two outstanding studies of Shitao in English, see Richard Edwards, *The Painting of Tao-Chi* (Ann Arbor, MI, 1967) and Jonathan Hay, *Shitao: Painting and Modernity in Early Qing China* (Cambridge, 2001). Shitao's original name was Zhu Ruoji. He is also known as Daoji or Yuanji.

[2] To my knowledge, the only in-depth study of 'dynastic ruins' in Shitao's work is Jonathan Hay's 'Ming palace and tomb in early Qing Nanjing: a study in the poetics of dynastic memory', *Late Imperial China*, 20 (1999), 1–48. Hay's paper interprets specific paintings, whereas the present essay deals with the conception of ruins as a specific aesthetic category.

connection emerged in a project which I have pursued on and off for the past fifteen years. I started this project, a study of the conceptual and representational modes of ruins in Chinese art and visual culture, around the mid-1990s. At the time I reread Hans Frankel's and Stephen Owen's writings on the Chinese poetic genre *huaigu*, often translated into English as 'lamenting the past' or 'meditating on the past'.[3] Their writings inspired me to conduct a survey of ruin images in Chinese painting, because such images frequently appear in *huaigu* poems. The result surprised me: among all the examples I checked (which cover a chronological span from the fifth century BC to the mid-nineteenth century AD), fewer than five depict ruined buildings. Typically, the architectural structure in a painting shows no trace of damage, even if the artist has inscribed a poem next to the image that identifies it as a ruin. One such example is Shitao's *Qingliang Terrace* (Fig. 1). The painting bears a poem by the artist which includes these two sentences: 'Crows return to a ruined entrenchment—silent, silent the midnight; | Flowers bloom in an abandoned garden—long, long is my thought.' But the buildings at the centre of the composition, supposedly the 'ruined entrenchment' and 'abandoned garden', show no signs of physical decay.

I was no less astonished when I turned to actual architecture: there was not a single case in pre-twentieth-century China in which the ruined appearance of an old building was purposefully preserved to evoke what Alois Riegl has theorised in the West as the 'age value' of a manufactured form.[4] Many ancient timber structures do exist, but most of them have been repeatedly renovated or even completely rebuilt. Each renovation and restoration aims to bring the building back to its original brilliance, while freely incorporating current architectural and decorative elements.

Although I can still continue my search, these initial findings were forceful enough to prompt me to ponder on their implications. Logically, I first questioned why I was so surprised by such findings: clearly I, like many other people, had presumed that ruins were an integral element of traditional Chinese culture and existed in both architectural and pictorial forms. It is also clear that in such a presumption I was unconsciously following a cultural/artistic convention which is at odds with the traditional

---

[3] Hans H. Frankel, *The Flowering Plum and the Palace Lady: Interpretations of Chinese Poetry* (New Haven, CT, 1976), especially the chapter 'Contemplation of the past', pp. 104–27; Stephen Owen, *Remembrances: the Experience of the Past in Classical Chinese Literature* (Cambridge, MA, 1986), especially pp. 16–32.

[4] Alois Riegl, 'The modern cult of monuments: its character and its origin' (1903) (trans.) K. W. Forster and D. Chirardo, in W. W. Forster (ed.), *Monument/Memory, Oppositions*, special issue, 25 (1982), 20–51; especially, 31–34.

Figure 1.   Shitao, *Qingliang Terrace*, hanging scroll, ink and colour on paper, Nanjing Museum.

Chinese ways of representing ruins—if such representations indeed existed in art. This realisation led to two kinds of reflections, about the origin of such misconception and about indigenous concepts and representational modes of Chinese ruins.

So I started to read scholarship on European ruin images and architecture, whose abundance and global reach may have shaped a modern Chinese observer's imagination of ruins in premodern China. I also started to think about alternative visual modes in Chinese art, which might express a 'ruin aesthetic' through non-architectural forms. This second inquiry led me to discover some interesting examples and also to see many familiar images in a different light. When I finally began to write on the topic, I naturally selected the examples I found most compelling to illuminate my findings. Only then did I realise that many examples I had selected came from a single person: Shitao. This essay utilises this realisation for two interrelated purposes: first, I want to define some basic modes of ruin representations in traditional Chinese art for which I will use Shitao's work as the main visual evidence; second, in so doing I also hope to explore some unnoticed dimensions in Shitao's art, and to demonstrate that the ancient conception of ruins can help us see some familiar images anew.

Qiu: a mound of rubble

The oldest term used for ruins in the Chinese language is *qiu* 丘. Meaning originally a natural mound or hillock, it also came to denote the ruined site of a village, town, or dynastic capital. We do not know when this second usage began, but it is quite explicit in a third-century BC poem called 'A Lament for Ying' (Ai Ying), which Qu Yuan (340 BC–278 BC) composed before casting himself into the Miluo River:

> . . .
> I climbed a steep islet's height and looked into the distance,
> Thinking to ease the sorrow in my heart:
> But only grief came for the rich, blest River Kingdom,
> For its cherished ways, now lost beyond recall.
> I may not traverse the surging waves to return there,
> Or cross south over the watery waste to reach it.
> *To think that its tall palaces (xia) should be mounds of rubble (qiu),*
> *And its two East Gates a wilderness of woods!*[5]   (italics added)

[5] David Hawkes (trans.), *The Songs of the South: an Anthology of Ancient Chinese Poems by Qu Yuan and Other Poets* (London, 1985), p. 165. The original translation of the seventh line in this

There has been much discussion about the subject of Qu Yuan's lament. My interest here lies instead in its definition of *qiu* as remains of former palatial halls. Unlike a stone Classic or Gothic ruin in Europe, such remains no longer convey the grandeur of the original building: the timber superstructures had disappeared, and only their foundations remained in the form of 'mounds of rubble'. A *qiu*, therefore, indicates the location of a former building but does not preserve its shape. This conception of ruins is therefore dependent on the notion of erasure: frequently, it was the 'void' left by a destroyed timber structure that stimulated a lament for the past. Significantly, in addition to a natural or artificial mound *qiu* has a second meaning. An entry in the earliest Chinese encyclopedia *Guang ya* reads: '*Qiu* means emptiness'.[6] These two significations of *qiu*—as architectural remains and as signifiers of emptiness—together construct an indigenous concept of ruins in China.

This is an enduring concept, because we find it underlying images created nearly two thousand years later, as exemplified by two of Shitao's (1642–1707) 'memory paintings'.[7] A descendant of the Ming royal house which surrendered its power to the Qing in 1644, Shitao developed a complex psychology toward the past, both longing for it and hoping to escape its grip.[8] The two paintings in question belong to two albums he painted in the last years of the 1690s, both depicting his earlier journeys around Jinling (the present-day Nanjing), the first Ming capital and Shitao's residence from 1680 to 1687. The first image, from the album *Reminiscences of Qinhuai River*, has an unusual composition even among Shitao's own works. Without a larger landscape setting and human traces, the leaf is filled with the image of a desolate *qiu*: a mound of rubble on which brambles grow (Fig. 2). Jonathan Hay has connected this image with contemporary descriptions of ruins.[9] One such description comments on the Hall of the Great Foundation (Daben tang), a Ming palace whose name Shitao adopted as one of his many studio names. After recalling its history and

---

stanza reads: 'To think that its palace walls should be mounds of rubble.' I changed 'palace walls' to 'tall palaces' because the character *xia* means 'large halls.'

[6] *Guang ya*, 'shigu' 3. This encyclopaedia was compiled by Zhang Ji of the third century.

[7] There are other related examples. An album in the Los Angeles County Museum dated to 1694, for instance, contains a similar scene. For an illustration of this painting, see Stephanie Barron, et al., *Los Angeles County Museum of Art* (New York, 2003), p. 66.

[8] For a detailed investigation into Shitao's attitude toward the past and the present, see Jonathan Hay, *Shitao: Painting and Modernity in Early Qing China* (Cambridge, 2001).

[9] Ibid., p. 120; also Jonathan Hay, 'Ming palace and tomb in Early Qing Jiangnan', especially pp. 41–2.

Figure 2.   Shitao, 'An Overgrown Hillock', a leaf in *Reminiscences of Qin-Huai*, album of 8 leaves,
ink and light colour on paper, Cleveland Museum of Art.

glorious days, the seventeenth-century commentator Yu Binshuo turned
to the building's present condition: 'Today the former palace is planted
with millet. Seekers after history pass through the ruins, the misty waste
spotted with white dew, squirrels amid the clumps of brambles. With a

single breath, they all sigh.'[10] Readers cannot miss the similarity between these words and Qu Yuan's 'Lament for Ying'.

The second image, less politically oriented but authenticated as a 'ruin image' by Shitao himself, depicts his journey to the Flower-Rain Terrace (Yuhua tai) when he lived in Nanjing (Fig. 3). According to local lore, the place became a popular scenic spot beginning in the third century and gained its name in 507 from a miraculous event: when the eminent monk Yunguang constructed a platform and lectured on Buddhist Dharma there, flowers fell from the sky. In the album leaf, Shitao has painted himself standing on a large, cone-shaped earthen mound, which contrasts the surrounding landscape with its strange form, soft contour, and unnatural bareness. Clearly the painter intends to tell the viewer that it is a man-made mound, not a natural rocky hill. This impression is supported by the poem Shitao has inscribed on the page, which begins with these two lines: 'Outside the city walls stands an ancient terrace in wilderness. | Today's folks still tell the legend of the flower rain.' He also appended a narrative

Figure 3.   Shitao 'Flower-Rain Terrace', *Eight Views of the South*, album of 8 leaves, ink and light colour on paper, British Museum, London.

[10] Translation from ibid., p. 137.

account to the poem: 'The Flower-Rain Terrace: When I was living in the Qin-Huai region [south of Nanjing], in the evening at sunset, I often climbed this terrace (*tai*) after people had left. Sometimes I also painted it after chanting poems.' The painting shows that the 'platform' he climbed is a naked earthen hill devoid of human construction; it is its barren desolation—its emptiness—that evokes the painter–poet's remembrance of the past.

Xu: emptiness

As these two paintings demonstrate, *qiu* as a particular concept and imagery of ruins never disappeared in traditional China. An important change, however, took place during the Eastern Zhou and significantly enriched people's imagination of the ruin: during this period, another character, *xu* 墟, gained currency to become the main term for ruins. The reasons for this development are complex; but a main factor must be the different root meanings of the two characters: although their dictionary definitions overlap and the two terms are often used interchangeably, *qiu* means, first of all, a concrete topographic feature, whereas *xu*'s primary significance is 'emptiness'.[11] The introduction of *xu* as a second—and eventually the main—term for ruins, therefore, signifies a subtle shift in the conception and perception of ruins. We can describe this shift as an 'internalisation' of ruins, through which ruin representations were increasingly freed from external signs, and also increasingly relied on the observer's subjective response to particular places.

No Eastern Zhou picture depicts a *xu*. But some old poems offer a clear image of these spaces. Whereas a *qiu* was distinguished, as we have read in Qu Yuan's 'Lament for Ying', by a 'mound of rubble', a *xu* was envisioned as a vast, empty space where the capital of a former dynasty once stood. As an empty site, a *xu* generated visitors' mental and emotional responses not through tangible remains: it is the *site*, not dilapidated structures or surviving platforms, that crystallises historical memory. This, in turn, means that a *xu* is not identified by external signs but is given

---

[11] This is the definition given in *Er ya*. See Xu Zhaohua, *Er ya jinzhu* (A modern annotated version of *Er ya*) (Tianjin, 1987), pp. 34 and 48. Bernhard Karlgren dates *Er ya* to the third century BC in 'The early history of the *Chou Li* and *Tso Chuan* texts', *Bulletin of the Museum of Far Eastern Antiquities*, 3 (1931), 1–59. The Han dictionary *Shuo wen* defines *xu* as 'a large mound' (*Da qiu*). See Duan Yucai (compiler), *Shuo wen jie zi zhu* (Annotated interpretations of characters and words) (Shanghai, 1981), p. 386.

a subjective reality: it is the visitor's recognition of a place as a *xu* that stimulates emotion and thought. The ancient worthy Zhou Feng thus teaches in *The Book of Rites* (*Li ji*): 'Ruins [*xu*] and graves express no mournfulness; it is people who mourn amidst them.'[12]

This particular conception of ruins underlies two early examples of *huaigu* poetry. The first, recorded by Sima Qian (*c*.145–86 BC) in the *Shi ji* (Historical records), was supposedly written by Jizi, a former prince of the perished Shang dynasty. According to Sima, when Jizi passed the Ruins of Yin (Yin Xu) at the beginning of the Zhou, he was 'moved by the destruction of the [Shang] palaces, where the grain and millet now grew. Distressed, he could neither cry out nor weep like a woman. He thus composed the poem "Ears of Wheat" (Mai xiu) to express his inner feeling.'[13] The poem does not mention any abandoned buildings. The only image it evokes is a field of wheat and millet, which conceal the old capital under their lush leaves. The same imagery is also employed in 'There the millet is Lush' (Shu li), a poem in the *Book of Songs*:

> There the millet is lush,
> There the grain is sprouting.
> I walk here with slow, slow steps,
> My heart shaken within me.
> Those who know me
> Would say my heart is grieved;
> Those who know me not
> Would ask what I seek here.
> Gray and everlasting Heaven—
> What man did this?[14]

This stanza is repeated twice more; only the second and fourth lines change: the millet sprouts and then produces seeds, while the traveller's grief grows darker and deeper. Again, the poem identifies neither the place nor the reason for the traveller's sorrow, which are provided later by the Han commentator Mao Heng in a preface: ' "There the Millet Is Lush" is a lament for the Zhou ancestral capital. A great officer of Zhou was passing the former ancestral temples and palace buildings, which were entirely covered by millet. He lamented the collapse of the Zhou royal house and lingered there, unable to bring himself to leave.'[15]

---

[12] Ruan Yuan (compiler and ed.), *Shisanjing zhushu* (Annotated thirteen classics), 2 vols. (Beijing, 1979), p. 1313; see James Legge (trans.), *Li Chi: Book of Rites*, 2 vols. (New York, 1967), vol. 1, p. 191.
[13] Sima Qian, *Shi ji* (Beijing, 1959), pp. 1620–1.
[14] Translation from Owen, *Remembrances*, p. 20.
[15] Ibid., p. 20.

Owen suggests that, in providing this exegesis, Mao Heng 'discovered a *huaigu*' in this poem.[16] To Mao, the grief of the traveller must have been caused by a direct encounter with the past: what triggered his emotional response was not the field of millet, but the buried Zhou capital which was absent to view. His discovery of a *huaigu* in the poem thus amounts to identifying the field of millet as a *xu*—the site of 'the former ancestral temples and palace buildings, which were entirely covered by millet'. In other words, the Han commentator spelled out the unspoken message in the poem, as his 'preface' constructs a narrative framework to specify the occasion of the poetic expression. Sima Qian supplied a similar framework to 'Ears of Wheat': only because of his explanation can we identify the poem as a *huaigu* lamenting the ruined Shang capital.

We find a parallel situation in art: many traditional Chinese paintings depict a traveller in a landscape. The scenes are often charged with intense emotion, but both the traveller and the landscape remain anonymous unless a narrative framework is given. In the latter case, although the artist still rejects a literal portrayal of physical ruins, he identifies the place in the painting as a *xu* and the painting as an expression of *huaigu*. We can again find a typical example of this type of ruin representation in Shitao's *Reminiscences of Qinhuai River*. Scholars agree that Shitao created this album in 1695, for a friend with whom he had travelled along the Qinhuai River near Nanjing a decade earlier.[17] It is uncertain whether the album's eight leaves depict a continuous journey, but from Shitao's inscription on the last leaf (Fig. 4) we know that this particular scene at least conveys the artist's reminiscences of an earlier pleasure trip, and that the purpose of that previous trip was *fanggu* and *huaigu*—searching for and contemplating ancient sites. In this case, Shitao and his friend were searching for and contemplating sites of the Six Dynasties (220–589), which established their capitals in Nanjing. We can thus describe the painting's theme as 'the rememberer being remembered':[18] the album is Shitao's reminiscence of one of his previous *huaigu* experiences. As the artist recounts:

> Along the river with its forty-nine bends,
> I search for every marvel of the Six Dynasties.
> Who has walked in wooden clogs after the snow has cleared on the East
>   Mountain?

---

[16] Translation from Owen, *Remembrances*, p. 21.
[17] Richard Vinograd, 'Reminiscences of Ch'in-huai: Tao-chi and the Nanking School', *Archives of Asian Art*, 31 (1977–8), 6–31.
[18] Owen, *Remembrances*, p. 19.

Figure 4.   Shitao, 'Searching for Plum Blossom along the Qin-Quai River', a leaf in *Reminiscences of Qin-Huai*, album of 8 leaves, ink and light colour on paper, Cleveland Museum of Art.

Who has composed poems while the wind roars through the west chasm?
Please have sympathy with the lonely plum trees,
A few of their bare branches are left;
Their flowers have all fallen even before Spring is over ...[19]

[19] Based on the translation in *Eight Dynasties of Chinese Painting* (Cleveland, OH, 1980), p. 323.

Like 'There the Millet is Lush', this poem does not describe any physical remains from the Six Dynasties, and only uses a plant (in this case the
plum trees) to allude to passage of time. The scene accompanying this
poem employs the same strategy but forges a powerful encounter between
the painter/poet with an empty *xu*. In the picture Shitao stands in a tiny
boat on a winding river, looking upwards. Responding to his gaze, the
mountain above him seems suddenly to bend over toward him, forming a
massive cliff like an enormous lobed overhang, on which bony plum trees
grow downward. Far more than a straightforward record of his visit to an
ancient site, this painting conveys the sense of a spontaneous 'spiritual
meeting' (*shen hui*) between the artist and the ancients, who once wandered
there and composed their own poems a thousand years before.

Withered trees as living ruins

Here we begin to detect an interesting connection between the 'wheat' and
'millet' in the two early *huaigu* poems, and the 'lonely plum trees' in
Shitao's painting. Far from innocent natural plants or flowers, these
images are charged with rich cultural meaning and play crucial roles in
forging a unique ruin aesthetic. Even today, old trees, as living ruins, are
revered in gardens and temples; but it is still taboo to keep functioning
buildings in disrepair. It is not rare for a temple's age to be measured by its
trees: the buildings have been rebuilt too many times to serve as an index
of time (Fig. 5).

From the same cultural tradition emerged a major pictorial image in
traditional Chinese art, referred to either generally as 'ancient trees' (*gu mu*)
or more specifically as 'withered trees' (*ku shu*). Figure 6 shows an early example of this image attributed to the Song painter Xu Daoning (*c*.970–1051/53).
Five gnarled pines grow from fissures in the rocks and reach the upper
edge of the picture, filling out the entire composition with their twisting
and turning branches. To Max Loehr, 'there is an air of mystery and sad-
ness about these trees, deepened rather than lessened by the elegance of
form given to their hoary shapes'.[20] It is impossible in this short lecture to
even outline the development of this image; readers interested in these
images may consult two excellent studies by John Hay and Richard
Barnhart.[21] An argument I want to advance here, however, concerns the

---

[20] Max Loehr, *The Great Painters of China* (New York, 1980), p. 142.
[21] John Hay, 'Pine and rock, wintry tree, old tree and bamboo and rock—the development of a
theme', *National Palace Museum Bulletin*, 4(6) (1970), 8–11; Richard Barnhart, *Wintry Forests,
Old Trees: some Landscape Themes in Chinese Painting* (New York, 1972).

Figure 5.   Ancient tree and newly renovated hall in the Forbidden City, Beijing.

relationship between such trees and the notion of *memory*. These tortured natural forms are associated with memory because they embody the experiences of decay, death, and rebirth, but never lend themselves to the construction of a teleological historical process.[22]

Long before the Song, Chinese writers had developed an intense interest in this image. This interest found its first major literary expression in Yu Xin's (513–81) 'Poetic disposition on withered trees' (Ku shu fu). Stimulated by a dying locust tree in the courtyard, Yu recalled some beautiful and awe-inspiring trees in their prime, whose trunks were like sculptures created by master artists, whose flowers were like multi-coloured embroidery, and who were even bestowed with honorable titles by emperors and princes. But in time,

> ... none of them could avoid a tragic fate: moss and fungus obscured their shape; birds and worms destroyed their appearance. Frost and dew lowered their branches; dusty winds shook their body and spirit. [This is why] a temple was dedicated to a Pale Tree (Baimu) at Donghan, and a sacrificial altar was built for a Withered Mulberry Tree (Kusang) near Xihe ...[23]

Yu Xin's exposition on withered trees closely resembles a ruin poem such as Bao Zhao's (414?–66) 'Ruined city', in which the poet always recalls a place's former splendour and then laments its fatal destruction. A withered tree is a particular kind of ruin, however: it is withered but not necessarily destroyed. Indeed, the power and mystery of such trees in Chinese painting is rooted in a visual and conceptual ambiguity: their ruinous forms possess at the same time an extraordinary energy and spirit.[24] While displaying signs of death and winter, they also offer hope for rebirth and spring. Rather than an image of *finality*, a withered tree pertains to a chain of perpetual transformation. Borrowing Pierre Nora's words on memory, a withered tree 'remains in permanent evolution, open to the dialectic of remembering and forgetting, unconscious of its successive deformations, vulnerable to manipulation and appropriation, susceptible to being long dormant and periodically revived'.[25]

---

[22] I say 'rarely' because in some cases withered trees gained the significance of political omens and were used to construct dynastic history.

[23] Yu Xin, 'Ku shu fu' (Poetic disposition on withered trees).

[24] For an interesting discussion of *ku shu* in Chinese philosophy, religion, and art, see Zhu Liangzhi, *Quyuan fenghe* (Lotus blown by wind in a winding courtyard) (Hefeng, 2004), pp. 113–42.

[25] Pierre Nora, 'Between memory and history: les lieux de mémoire,' *Representations*, 20 (Spring 1989), 7–26, quotation from 8–9.

Figure 6. Attributed to Xu Daoning, *Old Trees*, ink on silk, National Palace Museum, Taipei.

Shitao was likewise fascinated by the idea of ancient trees. Unique among Chinese painters, however, he bestowed such images with an auto-biographical significance, and especially emphasised their symbolism in conveying the notion of 'rebirth'. I want to focus on two groups of his works. The first group was likely created around 1695 and 1696, when Shitao was about 53 or 54 years old. The most important image in this group is found in the last scene in a complex handscroll known as *Calligraphy and Sketches by Qingxiang*.[26] Concluding a series of scenes and poems, this image shows, in Richard Vinograd's words, 'a withered but beatific figure, with protruding ribs and wrinkled face and neck, wearing a monk's robe, and meditating with a blissful smile within the hollow trunk of a tree' (Fig. 7).[27] Next to the image Shitao inscribed in large, formal characters: 'An old tree in the empty mountains: He sits within it for forty small-*jie* cycles.' Following these words is a passage written in smaller characters, which ends with a rhetorical question: 'The man in the picture—can he be called the future incarnation of Blind Abbot or not? Ha, ha!' Since Blind Abbot (Xia Zunzhe) is one of Shitao's adopted names, we know that the meditating monk inside the old tree is a pseudo-self-portrait, representing himself sixty-seven million years from 1696, the year he painted the image. (In Buddhist numerology one small-*jie* cycle equals about seventeen million years).

Iconographically, this pseudo-self-portrait of Shitao is related to a type of Arhat (Ch. Luohan) image, invented several hundred years ago by Guanxiu (832–912), a famous poet–painter who lived in the late Tang and early Five Dynasties period. Several series of Arhat paintings attributed to Guanxiu depict strange-looking monastic figures seated in deep medi-tation. Some of them dwell in caves while others sit beneath withered old trees; both their dried-up bodies and their landscape environment seem worn away by the passing of countless eons (Fig. 8). Scholars suspect that these images are Song copies of Guanxiu's work. An imprint that origin-ated in the Song shows a further development of this visual tradition. This is one of the famous *Five Hundred Luohans at Mt. Tiantai*, com-pleted by Lin Tinggui and Zhou Jichang in 1178 (Fig. 9). The composi-tion is roughly divided into two vertical halves. The lower half is occupied by a group of figures in vivid clothes, including four monks and an armoured man resembling Skanda (Chi. Wei Tuo), the Dharma guardian. Some of them look upward. Following their gaze we find a withered tree

---

[26] For a description and analysis of this scroll, see Hay, *Shitao*, pp. 122–3.
[27] Richard Vinograd, *Boundaries of the Self: Chinese Portraits, 1600–1900* (Cambridge, 1992), p. 62.

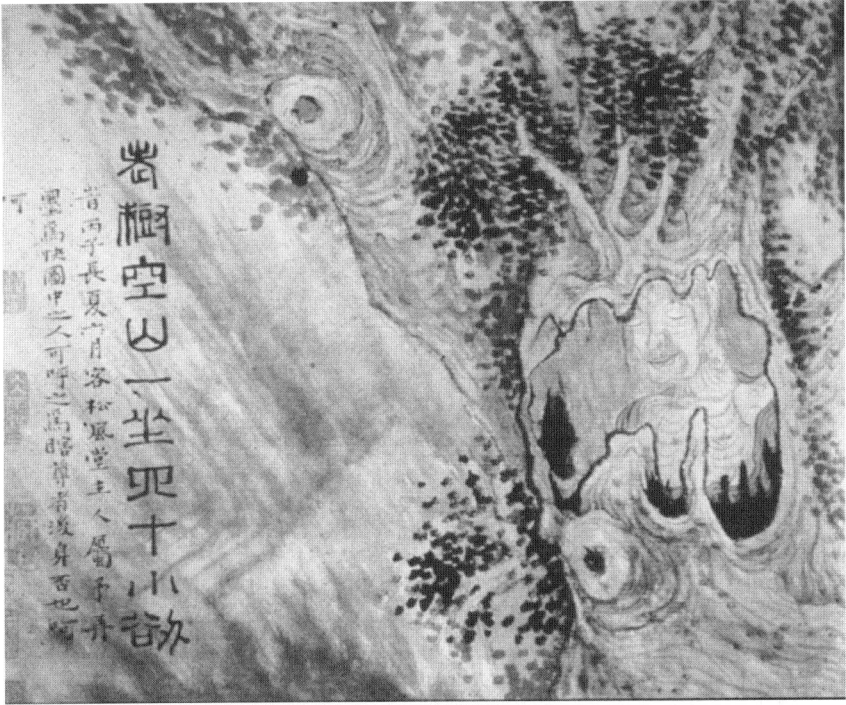

Figure 7.   Shitao, *Calligraphies and Sketches by Qingxiang*, dated 1696, handscroll (detail of final section), ink and colour on paper, Palace Museum, Beijing.

growing out of water and mist. Painted entirely in ink like the landscape, an old monk is sitting inside the tree trunk in meditation. His unusual setting, as well as his protruding ribs and wrinkled face, connects the image with Shitao's painting, and in turn links Shitao's self-imagination with the idea of an Arhat—a holy man who has achieved nirvana through gaining insight into the true nature of existence.

This painting can be linked with two other works by Shitao. One of them, a double album leaf created a year earlier, again portrays a figure sitting inside a tree trunk (Fig. 10). Because I have serious questions about the authenticity of this work, however, I will omit it from this discussion.[28] The other painting is undated; but the signature Blind Abbot places it before 1697, when Shitao abandoned his Buddhist identity and formally presented himself as a Taoist. One of the eight leaves in a large album, it represents what is at first sight an unremarkable mountain view, with a

[28] Judging from the brushwork, especially the calligraphy of the inscription, it is likely that this work was made by Zhang Daqian, a famous forger of Shitao's work.

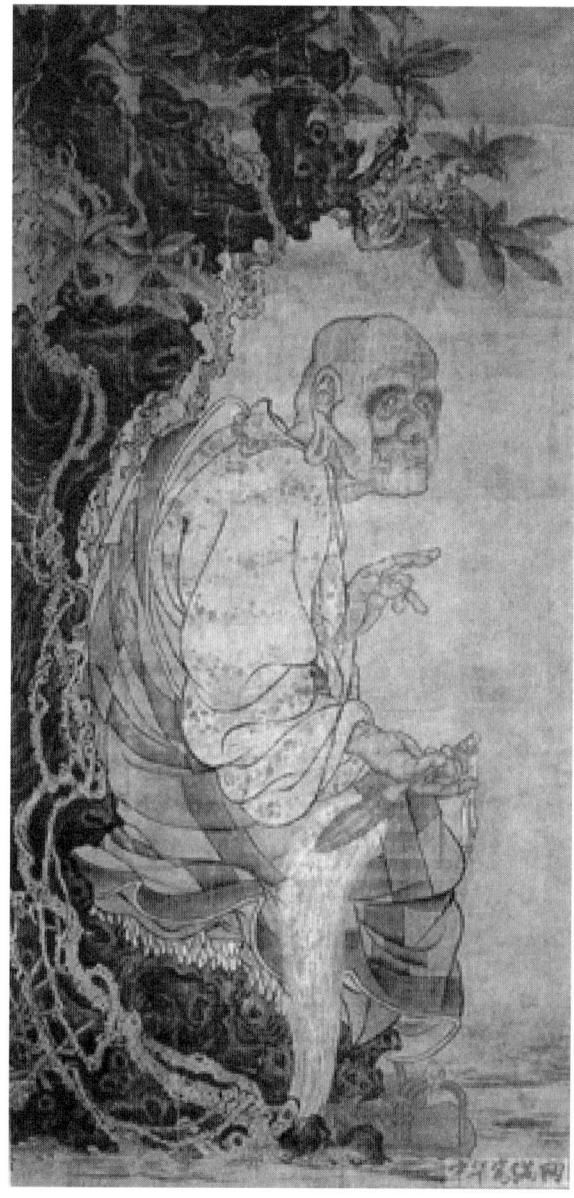

Figure 8. Attributed to Guanxiu, *Arhat*, ink and colour on silk, hanging scroll, Kodaiji Temple, Kyoto.

70　樹中坐禅

Figure 9. Lin Tinggui, *Luohan Meditating in a Tree*, 1178, hanging scroll, ink and colour on silk, Daitokuji Temple, Kyoto.

Figure 10. Shitao, 'Hermit within a Hollow Tree Trunk', a leaf in an album of 5 leaves, dated 1695, mounted as a handscroll, Sichuan Provincial Museum.

variety of trees growing in the mid-ground (Fig. 11). The uniqueness of the painting lies in its focal image, a leafless young tree with underdeveloped branches. It differs from all other trees in the painting in its stiff posture and striking bareness. With its straight trunk placed exactly on the painting's

Figure 11. Shitao, 'This Is My Former Incarnation', a leaf in *Landscape and Flowers*, album of 8 leaves, ink on paper, Tianjin Art Museum.

vertical axis, this humble image is given an iconic status and connected to Shitao's inscription on the painting: 'This is my former incarnation.'

While any relationship between the two images in Figures 7 and 11 can only be speculative, it is significant that their creation coincided with a major change in Shitao's life: after moving back to the south from the capital, he would soon abandon his long-time Buddhist identity. Relating this second change with the 1696 pseudo-self-portrait, Vinoglad has interpreted the image as a 'final, somewhat wistful letting-go of a long-maintained role and identity, with its spiritual attainment deferred to a possible future incarnation'.[29] But my interest here is not about the religious implications of these pictures, but about the role of the trees in Shitao's conceptualisation of selfhood: from the undernourished young tree to the hollowed but still energetic juniper, these images encompass millions of years in an imagined lifespan, and embrace conflicting religious and intellectual identities of the artist.

A decade later, Shitao created another group of tree images with the deepening theme of rebirth. An album which he created around 1705 to 1707 is completely devoted to flowering plum trees. Never before have we seen death and rebirth represented in such a succinct and dramatic manner. Opening the album we see a plum tree broken into several pieces, but continuing to produce abundant blossoms (Fig. 12). The poem about the picture identifies the plum as a relic from the past, but a relic which is full of life:

> Seeing ancient plum blossom is like meeting a 'leftover man' from the past—
> But who sent the plum to mirror the ancients?
> Having witnessed the up-and-down of the Six Dynasties, it hides itself in aloof retirement;
> Though broken, it doubles its spirit at the year's end.[30]

Then there is a painting from his 1707 album *Reminiscences of Nanjing*, which shows a close-up of an ancient gingko tree, whose ruinous state is emphasised by the broken and hollowed trunk (Fig. 13). Shitao gives this tortured form an ironic sense of monumentality, portraying it as a powerful pillar connecting heaven and earth (Chi. *ding tian li di*). According to

---

[29] Vinograd, *Boundaries of the Self*, p. 62.

[30] Marilyn and Shen Fu, *Studies in Connoisseurship: Chinese Paintings from the Arthur M. Sackler Collection in New York and Princeton* (Princeton, NJ, 1987), p. 299. The original translation of the first line is: 'Seeing an old plum is like meeting a "leftover man" from the past.' I changed 'an old plum' to 'ancient plum blossom' because this is closer to the meaning of *gu hua*—ancient flowers.

Figure 12.   Shitao, 'Plum of Baocheng', a leaf in *Plum Blossom: Poetry and Painting*, album of
8 leaves, ink on paper, Princeton University Art Museum.

his poem on the painting, the gingko grows on top of the Green Dragon
Mountains near Nanjing. During the Six Dynasties it was maimed by a
bolt of lightning, but later defied death and sprouted a new growth.[31] The
idea of death and rebirth in this legend clearly fascinated the artist: while
stressing the tree's physical damage, Shitao also painted new leaves growing on a lower branch and on the broken trunk itself. It is difficult to find
a stronger proof of the artist's enduring desire for life and art, because
when he created this image he had been seriously ill and would die before
the year's end.

Qi: ruins as extraordinary phenomena

I can now summarise the representational modes discussed so far, each
linked with a different aspect of Shitao's perception of the past. His depictions of ruins of Ming palaces represent *yi ji*, 'leftover traces' of a recently

---

[31] See ibid., p. 311.

Figure 13. Shitao, 'Old Gingko at Mt. Qinglong', a leaf in *Reminiscences of Jinling*, album of 12 leaves, dated 1707, ink and colour on paper, Arthur M. Sackler Gallery, Smithsonian Institution, Washington, DC.

perished dynasty with which he identified himself as a 'leftover subject' (*yi min*). He portrayed himself wandering in the areas near Nanjing, where the ancient Six Dynasties had established their capitals. His images of old trees betray a Buddhist belief in endless cycle of rebirth, which extend one's life back to an infinite past and forward to an infinite future. In all

these cases, ruins are not conceived as an external existence with independent historical and aesthetic value, but are internalised into a pictorial
language to express his experiences, feelings, and ideas.

This understanding prepares a basis for us to examine the last group
of 'ruin' images in Shitao's work, which seems at first glance to contradict
the interpretation I have just proposed. At the beginning of this lecture I
mentioned that my search for 'ruin' pictures in traditional Chinese painting—that is, pictures that represent not ancient but 'ruined' buildings—
had yielded fewer than five examples. Quite amazingly, the two most
convincing examples in this group come from Shitao's hand. One showing
a ruined stone archway and the other a stone pagoda, both pictures belong
to an album depicting views of the Yellow Mountain (Figs. 14*a–b*). To
modern people exposed to various kinds of ruin images on a daily basis,
these pictures may seem nothing special—they simply represent two
decaying structures Shitao found on his trips to the famous mountain.
But I believe that to a seventeenth-century Chinese viewer they must have
evoked the notion of *qi*—strange and extraordinary phenomena which
transcend the ordinary. This is not only because the two images were virtually unique in traditional Chinese painting, but also because Shitao's
purpose in creating the album *is* to transcend the ordinary: mingled with
these two seemingly realistic pictures are images of strange peaks, rocks,
and trees, as well as legends of immortals (Figs. 15*a–d*). Taken together,
these images depict the Yellow Mountains as a realm of marvels, in which
nature and culture, past and present, human and divine no longer follow
any conventional definitions.[32]

In this way, the ruined pagoda and stone gate are both *gu shi* and *shen
ji*—historical traces and divine traces. Here I will use another of Shitao's
Yellow Mountain pictures to illustrate this double meaning and to conclude this lecture. It is from another album in which Shitao recorded one
of his journeys to the famous mountain.[33] Each of the eight pictures in the

---

[32] Many scholars have discussed the importance of the Yellow Mountain to traditional Chinese
painting. For general discussions, see James Cahill (ed.), *Shadows of Mt. Huang: Painting and
Printing of the Anhui School* (Berkeley, CA, 1981); idem, 'Huang Shan paintings as pilgrimage
pictures', in Susan Naquin and Chünfang Yü (eds.), *Pilgrims and Sacred Sites in China* (Berkeley,
CA, 1992), pp. 246–92; Flora Fu, *Framing Famous Mountains: Grand Tour and Mingshan Paintings
in Sixteenth-century China* (Hong Kong, 2009).

[33] There are different opinions about the date of the album. Richard Edwards suggests that it was
probably made around 1670, when Shitao was thirty years old. But he also cautions that Shitao
often depicted a journey long after the event. See Richard Edwards, *The Painting of Tao-chi,
1641–ca. 1720* (Ann Arbor, MI, 1967), pp. 31–2, 45–6. Other scholars have dated the album to the
1680s based on stylistic evidence.

Figure 14(*a*). Shitao, *Huangshan Album*, Leaf 1, ink or ink and colour on paper. Palace
Museum, Beijing.

album shows the artist travelling through the mountain's famous scenic
spots while discovering its secrets. The leaf in question represents his
ascent of the mountain's central peak, called Tiandu Feng or the Heavenly
Capital Peak (Fig. 16). Near the centre of the composition, rock boulders

Figure 14(*b*).   Shitao, *Huangshan Album*, Leaf 4, ink or ink and colour on paper. Palace Museum, Beijing.

configure a stone giant. Shitao wrote an inscription next to it: 'Ice his heart and jade his bones, stone and iron makes this man. He is the master of the Yellow Mountain and the minister to Xuanyuan.' Here Xuanyuan refers to the Yellow Emperor, China's mythical founder, who had gone to

Figure 15(*a*).   Shitao, *Huangshan Album*, Leaf 6, ink or ink and colour on paper. Palace
Museum, Beijing.

the Yellow Mountain thousands of years before to collect herbs for
making an elixir of immortality. In the picture, the stone giant's head and
shoulders are covered with vegetation; cracks and erosion on his rock
body further betray the endless years which have passed: this is indeed a

Figure 15(*b*).   Shitao, *Huangshan Album*, Leaf 12, ink or ink and colour on paper. Palace Museum, Beijing.

'ruin' left from the remote past. Interestingly, Shitao also portrayed himself as a traveller below the stone giant in the same pose, thus making himself an incarnation of the master of the immortal mountain.

* * *

Figure 15(c). Shitao, *Huangshan Album*, Leaf 15, ink or ink and colour on paper. Palace Museum, Beijing.

Taking Shitao's work as my main examples, this lecture investigates the conception of ruins in traditional Chinese pictorial art. But my goal is neither to demonstrate an unchanging mode of conceptualisation nor a teleological progression of visual forms. Instead, I start by tracking down

Figure 15(*d*).   Shitao, *Huangshan Album*, Leaf 19, ink or ink and colour on paper. Palace Museum, Beijing.

the indigenous definitions of ruins as well as a broad variety of images related to the idea of ruination. An exploration of the historical, cultural, artistic and technological conditions of these definitions and images in turn raises a range of issues, including the relationship between the concept of

Figure 16. Shitao, 'Heavenly Capital Peak', a leaf from *Eight Scenic Spots in Huangshan*, album
of 8 leaves, ink and colour on paper, Sen-oku Hakuko Kan, Kyoto.

ruins and timber architecture, the idea of the 'trace' and its visual manifestations, the metaphorical use of images in representing time, and
indigenous methods for recording damage and decay. The subtly divergent meanings of two archaic characters for ruins, *qiu* and *xu*, provide this
study with a semantic basis, revealing different ways of imagining and
constructing 'memory sites' in literature and art. Images of 'withered
trees' then offer visual testimonies to understand how various temporalities—past, present, and rebirth—are realised in pictorial forms. The final
section studies several of Shitao's Yellow Mountain paintings, and links
his depictions of architectural ruins with the idea of *qi*—strange or
extraordinary phenomena. Although my lecture focuses on the traditional
period, it will help identify new, 'modern' concepts and representations of
ruins in the nineteenth and early twentieth century, when the aesthetic of
picturesque ruins reached China from Europe and when war ruins became
a frequent subject in the newly invented medium of photography. But this
must be the topic of another study.

Timely Images:
Chinese Art and Festival Display

JAN STUART
The British Museum

Introduction

LOOKING AT A WORK OF ART brings pleasure, but if created long ago or in a civilisation different from the viewers' own, then some of the original nuances are invariably lost or even misunderstood by the audience. A body of literature exists that explores some of the unintended meanings and miscommunications that are conveyed when paintings and three-dimensional objects from times past and places faraway are put on display in museums, but the issue of 'time' itself in the creation and viewing of art—its connections with seasons, rites, and festival events—has not been addressed adequately, especially in the case of China which is the focus of this study.[1] As a step toward redressing this lacuna, the importance of time in the production and display of art and artefacts in late imperial China, with an emphasis given to the Ming (1368–1644) and Qing (1644–1911) dynasties, is presented here. The goal is to draw attention to the significant, yet often overlooked bond between Chinese visual culture and its temporal conventions in order to expand the interpretive framework for understanding Chinese pictorial art.

Before examining 'time' as one of the key motivations in the production and viewing of Chinese art, an example with global familiarity can

Read at the Academy 3 December 2009.
[1] For museum studies, see Ivan Karp and Steven D. Lavine, *Exhibiting Cultures: the Poetics and Politics of Museum Display* (Washington, DC, 1991).

Proceedings of the British Academy, **167**, 295–348. © The British Academy 2010.

help introduce the point. This is the Christmas tree that while originally associated only with a Christian holiday, has come to have an international presence as a beacon of wintertime joy and harbinger of consumer spending. Every year a spectacular twenty-foot blue spruce decorated with Neapolitan angels goes on view at the Metropolitan Museum of Art in New York and exemplifies viewers' expectations about the display of a Christmas tree. This tree and its superb eighteenth-century figurines go on exhibition during the winter holiday season in a large interior courtyard where Christmas music is piped in. Visiting the tree is an annual ritual for adults and children from around the world but, despite the joy the display engenders, it is always taken down in January around the time of Epiphany (6 January). To even imagine this display in the summer months would be comical. People only expect to see the tree and angels at a certain time of year. However delightful as works of art the modelled figurines are, custom dictates that they and the great tree be on view only at a specific time of year for about a month before they are returned to the storage vaults of the museum.

In contrast, museum displays of Chinese art seldom demonstrate a similar sensitivity to the dimension of time. Take, for example, a subtly elegant flower painting by the Ming dynasty artist Lu Zhi (1496–1576), in the National Palace Museum, Taipei, illustrating a bouquet of branches of pomegranate blossoms, moxa, and loquat, a lily, and calamus leaves (Fig. 1). Imagine it on display in December in an exhibition of floral paintings; or consider the case of a Wanli-period (1572–1620) porcelain dish that brandishes the same triad of pomegranate flowers, calamus and moxa arrayed around the cavetto, which is on permanent view at the British Museum in a gallery dedicated to the Sir Percival David Collection of Chinese ceramics (Fig. 2). The well of the dish is decorated with boats that resemble a floating dragon, phoenix, and peacock; the unillustrated reverse side pictures five poisonous creatures.

For their original community of viewers, encountering either the dish or the hanging scroll in the winter would have produced a state of cognitive dissonance not dissimilar to that of the New Yorkers if they were to encounter the Christmas tree on view during the summer in the Metropolitan Museum. This is because the combination of pomegranate flowers, calamus, and moxa is instantly recognisable as appropriate for one moment in time only, the Double Fifth Festival, which falls on the fifth day of the fifth lunar month corresponding to the period between the end of May to late June in the Western calendar. Lu Zhi's inscription on the painting makes this association explicit as it names the holiday, *Tianzhong jie*,

Figure 1.   Lu Zhi (1496–1576), *Bouquet for Double Fifth*; Ming dynasty, 1570; hanging scroll; ink and colour on paper; National Palace Museum, Taiwan, Republic of China. Photograph © The National Palace Museum.

Figure 2. Porcelain dish with *wucai* decoration for Double Fifth; Ming dynasty; Wanli (1573–1620) mark and period; Jingdezhen, Jiangxi province; Height: 3.8 cm, Dia. 21 cm; Sir Percival David Collection at the British Museum; PDF. 750. Photograph © SOAS, all rights reserved.

which along with the names *Duanwu jie* and *Duanyang jie*, all literally meaning Solar Maximus, are the most common Chinese terms for the occasion. The event is known most widely in English as Dragon Boat Festival because of boat races that take place on the day and are referenced in the image on the dish. The poisonous creatures on the dish are apotropaic images also specific to Double Fifth. Yet despite the highly specific nature of the imagery discussed, museum curators often display such works at any time of the year in order to illustrate other points about the history of art in China, such as the artistic attributes of late Ming porcelain or the subtlety of Chinese brushwork.[2]

---

[2] Curators around the world, including in China, freely use festival images out of season if there is a larger art historical point to make. For example, an exhibition of bird-and-flower paintings at

Double Fifth is traditionally believed to be the most pernicious day of the year, when noxious vapours and pestilences peak in the stifling summer heat that coincides with the summer solstice which occurs close in date to Double Fifth. This is the season when pomegranate blossoms explode in full bloom and calamus and moxa peak at their most verdant. All three are traditionally credited with warding off evil. The dazzling red of the pomegranate blossoms imbues them with auspiciousness because of a long-established belief in the power of this fiery colour to deflect evil and attract joy. Positive associations are also lodged in the flowers because they are harbingers of the tree's many-seeded fruits. The words 'son' and 'seed' are homonyms and thus pomegranates are one of most common Chinese symbols to represent giving birth to many heirs, a blessing all families sought. Both the hot colour red and the wish for male progeny are especially appropriate for Double Fifth because of their association with the principle of yang—the bright, fiery, dry, male values—in the Chinese yin-yang cosmology of complementary bipolar forces that generate the cosmic phenomenon. At noon on Double Fifth the yang forces reach their zenith in the annual cycle, followed by the ascendancy of the yin forces.

The odiferous qualities of calamus and moxa are said to repel insects and disease, and lily flowers can be used in medicines explaining their choice in Double Fifth imagery. Moreover, calamus leaves resemble a sword, while moxa leaves, perhaps in what takes a greater feat of imagination, are said to resemble a tiger, thus imbuing these plants with additional symbolic qualities to fend off evil.[3] Tigers, the King of Beasts in Chinese lore, are noted for martial spirit and paired with a sword signify the ability to slay malevolent forces. To anyone familiar with Chinese tradition, the festival association of the trio of pomegranate, calamus, and moxa is readily apparent and so to display an artwork with this motif out of season would seem weirdly inappropriate.

The Metropolitan Museum's Christmas tree and the Chinese painting by Lu Zhi or the Wanli-period dish or, more precisely, the circumstances of their display, demonstrate a truth so elemental that it is rarely mentioned

---

the Art Museum of the Chinese University of Hong Kong included a painting by Wang Shimin, dated to the Double Fifth festival of 1661, as an example of top quality work, but without mentioning its place in a yearly cycle of imagery. This scroll, which is in the Guangdong Provincial Museum, presents a bouquet with pomegranate blossoms, calamus, and moxa. See Zhu Wanzhang *et al.*, *Flower and Bird Painting of the Ming and Qing Periods, Jointly Presented by the Guandong Provincial Museum and the Art Museum, The Chinese University of Hong Kong* (Hong Kong, 2001), no. 29.

[3] The leaves were sometimes plaited into tiger-shaped emblems to make the association clearer.

or thought about within the context of curatorial practice in the world of museums. It is simply this: when an object is seen can radically change its meaning and its power over the viewer's imagination; not everything was made to be seen all the time. Although it is a commonplace of cultural criticism and art historical writing to note that the artefacts that fill museums have been displaced from their original spatial, social, and ritual contexts, what is thought of less often, if at all, is how these objects have been snatched from their original temporal contexts in the societies that produced them. Placed on more or less permanent view in museums or displayed in exhibitions that have no regard for the time-specific nature of the works, the painting by Lu Zhi or the Wanli-period dish, here exemplifying a larger curatorial practice, provide year-round pleasure and edification, which, however, comes at the cost of obscuring their position within the grand rhythms of life that governed their production and original display, and imbued them with significance and performative functions in the lives of the viewers. The association between seasonality and the Christmas tree is universally known and respected, but with regard to displays of Chinese art (even including in some Chinese museums), their connection with the time of year is all too often ignored.

Any examination of how the concept of time has been made manifest in Chinese visual and material culture will first recognise the importance of the four seasons, which are a macro-level and fundamental organising principle in Chinese art and culture as has been addressed by several scholars, including Jessica Rawson in a study of cosmological systems as a source of ornament and Ogawa Hiromitsu in an analysis of flower paintings that mark the passage of time through the display of seasonal blossoms.[4] Another way to analyse the role of time in Chinese art is to drill down to the micro-level of the celebration of festivals, both large and small, which reveals the extent to which China's visual culture has been generated in their service as markers of the annual cycle, especially in imperial, or pre-1912, China.[5] While many practices have changed or been diminished in modern China, a link between major festival dates and specific imagery still exists.

[4] Jessica Rawson, 'Cosmological systems as sources of art, ornament and design', *Bulletin of the Museum of Far Eastern Antiquities, Stockholm*, 72 (2000), 133–89; and Ogawa Hiromitsu, 'Chū goku kachōga no jikū–kachōga kara kakizatsuga e' ('Space and time in Chinese bird and flower painting'), in Teisuke Toda and Ogawa Hiromitsu (ed.), *Chūgoku no Kachōga to Nihon* (Tokyo, 1983), pp. 92–107.
[5] One of the first English sources to draw attention to the subject of festivals is Tun Li-ch'en, translated and annotated by Derk Bodde, *Annual Customs and Festivals in Peking as recorded in*

The calendar and marking the passage of time

The Chinese festival calendar—a term here used to refer to decorous rites and more boisterous, communal festivals—is extremely full, with more than one occasion to be marked each month. A tabulation of large and small annual events in the Qing dynasty yields nearly one hundred and fifty rites that required some form of observation, which could have been as simple as placing a vase of flowers or an offering of incense and wine on a domestic altar, or far more elaborate entailing exuberant public and family festivities.[6]

The number of major festivals for which the imperial court granted time off from work—from one to seven consecutive days—and which were celebrated with street parades, extended family visits, and elaborate social dining, differed over time. In the Tang dynasty (618–907) fifty-three such festivals were listed, while in the Ming and Qing dynasties the number was reduced to three—the Winter Solstice, New Year, and the Emperor's Birthday.[7] Yet, in actual practice, Double Fifth and the autumnal Moon Festival also were major events in late imperial China and together with the New Year holiday served as the nexus for the most exuberant festivities and engendered the greatest production of objects for festival use and display. A reduction in the number of days off from work in the Ming and Qing dynasties compared to earlier times stands in an inverse relationship to the growing enthusiasm in the late period for observing holiday celebrations with elaborate preparations. Yet, many of the Ming and Qing events, while splendidly marked by displays of goods, were in fact nonetheless small holiday observances. Yet the culture of the

---

the *Yen-ching Sui-shi-ji* (Beiping[Beijing], 1936); another source that similarly focuses on late imperial festivals in Beijing is Zhang Jiangcai (comp.), *Beiping sui shi zhi* (*An Historical Account of Annual Customs and Festivals in Beiping*) (Guoli Beiping yanjiuyuan shixue yanjiu hui, 1936); more recently, see Yuan Hongqi, 'Qianlong shiqi de gongting jieqing huodong' ('Festival Activities at the Imperial Court during the Qialong period'), *Gugong Bowuyuan yuankan*, 53(3) (1991), 81–7. For references to earlier festivals see Derk Bodde, *Festivals in Classical China: New Year and Other Annual Observances during the Han Dynasty 206 B.C.–A.D. 220* (Princeton, NJ, 1975); Meng Yuanlao (1147), *Dongjing menghua lu* (Jinan, 2000); Jacques Gernet (trans. from the French by H. M. Wright), *Daily Life in China on the Eve of the Mongol Invasion 1250–1276* (Stanford, CA, 1970, from the French 1959).

[6] Tun and Bodde, *Annual Customs and Festivals in Peking*. For detailed descriptions of some court festival observed during the Qianlong emperor's reign, see Yuan Hongqi, 'Qianlong shiqi de gongting jieqing huodong', pp. 81–7.

[7] Lien-sheng Yang, 'Schedules of work and rest in Imperial China', *Harvard Journal of Asiatic Studies*, 18 (1955), 305.

period that promoted public displays of wealth was well suited to a mind-set that deemed it essential to have special decorations, clothing, and foods for each different rite and festival.

Given the fullness of the festival calendar only a small subset has been chosen here to elucidate some connections between art and annual celebrations. As it is important to consider how both major and minor festivals impacted the visual culture of China, the events examined in this study include two major holidays—the opposing pair of the wintertime New Year celebration and the summertime Double Fifth—and a few minor festivals, notably Spring's Beginning and the slightly later springtime Flower Festival.

It is worth noting at the outset that one of the distinctive features of Chinese festival customs and imagery is their inclusive nature. Commoners and the elite, including members of the imperial court, mostly celebrated the same holiday events with the same entertainments and foods, and sharing a consistent visual vocabulary across all social boundaries.[8] The greatest difference was the degree of lavishness of any given celebration, which was linked to social position and personal wealth. Another point of consistency was across time: festivals and their routine practices naturally changed over time, and yet many precedents for late imperial customs are observed in the Han dynasty (206 BC–AD 220) that itself continued and expanded upon seasonal rites practiced in the Zhou dynasty (*c.*1046–221 BC).

The period of greatest interest for studies of material cultural and art history, however, is the Ming and Qing dynasties. Craig Clunas has pointed out that time arguably had a greater visual presence in Ming culture than at any previous period, thus ensuring we can find many links between art and festival occasions.[9] This trend continued to build momentum in the succeeding Qing dynasty, whose emperors carefully observed Chinese and Manchu rites. They also placed greater emphasis than before on charting festivals through sets of artworks consisting of twelve monthly images.[10] The new emphasis on twelve may be in reference to Western calendrical traditions, although it is also a number with Chinese precedents.

---

[8] Maggie Bickford brings attention to the inclusiveness of festival imagery in 'The symbolic seasonal round in house and palace: counting the auspicious nines in Traditional China', in Ronald G. Knapp and Kai-Yin Lo (eds.), *House, Home, Family: Living and Being Chinese* (Honolulu, HI, 2005), pp. 349–71.

[9] Craig Clunas, *Empire of Great Brightness: Visual and Material Cultures of Ming China, 1368–1644* (London, 2007), p. 24.

[10] Chen Yunru, 'Shijian de xingzhuang: Qing yuan hua shier yue ling tu de yanjiu' ('The Shape of Time: A Study of Twelve Months in the Qing Court'), *Gugong xueshu jikan*, vol. 22, no. 4 (summer 2005), 103–39. For a more general study of the importance of paintings created for annual festival

The rites and festivals that inspired the production of paintings, prints, ceramics, textiles, and many other types of artefact, as well as some of the buildings and gardens in which they were used, gave expression to a profound concern with correctly measuring and regulating time in imperial China, which was directly tied to the importance of the agrarian calendar.[11] One example that draws attention to the importance of measuring time for agricultural concerns and shows how such an exercise can be given a festive, visual form is the practice of counting off the eighty-one days that lay between the Winter Solstice and the beginning of warm weather for planting—a counting system that is measured in nine units of nine days each. This tradition of 'counting the nines' has been thoroughly studied by Maggie Bickford who illustrates examples of similar visual aids used by semi- or illiterate farmers and by courtiers alike to count off the days and bring good fortune to their families.[12] Both text-based and purely pictorial systems to count off these eighty-one days were employed. A clever example of word-based imagery was the practice of writing a poem that alluded to spring imagery and ensuring that the poem consisted of exactly eighty-one brushstrokes, or nine characters, each of nine strokes. Such a poem was prepared in advance by writing the words in outline form, and then beginning on the Winter Solstice, filling in one brushstroke a day. An example of such a work from the hand of the Daoguang Emperor (1820–50) is displayed in the Palace Museum, Beijing.[13] The practice of an

---

dates at the Qing court, see a study on the works ordered by the Yongzheng and Qianlong emperors by Giuseppe Castiglione: Wei Dong, 'Lang Shining yu Qing gong jieling hua', *Gugong bowuyuan yuankan*, 2 (1988), no. 40, pp. 80–7.

[11] That architectural settings were sometimes directly inspired by festivals is less often acknowledged than recognition of links with paintings, porcelains, and other portable art forms. One example of architecture relates to the Spring Purification Festival (*fuchu*) which is celebrated in the third lunar month. During the Ming and Qing dynasties, gardens—in the palace, temple compounds, and owned by private scholars—were sometimes embellished with man-made, decorative watercourses for use during this festival occasion. Originally the festival was a day for expelling evil and praying for fertility, but by the Ming dynasty it was widely celebrated as a day to compose poetry. This association can be traced to a link with China's celebrated calligrapher, Wang Xizhi (AD 303–61), who on this day in 353 wrote the most highly admired calligraphic work in China, the *Preface to the Gathering at the Orchid Pavilion*. The setting for Wang's composition was an outing of scholarly friends on Spring Purification Festival. They sat beside a meandering stream on which wine cups were floated with each participant compelled to compose a poem before the cup reached him, or he had to drink a forfeit. Ming and Qing garden designers made artificial watercourses for this purpose. One of the courtyards in the residential section of the Forbidden City boasts an example; see *Zijincheng* (Forbidden City Magazine) (2006), 3. 136, p. 56.

[12] Bickford, 'The symbolic seasonal round', p. 351.

[13] See the cover of *Zijincheng* (Forbidden City Magazine) (2006), 3. 136.

emperor 'counting the nines' brings attention to the fundamental principle in imperial China that it was the Son of Heaven, the emperor himself,
at the summit of the enterprise of keeping time and regulating the calendar
in order to ensure the collective prosperity of his vast agrarian empire.[14]

The correct calculation of the calendar marked by festival observances
provided practical guidance for timing the labours of the agricultural year.
This was a complicated task given that the lunar calendar fluctuated as
much as a month from one year to another and required a parallel system
fixed to solar reckoning in order to bring it into accord with the seasonal
dates for agriculture. The Chinese calendar is complex precisely because it
is a luni-solar system. Months—or technically 'lunations'—lasted either
twenty-nine or thirty days and the Chinese year consisted of either 354 or
355 days, which thus required the periodic insertion of an intercalary
month to align the lunar cycle with solar reckoning.[15]

The first day of the lunar year was set by court astronomers to fall on
the first day of the second new moon after the Winter Solstice (fixed by
the solar calendar), reflecting the close coordination between lunar and
solar calculations. In understanding the intricacies of the Chinese lunar
system, it is worth noting that equinoxes and solstices marked the zenith,
or middle, of each season, unlike in the West where these four divisions
herald the beginning of a season. Thus, the first, second, and third lunar
months that comprise spring and embrace the spring equinox also encompass the extremely cold weather that corresponds to the month of February
in the Western calendar, and likewise Chinese autumn begins with the hot
weather that corresponds by Western calculation to August. The complexity of reconciling the lunar and solar systems is little less than a struggle
which explains why devices, including pictures, charts, and poems that
allow one to 'count the nines' and to determine when to plant seeds, were
immensely important and popular.[16]

---

[14] The emperor's role in keeping time that is well expressed by Jacques Gernet in his study of the
Yuan dynasty (1279–1368) in *Daily Life in China* applies to later times as well: 'It was the court
that fixed, printed and circulated throughout the empire the official annual calendar for the year: the
Emperor was still, according to most ancient traditions, the master and regulator of Time' (p. 181).
[15] For greater detail about Chinese calendars see Helmer Aslaksen, 'The mathematics of the Chinese
Calendar' (preprint, National Univ. of Singapore at <http://www.math.nus.edu.sg/aslaksen/
calendar>, 'Chinese calendar', 1999); Bodde, *Festivals in Classical China*, pp. 26–34 and 106–10;
Joseph Needham with the collaboration of Wang Ling *et al.*, *Science and Civilisation in China:
Volume 3: Mathematics and the Sciences of the Heavens and the Earth* (Cambridge, 1959),
pp. 390–408.
[16] Ellen Johnston Laing, *Art & Aesthetics in Chinese Popular Prints: Selections from the Muban
Foundation Collection* (Ann Arbor, MI, 2002) illustrates a number of prints that were of aid to
farmers.

As the Grand Master of Time, the emperor took part in all the rites and festivals set by the Ministry of Rites that helped to regulate people's lives and their agricultural endeavours, including his ploughing the first furrow of the planting season. This imperial duty, which had been in place since the Zhou dynasty and lasted until the fall of the Qing, was predicated on a general understanding that the emperor's expansive virtue would ensure the success of the harvest and, while details of the practice changed over time, the basic outline was the same.[17]

Qing dynasty records indicate that the ceremony was practised with the emperor holding a yellow trowel and the reigns of a yellow ox attached to a plough of the same colour. Yellow was both the colour of the earth and emblematic of the emperor. During the rite, the emperor dug three furrows to plant seeds, and then his officials made further furrows and finally peasant farmers finished the job.[18] This imperial spectacle took place in suburban Beijing at the Temple of Agriculture (Xiannong tan) on the day that corresponded to the first conjunction of the sun and the moon in the year, usually around 5 or 6 February, which is the Chinese festival called 'lichun', or Spring's Beginning. In concert with the emperor ploughing the ground in the empire's capital, the local officials repeated the same act throughout the rest of the country signalling the farmers to begin work in earnest.

The imperial connection with tilling is recognised in two types of artwork associated with the court. The more unusual case consists of paintings that depict a member of the imperial family in the act of farming. Prince Yinzhen, who took the throne as the Yongzheng Emperor in 1723, was the innovator for this kind of personal image and had himself painted enacting several stages of rice cultivation and also preparing silk. These self-referential commissions may have reflected an anxious desire to demonstrate his lofty character and thorough understanding of imperial duty since Yongzheng's rise to the throne was shrouded by court intrigue. Ideal depictions of him such as this may have played into some machinations useful to demonstrate his suitability as a ruler.[19]

---

[17] For reference to the Zhou dynasty, see Robert Eno, 'Chapter 1: Deities and ancestors in early oracle inscriptions', in Donald S. Lopez (ed.), *Religions of China in Practice* (Princeton, NJ, 1996), entry no. 57. A broader study is found in E. A. Armstrong, 'The ritual of the plough', *Folklore*, 54 (1943), 250–7.

[18] Rice seems to have been the general crop but the emperor also seeded corn according to Armstrong, 'The ritual of the plough'. Some Qing imperial paintings depict planting rice; see Frances Wood, *China: The Three Emperors, 1662–1795*, Guide for Teachers and Students, Royal Academy of Arts, 2006.

[19] Yinzhen is depicted in acts of farming and sericulture in the album *Pictures of Tilling and Weaving Portraying Yinzhen*, painted in the late Kangxi period (ink and colour on silk) in the

More conventional court practice was an imperial desire to assemble important paintings on the theme of tilling and weaving and reproduce these images through the media of stone rubbings, woodblock prints, and paintings on porcelains. The Kangxi Emperor (r. 1662–1722) sponsored sets of these images for wide distribution (Fig. 3). His grandson, the Qianlong Emperor (r. 1736–95), continued the enthusiasm for the theme and one of his inscriptions on a painting demonstrates the appropriateness of viewing images of tilling at the right time of year, bringing us to the point that in imperial China the act of viewing art was often coded by time of year. The date of his inscription on the antique scroll in his collection, *Tilling Rice, after Lou Shou*, illustrates this. When the painting entered Qianlong's possession it was attributed to the famous Song dynasty artist Liu Songnian (from *c.*1150 until after 1225) but, deploying his (or a courtier's?) skill as a connoisseur, he offered a more fitting assessment by reassigning the painting to Cheng Qi (active mid- to late thirteenth century).[20]

Qianlong inscribed the work several times while it was in his collection, but the first instance was on the fifth day after *shangyuan* (fifteenth day of the first lunar month) in the *yichou* year (corresponding to 26 February 1769). He likely chose this time because of its proximity to *lichun*, making the date appropriate, or even auspicious, as a time for an emperor to view and discuss a painting about agriculture. The emperor's symbolic enacting of the practice of ploughing or, one step more removed, viewing the labour of tilling through artwork were both actions that took meaning from their timely practice.

The Chinese festival calendar is filled with business-like occasions, such as making the first furrows of the year, that mark the flow of time and establish proper behaviour for each season, but which do not entail communal, boisterous celebrations that are limited to a smaller number of major holidays. But many of these small annual rites engendered the creation of objects or dictated what should be displayed or worn. An example was the event every year in the third lunar month when the emperor inaugurated the change from wearing warm to cool hats (or the change from gold to jade hairpins for women) and in the eighth lunar month he marked the change back to wearing fur hats and gold hair ornaments.[21]

Palace Museum, Beijing. One leaf is reproduced in Evelyn Rawski and Jessica Rawson (eds.) *The Three Emperors 1662–1795* (London, 2005), figure 60, p. 242.

[20] The painting in the Freer Gallery of Art, Smithsonian Institution, Washington, DC (accession no. F1954.21), is illustrated with translations of the poems and colophons at <http://www.asia.si.edu/songyuan/default.asp.>, entry no. 13.

[21] Tun and Bodde, *Annual Customs and Festivals*, p. 35.

Figure 3. *Scene of Tilling* from *Imperially Commissioned Illustrations of Agriculture and Sericulture in 46 leaves (Yuzhi gengzhi tu)*; illustration by Jiao Bingzhen, poetic inscription by Shengzu, the Kangxi Emperor; engravers: Zhu Gui and Mei Yufeng; printer, Imperial press Wuyingdian, Beijing; preface dated 1696; woodblock print in ink on paper, watercolours added by brush; 24 × 24 cm (impression); 1949,0709.0.1. © The Trustees of the British Museum.

Communal festival celebrations

Anthropologists and philosophers have argued for the universal importance of festivals and given perspective to some of the functions they fulfil
around the world. Roger Caillois in his seminal work notes that at their
most basic level festivals are periods in which the boundaries between the
sacred and profane become permeable, the human and spirit worlds inter-
act, and communities and families draw together to find release from routine in forms of social catharsis that include communal entertainments,
pageantry, feasting, and revelry.[22] Caillois sees the importance of the festival lying its role as a paroxysm of life; an aspect that seems to be diminishing in celebrations in modern, industrial societies that become ever
more regulated or sober as Charles Dickens presciently observed in 1831
when he noted that his fellow citizens were becoming so serious they no
longer enjoyed dancing around the May Pole.[23]

In the case of China, major festivals celebrate the complementary
totality of gods, ghosts, ancestors, and family members reunited, confirm
key agricultural dates, and provide social cohesion that links the imperial
and commoners' realms through relentlessly inclusive practices and
imagery. Festival activities provide the opportunity for grand ceremonies
to expel evil influences and make the world ready for a new beginning.[24]

In Chinese festival imagery flowers and children dominate the visual
field and their importance is linked to notions of cosmic renewal. The pre-
dictability of flowers to regenerate and appear on seasonal cue as well as to
grow quickly and luxuriantly is auspicious and easily linked to images of
fertility, while plump male children whose vigour and presence in a family
ensures the continuation of the lineage are considered to be the highest
blessing in the Chinese hierarchy of wishes. Images of healthy boys and
a profusion of flowers indicate a state of harmony and the promise of
unlimited new beginnings; thus these two motifs, either singly or together,
appear in the majority of pictorial images designed for festival use.

Another point about the importance of festivals is the necessary respite from work they provide. The dual nature of festivals as celebration

---

[22] For general comments on festivals see Roger Caillois, *Man and the Sacred*, translated by Meyer
Barash (Glencoe, IL, 1959); for views linked to Asia, see A. W. Sadler, 'The form and meaning of
the festival', *Asian Folklore Studies*, 28 (1969), 1–16, and Charles Stafford, *Separation and Reunion*
(Cambridge, 2001), chapter one on Chinese New Year and Mid-Autumn Festival.
[23] Charles Dickens, 'The "Clergy" on May Day', published in *All the Year Round*, 30 April 1881.
[24] See Caillois, *Man and the Sacred*; and Sadler, 'The form and meaning of the festival' for
considerations of festivals as markers of a new beginning.

and rest is cited as early as the *Li Ji*, or the *Book of Rites*, attributed to Confucius (551–479 BC) and redacted in the Han dynasty. Comment on a festival to drive away evil spirits resulted in endorsement of the celebration solely on the grounds that it provided needed rest and pleasure.[25] In China, farmers, labourers, and government officials all organised their lives around festival dates, something that was increasingly the case for the social and political elite in the Ming and Qing dynasties, when frequent, minor breaks common in ancient work schedules were replaced by granting officials longer periods off at the major breaks, especially the New Year.

Mention of the term 'festival calendar' draws attention to a parallel calendar that explicitly demonstrates the thesis that by Ming times many artworks were intended only for brief display in synch with festival occasions. In the seventeenth century, Wen Zhenheng (1585–1645), a scholar, artist, and arbiter of taste, wrote the manual *Zhangwu zhi* (*Superfluous Things*) to provide detailed information about garden design and interior decoration appropriate for anyone trying to position themselves among China's social elite. It included a 'Calendar for the Display of Scrolls' that advises on the appropriate images for paintings to hang on major holidays.[26] As with the rest of his advice to his readers, he emphasises the vulgarity of disregarding the guidelines he sets out. Living in an age of showmanship when the scholar-class competed to make certain their own good taste was known, his suggestions were widely followed. Wen Zhenheng appealed to a sort of snobbishness of the time by including the suggestion in his calendar that the paintings displayed are best if they date to the Song dynasty (960–1279)—works that were rare and expensive in the Ming dynasty.

> On New Year morning you should display Song paintings of the Gods of Happiness and images of the Sages of olden times. Round the 15th of the first moon you should suspend on your wall paintings showing the Lantern Festival or marionette performances.

The Lantern Festival that occurs with the full moon fifteen days after the New Year is the concluding event of the New Year holiday season. Wen's statement offers some insight into a little studied theme and helps explain

---

[25] The seminal article on work and festival breaks in China is Lien-sheng Yang, 'Schedules of work and rest in Imperial China'; Yang's writing also brings attention to the comment in the *Li Ji*, see James Legge (trans.), *The Li Ki*, vol. 2, p. 167 (Oxford, 1885).
[26] A comprehensive study of *Superfluous Things* is found in Craig Clunas, *Superfluous Things: Material Culture and Social Status in Early Modern China* (Cambridge, 1991). For the calendar itself, see a translation in R. H. van Gulik, *Chinese Pictorial Art as Viewed by the Connoisseur* (Rome, 1958), pp. 4–6.

a relatively large number of unsigned, untitled paintings depicting boys playing with marionettes in the Chinese repertoire. It is worth examining all of Wen's prescriptions to discover reasons for the popularity of certain themes, which were in fact images to be hung for short duration and useful for charting the passage of the year.

Wen Zhenheng's list continues:

> In the second moon there should be representations of ladies enjoying spring walks, of plum blossoms, apricots, camellia, orchids, and peach and pear blossoms. On the third day of the third moon there should be shown Song pictures of the Dark Warrior, while round the Qingming Festival there should be shown pictures of peonies and *paeonia albiflora*. On the eighth day of the fourth moon, the birthday of Buddha, you should display representations of Buddha by Song and Yuan [dynasty (1279–1368)] artists ... On the fifth day of the fifth moon there should be charms written by Daoist masters and calligraphic specimens by famous men of the Song and Yuan dynasties; further scrolls depicting the Duanyang Festival, the Dragon Boat races, tigers made of artemisia [moxa] and the Five Poisonous Creatures ...

His stipulations clearly drew upon practices already in use before he wrote his treatise. His reference to displaying Song and Yuan paintings on these themes was completely plausible since a corpus of works with these themes exists suggesting that already by the Song preferences for specific festival imagery were under development, which is also borne out by writings of the period detailing holiday practices and displays.[27]

James Cahill has made the point that already in the mid-Ming period before Wen Zhenheng the themes of paintings he mentions were important to collectors of the period to amass. The inventory list of belongings confiscated from the disgraced Ming prime minister Yan Song (1481–1568) match up closely with Wen Zhenheng's calendar for a year's worth of seasonal art display: 'Together, they [Wen's calendar and the Yan inventory] provide a good indication of the demands that were placed on professional painters, as well as on the antique market and the studios of forgers, who supplied "Song paintings" (such as are stipulated in Wen Zhenheng's list) for a demand that must have vastly exceeded the supply.'[28]

---

[27] Song dynasty writings packed with information on festival practices and goods include Wu Zimu, 1274, *Mengliang lu* (Records of Dreams); Meng Yanlao (from *c*.1080 until after 1147), *Dongjing menghua lu* (Prosperity in the Capital), and Zhou Mi (1232–1308), *Wulin jiushi* (Things of the Past from Wulin).

[28] See 'The Writings of James Cahill' at <http://jamescahill.info/rll.169.145.shtml#_ftnt1>, Cahill Lectures and Papers, CPL 30:1999, Columbia University Lecture, 3 March 1999: 'Is there a Chinese equivalent to Ukiyo-e?'

Chinese New Year

The best known category of seasonal imagery is that prepared for the Chinese New Year, including *nianhua*, or New Year prints, that appear as single-sheet wood-block prints used for display on doors and around the home.[29] One type of New Year print—images of protective Door Gods, or Guardians, which appear in pairs, one for each leaf of the traditional two part door—offer an obvious exception to the rule of short-term, timely display because they typically are left on view for an entire year (Fig. 4). But this practice is also rooted in the importance of the seasonal round and the need to change particular images on particular days. Custom dictated that the Door God images should be replaced every New Year's eve because faded, tattered images have little or no power; yet, their protective function was so important that it seemed best to leave the prints in place as a reminder to evil forces that the household was under a watchful eye. However, the images only possessed power if in the first instance, when they were fresh and brightly coloured, they had been pasted on a door in a timely manner, which meant New Year's eve. If so, the images of fierce, axe-wielding, bushy-bearded warriors dressed in armour were empowered to repel evil. In addition to military Door Guardians, pictures of civil officials also exist, and both the warriors and officials are sometimes pictured holding symbols emblematic of emolument and good fortune, wishes deemed especially appropriate for the new beginning of the year.

While Door Guardians are probably the most familiar Chinese auspicious images around the world because of their annual display every year by restaurant owners in Chinatowns across the world, there is a far more extensive list of New Year images all with a long history. The lunar New Year is both the most joyous and the longest holiday in the festival calendar because it falls at a fallow time of year when farmers could best afford to rest. It therefore was logical to make this the seasonal holiday with the most entertainments and visits to friends and family and, with so much social intercourse, it was also a perfect time to display special wares, including clothing, tableware, decorations and toys, each of which was encoded with auspicious wishes appropriate to new beginnings.

---

[29] See Ellen Johnston Laing, 'Picture Calendars in Late Imperial China: art and commerce', in Jennifer Purtle and Hans Bjarne Thomsen (eds.), *Looking Modern: East Asian Visual Culture from Treaty Ports to World War II* (Chicago, IL 2009), pp. 62–84; and Laing, *Art & Aesthetics in Chinese Popular Prints: Selections from the Muban Foundation Collection*.

Figure 4. *New Year Print of Door-god in Military Dress;* twentieth century; Yanzhou, Shandong province; woodblock print in ink and colours on paper; 45 × 28 cm; 1982,1217,0.133; © The Trustees of the British Museum.

The traditional name for the festival is 'Passing over into the Year' or *guonian*; however, in 1914, Yuan Shikai (1859–1916), as the first president of the newly founded Republic of China, changed the name to 'Spring Festival', or *chun jie*. This momentous decision was in order to differentiate the holiday from 1 January, which had recently been authorised as a government holiday in a move to demonstrate modernisation through acceptance of the Western, or so-called international, calendar.[30] People continued, however, to frame family and social life around the lunar New Year and merchants, too, persisted in using the familiar lunar holiday as the day of reckoning for accounts. A tense co-existence between the two New Year holidays ensued with the traditional date, now called *chun jie*, continuing to have the greater importance. This recent postscript to the ancient and continuous history of the Chinese New Year festival reconfirms in modern times the explicit political authority that is held by the person who controls and imposes the festival calendar. Just as the emperor's court determined the first day of the New Year in imperial times, the President was showing his power by imposing a new regime of time and by adding the Western New Year into the list of annual celebrations.

Regardless of the relatively recent adoption of the nomenclature 'Spring Festival', the word 'spring' (*chun*) has in fact always been associated with the Chinese lunar New Year, or *guonian*. Images and the word for 'spring' figured prominently in traditional literature and visual imagery dedicated to the lunar New Year festival. In this paper the term 'New Year' is used to refer to the Chinese lunar date.

In imperial China (as now) the New Year was (and is) a time to display images that embody and broadcast wishes for long life, wealth, social and professional distinction for oneself and one's progeny. Popular images can take many forms and often rely on a combination of sources, for example drawing on folklore and also often employing the device of the rebus to make their point. To exemplify this point a common image printed for the New Year depicts a boy dressed as a high-ranking official sitting astride a giant rooster prancing about on a ground laden with auspicious objects. The print bears characters that read 'New Spring'—a reference to the New Year—and also provides the name of the workshop in Henan where it was produced in the early twentieth century.[31]

---

[30] Henrietta Harrison, *China* (New York, 2001), pp. 158–61 and 200–1 describes various attempts to convert from the lunar to solar calendar during the early Republic.

[31] For this and other New Year prints see Clarissa von Spee (ed.), *The Printed Image in China: Eighth to Twenty-first Centuries* (London, 2010). My understanding of this print is indebted to Ellen Johnston Laing (see pp. 106–7).

The key to understanding the design lies in deconstructing it as a rebus. Lying on the ground are a music chime, a *ruyi* (as you wish) sceptre and three citrons. Through the value of these objects used as homophones it is possible to construct the phrase, 'may you celebrate wishes for top rank in all three examinations [that will bring you official rank]'. 'Three citrons' (*san yuan*) sounds like 'top candidate three times', which is the number of exams a scholar must pass on his path to obtaining entrance to Chinese official-dom, a career aspiration that explains the boy's costume. The music chime sounds like the word 'to celebrate'. To say 'big rooster' sounds like another phrase that means 'great good fortune'. The print also invokes folk tradi-tions that extend back to at least to the sixth century CE, when it was cus-tomary to put an image of a rooster on the door on the first day of the New Year because the cockerel's morning call dissipates the darkness of evil.

New Year prints, including Door Guardians and the above described image of a rooster, were displayed at the British Museum in an exhibition of wide-ranging print themes, entitled *The Printed Image in China: Eighth to Twenty-first Centuries,* which was on view from May to September 2010. The display certainly did not coincide with the New Year and rather was fixed according to other conveniences. Therefore, however engaging, attractive, and technically well-made the New Year prints are, when viewed like this, out of season and thus transformed into art in a formal sense, they lose their original performative power. The visitor is allowed to forget that the impetus for their creation was as working images with time-delimited powers.

In addition to prints, wealthy households and the court also commis-sioned all manner of expensive luxury goods for the New Year, including what James Cahill among others calls 'functional paintings'.[32] A delicate, exquisitely detailed hanging scroll painted on silk, which dates to the late thirteenth to early fifteenth century, now in the Freer Gallery of Art, Washington, DC, represents a fine example of a popular type of image made for seasonal display (Fig. 5). The image depicts a princely house-hold, and may have been made for such an establishment or at least for a distinguished household.[33] Conveniently for the modern viewer, it is a

---

[32] James Cahill, *Pictures for Use and Pleasure: Vernacular Painting in High Qing China* (Berkeley, CA, 2010).

[33] *Palace Women and Children Celebrating the New Year* (*F1916.403*) is illustrated on the Freer's website at <http://www.asia.si.edu/collections/singleObject.cfm?ObjectNumber=F1916.403>, which gives the date as sixteenth century. This author believes the work is earlier—Yuan to early Ming in date, an opinion shared by James Cahill when we viewed the painting together many years ago in the Freer storage vaults, and who has recently published the painting in *Pictures for Use and Pleasure*, p. 105, also with a Yuan to early Ming date.

Figure 5. *Palace Women and Children Celebrating the New Year*; anonymous; Yuan-Ming dynasty (thirteenth to early fifteenth century); panel mounted hanging scroll; ink and colours on silk; 228.2 × 3.5 cm; Freer Gallery of Art, Smithsonian Institution, Washington, DC; Gift of Charles Lang Freer (F1916.403) © Freer–Sackler.

self-referential view of the New Year illustrating several of the key celebratory activities enjoyed during the two-week holiday period telescoped
together into a single pictorial scene. This type of image and variations on
it became extremely popular in the Qing dynasty, both at the court and
among the wealthy in large cities.

The anonymous artist of the Freer Gallery's painting was a master of
the style known as 'ruler, or boundary painting' (*jiehua*) and deployed
fine-line brushwork and ruler precision to execute the scene. It presents
the activities of women and children set within a splendid, walled-in compound of a two-story pavilion and several lower buildings constructed
with bright red pillars, airy verandas and marble stairs. A towering pine
and blossoming plum and camellia trees add natural beauty to the grand
residence. Their open flowers at this time of year suggest the setting is in
the Jiangnan region, perhaps near Nanjing, the first Ming capital, as the
plum does not usually flower in time for the New Year further north.

The artist provides a bird's eye view into the compound and the first
detail to catch a viewer's attention is a woman standing on a table to pin
up an inexpensive print of a dishevelled figure. This is Zhong Kui, the
Demon Queller—a legendary hero associated with the New Year since the
eighth century. He is the subject of a huge number of popular, low-to-
moderately priced prints that were widely distributed around villages during the twelfth month and for the New Year itself at the beginning of the
first month. Many such prints have survived, including in the collection of
the British Museum (Fig. 6). To see such a print being pasted on the wall
of a princely household in this Yuan-to-early-Ming painting reinforces the
point about the inclusive nature of festival imagery across social lines in
imperial China. Such protective images were put up on New Year's eve
when sacrifices of food and wine were being made to the family ancestors
and also to guardian spirits, including the gods of the door, stove, bed,
courtyard, and the earth. However, some traditions indicate images of
Zhong Kui could be hung earlier as well, any time during the twelfth
month.[34]

Zhong Kui was also the subject of much more elaborate and expensive
artworks intended for seasonal display, as seen in a sixteenth-century silk
scroll painted for the New Year that depicts a humorous debacle (Fig. 7).
Zhong Kui on donkey-back is shown trying to cross a snowy bridge at a
moment when disaster befalls one of his supplicant demons. The grotesque

---

[34] See Wen Zhenheng as translated by R. H. van Gulik, *Chinese Pictorial Art as Viewed by the
Connoisseur*, p. 5.

Figure 6. *Demon-Queller Zhong Kui with wintertime plum bough and demon with tray of jewels*;
Qing dynasty, eighteenth century; Suzhou, Jiangsu province; woodblock print in ink and colours
on paper, 29.4 × 21.2 cm; 1964,0411,0.12; © The Trustees of the British Museum.

Figure 7. *Zhong Kui and Demons Crossing a Bridge*; Ming dynasty; close copy of Dai Jin (1388–1462); sixteenth century; panel mounted hanging scroll; ink and colours on silk; 197.4 × 118.6 cm; Freer Gallery of Art, Smithsonian Institution, Washington, DC; Gift of Charles Lang Freer (1911. 283); © Freer–Sackler.

little creature has just crashed through the bridge's sodden planks into the icy water below; pandemonium ensues and Zhong Kui's donkey balks.[35] This painting is signed as Dai Jin (1388–1462), but probably is instead an extremely close copy of his original work. Dai Jin, one of the most inventive talents of the Ming, served briefly as a court painter and then subsequently worked outside the imperial sphere, but his work in both the imperial and private realms points up the close connections in imagery and approach an artist could bring to festival paintings throughout the empire.

Zhong Kui Crossing a Bridge exemplifies the practice of major artists to create impressive works of him for display at court and in wealthy homes, or for gift giving. At the same time inexpensive wood block prints were also in demand by all social classes. The principle of production of a wide range of quality and prices of festival imagery applies to all holiday occasions.

The story of Zhong Kui that led to the proliferation of his image is rooted in an event said to have occurred in the eighth century, but which was first recounted in the Song dynasty.[36] Popular convention records that when the Tang Dynasty Emperor Xuanzong (r. 713–56) was suffering from a feverish delirium, he dreamt that his palace was besieged by demons. Suddenly a large, grotesque man appeared and devoured the miscreants. The delighted emperor sought to discover his protector's identity and learned it was Zhong Kui, a failed scholar from a previous era who had committed suicide out of shame for not being allowed to pass the palace examination because the emperor had declared him too unseemly for the honour. Xuanzong granted him special posthumous privileges and in return Zhong Kui's spirit vowed to protect the imperial household eternally.

Upon waking the emperor's health was miraculously restored and he summoned the court's most famous painter Wu Daozi (from 689 until after 755) to depict the imposing, dream-hero on a door to scare away evil.

---

[35] For more about *Zhong Kui and Demons Crossing a Bridge*, attributed to Dai Jin (1388–1462), F1911.283, see Shen C. Y. Fu, 'Puns and playfulness in Chinese painting', *Asian Art and Culture* (Autumn 1994), 58.

[36] General information about Zhong Kui is found in Hu Wan-ch'uan [Hu Wanquan], *Zhong Kui shenhua yu xiaoshuo zhi yanjiu* (Research on the Mythology and Stories of Zhong Kui) (Taipei: Wenshizhe, 1980); Ginger Cheng-chi Hsu, 'The Drunken Demon-Queller: Chung K'uei [Zhong Kui] in Eighteenth-Century Chinese Painting', Meishu shi yanjiu jikan, no. 3, 1996, pp. 144–62; and Mary H. Fong, 'A Probable Second "Chung Kuei [Zhong kui]" by Emperor Shun-chih [Xun zhi] of the Ch'ing [Qing] Dynasty', *Oriental Art*, XXIII, no. 4 (Winter 1977), 423–37.

Over time, Zhong Kui's conventional image came to show him as a wine-loving, swashbuckling gallant who, ugly and dishevelled, usually wields a sword and is accompanied by subservient demon helpers. Symbols of wealth and luck were also associated with him. By the Northern Song, his image was becoming indelibly linked to the New Year as a talisman to ward off evil and prints of Zhong Kui were sent along with almanacs to court officials at the end of the year.[37]

The association between Zhong Kui and the New Year continues into contemporary times, as seen in paintings by several modern masters, including Zhang Daqian (1899–1983). A scroll in the Arthur M. Sackler Gallery, Washington, DC, dated to 1926, depicts Zhong Kui receiving an offering of a blossoming plum branch, which indicates the New Year season, from an attendant demon.[38] In a surprising twist Zhang Daqian's inscription reveals his plan to hang the painting for the summertime festival of Double Fifth. This points to a great jump in the power of Zhong Kui's image in popular imagination that began to occur gradually from the late fifteenth century on, so that eventually his powers of exorcism associated with the New Year expanded to be appropriate for the summertime holiday.[39] This transformation became deeply rooted in the late seventeenth and eighteenth centuries, when it became standard to place Zhong Kui at the centre of Double Fifth celebrations. His image replaced that of the Daoist Celestial Master, another supernatural figure capable of exorcising evil who had had a long association with Double Fifth. Wen Zhenheng, in his late Ming dynasty calendar of paintings to display for different festivals, only mentions Zhong Kui for the twelfth month in advance of the New Year, suggesting that the link with the summer festival was not yet important during his lifetime.

The reasons for this change in Zhong Kui imagery are complicated, but as the New Year and Double Fifth festivals exactly mirror each other, occurring at the two times in the annual cycle when the balance of yin and yang shifts dramatically from the peak of one to the ascendancy of the other, they mark a dangerous temporary instability that calls for protective forces. It was presumably comforting in its symmetry to call upon the

---

[37] Ginger Hsu, 'The drunken demon queller', p. 142

[38] For the image, see <http://www.asia.si.edu/collections/singleObject.cfm?ObjectNumber=S1988 .49>, *Demon Presenting a Plum Bough*, by Zhang Daqian, 1926, museum purchase, 1988.49 and for fuller treatment see, Shen C. Y. Fu and Jan Stuart, *Challenging the Past: The Paintings of Chang Dai-chien* [Zhang Daqian] (Washington, DC, 1991).

[39] National Museum of History (comp.), *Chung K'uei [Zhong Kui] Paintings on the Fifth Day of the Fifth Month* (Taipei, 1996).

same popular figure of Zhong Kui to rein in evil on both of these major holidays. What is surprising then in Zhang Daqian's desire to hang up a picture of Zhong Kui on Double Fifth is not the reference to Zhong Kui but that he used an image with explicit New Year imagery—the plum—to put on the wall out of season. He wrote 'I playfully hang up the scroll', perhaps in reference to his subversion of the normal rules about seasonality for it would have been perfectly easy for Zhang to follow modern convention and hang up one of the many images produced from Qing times onwards of Zhong Kui pictured with pomegranate blossoms that were specially made for Double Fifth.

Putting up protective images of Door Guardians and portraits of Zhong Kui, as well as displaying prints to ensure good fortune such as the image of a boy astride a giant rooster, was only a small part of the New Year festivities. Wearing appropriate clothing and setting off firecrackers to scare away evil spirits were also typical rites and special delights. In the painting in the Freer Gallery under discussion, the princely child, who wears an auspiciously coloured red robe, bears witness to one of the key events of the New Year. He covers his ears in anticipation of the bang from a firecracker being lit by the maid.

Clothing was coded for holiday celebrations, and for the New Year it was always important to wear new garments. During the Ming dynasty the court developed fastidious rules to match their dress to the yearly cycle of festivals and individuals wore special cloth badges decorated with imagery appropriate to each of the annual occasions. The badges worn on the front and back of a robe could either be woven into the garment itself or be made separately and sewn onto a garment. Wearing of festival badges at the Ming court built upon precedents established in the Jin (1115–1234) and Yuan dynasties that, however, did not develop into an elaborate set of conventions until the Ming, reaching a crescendo of popularity during the latter part of the dynasty. These badges have been the subject of much study, initially and notably by Schuyler Cammann, to whose work the reader is referred for more information.[40]

In association with the long New Year celebration, the imperial family and courtiers wore two badges, one for the period extending from the Winter Solstice until the Lantern Festival, when a different badge was affixed to their clothing.[41] The imagery on the Ming badges appeared on

[40] Schuyler Cammann, 'Ming festival symbols', *Archives of the Chinese Art Society of America*, 7 (1953), 66–70.

[41] Information about many Ming imperial customs, including festival badges is found in Liu Ruoyu (*fl. c.*1572–1620), *Ming gong shi* (History of the Ming Palace) (Beijing, 1981). For examples

paintings, porcelains and other objects of the season. The badge put on clothing at the time of the Winter Solstice displays nine phoenixes as a main image in reference to the custom of 'Counting the Nines' to pace off the time until warmer weather for planting arrives. Seasonally appropriate plants—the plum, pine, and bamboo (the so-called Three Friends of Winter)—are typically worked into the design and carry wishes for longevity because of the hardiness of the plants to bloom and remain green in frigid weather. In addition to the phoenixes, the Winter Solstice/ New Year badges also typically depict three rams standing on red sunlike disks. Through the device of homophones this image creates a rebus for the common New Year expression, *sanyang kai tai*, that welcomes the blessings of the New Year, which has been explored in the work of Maggie Bickford.[42]

As the New Year season is the time when the yang forces begin their cyclical ascent after the yin forces have crested, the pairing of images of phoenixes and rams takes on additional poignancy to draw attention to this important cosmic shift. The image of the ram (also pronounced *yang*) is a useful device to draw attention to the propitious rise of this element, and the phoenix—an emblem of yin forces—appears larger than the rams in the design for the reason that it is the time of their peak, just before the yin/yang balance shifts.

After the fall of the Ming, the popularity of badges declined, but in the Qing, just as during the Ming, the colours of robes, their patterns and the details of the imperial headgear continued to be coded for each festival date. The annals from the Qianlong Emperor's reign bear punctilious record of his costume changes for each major event in the annual calendar.[43]

Returning to discussion of the Freer Gallery painting, it illustrates many of the joyous New Year's activities. In the courtyard a maid is pictured holding aloft a tray strewn with trinkets that suggest the abundance of merchandise available in special holiday markets set up just before the New Year, that overflowed with baubles, including glass balls, strings of pearls and beads, and toys, especially puppets, all of which are present here.

---

of badges see Urban Council of Hong Kong, *Heaven's Embroidered Cloths: One Thousand Years of Chinese Textiles* (Hong Kong, 1995), pp. 278 and 286. The section on rank badges, pp. 254–98, includes a number of festival badges for various of the annual celebrations.

[42] Maggie Bickford has written on the theme of the three rams; see 'Three rams and three friends: the working lives of Chinese auspicious motifs', *Asia Major*, 3rd series, 12 (1999), 127–58.

[43] Yuan Hongqi, 'Qianlong shiqi de gongting jieqing huodong', p. 83.

A woman arriving at the gate of the compound holds up a large ball of a type popular at the Lantern Festival. Its roundness recalls the full moon that is celebrated on that night and coloured balls, large and small, were tossed about in games throughout the empire during the New Year and Lantern Festival break. Some of the larger ones were intended for use as lanterns and were placed on stands as shades for burning candles. Lanterns of this construction are pictured in a section of the long hand-scroll, *Xianzong Enjoying Pleasures*, that depicts the Ming Emperor Zhu Jianshen, (temple name Xianzong; r. 1465–1487) delighting in seasonal entertainments.

Produced by court artists, this colourful painting now in the National Museum depicts the emperor at several moments in time, including his tour of the palace surveying the elaborate festivities he ordered for the Lantern Festival.[44] Court records supply lively descriptions of the New Year festivities he orchestrated several times during his reign, including grand feasts and ball games. On more than one occasion he directed the palace staff to reproduce folk celebrations within the palace grounds—a practice indebted to Song dynasty precedents which continued uninter-rupted into Qing times, especially under the Qianlong Emperor, who expanded the scale of festival celebrations.[45]

Emperor Xianzong converted a spacious courtyard in the private area of the palace into a lantern fair filled with archways constructed from branches and bedecked with row upon row of brilliantly blazing lanterns. The court set up booths with vendors hawking wares, and folk artists, acro-bats and performers demonstrated their skills. The cost was considerable which, more than merely suggesting a capacious appetite for pleasure, also demonstrates the importance emperors placed on festival celebrations.

In the Qing dynasty, the Manchu rulers continued most of the previ-ous dynasty's New Year and Lantern Festival customs, while also adding some of their own ethnic celebrations or intermixing the two. Court art-ists, like those outside the palace as well, produced a copious number of

[44] A detail of the New Year scene is reproduced in Craig Clunas, *Empire of Great Brightness*, p. 140.
[45] Jacques Gernet, *Daily Life in China*, p. 189–90 discusses the Song precedents. For a view of an elaborate Lantern Festival presentation at the Qing court, see the painting by Ding Guangpeng (active 1708–71) entitled *Taicu shi he* (Peace for the New Year); illustrated on the National Palace Museum, Taipei, website: <http://www.npm.edu.tw/exh99/palace/>. A letter by the Jesuit Jean-Denis Attiret (1702–68) offers some evidence of the practice of using the imperial garden in the Yuanming Yuan for festival celebrations in which eunuchs set up markets and re-enacted popular celebrations for the emperor's entertainment. See, a translation from the French by Sir Harry Beaumont (pseudonym of Joseph Spence) included in R. Dodsley and J. Dodsley, *Fugitive Pieces, on Various Subjects V1* (London: 1765), repr. Kessinger Publishing (Whitefish, MT, 2008).

paintings for each holiday. One of the common themes was to present a holiday-time domestic interior that showed family harmony, which was emblematic of the theme of cosmic harmony associated with festival events. This type of visual programme is represented by the New Year painting in the Freer Gallery of Art.

Another popular presentation was to picture boys—symbols of fecundity and cosmic harmony—gaily engaged in holiday games and typically in a garden setting effulgent with blossoming flowers appropriate to the season, thus bringing into play another motif to reinforce the image of fertility and abundance. The children's activities should not be interpreted as snapshots of actual events, but rather present carefully contrived images created to broadcast auspicious messages. In some ways these paintings were analogous to the modern Hallmark greeting card that employs conventional, even hackneyed, imagery to convey well wishes for the recipient. However, unlike the modern card, the Chinese paintings were understood to have agency to attract the very messages of good fortune to which they alluded and just as importantly to repel the evil forces that circulated at times like the New Year and Double Fifth when the balance of yin and yang was shifting and the boundary between the mortal world and that of gods and ghosts was porous.

Qing festival imagery drew heavily upon Chinese Han customs, but also incorporated occasional references to Manchu heritage.[46] An album leaf in the National Palace Museum, Taipei, of chubby boys playfully engaging in a mock hunt with lanterns as their props makes this point (Fig. 8). One of the rascals tugs at two wheel-mounted lanterns shaped like a rabbit and a deer, each of which sports a burning red candle in a cavity in the animal's back. His aim is to wheel them out of the danger posed by a companion boy mounted on a hobby horse—also a lantern with lit candle—who pulls taut a toy bow ready to release its arrow. Another fellow gleefully lunges towards the boy with the rabbit and deer, menacingly shaking his own lantern which is fashioned as a predator falcon and standing next to a hunting-dog lantern. The boys are enacting a Manchu hunting festival of *Xijing jie*, during which mounted archers skilfully pursue game in the wilds of Manchuria.[47]

---

[46] For discussion of intermixing Han and Manchu foods and feasting customs at the Qianlong court, see Yuan Hongqi, 'Qianlong shiqi de gongting jieqing huodong', p. 85.

[47] See National Palace Museum (ed.), *Yingxi tu* (Children at Play) (Taipei: National Palace Museum, 1990), p. 44. This leaf is from a Qianlong-period album entitled *Shengping leshi* (Peaceful Entertainments).

Figure 8. *Lantern Festival* from 12-leaf album of *Peace and Prosperity at the New Year*; Qing dynasty, Qianlong reign period (1736–95); album leaf in ink and colours on silk; National Palace Museum, Taiwan, Republic of China; © National Palace Museum.

It would be misleading to suggest that prints and paintings are the only, or even the main, type of New Year and Lantern Festival objects, at court or in the realm beyond. All nature of materials were pressed into service, including textiles and luxury goods fashioned of lacquer, porcelain, metalwork, jade and ivory carvings. Tableware and gift boxes used to present holiday foodstuffs comprised major categories of festival decorations because of deeply entrenched associations between feasting and seasonal celebrations.

Many of the popular designs for New Year food boxes used at the Ming court continued in use throughout the Qing. One of the favourites in the Qianlong period was first used on carved lacquer boxes at the mid-Ming court of the Jiajing Emperor (1521–67). The success of the design is seen in the complex interweaving and overlaying of multiple motifs that together proclaim the power of the New Year to bring wishes of springtime rebirth and bounty. The Chinese word for spring (*chun*) is written large at the centre of the round box lid, positioned above a bowl overflowing with gems and symbols of prosperity from which bands of radiant light emanate.[48] Shoulao, the star god of longevity, is superimposed over the top part of the word *chun*, which is flanked by images of dragons. The one on the right is depicted with subtly carved scales suggesting he represents the directional animal the Dragon of the East, while the dragon on the left, oddly enough for his species, has been given a treatment that suggests soft fur, creating a dragon motif that incorporates a reference to the Tiger of the West. The presence of directional coordinates imbues the design with a greater cosmological symbolism appropriate to the New Year and Lantern Festival as a time for the emperor to reassert his central role in coordinating the calendar and announcing the arrival of spring and a time of rebirth.

The Qing emperors produced more festival-specific objects than in any previous court, perhaps because of the great prosperity of the eighteenth century, but also because of their desire to broadcast publicly their full command of the festival calendar in demonstration of the ruler's position at the apex of time; thusly impressing upon the Han population the legitimacy and propriety of their authority despite their own foreign origins. The Yongzheng Emperor (r. 1723–35), who among the Qing emperors had the most artistic eye, was fastidious in his orders for festival tableware, including for the Lantern Festival. One of his edicts concerns instructions for the imperial workshop to follow in producing a set of porcelain bowls. All subsequent Qing emperors continued these patterns, making only technical updates to employ newly developed enamel palettes for ceramic decoration.

Yongzheng instructed the court eunuch Hu Shijie to present to him a blue-and-white food bowl and then issued the imperial command:

> By imperial edict send the bowl to Tang Ying [supervisor of the imperial kilns at Jingdezhen] to make bowls according to the size, thickness, depth, and design of this bowl. The exterior of the bowls should be decorated in designs using all colours of *wucai* [a palette of translucent overglaze enamel colours and underglaze cobalt blue]. Each pattern should be auspicious according to the seasonal festivals. The inside of the bowls should accord with the exterior pattern, but should be rendered in the blue-and-white technique. For New Year use '*sanyang kaitai*' [the 'three yang force heralds prosperity' represented by a rebus picturing three goats and a sun]; for the Upper Primordial Festival [Lantern Festival] use 'abundant harvest of the five grains ...'[49]

[48] An example from the collection of the Freer Gallery of Art is illustrated at <http://www.asia.si.edu/collections/singleObject.cfm?ObjectNumber=F1990.15a–e>.

[49] Forbidden City (comp.), *Qing gong neiwufu zaobanchu dan'an huizhuan* (Collection of Qing dynasty palace archives from the Office of the Imperial Household), in Zhang Faying (comp.),

At the end of the edict Yongzheng demanded ten examples of each festival bowl to be brought to him for close inspection. The emperor's order mentioned five other festival designs, designating an iconic image for each. His design choices were not innovative but, by codifying and applying them for use on festival tableware, his gesture was one step toward an ever greater elaboration of holiday display that accompanied his reign.

The Lantern Festival design mentioned is another rebus. The motif consists of a lantern with hanging streamers that consist of strings of decorative baubles, including small ornaments shaped like wasps. The words 'lantern' and 'wasp' said together sound like the word *fengdeng* meaning 'bumper harvest', a wish especially appropriate to emanate from the emperor whose virtue and righteousness in theory enabled such a result.

Flower festival

After the double-barrelled holiday of New Year and the associated Lantern Festival, the next truly joyous celebration in the traditional Festival Calendar is the Flower Festival that was marked in late imperial times by visits to temples, picnics, flower shows and competitions, poetry writing, and the creation and display of pictorial arts, especially paintings and statuettes of figures holding or in close proximity to flowers.[50] By the mid-Qing, the temples visited were usually specifically dedicated to Flower Spirits, and altars, often set up in outdoor courtyards, held candles, fruits, and sweets. Although Flower Festival belongs to the category of a lesser festival in the sense that people were not granted leave from work nor were there large family reunions or street parades, it was nonetheless widely celebrated both inside and outside the court.

Tang Ying quanqi (Beijing: Xueyuan chubanshe, 2008), vol. 4, 1252. For an illustration of such a bowl see Louise Alison Cort and Jan Stuart, *Joined Colours: Decoration and Meaning in Chinese Porcelain* (Washington, DC, 1993), p. 131.

[50] The most comprehensive study of the festival is Gōyama Kiwamu, 'Min Shin jidai ni okeru hana no bunka to shūzoku' (Flowers in the Culture and Conventions of the Ming and Qing dynasties), in Chūgoku bungaku ronshū, no. 13, pp. 142–86 (Dec. 1984), or see <https://qir.kyushu-u.ac.jp/dspace/handle/2324/9744> for a pdf file. The article quotes a number of Chinese sources, including descriptions of temples furnished with Flower Spirit statues. A major Chinese source is Chen Meng-lei (comp.), *Gujin tushu jicheng* (The Complete Collection of Illustrations and Writing from Ancient to Contemporary Times, published 1725–8), repr. (Shanghai, 1934), fol. 18, 4–5. The best English studies are by Ellen Johnston Laing, 'Picture calendars', pp. 76–81, and Laing, 'Notes on ladies wearing flowers in their hair', *Orientations* (Feb. 1990), 32–9.

The most common name for the festival is '*huazhao*' (flower morning), but it is also known as *huashen jie*, Festival of the Flower Spirits, and *baihua shengri* (Birthday of the Flowers). Each lunar month was assigned a Flower Spirit but as this group of figures is complex with frequently shifting values, it is not addressed here.[51] The words *hua zhao* appear together in some ancient agricultural texts, but do not seem to refer to a special event, and Han dynasty (206 BC–AD 220) lists of festivals do not include this occasion. Gōyama Kiwamu suggests that the occasional appearance of the term in Song dynasty texts may presage a formal cele-bration of Flower Festival, but there is no secure evidence for it being a true holiday celebration until the late Ming dynasty. Certainly its most enthusiastic commemoration was during the Qing period.[52]

It should be acknowledged that there are many contradictory state-ments in popular literature, including on both English-language and Chinese-language websites, about the origin of the holiday. Numerous references point to celebrations held in the Tang dynasty; however, such stories all post date the Tang and were applied retrospectively. The festival corresponds perfectly with new concerns in the Ming and Qing when com-mercial flower growing and ardent interest in flower arranging, including books dedicated to the subject, reached a crescendo among the educated elite and the imperial court.[53]

With the gradual decline of the glory of the Qing dynasty beginning in the nineteenth century, celebration of the Flower Festival gradually faded, but at least through the 1930s Japanese and Western observers were still being impressed by the festival to write accounts of it before its total eclipse in the struggles of mid-twentieth-century China. Today Flower Festival is enjoying a beginning resurgence, even if only as a tourist event. Women re-enact the custom of cutting red and yellow silk ribbons to tie them on the stems of peonies and tree boughs in order to encourage the blossoming of the plants. This custom was one of the most popular practices of the festival in Qing times.

The annual date for the Flower Festival varies by region. It always falls during the second lunar month, but depending on place can be cele-brated on the second, twelfth, or fifteenth day (usually corresponding to a time in March). The Qing dynasty court, perhaps because of its base in

---

[51] See Ellen Johnston Laing, 'Picture calendars', pp. 76–9.
[52] Gōyama Kiwamu, 'Min Shin jidai ni okeru hana no bunka to shūzoku', pp. 142–6.
[53] See for example, Yuan Hongdao, *Ping shi* (*A History of the Vase*), written in 1599; translated by Duncan Campbell in *New Zealand Journal of Asian Studies*, 5(2) (Dec. 2003), 77–93.

cold Beijing and with another palace still further north, chose to celebrate on the fifteenth when more flowers were in bloom as it is supposed to be a day to greet all the flowers. However, in reality, the court relied heavily on the ability of the gardeners to force hothouse flowers for use in decorating the imperial temples they had built and dedicated to the Flower Spirits.

The Qing court's decision to officially celebrate *huazhao* on the fifteenth had the advantage of creating a symmetrically balanced nodal point with the Mid-Autumn Festival celebrated on the fifteenth day of the eighth lunar month (usually September). Together these holidays were described as *huazhao yuexi*—Flower Morning and Moon Evening.[54] The three most significant festivals of the year are New Year, Double Fifth and the Mid-Autumn Festival, thus the pairing of the Flower and Mid-Autumn festivals is an endorsement of Flower Festival's importance.

Another reflection of its status and the attention devoted to the Flower Spirits venerated on this day is seen in a minor rite practiced in the Qing with the purpose of sending away the Flower Spirits. A passage in the celebrated Qing dynasty novel, *Honglou meng*, recounts that during the sixth lunar month offerings of wine and flowers were placed on a domestic altar and a ceremony held to send the Flower Spirits into retirement until their return the following year at Flower Festival. This observance is all the more poignant given the close association in the novel between the beautiful young women who occupy the attentions of the male protagonist, Jia Baoyu, and individual flowers; as well as the significance that the female protagonist Lin Daiyu, who deeply loves Jia Baoyu, was born on the day of the Flower Festival.

Particular flowers have a long history of being associated with each month, and references to flower calendars can be found in texts of the Spring and Autumn Period (722–481 BC).[55] Yet, the floral assignments changed by place and over time, making it no surprise that the identities of the Flower Spirits (themselves probably a Ming phenomenon) never became fully standardised. It was not even agreed whether there were twelve Flower Spirits, or thirteen in order to provide for years with an intercalary month. The most commonly invoked lists of monthly flowers overlap in their choices, and certain flowers such as the lotus appear in

---

[54] This phrase appears at least as early as the second half of the Ming dynasty in a poem by Tian Rucheng, 'Xihu youlan zhiyu' (Record of sights while travelling around West Lake). See Gōyama Kiwamu, 'Min Shin jidai ni okeru hana no bunka to shūzoku'.
[55] See Xiaoxiazheng zhuan (Comments on the Lesser Annuary of the Xia dynasty).

invariable positions, such as the sixth month in this case; or for apricot blossoms in the second month, but there was considerable latitude, usually correlated with regional climates. By the Qing two more or less standard lists existed, one for the south (the Jiangnan region) and one for the north (Beijing). For example, in the Jiangnan list the flowering plum represents the first month, while in the north it represents the twelfth month. In the Beijing calendar winter jasmine is assigned to the first month, but is not included at all in the Jiangnan list.[56] Because of regional discrepancies there is often some ambiguity in which month is suggested by the appearance of a particular flower in an artwork.

The enthusiastic celebration of Flower Festival during the Ming and Qing dynasties engendered the creation of many objects, including paintings, figurines, imitation *pengjing* made with gemstone trees, and porcelains for display at this time of year; yet in contemporary times these associations have often been forgotten. The desire for floral decorations on this day recalls Wen Zhenheng's Calendar for Scrolls in which he advised displaying paintings of ladies walking beneath blossoming trees during the second moon.

By examining paintings with inscriptions that mention *huazhao* it is clear that the images suitable for display at this time of year are broader than Wen Zhenheng mentioned, nor do they need to be directly connected with the concept of Flower Spirits. A painting by Wang Wu (1632–90) of a rock, peonies, and butterfly bears the date '*huazhao*' and the cyclical year corresponding to 1677; while a fan painting of hydrangea, azaleas and butterflies by Wu Shangxi dated to the Flower Festival of 1854 presents a related theme but with different choices of flower.[57]

The presence of the butterfly is appropriate for Flower Festival but its use in Chinese motifs is also much wider because of its value in various rebuses, where it can be used to sound like a word for an octogenarian or a word meaning to multiply and reduplicate. Association with Flower Festival in particular was first pointed to by Ellen Laing who traces it to a Flower Festival custom apocryphally ascribed to the Tang Emperor Minghuang (r. 712–56), who allegedly instructed the court women to visit his palace garden wearing flowers in their hair and holding peony-decorated fans to

---

[56] Yang, Boda (intro.); *The Tsui Museum of Art: Chinese Ceramics IV, Qing Dynasty* (Tsui Museum of Art, 1995).

[57] Wu Shangxi's painting in the Guangdong Provincial Museum is illustrated in Zhu Wanzhang *et al.*, *Flower and Bird Painting of the Ming and Qing Periods*, entry no. 40. For Wu Shangxi, see Ellen Johnston Laing, 'Notes on ladies wearing flowers'.

attract butterflies. The beauty first visited by a butterfly was the emperor's choice for the night. The flower and butterfly paintings by Wang Wu and Wu Shangxi would no doubt be treated as generic floral motifs in contemporary painting studies if they were not specifically dated to Flower Festival as a reminder of their place in the Chinese custom of creating works of art for specific, timely displays. Many other paintings of an identical theme exist without any date or inscription and it is worth considering them afresh as works very possibly painted as gifts for Flower Festival. At home, families offered fruit and wine to the Flower Spirits and if they hung a suitable scroll above the offering table the setting was presumably enhanced.

Paintings of flowers could also change meaning in association with the Flower Festival, which was the one time of year that embraced all flowers. A chrysanthemum painting dated to the twenty-fourth day of the ninth lunar month painted by Ren Bonian (1840–96) for his close friend, the artist Wu Changshi (1844–1927), was judging from the date probably made in association with either the Mid-Autumn Festival or the Double Nine, when chrysanthemum imagery was appropriate. But the painting took on new life when Wu Changshi subsequently presented it to another friend and inscribed it as a gift for *huazhao*, indicating pleasure for Flower Festival in creating broad, inclusive displays of seasonal flowers.[58]

Many fewer three-dimensional objects carry a date than do paintings, except for those with an imperial reign mark, which in any case provides only the year and not a month or day. Thus when considering gem-trees, porcelains, and ivory carvings it is not easy once they have been removed from their original context and placed in the art market to identify whether they were made for a specific calendrical observance. The Qing emperors constructed temples dedicated to the Flower Spirits at the Chengde Summer Villa for Escaping Heat and at the Yuanming Yuan palace, or Garden of Perfect Brightness. These edifices must have required specific decorations for Flower Festival, but if such images are circulating today it is difficult to separate the generic types from images of Flower Spirits. Although women are more closely linked in popular imagination to flowers, each month had both a male and female incarnation of a Flower Spirit.[59] Thus many figures, including images of men wearing a scholar's

[58] I thank Yu Ping Luk for bringing this reference in Ding Xiyuan, *Ren Bonian nianpu* (The Annual Record of Ren Bonain) (Shanghai, 1989), p. 87 to my attention.
[59] See Ellen Johnston Laing, 'Picture calendars', p. 77, for some of the most common designations, including the beauty Yang Guifei (717–55) and the poet Bai Juyi (722–846).

robes and holding a flower, may likely have been made for the Flower Festival in the second lunar month or perhaps for display in the specific month that the Flower Spirit represents, but such figures were not intended for long term display.

Among the most exquisite sets of twelve images of flowers are sets of small porcelain wine cups made in the Kangxi period, beginning in the early 1680s, and each bearing a reign mark on the base (Fig. 9).[60] The vessels are extremely thin, painted on one side with a flower rendered in overglaze enamel colours and inscribed on the other with a poetic couplet written in underglaze blue. Ten of the twelve stanzas are from identifiable Tang poems, but two have not yet had their source successfully identified. Each cup is inscribed with the square seal legend '*shang*' following the poem. Usually translated as 'admired', it correctly means 'awarded to' in reference to receiving a cup of wine as a winner in a drinking game in which these cups were used.[61]

The use of the cups has given rise to different interpretations, including that the emperor used the one appropriate to each month in cyclical succession for his private dining. Described in the Qing imperial household records of the Zhaobanchu under the rubric 'yueling bei' (cups for the months), their association with specific months is clear and some scholars equate them also with the Flower Spirits, although there is no secure evidence for the later point.[62] Since they are imperial commissions and include an image of winter jasmine among the flowers, it is clear the monthly association for each flower should follow the Beijing calendar and thus the plum blossom should be assigned to the twelfth month, although various publications have positioned this flower as the first month.[63]

The exact use of the cups is somewhat nebulous but they were used in drinking games to test participants' knowledge of poetry by the inscriptions.

---

[60] I thank Peter Lam for this information in personal correspondence and much insight about the month cups. He notes that Liu Yuan was the designer of the cups.
[61] Peter Lam provided the reference in personal correspondence for the association with wine games found in a small booklet called *Jiuling* (Drinking for the months) produced by the Imperial Porcelain Factory supervisor, Lang Tingji (1663–1715), in *Sheng yin Bian* (repr. Yuan Fuzheng (ed.), Beijing: Zhonghua shuju, 1991).
[62] Xuan Caoyuan, 'Qiantan Kangxi shier yueling huashen bei' ('Notes on the Kangxi-period month cups of Flower Spirits'), *Shoucangjie*, 2006, no. 6, p. 62.
[63] The Percival David Month cups have been previously published with the plum denoting the first month. Rosemary Scott, 'Fine porcelain and delicate brushwork: a group of Qing dynasty wares with overglaze enamel decoration from the Percival David Foundation', *Orientations*, 11 (1986), 22–35.

Figure 9. Set of twelve porcelain wine cups with underglaze cobalt oxide and overglaze enamels; Qing dynasty, Kangxi period (1662–1722); Jingdezhen, Jiangxi province; H. 5 cm; Sir Percival David Collection at the British Museum; PDF 815; photograph © The Trustees of the British Museum.

Peter Lam also points out the analogy between these cups and sets of eight cups of the Drunken Immortals used in drinking games. At present there is no evidence to suggest when one set of drinking cups was used instead of the other. The month cups were perhaps brought out more often at the time of the Flower Festival as expression of the court's delight in this holiday which was celebrated at all three of the imperial palaces—the Forbidden City, Yuanming Yuan, and at Jehol, each of which had dedicated flower temples. It is worth noting that the Kangxi Emperor's commission for the twelve month cups seems to be the first order for a set of twelve porcelain vessels each decorated with a specific monthly indicator and this draws attention to Qing court practice to focus on charting time in twelve monthly units, which is discussed below.

Double Fifth

This presentation began with mention of the Double Fifth Festival, to which I return as a last case study in this examination of the time-specific nature of Chinese art. A wide variety of objects was commissioned for this day because its dangerous aura mandated that a multitude of apotropaic devices should be put on display to avert evil; and like the other festival days of the year, it was also an occasion for social communion. The New Year season was very clearly set aside for family reunions, while the Double Fifth was not as much of a family day and therefore provided a good focus for social intercourse among friends. Paintings themselves provide the evidence for some of these outings, such as a handscroll by the Qing artist Fang Xun (1736–99), who painted such a gathering on the fifth day of the fifth lunar month in 1782. The setting was the waterside garden-residence of his patron Jin Deyu.[64]

Similar gatherings occurred across China, for some of which there are entertaining records that outline the activities of the festival day, while also tellingly revealing the social anxieties of the participants—a group of wealthy merchants in eighteenth-century Yangzhou. The Double Fifth described by Ginger Chengchi Hsü in her study of Yangzhou points to the event as a combination of expelling evil, commemorating friendships, and

---

[64] A. Kerlan-Stephens, ' "Glimpses of the Duanwu Festival" by Fang Xun (1736–99): commemorative painting or private souvenir?', *Phoebus, A Journal of Art History*, 9 (2001). The painting is illustrated in Claudia Brown, *Myriad Points of View: New Research on Ming and Qing Paintings in the Roy and Marilyn Papp Collection* (Phoenix, AZ, 2006).

engaging in social climbing all in the one holiday activity.[65] On the occasion in question the locally famous Ma brothers invited their influential townsmen to view a collection they had assembled of paintings depicting Zhong Kui, the Demon Queller. They were quick to promote the thirteen artworks dated from the Ming dynasty or earlier showing their acumen and status as serious and wealthy collectors. This anecdote also reveals that Wen Zhenheng's instruction to display works by early artists for Double Fifth still held currency as a key for advancing one's social reputation.

Fang Xun's painting belongs to the self-referential genre that we have seen for the New Year in which an artist describes the events of the festival and people display it on the holiday itself. In Fang's work he shows a portrait of Zhong Kui hanging in the main pavilion over a table set with a vase of pomegranate flowers. Outside, a pomegranate tree is in full bloom. Lush loquat, hollyhock and calamus plants on the shore also confirm the time of year. The familiar trope of depicting male children as part of a festival image is here presented in a believable manner since the painting is constructed to read as a real-time family gathering. A woman, presumably Jin Deyu's wife, with a baby in her arms, is watching two toddlers. One of them amuses himself with a toy shaped like a three-legged toad, one of the poisonous creatures feared on the day that is replicated and displayed following the principle of apotropaic magic.

Many paintings are easily associated with Double Fifth because they invoke obvious devices such as Zhong Kui in proximity to pomegranate flowers, but other images can easily be subsumed into the category of generic flower paintings unless they are inscribed. Only if they bear a dated inscription do we become alert to the time-sensitive nature of the iconography, as was seen in the case of paintings of peonies and butterflies. It is important to take account that certain 'generic' looking floral scenes were actually made for time-linked displays in the yearly cycle and they serve as functional markers of time and were appropriate for seasonal gift giving.

A good example is a scroll by Gao Jian dated to 1662 in the Arthur M. Sackler Gallery, Washington, DC. The scene presents a scholar, perhaps the artist himself, with a jar of wine at his side, loosely robed, lolling by the side of a stream to catch the summer breeze and perhaps compose a poem (Fig. 10). Pomegranate flowers blossom overhead and tall blades of calamus follow the watercourse, which are seasonal clues to Double Fifth,

---

[65] See Ginger Chengchi Hsü, *A Bushel of Pearls: Painting for Sale in Eighteenth-Century Yangchow* (Stanford, CA, 2001).

but the association is clear to the modern viewer because the artist's inscription dates the painting to four days in advance of the day of Double Fifth. In the original context, viewers would have judged any similar painting even if it was uninscribed as appropriate only for the season of Double Fifth, but modern viewers often disregard such clues and erroneously assume that Chinese paintings like many works in the Western canon could be displayed without strict observance to the time of year.

Since Double Fifth was a potentially dangerous time it required the display of apotropaic devices equally at the court and in humble households. It was only the elaborateness and expense of the objects that differed. Many images invoke the power of tigers to protect children. A common practice was to write the word for 'tiger' on their foreheads using a special combination of realgar (an arsenic sulphide used for medicine) and powdered dregs of wine that had been evaporated under a noontime sun, which represented the strength of the strong 'yang', or positive forces.

Double Fifth was viewed with such trepidation because it was a double whammy of dangers: on noon of the day the yang forces peaked and if they became too potent they could turn destructive. Large fires, even in home hearths, and all smelting operations were banned for the day. As soon as the yang forces crested, yin began its ascendancy bringing with it vexatious vapours, chills, and poisonous creatures. This led to the commission of pictures and decorated tableware and household goods that could avert evil forces. At least as early as the Song dynasty records show that such gifts were appropriate to give for Double Fifth, including a preference for giving round fans with apotropaic images. Archives from the Qing imperial household reveal Double Fifth as an important occasion to give gifts to the nobility and high officials, and likewise courtiers sent seasonally coded tribute gifts to Beijing in advance of the holiday for imperial enjoyment.

Some of the best descriptions of practices for the Double Fifth are found in early twentieth-century writings. At the time there was a sense of urgency and national pride among some Chinese scholars to record as much folklore as they could in the face of the escalating adoption of Western customs and loss of tradition. Most of these documents corroborate and amplify practices recorded in earlier records. The early twentieth-century *Record of Annual Festivals in the Capital* by Guo Lichen records that for Double Fifth shops churned out a large number of inexpensive stamped prints made on yellow paper as protective devices. Some of these depicted an imposing figure called the 'Heavenly Master, Zhong Kui',

Figure 10. *Enjoying Pomegranate and Hollyhock Flowers*; by Gao Jian; Qing dynasty, 1662; Suzhou, China; hanging scroll in ink and colours on paper; 239 × 83.2 cm; Arthur M. Sackler Gallery, Smithsonian Institution, Washington, DC; Gift of Arthur M. Sackler (S1987.271); © Freer–Sackler.

which is a name that conflates the two identities of the Daoist Celestial Master and Zhong Kui, both of whom repelled evil. Some strips were decorated with the five poisonous creatures (spider, scorpion, snake, three-legged toad, and centipede)—the same group on the back of the imperial Wanli-period porcelain discussed in the beginning of this paper. Guo described people in the capital almost fighting to buy the lucky paper strips in order to paste them on their main doors to repel evil spirits.[66]

A record composed around the fall of the Qing dynasty by Dun Lizhen provides another view of the festival by describing the offerings for placement in local temples and on altars dedicated to the ancestors in individual homes. The list is headed by glutinous rice dumplings, or *zongzi*, and continues with cherries, mulberries, peaches, water chestnuts, and cakes known as the Five Poisons. Only the first two were deemed suitable for temple offerings, while the other foods made appropriate gifts to friends and family. The presence of these foods in earlier paintings attests to the traditional nature of this list.

Two similar paintings—one in the Palace Museum, Beijing, and one in the National Palace Museum, Taipei—are good examples of imagery suited for display in the palace and elite homes for Double Fifth (Fig. 11). The version in the Palace Museum, Beijing was executed by Giuseppe Castiglione (Lang Shining 1688–1796) in a dazzlingly beautiful and precisely naturalistic style, while the anonymous version in Taipei, less assured in its command of Western descriptive techniques, offers a more complete iconography. Palace archives record that the Yongzheng Emperor ordered Castiglione on the twenty-ninth day of the fourth lunar month of 1732 to prepare a painting on silk that could be hung for the *Duanyang* festival.[67] The nearly identical work should date close in time.

The main subject is a ceramic vase filled with effulgent flowers: pomegranate, calamus, moxa, and the seasonal rose mallow flower. Hanging from one of the flower branches is a decorative sachet pouch filled with pungent herbs that ward off illnesses, which is another common symbol of the holiday season. Both paintings also depict the seasonal foods, including *zhongzi*, that were appropriate for offerings and gifts.

The top edge of the painting in Taipei provides one more reference to Double Fifth and in particular to the need for protective symbols. It is embellished by a series of rectangles that resemble the lappets at the top

---

[66] Guo Lichen, *Yanjing suishi ji* (*Record of Annual Customs in the Capital*) (repr. Taipei: Guangwen shuju, 1969), pp. 62–3.
[67] Wei Dong, 'Lang Shining yu Qing gong jieling hua', p. 81.

Figure 11.   *Vase with Bouquet for Double Fifth*; unknown artists in style of Giuseppe Castiglione; Qing dynasty, eighteenth century; hanging scroll in ink and colours on silk; National Palace Museum, Taiwan, Republic of China; © National Palace Museum.

of a temple cloth banner, each with a wildly written seal-style character of a type associated with Daoist talismans, and with an image of Zhong Kui. This version of the painting is more traditionally Chinese and was perhaps even a draft or first version created for the purpose of Castiglione to consult when creating his more Westernised presentation of the subject.

The prominence of the *zongzi* introduces a second layer of associations that the Double Fifth festival carries, which is the story of the famous statesman and poet Qu Yuan, who lived in the third century BC. A trusted and forthright advisor to his ruler, Qu Yuan was maliciously slandered by jealous opponents who caught the ear of the emperor and had him banished. Qu Yuan produced poetry of indescribable beauty and emotion during his exile, but the depth of his disillusionment at having been wronged by his king, now forever tainted by corruptibility, led Qu Yuan to drown himself. According to popular legend, villagers raced into the water to save him, but failing they instead threw their lunch of rice dumplings into the river as a decoy to keep the fish from devouring his corpse. They also beat drums to fend off evil. This is the rationalisation invariably given to explain the dragon boat races held on Double Fifth, but the boat races with wild drumming predate any link between the festival and the story of Qu Yuan's death. The races were timed with ancient practices at the Summer Solstice to attract rain-bringing dragons to quench the dry lands.[68] A sort of amalgamation or blend of practices associated with the Summer Solstice and with Double Fifth reflects on the the luni-solar nature of the Chinese calendar.

During the Ming and Qing the Chinese courts produced a large array of luxury objects to celebrate Double Fifth which often featured the boat races, as already seen with the Wanli-period dish. They also commissioned paintings, textile hangings, and small trinkets, such as a rooster-shaped box in the National Palace Museum that opens to reveal a delicate ivory carving of swiftly racing boats. The rooster appears for its value as a homophone for 'good fortune', a meaningful wish at any of the seasonal festivals. But since the rooster was widely associated with the New Year festival, its use at the opposite holiday of Double Fifth is another example like the invocation of Zhong Kui at both the winter and summer festivals of a desire to impose a degree of symmetrical balance on the festival calendar.

---

[68] Bodde, *Chinese Festivals*, pp. 314–15.

Sets of twelve

In the Qing, especially during the Yongzheng and Qianlong reigns, the number twelve and its association with charting time through seasonal and festival activities became more deeply entrenched than before in the court's practice of commissioning artworks.[69] An important subcategory of Qing court art is known as 'nian jie bei yong hua' (paintings for annual festivals prepared in advance (to have in reserve for the day)), and among this group of images two nearly identical sets of twelve paintings deserve consideration in this light.

The sovereign would never risk being without exquisitely prepared artworks of seasonal imagery to use for display or give as gifts at the opportune moment in the annual cycle. Judging from court records it seems that painters were called in from one to several months before a festival to produce an appropriate work.[70] Given the weeks it takes to mount a hanging scroll it was typically necessary to order scrolls a few months in advance, but some of the orders seem to have been placed unnervingly close to the display date, as was the case with the Castiglione commission for Double Fifth mentioned above. Perhaps it was efficacious to commission certain subjects in the appropriate season and once approved by the emperor the scrolls could be mounted in studios out of sight and stored for display the following year. This fits into the practice of having festival objects made in advance to avoid what would have been understood as a calamity if the palace room were not properly decorated.

The 'twin' sets of twelve paintings under consideration were produced during the consecutive reigns of the Yongzheng Emperor between 1723 and 1735 and by the Qianlong Emperor, early in his reign around 1736. It is clear in each case that the works were produced as a set, each set having the same dimensions and materials of production, including the silks used to mount the scrolls for display. Both sets are entitled *yueling*, or *Monthly Activities*, a term that appears in the Book of Rites rooted in practices of the Zhou dynasty and redacted in the Han dynasty, in a chapter devoted to instructions developed to attune the ruler's behaviour to coordinate with the seasons. The Qing paintings are unrelated to the abstruse instructions recorded in the Book of Rites, but instead record in precise visual detail a wide array of festival activities practiced in Qing times.

[69] Chen Yunru, 'Shijian de xingzhuang: Qing yuan hua shier yueling tu yanjiu' (The 'Shape of Time: a Study of Twelve Months in the Qing Court'), *Gugong xue shu jikan*, vol. 22, no. 4 (2005), 103–39.

[70] Chen Yunru, 'Shijian de xingzhuang: Qing yuan hua shier yueling tu yanjiu', p. 124.

When the Yongzheng Emperor commissioned the first set of *Twelve Monthly Activities* he was drawing upon a precedent established in the late Ming dynasty that gave pictorial expression to monthly festivals. The court painter Wu Bin (died *c.*1627) produced twelve album leaves representing annual ceremonies and festivals, which are now in the National Palace Museum. Each painting features a major activity of the month. For example, the fourth leaf presents the rite of 'Washing the Buddha' to commemorate the festival celebrating his birthday, a subject matter that would have been acceptable according to Wen Zhengheng's calendar for the scroll discussed above (Fig. 12). A large temple complex dominates the painting and, within the inner recesses of the main hall, a small standing figure of the baby Buddha (standing because he took seven steps at birth) is depicted in the centre of a basin on the altar. A bird's eye view into the temple allows the viewer to witness the custom of believers ladling water over the statue to ritually wash the infant Buddha as a declaration of faith.

The late Ming was a time of imperial anxiety as the Wanli Emperor struggled to hold on to his ever diminishing power. In this climate he may have felt it especially important to place renewed emphasis on observing all the rites and festivals in order to assert his sovereignty and domination over his realm in time and space. It was during his reign that the greatest number of festival badges were made for court robes and his was the first commission of a set of twelve monthly activity paintings, which provide much more detailed information about customs than earlier court paintings produced on festival themes. The creation of a set of twelve caught the Yongzheng Emperor's attention as an appropriate model to follow.

Perhaps the completeness of such a set to record annual customs suited his own concerns to portray his legitimacy as the Grand Master of time and local custom. A fascination with the phenomena used to calculate time and space, such as astrolabes and Western clocks, also manifests this emperor's deep concern with charting time. These instruments appear as palace decorations in several court paintings of his era revealing that such tools were not stored away with the court astronomers, but held pride of place as palace decorations. During the Qianlong reign, this trend, especially for collecting Western timepieces, continued to accelerate.

Yongzheng's commission for the *Twelve Monthly Scrolls* incorporated three significant changes from the Wanli precedent—the format of the paintings was shifted from an album to a large hanging scroll in order to give them greater potential for highly visible display. He also inserted his own portrait image into each of the monthly activities, thereby announcing the centrality of his role in the annual cycle. He also had the subject

Figure 12.   *Washing an Image of the Buddha* from *Album of Seasonal Paintings*; by Wu Bin (active *c.*1583–1626), Ming dynasty; album leaf in ink and colours on paper; National Palace Museum, Taiwan, Republic of China; © National Palace Museum.

matter widened. Wu Bin's Ming paintings each depict the single most important festival activity for a month, while Yongzheng had his court artists create composite images that combine in a single scene the monthly customs of different regions in his realm. An example is the scroll for the Fifth Month which features dragon boats and highlights this empire-wide custom, but he also had inserted in the lower portion of the scroll the arrival of a mendicant with his acolyte who carries a medicine gourd, alluding to a day after Double Fifth that in some parts of China commemorates those skilled at compounding medicines.[71] The same iconography appears in the Qianlong version of the fifth month scroll (Fig. 13).

The Yongzheng Emperor's changes to *Twelve Monthly Activities* made his set a much stronger testimony of imperial authority and domination over the Chinese festival calendar than the Wanli period exercise. Qianlong repeated the model Yongzheng pioneered with one major exception. He did not have his own image represented, probably in deference to his father's memory as it would have been improper to substitute his own visage in the place of the recently deceased imperial ancestor. The Qianlong Emperor was not shy about having himself depicted and brought the genre of imperial portraits of the emperor in leisure-time activities to grand heights; thus it may have come as a disappointment that he could not appropriately have his physical presence inserted into the *Twelve Monthly Activity* scrolls. That he repeated the compositions so closely attests to their perceived efficacy, and since Qianlong commissioned his version early in his reign, he may have felt pressured to begin his rule with a proper representation of the calendar, while he had not yet had time to explore other visual presentations of the subject.

Both sets of *Twelve Paintings of Monthly Activities* were created collaboratively in the imperial workshop, and although not signed some of the same artists worked on both sets, notably Tang Dai (from 1673 until after 1752), Ding Guanpeng (active 1708–71), and Chen Mei (1697–1745). The artists incorporated selective details of foreign style taking advantage of chiaroscuro and Western descriptive techniques in these paintings to create highly detailed, so-called 'realistic' images. It is more appropriate, however, to read them as a mixture of fact and idealised fantasy blended together. They can perhaps best be described as 'believable' rather than as 'realistic'.

A look at the First Lunar Month exemplifies the programme that each of the twelve scrolls follows. While we do not have a record from the

---

[71] Chen Yunru, 'Shijian de xingzhuang: Qing yuan hua shier yueling tu yanjiu', pp. 125–6.

Figure 13. *Painting of the Fifth Lunar Month* from a set of 12 *Paintings of the Months*; court painters, Qing dynasty, Qianlong period (1736–95); hanging scroll in ink and colours on silk; National Palace Museum, Taiwan, Republic of China; © National Palace Museum.

Yongzheng-period archives that states when the scrolls were to be displayed, references to various of the individual month scrolls appear in the household archives about the Qianlong-period set, including edicts commanding which painters should be assigned to the task and references about getting the scrolls mounted. From these comments it is clear the emperor intended that each of the twelve scrolls should be displayed one by one during the month referenced in the painting.[72] The scrolls thus at first seem akin to modern wall calendars; however, the purpose is not for charting time day by day, but rather to represent in a holistic fashion the calendar of festivals of each month. Since the beginning of imperial times festival observances had always been a primary concern of the emperor if he was to keep his behaviour in sync with the seasonal life of his subjects.

The imperative to represent multiple festival activities in one scene reflects the Qing emperors' notion of the imperial self as grand master, whose rule was extensive in its physical reach encompassing diverse peoples and customs. By the display of the *Twelve Monthly Activities,* mostly rooted in Han customs, on the one hand, and of paintings illustrating imperial hunts, a quintessentially Manchu activity, on the other, the emperors made manifest in visual form the universality of their power.

In the scroll of the First Month, the New Year and Lantern Festival are amalgamated (a practice already seen in the scroll in the Freer Gallery discussed above). For the imperial commission, the Yongzheng Emperor had himself shown dressed as a Chinese scholar standing in an ornate doorway, watching his sons explode a firecracker. In the lower corner of the painting, men observe tall, dancing sprays of water, which can be interpreted as the far away Hangzhou tidal bore that was observed annually during the first lunar month (and also later in the year when the bore arrived for a second more spectacular display). Surely the man-made pond in the imperial Yuanming Yuan garden, which is the identifiable setting of the painting, could not have produced such a geyser in the frigid Beijing weather of the New Year. But in the medium of painting, it was easy to turn the imperial garden into a simulacrum of all of China, with the Yongzheng Emperor presiding as the grand master of ceremonies.

Some of the ancillary figures in the *Twelve Monthly Activities* corroborate the theatrical flair of the paintings. As mentioned above, emperors were known to have palace staff imitate folk customs or to invite pedlars and acrobats to come into their private confines at the New Year. The

---

[72] Chen Yunru, 'Shijian de xingzhuang', pp. 108 and 124.

wide variety of figures represented in the First Month scroll are meant to illustrate all the stereotypical peoples of the empire, and whether they are represented by actors or real commoners is beside the point. Their presence indicates that both in the actual practice of court New Year celebrations and in the permanent record given in paintings, it was important for the emperor to be inclusive and show his sovereignty over a diverse domain.

The popularity of sets of twelve to depict festival activities reached a new height in the Qing. Beside the sets of scrolls under discussion, many court albums depicting children enacting festival rites (including the Lantern Festival image in Figure 8) were created in sets of twelve, as was a set of images of women engaged in monthly festivities. Chen Yunru persuasively argues a connection between measuring a complete yearly cycle in units of twelve with new Qing court interest in Western systems of time keeping. But regardless of how the Qing emperors perceived and divided the yearly calendar, the individual festival dates were always the most critical unit of time in imperial China. A list from the end of the Qing dynasty records some 155 major and minor festival events in the annual cycle for the Emperor to preside over, and each of these generated a vast production of visual materials, which have in modern time often become jumbled together and read out of context.[73]

Conclusion

China's many festivals, especially the popular examples discussed here of the New Year, Lantern Festival, and Double Fifth celebrations, if not as much the less-known Flower Festival, are subjects that have been studied by anthropologists aiming to understand and explicate the customs that underpin the rhythm of Chinese life. However, not enough attention has been devoted to the interplay between festivals and China's rich visual culture. We can better understand Chinese culture if we attempt to recover, whenever possible, the positions in time originally occupied by objects and reassign to them the power and special qualities they embody precisely because they are meant for limited use only. Time, our old enemy, eats away at all things; it obscures and erases both geological formations and the artefacts of human hands, but only by acknowledging that the significance

[73] See Tun Li-ch'en, translated by Derk Bodde, *Annual Customs and Festivals in Peking as recorded in the Yen-ching Sui-shi-ji*.

of countless works of art in China was shaped by the temporality of their production and perception do we recover, however fleetingly, the meanings they conveyed during the brief lifetimes of those who made and viewed them.

Note. With warmth and gratitude I thank Robert E. Harrist, Jr., Columbia University, for offering sage advice at many stages in this project and I thank the anonymous reader for improvements to the work. It is also a pleasure to acknowledge two museum interns, Yu Ping Luk and Gabby Jiayin She, for help in identifying key Chinese and Japanese sources and consulting on some translations.

Gaelic in Medieval Scotland: Advent and Expansion

THOMAS OWEN CLANCY

University of Glasgow

OVER THE PAST TWENTY-FIVE years, there has been a very considerable amount of change in the way scholars regard the evolution of Scotland in the early Middle Ages, and in particular the Celtic aspects of the Scottish past. Many of the views which I inherited on entry into the field in the mid-1980s have gradually been overturned, or shaken up; paradigms have been shifted, terminology reviewed and refined; new perspectives opened up. All of this has been for the better, even if not every challenge should be sustained or even welcomed. It speaks of a healthier field of enquiry, in which a much greater number of voices than before, new and old, have been prepared to debate and reconsider this most perplexing of times and locations. For let us be clear, this is a perplexing area of study. Only for a few brief periods of time—the seventh and eighth centuries, and then the later eleventh and twelfth—do we have anything approaching good historical data for early medieval Scotland, and many of the major developments happen in the shadows of a virtual evidence blackout. For certain areas, like the island of Lewis, that blackout is pretty much total. I note here Sir John Rhŷs's still valid description of working on this period: 'The difficulty of writing anything intelligible on the subject arises not only from the scarcity of the data ... but also in a great measure from the absence of the information necessary to enable one rightly to connect those data with one another.'[1]

Read at the Academy 4 March 2009.

[1] J. Rhŷs, *Celtic Britain*, 3rd edn. (London, 1904), pp. iii–iv.

Proceedings of the British Academy, **167**, 349–392. © The British Academy 2010.

The topic of this lecture pays tribute to the interests—capacious as they were—of Sir John Rhŷs himself. The lecture engages with some of his keen, if understandably preliminary and often problematic, interests in the early languages and ethnology of Britain; in particular those which gave rise to his 1890 Rhind Lectures to the Society of Antiquaries of Scotland on that subject, and especially the Fifth Rhind Lecture, 'The spread of Gaelic in Scotland'.[2] My main focus will be the study of Celtic place-names, another area in which Rhŷs was a pioneer, out there before the great Gaelic scholars Alexander MacBain or William J. Watson, and a frequent, often flawed predecessor against whom they could sharpen their tools.[3] Unlike many other authors on place-names, for whom neither had much time, Rhŷs was a linguist at the forefront of his field, and his mistakes, as MacBain and Watson often rightly saw them, were of a different order than some others who came under their fire. As Sir Ifor Williams put it:

> He was a pioneer hacking his way through virgin forests. There was for him no abiding city of a final conclusion: an open mind had to be kept, and he had to push on into a second theory, and then into a third. Flexibility and a readiness to learn—these were his virtues, the indispensable requisites of a pioneer. It was easy for another generation, which profited by his labours, to complain of his changes of mind. The experience of those who have attempted to carry on his research is that the marks of his axe are to be found in every part of the forest.[4]

An awareness of the way in which in the 1880s and 1890s someone of the intellect of Rhŷs could still be casting about trying to find a clear path through the mirkwood of Scotland's early languages and history is a necessary preparation for this lecture, since it addresses the establishing of paradigms, of consensual academic approaches to the Scottish past, and the gradual crumbling of these in the face of uncertainties and new perspectives. During the 1950s, 1960s and 1970s, building on the bedrock of the linguistic and textual advances of the late nineteenth and early twentieth centuries, two generations of Celtic scholars of great status, and their

---

[2] Published in *The Scottish Review*, 1890–1, and later under one cover as *The Rhind Lectures in Archæology in connection with the Society of Antiquaries of Scotland, delivered in December, 1889, on the Early Ethnology of the British Isles* (s.l., s.n, [1891?]), repr. as *The Early Ethnology of the British Isles* (Lampeter, 1990); Fifth Rhind, 'The spread of Gaelic in Scotland', *The Scottish Review*, 17 (1891), 60–84; for related work by Rhŷs, see his *Celtic Britain*.

[3] A. MacBain, *Place Names of the Highlands & Islands of Scotland*, with notes and a foreword by William J. Watson (Stirling, 1922); W. J. Watson, *A History of the Celtic Place-Names of Scotland* (Edinburgh, 1926); idem, *Scottish Place-Name Papers* (London, 2002).

[4] Ifor Williams, 'Rhŷs, Sir John (1840–1915), Celtic scholar', *Dictionary of Welsh Biography*, accessed through National Library of Wales, 'Welsh Biography Online' <http://wbo.llgc.org.uk>.

allies in fields such as history and archaeology, laid the foundations for a certain level of 'consensus' on aspects of early medieval Scotland. The Rhŷs lectures played some part in this: I think here particularly of Kenneth Jackson's important 1951 Lecture on 'Common Gaelic' to which the current contribution obliquely responds.[5] Here, as with so much of Jackson's prodigious scholarship, his views came to colour all that was subsequently written on the subject. Younger colleagues of Jackson's in the University of Edinburgh, such as John MacQueen, W. F. H. Nicolaisen and John Bannerman, would later be particularly influential in shaping our understanding of how Gaelic came to be in Scotland, how it related to the languages round about it, and the chronology and nature of its expansion. The world-view they helped to create (which included nostrums on, for instance, the Pictish language, which are not the subject of our scrutiny but which have also been subject to sweeping review in recent years[6]) held and to some extent still holds sway.

What I intend to do in what follows is first to outline—no doubt too starkly and with less nuance than one might like—the prevailing paradigms within which the arrival of Gaelic in Scotland and its expansion throughout it during the course of the early Middle Ages has been envisaged; then to explain, necessarily briefly, some of the challenges that have been put to the foundations of these paradigms over the past quarter century; and then finally to focus in on four main topics within the overall problem of understanding the development of Gaelic in early medieval Scotland by way of finding new ways forward.[7]

---

[5] K. H. Jackson, ' "Common Gaelic": the evolution of the Goidelic languages' (The Sir John Rhŷs Memorial Lecture 1951), *Proceedings of the British Academy*, 37 (1951), 71–97.

[6] See for instance, K. Forsyth, *Language in Pictland: the Case against 'Non-Indo-European Pictish'* (Utrecht, 1997); S. Driscoll, J. Geddes and M. Hall (eds.), *Pictish Progress: New Studies on Northern Britain in the Early Middle Ages* (Leiden and Boston, 2011).

[7] Some of the noticeably shifting paradigms have been received quizzically and perhaps misinterpreted outwith Scotland. One such is the increasing use within Scottish scholarship of the term 'Gaelic', as I have employed it in my title and throughout this lecture. Over the course of the past two decades, scholars in Scotland, particularly of a younger generation, have taken to using the terms 'Gaels' (in preference to 'Scots' or 'Irish') and 'Gaelic' (in preference to 'Irish') in relation respectively to the people and language during this period. The reason has been to avoid the confusion and potential political charge of modern, ambiguous or too unambiguous terminology, such as Scots or Irish, to say nothing of the confusion inherent in descriptions of the period which have the 'Irish' turn into the 'Scots' after c. 850, who speak Gaelic (but then start speaking 'Scots' in the later middle ages!); or have the same essential people referred to as 'Scots' when in Britain but 'Irish' when in Ireland (all memorably sent up by W. C. Sellar and R. J. Yeatman, *1066 and all that* (London, 1936), p. 5). 'Gaelic' works reasonably well in print, but orally one is

Review

The basic outline of the arrival and expansion of Gaelic in Scotland as traditionally received can be briefly described: in AD 500, the Irish Fergus Mór mac Eirc arrived as king of Dál Riata in northern Britain, effectively shifting the centre of gravity of this early medieval cross-channel kingdom from Ireland to Scotland. Dál Riata may have been in existence for some time; Argyll may have been Gaelic-speaking for some time, but in this year the dynasty moved east.[8] Whenever it had been first established, though, this was a Gaelic colony, like those in southern Wales and Cornwall and Devon to which some historical data and a considerable number of ogham inscriptions in the south-west of Britain testify. The advent of Gaelic in Scotland can thus be described in terms of a migration, though that could be placed any time in the early centuries AD.[9] Dál Riata was one of four different linguistically determined polities in early medieval northern Britain, and lasted up to the ninth century, when a Gael, Cinaed mac Ailpín (usually referred to as Kenneth mac Alpine), effected what has come to be known as 'the Union of the Picts and Scots'. Cinaed's descendants continued to rule their new joint-kingdom of Alba until and beyond the great changes of the twelfth century. Their ninth-century 'Union', with Gaelic as the upper partner, led inevitably to the demise of Pictish, certainly by 1100, and most probably by 1000.[10] Gaelic continued to expand, as did the core kingdom of the Scots; first intruding

---

forced to choose a pronunciation, and this has caused some problems. Irish scholars have increasingly seen this as a sort of Scottish imperialism, a colonising of the Irish past with an implicit Scottishness, or at the very least an attempt to divest the Scottish past of its Irish roots. Pronouncing 'Gaelic' as it is pronounced in Ireland does not help, as the term has largely negative or old-fashioned resonances in Ireland. Despite this, I, and others, have seen it rather as an attempt to keep terminology clear, and to shy away from the straightjackets of 'Scots', 'Irish'. I will use 'Gaelic' and 'Gaels' throughout this lecture, except where I wish to refer only to Ireland or only to the high medieval Scottish kingdom.

[8] See for instance, John Bannerman, *Studies in the History of Dalriada* (Edinburgh and London, 1974), p. 1, and also *passim*.

[9] See for instance Charles Thomas, 'The Irish settlements in post-Roman western Britain: a survey of the evidence', *Journal of the Royal Institution of Cornwall*, NS 6 (1969–72), 251–74; *idem, Britain and Ireland in Early Christian Times, A.D. 400–800* (London, 1971), pp. 53–70.

[10] See for instance E. James, *Britain in the First Millenium* (London, 2001), pp. 138, 230. For a review of further literature on this topic, see D. Broun, 'Alba: Pictish homeland or Irish offshoot?', in P. O'Neill (ed.), *Exile and Homecoming. Papers from the 5th Australian Conference of Celtic Studies* (Sydney, 2005), pp. 234–75, at 236–8. This article is now revised and republished, minus the section just noted, in *Scottish Independence and the Idea of Britain from the Picts to Alexander III* (Edinburgh, 2007), pp. 71–97; subsequent references are to the later version, where possible.

their power into Strathclyde; then making conquest of the Lothians; and Gaelic place-names in these areas are a natural consequence of this.[11] The twelfth century saw a gradual infiltration of French and English influence into the Scottish court, and the establishment of burghs and new monasteries, and these began to have a strong and negative effect on the Gaelic language, which began to recede from the eastern and southern lowlands during the twelfth, thirteenth and fourteenth centuries; a relatively stable 'highland line' roughly coterminous with the area of Gaelic speech had emerged by c.1400.[12] The 'heartland' of Gaelic increasingly became the Western Highlands and Islands; the latter, though conquered and settled by Scandinavians and under Norwegian rule until 1266, saw a re-emergence of Gaelic under the descendants of Somerled, the future 'Lords of the Isles', who were to provide the main prop for the continuance of Gaelic language and culture into the early modern period.[13]

To this overall scenario, leading Scottish academics, including language specialists, of the 1950s and 1960s added some considerable definition. First, Kenneth Jackson in 1951 made a strong case, only really challenged directly nearly fifty years later by Roibeard Ó Maolalaigh and Breandán Ó Buachalla, for the notion that the Gaelic of Scotland was the 'Common Gaelic' of Ireland, and that there was no sign of differentiation until at least the tenth century, and more probably the thirteenth: well into the later Middle Ages.[14] It should be said that in so doing Jackson was laying to rest definitively some long-standing red herrings, in particular the idea that Scottish Gaelic had grown up indigenously and had no real linguistic connection with Irish or Ireland. It is easy now to forget how prevalent this view had been amongst respected scholars in the previous century.

[11] See for instance W. F. H. Nicolaisen, *Scottish Place-Names: their Study and Significance* (London, 1975; rev. edn., Edinburgh, 2001), pp. 173–5; M. O. Anderson, 'Lothian and the Early Scottish Kings', *Scottish Historical Review*, 39 (1960), 98–112.

[12] See for instance T. C. Smout, *A History of the Scottish People 1560–1830* (London, 1969), pp. 39–46, and map p. 518; Charles W. J. Withers, *Gaelic in Scotland, 1698–1981: the Geographical History of a Language* (Edinburgh, 1984), pp. 16–27.

[13] See for instance John Bannerman, 'Historical background', in K. Steer and J. Bannerman, *Late Medieval Monumental Sculpture in the West Highlands* (Edinburgh, 1977), pp. 201–2; R. Andrew McDonald, *The Kingdom of the Isles: Scotland's Western Seaboard, c.1100–c.1336* (East Linton, 1997).

[14] Jackson, 'Common Gaelic'; R. Ó Maolalaigh, 'The Scotticisation of Gaelic: a reassessment of the language and orthography of the Gaelic notes in the Book of Deer', in K. Forsyth (ed.), *Studies on the Book of Deer* (Dublin, 2008), pp. 179–274; B. Ó Buachalla, '"Common Gaelic" revisited', in C. Ó Baoill and N. McGuire (eds.), *Rannsachadh na Gàidhlig 2000. Papers read at the Conference of Scottish Gaelic Studies 2000 held at the University of Aberdeen 2–4 August 2000* (Aberdeen, 2002), pp. 1–12.

Second, John MacQueen began a process of seeing place-name elements, in their distribution, as barometers of linguistic expansion, in particular in his influential work on Gaelic in the south-west of Scotland.[15] This process was brought to fruition by W. F. H. Nicolaisen, the dominant Scottish place-name scholar of the past fifty years, whose pioneering use of distribution maps allowed for a sense of 'seeing' Gaelic emerge and expand on the map.[16] MacQueen and Nicolaisen both also produced work that was influential in seeing the south-west of Scotland as having played host to a very early colony in the Rhinns of Galloway (as evidenced above all by place-names containing the Gaelic place-name element *sliabh* 'moor, hill'), with a subsequent small-scale infiltration of the south-west through the medium of the church (borne out by the smattering of Gaelic place-names employing *cill* 'church').[17] Nicolaisen was also influential in seeing the language situation of some of the Hebrides and western seaboard being one in which Norse place-names show in many places only a transitory connection, not permanent settlement. A great number of place-name scholars have viewed Gaelic in the Hebrides and elsewhere as a survivor language, one which *re-emerged* consequent on political distractions elsewhere. And this has been the prevailing view underlying much research by, for instance, scholars of Norse place-names in Britain.[18] It is worth noting the straightforward eastwards and southwards expansion of

---

[15] J. MacQueen, 'Welsh and Gaelic in Galloway', *Transactions of the Dumfriesshire and Galloway Natural History and Antiquarian Society*, 32 (1953–4), 77–92; 'Kirk- and Kil- in Galloway place-names', *Archivum Linguisticum*, 8 (1956), 135–49; *idem*, *St Nynia* (Edinburgh, 1961), pp. 45–7; 'The Gaelic speakers of Galloway and Carrick', *Scottish Studies*, 17 (1973), 17–33.

[16] See his *Scottish Place-Names* and his own earlier work there cited, pp. xi–xiii. See also *idem*, 'Place-names, Gaelic in Scotland', in D. S. Thomson (ed.), *The Companion to Gaelic Scotland*, rev. edn. (Glasgow, 1994), pp. 231–3, with maps on p. 232; also P. G. B. McNeill and H. L. MacQueen (eds.), *Atlas of Scottish History to 1707* (Edinburgh, 1996), pp. 58–60, and for '*pit*', 50–1.

[17] Nicolaisen, *Scottish Place-Names*, pp. 51–60, and see his earlier 'Scottish Place-Names: 24. Slew- and *sliabh*', *Scottish Studies*, 9 (1965), 91–106; MacQueen, 'Welsh and Gaelic'. MacQueen's case also drew on the evidence of the element *carraig*, 'rock', which, though a highly localised toponymic element in Scotland, cannot be shown to be early, rather than just limited in extent (see below).

[18] Nicolaisen, *Scottish Place-Names*, pp. 109–55, esp. 122; Ian A. Fraser, *The Place-Names of Arran* (Glasgow, 1999), pp. 52–60, esp. 59 for Nicolaisen's description of Norse names there as 'onomastic graffiti'; for argument for Gaelic survival in Manx context, see G. Fellows-Jensen, 'Scandinavian settlement in the Isle of Man and north-west England: the place-name evidence', in C. Fell, P. Foote, J. Graham-Campbell and R. Thomson (eds.), *The Viking Age in the Isle of Man* (London, 1983), pp. 37–52, who there summarises the earlier debate between Basil Megaw and Margaret Gelling about survival. I should note that there has been considerable awareness of the potential for complete Scandinavian linguistic dominance, at least in Lewis, among scholars: see, e.g. B. E. Crawford, *Scandinavian Scotland* (Leicester, 1987), p. 97.

Gaelic these researches and the maps derived from them seem to imply. With the exception of the seemingly proleptic 'colony' in Galloway, Gaelic in this analysis proceeds from Dál Riata up and out and down.

Revisions

At both micro- and macro-level, these paradigms have been subjected to considerable scrutiny over the past twenty-five years. This lecture cannot cover every challenge in depth, but I will discuss a number of the major ones.

The origins and nature of Dál Riata

Recent years have seen considerable challenges to the received notion of a Gaelic colony in Argyll, from a number of angles. The political nature of Dál Riata, as a single kingdom ruled over by a series of related and competing kindreds, established by John Bannerman in his important studies of the late 1960s, has been subjected to considerable scrutiny recently.[19] The fundamental text on which Bannerman's model was built, the text formerly known as *Senchus Fer nAlban*, has been vigorously dismantled by David Dumville.[20] Dauvit Broun, in as yet unpublished work, has recently supported that act of deconstruction, while arguing strongly that one can, nonetheless, trace at least some of the stages by which this complex text was assembled into the form we now have, and returning cautiously towards Bannerman's original formulation of a core dating from the 640s and a final phase in the tenth century, but with key and identifiable modifications in between.[21] The result is that the text becomes a window on the shifting

---

[19] See Bannerman, *Studies*; and see also R. Sharpe, 'The thriving of Dalriada', in S. Taylor (ed.), *Kings, Clerics and Chronicles in Scotland, 500–1297* (Dublin, 2000), pp. 47–61.

[20] David N. Dumville, 'Ireland and North Britain in the earlier Middle Ages: contexts for *Míniugud senchasa fher nAlban*', in Ó Baoill & McGuire, *Rannsachadh na Gàidhlig 2000*, pp. 185–211, republished in D. N. Dumville, *Celtic Essays, 2001–2007*, vol. II (Aberdeen, 2007), pp. 35–71. Page numbers are cited from the republished article. Although I accept Dumville's argument that the description of the text as '*Míniugud Senchasa Fher nAlban*' ('The relating of the [genealogical] lore of the men of Alba') is significant, I have nonetheless opted to use the title that had previously been conventional.

[21] D. Broun, '*Míniugud Senchusa fher nAlban* and the History of Dál Riata', Morgyn Wagner Memorial Lecture, University of Edinburgh, 11 Feb. 2009; 'The Arrival of the Gaels in Pictland', unpublished conference lecture, Scotland's Global Impact, Inverness 21 Oct. 2009. I am grateful to Professor Broun for allowing me to see a copy of the text of this material.

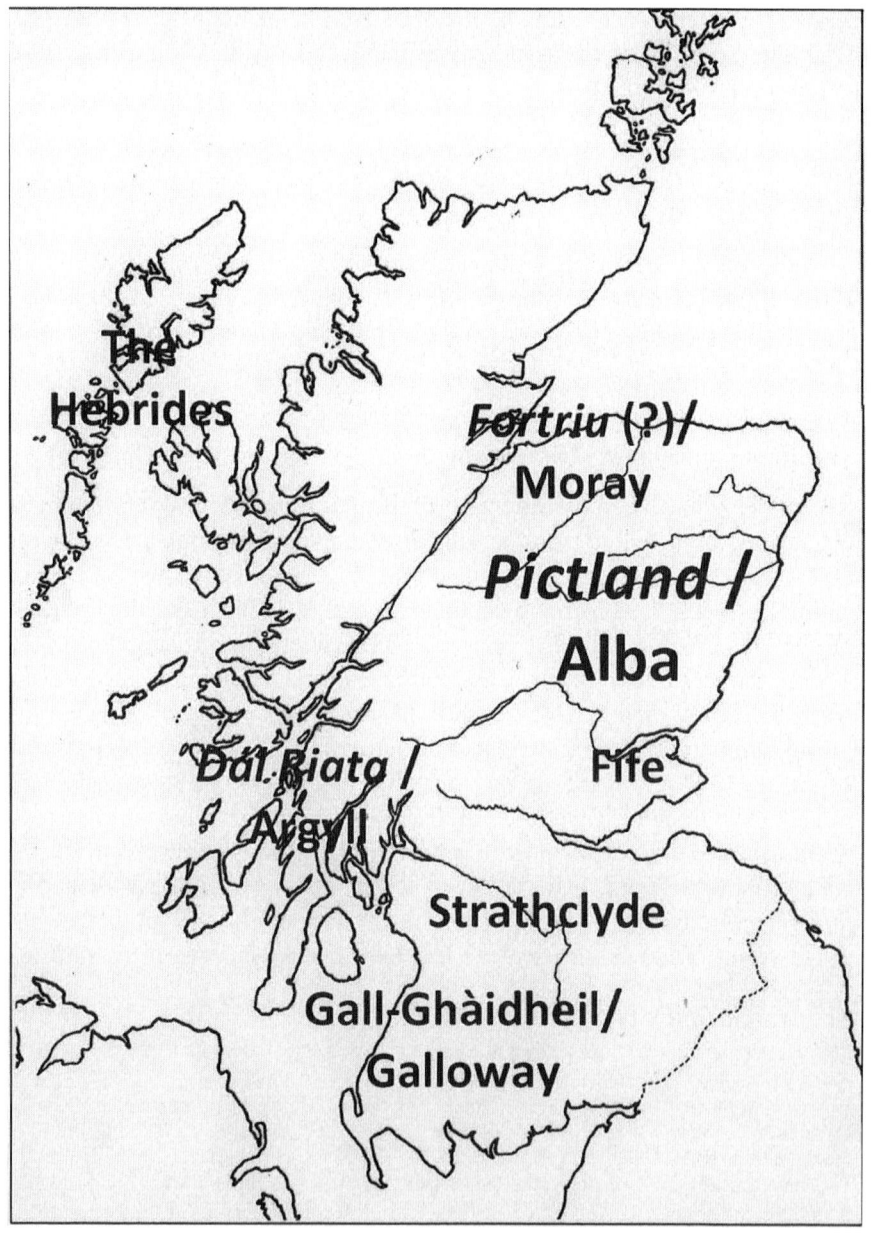

Figure 1.   Regions mentioned frequently in the text. Names in italic obsolete by *c*.900; non-italic names occur from 900 onwards.

political fortunes over time of the kindreds it describes, rather than a freeze-frame political geography of Dál Riata. Most radically Broun has recently and tentatively proposed it as a text reflecting in one phase the interests of overlords under whose sway Dál Riata had fallen by the mid-eighth century.

Following a related line of enquiry, James Fraser, in a series of probing articles and in his recent book, has argued against reading Dál Riata as a unified kingdom or strong polity, and has tried to deconstruct some of the terminology with which modern scholars have become perhaps too familiar. He has pointed cogently to the fact that our sources are much more heterogeneous in terms of the kindreds they think are important at any given time, and indeed the names they give them; and Dál Riata itself is by no means a constant either in its appearance in sources, or in its meaning. In his view we are dealing with a collection of kindreds, with their own kingships, who only fitfully coalesce into anything we might wish to term an over-kingdom.[22]

Of greatest relevance for our current purpose is the argument put forward by the Glasgow archaeologist Ewan Campbell, first in 1999 and then more fully in 2001, that most of the received view of the Gaelic 'colony' cannot be demonstrated from reliable evidence. Fergus Mór's emigration from Ireland looks to be an origin-legend[23] (and indeed, as Dumville and Broun have subsequently shown, Fergus Mór himself seems to be a late entrant into the traditions of the region in any case). The migrationist paradigm has come under attack in archaeological circles in general. In the case of Dál Riata, there is no archaeological evidence for any migration at all; and there is no reason linguistically why Gaelic could not have developed concurrently on both sides of Sruth na Maoile. As Campbell shows, there is no reason why the cultural and linguistic dividing line should not have been at Drumalban, the mountainous massif of the central highlands, rather than at the North Channel. Languages are not afraid of the water, and the role of the North Channel in particular as a uniter rather than a

---

[22] James E. Fraser, 'The Iona Chronicle, the descendants of Áedán mac Gabráin, and the "Principal Kindreds of Dál Riata"', *Northern Studies*, 38 (2004), 77–96; *idem*, '*Dux Reuda* and the Corcu Réti', in W. McLeod, J. E. Fraser and A. Gunderloch (eds.), *Cànan & Cultar / Language and Culture: Rannsachadh na Gàidhlig 3* (Edinburgh, 2006), pp. 1–9; *idem, From Caledonia to Pictland: Scotland to 795* (Edinburgh, 2009); *idem*, 'The Three Thirds of Cenél Loairn, 678–733', in W. McLeod *et al.* (eds.), *Bile ós Chrannaibh. A Festschrift for William Gillies* (Ceann Drochaid, 2010), pp. 135–66.

[23] E. Campbell, *Saints and Sea-Kings: the First Kingdom of the Scots* (Edinburgh, 1999), pp. 11–15; *idem*, 'Were the Scots Irish?', *Antiquity*, 75 (2001), 285–92.

divider of culture is well known from the early Middle Ages at least. Although Dumville, badly misreading I think both the scholar and the argument, castigated Campbell's viewpoint as 'a strongly nationalist account', in the same work he himself went on to espouse most of these main points, though to some extent on other grounds.[24]

We are thus left with the bare fact of Argyll in the sixth, seventh and eighth centuries as a region of Gaelic-speakers with intense and important connections to Ireland through both political and ecclesiastical channels. It is emerging as a much more diverse and dynamic polity than in the previous formulation, and the recent work on the *Senchus Fer nAlban* indeed reads that text as a representation of that dynamism, an attempt to sort out a complex collection of traditions from different sources. We can no longer be sure when Gaelic 'arrived' in Scotland, and increasingly one feels that even to pose the question may be to anticipate a wrong answer.

'The Union of Picts and Scots'

Despite its longevity in the popular imagination, the so-called 'Union of the Picts and Scots' is a modern (or perhaps early modern) confection;[25] scholars have long since abandoned seeing the reign of Cinaed mac Ailpín (Kenneth mac Alpine) as in and of itself a turning point in Scottish his-

---

[24] Dumville, 'Ireland and North Britain', pp. 49, 68–9. Dumville's text is worth quoting *in extenso*, as many of the views here expressed have become so closely associated with Campbell's thesis and with archaeological methodology, and it is important to stress their bolstering from this different quarter: 'Thanks to the questions being asked nowadays, we find ourselves liberated from following literally the discourse of our source-texts. ... [W]e have no reason to place the gaelicisation of what we know as Dál Riata in Britain in close proximity to the first historical notices of its existence; there is nothing in the written or, apparently, the archaeological evidence to cause us to separate the gaelicisation of that part of western Scotland from the gaelicisation of northern Ireland. I therefore reject absolutely the following proposals advanced by John Bannerman as at the time of writing essentially uncontroversial: that someone called Fergus Mór mac Eirc was the founder of Dál Riata; that "in the person of Fergus Mór ... the Dalriadic dynasty removed from Ireland to Scotland"; that "Fergus Mór may be considered the earliest historically authenticated figure" mentioned in *Míniugud senchasa fher nAlban* (Bannerman 1974, 73) and that "Fergus himself flourished towards the end of the fifth century" (Bannerman 1974, 70). Further, concerning what was in the 1960s and 1970s a slightly less uncontroversial issue, I reject the need to argue for a political separation of Irish and British Dál Riata in the seventh century. ...' To be fair, it does seem that Dumville's initial criticism of Campbell's thesis, with which he then conversely agreed in spirit, was advanced without his having yet been able to read the main article on which Campbell's arguments were based (only the popular précis in Campbell, *Saints and Sea-Kings*, was cited).

[25] On this topic, see Broun, 'Alba: Pictish homeland or Irish offshoot?', esp. pp. 236–43; C. Kidd, 'The Ideological Uses of the Picts, 1707–*c.*1990', in E. J. Cowan and R. J. Finlay (eds.), *Scottish History: the Power of the Past* (Edinburgh, 2002), pp. 169–90.

tory. What gives him his key significance is as an ancestor figure for the rulers of Pictland in the late ninth century, rulers whose kingdom would be 'rebranded' Alba by *c*.900.[26] It is in such a context that collocations such as 'the MacAlpine dynasty' and more recently, courtesy of Alex Woolf's taste for exoticism, 'the Alpínids', have been formed—none of these has any historical attestation in their current meaning, it should be cautioned.[27] Scholarly attention, best exemplified perhaps by Alex Woolf's superb and stimulating recent history of the period, has begun to focus instead on the reigns of Cinaed's grandsons, Domnall and Consantín (particularly the latter), as well as the period in between (a period of considerable upheaval), as providing the context for the creation of a 'new order' benorth the Forth. That new order was a new kingdom territorially based on the old Pictland, but now named Alba, and possessed of rulers with Gaelic names, who seem to have espoused Gaelic language and laws.[28]

That said, prior to 1998 a great variety of scholars, such as A. A. M. Duncan, Marjorie Anderson, Alfred P. Smyth, Benjamin Hudson and John Bannerman, were urging that the Gaelicisation of the Pictish polity began *before* Cinaed's time, indeed, that a series of kings from Gaelic Dál Riata, starting with one Custantin son of Fergus (†820), had imposed their power over the strongest of the Pictish polities, Fortriu.[29] For those

---

[26] See for instance D. N. Dumville, *The Churches of North Britain in the First Viking-Age*. Fifth Whithorn Lecture (Whithorn, 1997), pp. 34–6; D. Broun, 'The Origin of Scottish identity in its European context', in B. E. Crawford (ed.), *Scotland in Dark-Age Europe* (St Andrews, 1994), pp. 21–31, esp. 33. Note, however, his change of mind on the significance of the name-change to *Alba*, in his article 'Alba', p. 243; and in *Scottish Independence*, p. 74, and his apology to authors who have followed him in his earlier view. As one of those apologised to, I should note that I concur with his earlier view, and with other scholars, in seeing the name-change of *c.*900 as highly significant, and an alteration of meaning (see below). I am unconvinced by his more recent arguments concerning it.

[27] For Alpínids, see A. Woolf, *From Pictland to Alba, 789–1070* (Edinburgh, 2007). We might wish to begin to use the term employed in the *Genelogia Albanensium* in the Book of Lecan (f. 110r39–41), *Clann Chinaeda meic Ailpín*, also referred to as *in rígrad* 'the royal line' (text also in Book of Ballymote, 149a31–2). I am grateful to Dauvit Broun for access to his edition and translation of this text; see also his *The Irish Identity of the Kingdom of the Scots* (Woodbridge, 1999), p. 173, n. 35. Thomas Charles-Edwards has made a start on employing the term 'Clann Chinaeda': 'Picts and Scots', *Innes Review*, 59 (2008), 168–88.

[28] See Woolf, *From Pictland to Alba*, esp. pp. 126–76; and sources cited above, n. 26. For Consantín as the 'new Cinaed' in modern scholarship, see Broun, *Scottish Independence*, p. 73, and n. 14, who credits Ted Cowan as the first to spot Consantín's pivotal status: 'Myth and identity in early medieval Scotland', *Scottish Historical Review*, 63 (1984), 111–35.

[29] A. A. M. Duncan, *Scotland: the Making of the Kingdom* (Edinburgh, 1975), pp. 54–9; Marjorie Anderson, 'Dalriada and the Creation of the Kingdom of the Scots', in D. Whitelock, R. McKitterick and D. Dumville (eds.), *Ireland in Early Medieval Europe: Studies in Memory of Kathleen Hughes*

seeking a founding 'moment' for the Gaelicisation of the Scottish kingdom, attention had shifted back before Cinaed's time. Taking a prompt
from Patrick Wormald, Dauvit Broun challenged this view in 1998 in the
conference on the St Andrews Sarcophagus, and his elegant solution to
the contradictions of the frankly pretty messy and measly evidence was to
see Custantin and his offspring as first and foremost Pictish kings of
Fortriu, and only secondarily kings over Dál Riata.[30] This solution seems
to have found very rapid favour, but has recently been subject to an implicit
challenge in a recent review article by Thomas Charles-Edwards.[31] As I
will explain below, in some sense it does not matter who is right about the
ancestry of the individuals concerned. Whether Gael or Pict or both by
descent, Custantin and his family drew their power from their control of
Pictish territory. The main thing we take away from the evidence, and
there seem to be few folk now willing to disagree on this point, is that Dál
Riata had become inextricably linked with, indeed absorbed into, Pictland,
at least in political terms, by the period around 800.[32] Crucial here has been
a parallel process of revision within Scottish historiography, by which the
kingdom of the Picts has become recognised as by far the dominant power
in northern Britain after 685, and an expansionist one at that. In this context, whatever Cinaed mac Ailpín's ancestry (Dumville has suggested,
without to date providing supporting discussion, that he was a Pict; recent
work has supported the perspective of the chronicles at least that he was
king of Picts, and that Gaelic ancestry is not an overt feature of his profile
at the time, though it would be a feature during his descendants' time[33]),

---

(Cambridge, 1982), pp. 106–32; A. P. Smyth, *Warlords and Holy Men. Scotland* AD *80–1000*
(London, 1984), pp. 177–85; B. T. Hudson, *Kings of Celtic Scotland* (Westport, CT, 1994), pp. 34–6;
John Bannerman, 'The Scottish takeover of Pictland and the Relics of Columba', in D. Broun
and T. O. Clancy (eds.), *Spes Scotorum, Hope of Scots. Saint Columba, Iona and Scotland*
(Edinburgh, 1999), pp. 71–94.

[30] D. Broun, 'Pictish kings 761–839: integration with Dál Riata or separate development?', in S. Foster
(ed.), *The St Andrews Sarcophagus: a Pictish Masterpiece and its International Connections*
(Dublin, 1998), pp. 71–83; and see P. Wormald, 'The emergence of the *Regnum Scottorum*: a
Carolingian hegemony?', in B. E. Crawford (ed.), *Scotland in Dark-Age Britain* (St Andrews/
Aberdeen, 1996), pp. 131–53.

[31] Charles-Edwards, 'Picts and Scots'; and see my own anxieties about the swift consensus that
had grown around Broun's argument: T. O. Clancy, 'Review of Sally Foster (ed.), *The St Andrews
Sarcophagus*', in *Innes Review*, 52 (2001), 109.

[32] For instance, Duncan, *Scotland: the Making of the Kingdom*, p. 54; Dumville, *Churches of North
Britain*, pp. 35–6.

[33] Dumville, *Churches of North Britain*, pp. 35–6; Woolf, *From Pictland to Alba*, pp. 93–6 explores
the possibility further on his own terms. See however the references to Cinaed in 'The Chronicle
of the Kings of Alba', as *primus Scottorum* (M. O. Anderson, *Kings and Kingship in Early Scotland*

he was ruling over a Pictish kingdom that had expanded its domination to include the formerly Gaelic polity of Dál Riata. It is also worth noting at this juncture the most momentous paradigm shift of recent years, Alex Woolf's bold and convincing suggestion that the kingdom or region of Fortriu, to judge by the Irish annals the most important part of the Pictish kingdom(s) from the late seventh to the ninth centuries, was not, as previously envisaged, in Strathearn, but was rather north of the Grampians. This 'turning of the world upside down' has implications that are still being worked out, but it has been conducive to much recent free-thinking.[34]

The most important historical text to bear witness to the Gaelicisation of Pictland remains the text known amongst different scholars as 'The Chronicle of the Kings of Alba' (Dumville's term, followed by the majority of Scottish historians since he proposed it) or as 'The Scottish Chronicle', a term used by Ben Hudson and recently championed anew by Thomas Charles-Edwards.[35] The last word has not yet been said on this crucial but complex text, preserved in a fourteenth-century manuscript now in Paris. Although both Dumville and Woolf have rightly cautioned that this text may contain adaptations and insertions as late as the reign of William the Lion (1165–1214),[36] the text on the whole seems to have been composed during the reign of King Illulb (954–62), and updated up to the reign of Cinaed mac Maíle Choluim (971–95).[37] At any rate, its perspective may be held to be largely that of the rulers of tenth-century eastern Scotland, of the kingdom called *Alba*, named as such (taking over in terminology from *Pictavia*) around 900 in the text. This is a name-change known also from

---

(Edinburgh and London, 1980), p. 249), and in the 'Syncronisms' as *in cétríg rogab ríge Sgóinde do Gaidhelaib*, a slightly ambiguous phrase, perhaps to be translated 'the first king to have taken the kingship of Scone for the Gaels' (alternatively, 'the first king of the Gaels ...'): Broun, *Irish Identity*, p. 173, n. 35.

[34] A. Woolf, 'Dún Nechtain, Fortriu and the geography of the Picts', *Scottish Historical Review*, 85 (2006), 182–201.

[35] For the text, see Anderson, *Kings and Kingship*, pp. 249–53; Dauvit Broun has provided a good translation in C. Erskine, A. R. MacDonald and M. Penman (eds.), *Scotland: the Making and Unmaking of the Nation c.1100– 1707, vol. v, Major Documents* (Dundee, 2007), pp. 8–14. There is also an edition and translation in B. T. Hudson, 'The Scottish Chronicle', *Scottish Historical Review*, 77 (1998), 129–61. For comment, see D. Broun, 'Dunkeld and the origin of Scottish identity', in Broun and Clancy, *Spes Scotorum*, pp. 95–111; D. N. Dumville, *Churches of North Britain*, p. 36, n. 107; *idem*, 'The Chronicle of the Kings of Alba', in Taylor, *Kings, Clerics and Chronicles*, pp. 73–86; Charles-Edwards, 'Picts and Scots', 174–5; and the astute discussion, tinged with despair, of Alex Woolf, *From Pictland to Alba*, pp. 88–91, and elsewhere.

[36] Woolf, *From Pictland to Alba*, p. 90; Dumville, 'Chronicle', p. 86, and 84 for an example of potential late aspects to the text.

[37] Broun, 'Dunkeld', 98.

contemporary Irish annals. As Thomas Charles-Edwards has recently emphasised, whatever the origins of the term Alba, this name change is also roughly coincident with a shift of terminology amongst English chroniclers, who begin to use the term *Scottas* 'Scots' for the inhabitants of Alba from the 920s; Archie Duncan has noted that poetic evidence from Æthelstan's reign suggests they were using the Latin term *Scotti* as well.[38] All of this fits the avowedly Gaelic perspective of the Chronicle, even if we cannot determine when some of that perspective dates from. It is pretty clear that, at least among the rulers of Alba and also the arbiters of information among their neighbours, things had changed. The tenth century may be seen, then, as the century during which we may be certain that a necessary component of the Gaelicisation of the east had occurred: the reorientation of the ruling elite in terms of language and identity. It bears emphasising, as Alex Woolf has repeatedly done, that this in itself is, however, not sufficient to explain the linguistic change of the period.

The use of distribution maps and dating horizons

So far the perspective of this discussion has been largely that generated by the historical sources, such as they are. These sources can tell us about the shifting fortunes of kings belonging to Gaelic and Pictish elites. To a certain extent they shed light on the ideologies of these elites, and as we can see they also include some crucial comment on shifting identities, linguistic and ethnic as well as political. They are, however, not a precise witness to the progress of Gaelic as it spread into eastern Scotland, or the means by which this happened.

Into this breach the study of place-names has stepped, and has been a mainstay of Scottish historical enquiry for some considerable time. The reasons why place-names have been seen in a Scottish context as being capable of providing a substitute for a historical narrative of the interaction among language groups are not hard to find: Scotland is almost uniquely possessed of a linguistic history of great complexity, and that complexity is displayed overtly in the stratigraphy of our place-names. In several recent introductory articles Simon Taylor has helpfully clarified that linguistic complexity as it relates to place-names, dividing Scotland into zones of linguistic content: mapped, this allows us to see the different linguistic layers one might expect in any given region, though the precise

---

[38] Charles-Edwards, 'Picts and Scots', 170; A. A. M. Duncan, *The Kingship of the Scots 842–1292: Succession and Independence* (Edinburgh, 2002), pp. 3–4; see also Dumville, 'Chronicle', p. 85.

nature of the layers and interactions among the languages in certain regions remain to be determined.[39] Bill Nicolaisen's pioneering distribution maps seemed to promise the ability to see the spread of Gaelic through the use of particular common generic elements, that is, the key referent noun in a place-name. In particular, in his work on the generic element *sliabh*, 'moor, hill', following John MacQueen, he seemed to have identified, solely through the use of toponymy, an otherwise unknown early Gaelic settlement in south-west Scotland: this argument staked the claim, more than any other, for the study of place-names as able to contribute independently of textual histories or archaeology, to the history of Scotland.[40]

Nicolaisen's work has been frequently republished and remains the mainstay for the study of Scottish place-names. And yet the methodological flaws of these distribution maps, acknowledged by Nicolaisen in a number of places, as artefacts in themselves, and in the way they have been employed as tools in the construction of historical narratives, have not really hit home as yet.[41] Without doubt we can concur that the distribution maps of *achadh,* 'field, farm', and *baile*, 'farm(toun)', are crucial in mapping, through the use of Gaelic place-names, those parts of Scotland where Gaelic was at some stage spoken sufficiently to leave behind it a toponymic footprint. But there are problems with using these distributions to construct a narrative of linguistic change. To give an illustration of the problems, we may take each of Nicolaisen's key Gaelic elements in turn.

Sliabh

As noted already, John MacQueen proposed in 1954 that the highly restricted, but very productive use of *sliabh* as a place-name generic in the Rhinns of Galloway (in names like Slewfad, Slewhabble) suggested a Gaelic settlement there of very early date, contemporary with the migration of Gaels to Dál Riata.[42] The argument was developed by Nicolaisen,

[39] S. Taylor, 'Place-names', in M. Lynch (ed.), *The Oxford Companion to Scottish History* (Oxford, 2001), pp. 479–84; *idem*, 'Reading the map: understanding Scottish place-names', *History Scotland*, vol. 2, no. 1 (Jan./Feb. 2002), 13.

[40] Nicolaisen, *Scottish Place-Names*, pp. 51–60, esp. 59–60.

[41] For Nicolaisen's notes of caution, see, e.g. ibid., p. 45; see especially his 'Place-name maps: how reliable are they?', *Namn och Bygd*, 79 (1991), 43–50.

[42] He also proposed the element *carraig* 'rock' as being also early, something he has recently restated (*Place-Names in the Rhinns of Galloway and Luce Valley* (Stranraer, 2002), pp. 33–7; *Place-Names of the Wigtownshire Moors and Machars* (Stranraer, 2008), pp. 68–73). The proposal regarding *carraig* has yet to be further discussed by other scholars, but many of the names cited

and became a point in favour of seeing the difference between the representation of Gaelic generics on distribution maps as being one of time. Yet in a recent article Simon Taylor has comprehensively dismantled this argument, both on methodological grounds (for instance the data collection underlying the distribution map of *sliabh* used the Ordnance Survey 6-inch map for the Rhinns, but the 1-inch for the rest of Scotland), and on the grounds that *sliabh* is, in fact, more widely distributed, once the record is combed more widely (see Fig. 2). Most cogently, however, he disputed a key plank in the argument: that the meaning of the term in the Rhinns was closer to Irish than to later Scottish Gaelic usage.[43] Despite some rearguard action by both Nicolaisen and MacQueen, it is hard to see how the argument can now be sustained, particularly in the absence of any other reason to expect a Gaelic colony in the Rhinns this early.[44] Of course, it will be impossible to completely dismiss Gaelic settlement in the Rhinns at any point in history, since they are so close to Ireland. Gaelic settlement in the south-west seems logical, and that logic may, after all, turn out to be correct. But the *sliabh* names simply do not demonstrate this. It is worth remembering that before the 1950s no one much thought that there had been Gaelic settlement in the south-west at an early period: it would be good to return to that situation.

Cill

For the Gaelic place-name element *cill*, 'a church' (originally *cell*, from Latin *cella*), it was proposed that we were seeing, by and large, the infiltration of Gaelic during a missionary phase, stretching eastwards, but only fitfully. Nicolaisen put more precision on this, noting that such names

---

are manifestly late, containing syntax (noun plus article plus noun formations), personal or kindred names, and perhaps items of vocabulary which belong in some cases to the later middle ages.

[43] Simon Taylor, '*Sliabh* in Scottish place-names: its meaning and chronology', *Journal of Scottish Name Studies*, 1 (2007), 99–13. See also now Paul Tempan, '*Sliabh* in Irish place-names: its meaning, distribution, chronology, and some implications for Scotland and the Isle of Man', *Scottish Place-Name News*, 27 (Autumn, 2009), 3–8; *idem*, '*Sliabh* in Irish place-names' *Nomina*, 32 (2009), 19–41.

[44] W. F. H. Nicolaisen, 'Gaelic *Sliabh* revisited', in S. Arbuthnott and K. Hollo (eds.), *Fil súil nglais, A Grey Eye Looks Back: a Festschrift in honour of Colm Ó Baoill* (Ceann Drochaid, 2007), pp. 175–86; J. MacQueen, *Place-Names of the Moors and Machars*, p. 69. The most cogent rebuttal regards Taylor's use of some names in which *sliabh* is the specific element, rather than the generic. This, to be fair, makes his own new map not a direct comparison with Nicolaisen's, but omitting these names does not substantially change the force of his argument.

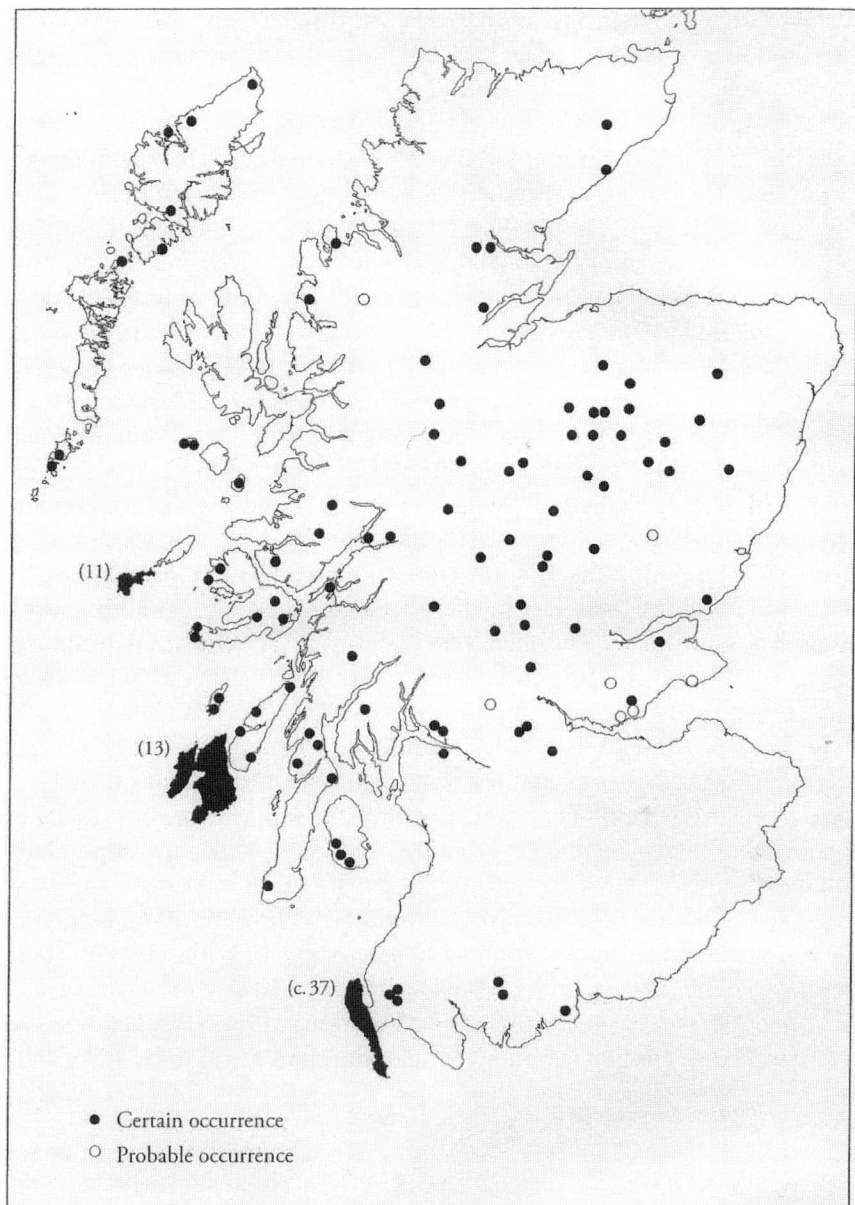

Figure 2. Distribution map of Gaelic element *sliabh* 'hill or moor, upland' in Scottish place-names. (From S. Taylor, '*Sliabh* in Scottish place-names: its meaning and chronology', *Journal of Scottish Name Studies*, 1 (2007), 102. Reproduced by permission of the author.)

demanded more than just individuals; they demanded Gaelic-speaking communities to establish them.[45] Again, more detailed analysis of sources by Simon Taylor changed the overall pattern of distribution significantly, revealing in particular three clusters of *cill* place-names in eastern Scotland (see Fig. 3).[46] In Nicolaisen's view the distribution of *cill* in eastern Scotland suggested that the term must have died out of use before the Gaelic take-over of Pictland, or else it would be more widespread; therefore it has a rough *terminus ante quem* of *c*.800.[47] This reasoned date of *c*.800 was subsequently transferred from eastern Scotland onto the presence of *cill* in other regions, to some extent by Nicolaisen, but more often and more bluntly by other writers; it influenced Taylor's analysis of *cill* names in 1996. Neither the date for the east, nor its imposition elsewhere, can be sustained. We know of names in *cill* being coined in the west much later: as Aidan Macdonald pointed out in 1979, Killantringan in Ayrshire was shown by Watson to be later medieval; the date of the death of its referent, King Olaf of Norway, makes Cill Amhlaigh in Lewis and Uist no earlier than 1030, and more likely some considerable time after. The cult of St Catherine looks to be a late medieval phenomenon in Scotland, and so churches named *Cill Chaitriona* (on Colonsay and Loch Fyne) are almost certainly fifteenth-century in coinage.[48] The point is that in those areas that remained Gaelic-speaking into the later Middle Ages it appears to have been possible to use *cill* for naming new churches all through that period. If this is so, we cannot tell when a given name has been created—it could be fairly recent. That said, I would still support the view that the majority of *cill* names were generated before 1100, in the west as in the east.

There is another way to look at the problem, however. Why is *cill* not as widespread in eastern Scotland as it is in Argyll or the south-west? Is it because neither Christianity nor Gaelic had reached that far to the east at the time they were coined (the received wisdom)? Or is it rather because there were other available options for naming churches in the east; indeed,

---

[45] Nicolaisen, *Scottish Place-Names*, pp. 165–7, 183–6; see also A. Macdonald, 'Gaelic *Cill* (*Kil(l)-*) in Scottish place-names', *Bulletin of the Ulster Place-Name Society*, Series 2, 2 (1979), 9–19.

[46] S. Taylor, 'Place-names and the early church in Eastern Scotland', in Crawford, *Scotland in Dark-Age Britain*, pp. 93–110.

[47] Nicolaisen, *Scottish Place-Names*, pp. 167, 183.

[48] See Macdonald, 'Gaelic *Cill*', 16. For further explorations of the problems of the element, see Rachel Butter, 'Cill- names and saints in Argyll: a way towards understanding the early church in Dál Riata?', Ph.D. thesis, University of Glasgow, 2007, p. 207.

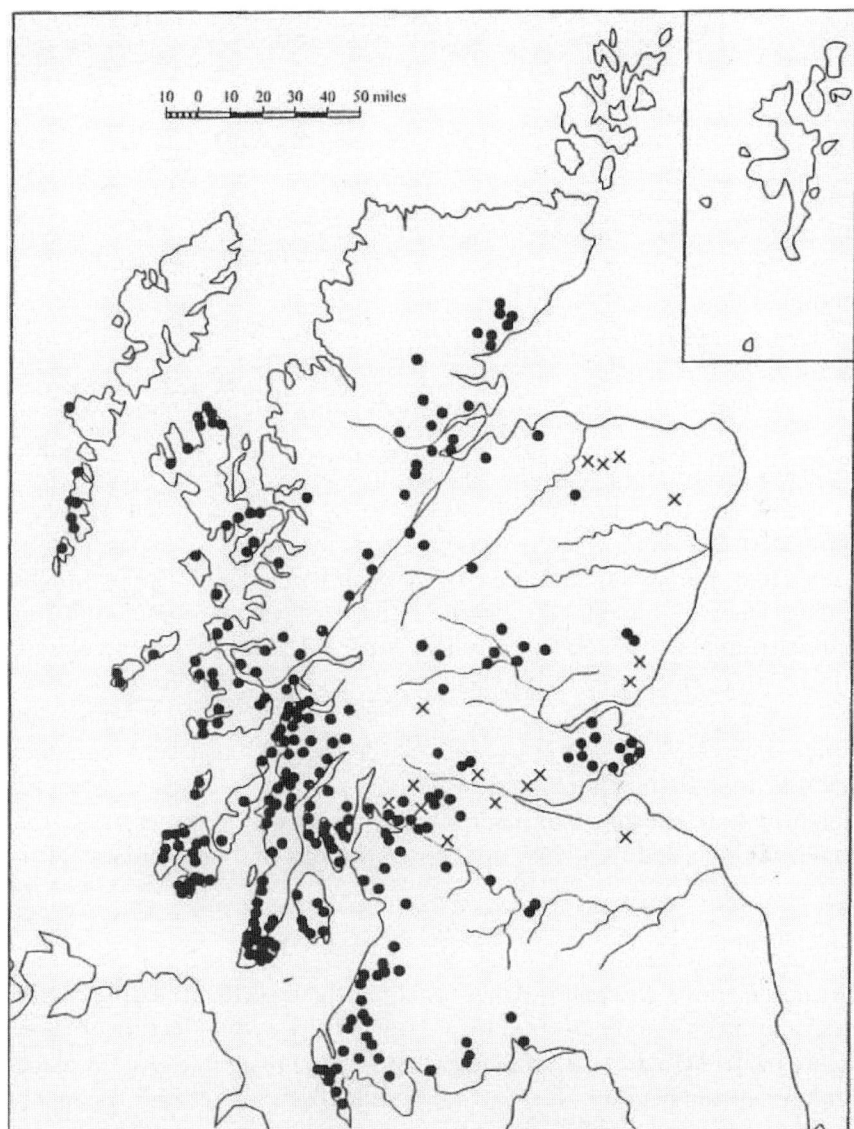

Figure 3.   Distribution map of Gaelic elements *cill* 'church' and *both* 'hut, church' (×) in Scottish place-names. (From S. Taylor, 'Place-Names and the Early Church in Eastern Scotland', in B. E. Crawford (ed.), *Scotland in Dark-Age Britain* (St John's House, St Andrews, 1996), p. 96. Reproduced by permission of the author and editor.)

because many other churches had already been named, using other ecclesiastical place-name generics? Here we must consider the presence in the
east, though not in the Gaelic west or in the south-west, of a range of
ecclesiastical place-name generics. Some of these have been explored in
detail by Simon Taylor. They include the Gaelic element *both*, usually
'hut', but in many instances in the east clearly 'church', perhaps a calque
on a Pictish term; and the word *lann*, 'enclosed ground > church site'.
Both terms are distinguished by their broadly 'Pictish' distribution, *lann*
more so than *both*.[49] A further term **eclés* is more complex, but in its
usage north of the Forth it is comparable to these others.[50] In addition, in
a forthcoming article I explore a further ecclesiastical generic, **locin*,
'(holy) place > church', an element which contributes the names of fourteen parishes in eastern Scotland (examples include Logierait, Logie-
Murdo).[51] Superimposing the distribution of these other ecclesiastical
generics over the map of *cill* allows one to see a fairly crowded landscape
in eastern Scotland of churches with a variety of name types. Factors
other than purely linguistic may be at work here, manifestly. Two possibilities emerge from this consideration: the employment of *cill* for naming
churches might be generated in eastern Scotland from particular ecclesiastical centres, employing distinct naming strategies (this has been suggested
by Taylor as a cause of his notable *cill* clusters in Easter Ross, Atholl, and
Fife). It may well be that those centres which gave rise to *cill* were dominated
by Gaelic-speaking churchmen. A second possibility, however, is that it
might instead have something to do with the type of church the term describes
(*cill*, *both*, *lann* and **eclés* may not be synonymous, in other words).[52]

Achadh and *baile*

As noted above, we can probably concur at the least that the distribution
maps of *achadh* and *baile* (see Figs. 4 and 5) give a vivid picture of those
places where Gaelic was spoken sufficiently to create and sustain place-
names at some point during the Middle Ages. After this there are

---

[49] Taylor, 'Place-names and the early church in Eastern Scotland', pp. 95–8, map at p. 96; *idem*,
'Place-names and the early church in Scotland', *Records of the Scottish Church History Society*,
28 (1998), 1–22, map at 22.
[50] See ibid., pp. 3–7.
[51] T. O. Clancy, 'Logie: an ecclesiastical place-name element in eastern Scotland', *Journal of
Scottish Name Studies* (forthcoming).
[52] I will explore some of these issues in the published version of my 2004 *Groam House Lecture*
(forthcoming).

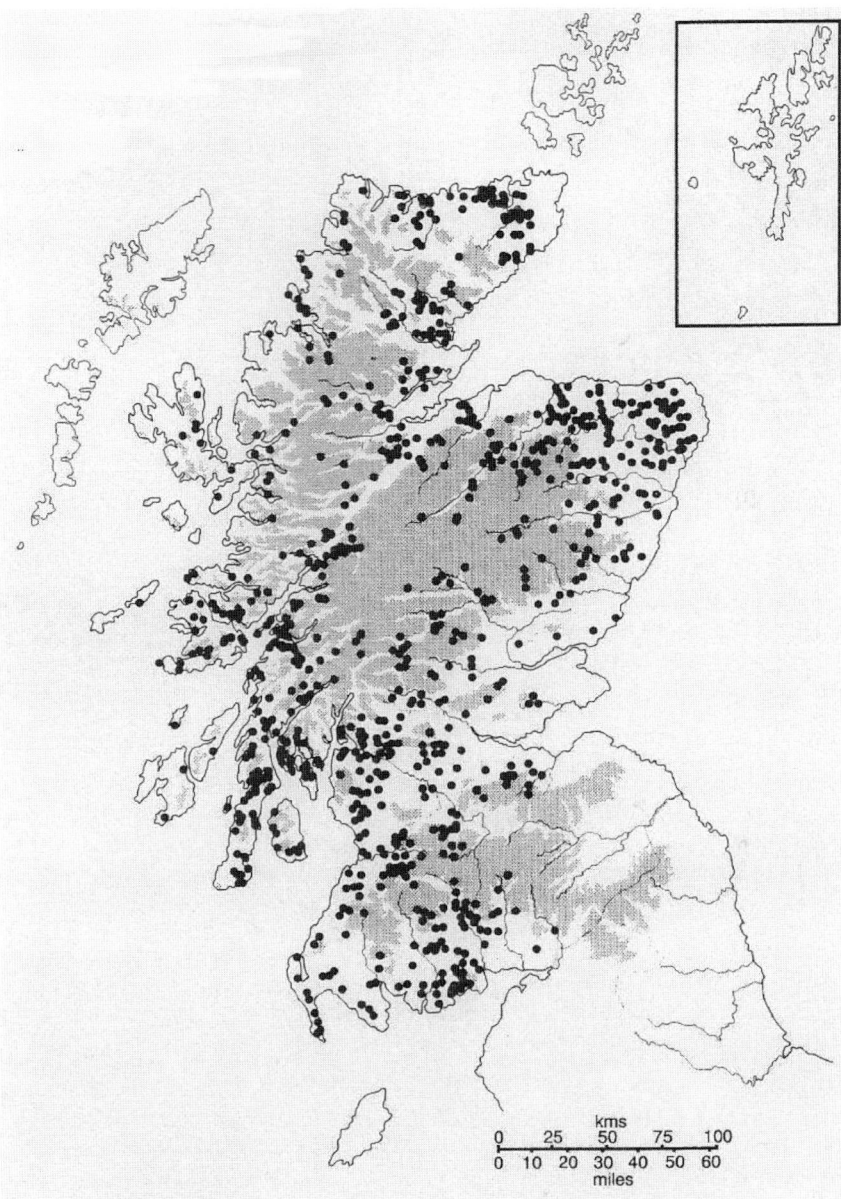

Figure 4.   Distribution map of Gaelic element *achadh*, 'field, settlement, fermtoun', by W. F. H. Nicolaisen. (From P. G. B. McNeill and H. L. MacQueen (eds.), *Atlas of Scottish History to 1707* (Edinburgh, Scottish Medievalists and Department of Geography, University of Edinburgh, 1996), p. 60. Reproduced by permission of the editors.)

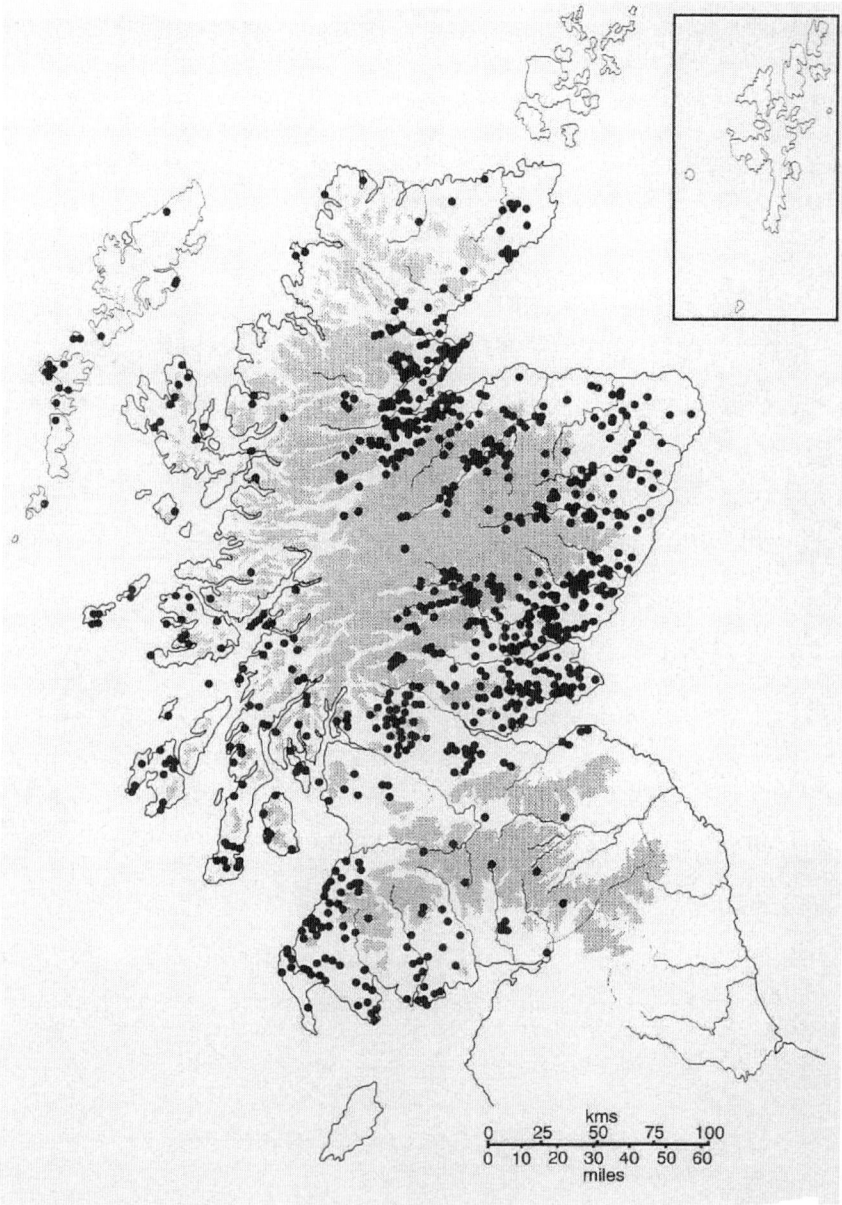

Figure 5. Distribution map of Gaelic element *baile*, 'settlement, fermtoun', by W. F. H. Nicolaisen. (From P. G. B. McNeill and H. L. MacQueen (eds.), *Atlas of Scottish History to 1707* (Edinburgh, Scottish Medievalists and Department of Geography, University of Edinburgh, 1996), p. 60. Reproduced by permission of the editors.)

considerable problems with the received view of these, only a few of which can be explored here. The distribution patterns need some revisiting as has been shown in the case of Fife by Simon Taylor (there are no certain *achadh* names in Fife), and as is also the case in Cunninghame in northern Ayrshire, where all the supposed *baile* names that have been mapped have proved to be misleading. The new gaps that appear create evident problems of interpreting what the distribution means, problems that the previous understanding of the terms did not cover. We need to add to these problems issues with dating. For instance, *achadh* as an active element in creating new names can be shown to be post-Norse in Caithness (a series of *achadh* place-names incorporate existing Norse place-names such as Achvarasdal and Achsteenclate[53]) and so probably here belongs, at the earliest, to the thirteenth century. There are a number of *baile* names in the south-west, in the Western Isles, and other places which may be shown to be later medieval, or modern. Ian Fraser's sensitive discussion of the *baile* names on the Isle of Arran is sobering: in his view they 'all date from the period post 1600'. The main reasons behind this late development are the conservatism of land-holding, and a late flourish of the division of farms.[54] Peter McNiven discusses in his forthcoming doctoral dissertation one *baile* name in Kilmadock parish in Menteith that can be securely dated to the 1480s.[55] Equally important, scholarship has gradually realised that the coining of most *baile* names can scarcely be much older than 1100, though at least one, Balchrystie, dates to 1058×1093.[56] In Ireland, such names are thought to belong to the twelfth century and later; in Fife, the data suggest that most of those that can be dated belong to the later twelfth and early thirteenth centuries.[57] What I would suggest is that we are dealing here with social contingency, not chronological or linguistic factors as such. The creation of *baile* and *achadh* names represents a change in the landholding patterns of the locale they are in, sufficient to create new farm names. That change was put into effect in a Gaelic-speaking environment, but it does not need to have been consequent on

[53] Doreen Waugh, 'Settlement names in Caithness with particular reference to Reay Parish', in B. E. Crawford (ed.), *Scandinavian Settlement in Northern Britain* (London, 1995), pp. 64–79, at 77–8.

[54] Fraser, *Place-Names of Arran*, p. 21.

[55] P. McNiven, 'Gaelic settlement-names of Menteith' (University of Glasgow).

[56] Simon Taylor with Gilbert Márkus, *The Place-Names of Fife*, vol. 2: *Central Fife between the Rivers Leven and Eden* (Donington, 2008), pp. 477–8.

[57] Liam Price, 'A note on the use of the word *baile* in place-names' *Celtica*, 6 (1963), 119–126; D. Flanagan and L. Flanagan, *Irish Place Names* (Dublin, 1994), pp. 20–6. S. Taylor with G. Márkus, *The Place-Names of Fife*, vol. 5 (Donington, 2011: forthcoming).

the *introduction* of Gaelic. The different patterns of *baile* v. *achadh* may indeed have some chronological dimension, but this may just as easily be to do with the type of land, or the type of land-holding, involved.

Recent research on the Gaelic place-name element *gart*, 'enclosed field', gives a flavour of this change in perspective, from the chronological to the social and contextual. Peter McNiven has advanced the view that *gart*, which has a very constrained distribution pattern within central Scotland, is a record not of the Gaelicisation of that region, but rather of the socio-economic changes implied by the clearing of woods to make new fields. He associates the *gart* names of Clackmannanshire particularly with the activities of forestry and assarting within Clackmannanshire.[58] He is not proposing this as a global solution, but his perspective points the way forward to a way of approaching distribution maps partly as a record of social developments, rather than simply linguistic ones.

In fact, if one were to seek for a distribution map to tell a narrative of Gaelic expansion into eastern Scotland, the one which does this most eloquently is the map of the place-name generic *pett*, 'a portion of an estate' (in names like Pitlochry, Pittenweem), which misleadingly continues to be used by scholars as a map displaying the extent of Pictish.[59] This is a word borrowed from Pictish into Gaelic to describe, as it would seem, a specific type of landholding unit. The context of that borrowing is almost certainly the centuries during which Gaelic superseded Pictish in the east, and this map bears testimony to one of the vectors by which it did so: the takeover of the major productive properties in the east by Gaelic-speakers. For almost all the *pit-* names on this map were coined by Gaels: they have Gaelic specifics, and these are frequently personal names or family names. It may be important also that the use of this element has been closely associated with major ecclesiastical establishments.[60]

The purpose of my discussing these distribution maps has not been to denigrate the advances they undoubtedly made, but rather to indicate that we must be alive to the different ways in which the data might be interpreted, and that, except at a very general level, we are hard pressed to use them to create models of Gaelicisation over time.

---

[58] P. McNiven, 'The *Gart-* names of Clackmannanshire', *Journal of Scottish Name Studies*, 1 (2007), 61–76.
[59] See, e.g. *Atlas of Scottish History*, p. 51 where it is listed under 'British and Pictish Place-Names'.
[60] For full discussion, see Taylor, *Place-Names of Fife*, vol. 5, forthcoming; *idem*, 'Pictish place-names revisited', in Driscoll, Geddes and Hall, *Pictish Progress*, pp. 67–118, at 77–80.

Before leaving this aspect of my lecture, I should simply note that many of our problems are caused by the absence of a full and detailed historical survey of Scottish place-names. Although such a survey is a long way off, advances have been made on this front, most notably, recently, by Simon Taylor in the five-volume *The Place-Names of Fife*, produced with Gilbert Márkus, the first three volumes of which have already appeared.[61]

Gaelic and Southern Scotland

It is clear that the extension of Gaelic speech into south-eastern Scotland, probably never in any magnitude, happened on the heels of conquest of the region by the kings of Alba, the staging-posts for which are usually seen as the seizure of Edinburgh in the 960s and the battle of Carham in 1018.[62] For a long time it was thought that the most reasonable explanation for the expansion of the Gaelic language into other parts of the south, those parts that had once formed the kingdom of Strathclyde, likewise owed something to the takeover by kings of Alba of the kingdom of Strathclyde, something held to have happened from the early tenth century. This has been shown to be wrong on several counts; the basic narrative derives from a later medieval source seeking to mirror later power relationships in the distant past.[63] The only fundamental piece of contemporary evidence on which modern scholars depended for the whole episode, a brief entry in the Chronicle of the Kings of Alba, was shown by Ben Hudson in a still neglected article in 1988 to have been a misreading.[64] Strathclyde clearly did come under the sway of the kings of Alba sometime in the eleventh century, but it seems likely that Gaelic had already made inroads in parts of the kingdom through other means. There may well, nonetheless, have been some influence on the linguistic balance of this region accruing from the takeover.

As already noted, the dismantling of the argument for an early colony of Gaelic-speakers in the Rhinns of Galloway, as well as the need for caution in exporting a false horizon of before *c*.800 for *cill* place names, means

---

[61] This was work conducted as the major tranche of an AHRC-funded project for which I was the Principal Investigator, which will attempt also to use the evidence made available by the Fife volumes to try to understand better the situation of the rest of Scotland. We are grateful to the AHRC for its support for this project.

[62] For the problems associated with Carham, see Duncan, *Kingship*, pp. 28–31.

[63] D. Broun, 'The Welsh identity of the kingdom of Strathclyde, c.900–c.1200', *Innes Review*, 55 (2004), 111–80, at 125–35.

[64] B. T. Hudson, 'Elech and the kings of Strathclyde', *Scottish Gaelic Studies*, 15 (1988), 145–9.

that we are no longer certain of how Gaelic came to south-western Scotland. In any case, the apparent history of the area, as a British zone subject to Northumbrian English conquest and settlement during the late seventh and eighth centuries, has left little room for Gaelic development, even were its roots to be early. I have recently argued, carrying forward work by Andrew Jennings and others, that Gaelic receives its first substantial foot in the south-west with the Gall-Ghaidheil.[65] These are the people or polity who gave their name ultimately to Galloway. Initially, *c*.900, we can see them as located in the Firth of Clyde area. The expansion from there, probably over the course of the tenth and more probably the eleventh centuries, to take over the south-west, so that '*Galwedia*' and variants are used of places as diverse as Renfrewshire and Annandale in the twelfth century,[66] takes place in unknown circumstances, but by the time we begin to have access to decent documentation, in the later twelfth century, Gaelic is demonstrably the major underlying language in the landscape of the south-west. Galloway becomes fixed as a name for what is now Wigtownshire and Kirkcudbrightshire only really around 1200, owing to the royal conquest and settlement of Kyle, Cunninghame and Renfrewshire, the solidifying of the core assets of the Lords of Galloway, and the hiving off of the earldom of Carrick. The significance of all this is that we must readdress the sequencing of languages in the south-west, allowing now for Gaelic as a successor language to British and English, and thus probably only on the scene from *c*.900.

In this context the Irish Sea dimension is crucial, as scholars such as Seán Duffy, Ben Hudson and Fiona Edmonds have shown that Galloway is part of that world, with the Rhinns at least being a segment of a multi-site kingship during the eleventh century.[67] One ruler of this world, Echmarcach mac Ragnaill, has been seen as emblematic in several respects: he ruled only briefly over Dublin, Man, the Isles and the Rhinns, but his

---

[65] T. O. Clancy, 'The Gall-Ghàidheil and Galloway', *Journal of Scottish Name Studies*, 2 (2008), 19–50. See also A. Jennings, 'Galloway, origins of', in Lynch, *Oxford Companion*, pp. 257–8.
[66] On which see G. W. S. Barrow, *Regesta Regum Scotorum, vol. I: The Acts of Malcolm IV, King of Scots 1153–1165* (Edinburgh, 1960), p. 38.
[67] S. Duffy, 'Irishmen and Islesmen in the kingdoms of Dublin and Man, 1052–1171', *Ériu*, 43 (1992), 93–133; B. T. Hudson, 'The changing economy of the Irish Sea province, AD 900–1300', in B. Smith (ed.), *Britain and Ireland 900–1300: Insular Responses to Medieval European Change* (Cambridge, 1999), pp. 39–66; and also his *Irish Sea Studies* (Dublin, 2006); F. Edmonds, 'Hiberno-Saxon and Hiberno-Scandinavian Contact in the West of the Northumbrian Kingdom: A Focus on the Church', D.Phil. thesis, University of Oxford, 2005; *eadem*, 'Saints' Cults and Gaelic-Scandinavian influence around the Cumberland coast and north of the Solway Firth', in T. Bolton (ed.), *Celtic/Scandinavian Interaction by the Irish Sea* (Leiden, forthcoming).

career saw his territory expand and contract, and he was ruler over differ-ent combinations of these regions at different times. His own name was a Gaelic one, his father's Norse, and so he bears testimony to the rise of Gaelic by the early eleventh century as a status language within the Scandinavian dominated Irish Sea world.[68]

Norse and the Hebrides; the 'Irish Sea World'

It is of course a fact that Gaelic is now most widely spoken as a commu-nity language throughout the Hebrides; and in the later Middle Ages the western seaboard and the Isles became most closely associated with Gaelic. I suspect that it is partly because of this that scholars have had difficulty dissociating the zones of later medieval Gaelic speech from those areas likely to have been Gaelic-speaking in the early Middle Ages. There is no doubt that Argyll, including the islands of the southern Hebrides (that is from Ardnamurchan south), was Gaelic in speech from the seventh cen-tury at the latest; but equally there is good reason to exclude what became northern Argyll, Sutherland and Caithness, and the Western Isles, from any *assumption* of Gaelic having been spoken there in the period before the arrival of Scandinavians, the Vikings, in the period around 800. Increasingly, spearheaded lately by the joint work of Andrew Jennings and Arne Kruse, scholars have been emphasising the lack of any good evidence for Gaelic having been the language of the Outer Hebrides during this earlier period.[69] The same holds good for large parts of the northern mainland, especially Sutherland and Caithness, conquered by Scandinavians before there is any reason to believe Gaelic can have made inroads on them. We should rather presume that these areas were Pictish-speaking for the most part: certainly the name-evidence from Ptolemy suggests these areas were Celtic, and probably Brittonic, in speech in the second century AD, and there are good suggestions of cultural affinities

---

[68] Echmarcach has been much commented upon, but see my summary in 'Gall-Ghàidheil and Galloway', 28–9, and references there cited.

[69] A. Jennings and A. Kruse, 'An Ethnic Enigma—Norse, Pict and Gael in the Western Isles', in A. Mortensen and S. V. Arge (eds.), *Viking and Norse in the North Atlantic: selected papers from the Proceedings of the Fourteenth Viking Congress, Tórshavn, 19–30 July 2001* (Tórshavn, 2005), pp. 284–95; A. Kruse, 'Explorers, raiders and settlers. The Norse impact on Hebridean place-names', in P. Gammeltoft, C. Hough and D. Waugh (eds.), *Cultural Contacts in the North Atlantic Region: the Evidence of Names* (Lerwick, 2005), pp. 141–56; Jennings and Kruse, 'One coast—three peoples: names and ethnicity in the Scottish West during the early Viking period', in A. Woolf (ed.), *Scandinavian Scotland—Twenty Years After* (St Andrews, 2009), pp. 75–102.

thereafter. We can be less sure of Lewis and Harris, having really no evidence on which to go. But Gaelic was probably not what they were speaking, at any time before (and probably for some considerable time after) the settlement of Scandinavians there. I should note here that Richard Cox has pointed to some evidence for Gaelic-Norse contact in the form of Gaelic loan-words into Norse and Norse names loaned into Gaelic at an early stage, as well as suggesting taxonomies that would allow certain Gaelic names to be classified as early.[70] Part of the problem with the first of these proposals is that the location of the loaning activity cannot be securely determined, only their application to Lewis nomenclature. The 'early Gaelic names' likewise depend on a presumption of early syntax which is far from certain. Nonetheless, a number of his examples are worth bearing in mind as a caution that things may be more complex than they currently seem and, as Cox rightly points out, if it cannot be proven that Gaelic was spoken in the Western Isles before the Scandinavian settlements, neither can it be definitively proven that it was not. Likewise, the cult of saints and the seeming continuity of church-sites with Gaelic names from the earlier through to the later Middle Ages hold out one venue in which Gaelic speech might have been introduced and sustained prior to and during Scandinavian dominance of the region.[71]

No matter what language was spoken originally in the Western Isles, Scandinavians may still have created a 'tabula rasa' linguistic effect: the lack of clear evidence of linguistic continuity remains striking, and even Cox admits 'there is general agreement that no Gaelic names can be shown to be pre-Norse creations'.[72] It should be noted that Alan Macniven in his 2006 doctoral thesis has argued that Islay, too, suffered almost total linguistic replacement of Gaelic by Norse, before the gradual reintroduction of Gaelic.[73] Whether Gaelic is a new introduction, or whether it was starting afresh, the proposal then is that Norse represents a clear linguistic line after which the Gaelic of the Hebrides predominantly dates.

[70] R. Cox, 'Notes on the Norse impact on Hebridean place-names', *Journal of Scottish Name Studies*, 1 (2007), 139–44; idem, *The Gaelic Place-Names of Carloway, Isle of Lewis: their Structure and Significance* (Dublin, 2002), pp. 111–18.
[71] Cf. Cox, *Gaelic Place-Names*, p. 115 for some examples. See also the comments of Nicolaisen, *Scottish Place-Names*, pp. 185–6, though this is also a good example where the reasoned date of 'before 800' devised for eastern Scotland is invoked inappropriately elsewhere.
[72] Cox, 'Notes on the Norse impact', 142. See also Barbara Crawford's earlier comments, *Scandinavian Scotland*, p. 97.
[73] A. Macniven, 'The Norse in Islay. A settlement historical case-study for medieval Scandinavian activity in western maritime Scotland', Ph.D. thesis, University of Edinburgh, 2006.

The effect of this realignment is dramatic, and has I think still not been sufficiently absorbed. If it was either not already there, or had been extinguished, where, then, did the Gaelic later spoken in these areas come from? This, it seems to me, is not a question that has been posed as yet. We cannot resort, as one perhaps can in other areas such as the Argyll mainland, or possibly further south in the Isle of Man, to the notion that Gaelic 're-emerged' autochthonously after Norwegian rule came to an end.

A further and very important development that space does not allow me to explore properly here was sparked by Barbara Crawford's observation that topographical names employing elements like *dalr*, 'dale, strath', which Nicolaisen took to be evidence only of a very fleeting and tenuous connection between Scandinavians and certain parts of Scotland, were elsewhere (as in Iceland and Orkney) given to early and important farms or landholding units. This observation has been developed by her in respect of the north and north-east of Scotland, and recently by Andrew Jennings in an important article on Norse names in Kintyre.[74] This work leads to the possibility that we may be seeing Norse topographical nomenclature at work identifying primary settlements within areas where Gaelic remained the predominant language of those who worked the land: a situation which then may have applied to much of Argyll and the north-west seaboard, for instance, if we may go by the distribution of *dalr* names.[75] There is much further work to do in this area: a Glasgow doctoral student, Anne Bankier, is at present working on trying to wed these insights to archaeological evidence on the western Scottish mainland.[76]

An important feature of our changed understanding of the situation of the Hebrides during the Viking ages is a very profound augmentation

---

[74] B. Crawford, 'Introduction', in Crawford, *Scandinavian Settlement*, pp. 12–13; see also in general her *Earl and Mormaer. Norse-Pictish Relations in Northern Scotland* (Rosemarkie, 1995); *eadem*, 'Earldom strategies in north Scotland and the signifcance of place-names', in G. Williams and P. Bibire (eds.), *Sagas, Saints and Settlements* (Leiden, 2004), pp. 105–24; B. E. Crawford and S. Taylor, 'The southern frontier of Norse settlement in north Scotland', *Northern Scotland*, 23 (2003), 1–76; A. Jennings, 'The Norse place-names of Kintyre', in J. Adams and K. Holman (eds.), *Scandinavia and Europe 800–1350. Contact, Conflict and Coexistence* (Turnhout, 2004), pp. 109–19. See also A. Kruse, 'Norse topographical settlement names on the western littoral of Scotland', in Adams and Holman, *Scandinavia and Europe*, pp. 109–19. For a an important cautionary view, see James Graham-Campbell, 'Some reflections on the distribution and significance of Norse place-names in northern Scotland', in P. Gammeltoft and B. Jørgensen (eds.), *Names through the Looking Glass. Festschrift in honour of Gillian Fellows-Jensen* (Copenhagen, 2006), pp. 94–118.

[75] See Nicolaisen, *Scottish Place-Names*, p. 123 for distribution map.

[76] A. Bankier, 'Norse settlement in Western Argyll and Ardnamurchan, Scotland' (University of Glasgow).

and revision of our understanding of the interaction of the Irish Sea zone. Scholarship in this area was probably heralded by the work of A. P. Smyth in the late 1970s and 1980s, but it has been the considerable volume of work carried out from 1992 to the present by scholars such as Seán Duffy, Colmán Etchingham and Ben Hudson, and more recently Alex Woolf, Clare Downham and Fiona Edmonds, that has really transformed our perspectives.[77] While this has, as we have seen, some profound implications for our analysis of the evolution of south-west Scotland, it also has an impact on how we see the Isles evolving. The Isles are ostensibly ruled by kings based in Dublin for large parts of the tenth and eleventh centuries. In the eleventh and even the twelfth century Irish kings, even ones based in Munster, attempted to exert their domination over Dublin and the Isle of Man, and also over the Hebrides.[78] The need to have a weather-eye on all sides of the Irish Sea in order to achieve a significant integration of knowledge has been amply demonstrated by the work of Duffy and Etchingham, and most recently Downham; and the well-known case of Echmarcach mac Ragnaill (†1064), mentioned above, ruler at various points in the Rhinns of Galloway, the Isles, Dublin and Man, illustrates it well. The porousness of this zone politically has far-reaching implications for our understanding of its development in linguistic and in ethnic terms.

The twelfth-century 'native v. newcomer' model

Echmarcach mac Ragnaill's ultimate successors in the south-west were the kings and Lords of Galloway, starting in mid-twelfth century with Fergus, and continuing with his sons and grandsons.[79] This family of Gaelic-speaking nobility, of unknown origins but with widespread and multi-cultural marital links over several generations subsequently, illustrates

---

[77] A. P. Smyth, *Scandinavian York and Dublin: the History and Archaeology of Two Related Viking Kingdoms* (Dublin, c.1975–9); *idem, Warlords and Holy Men*, ch. 5; Duffy, 'Irishmen and islesmen'; C. Etchingham, 'North Wales, Ireland and the Isles: the insular Viking zone', *Peritia*, 15 (2001), 145–87; Hudson, *Irish Sea Studies*; A. Woolf, 'Amlaíb Cuarán and the Gael, 941–81', in S. Duffy (ed.), *Medieval Dublin III: Proceedings of the Friends of Medieval Dublin Symposium 2001* (Dublin, 2002), pp. 34–43; *idem, From Pictland to Alba*; C. Downham, *Viking Kings of Britain and Ireland. The Dynasty of Ívarr to A.D. 1014* (Edinburgh, 2007); Edmonds, 'Hiberno-Saxon and Hiberno-Scandinavian contact'; *eadem*, 'History and names', in J. Graham-Campbell and R. Philpott (eds.), *The Huxley Viking Hoard. Scandinavian Settlement in the North West* (Liverpool, 2010), pp. 3–12.
[78] See Duffy, 'Irishmen and islesmen'.
[79] R. Oram, *The Lordship of Galloway* (Edinburgh, 2000), is the most thorough survey.

well the problems with one further dominant paradigm for examining the history of Scotland, this time in the twelfth century: the seeming polar opposition between 'native' and 'newcomer', between 'Celtic' and 'Norman' attributes. This essentialist paradigm relies on inherent Celtic conservatism and opposition to Anglo-Norman social and cultural changes, and leaves little room for the complex and nuanced world of negotiated identities and porous language zones that was twelfth-century Scotland.[80] The Lords of Galloway were major landholders in the late twelfth and early thirteenth centuries; they adopted many of the distinctive attributes of the Europeanised world of Scotland during those centuries; and yet their charters for certain areas, such as properties in Kirkcudbrightshire, show them to be Gaelic-speaking lords, even down to the coining of a new Gaelic place-name during the settlement of a boundary dispute in the early thirteenth century.[81] This situation, and analogous ones, can be replicated in various other parts of Scotland. We owe to Geoffrey Barrow's research a much more complex understanding of where the 'Gàidhealtachd' of the Scottish Middle Ages in fact was; as well as to Steve Boardman's recent research a much more nuanced picture of the Scottish Crown's relationship with Gaelic Scotland in the fourteenth and fifteenth centuries, and of the multifaceted background of emergent Gaelic kindreds like the Campbells.[82] Matthew Hammond has recently written of the need to abandon unhelpful polarisations in our approach to the period, and the recently completed AHRC-funded project on 'The Paradox of Medieval Scotland', through its prosopographical approach to the period,

---

[80] Two recent bodies of otherwise important scholarship seem to me to be beset by the problems of seeing the world through this paradigm: the work of R. Andrew McDonald, e.g. *The Kingdom of the Isles*, and *idem, Outlaws of Medieval Scotland: Challenges to the Canmore Kings, 1058–1266* (East Linton, 2003); and that of Cynthia Neville, *Native Lordship in Medieval Scotland: the Earldoms of Strathearn and Lennox, c.1140–1365* (Dublin, 2005).

[81] For the Lords of Galloway's charters, see K. J. Stringer, 'Periphery and core in thirteenth-century Scotland: Alan son of Roland, Lord of Galloway and Constable of Scotland', in A. Grant and K. J. Stringer (eds.), *Medieval Scotland: Crown, Lordship and Community. Essays Presented to G. W. S. Barrow* (Edinburgh, 1993), pp. 82–113; 'Acts of Lordship: the records of the Lords of Galloway to 1234', in T. Brotherstone and D. Ditchburn (eds.), *Freedom and Authority: Historical and Historiographical Essays presented to Grant G. Simpson* (East Linton, 2000), pp. 203–34. For the new name of the burn, see ibid., §50, issued 1209 × 1234 (p. 229): 'qui rivulus de nouo a nobis propter prehabitam contencionem uocatus est Pollenchosnewa'.

[82] G. W. S. Barrow, 'The lost Gàidhealtachd of medieval Scotland', in W. Gillies (ed.), *Gaelic and Scotland/Alba agus a' Ghàidhlig* (Edinburgh, 1989), pp. 67–88; S. Boardman, 'The Gaelic world and the early Stewart court', in D. Broun and M. MacGregor (eds.), *Miorun Mor nan Gall, The Great Ill-Will of the Lowlander: Lowland Perceptions of the Scottish Highlands* (Glasgow, 2005), pp. 83–109; *idem, The Campbells, 1250–1513* (Edinburgh, 2006).

should shed much needed light on these issues of identity, language and status.[83]

'Common Gaelic'

As one final note on shifting paradigms, there has been considerable, though not greatly noticed, movement on the question of the relationship of Scottish Gaelic and Irish. I have alluded already to Kenneth Jackson's influential Rhŷs Lecture on 'Common Gaelic', which held sway for half a century. Along the way there was some fretting about the approach he took, most notably by David Greene and Donald MacAulay.[84] Roibeard Ó Maolalaigh cogently laid out the linguistic case for revisiting the received view in 1998, and consolidated further thinking along these lines in his work on the Gaelic notes in the Book of Deer.[85] In 2000, Professor Breandán Ó Buachalla launched a devastating critique on the premises and conclusions of Jackson's paper.[86] In a nutshell, these critiques made it clear that the principal dialectal division in the Gaelic languages was north–south, not east–west; that linguistic analysis makes it necessary for the medieval and modern dialects to be have been evolving out of a common ancestor all the time—aside from the standardised written form of the language, there was no linguistic stasis during our period. Fundamental changes in Scottish Gaelic must predate the twelfth century, and not be later developments. Scottish Gaelic therefore has much to tell us about the evolution of Gaelic as a whole—it is not just a late offshoot, but rather can help explain features of the earlier language that were subsequently lost in the major dialects of Irish, for instance.[87]

---

[83] M. Hammond, 'Ethnicity and the writing of medieval Scottish history', *Scottish Historical Review*, 85 (2006), 1–29; idem, 'Ethnicity, personal names, and the nature of Scottish Europeanization', *Thirteenth-Century England*, 11 (Woodbridge, 2007), 82–93; idem, 'Domination and conquest? The Scottish experience, 1100–1286', in S. Duffy and S. Foran (eds.), *The First English Empire?* (Dublin, forthcoming). See <www.poms.ac.uk> for further details of this project, and the online prosopographical database.

[84] D. Greene, 'Review of K. Jackson, *Gaelic Notes in the Book of Deer*', *Studia Hibernica*, 12 (1972), pp. 167–70; D. MacAulay, 'Review of K. Jackson, *Gaelic Notes*', *Scottish Historical Review*, 54 (1975), pp. 84–7.

[85] R. Ó Maolalaigh, 'Place-names as a resource for the historical linguist', in S. Taylor (ed.), *The Uses of Place-Names* (Edinburgh, 1998), pp. 12–53, esp. 12–15; 'Scotticisation of Gaelic'.

[86] Ó Buachalla, ' "Common Gaelic" revisited'.

[87] For detailed work in this direction, see for instance articles cited in Ó Buachalla, ' "Common Gaelic" revisited', p. 10, n. 7; Ó Maolalaigh, 'Scotticisation of Gaelic'.

Looking forward

I hope that up to this point this review has demonstrated, if nothing else, that the previous narrative of Gaelic expansion simply will no longer do. At several points most scholars working in the field have probably shifted ground, though the implications for the whole picture have not sufficiently been spelled out as yet. In what remains of this lecture, I will try to provide some sense from my perspective of what we can and should say about the advent and expansion of Gaelic. I will focus on four main issues, but my emphasis here is on one prevailing approach: we should be prepared for the expansion of Gaelic to be complex, multidirectional and multiphased, and to have lasted longer than has usually been allowed for.

Origins

Gaelic was the language of Argyll by *c.* AD 600, so much we can probably agree. There is not room to explore this issue here, but our understanding of how it got there must take into account the recent views of some linguists that up until, say, the first century AD there is no clear evidence of formal distinction between Goidelic and Brittonic: the P-Celtic/Q-Celtic divide so often cited as a major distinctive feature is effectively merely an isogloss. The major developments which separate Brittonic from Goidelic belong largely to the next six centuries or so, and there is no good reason to imagine that Argyll's linguistic development would have followed that of eastern Scotland rather than that of the north of Ireland. Admittedly, Ptolemy shows us a polity with what looks to be a Brittonic name, the Epidii, present in Kintyre in the second century AD, but then he has ostensibly Brittonic tribes in Ireland too, and not in peripheral areas.[88] Of course, it would be surprising if there were not political and social change in Argyll, with concomitant linguistic development, in the period 400–600, since the whole of Britain and Ireland manifests this.[89] But there is no

[88] See A. L. F. Rivet and C. Smith, *The Place-Names of Roman Britain* (London, 1979), pp. 360–1; and see G. R. Isaac, 'Scotland', in J. de Hoz, E. R. Lujan and P. Sims-Williams (eds.), *New Approaches to Celtic Place-Names in Ptolemy's Geography* (Madrid, 2005), pp. 189–214; on Brittonic and other names in Ireland, see Patrizia de Bernardo Stempel, 'Pre-Celtic, Old Celtic layers, Britonic and Goidelic in ancient Ireland', in P. Cavill and G. Broderick (eds.), *Language Contact in the Place-Names of Great Britain and Ireland* (Nottingham, 2007), pp. 137–63.
[89] See various studies in A. Bammesberger and A. Wollmann (eds.), *Britain 400–600: Language and History*, Anglistische Forschungen 205 (Heidelberg, 1990); T. Charles-Edwards, 'Language and society among the Insular Celts AD 400–1000', in M. J. Green (ed.), *The Celtic World* (London, 1995), pp. 703–36.

good reason to posit migration even of elites, in order to see a Gaelic-speaking Argyll come into being. Having said this, my own recent work on the earliest attested Gaelic place-names in the Scottish record does seem to suggest a more linguistically 'shallow' place-name landscape, one suggestive of a recent, and not very deep or developed, relationship between Gaelic and Argyll. It may be that here, as elsewhere, the study of place-names will cause us once more to revise our understanding.

The Gaelicisation of Pictland

We are no longer at liberty to ascribe the Gaelicisation of Pictland to the 'unionising' activities of Cinaed mac Ailpín, or indeed to his predecessors. That said, the ruling elite of eastern Scotland, of the former Pictland, seems to have adopted Gaelic language and identity by the tenth century, and this was being observed by their neighbours as well, the English referring to them as *Scottas* and *Scotti*. Alex Woolf has made a cogent case for not thinking that elite emulation alone works as a vector for linguistic change.[90] His two alternative suggestions in his recent book seem to pull in different directions. One proposes an 'Albanian' language which emerged from the Gaelicisation of an underlying but fairly similar Brittonic language, Pictish: 'the Gaelic and British dialects of Albania probably influenced each other enormously and probably began to converge into a single Albanian language'.[91] There seem to me a number of deep-seated difficulties with this proposal, not least of which is its downplaying of the very fundamental linguistic relationship between Irish and Scottish Gaelic; there is a drift eastwards here that is reminiscent of the work that Jackson was at pains to refute in his Rhŷs Lecture in 1951. Ultimately, although we can point to significant lexical import from Pictish into Gaelic, and suggest some other substrate influence of the sort that might be caused by Brittonic speakers adopting Gaelic as their language, it is this latter phenomenon which surely occurred in central medieval Scotland, rather than 'convergence'.[92] Conversely, however, Woolf argued for political displacement and territorial redistribution on a very significant scale owing to the disruption of the first Viking age as the main underlying cause of the 'Gaelic

---

[90] Woolf, *From Pictland to Alba*, pp. 291–2.
[91] Ibid., p. 340: the full discussion is pp. 322–40.
[92] For a further critique of this aspect of Woolf's book, see Charles-Edwards, 'Picts and Scots', 186–7.

conquest of Pictavia'.[93] To my mind neither scenario seems sufficient as an explanation.

I would suggest a series of ways in which Gaelic was introduced into eastern Scotland in the period 550–900, at multiple social levels, preparing the ground for its dominance over Pictish. Prime among these from early on was the church. The conversion of Pictland, though not produced solely by Gaelic missionaries by any means, led to dominance over the Pictish church by Gaelic churchmen, and not just 'Columban' clergy, and this sort of influence can be seen at various points during the seventh and early eighth centuries.[94] One reflection of this may be the predominance of Gaelic saints in the dedications even of seemingly Pictish church place names such as those in *eccles*.[95] While this is hardly a transformative thing in itself, we should not underestimate the importance of Gaelic church culture. Most significant in this respect is the place accorded the Gaelic language within its church: already by the early seventh century we have ecclesiastical writing in the vernacular.[96] In Europe, the status of the vernacular within Gaelic Christian culture is only paralleled, and that partially, by the role of Anglo-Saxon in England. This gave Gaelic a status not shared by any of the Brittonic languages at this date. Within certain circles in Pictland, then, from the seventh century on, the order of status of languages may well have been Latin, Gaelic, and then Pictish (Thomas Charles-Edwards has argued something similar for the status of Welsh in Wales during the sixth and early seventh centuries).[97] This is far from saying Pictish had no status, of course, but the, admittedly very limited, evidence available to us makes it seem quite restricted. We may even wish to consider the fact that, even if some or most of the 'Pictish ogham' inscriptions should prove to be in the Pictish language, nonetheless the script chosen in which to write it was one with overt Irish associations.

There is also a whole series of minor incidents of interaction which we might see as reinforcing Gaelic's status within Pictland over this period:

---

[93] Woolf, *From Pictland to Alba*, pp. 340–2.

[94] For some preliminary discussion on these lines, see T. O. Clancy, 'Deer and the early church in the North-East', in Forsyth, *Studies in the Book of Deer*, pp. 363–97.

[95] On which see e.g. Taylor, 'Place-names and the early church'; G. W. S. Barrow, 'The childhood of Scottish Christianity: a note on some place-name evidence', *Scottish Studies*, 27 (1983), 1–15.

[96] See for instance T. O. Clancy and G. Márkus, *Iona: The Earliest Poetry of a Celtic Monastery* (Edinburgh, 1995). By the first half of the ninth century religious texts in Gaelic included hymns, prayers, sermons, commentaries, ecclesiastical legislation, monastic rules, advice literature, martyrologies, hagiographical texts and creative Christian literature. This was a powerful vernacular religious culture.

[97] Charles-Edwards, 'Language and society'.

marriage alliances, the potential exile of Pictish kings in Ireland and subsequent return. We should by no means think links with Gaelic need be
confined to links with Argyll—the foundation legend of Abernethy suggests otherwise. There also may have been pockets of significant Gaelic
settlement all through this period, allied either to the church, or to the
introduction of Gaelic nobles into areas by Pictish kings as a means of
dealing with opponents, or both. The region, probably at the time a kingdom or subkingdom, of Atholl springs to mind here. Although the derivation of the name as 'New Ireland' has been questioned from time to time,
most recently by James Fraser, I find it difficult to see another clear
explanation for the name.[98] It is probably no accident that this area has the
clearest evidence of the cults of Iona personnel, both famous and obscure,
as saints; and that it hosts one of the eastern clusters of *cill* names. I have
also argued that a major sept of the Cenél Comgaill of Argyll were given
land in what became Strathearn in the aftermath of the shattering of
Northumbrian overlordship of southern Pictland in 685. This may have
introduced Gaelic into this area: indeed, it is one potential explanation
behind the term 'Strathearn' for the area (not, in fact, a contiguous block
of territory) they seem to have controlled.[99]

Alex Woolf has additionally proposed that at some point between 700
and 900 we see an introduction of Gaelic kindreds into southern Pictland,
those who would give rise to areas such as 'Angus' and 'Gowrie'.[100]
Certainly by the tenth century there is clear evidence that a series of Gaelic
kindreds in the east were thought of as being descended from Argyll kindreds. Dauvit Broun has recently proposed the early ninth century as a
significant moment in which we might imagine this happening: this makes
more sense if we can see the dominant rulers of Pictland at the period, the
rulers of Fortriu, being based north of the Mounth, as Alex Woolf has
convincingly argued.[101] Introduction of Gaelic kindreds in order to settle

---

[98] Fraser, *From Caledonia to Pictland*, pp. 101–2; I explore the name in 'Atholl, Banff, Earn and
Elgin: "New Irelands" in the East revisited', in McLeod *et al.*, *Bile ós Chrannaibh*, pp. 79–102. By
a regrettable oversight I neglected to discuss Dr Fraser's proposal for the name in this article. The
suggestion merits deeper consideration than I can give here. He proposes, interestingly, an
underlying Brittonic *Atui Guocled* via a Gaelic *Áth Fochla*, 'north pass' or 'north way'. As I
discuss, however (without direct reference to this proposal), the initial-stress pattern of the name
probably rules this sort of derivation out; as also the unlikelihood of scribes mangling a familiar
word like *fochla*, 'north', in the many ways they have—to say nothing of the modern form of the
name.
[99] T. O. Clancy, 'Philosopher-king: Nechtan mac Der-Ilei', *Scottish Historical Review*, 83 (2004),
125–49, at 138–42; *idem*, 'Atholl, Banff, Earn and Elgin', pp. 88–90.
[100] Woolf, *From Pictland to Alba*, pp. 226–30.
[101] Broun, 'Arrival of the Gaels'.

a problematic region after the round-robin warfare of the early eighth century has much to recommend it as a hypothesis. Such movement also makes a great deal of sense within the context of the incorporation of Argyll within the Pictish kingdom: by the early ninth century Loch Lomond and Iona could be described as being within or off the coast of Pictish territory.[102] As David Dumville has suggested, Pictland may have become completely porous to Gaels—a feature that undoubtedly would have had consequences in the period after the Viking incursions and settlements in the west, from c.800.[103] Whatever we conclude about this, we must leave room for the expansion of such kindreds, for 'predatory kinship', to borrow the term of Eleanor Searle, describing Norman expansion in Normandy,[104] leading to the displacement of previous landholders by Gaelic kindreds.

Finally, we should consider the role of ideology. Though its contemporaneousness has been cast into some doubt, 'The Chronicle of the Kings of Alba' displays a denigration of Pictishness, a linkage with injustice and unchristian activity that is easy to credit as belonging to the period. 'The Chronicle of the Kings of Alba' seems to suggest that, ideologically, Pictishness became equated with injustice and failings towards the church. Given the ravaging of Pictland in the mid- to late ninth century it is easy to see how this might be the case. Lest we forget in our focus on 'the Pictish heartland': a series of areas that had been, as far as we can see, prosperous and integral parts of the Pictish culture-zone (Shetland, Orkney, the northern mainland) had by c.900 been seized by Viking lords, and perhaps had been under Scandinavian dominance in some cases for some considerable time. These losses only increase if we think that Pictish kings had controlled Argyll for over half a century as well.

My solution then to the Gaelicisation of eastern Scotland is to see it as resulting from a combination of factors: church influence (giving the language significant status amongst Pictish elites from an early stage); the settling of and subsequent predatory expansion of landholding by important Gaelic kindreds in swordland over the course of the late seventh,

---

[102] T. O. Clancy, 'Iona in the kingdom of the Picts: a note', *Innes Review*, 55 (2004), 73–6.

[103] See Dumville, *Churches of North Britain*, pp. 35–6: 'Pictland, by virtue of containing a Gaelic subkingdom, was open to Gaelic influence and settlement to a degree previously unimaginable.' There is clearly convergence here with the views of Woolf and Broun, even if all three disagree with each other about particulars.

[104] E. Searle, *Predatory Kinship and the Creation of Norman Power 840–1066* (Berkeley, CA, 1988). I owe my awareness of this work to Alex Woolf. Woolf's proposal, *From Pictland to Alba*, pp. 340–2, has this paradigm partially in mind.

eighth and perhaps early ninth centuries; the Pictish conquest of Dál Riata, and its consequent creation of a porous zone of movement for Gaelic-speakers within the same kingdom as Picts; the collapse of the status quo in the middle decades of the eighth century; and, ultimately, the domination of the Pictish kingship by a dynasty who espoused Gaelic language, law and identity, and within whose ideology Pictish attributes were rejected as having led to the mess that was the first part of the Viking age. This explanation feeds off breadcrumbs of information, but allows for multiple phases, multiple vectors, and a series of reinforcing mechanisms. This is not, I would stress, Gaelicisation by elite emulation, osmosis or trickle-down. It has teeth. People get hurt: they are displaced, disinherited and disenfranchised as part of the process of linguistic transformation. But it happens over an extended period, and the linguistic shift is adequately underpinned by a variety of transformations in the sociolinguistic context. This, I think, best accounts for the long-term interchange between Pictish and Gaelic that the place-name evidence of the east gives witness to.

That said, the distribution maps we have used probably do not map that process (although the map of place-names in *pett* may reflect it more than any other). Rather, what we see in the distribution maps of, for instance, *achadh* and *baile* are the consequences of a much longer period of Gaelic *internal* expansion and reinforcement, and landholding changes that belong to a later period. The map of *baile*, for instance, probably shows multiple, multiphased processes of reorganisation of landholding, the creation of the fermtouns in Gaelic-speaking contexts that necessitated use of the term *baile*. For my money, in eastern and central Scotland this is a phenomenon of the period 1050–1250, by and large; elsewhere it is something that could still be occurring in the fifteenth century, or indeed, as in Arran, much later.

The transformation of the south-west

I have noted already some of the ways in which the south-west has come to be viewed in a very different light in recent years. The way is clear now to see the Gaelicisation of the south-west occurring from two distinct impetuses. First, the evidence of saints' cults suggests that Carrick was settled significantly from Kintyre. A series of dedications to saints in Kintyre is closely mirrored by the parish churches and other dedications of Carrick. This fed into my recent arguments for situating the Gall-

Ghàidheil in the Firth of Clyde region in the period around 900.[105] Second, Fiona Edmonds has recently argued convincingly, on the basis of evidence such as the culting in church dedications of localised Dublin and Leinster saints, that the Hiberno-Norse culture of Dublin and its hinterland had a strong effect on the settlement and toponymy of the Solway Firth littoral.[106] Although more investigation will no doubt solidify or refine these issues, this chimes well with linguistic evidence that the Gaelic of Galloway aligns itself with Irish in a number of key ways (notably eclipsis).[107] On the other hand we should not rule out influence from the Gaelic kingdom of Alba itself at various periods: clusters of names in Galloway employing elements like *dabach* and *earann* (both land-holding terms of different sorts, one associated with eastern Scotland, the other predominantly with the area of Menteith) suggest some such influences. These must be set against the manifest and fairly widespread use in the south-west of place-name terminology, such as land-assessment terms like *peighinn*, 'pennyland', or *ceathramh*, 'quarterland', terms associated strongly with the western seaboard, and not common in eastern Scotland (unknown indeed, for instance, in Fife).

We cannot determine when between 900 and *c.*1050 the south-west came under the sway of Gaelic-speaking rulers, but by the twelfth century it is clear that Gaelic had been in the region long enough to give it a corporate identity ('Galloway'), and to lay down a major infrastructure of Gaelic place-names.[108] It may not have been the only language in the region, however: Alex Woolf has proposed a linguistic 'balkanisation' of the region—the term may be problematic, but the idea has some force.[109] It might explain the clusters of distinct settlement name types in Ayrshire, for instance: Norse *bý* names in Cunninghame; Brittonic **trev* names in Carrick; and Gaelic *baile* names in Kyle and Carrick.[110]

---

[105] Clancy, 'Gall-Ghàidheil and Galloway', 44–5.

[106] Edmonds, 'Saints' cults and Gaelic-Scandinavian influence'.

[107] See Roibeard Ó Maolalaigh, 'Place-names as a resource', p. 30.

[108] See Clancy, 'Gall-Ghàidheil and Galloway'; MacQueen, *Place-Names in the Rhinns*; idem, *Place-Names of the Moors and Machars*; and my forthcoming Whithorn Lecture for 2010, 'Gaelic in Medieval Galloway: the Evidence of Names'.

[109] Woolf, *From Pictland to Alba*, p. 297.

[110] On the *bý* names, see Simon Taylor, 'Scandinavians in central Scotland: *bý*-place-names and their context', in Williams and Bibire, *Sagas, Saints and Settlements*, pp. 125–45; Alison Grant, 'The origin of the Ayrshire *Bý* names', in Gammeltoft, Hough and Waugh, *Cultural Contacts*, pp. 127–40; on **trev*, see recently Bethany Fox, 'The P-Celtic Place-Names of North-East England and South-East Scotland', *The Heroic Age (An on-line Journal of Early Medieval Northwestern Europe)*, 10 (2007), <http://www.mun.ca/mst/heroicage/issues/10/fox.html>; Carole

Parts of the south-west were to be strongly and permanently affected by the settlement of the area by Anglo-Norman nobles from King David I's time as Prince of Cumbria: this was particularly significant in Cunninghame, Renfrewshire and Annandale.[111] These regions seem to begin their reception of Older Scots during this period, a process that was never reversed. We should, of course, remember that in Annandale as perhaps in northern parts of Ayrshire, and indeed in Galloway proper, Scots was coming into an area which had had English settlements since the eighth century. We should allow for potential continuities from Old English to Older Scots in these areas, deepening the linguistic complexity of the region as a whole.

But this is not the full story of Gaelic in the south-west: we must leave room here, as elsewhere, for periods of internal expansion or re-expansion of Gaelic, the reinforcement of its standing amongst the local landholding elite with consequent effects on the place-nomenclature. The evidence is there, if as yet not studied sufficiently to bring it into focus, to suggest that this is precisely what happened in the south-west during the course of the thirteenth to fourteenth centuries, particularly in areas like Carrick and Kirkcudbrightshire, and Fiona Edmonds's recent work on Nithsdale suggests it was the case there too.[112] An example may be seen in one record from Kirkcudbrightshire of the settlement of a boundary dispute between Colvend and Kirkgunzeon, on 21 February 1289. The list of those present includes a fair slice of the 'Anglo-Norman' aristocracy of the area (Sir Thomas son of Gilbert de Culwenne, Michael son of Durand), but also a large number of individuals from Gaelic-speaking backgrounds (Patrick mac Coffoc, Patrick Magilboythin, Gilchrist mac Karnachan, Achyne mac Nele, Monc Macgilherine).[113] Many of these latter families came to prominence in this area in the period of the Wars of Independence, and their rise sees a concomitant rise in the landholding—and thus we might propose, land-naming—status of Gaelic families.

Hough, 'P-Celtic *tref* in Scottish place-names', *Notes and Queries*, 48/3 (Sept. 2001), 213–15; Alan G. James, 'A Cumbric diaspora?', in O. J. Padel and D. N. Parsons (eds.), *A Commodity of Good Names: Essays in Honour of Margaret Gelling* (Donington, 2008), pp. 187–203.

[111] See for instance G. W. S. Barrow, *The Kingdom of the Scots* (London, 1973; repr. Edinburgh, 2003), chaps. 12, 15.

[112] F. Edmonds, pers. comm. I explore this issue further in my forthcoming Whithorn Lecture.

[113] F. Grainger and W. G. Collingwood (eds.), *Register and Records of Holm Cultram* (Cumberland & Westmorland Antiquarian & Archaeological Society, Record Series, 7: Kendal, 1929), no. 255. One might render these names Pádraig mac Gufóg, Pádraig mac Gille Baoithín, Gille Críst mac Carnacháin, Eachainn mac Néill, Mungo (?) mac Gille Chíaráin. Some of the patronymics may be surnames.

The Hebrides and northern Scotland

Finally, we must turn to the west and the north. Earlier, I noted that recent scholarship has presented us with a conundrum: if Gaelic was not spoken in the Western Isles or in Sutherland and Caithness before the Viking age (or even if it only had a limited presence there, for instance, in the form of the church) then where did the Gaelic spoken in these areas come from? Arne Kruse has presented us with the interesting notion that Gaelic was first spoken on Lewis by Gaelic slaves, introduced there by the Viking settlers just as they were introduced to the Faroes and Iceland (and presumably speaking a wide variety of Gaelic dialects).[114] I do not think these slaves will, however, provide the explanation for the Gaelicisation of the area. We have good evidence for the rising status of Gaelic amongst the Scandinavian elite of the Irish Sea zone: many of these men had Gaelic by-names, Gaelic foster-brothers, Gaelic forenames and by the late tenth century were having poetry composed for them in Gaelic. This is surely of great significance, but once again, though, this falls short of a full explanation. The engine-rooms for this elite Gaelicisation seem to be Dublin and Man, the key sites of dominance within the Scandinavian Irish Sea zone. This then may suggest Gaelic continuity in certain regions, like the Isle of Man and Islay, where a hiatus has been proposed. Argyll may be one key to the problem: Jennings' arguments anent Kintyre could be applied to much of Argyll, allowing us to see here prominent Scandinavian settlements amongst a majority Gaelic population. From Argyll was drawn one segment of the twelfth-century elite of the Irish Sea zone, that segment, with Somerled mac Gille Brighde at its head, which would progress to dominance of the Hebrides from the mid-twelfth century on. It may be that under this family and its allies, as it ramified and extended its control of the Isles, Gaelic speech from the mainland was brought to, or back to, the Hebrides.

Some indicators that actual westward migration of Gaelic-speaking settlers might be involved in the process comes from Caithness. Here a series of little signs seems to point to Gaelic, which here clearly was subsequent to Norse in Caithness and never completely replaced it throughout the territory, having come from the north-east mainland, from Moray. Doreen Waugh has suggested this tentatively, and it has considerable plausibility.[115] The evidence, which remains to be explored fully, includes

---

[114] Kruse, 'Explorers, raiders and traders'.

[115] Waugh, 'Settlement names in Caithness'; *eadem*, 'Caithness: another dip in the Sweerag well', in Woolf, *Scandinavian Scotland—Twenty Years After*, pp. 31–48, esp. p. 39. See also W. F. H. Nicolaisen,

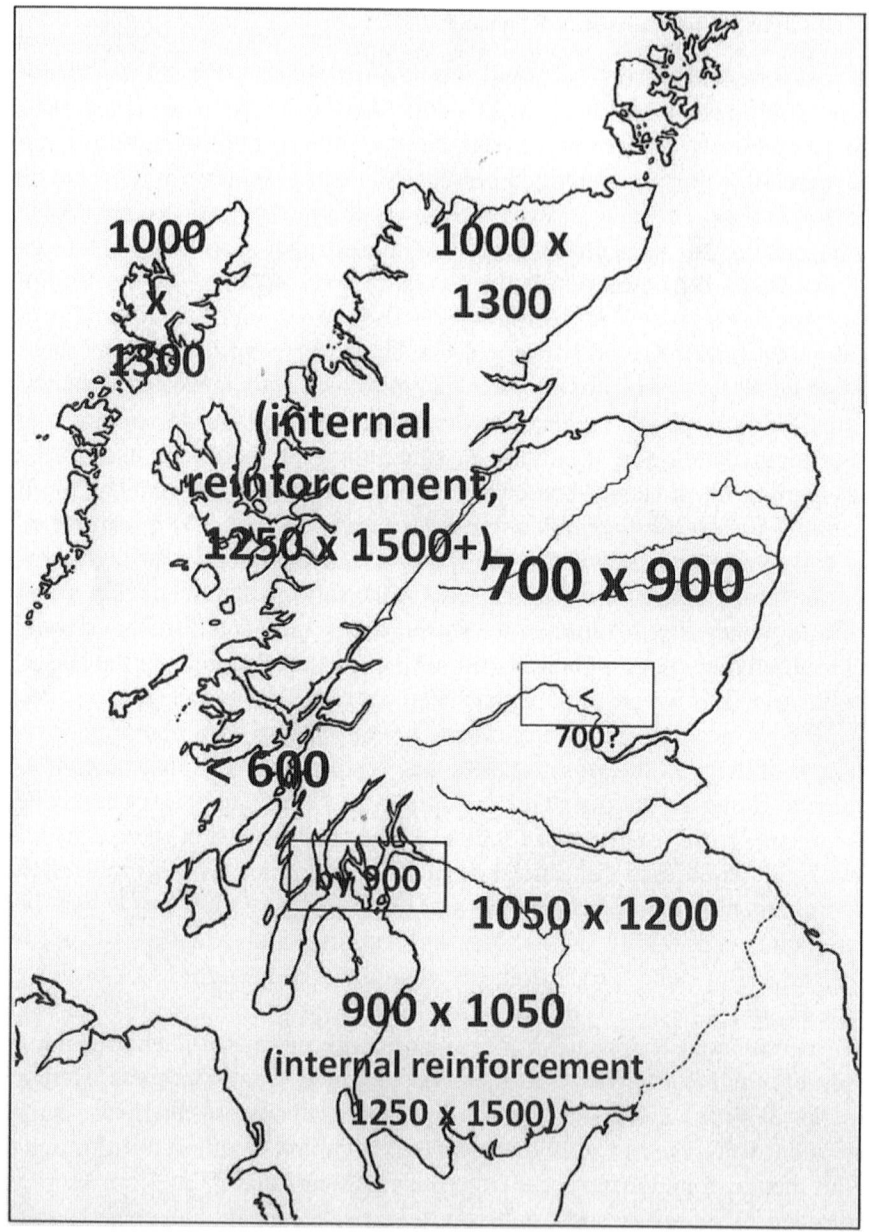

Figure 6. Advent and expansion of Gaelic. Dates and date-ranges are estimates of when Gaelic became a major language in each region.

distinctive saints' cults shared between the regions (Drostan, Fergus), the presence in Caithness place- and kindred-names of rare personal names associated closely with major kindreds in Moray (Cano in Canisbay, Morgan in the eponym of the MacKays, the Clann Mhorgainn); and the historically attested fact that this was swordland given to the de Moravia family in the late twelfth century.[116]

As was the case with the south-west, however, we should make room for the incremental reinforcement of the status of Gaelic amongst the landholding classes in these areas during the course of the thirteenth to fifteenth centuries, and, indeed, beyond. A key point I am trying to make here is that linguistic 'expansion' happens internally within a region, as well as laterally, as the landscape becomes ever more filled-in with features named in that language, as the internal history of a region becomes tied ever more to people from a particular linguistic set, and the duration of settlement turns swordland into *dùthchas* (see Fig. 6).

Conclusion

Our maps have tended to teach us that Gaelic's decline in Scotland began around 1093, never to be reversed. What I have been arguing in this lecture is that it was not so. The great, long century between 1093 and 1215 so closely identified with Gaelic's demise in fact sees Gaelic playing a major part in the naming of lands whose use and ownership was changing during the 'feudal' land redistribution of the period, in places such as Fife and Galloway. The twelfth century and later saw significant expansion of Gaelic into a number of areas later considered to be Gaelic heartlands, such as the Western Isles, Sutherland and parts of Caithness. This was a process which, if we consider the notion of internal Gaelicisation within regions, may well have been continuing into the fifteenth century and, perhaps in some areas like Sutherland, beyond. That makes the high Middle Ages, usually associated with Gaelic's decline, instead key centuries for Gaelic's expansion. This is a fundamentally different way to envisage the period.

'Scandinavians and Celts in Caithness: the place-name evidence', in J. Baldwin (ed.), *Caithness: a Cultural Crossroads* (Edinburgh, 1982), pp. 75–85.

[116] Barbara Crawford, 'The Earldom of Caithness and the Kingdom of Scotland, 1150–1266', in Keith Stringer (ed.), *Essays on the Nobility of Medieval Scotland* (Edinburgh, 1985), pp. 25–43.

Sir John Rhŷs was as active in tracing the contemporary decline of the Celtic languages as he was involved in understanding their earliest presence and interaction in Britain and Ireland. What I hope I have managed to demonstrate in this lecture is that the way is open for us to have a different and more complex understanding of Gaelic and Gaelic-speakers in medieval Scotland, of mechanisms of expansion as well as contraction. We have by no means achieved a full understanding, but the shifting paradigms of the last quarter century have all had their part to play in allowing us to see more clearly what the most crucial questions are. Without doubt the greatest contribution to the expansion of our understanding will be made by the careful survey and analysis of the place-names of Scotland: there is rich evidence here, waiting to be worked through. Work like this demands the fruitful exchange of ideas between historians, linguists, onomasticians, archaeologists. If this lecture has demonstrated nothing else, I hope it has given a sense of the fertility of such interaction in early medieval Scottish studies. There is much to do.

Note. I am most grateful to the British Academy for their invitation to give this lecture, as also to the Society of Antiquaries of Scotland who hosted two further events, in the Royal Society of Edinburgh, and at the University of Aberdeen, at which it was delivered. Audiences at all these events, as also at Comann Gàidhlig Ghlaschu in 2009, gave some stimulating and helpful feedback. The Arts and Humanities Research Council funded the four-year project 'The Expansion and Contraction of Gaelic in Medieval Scotland: The Onomastic Evidence' which prompted the topic of the lecture. I owe a particular debt of gratitude to my colleagues on that project, Dr Simon Taylor, Gilbert Márkus, and Peter McNiven; and to colleagues who commented on aspects of this work in draft, or provided other forms of encouragement: Professor Roibeard Ó Maolalaigh, Professor Dauvit Broun, Bronagh Ní Chonaill and especially Simon Taylor for reading the final draft. Inevitably the lecture bears the stamp of many inspiring conversations with Dr Alex Woolf. The lecture is dedicated to the memory of my former teacher, colleague and friend, Dr John Bannerman.

Surrealism and its Legacies in Latin America

DAWN ADÈS
Fellow of the Academy

SURREALISM IN LATIN AMERICA has a history peppered with lacunae, misunderstandings and bad faith, not least in the ways this history has been told; it has also had strong adherents and defenders and some of the movement's greatest poets and artists, such as Roberto Matta from Chile, who made his career exclusively outside the continent, and César Moro, who has been described as 'the only person who fully deserves the epithet surrealist in Latin America'.[1]

Surrealism has played an important but contentious role in the development of modern Latin American art. The history of the reception of surrealist ideas and practices in Latin America has often been distorted by cultural nationalism and also needs to be disentangled from Magic Realism. Surrealism was nonetheless a potent influence or chosen affiliation for many artists and its legacies can still be detected in the work of the contemporary artists from Latin America who now dominate the international scene.

Read at the Academy 27 May 2009.

[1] Camilo Fernandez Cozman, 'La concepción del surrealismo en los ensayos de Westphalen', in *César Moro y el surrealismo en América Latina*, ed. Yolanda Westphalen (Lima, 2005), p. 44. See also Jason Wilson, 'The sole surrealist poet: César Moro (1903–1956)', in S. M. Hart and D. Wood (eds), *Essays on Alfredo Bryce Echenique, Peruvian Literature and Culture* (London: 2010), pp. 77–90. César Moro, the pseudonym for Alfredo Quispez Asin, was born in Peru, lived in Paris for eight years from 1925 to 1933, encountered the surrealists in 1928, chose to write in French and published his encantatory celebration of love, 'Renommée d'amour', in S*ASDLR* in 1933. See also Dawn Adès, 'César Moro and surrealism in Latin America' (Getty Research Papers, forthcoming).

Proceedings of the British Academy, **167**, 393–422. © The British Academy 2010.

Some of the key issues and questions that arise in trying to give an account of Surrealism in Latin America would be pertinent to its reception anywhere outside its home base, Paris, but others have a special relevance to Latin America. Often adherents to surrealism were or felt themselves to be outsiders in their own communities, marginalised for social, political or sexual reasons. Surrealism's strong stance against *père, patron, patrie* and absolute refusal of religion attracted like-minded people in many countries, but questions of faith and of nationalism loom especially large in Latin America. How could the cultural nationalism rife in many of the relatively newly independent countries in Latin America co-exist with the anti-nationalism and internationalism of the surrealists? Another important question is the relationship between surrealism and the local avant-gardes. How were the latter manifested and how far were they already linked to the new developments in Europe? The strength of local art and cultural groups varied a great deal, as did the response to surrealism. There was extensive two-way traffic and this took very interesting forms in the encounters between surrealism and Latin America, especially following the dispersal of many of the surrealists to the Americas following the Fall of France to the Germans in 1940.

During the Second World War the surrealist headquarters moved to New York, with Breton, Tanguy, Matta, Ernst and Duchamp; another group settled in Mexico: Péret, Leonora Carrington, Remedios Varo, Wolfgang Paalen, Alice Rahon, and César Moro, who had already taken refuge there from Peru. While Europe was being torn apart by the rise of Fascism and then the war, surrealist networks strengthened in the New World. In recognition of the importance to the surrealist movement of artists and poets from Latin America, Breton, contrasting the 'warm south' with the cold ruins of Europe, wrote, with regard to the Brazilian sculptor Maria Martins: 'L'esprit, durant ces dernières années, n'a cessé de souffler des terres chaudes.'[2] On Marcel Duchamp's cover of the New York surrealist review, *VVV*, in 1943, the rider on the globe points south.

'Latin America', a designation based on geography and race, was long thought to date from the French intervention in Mexico in the 1860s, invented by pan-Latinist intellectuals around the parvenu emperor Napoleon III to disguise his hunger for *la gloire* (military glory) with appeals to a shared Latin heritage between France and Mexico. However, recent research has shown that the term was widely in use by Spanish-speaking intellectuals in the Americas in the previous decade, the 1850s; it

---

[2] André Breton, 'Maria' ex. cat., *Maria* (Julien Levy Gallery, New York, 1945).

appears in an 1856 poem by Tomas Calcedo of New Granada (now Colombia) 'Las dos Américas' and elsewhere.[3] The Latin American source of the term originated in the context of racial, political and commercial tensions with the United States, with its expansionist aims and the incursions of the filibusterer William Walker who sought to reintroduce slavery in Central America.

The rivalry between the two Americas has continued, not just in the political but also the cultural arena; in seeking to establish an identity over and above the national and to fight cultural colonialism, critics and artists in Latin America have pursued various essentialist notions—from the Cuban writer Alejo Carpentier's '*lo real maravilloso*', 'marvellous reality', to Cesar Paternosto's *Abstraction: the AmerIndian Paradigm*,[4] fuelled by a sense of being marginalised in relation to the USA. In the context of Latin America, surrealism has been accused of neocolonialism, of being too fantastic or not fantastic enough, too irrational or not irrational enough. For the one-time surrealist, Carpentier, its 'mysteries' were manufactured, and for the curators of the controversial exhibition of 1987, *Art of the Fantastic*, the 'fantastic' in Latin America 'is more spontaneous and direct than programmatically surrealist'.[5] The surrealists have been described as the latest in a long line of European visitors who, 'since Columbus, have invented an America at the service of their own desires and interests'.[6]

Surrealism has been the victim of its own success, the word passing into common currency with its meanings and histories debased and trivialised. So the first part of my lecture is a job of historical retrieval, to counter some of these assumptions and explore the reception of surrealism in Latin America, from the foundation of the movement in Paris in 1924 to *c*.1944. The second part of the lecture will focus on two artists working in Mexico with surrealist connections of different kinds: Frida Kahlo and Gunther Gerzso.

---

[3] See Aims McGuiness, 'Searching for "Latin America"; race and sovereignty in the Americas in the 1850s', in N. Appelbaum, A. S. Macpherson and K. Rosenblatt (eds.), *Race and Nation in Modern Latin America* (Chapel Hill, NC, 2003). 'Latin America', which includes Central America, parts of the Caribbean and Mexico, which is part of the North American continent, should never be confused with 'South America'.

[4] César Paternosto, *Abstraction: the AmerIndian Paradigm* (Palais des Beaux-Arts, Brussels and IVAM, Valencia, 2001).

[5] Holliday T. Day and Hollister Sturges, *Art of the Fantastic: Latin America 1920–1987* (Indianapolis Museum of Art, 1987).

[6] Ida Rodriguez Prampolini, 'El surrealismo y la Fantasia Mexicana', *Los Surrealistas en México* (Mexico City, 1986), p. 17.

Rather than offering a definition of surrealism and then applying it to the diverse manifestations of the movement and to creative individuals in Latin America, I shall follow another methodology, which aims to chart the self-defined surrealist groups and individuals active in Latin America, taking firstly reviews and then exhibitions as key markers of surrealist activity, and through them assess the attitudes to and responses to surrealism within Latin America. I have chosen this approach rather than one based on country ('Surrealism in Argentina', or 'in Chile', etc.), as a matter of principle, because surrealism itself and its major protagonists, like César Moro, shared the sentiment expressed so succinctly in the 1920s by Salarrué: 'Yo no tengo patria' ('I have no fatherland').[7] In some respects this goes against the grain from a practical point of view, as many of the surrealist initiatives were perforce circumscribed by their location at the time, and subsequent critical histories all too often define themselves nationally. The only 'country' Breton acknowledged as such was Mexico, and the relationship between surrealism and Mexico will inevitably dominate my lecture, though it will be threaded through it thematically and treated critically.[8]

There are several areas where surrealism's encounters with Latin America were articulated in particularly interesting ways: the tensions with cultural nationalism, the clash with the Roman Catholic church, the question of the 'fantastic' vs. the 'marvellous', the problem of modernity vs. indigenous cultures and the enduring surrealist fascination with Pre-Columbian art, architecture and literature. These topics emerge during the investigation of reviews, and will then be explored in relation to the works of artists related to surrealism.

Surrealist journals in Latin America

Reviews have been the life-blood of the movement, since its inception in 1924 and the founding of its first journal, *La Révolution surréaliste* (1924–9). This and its successor *Le surréalisme au service de la révolution* (1930–3) were its prime means of communication, expressed the collective nature

---

[7] Salarrué 'Yo no tengo patria', *Repertorio Americano* (Costa Rica, 1929).
[8] André Breton, 'Souvenir du Mexique', *Minotaure* nos. 11/12 (Paris, 1939). A strong case could be put for 'Argentina' as also of special interest. Julio Cortàzar was a major heir of surrealism, while Borges thoroughly disliked its irrationality and interest in the unconscious; but both drew on Duchamp, who happened to go there in 1918, see Graciela Speranza, *Fuera de Campo: Literature y arte argentinos despues de Duchamp* (Barcelona, 2006).

of the movement, and were the principal forum for its multidimensional ideas and activities. Through the 1920s and 1930s there was vigorous debate about poetry, art and politics, a fractious relationship with the communist party, which Breton and others joined in 1926, a flow of writings of extraordinary originality and experiments in the visual field that carried across the globe. As Walter Benjamin, writing from Weimar Germany, acknowledged in his 1929 essay, 'Surrealism: latest snapshot of the European intelligentsia', surrealism was the most powerful cultural force in Europe: 'The sphere of poetry was here explored from within by a closely knit circle of people pushing the "poetic life" to the utmost limits of possibility.'[9] It was a small group, held together by daily meetings in the café, loving Paris but otherwise resistant to nationalist sentiments. As the movement expanded from its Paris centre, it was often through international and local avant-garde reviews that surrealist ideas and their expression in writing, painting, photography and film had spread. The surrealists themselves could not, however, necessarily control their presentation in these foreign contexts and while eager for surrealism to become international there was always a question of how fully the movement had been understood. This was to remain a cause of tension, exacerbated by the nature of surrealism, which was neither monolithic nor static, nor reducible to a style. On the one hand, surrealism was centred on Breton and his circle in Paris; on the other hand, it offered a message of liberation, the freedom of desire, a nonconformist model of the relationship between politics and art of increasing value as the totalitarian regimes closed in, all of which drew adherents from round the world. The reviews that were associated with, identified with, or just included surrealism in Latin America highlight some of the key issues in the movement's internationalism as well as the question of individual or group involvement.

There was an explosion of reviews in Latin American countries through the 1920s and 1930s. Some have a specific affiliation with surrealism, some respond to its radical ideas in so far as they relate to their own cultural and political positions and others drop in on surrealism—artists in particular—as part of an eclectic survey of contemporary art and poetry. It is beyond the scope of this lecture to cover them all; I have selected some of the most important, as representative of these different aspects and bearing in mind the broader history of surrealism's impact in the continent.

[9] Walter Benjamin, 'Surrealism: The last [*sic*] snapshot of the European intelligentsia' (1929), *Reflections* (New York, 1986), p. 178.

The first review explicitly announcing its adherence to surrealism was the aptly named *Qué* (What). The circumstances in which the first surrealist group, responsible for this review, was formed in Argentina are curious; in October 1924 the Buenos Aires newspaper *Critica* dedicated an entire issue to the death of Anatole France. Slipped into the issue was the announcement of a pamphlet attacking the great old man of French culture: *Un cadavre*. Aldo Pellegrini, a student in Buenos Aires, was fascinated by the outspoken attack on this representative of the pure French genius, and immediately sent for all the publications of this disrespectful group. So he acquired Breton's *Manifesto of Surrealism* of 1924, and the first issue of *La Révolution surréaliste*, started a small 'surrealist fraternity' with like-minded fellow students seeking a new language for poetry, experimented with automatic writing and eventually published two numbers of the review *Qué*, in 1928 and 1930.[10] As well as poems and texts declaring firstly limitless freedom, followed by the use of psychoanalysis for self-knowledge, the review had articles on Charlie Chaplin and Harry Langdon—a taste shared by other avant-garde reviews such as the catalan *L'Amic de les arts*, which may well have been an important conduit between Spain and South America. *Qué* was austere in appearance, with no illustrations and a hard, clean typeface with the name on its cover; the next issue, it announced, would deal with 'El problema de la muerte', the problem of death. This was in tune with if not directly influenced by recent issues of *La Révolution surréaliste*, such as no. 7, June 1926, which had a succession of articles on death: Benjamin Péret's 'La dernière nuit du condamné à mort', and René Crevel's 'Le pont de la mort'.

But after the second issue of *Qué* there was no further evidence of group activity and Pellegrini fell silent until 1947. There seems to have been no connection between the Qué group and the painter Antonio Berni, who fraternised with the surrealists while in Paris in the 1920s, and in 1932 exhibited works from his surrealist period at the Amigos del Arte in Buenos Aires, before inventing his own collage-form of social realism. Pellegrini contacted César Moro and the Peruvian poet Emilio Westphalen after the war to try to establish a broad surrealist front in Latin America but received little encouragement. He translated one of the surrealists' chosen books, *Les chants de Maldoror* by Lautréamont (originally from Uruguay), and then, in 1952, he joined forces with the poet Enrique Molina to publish in Buenos Aires what was undoubtedly one of the high

---

[10] See Ruben Daniel Méndez Catiglioni, 'Aldo Pellegrini y el surrealismo en Argentina', *César Moro y el surrealismo en América Latina*, pp. 47–59.

points of surrealism in Latin America: *A partir de cero*. The front cover of the final issue in 1956 has a disturbingly effective photo-collage by Juan E. Fassio, playing on a Baudelaire quotation, 'Le bonheur vomitif'. Nonetheless, *A partir de cero* was, as Molina says, important but at the same time quite 'intimate', 'porque si bien en America hubo influencias surrealistas, no hubo verdaderos grupos de acción. Excepto en Chile: Mandragora si era mas coherente y trataba de hacer intervenciones, como la famosa anecdota de Braulio Arenas, que rompió el discurso de Neruda en un teatro ...'[11] It was not linked to wider public and political action. The very title, 'starting from zero', expresses an often voiced concern within Latin America about the avant-gardes—that there was little continuity, little sense of an internal tradition of modernism, even of the 'art and anti-art' tensions, but rather repeated 'ruptures' and a tendency to respond to external initiatives in art and culture. Molina recognised that surrealism was 'not a literary school but a total conception of man and the universe'. Like César Moro, he believed that 'ningún poeta puede dejar de querer al surrealismo. De algun modo es la encarnación de un mito de la poesía, que perdura y le da un sentido muy especial a la tarea del poeta.'[12] But also like César Moro, by the 1950s he had ceased to believe that the initial commitment of surrealism to automatism, which had been reasserted during the surrealist exile in America, could be the sole key to poetry.

Automatism had been the basic principle in the definition of surrealism in Breton's *Manifesto* of 1924: 'Pure psychic automatism, by which we intend to express, whether verbally, in writing, or in any other way, the true functioning of thought. The dictation of thought in the absence of any control exerted by reason, and outside all aesthetic or moral considerations.'[13] Surrealism had grown and flowered beyond this definition, whose strict application had been interpreted freely by artists like Max Ernst and André Masson, but had been relatively disappointing so far as texts were concerned. The greatest writings by the surrealists were not strictly automatic—Breton's *Nadja* (1928) and Louis Aragon's *Paris*

[11] '... because if it is true that there were surrealist influences in America, there were not really active groups. Except in Chile: Mandragora was more coherent and tried to make interventions, like the famous anecdote when Braulio Arenas interrupted Neruda's lecture in a theatre ...', Enrique Molina, *A Partir de Cero* (Entrevista, 1997), *Surrealismo: Poesia & liberdade* <www. triplov.com>.

[12] 'no poet can fail to love surrealism. It is, in any case, the incarnation of a myth of poetry, which endures and gives the poet a very special sense of his task.' Ibid.

[13] André Breton, *Manifeste du surréalisme* (Paris, 1924), p. 42 (author's translation).

Peasant (1926) were the works that had convinced Benjamin that surrealism was the source of the most powerful creative current of the time. Writing in 1929, he described them as a completely new genre of expression. The reassertion of automatism by Breton in the 1940s, with the admission that it might run 'underground', had partly been a defence against the wildfire success of Salvador Dalí's 'dream paintings' which had given the public a simplistic view of surrealism. Despite the fact that Molina had a sophisticated understanding of surrealism and its wider significance, it is the specific failure of automatism that he focuses on: 'Yo sigo creyendo en el surrealismo, pero no creo en la cosa formal ... Se imita la escritura automàtica, la forma y las imàgenes surreales, pero yo creo que el poema es un campo cerrado, neto, de tensiones y de lucidez. No es una cosa interminable, como sería la pretension del automatismo ... Como hipótesis es interesante, pero el inconsciente no es todo el hombre.'[14] Molina is quite right in saying that automatism had not produced the literary crop it had promised, but in a sense to focus his critique on this point is a relatively mild form of rejection. It is in line with that of Moro, who became disillusioned with surrealism in the early 1940s, and earlier of the Mexican poet Villarutia,[15] as well as poets of the first surrealist hour such as Robert Desnos, who came to believe that poetry could not come of unrestrained verbiage but needed shape, tension and clarity. Moro was associated in Mexico with the artist Wolfgang Paalen and contributed to his review, *Dyn,* which announced itself as moving on beyond surrealism. Moro wrote to Westphalen in 1944: 'je garde une admiration définitive pour le surréalisme en ce qu'il a fait du positif dans le domaine poétique, mais il y a tout un coté dogmatique qui réellement m'emmerde ... Je ne crois pas non plus que "Dyn" puisse remplacer le surréalisme ... le temps est trop au cataclysme pour qu'on puisse voir clair.'[16]

The problem Molina faces here, speaking many years later, after surrealism had been pronounced dead many times, reflects a paradox at the heart of surrealism: on the one hand the movement was, constituted itself as, a collective; on the other, it promulgated a practice—automatism—

---

[14] 'I continue to believe in surrealism, but not in its formal side ... Automatic writing, surrealist forms and images are imitated, but I believe that poetry is a closed arena ... It is not an interminable thing, as automatism would like to believe ... It is interesting as an hypothesis, but the unconscious is not the total of the human being.' Molina, *A Partir de Cero.*

[15] See Kent Dickson, 'César Moro and Xavier Villaruria: the politics of Eros', Ph.D. thesis, University of California at Los Angeles, 2005.

[16] Moro, letter to Westphalen, 26 Nov. 1944, Westphalen Archive, W Box 1, f 8, Getty Research Institute.

which was in-turned on the individual psyche. What was automatism for? Was it the seedbed for wonderful poetic images? Or was it a means of exploring the hidden depths of the unconscious, the mystery of the individual 'I'. Both are suggested in the first *Manifesto*. Among the diverse and distinctive responses of surrealist groups in North and South America to the idea of automatism in the post-war years was an interest in the potential of music, especially improvisation in jazz.[17]

By the late 1920s, at the same time that *Qué* had its short-lived and largely unnoticed moment in Argentina, surrealism had already come to the notice of established journals which provided an important conduit within the continent for new ideas without having a specific affiliation. Some, like the Mexican *Los Contemporaneos*, adopted a broad cultural modernism (itself quite confrontational in a Mexican context); poems by the 'super-realista' group were published in 1929 (vol. 4) together with Rayographs from Man Ray's *Champs délicieux*, which had been published in Paris in 1922, and a still from his film *Etoile de mer*. The following year recent paintings by Salvador Dalí and Joan Miró were reproduced, demonstrating the close contacts with contemporary art in Spain and Catalunya as well as Paris, but there was no special recognition of the movement, as the stance of the journal was to present a broad anthology of 'modern movements'.

The Peruvian review *Amauta*, founded in 1926 by José Carlos Mariátegui, had a very different relationship with surrealism, with which it was in contact as part of a broad network of leftist intellectuals and artists. Mariátegui also founded the Peruvian Socialist Party, for which he took as model not the USSR but the Andean commune, or *ayllu*, based on pre-Conquest social and economic structures. Poems and articles by surrealists were published: a poem by César Moro, in Paris and about to join the movement (no. 14, April 1928), and Xavier Abril's 'Poema surrealista' (no. 18, 1928). The texts and interviews translated for *Amauta*, including Aragon's 'El proletariado del espiritu' and a questionnaire 'Existe una literatura proletaria?' in which Breton was a respondent, reflect the recent adherence of leading surrealists to the communist party. *Amauta* welcomed the connection between *La Révolution surréaliste* and the communist

---

[17] Westphalen in Lima as well as the Chicago group were keen on the link between surrealism and jazz. The Chilean poet Jorge Cáceres founded the Club de Jazz de Chile. See Franklin Rosemont, 'Black Music and the surrealist revolution', *Arsenal*, 3 (Chicago, Spring 1976), p. 17. This is a topic that needs further investigation; there might for instance be an interesting connection with the close friendships between the Latin American and the Belgian surrealists. The latter, unlike the Paris group, liked music.

review *Clarté*, hoping for a merger in a new review to be called *La Guerre civile*, as announced in *La Révolution surréaliste* (no. 6, March 1926). Like the surrealists, Mariátegui encouraged debate about the ways Marxism should be understood and interpreted in the cultural and literary spheres. Surrealism was a controversial subject in *Amauta*, with doubts expressed about Breton's homage to Jacques Vaché (who was described as a criminal and drug-addict), but Mariátegui saw surrealism not just as a symptom of the decadence of capitalist civilisation, evident in the atomisation and dissolution of its art, but as active rejection of bourgeois culture, constituting a necessary break with it. Mariátegui wrote in *Variedades* in 1930 of Breton's *Nadja* that it had 'superado al realismo mediante el descubrimiento del mundo de la locura y lo irracional, con lo que "*Nadja* preludia, tal vez, bajo este aspecto de procedimiento, una revolución de la novella"'.[18] *Nadja* was, apparently, one of the very few avant-garde books in Mariátegui's private library, and Breton was one of the few contemporary figures to be honoured with a full-page portrait in *Amauta*. The publication of the *Second Manifesto of Surrealism* in *La Révolution surréaliste* in 1929 seemed to Mariátegui to affirm the movement's commitment to Marxism, though difficulties with the PCF were already threatening the partnership as the surrealists refused to sacrifice their own poetic and visual experiments in the interests of political action. Mariátegui's articles on surrealism always expressed 'sympathy and hope', but his early death in 1930 brought to an end the relationship with the leading Latin American intellectual of his time.

It is possible that he would have retained greater sympathy for the movement during its intransigeant refusal in the 1930s to give in to the Parti communiste français's (PCF) demands that it decide once and for all whether it put itself or the party first, and back the programme of socialist realism, as opposed to its own experiments with language and object, than César Vallejo. Vallejo, who visited the Soviet Union in 1928 and 1929, responded to the *Second Manifesto* and to the notorious attack on Breton, *Un cadavre*, by announcing the death of the movement. Their adherence to Marxism had been promising, he wrote in 'Autopsy on Surrealism', but in the end they remained wedded to anarchism, 'the most abstract, mystical, cerebral form of politics', and in 'perpetual breach with

---

[18] ('… added the discovery of the worlds of madness and the irrational to realism, so that "*Nadja* is a prelude to a revolution in the novel"') José Carlos Mariátegui quoted in Milagros Carazas, 'El discreto (des)encanto del surrealismo francés. Reacciones y posturas críticas del intelectual peruano (1924–1930)', in Westphalen, *César Moro y el surrealismo en América Latina*, p. 84.

the great Marxist directives'.[19] 'Adherence to communism', he continued, 'had no reflection whatever in the sense or essential forms of their works.' (Indeed, this classic example of Marxist aesthetics, reflection theory, reveals the fundamental gap with surrealism.) Vallejo pinpoints Breton's claim in the *Second Manifesto* that surrealism's success lay in 'the crisis of consciousness' it had stirred up. This, Vallejo argues, following the party line, does not conform to Marxist doctrine. Moral and intellectual crises are chimaerae, promising revolution 'from above', whereas true revolution can only be made from below: 'there is only one revolution, the proletarian, and the workers will make this revolution with action. Not the intellectuals with their "crisis of consciousness".'

The three final reviews I shall introduce all have a clear, if not exclusive, affiliation with surrealism. The first is the only review in which Moro had an editorial role: *El Uso de la Palabra*, a single issue published in Lima, late in 1939. It was long-planned by its editors, the Peruvian poet Emilio Westphalen and Moro, the latter at long-distance, from Mexico, where he was resident from 1938 to 1948. It finally reached Moro in Mexico City just too late to coincide with the opening of the International Exhibition of Surrealism in Mexico City. Moro was passionately committed to surrealism and made strenuous efforts, following his return from Paris in 1933, to animate it in Latin America, but *El Uso de la Palabra* was a disappointment. For one thing, by mischance the title was identical with that of a review that appeared at almost the same time, in Paris—*L'usage de la parole*. Moro wrote to Westphalen that they would have to change the title for any future issues: although they thought of it first—the title was advertised in the Paris journal *Minotaure* in 1936—they would be accused of plagiarism again.[20] Moreover, Moro did not wish to be associated with contributors to *L'usage de la parole*, surrealist dissidents who were 'en froid avec Breton'. More seriously, the review itself did not match Moro's expectations. Being in Mexico, he had been unable to oversee the layout, which he found awkward and inelegant, the typography boring and the photographs that he had chosen and sent with great care and some satisfaction at their subversive character badly reproduced. He had commissioned his friend Eva Sulzer to photograph a nude sculpture: 'a very lovely and obscene statue in the main gardens of the Avenida Juarez'.[21]

[19] César Vallejo, 'Autopsy on surrealism', in Jack Hirschman (ed.), *Art on the Line* (New Haven, CT, 2002). Originally published as 'Autopsia del surrealismo', *Variedades*, 1151 (26 March 1930).
[20] César Moro letter to Westphalen, 1 March 1940, Westphalen archive, W Box 1 GRI.
[21] Moro letter to Westphalen, 16 Oct. 1939, W Box 1 f 4, Getty Research Institute.

This and two photographs of Indian women by Lola and Manuel Alvarez Bravo were clearly intended to signify in their own right, rather than mere illustrations; despite Moro's disappointment they retain something of the punch of the illustrations in *La Révolution surréaliste*.

The main thrust of *El Uso de la Palabra* was an attack on contemporary Peruvian art, poetry and culture. The two photographs of Indian women, by Lola Alvarez Bravo and her then husband Manuel Alvarez Bravo, are ripostes against the indigenist painting that Moro describes in his text 'About painting in Peru' as odious and spreading like a virulent plague. He attacks the fashion for images of the 'Indian' (the term then common) 'which the ruling class accepts in its houses of appallingly bad taste, as long as they come framed and without the peculiar smell of wool which, according to this class, characterises the Indians. They really prefer the smell of the little crucifixes ... These paintings serve Aryan fat cats as proof of the supposed inferiority of the races of colour.' Anyone who 'dares to look at the world with eyes that are not those of a brave indigenist painter or of a folkloric writer is immediately treated as foreign-loving, frenchified and bitter enemy of the Indian, of this fabulous cardboard myth that gives them a living'.[22] Such picturesque images are examples of the real cruelty with which the great misery of the indigenous peoples, their complete ostracism and exploitation, is traduced on canvas or on the pottery knickknacks sold to tourists. Like Mariátegui in *Amauta*, though with less faith in social and political reform, Moro contrasts the picturesque with the actuality of the Indian 'who works tirelessly in implacable climates with a pathetic handful of maize for food, [or] drowns in the refuge of cocaine and alcohol'. The fashion for indigenism is, moreover, paired with ignorance of history; the indigenist painters and their collectors are conscious only of the Inca period and know nothing of the ancient and highly refined coastal civilisations, preferring if anything 'coastal primitivism' such as processions of 'Our Lord of the Miracles'.

The promised second issue of *El Uso de la Palabra* never materialised, but after the war Westphalen edited a new journal, *Las Moradas*, to which Moro frequently sent contributions from Mexico, including a translation of Leonora Carrington's *Abajo* (En Bas, Down Below), an account of her escape from France in 1940 and incarceration in a lunatic asylum (no. 5, July 1948).

---

[22] César Moro, 'A propósito de la pintura en el Peru', *El Uso de la Palabra* (Lima, Dec. 1939), 3, 7.

There was a surprising lack of coordination and collaboration between Moro and the group that launched the review *Mandragora* in Santiago de Chile in December 1938. The review, edited by the poets Braulio Arenas, Teofilo Cid and Enrique Gomez-Correa, initially affiliated itself with surrealism because this was still where 'the most vital developments in poetry, philosophy and art' were originating; its rubric was 'Poetry, Philosophy, Painting, Science, Documents'. The first issue published reviews of Eluard's latest book of poems, *Cours naturel*, and of Breton's *L'amour fou* which 'does no more than ratify us in our old, known positions. It unites us to the cosmic rhythm, revealing the precious land where the words poetry, revolution and love acquire a more captivating and true meaning.' Gradually a split developed among the editors. By 1943 Gomez-Correa, in his article for the seventh and final issue of *Mandragora*, 'Testimony of a black poet', is more ambivalent towards surrealism: it was, he wrote, engaged in a process of recapitulation and, although it remained the best strategy, could no longer be the sole and sufficient goal for our thinking. Like Wolfgang Paalen in *Dyn*, the editors of *Mandragora* felt the need to go beyond surrealism while taking it as the necessary starting point. Braulio Arenas, however, in a letter to the New York surrealists published in *VVV* in 1943, affirmed his allegiance to international surrealism, complained bitterly of the hostility and incomprehension they met in Chile, announced the end of *Mandragora* and the forthcoming appearance of a new review.[23] Particular venom was reserved for the Chilean writer Vicente Huidobro, 'el sembrador de escarcha'—sower of frost, who was interested only in solving purely aesthetic problems in a simplistic manner, who attacked surrealist automatism without understanding it and confused in the grossest fashion poetic activity, pure poetry and poetic concretion or crystallisation (the poem itself).

Mandragora contained some interesting visual material, notably the collages and photomontages from Jorge Cáceres' book of poems *Monument to the Birds*. Cáceres sent copies to Benjamin Péret in Mexico, who responded with friendly critique, and a warning:

> Everyone at some time has been more or less influenced by the works of his predecessors ... In Monument to the Birds, I think the influence of Max Ernst is so invasive that it hides entirely Jorge Caceres. This is serious. At any price, you must forget Max Ernst and the other surrealists in order to find yourself; otherwise you risk paraphrasing someone or other without the personality of Jorge Caceres managing to detach itself. I think, too, that collage has become

---

[23] Braulio Arenas, 'Letter from Chile', *VVV*, nos. 2/3 (March 1943), 124.

very difficult to use as a means of expression unless its elements can be completely renewed. Those used by Max Ernst have become, obviously, unusable by anyone else. The best thing would be, in my opinion, to look for new automatic procedures. Surely there are some that no-one has thought of yet ...[24]

The final review in this selective survey, *Tropiques,* is one of the most remarkable to be associated with surrealism, and one of the most important in the history of surrealism's international contacts. *Tropiques* first appeared in April 1941 in Vichy-controlled Martinique. In the same month Breton, Lam, Lévi-Strauss and Masson arrived as refugees on the Caribbean island. Breton, temporarily released from what was effectively a prisoner-of-war camp to visit Fort-de-France, picked up the first issue of a new review that to his astonishment referenced surrealism. Its voice 'said exactly what needed to be said ... Aimé Césaire was the name of the one speaking.'[25] This was the French language review *Tropiques,* edited by Aimé and Suzanne Césaire and René Menil. In this home-grown review the refugee surrealists, who quickly made contact with the editors, found not only independent references to their own poetic universe—Rimbaud and Lautréamont—but also a political voice that believed in poetry. Césaire's opening text was a passionate protest against a colonial power subservient to fascism and expressed horror at the cultural void of his country: 'A silent and sterile land. I am speaking about ours. And my hearing measures by the Caribbean sea the terrifying silence of man ... [but] we are the kind who refuse the shadow.' The surrealists in Paris had long campaigned against European colonialism, as in the 1931 exhibition 'The Truth about the Colonies', organised by Louis Aragon and André Thirion in association with the PCF. With *Tropiques* the surrealists encountered a movement of a new kind which championed the black population and cultures from within and which reciprocated the surrealists' admiration. 'Breton', Césaire said in a 1978 interview, 'brought us boldness; he cut short our uncertainties ... I would say that the meeting with Breton was a confirmation of the truth of what I had discovered by my own reflections.'[26] He had coined the term *négritude* in the review *L'étudiant noir* in 1934, while at the Ecole Normale Supérieur in Paris, and

[24] Benjamin Péret, letter to Cáceres, 15 Dec. 1942, Gomez-Correa Archive, Box 1, Getty Research Institute.

[25] André Breton, 'Martinique charmeuse de serpents: Un grand poète noir', *Tropiques,* no. 11 (May 1944), 119. See also Dawn Adès, 'Wifredo Lam and surrealism', in *Wifredo Lam in North America: the Making of an Exhibition* (Milwaukee, WI, 2008), pp. 37–47.

[26] 'Entretiens avec Aimé Césaire par Jacqueline Leiner', Introduction to the facsimile edition of *Tropiques* (Paris, Jean-Michel Place, 1978), p. VI.

remained its greatest exponent. Menil, however, became, 'one of its more trenchant critics'.[27] For Menil, it became a reductive political ideology based on an essentialist notion of identity that merely inverted black/white values. Wifredo Lam, whose famous painting *The Jungle* (1943) depicts personages from the Afro-Cuban religion *santería* as well as satirising the sentimental and sexualised depictions of blacks came to agree with Menil: 'The personages in my paintings are neither white nor black, they lack race ...'[28]

Surrealist exhibitions in Latin America

Exhibitions, like reviews, played a major role in the internationalisation of surrealism. Reviews were the best site for the movement's dynamic and multidimensional activities, but the surrealists expected exhibitions, too, to be more than a collection of pictures hung on the wall. In Paris, the 1938 *Exposition internationale du surréalisme* was a complete, other-worldly environment, with pools and foliage in an underground cavern, confounding the visitor's sense of divisions between art and life, inside and outside, night and day. Few surrealist exhibitions outside Paris achieved this degree of inventive disorientation, but most nonetheless tried to go beyond the regular 'art exhibition'. Aside from one-person exhibitions by surrealist artists relatively few surrealist group exhibitions were organised within Latin America. Factors to take into account include the comparative paucity of exhibition spaces and of commercial art galleries through the 1930s and 1940s, and the conservative character of the national fine art academies. César Moro, again, sought to animate surrealism through exhibitions. He organised the first surrealist exhibition in Latin America, in Lima in May 1935, as well as the International Exhibition of Surrealism in Mexico City in 1940. The cover of the 1935 catalogue was included in the double page spread 'Surrealism around the World' in the Paris journal *Minotaure,* to demonstrate the global sweep of the movement.

The 1935 exhibition was restricted in scope, as Moro lacked the resources to put on a truly international show; it was titled 'Exposición de las obras de Jaime Dvor, César Moro, Waldo Parraguez, Gabriela

---

[27] Michael Richardson, 'Introduction', *Refusal of the Shadow: Surrealism and the Caribbean* (London, 1996), p. 8.
[28] Wifredo Lam, 'Mi pintura es un acto de descolonizacion', interview with Gerardo Mosquera, *Exploraciones en la plástica cubana* (Havana, 1983), p. 189.

Rivadeneira, Carlos Sotomayor and Maria Valencia'. The show announced as *Exposición surrealista* in Chile, 1941, similarly showed only the work of the Mandragora group immediately to hand: Jorge Cáceres and Braulio Arenas. Most of the works in the 1935 Lima exhibition were by Moro himself—paintings, drawings, and collages, some of whose titles read like automatic texts: 'L'oeil anthropophage au dessus de ciel cherche un oeil nu nez de platre un ciel nu né du platre ...'[29] The pun on 'nu nez' and 'nu né' is characteristic of Moro's writing and relates to the curious system of generating images adopted by Raymond Roussel. Four of the other artists had exhibited a couple of years earlier in Santiago de Chile (Dvor, Parraguez, Rivadeneira and Valencia) and showed some of the same work in Lima. Interestingly, this work had been presented in a very different way in the 1933 exhibition. The Chilean poet and critic Vicente Huidobro supplied a celebratory preface, 'Una nueva constelación en el cielo de America'. Normally, he writes, he returns to America from Europe with a sinking heart and finds nothing but fields and mountains;[30] this time, in the four artists, he recognised true originality and works worthy of international success. Various as they are, he goes on, they share the use of poor materials, simple, overlooked things from which they conjure poetry. But there is no attempt to link this practice of collage/constructions and objects to surrealism. Moro, by contrast, in his 1935 catalogue surrounds his own and some of the same works as those celebrated by Huidobro with inflammatory dada and surrealist quotations, with a strong anti-art flavour, such as Picabia's 'Art is a pharmaceutical product for fools'. The preface, unsigned but almost certainly by Moro, is in the most violent surrealist vein of announcing the supercession of art. Far from nourishing the human spirit with their lyrical effects, as Huidobro claimed, these works were to sow disillusionment and bring an end to painting altogether: 'En el Peru, donde todo se cierra, donde todo adquiere, mas y mas, un color de iglesia al crepúsculo, color particularmente horripilante, tenemos nosotros la simple temeridad de querer cerrar definitivamente las posibilidades de éxito a todo joven que desee pintar; esperamos desacreditar en tal forma la pintura en América ...'[31] Not only do they intend to

---

[29] Since his stay in Paris (1926–33) Moro wrote almost exclusively in French, perhaps to distance himself from Hispanic culture as well as to affirm his solidarity with the surrealists. French was, of course, the international language of the time.

[30] *Exposición de Diciembre*, Huerfanos 920 (Santiago de Chile, 1933).

[31] 'In Peru, where everything is closed in, where everything acquires, more or less, the colour of a church at dusk, a particularly horrific colour, we have the simple temerity to wish to close off definitively the possibilities of success for any young person who wishes to paint; we intend to

undermine painting, which Breton had once called a 'lamentable expedient', but they also express their disdain for good taste and for bourgeois art lovers, and their refusal to please: 'Esta exposición muestra ... por la primera vez en el Peru, una colección sin elección de obras destinadas a provocar el desprecio y la colera de las gentes que despreciamos y que detestamos ...'[32] The final text in the catalogue is an outspoken attack by Moro on Huidobro himself, a personal diatribe calling him an arriviste and plagiarist, which led to a high profile polemical exchange between the two.[33] Moro's attack on Huidobro—who also came under fire from the Mandragora group—is a striking example of the desire both in dada and surrealism to distance themselves from what Aragon described as the 'accredited avant-garde'. It was this, quite as much as the academic and conservative art world, that these more radical and subversive movements rejected. They wanted to bring an end to the idea of art as a spiritual alibi, remote from reality, at the same time as asserting the distinct character of their ideas, and wanted to avoid at all costs getting absorbed into a general notion of 'modernism'. Huidobro, who had extensive contacts with the European avant-garde, collaborating, for example, with Hans Arp, represented exactly the kind of flaccid acceptance of all and every modern trend that they rejected.

The most important international surrealist exhibition in Latin America was also organised by Moro. Following his involvement in political protests against an increasingly fascist government in Peru, which was allied to Franco's nationalist rebellion in Spain, Moro was obliged to leave the country and in 1938 settled in Mexico City.[34] Here he saw André Breton again on the latter's five month visit, and became friends with local artists and poets, such as Villarutia, as well as the surrealist exiles—Wolfgang Paalen, Alice Rahon, Leonora Carrington, Remedios Varo and

---

discredit in this way painting in America ...' After his return to Lima in 1933, Moro wrote *Los anteojos de azufre*, Sulphur Goggles, which was not published until 1958, after his death. Here Moro attacks the stultified, provincial art and poetry of Peru; the only poetry he finds worthy of the name is by the inmates of the mental asylum, the Hospital Larco Herrera, where he worked as librarian.

[32] 'This exhibition shows for the first time in Peru a collection, unselected, of works destined to provoke the scorn and anger of the people we scorn and hate ...'

[33] Huidobro responded in his little magazine *Vital* (June 1935) with a vicious article calling Moro among other things a 'piojo homosexual'; in February 1936 Moro hit back with 'Vicente Huidobro o el Obispo embotellado' (the bottled bishop), calling him a cretin whose work was a brothel. See also Wilson, 'The sole surrealist poet: César Moro (1903–1956)'.

[34] See Dickson, 'César Moro and Xavier Villaruria', for an account of Moro's activities in Lima with CADRE, the Comité de Amigos de los Defensores de la Republica Española (1936).

Benjamin Péret. Despite the misery of his personal circumstances his commitment to promoting surrealism was undimmed. In 1940 he and Paalen, with the collaboration of Breton from a distance, organised the International Exhibition of Surrealism at the Galería de Arte Mexicano— at the time the only commercial gallery in Mexico City. The exhibition was intended as the latest in the series of international surrealist exhibitions that had taken place previously in Prague, London, Tenerife and Japan, as well as Paris. Moro had to contend, however, with a very powerful local art world, as well as with the practical transport problems following the outbreak of the Second World War. These, as Paalen noted in the catalogue, prevented them from showing adequately the work of surrealist sculptors Arp, Giacometti and Moore, and deprived them of the sculptures of Picasso and Ernst altogether, as well as of surrealist and found objects. But the exhibition nonetheless continued the surrealist tradition by including non-Western objects—ancient Mexican art, dance masks from Guerrero and Guadalajara, 'Arte Salvaje' (masks from New Guinea) —and drawings by the insane. It also included a section of 'Pintores de México'; the most famous Mexican artist, however, Diego Rivera, together with Frida Kahlo and the photographer Manuel Alvarez Bravo, was included in the 'surrealist artists' section. Rivera had hosted Breton and Lamba during their visit to Mexico, and Kahlo had stayed with Breton in Paris in 1939. Moro was sceptical of Rivera's affiliation to surrealism, as he wrote to Westphalen: 'Nobody believes in his surrealism; it's his thousandth attempt to re-make his reputation, which he really has no need to do, as in the United States he earns fabulous sums and is regarded as a matchless genius.'[35] There is a suggestion in Moro's letter that Rivera had hoped through Breton to establish his reputation in France—several canvases had been reproduced in the special section on Mexico in *Minotaure*—but without success: 'A Paris, cela n'a pas marché, malgré Minotaure; tu comprends les gens ont un instinct assez fin et connaissent la peinture. Il fallait mille circonstances pour que Breton soit tombé dans le piège qui lui tendait Rivera, lui si lucide a été roulé comme un enfant.'[36] Rivera and Kahlo, Moro confided, insisted on their paintings hanging in the most prominent places, as is confirmed from installation shots.

[35] Moro, letter to Westphalen, 28 Jan. 1940, Westphalen Archive, Box 1, GRI.
[36] Ibid. 'In Paris, it didn't work, in spite of *Minotaure*; you know, people there have a refined instinct and understand painting. There were a thousand reasons why Breton fell into the trap prepared for him by Rivera, though so lucid he was tumbled like a child.'

An incident over the catalogue is revealing of sensitivities in Mexico over political and religious issues. Moro was asked by the gallery to suppress 'a paragraph on the Christian era, another on Aragon, another on intellectuals, and they don't want me to call the Spanish Conquerors "Barbarians"'. He was convinced the request came from the grand old man of Mexican letters, Alfonso Reyes, although this proved incorrect and he never did discover who was behind it. The attack on Aragon, who had chosen to stay in the Communist Party rather than surrealism and remained a Stalinist, stayed in (he was a traitor who had fallen 'to the lowest moral level of a provoker at the service of the darkness and confusion required to start docile masses on a new slaughter'), as did the reference to the 'invasion of the Spanish barbarians and their followers of today'. But the paragraph on the Christian era was censored. Moro wrote it out in the catalogue he sent to Westphalen:

> At this precise moment the Christian era ends. A great wind has been unleashed, at whose origin we see the moral, poignant support of Sigmund Freud, which has just dispersed for ever the props of Golgotha and death-loving ivy devours the crosses where birds would never live. Surrealist clairvoyance situated the end of the Christian Era in 1925; in 1939 we need to remember this.[37]

Moro's reference to '1925' relates to the photograph on the cover of *La révolution surréaliste*, no. 3 (15 April 1925) which showed Christian statuary—a Pieta, angels, a pope, a saint—grouped haphazardly in a double exposure against an ordinary house, as if discarded and desacralised, with the title '1925: Fin de l'Ère Chrétienne'.

Surrealism's unflagging battle against Christianity, and especially the Roman Catholic church, manifested for instance in the famous photograph in *La révolution surréaliste* of Benjamin Péret insulting a priest, in the display of 'European fetishes', including a statue of the Madonna and child, in the Anti-colonial exhibition in Paris of 1931, on the cover of the surrealist journal *Bief*, showing a nun with a gun (no. 1, November 1958), as well as in Moro's censored text, touched a nerve in many places in Latin America. In Brazil, for example, 'The polemic between Surrealism and Catholicism has been frequent in our culture.'[38]

---

[37] The copy of the catalogue with handwritten paragraph is in the Westphalen Archive, GRI.
[38] Floriano Martins 'Surrealismo & Brasil' <www.triplov.com>.

Surrealism and *lo real maravilloso*

Of the many initiatives aiming to stamp a distinctive, unique cultural identity on Latin America in the second half of the twentieth century, the Cuban writer Alejo Carpentier's '*lo real maravilloso*' has probably been the most influential. It has also had a disastrous effect on the understanding of surrealism in this context, as Carpentier's purpose was to distance surrealism from Latin America. The opposition he sets up between 'surrealist fantasy' and 'magic reality' is fictitious and misleading. Carpentier, who had been on the fringes of the surrealist movement in Paris in the late 1920s and contributed an article on Cuban music to Bataille's review *Documents*, announced his thesis in the 1949 prologue to his novel *Kingdom of this World*, one of the first of the so-called Magic Realist novels of Latin America. Carpentier draws a sharp distinction between what he presents as the surrealist marvellous, and the Latin American marvellous real. In surrealism, he claimed, '... the dream technicians became bureaucrats ... Poverty of the imagination, Unamuno said, is learning codes by heart. Today there are codes for the fantastic ...' Surrealism was no more than 'that old deceitful story of the fortuitous encounter of the umbrella and the sewing machine on the dissecting table that led to ermine spoons, the snail in a rainy taxi, the lion's head on the pelvis of a widow, the surrealist exhibitions'.[39] In Latin America, by contrast, Carpentier argues, reality itself is marvellous: 'What is the entire history of America if not a chronicle of the marvellous real?'[40] He claims to have had the revelation in Henri-Christoph's kingdom—Haiti, where a former cook became king. A 'marvellous reality' arises from 'an unexpected alteration of reality (the miracle), from a privileged revelation of reality ... [a nature that is untamed, living myths and ancient superstitions] ... an amplification of the scale and categories of reality, perceived with particular intensity by virtue of an exaltation of the spirit that leads it to a kind of extreme state'.[41] Carpentier's invective against surrealism and apparent exaltation of an alternative 'marvellous' have had far-reaching, but quite paradoxical, consequences.

Firstly, it consolidated, especially in Latin America, the identification of surrealism with 'fantasy' and a fantastic divorced from the real world.

---

[39] Alejo Carpentier, 'On the Marvelous Real in America', in Lois Parkinson Zamora and Wendy B. Faris (eds.), *Magical Realism: Theory, History, Community* (Durham, NC, 1995), p. 85.
[40] Ibid., p. 88.
[41] Ibid., p. 86.

The construction put on the terms 'fantastic' and 'marvellous' needs to be examined. If one looks at Breton's discussion of the marvellous and at the works he chooses to illustrate his ideas, they are in no sense the 'manufactured', 'fake' marvellous of Carpentier's caricature. Nothing, in fact, as Maria Bernal has said, 'goes against Breton's definition of the marvellous',[42] except the idea that it is an exclusively Latin American phenomenon and only Americans can express it and also, crucially, the notion that the marvellous presupposes faith.

The term Magical Realism, which has supplanted Carpentier's 'lo real maravilloso' in relation to the fiction that is the best-known twentieth-century cultural export of Latin America, was coined by Franz Roh in his 1925 book *Nach-Expressionismus: Magicher Realismus: Probleme des Neusten Europeanischen Malerei* (*Post Expressionism, Magic Realism: Problems of the Most Recent European Painting*), to define a quality common in post-war figurative paintings by such as de Chirico and Carra, as well as in Henri Rousseau. Carpentier was certainly aware of Roh's book, which had been translated into Spanish, but denied its influence on him for a long time, saying that 'What he called magical realism was simply painting where real forms are combined in a way that does not conform to daily reality ...'[43] That is not how Roh saw this kind of painting. For him, they had clarity, simplicity and objectivity, but with an underlying intention of approaching the ultimate enigmas of existence. Apparently familiar objects were imbued with a quality of strangeness: nearer to Freud's Uncanny than anything else.

Carpentier's ideas have had a profound effect on the post-war reception and historiography of surrealism, not least in Mexico. The exhibition *Los surrealistas en México* brought to a head, in the context of the visual arts, the controversy that had been rumbling for a while. Ida Rodriguez Prampolini, in her essay 'El Surrealismo y la fantasía mexicana', for the exhibition catalogue *Los surrealistas en México* (1986), wrote 'There is no doubt [Breton] was hypnotised by our country, but he did not understand that what he was postulating as surreality, among us functions in a different way, as real reality fertilised by a peculiar fantasy but not like unreal reality which is what he was after.'[44] Here again, the deliberate

---

[42] Maria Clara Bernal, *Mas allá de lo real maravilloso: El surrealismo y el Caribe* (Bogotá, 2006); see also *Realismo Magico: Fantastico e iperrealismo nell'arte e nella letteratura Latinoamericane, a cura di Mario Sartor* (Forum, Udine, 2005).

[43] Carpentier, 'The Baroque and the Marvelous real', in Zamora and Faris (eds.), *Magical Realism*, p. 102.

[44] Prampolini, 'El surrealismo y la Fantasía Mexicana', p. 19.

misconception that surrealism intended completely to override reality is
drawn into a specious argument primarily intended to distance Frida
Kahlo from surrealism: 'In México, Breton extended surrealism to pre-
Hispanic production, to the popular, and dubbed "surrealist" probably
the most realist of our painters, Frida Kahlo.'[45] This is now repeated in
most accounts of Kahlo, underpinned by her own late statement: 'They
thought I was a surrealist, but I wasn't. I never painted dreams. I painted
my own reality.'[46] I question this, not from the desire to pigeonhole Kahlo
again but to contrast it with the way she and others saw her painting in the
period after Breton's visit and also restore to surrealism its fuller meaning.
Las Dos Fridas was exhibited at the International Surrealist Exhibition in
Mexico City and at the MoMA New York *20 Centuries of Mexican Art* in
the same year, 1940. For the catalogue of the New York show, Kahlo's
friend Covarrubias dubbed her 'suprarrealista' and wrote: 'Almost all
Frida Kahlo's paintings are autobiographical, expressed in a dream language that is truly surrealist and motivated by the psychological states of
the artist's mind.'[47] Covarrubias certainly wrote this with Kahlo's approval.
Her own comment is entirely in line with surrealism: 'I never knew I was
a surrealist until André Breton came to Mexico and told me I was. The
only thing I know is that I paint because I need to, and I paint always
whatever passes through my head, without any other consideration.'[48] The
reference here to the definition of surrealism in the first manifesto is oblique
but knowing. That she was unaware of surrealism before is neither here
nor there. Surrealism was built on the recognition of like spirits from the
past and present regardless of their awareness of the movement itself, and
Kahlo was one of many artists—like the photographers Manuel and Lola
Alvarez Bravo, whose work was recognised as cognate with surrealism: 'At
this present point in the development of Mexican painting, which since
the beginning of the 19th century has remained largely free from foreign
influence and profoundly attached to its own resources, I was witnessing
here, at the other end of the earth, a spontaneous outpouring of our own
questioning spirit ... '[49] It was not for their 'unreal reality' that Kahlo's

[45] Prampolini, 'El surrealismo y la Fantasia Mexicana', p. 19.
[46] Frida Kahlo, Undated quotation in Hayden Herrera, *Frida: A Biography of Frida Kahlo* (New York, 1983), p. 266.
[47] Miguel Covarrubias, in *Twenty Centuries of Mexican Art* (New York, 1940), p. 160.
[48] Kahlo, undated quotation, Herrera, *Frida: a Biography of Frida Kahlo*, p. 254.
[49] André Breton 'Frida Kahlo de Rivera', in exhibition catalogue, *Méxique* (Paris 1939), repr. in Breton, *Le Surréalisme et la peinture* (Paris, 1965), English trans. by Simon Watson-Taylor, *Surrealism and Painting* (London, 1972), p. 144.

paintings and Bravo's photographs were so highly valued by the surrealists, but for a thoroughly grounded real resistant to pure fantasy, a real that included the psychic realities of dream, memory and the unconscious, the impulses of desire revealed in the imagination. The fact that Kahlo subsequently, in her diary, continued to experiment with automatic writing and drawing suggests that she found more resources in surrealism than she subsequently admitted openly.

Although Kahlo's paintings after 1938 betray an awareness of surrealism (*Las Dos Fridas* is a brilliant expression of uncanny doubling and a split self, and *What the Water told me*, reproduced by Breton in *Minotaure* in 1939, multiplies reveries and memories) her earlier works, such as the extraordinary *My Birth*, are no less convincingly surrealist. *My Birth* of 1932, like several of her works of this period, uses, as Diego Rivera wrote in his 1943 article which was intended to reclaim Kahlo for Mexican art, the *retablo*: 'In her *retablos*, Frida always paints her own life.'[50] The *retablo* is a traditional catholic offering, a tiny painted representation of a miracle owed to the intervention of a saint, Virgin or Christ. Kahlo's versions of the *retablos* nail precisely that ambiguous point where modernity and superstition clash, where the popular is harnessed to its opposite and survives. *My Birth* was painted just after Kahlo had a miscarriage, and her own mother had died. The Virgin of the Sorrows, at the head of the bed, was a precise memory of an object her devout mother cherished. It is not the magically hovering saint or virgin of the *retablos*. The empty scroll at the bottom of the painting is the most telling detail of all—in the traditional *retablo*, a text explains the circumstances of the miracle. Here there is no miracle—there are the deaths of the unborn baby and of her mother, embodied in her own birth. The directness of the image simply underlines a conundrum that cannot quite be put into words.

No doubt the surrealists, who had a horror of the catholic church, responded to the anticlerical sentiments of Kahlo's painting, while sharing an ambiguous appreciation of the visual treasures of the imagination that faith produced. This differs radically from Carpentier's incorporation of superstitious belief in his description of the Latin American marvellous real: 'The phenomenon of the marvellous presupposes faith', he wrote.[51] In Magic Realist novels, faith is often the instrument for the shift

---

[50] Diego Rivera, 'Frida Kahlo y el arte mexicano', *Boletin del Seminario de Cultura Mexicana*, 1/2 (Oct. 1943), repr. in Rivera *Arte y Politica* (Mexico, 1978), p. 246.
[51] Carpentier, 'On the marvellous real in America', in Zamora and Faris (eds.), *Magical Realism*, p. 86.

into the fantastic, which is articulated as a longing for an imaginary unity. The ways that novels like Gabriel Garcia Marquez's *One Hundred Years of Solitude* (1967) or Juan Rulfo's *Pedro Páramo* (1987) slide between dreams, daily realities and miracles, however, do have something in common with surrealism. There was 'a deep vein in Latin American culture, more apparent in literature than in the visual arts, that the surrealists recognised and claimed as kindred'.[52]

Prampolini, to underline the distinction she is trying to draw between 'surreality' (secret fantasies, dreams of a purely personal world) and Mexican artists (whose 'fantasy' is rooted in their real and irrational world), contrasts the work of Kahlo with that of Remedios Varo, who escaped to Mexico in 1941 with her partner the poet Benjamin Péret and stayed there until her death in 1963: 'Al ver su mundo, donde se extiende la belleza maravillosa de que hablaba Breton, uno se pregunta? como es possible que una realidad enormemente poderosa y estrujante como la mexicana, no haya podido tocar una sola cuerda sensible del alma de esta artista? El programa surrealista que conformó su talento le impidió ver la realidad?'[53] This is 'the tone of the Moscow Trials', the surrealist writer José Pierre suggests in his critique of Prampolini and her insistence on the 'Mexican School' and on 'Mexican reality'.[54] He wonders at the odd situation in which someone who evidently hates surrealism is invited to write the introductory essay in the catalogue of the exhibition, *Los surrealistas en México* at the National Museum of Art. Vigorously defending surrealism from Prampolini's misunderstanding, based on Carpentier, he identifies two powerful forces within official Mexican culture that inevitably clash with surrealism: the overriding 'mexicanidad', and the linked emphasis on representing the 'reality that surrounds us'. Pierre sniffs here a sulphurous hint of 'Stalin's and Jdanov's so-called "socialist realism"', rather than Carpentier's 'marvellous real', suggesting that the Stalinist mural painter Siqueiros would have approved her argument. Siqueiros, unlike Rivera, was an unwavering member of the Party and opponent of surrealism. He

---

[52] Martica Sawin, *Surrealism in Exile and the Beginning of the New York School* (Cambridge, MA, 1995), p. 255.
[53] 'Looking at her world, where we see the marvellous beauty Breton spoke of, one asks oneself? How is it possible, that a reality as enormously powerful and striking as the Mexican, has not touched a single cord in the soul of this artist? The surrealist programme that formed her talent prevented her from seeing reality.' Prampolini, 'El surrealismo y la Fantasía Mexicana', p. 20.
[54] José Pierre, 'A few disjointed reflections on the encounter between México and Surrealism', *El Surrealismo entre Viejo y Nuevo Mundo* (Las Palmas de Gran Canaria, 1989), p. 333.

accused Alvarez Bravo, whose photographs compose the cover of the 1940 International surrealist exhibition catalogue, of 'the aesthetic crime of Bretonism'.

Prampolini's comment betrays a fundamental misunderstanding of surrealism, which never tried to impose a programme on the artists, other than questioning a crude definition of reality. Surrealism could not be equated with any style, and the degree of 'reality' in the work of an artist was very variable. The surrealist belief in the interpenetration of dream and waking, the imagination and reality, exterior and interior, is expressed in Kahlo's work as convincingly as in any surrealist artist's work. Metaphors like that of the palette/heart, veins exposed and brushes dripping blood, capture the mental as much as the physical reality of her condition. What then should we make of the contrast Prampolini draws with Varo? Here the former surrealist Roger Caillois offers an interesting interpretation of Varo's 'fantasy' in 'Cases d'un echiquier'. Her world, Caillois writes, 'est entièrement insolite, en tout point incompatible avec le monde familier, cependant il tient du monde réel les divers éléments qui le composent ... Ils n'obéissent plus aux mêmes lois ... Les corps les plus durs, la pierre ou les metaux, sont devenus solubles et perméables ou froissables ... cet univers est identifiable et impossible à la fois. On n'y trouve pas de mons- tres, de larves ou d'engins venus de lointaines planètes, Tout y est terrestre et connu, mais répondant a une autre économie et pourvu d'autres pro- priétés. En outre, ce monde déconcertant possède, et c'est sa force, une incontestable unité: il ne consiste pas en mille démentis hétéroclites, infligés au monde réel.'[55] Caillois makes an analogy with Bosch, whose world was based on a complete if strange theology and iconography, to be in turn eclipsed by others, equally recondite and esoteric. The point is that Varo, like Bosch, creates a complete if uncertain and unpredictable world, informed not just by alchemical ideas but also by Varo's serious and pre- cise understanding of physics, and delight in the appearance of new scien- tific models of the universe and its physical properties.[56] The fact that these change and will continue to change reveals not just the results of scientific experiment but the role of the human imagination in the construction of models of 'reality'.

[55] Roger Caillois, 'Cases d'un echiquier', *Obliques* (Paris, 1977), p. 219.
[56] Alan Friedman, 'The serenity of science', *Remedios Varo: Catalogue raisonné* (Mexico, 2002), pp. 75–87.

Surrealism and Pre-Columbian America

When the surrealists redrew the map of the world in 1929 to express their own geosocial values, nations suffered a sea change; in America, only Mexico and Peru survive, together with Alaska, as the homes respectively of the Pre-Columbian civilisations of Mesoamerica—Maya, Aztec, etc, the Andean civilisations and those of the North West Coast. This view of America was reinforced when many of the surrealists were refugees in the United States during the war: a land 'that denies myth',[57] and turned to the indigenous present and the Pre-Columbian past. Their interest began in the 1920s; one of the earliest of the Paris surrealist exhibitions, in 1927, had paired the painter Yves Tanguy with 'Objets d'Amérique', and displayed a version of the great Aztec statue of Coatlicue. The collections of Breton and Eluard already included Mexican and North West Coast figures and objects by the late 1920s, and, once in America, Breton, Ernst and others amassed quantities of 'First Nations' art: Kachina dolls, Haida masks, Tlatilco figurines, even gigantic totem poles. But their interest extended well beyond art and artefacts, to myth, poetry and literature, which they helped to bring to wider appreciation. In Mexico, the surrealists were in contact with the major Americanist scholars like Alfonso Caso, the first person in the modern period to decipher the Mixtec-Toltec codices and whose article on the newly discovered 'Codices of Azoyu' was published by Wolfgang Paalen in his review *Dyn*.[58] The point I wish to make is that the surrealist interest was not limited to, say, the fantastic Aztec sculpture or animal masks, to the visibly marvellous but extended to the civilisations as a whole. The association with Claude Lévi-Strauss, who had travelled on the same boat as Breton to Martinique, and whose essays were published in *VVV*, is often discussed in connection with the surrealists' growing interest in myth, but in his research as an anthropologist he avoided the peoples who had scripts and a literature.

Benjamin Péret played a significant role in extending the West's knowledge of indigenous literatures. He was the first to publish a French translation of the Maya book *Chilam Balam of Chumayel*, in 1955, and spent years gathering material for his *Anthologie des Mythes, Légendes et contes*

---

[57] Anais Nin quoted in Sawin, *Surrealism in Exile*, p. 150. See also Fabrice Flahutez, *Nouveau monde et nouveau mythe: Mutations du surréalisme de l'exil américain à l'"Ecart absolu" (1941–1965)* (Paris, 2007)

[58] *Dyn*, 4–5, Amerindian Number (Mexico, Dec. 1943).

populaires d'Amerique.[59] He had started this in Brazil, and in Mexico set up an extensive network of contacts throughout the Americas to help him. Through Moro, he wrote to Westphalen explaining his project and asking for contacts in Ecuador, Colombia, Bolivia and Paraguay: 'je voudrais de véritables legends incaïques, des légendes des indiens actuels de l'Amazonie et des myths precolombiens ... un recueil de légendes d'Amérique bien choisis pourrait être fort intéressant et montre comment la poésie et le sens du merveilleux sont innés chez l'homme. Je suis persuadé que si actuellement il (le sens du merveilleux) est réfugié chez quelques artistes et étouffé par la vie moderne chez la plus grande partie du people civilisés, il n'est néanmoins pas disparu, les constructions délirants des fous en témoignent. Il est simplement réprimé et il réapparaîtra un jour dans toute sa splendeur.'[60]

Gunther Gerzso shared the surrealists' passion for the art and architecture of Pre-Columbian America. His work has been almost exclusively exhibited and commented upon in the context of Mexican twentieth-century art and within that as a pioneer of abstraction; *Risking the abstract: Mexican Modernism and the art of Gunther Gerzso* is the title of the largest exhibition so far dedicated to his work. Gerzso was born in Mexico in 1915, spent much of his youth in Switzerland, was a stage designer in Cleveland, Ohio, returning to Mexico frequently, and in 1941 finally settled there, working as set designer during the golden age of Mexican cinema, for the surrealist Luis Buñuel among others, and painting in his spare time. He finally dedicated himself to painting in 1962.

The polemics that split the Mexican art world, between the socialist realists like Siqueiros ('Abstraction? What trash!') and artists following modernist trends hardly touched him and he always denied his paintings were purely abstract: 'Today still, I am a surrealist ... what I do is a species of abstract surrealism.'[61] Abstract surrealism was not the oxymoron it might seem: painters like the Chilean Roberto Matta had been forging from the spontaneous gestures of automatism and biomorphism canvases of breathtaking originality, cellular caves on a cosmic scale, with titles like *Psychological morphology*. Gerzso, though, had little interest in automatism. The grid-like structures of his paintings, as he acknowledged, relate

---

[59] Benjamin Péret, *Anthologie des myths, legends et contes populaires d'Amérique* (Paris, 1959). See also Fabienne Bradu, *Benjamin Péret y México* (Mexico, 1995).

[60] Benjamin Péret, letter to Westphalen, 18 April 1942, Westphalen archive, Box 3, GRI.

[61] Gerzso, quoted in Diana C. Du Pont, 'Gerzso: pioneering the abstract in México', *Risking the Abstract: Mexican Modernism and the Art of Gunther Gerzso* (Santa Barbara, CA, 2003), p. 98.

to cubism: 'my work is a confluence of three things: Cubism, Surrealism and Pre-Columbian art and architecture'.[62]

Gerzso was close to the group of surrealist exiles in Mexico City, Leonora Carrington, Remedios Varo and Benjamin Péret, as well as to Wolfgang Paalen and the Mexican poet, critic and diplomat Octavio Paz. Early paintings, such as *El Descuartizado* (The Quartered) of 1944, were inspired by the French surrealist André Masson, and one notable canvas commemorates his friends transformed: Varo masked and surrounded by cats, Leonora a naked icon. From the mid-1950s, Gerzso's paintings develop an original pictorial language of overlapping planes, beautifully modulated surface that construct shallow spaces, behind which an unfathomable black is glimpsed. As Paz put it, Gerzso 'gave up figuration to explore non-figurative space. In this change Cardoza y Aragon saw a break with surrealism. I do not agree: Gerzso's work was no longer surrealistic, but surrealism was still his inspiration.'[63] Although without any obvious figuration, the paintings allude to architecture, to archaeological sites and their landscapes. It was the buildings of pre-conquest America that had the most profound impact on Gerzso's painting. He visited the old cities, like Labna and Chichen Itza, naming paintings after them, but also used/ appreciated photographs like those of Martin Chambi. The special issue of Wolfgang Paalen's review *Dyn*, dedicated to Amer-Indian art, contained fine photographs of Inca architecture, including that of the famous twelve-sided stone in a wall at the Inca capital, Cuzco, whose extraordinary form and modulated surface echo in Gerzso's painting. It was not just the structures of these walls and buildings that fascinated Gerzso, but the tragic past and hidden present of indigenous America of which they are dumb witnesses. The first line of Péret's poem 'The Swirl of Dust', written in Mexico, captures this effect:

> When stones slam their doors as a sign of despair ...

Cuauhtémoc Medina, in 'Gerzso and the Indo-American Gothic: from eccentric surrealism to parallel modernism', points to the violence and hauntings that 'stalk the fragments of Latin American art that deal with the indigenous and the modern at the same time', and identifies the

---

[62] Gerzso, quoted in Diana C. Du Pont, 'Gerzso: pioneering the abstract in México', *Risking the Abstract: Mexican Modernism and the Art of Gunther Gerzso* (Santa Barbara, CA, 2003), p. 98.
[63] Octavio Paz, 'Gerzso: the icy spark', in John Golding and Octavio Paz, *Gerzso* (Neuchâtel, 1983), quoted in Diana C. Du Pont, 'Gerzso: pioneering the abstract in México'.

role of surrealism in perceiving the continent in terms of layers of history and the uncanny return of an undead past.[64] Gerzso once said: 'When you try to look into one of my paintings, you'll always run into a wall that keeps you from going any further. It will stop you with the brilliance of its light, but at the back there's a black plane: it's fear.'[65] Fear of what? Fear of the dark, of ghosts, of the past, of the dead, or of a repressed, supposedly 'archaic' present that confronts modern Latin America at every turn. As Medina argues, the book that most brilliantly captures this fear, which Mexican intellectuals represented as a metaphysical threat, is *The Labyrinth of Solitude* by Gerzso's close friend, Octavio Paz. The ambiguity at the heart of *The Labyrinth of Solitude* is between 'we', the modern Mexican seeking to forge a fully modern society, and 'they', peasants, 'Indians': 'We ... struggle with imaginary entities, with vestiges of the past or self-engendered phantasms. These vestiges and phantasms are real, at least to us ... those ghosts are the vestiges of past realities. Their origins are in the Conquest, the Colonial period ...'[66] The peasant—'remote, somewhat archaic in his ways of dressing and speaking' embodies for everyone but himself 'the occult, the hidden ... an ancient wisdom hiding among the folds of the land'.[67] Paz romanticises the bitter reality of an indigenous present incommensurable, he believes, with the former civilisations, those who built Uxmal, Sacsahuayman, etc. In his 'Circulatory Poem (for general disorientation)' Paz suggested parallels between surrealism and the overlaying of eras, the co-existence of pasts and presents, alien to the normal, given periodisations of history:

> surrealism
> passed   will pass through México
> magnetic mirror . . .
> far away in México
> not this one
>   the other, ever buried ever living . . .[68]

---

[64] Cuauhtemoc Medina, 'Gerzso and the Indo-American Gothic: from eccentric surrealism to parallel modernism', in *Risking the Abstract: Mexican Modernism and the Art of Gunther Gerzso*, p. 212.

[65] Gerzso to Rita Eder, in Eder *Gunther Gerzso: El Esplendor de la muralla* (México 1994), quoted in Medina, 'Gerzso and the Indo-American Gothic', p. 195. Gerzso was close to the German art historian and critic Paul Westheim, who emigrated to Mexico in 1941. Westheim had worked with Carl Einstein, whose book *Negerplastik* had analysed the aesthetic qualities of African art. Westheim characterised Aztec sculpture as 'surrealist'.

[66] Octavio Paz, *The Labyrinth of Solitude* (1950; New York, 1961 edn.), p. 72–3.

[67] Ibid., p. 65.

[68] Octavio Paz, *The Collected Poems 1957–1987* (trans. and rev.) (Manchester, 1988), p. 399.

In his memoir of André Breton, Paz recalled a conversation in which he said to Breton that, to him, surrealism was the 'sacred malady of our world ...'; since it was a necessary negation in the West, it would remain alive as long as modern civilisation remained alive, whatever political systems and ideologies might prevail in the future. Breton answered that he doubted whether the world now dawning can be defined in terms of affirmation or negation: 'we are entering a neutral zone, and the surrealist rebellion will be obliged to express itself in forms that are neither negation nor affirmation'.[69] The contemporary Brazilian artist Cildo Meireles echoes this, in the context of a comment on the dangers of political and cultural nationalism: 'There is no possibility of collective survival if we stay with the notion of region or nation ... this is a question of national identity, the most perverse of cultural projects. The contribution [of Brazil] would be to demonstrate the impossibility of surviving if we do not understand the earth as something unique. There is no way of creating a perfect project that is marked out by its opposite. There is no way of avoiding social, economic and political entropy.'[70]

In the final part of my original lecture I looked at the work of Cildo Meireles, hoping to reignite debate about surrealism's legacies in contemporary art which I believe have been seriously underplayed and are especially interesting in a Latin American context. Recently the legacies of Dada, Duchamp and surrealism have shown up in the most refreshing trends in the both literature and the visual arts in Latin America: art that is suspicious of political boundaries and the limits of specific mediums, that explores alternative cartographies (Guillermo Kuitca and Jorge Macchi, for instance); that engages in unclassifiable urban interventions that nod to surrealist wanderings in the city, such as Francis Alÿs; renewing the readymade, montage, chance encounters, found objects, revisiting the old surrealist strategies of black humour and disorientation to express contemporary states of unrootedness, displacement and alienation; an art which alternately seduces and estranges. This art without fixed frontiers is flourishing everywhere, but nowhere with greater variety and conviction than in Latin America.

[69] Paz, 'André Breton or the Quest of the Beginning', *Alternating Current* (London, 1974), p. 54.
[70] Cildo Meireles (1994), in Nuria Enguita, 'Places for Digressions, an interview with Cildo Meireles', *Cildo Meireles*, ed. Nuria Enguita and Vicente Todolí (IVAM, 1995), p. 166.

'The Reason of this Preference': Sleeping, Flowing and Freezing in Pope's *Dunciad*

VALERIE RUMBOLD

University of Birmingham

I

WHEN, IN THE EARLY 1780s, forty years after Pope's death, Samuel Johnson was working on his *Lives of the Poets*, he declared that 'among the excellences of Pope ... must be mentioned the melody of his metre'; and this led him to introduce a striking anecdote:

> I have been told that the couplet by which he declared his own ear to be most gratified was this:
>
> > Lo, where Moeotis sleeps, and hardly flows
> > The freezing Tanais through a waste of snows.
>
> But the reason of this preference I cannot discover.[1]

Given the evidence now available to us about Pope's crafting of this couplet, the anecdote is particularly intriguing. This evidence of the revision process also illuminates the thematic as well as the aural development of the couplet, and opens up a range of suggestive links with the wider strategies of the *Dunciad* as a whole. 'Suggestive', however, remains the

---

Read at the Academy 4 May 2010.

[1] *Samuel Johnson: the Lives of the Poets*, ed. Roger Lonsdale, 4 vols. (Oxford, 2006), 4. 78–9, 347. For the purposes of this paper, diphthongs are spelled out as separate characters, and the spelling variants Ma'otis/Maeotis/Moeotis are reproduced but not discussed.

important word here: this cannot be a conclusive enquiry because we shall never know, in the absence of direct evidence, what reasons Pope himself might have given for choosing this couplet—if indeed his choice was accurately reported to Johnson in the first place; but Johnson's anecdote, if it does nothing else, effectively issues us with an invitation to contemplate, in more than usual detail, one exemplary instance of Pope's couplet art.

II

The couplet that Johnson singles out describes what is now called the Sea of Azov, and the River Don which flows into it. It forms part of a sequence in Book III of Pope's *Dunciad*, appearing first in the three-book poem of 1728, and remaining in place in all succeeding editions through to the enlarged *Dunciad in Four Books* of 1743.[2] This sequence introduces the northern tribes implicated, in Pope's account, in the fall of the Roman empire; and the couplet that Johnson quotes depicts the landscape from which their southwards journey begins.

> Lo where *Moeotis* sleeps, and hardly flows
> The freezing *Tanais* thro' a waste of snows,
> The North by myriads pours her mighty sons,
> Great nurse of *Goths*, of *Alans*, and of *Huns*.[3]

Although none of Pope's manuscripts has survived, the process of his composition and revision of this couplet can be reconstructed in part from transcriptions of manuscript readings made by his friend Jonathan Richardson the younger, who worked from two manuscripts now lost, transferring their variants into two printed copies, now in the New York Public Library.[4] The earlier of these manuscripts, the so-called First Broglio,

---

[2] For the 1728–9 versions of the *Dunciad*, see *The Poems of Alexander Pope*, ed. Julian Ferraro, Valerie Rumbold, Nigel Wood and Paul Baines, 5 vols. (Harlow, 2007–), 3, ed. Valerie Rumbold, pp. 4–5, 113–14; for the final lifetime version of 1743, see *Alexander Pope: The Dunciad in Four Books*, ed. Valerie Rumbold, rev. 1st edn., Longman Annotated English Texts (Harlow, 2009), pp. 1–2.

[3] Rumbold (ed.), *The Poems of Alexander Pope*, 3: *The Dunciad. A Heroic Poem*, 1728, III. 79–82.

[4] For Richardson's transcriptions from the so-called First Broglio and Second Broglio, see Rumbold (ed.), *The Poems of Alexander Pope*, 3. 2–4; for transcription of both sets of readings, see Maynard Mack, *The Last and Greatest Art: Some Unpublished Poetical Manuscripts of Alexander Pope* (London, 1984), pp. 97–155; for a facsimile of the 1728 copy into which Richardson copied the readings of the First Broglio, see David L. Vander Meulen, *Pope's Dunciad of 1728: a History and Facsimile* (London, 1991).

whose readings Richardson recorded in a copy of the 1728 edition, shows significant developments for this couplet.

Figure 1 shows the opening where the passage appears, with the relevant couplet printed towards the foot of the left-hand page.[5] Richardson's general procedure is to place the variants closest in time to the printed version as close as possible to the printed lines, moving further away as the versions go further back in time. The opening shows three stages of development for this particular couplet: (a), the earliest, is from the block of three couplets at the top of the right-hand page; (b) is the intermediate stage, from the margin and interlining around the couplet itself; and (c) is the version as printed:

> (a) Where dull Ma'otis sleeps, & hardly flows,
>   The frozen Tanais thro', a waste of snows …
>
> (b) Lo where *Moeotis* sleeps, and hardly flow
>   The streams of *Tanais* thro' a waste of snow …
>
> (c) Lo where *Moeotis* sleeps, and hardly flows
>   The freezing *Tanais* thro' a waste of snows …

Johnson states that it was specifically the poet's *ear* that was gratified by this couplet; but attention to these early stages of revision makes it clear that the development of *sound* in the process of revision was closely implicated also in the development of *sense*. That this was a consistent concern with Pope, and one that he associated particularly with his work on the *Dunciad*, is attested by a comment recorded by his friend Joseph Spence in 1744:

> I have followed that (the significance of the numbers and the adapting them to the sense) much more even than Dryden, and much oftener than anyone minds it: particularly in the translations of Homer, where 'twas most necessary to do so, and in the *Dunciad* often, and indeed in all my poems.[6]

Richardson's transcription shows that as Pope moved from the earliest recoverable version of the couplet (a) to the intermediate stage (b), he dropped two commas. These had probably been intended as rhetorically expressive rather than grammatical; but their removal usefully clarifies the syntax by steering the reader away from any preliminary assumption that 'Ma'otis' will be the subject of both 'sleeps' and 'flows', and towards the recognition, on beginning the second line, that it is '*Tanais*' that is the

---

[5] Vander Meulen, *Pope's Dunciad*, facsimile p. 41; Mack, *The Last and Greatest Art*, p. 123.
[6] Joseph Spence, *Observations, Anecdotes, and Characters of Books and Men*, ed. James M. Osborn, 2 vols. (Oxford, 1966), 1, no. 396, pp. 173–4.

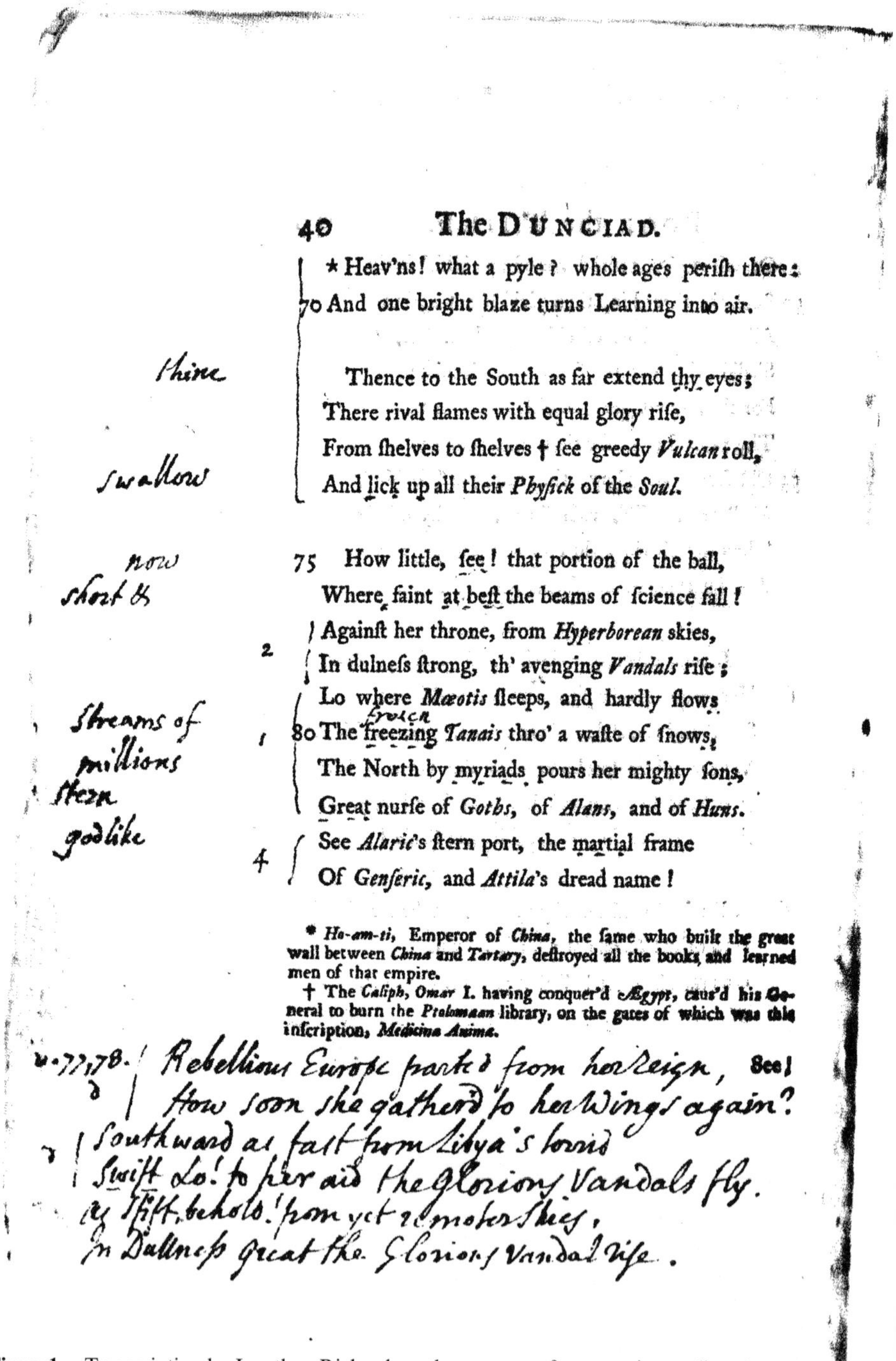

40   The DUNCIAD.

thine

> * Heav'ns! what a pyle? whole ages perish there:
> 70 And one bright blaze turns Learning into air.

swallow

> Thence to the South as far extend thy eyes;
> There rival flames with equal glory rise,
> From shelves to shelves † see greedy *Vulcan* roll,
> And lick up all their *Physick* of the *Soul*.

now
short &

> 75 How little, see! that portion of the ball,
>   Where faint at best the beams of science fall!
> 2   } Against her throne, from *Hyperborean* skies,
>   { In dulness strong, th' avenging *Vandals* rise;
>   { Lo where *Maeotis* sleeps, and hardly flows
> 1   80 The freezing *Tanais* thro' a waste of snows,
>   The North by myriads pours her mighty sons,
>   Great nurse of *Goths*, of *Alans*, and of *Huns*.
> 4   { See *Alaric*'s stern port, the martial frame
>   { Of *Genseric*, and *Attila*'s dread name!

streams of
millions
stern
godlike

> * *Ho-am-ti*, Emperor of *China*, the same who built the great
> wall between *China* and *Tartary*, destroyed all the books, and learned
> men of that empire.
> † The *Caliph*, *Omar* I. having conquer'd *Ægypt*, caus'd his Ge-
> neral to burn the *Ptolomaean* library, on the gates of which was this
> inscription, *Medicina Animæ*.

v.77,78. *Rebellious Europe parted from her Reign,* See |
How soon she gather'd to her Wings again?
Southward as fast from Libya's torrid
Swift Lo! to her aid the Glorious Vandals fly.
As swift, behold! from yet remoter skies,
In Dulness great the Glorious Vandals rise.

Figure 1.   Transcription by Jonathan Richardson the younger of manuscript readings in a copy
of Pope's *The Dunciad. A Heroic Poem* (1728) in the New York Public Library, from David L. Vander
Meulen, *Pope's Dunciad of 1728: a History and Facsimile*, London, University Press of Virginia,

Then from a Mountains Cloudy top the Guide
Shews all the Kingdoms of the Goddess wide
From whence the North first pour'd her mighty sons,
Stern Nurse of Alans, Visigoths, & Huns:
Where dull Mæotis sleeps, & hardly flows,
The frozen Tanaïs thro' a waste of snows.

BOOK the THIRD. 41.

85 See! the bold *Ostrogoths* on *Latium* fall ;   *Millions of*
   See! the fierce *Visigoths* on *Spain* and *Gaul*.   *Millions of*
   See! where the morning gilds the palmy shore,
   (The soil that arts and infant letters bore)
   His conqu'ring tribes th' *Arabian* prophet draws,
90 And saving Ignorance enthrones by Laws.   *restores*
   See *Christians*, *Jews*, one heavy sabbath keep ;   *a*
   And all the Western World believe and sleep.

   Behold this Scene, once in Science proud, that as Rome, in one foggy cloud ? | d

   Lo *Rome* herself, proud mistress how no more   *See   the*
   Of arts, but thund'ring against *Heathen* lore ;
95 Her gray-hair'd Synods damning books unread,
   And *Bacon* trembling for his brazen Head.
   Lo statues, temples, theatres o'erturn'd,
   (Oh glorious ruin!) and ✱ ✱ ✱ burn'd.   *La varius / Vigilius*

   See'st thou an *Isle*, by Palmers, Pilgrims trod,   *Beh. yon neighb'r. Isle, all over*
100 Men bearded, bald, cowl'd, uncowl'd, shod, unshod,   *In tracks of Pilgrim's by feet*
   Peel'd, patch'd, and piebald, linsey-woolsey brothers   *Oerrun with*
   Grave mummers, sleeveless some, and shirtless others.

Who ✱ ✱ ✱ ✱ bath'd in children's Blood,
Yet fought for Easter, of a ✱ of wood, that
Could weep devoutly when an Image spoke,
And groan in concert with a Saint of Oak.

Almighty Dullness! what a Sea of Blood
for early Easter, or a Stick of wood.
thus visit not ———— Oh spread — v. 108.

All this pursued the Line, was once our own,
now shorter limits bound her   Throne.

1991. Reproduced by kind permission of David Vander Meulen, the Bibliographical Society of the University of Virginia and the University Press of Virginia.

subject of 'flows', and that the 'waste' is what it flows through. This clarification helps focus a syntactic chiasmus in the relation between the two
subject–verb pairs (with '*Moeotis* sleeps' mirrored in reverse by 'flows |
The ... *Tanais*'). But however punctuated or not punctuated, the couplet
remains awkward to read: the transition between lines is both formally
elegant and expressively obstructive. The river 'hardly flows', and this is
true also of the reader's engagement with the syntax. That Pope was
acutely conscious of such expressive difficulty is borne out by a conversation he had with Spence about a line from his *Iliad* translation ('He lies, a
lifeless Load, along the Land'), of which Pope commented that the liquids
did 'not make it run on like a river-verse ... 'Tis as the thing described,
nerveless and yet stiff.'[7] The line in the *Iliad*, as Pope reads it, enacts not
flow but an encumbering dead weight: liquidity is arrested by the final
dead stops of 'Load' and 'Land'. Conversely, in the Maeotis couplet, what
'hardly flows' over the line-end audibly hangs momentarily suspended, at
the beginning of the second line, over the ice that awaits it.

The intermediate stage (b) also shows changes to the beginning of the
couplet; and in the change to 'Lo where *Moeotis*', a potentially important
word, 'dull', is lost from 'dull Ma'otis'. Yet although 'dull' is an important
word in a poem whose presiding goddess is Dulness, there may have been
a particular problem in using it here, because 'dull' could denote not only
sluggishness of motion, but also darkness of colour.[8] Once 'dull' is removed,
it is easier to visualise Maeotis as sleeping under ice, matched in with the
surrounding scene of unbroken whiteness. It is also suggestive that in the
miniature anthology of snow poems that Pope compiled in a letter to his
friend Caryll in 1712, prompted by the hard winter of that year, he had
included what he called a 'very *picturesque*' couplet from Ambrose Philips's
celebrated winter piece, the 'Epistle to the Earl of Dorset from Copenhagen',
in which Philips describes how all the usual attractions of landscape are
hidden under 'snow' that forms a prospect of 'waste':

> All hid in snow, in bright confusion lie,
> And with one dazling waste fatigue the eye.[9]

Philips renders the impact of unbroken brilliance not as radiant or uplift-
ing, but as chaotic and glaring (a kind of irony that Pope will often draw

---

[7] Spence, *Observations*, 1, no. 399, p. 175.
[8] *OED*.
[9] *The Correspondence of Alexander Pope*, ed. George Sherburn, 5 vols. (Oxford, 1956), 1. 168.

on in representing even the most inventive of Dulness's projects as point-
less and baleful; and it is particularly ironic to note parallels between
Philips's poem and the freezing and flowing of the *Dunciad*, given how
negative will be Pope's considered view of Philips, and how he will delight
to taunt him with his association with cold, lifeless writing).[10] But the
instance of the 'snow' that forms Philips's 'dazzling waste' certainly demonstrated the kind of effect that might be available without the ambiguous
'dull' of Pope's couplet: by removing it Pope eliminates any visual contrast
that might relieve the eye from the oppressive impact of his own 'waste of
snows'.

At the same time another epithet, this time in the second line of the
couplet, is also rejected. Pope is evidently unhappy with 'frozen Tanais'
(perhaps it seems illogical to claim that a river 'flows', even 'hardly', when it
is 'frozen') and he experiments instead with 'streams of *Tanais*'. But this too
is arguably unhelpful in terms of sense, since 'streams' tends to suggest a
volume and fulness incompatible with the 'hardly flows' of the previous
line. Moreover, being a plural, 'streams' entails losing the final 's' from the
rhyme word, which leaves 'flow' and 'snow' both inappropriately open,
underlining the potential copiousness of 'streams', and removing a particularly prominent pair of sibilants from the couplet's dozy and obstructive
symphony on that consonant.

It is at this point, evidently unhappy with both 'frozen' and 'streams of',
that Pope makes his decisive move towards the published version (c); and
this brings him to the heart of the paradox that he is on his way to articulat-
ing, the problem of the river that is at once flowing and ice-bound. 'Streams',
though now discarded, has perhaps suggested the desirability of an asso-
nance with 'sleeps' in the first line, for Pope's next and final attempt, a par-
tial reversion to his first thought of 'frozen', is 'freezing'. This foregrounds
the process, the liminal moment of movement in and out of the frozen state,
that will henceforth focus the couplet's enactment of obstructed flow.

In effect, once 'freezing' is in place, all the important changes have
been made. This is the form in which the couplet is published in 1728; and
thereafter it changes only in spelling, punctuation and styling. In the last
lifetime *Dunciad*, the *Dunciad in Four Books* of 1743, it appears as:

> Lo! where Maeotis sleeps, and hardly flows
> The freezing Tanais thro' a waste of snows ...[11]

---

[10] For a text of the poem, see David Fairer and Christine Gerrard (eds.), *Eighteenth-Century Poetry:
an Annotated Anthology*, 2nd edn. (Oxford, 2003), pp. 20–1.
[11] Rumbold (ed.), *The Dunciad in Four Books*, III. 87–8.

And, punctuation apart, this is very close to the form in which Johnson gives it:

> Lo, where Moeotis sleeps, and hardly flows
> The freezing Tanais through a waste of snows ...[12]

III

Slight as they may appear, the emphases of sound and sense highlighted by Pope's revisions to this couplet prompt a range of questions about the sources and implications of this imagined landscape of ice and snow. The area is certainly a part of his imaginative repertory as early as 1711, when in *The Critical Specimen*, a counterblast to attacks by John Dennis, Pope was characterising '*Maeotis*' Marsh' as the cold and windswept terrain of predatory birdlife, a fit setting for the 'baneful *Hunch-back'd Toad*, with look Malign' that served for an image of Dennis, waiting to spit his venom at the 'Traveller' whose 'unwary steps' lead him into 'those dark unwholesome, misty Fens'.[13] Here, Pope temporarily places himself, as well as Dennis, in the stagnant chill of Maeotis; but Dennis belongs there: Pope is just a visitor.

A more sustained instance of Pope's early absorption in scenes of snow and ice is the letter he wrote to Caryll in the hard winter of 1712, the letter in which he inserted his anthology of snow poems:

> My ill state of health ever since the cold weather began renders vain any such pleasing thoughts as of the enjoyments of your fireside: I cannot express how thoroughly I'm penetrated by the sharpness of it. I feel no thing alive but my heart and head; and my spirits, like those in a thermometer mount and fall thro' my thin delicate contexture just as the temper of the air is more benign or inclement.[14]

Yet the very experience of cold and restriction leads him to focus on the literary representation of such scenes:

> The severity of the cold has turned my studies to those books, which treat of the descriptions of the Arctic regions, Lapland, Nova Zembla and Spitsberg; deserts of snow, seas of ice and frozen skies might administer some odd kind of shiver-

---

[12] See above, n. 1.

[13] J. Butt *et al.* (eds.), *The Twickenham Edition of the Poems of Alexander Pope*, 11 vols. (London, 1939–69), 6, *Minor Poems*, ed. Norman Ault and John Butt (1964), pp. 79–80.

[14] Sherburn (ed.), *The Correspondence of Alexander Pope*, 1. 165.

ing satisfaction (or as the vulgar have it cold comfort), in the comparison with my own case. This, I say, some people would imagine ...[15]

He then goes on to copy out for Caryll 'several beautiful winter pieces of the poets, which have occurred to my memory on this occasion'; and he goes on:

> These are the scenes the season presents to me, and what can be more ridiculous than that in the midst of this bleak prospect that sets my very imagination a shivering, I am endeavouring to raise up round about me a painted scene of woods and forests in verdure and beauty, trees springing, fields flowering, Nature laughing. I am wandering thro' Bowers and Grottos in conceit, and while my trembling body is cowering o'er a fire, my mind is expatiating in an open sunshine.[16]

The keenness of the young Pope's engagement both with the reading that reflects the harshness of the actual weather and with the contrary task of summoning up the landscape in its summer beauty (probably in relation to prepublication revision of *Windsor Forest*) reflects a power of imaginative projection that, subtly and strategically disorganised as part of what Dulness takes to be a poetic sensibility, will indeed be rendered 'ridiculous' when, in the *Dunciad*, she encourages poets to describe places of whose situation, climate and flora they have only the vaguest idea:

> Here gay Description Aegypt glads with showers,
> Or gives to Zembla fruits, to Barca flow'rs;
> In cold December fragrant chaplets blow,
> And heavy harvests nod beneath the snow.[17]

The rock of ice on which the temple is placed in Pope's Chaucerian dream-vision *The Temple of Fame* (1715), and the comparison to Zembla that it evokes, with its never-setting Arctic sun, its Northern Lights, and its layers of accumulated snow, provides further testimony to Pope's extraordinary imaginative realisation of a sublimity that he had never witnessed and was never likely to witness:

> So *Zembla*'s Rocks (the beauteous Work of Frost)
> Rise white in Air, and glitter o'er the Coast;
> Pale Suns, unfelt, at distance roll away,

---

[15] Ibid., p. 166. For Nova Zembla in relation to Swift's *Battel of the Books*, see Dirk F. Passman and Hermann Real, 'Barbarism, witchcraft, and devil worship: cock-and-bull stories from several remote nations of the world', *Swift Studies*, 23 (2008), 94–110.

[16] Sherburn (ed.), *The Correspondence of Alexander Pope*, 1. 168.

[17] Rumbold (ed.), *The Dunciad in Four Books*, I. 75–8.

> And on th' impassive Ice the Lightnings play:
> Eternal Snows the growing Mass supply,
> Till the bright Mountains prop th' Incumbent Sky:
> As *Atlas* fix'd, each hoary Pile appears,
> The gather'd Winter of a thousand Years.[18]

He was characteristically enthralled, despite the physical fragility that debarred him even from crossing the Irish Sea or the English Channel, by the contrasts of 'Earths wide extreams'; and reading and imagination supplied, to a degree, what travel could not.[19] In particular, he owned an impressive folio atlas of ancient geography, the *Theatri geographiae veteris tomus prior* (1618) by Petrus Bertius, based on Ptolomey (Claudius Ptolemaeus), who, writing about AD 150, cited the work of Marinus of Tyre: images of both Ptolomey and Marinus appear on the engraved title (Fig. 2).[20] The Sea of Azov and the Don are clearly recognisable even on the globe displayed at the foot of the title; and later in the volume they appear in much more detail in the eighth of the fold-out maps devoted to Europe (Fig. 3).[21] On the right-hand side is 'Euxini maris pars' (part of the Black Sea) in the south, with, to the north, the 'Bosphorus Cimmericus' (Cimmerian Bosphorus) leading north into the Palus Maeotis (the Maeotian Marsh, or Sea of Azov); and flowing down into it from the north is the 'Tanais fluvius' (River Tanais, the Don). The image emphasises the status of the Don, which serves as a boundary between 'Sarmatia Europae' (European Sarmatia) and 'Sarmatiae Asiaticae pars' (part of Asian Sarmatia).[22] Not far to the north are the fabled 'Riphei montes' (Riphaean mountains—in the *Memoirs of Martinus Scriblerus* they are singled out by the hero's father as particularly worthy of his personal inspection);[23] and on the eastern bank of the Don are depicted spear-carrying tribesmen, posed with the tents, cart, bundled luggage, cattle and

---

[18] *The Twickenham Edition*, 2, *The Rape of the Lock and Other Poems*, ed. Geoffrey Tillotson (1962), lines 27–8, 53–60.

[19] Rumbold (ed.), *The Poems of Alexander Pope*, 3: *The Dunciad. A Heroic Poem* (1728), III. 63.

[20] For Pope's copy, see 'A Finding List of Books Surviving from Pope's Library with a Few That May Not Have Survived', in Maynard Mack, *Collected in Himself: Essays Critical, Biographical, and Bibliographical on Pope and Some of his Contemporaries* (London, 1982), pp. 394–460, no. 17 (p. 397). For Ptolemy, see J. Oliver Thomson, *History of Ancient Geography* (Cambridge, 1948), pp. 229–30.

[21] Bertius, *Theatri geographiae*, 'Europae tabula octava'.

[22] A map in the Asian sequence of Bertius's atlas shows this same region from the Asian perspective, again emphasising the status of Sarmatia, between the Don and the Vistula, as an intercontinental borderland ('Asiae tabula secunda').

[23] Charles Kerby Miller (ed.), *Memoirs of the Extraordinary Life, Works, and Discoveries of Martinus Scriblerus* (New Haven, CT, 1950), p. 101.

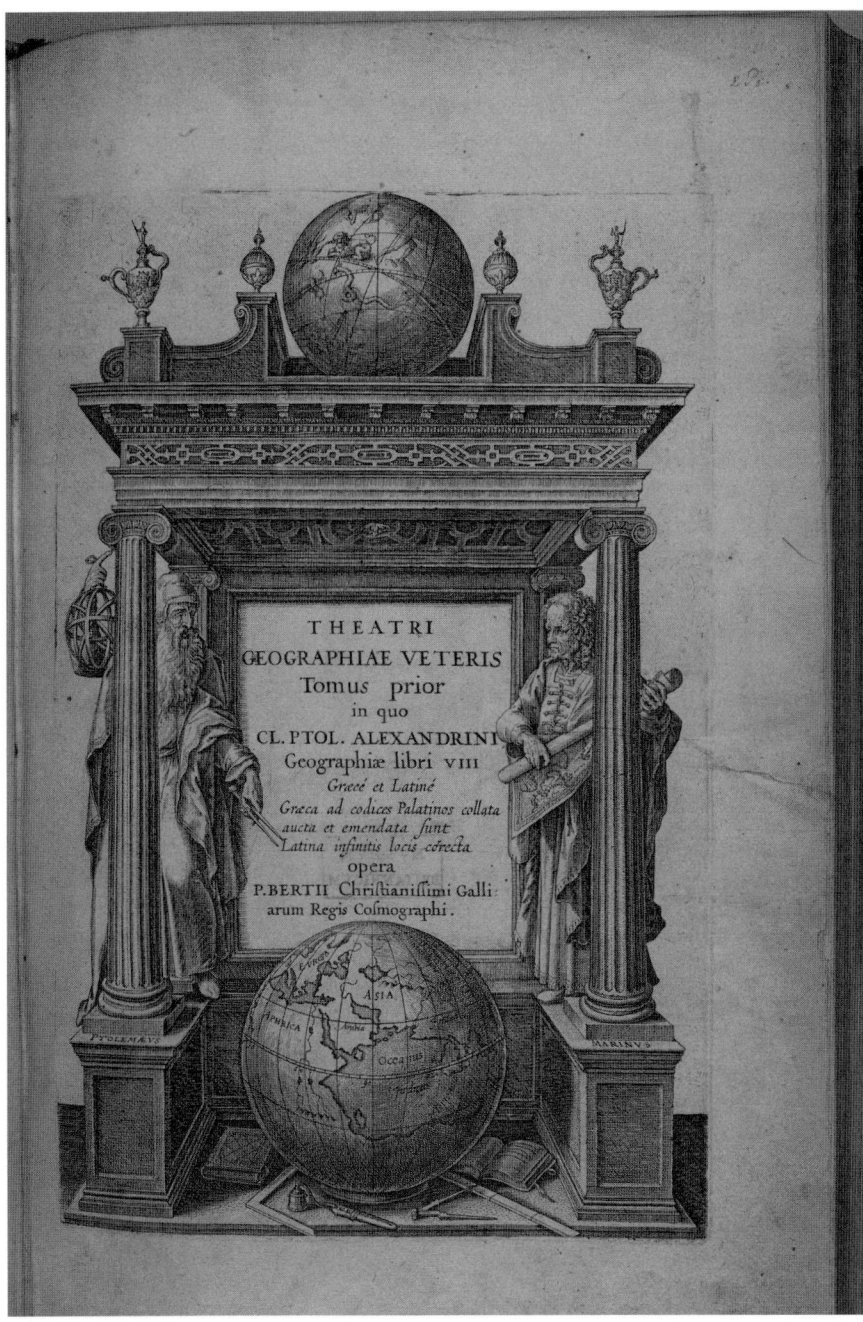

Figure 2. Title page of Petrus Bertius, *Theatri geographiae veteris tomus prior* (1618: British Library 210.h.4, reproduced by kind permission). © The British Library Board.

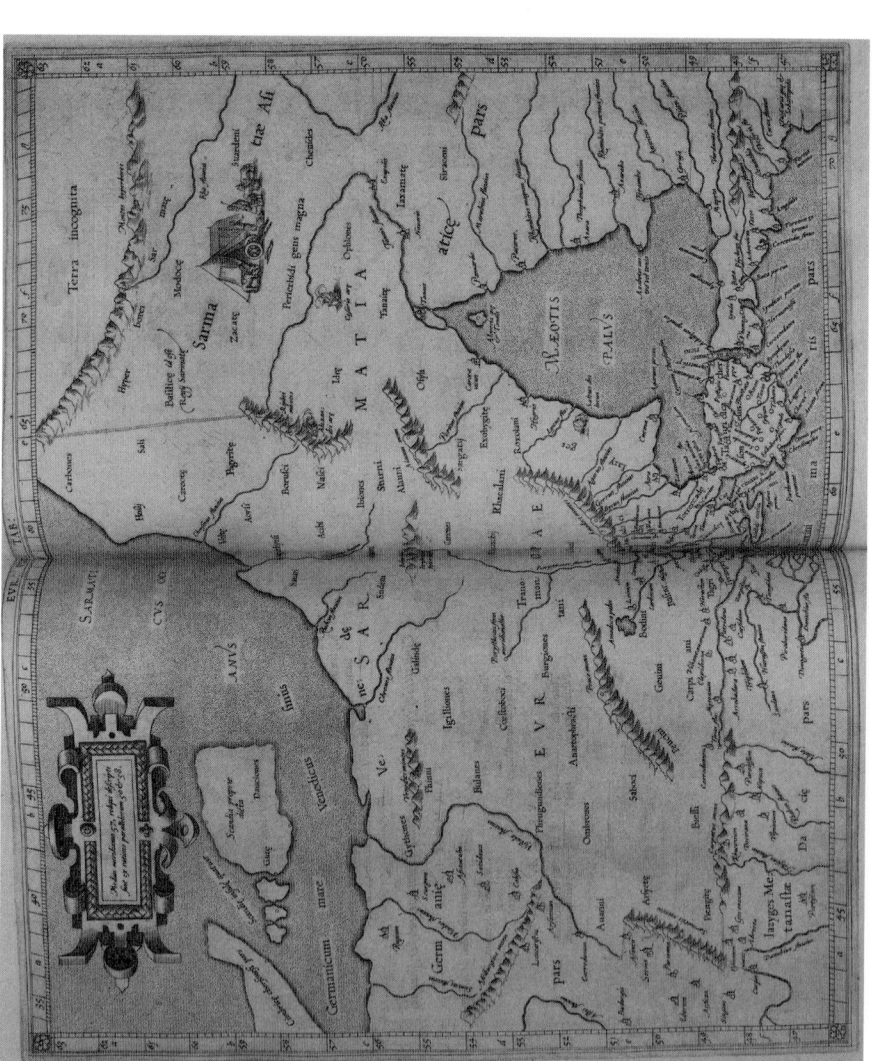

Figure 3. 'Europae tabula octava', from Petrus Bertius, *Theatri geographiae veteris tomus prior* (1618: British Library 210.h.4, reproduced by kind permission). © The British Library Board.

pack animals associated with their nomadic lifestyle. To the north again, it is not far to the 'Montes Hyperborei' (Mountains of the Hyperboreans, the people fabled to live beyond the north wind); and beyond that imposing barrier is nothing but 'Terra incognita' (an unknown land).

IV

There was no shortage of available accounts of this and other icy regions that Pope could have read; but the Roman poets, particularly Virgil and his recent English translators, were evidently particularly crucial in developing this aspect of his imaginative geography. This is plain from an examination of the phrase 'freezing Tanais', the crucial revision by which his supposedly favourite couplet reached its definitive form; for Pope's working towards this phrase reveals a very clear relation to familiar translations from Virgil. The phrase 'freezing Tanais' appears, in fact, to be something of a novelty: before Pope, there are precedents for the discarded phrase 'frozen Tanais', but none have been so far identified for 'freezing Tanais'.[24] Whereas this commoner form, 'frozen Tanais', would simply have represented the end point of freezing, Pope evidently decided, during his revisions, to represent freezing in process; and in so doing he comes very close to a formulation that would have been familiar to him from Dryden's *Sylvae* (1685).[25] In '*Part of* Virgils 4th. *Georgick, Englished by an unknown Hand*' ('A Table of the Poems'), the translator (actually Richard Maitland, later fourth Earl of Lauderdale) describes how Orpheus, having lost Eurydice a second time, roams by the Tanais:

> Alone he wander'd thro' the *Scythian* Snows,
> Where Icy *Tanais* freezeth as it flows ...[26]

[24] See searchable texts in Literature Online <http://lion.chadwyck.co.uk>, Early English Books Online <http://eebo.chadwyck.com/home> and Eighteenth-Century Collections Online <http://find.galegroup.com/ecco>. For 'frozen Tanais', see the first sonnet of 'Urania', by William Drummond of Hawthornden, in *Poems. The Second Impression* (Edinburgh, 1616), 'The Second Part', unpaginated ('From frozen *Tanais* to Sunne-gilded *Gange*'); and *Hippolitus translated out of Seneca by Edmund Prestwich; together with divers other poems of the same authors* (London, 1651), p. 17 ('Such was *Hippolita*, and as she guides | From frozen *Tanais*, and *Maeotis* sides | Her troops to Attick coasts ... | ... even so | Accoutred I, into the woods will goe': this passage is also cited below, see n. 34).

[25] *Sylvae, or, The Second Part of Poetical Miscellanies* (London, 1685).

[26] Ibid., p. 153, translating Virgil, *Georgics*, IV. 517. (This and other citations of Latin verse refer to the texts in the Loeb Classical Library). For Lauderdale's authorship, see *The Works of Virgil, translated into English Verse. By the Right Honourable Richard late Earl of Lauderdale* (London, 1709).

Here, developed from Virgil, is the *idea* of the liminal point between flowing and freezing, spelled out at length by Maitland in the line 'Where icy *Tanais* freezeth as it flows'. (And here also is the rather obvious 'snows' | 'flows' rhyme that Pope will use.) In fact it is Dryden who, in his own later translation of Virgil (which Pope owned in its third edition of 1709), does include the word 'freezing', but applies it to a different river:

> By *Strymon*'s freezing Streams he sate alone …[27]

Dryden's phrasing also brings into play the word 'Streams': in effect, both elements of Dryden's 'freezing Streams' had been considered in the process of Pope's characterisation of the Tanais, with 'freezing' in the end replacing 'Streams'. Furthermore, behind Maitland, Dryden and Pope also stands an account of the hard life of the Scythian inhabitants of this vaguely defined region that occurs earlier in Virgil's *Georgics*, in one of the passages that Pope had anthologised for Caryll in 1712.[28] According to Virgil it is always winter ('semper hiems'); and 'sudden crusts of ice form on the flowing river' ('concrescunt subitae currenti in flumine crustae').[29] Dryden, in rendering the hardships of the Scythian 'who treads the bleak *Meotian* Strand', translates this line as 'Swift Rivers are with sudden Ice constrain'd'.[30] Virgil's evocation of the sudden formation of ice, with its contrast, sharpened by alliteration, between 'currenti' and 'crustae', seems to be picked up in the formulations that Maitland and Dryden bring to the wintry rivers encountered by Orpheus in *Georgics* IV, offering a further precedent for Pope's concern with the liminal moment between motion and stasis, the in-between state in which the 'freezing' current 'hardly flows' through the 'waste of snows'.

It is also suggestive that the Virgilian passage that underlies Pope's 'freezing Tanais' should itself belong to an account of the death of Orpheus, the exemplary and mythic poet, who, having lost Euridice for the second time, wanders in a wintry landscape that mirrors his desolation. From this point of view, Pope's 'freezing Tanais' establishes a connection with a fundamental allusion to the myth of Orpheus in the *Dunciad*.[31] Indeed, among

[27] John Dryden (trans.), *The Works of Virgil … The Third Edition*, 3 vols. (London, 1709), 1. 208: *Georgics*, IV. 738. Pope's copy, which later belonged to Thomas Gray, is British Library C.28.f6: see Mack, 'A Finding List', no. 171, p. 459. The Strimon is on the Thracian/Macedonian border.
[28] Virgil, *Georgics*, III. 349–83; Sherburn (ed.), *The Correspondence of Alexander Pope*, 1. 167.
[29] Virgil, *Georgics*, III. 356, 360.
[30] Dryden, *The Works of Virgil*, 1. 169, *Georgics*, III. 554.
[31] Cp. the epigraph (Rumbold (ed.), *The Dunciad in Four Books*, p. 21), taken from Ovid's account of how, after the murder and dismemberment of Orpheus at the hands of the Maenads, Apollo

the allegations of violence and barbarism routinely made against the inhabitants of the region, the Roman poets laid particular stress on female bloodthirstiness; and Virgil's mention of the Tanais in connection with the Thracian women who dismember Orpheus in their Bacchic rites is just one instance of a well-established association. Ovid, from his exile in Tomis, some way to the south, explains that the Scythian cult of Diana, the moon-goddess, features human sacrifice, and that it is the specific role of well-born Scythian virgins to put strangers to death.[32] He also associates the area with the murderous Medea.[33] Horace too combines the notion of the Tanais as the limit of the known world with its association with female savagery; and both Seneca and Statius describe the area as the abode of fearsome Amazons.[34] Maeotis and the Tanais not only set limits to the Roman world, but also associated those limits with spectacularly bloody female transgressions against civilised custom.

This association also tends to align the region, in ways that Pope would not have had to spell out for his classically educated readers, with the dubious female cults and moon divinities so comprehensively shadowed in his creation, for the myth of the *Dunciad*, of his presiding goddess Dulness. Named in the first line of the poem as 'The Mighty Mother', she is associated by the poem's networks of mythological allusion with Aeneas's mother Venus, with the Great Mother Cybele worshipped in Asia Minor, with the Egyptian Isis, with the Greek patroness of agriculture Demeter and the Roman Ceres, and with Hecate, the goddess of the dead worshipped as a sinister aspect of the moon goddess Diana.[35] The reputation of Maeotis and the Tanais thus underlines the centrality of these mysterious and potentially sinister female cults to Pope's characterisation of his presiding goddess.

---

intervened to stop a serpent from devouring the dismembered poet's head. For a broadly positive interpretation in terms of the role of the head in providing for the continuance of poetry through its burial on Lesbos, see John V. Regan, 'Orpheus and the *Dunciad*'s narrator', *Eighteenth-Century Studies*, 9 (1975), 87–101; and for a darker reading, Howard Erskine-Hill's 'Pope's Epigraphic Practice' (forthcoming), discerning 'an affinity between Orpheus and the singer of the *Dunciad* as each sweeps into darkness'. For another comparison with Orpheus, see the episode of Doll's decapitation by falling through the frozen Thames in Gay's *Trivia*: Clare Brant and Susan E. Whyman (eds.), *Walking the Streets of Eighteenth-Century London: John Gay's Trivia (1716)* (Oxford, 2007), p. 188 (*Trivia*, II. 389–98).

[32] *Ex Ponto*, III. ii. 55–60; cp. *Tristia*, IV. iv. 63–4, 67–8.

[33] *Tristia*, III. ix. 33–4; *Heroides* VI. 107–8.

[34] Horace, *Odes*, III. x. i. 1–4. Seneca, *Hercules Furens*, 533–46; *Hippolytus*, 399–403. Statius, *Thebaid*, XII. 526; *Achilleid*, I. 758–60.

[35] Rumbold (ed.), *The Dunciad in Four Books*, p. 89.

Another vital aspect is the area's reputation for perpetual cold: though it actually enjoys warm summers, Virgil had claimed that it is 'always winter', and Ovid, lamenting his exile to the very ends of the earth, sees nothing to the north but uninhabitable cold.[36] The icy sea also offered an image for stasis: when Lucan describes Caesar's ships becalmed in a motionless sea, it is the frozen Maeotis that he invokes as a comparison: here, the absence of even a breath of wind suggests lack of inspiration in its most literal sense.[37] For the Christian reader this is also the antithesis of that primal scene of creation in which 'the Spirit of God moved upon the face of the waters', further intensifying the association between Maeotis and lack of creativity (Genesis 1.2). 'Cold' was in Pope's time a familiar term of dismissal for weak or uninteresting writing, further supporting the alignment of ice-bound landscape with blighted creativity.[38] (This imagery also recalls the 'lazy Lake' unpromisingly placed 'In fam'd *Hibernia* on the *Northern* Main' that Blackmore had chosen as the headquarters of his own temple of Dulness in his poem *The Kit-Cats*, the precursor of the *Dunciad* to which David Womersley drew our attention in his 2004 Warton Lecture.[39])

Yet another and perhaps more surprising angle on threats to poetry and the civilised order is suggested by Juvenal's episode of the monster turbot officiously presented to the emperor in *Satire* IV, which refers, for a comparison, to the apparently proverbial size of fish overwintered under the ice of Maeotis.[40] (And we may recall the venom-swollen toad of Maeotis to which Pope had likened Dennis, who 'swells his bloated Corps to largest size'.[41]) Ovid had written memorably about watching the fish trapped alive in the ice, inviting readers to make the analogy with his own confinement in exile; and Juvenal's sense of the ice as a trap in which fish grow fat and sluggish suggests another kind of threat to creativity.[42]

In the translation of Juvenal published by Dryden in 1693, this satire had been translated by his friend Richard Duke:

[36] Ovid, *Tristia*, III. ivb. 51–2.
[37] Lucan, *Pharsalia*, V. 436–46.
[38] Cp. *Tatler* no. 254 for words supposedly freezing as soon as uttered in Nova Zembla (*The Tatler*, ed. Donald F. Bond, 3 vols. (Oxford, 1987), 3. 288–92, and for earlier analogues, n. 10, p. 292).
[39] David Womersley, 'Dulness and Pope', *Proceedings of the British Academy*, 131: *2004 Lectures* (Oxford, 2005), pp. 229–50 at 245.
[40] Juvenal, *Satires*, IV. 37–44.
[41] See above, n. 13.
[42] Ovid, *Tristia*, III. x. 49–50.

> Where *Venus* Shrine does fair *Ancona* grace,
> A Turbut taken of prodigious Space,
> Fill'd the extended Net, not less than those
> That dull *Maeotis* does with Ice enclose,
> Till conquer'd by the Sun's prevailing Ray,
> It opens to the *Pontick* Sea their way;
> And throws them out unweildy with their Growth,
> Fat with long ease, and a whole Winter's sloth.[43]

(It is noteworthy, by the way, that Duke here uses the phrase 'dull *Maeotis*', which had been included in Pope's early draft of his couplet, but was discarded during revision.) Duke also comments on the flattering terms in which the huge fish is presented to the emperor:

> How fulsom this! how gross! yet this takes well,
> And the vain Prince with empty Pride does swell.[44]

This is all too reminiscent of a description of the king of the dunces that Pope had drafted for the *Dunciad*, but never published in any version of the poem, since it reflected so obviously on the similiarities between Dulness's chosen king and George II himself: the king of the dunces is characterised by 'His Strut his Grin, and his dead Stare' and 'his stupid Eye', and is surrounded by a 'Laurelld Train' of poetic flatterers, as 'With Kingly Joy he hears their Loyal Lies'.[45] Although the fat fish of Maeotis evokes a threat to civilised culture very different from that of the female violence that befell Orpheus, it is one undeniably relevant to Pope's vision of England under George II.

V

When we come to relate Pope's couplet on Maeotis and the Tanais to the poem of which it forms part (and I shall be referring throughout to the poem in its final lifetime form, *The Dunciad in Four Books* of 1743), it becomes clear that the three actions of sleeping, freezing and flowing are crucial to his imagining of what Dulness is and does in the world. Sleeping

---

[43] *The Satires of Decimus Junius Juvenalis: and of Aulus Persius Flaccus. Translated into English Verse by Mr. Dryden and other Eminent Hands. To which is Prefix'd a Discourse concerning the Original and Progress of Satir* [sic] ... *The Fourth Edition* (London, 1711): Juvenal, *Satires*, IV. 150–1. For Pope's copy of Dryden's Juvenal, see Mack, 'A Finding List', no. 102, p. 422.
[44] *The Satires of Decimus Junius Juvenalis*, p. 153, translating Juvenal, *Satires*, IV. 69–71.
[45] Rumbold (ed.), *The Dunciad in Four Books*, p. 148.

and freezing, while each replete with a different range of literal and metaphorical potential, work in this particular couplet as parallel terms for
inactivity:

> Lo! where Maeotis sleeps, and hardly flows
> The freezing Tanais thro' a waste of snows ...[46]

Sleeping is characteristically associated in the *Dunciad*s with torpor rather
than refreshment: Claude Rawson aptly contrasts it with what he calls 'the
hearty sleep of heroes', the refreshing and well-earned sleep enjoyed by
Homer's heroes.[47] Falling asleep out of laziness, boredom or futile exhaustion is what characters in the poem literally do on several occasions; and
it is also what other entities, including other bodies of water like Maeotis,
are said to do metaphorically: indeed, when characters sleep literally in
the poem, they enact in allegory the metaphor of sleep as inactivity. In
addition, the habitual sleep of babies and the final sleep of death are both
specifically invoked in the poem as aspects of the state into which Dulness,
characterised as an irresponsible nurse or mother, invites her protégés to
relapse. Freezing, however, apart from its relation to the warm/cold contrast conventionally applied to creativity or its absence (which Pope draws
on more than once in the poem), works in this particular couplet to suggest the fragility of motion, the instant-by-instant risk of losing momentum and lapsing into stasis; and in this respect the trickling of almost
frozen water into a shallow, silty sea is emblematic of the obstruction that
literally congests other bodies of water in the poem, and metaphorically
afflicts entities that can be likened to such bodies of water.

Flowing, on the other hand, is different. Because of the inversion of
verb and subject in Pope's description of the Tanais, 'flows' intervenes
between 'sleeps' and 'freezing', opening up, with an open vowel emphasised
by enjambement, a sense of space beween the repeated narrow 'ee' of the
two words associated with torpor, cold and inertia:

> Lo! where Maeotis sleeps, and hardly flows
> The freezing Tanais thro' a waste of snows ...[48]

Flowing would thus seem, at first sight, to be the positive term between
two negatives, with the implication that to be torpid, cold and inert is bad,

[46] Rumbold (ed.), *The Dunciad in Four Books*, III. 87–8.
[47] Claude Rawson, 'The Sleep of the Dunces', in David Womersley and Richard McCabe (eds.),
Literary Milieux: Essays in Text and Context Presented to Howard Erskine-Hill (Newark, DE,
2008), pp. 258–83 (pp. 258, 270).
[48] Rumbold (ed.), *The Dunciad in Four Books*, III. 87–8.

while the energy of flow is good. After all, Denham had in a famous and much-imitated passage from his poem *Cooper's Hill* made the flow of the Thames a model for good writing:

> O could I flow like thee, and make thy stream
> My great example, as it is my theme!
> Though deep, yet clear, Though gentle, yet not Dull;
> Strong without rage, without ore-flowing, full.[49]

But it is equally well known what Pope makes of this in his *Dunciad*:

> Flow Welsted, flow! like thine inspirer, Beer,
> Tho' stale, not ripe; tho' thin, yet never clear;
> So sweetly mawkish, and so smoothly dull;
> Heady; not strong; o'erflowing, tho' not full.[50]

The power of flow as an enabling image of creativity is here radically undercut—as we might expect in a poem that, whatever its beauty, complexity and mystery, has satire at its heart. (Indeed, David Fairer's sense of the centrality of mud and slime to Pope's imagery of Dulness is highly relevant here.[51]) Flowing is thus not always good. It depends what is flowing and how. So to succumb to the encouraging thought of flow as an enabling metaphor, a positive allusion, whether to the spring of Helicon or to the reviving and sanctifying waters of Scripture, may be to risk tumbling into the irony that Pope holds open for our perplexity in the very setting up of his poem, the irony by which, although torpor is the final end of Dulness's perverse providence, the often frenetic activity of the poem's human characters is not an opposite but merely a contributory force, advancing only the causes of perversity, exhaustion and entropy.[52] For

---

[49] *The Poetical Works of Sir John Denham*, ed. Theodore Howard Banks, 2nd edn. (Hamden, CT, 1969), 'Cooper's Hill', lines 189–92.

[50] Rumbold (ed.), *The Dunciad in Four Books*, III. 169–72.

[51] David Fairer, *Pope's Imagination* (Manchester, 1984), pp. 113–52; see also index under 'Imagination' and 'Sleep and dreams'. Cp. also Patricia Meyer Spacks, *An Argument of Images* (Cambridge, MA, 1972), for 'the image of life as a river' as one of Pope's reworkings of 'traditional, even hackneyed images' (pp. 2–4); also for the *Dunciad*'s 'elaborate structure of physical images for moral conditions' (p. 86); and for its 'lack of clarity about where description stops and metaphor begins' (p. 108).

[52] Cp., on entropy, Thomas Robert Edwards, *This Dark Estate: a Reading of Pope* (Berkeley, CA, 1963): the dunces 'yield happily to the tendency of life to run downhill towards darkness, sameness and sleep' (pp. 127–30). John E. Sitter, *The Poetry of Pope's Dunciad* (London, 1971), draws on the notion of circularity: 'images of circular motion ... become an important means of resolving a conceptual paradox—namely, that the dunces exhibit a nonproductive energy (one which does not "go anywhere") and yet are part of an energy which progresses steadily like the

Dulness, in a formulation that Pope's authorised editor, William Warburton, evidently found sufficiently paradoxical to require explanation, is introduced to us at the outset not simply as idle or lazy, but as 'Laborious, heavy, busy, bold and blind.'[53] Perhaps anticipating the criticism that Pope is arbitrarily assigning everything he dislikes, whether inert or active, idle or productive, derivative or inventive, to the realm of Dulness, Warburton insists:

> Dulness here is not to be taken contractedly for mere Stupidity, but in the enlarged sense of the word, for all Slowness of Apprehension, Shortness of Sight, or imperfect Sense of things. It includes (as we see by the Poet's own words) Labour, Industry, and some degree of Activity and Boldness: a ruling principle not inert, but turning topsy-turvy the Understanding, and inducing an Anarchy or confused State of Mind. This remark ought to be carried along with the reader throughout the work; and without this caution he will be apt to mistake the Importance of many of the Characters, as well as of the Design of the Poet.[54]

Pope's verse relentlessly stages what he seeks to ridicule as the futility of exertions, however heroic in scale and cost, that end only in the boredom, exhaustion and, ultimately, sleep into which Dulness lulls her followers. Indeed, there is a precedent for part of the passage in which he embeds his couplet on Maeotis and the Tanais that points this irony particularly. In Pope's account

> The North by myriads pours her mighty sons,
> Great nurse of Goths, of Alans, and of Huns![55]

This pouring, like the 'freezing Tanais', defies the apparently ice-bound landscape, but the personification of the paradoxically prolific North as 'Great nurse' echoes the sinister awe evoked by Milton's headcount of fallen angels:

> A multitude, like which the populous north
> Poured never from her frozen loins, to pass
> Rhene or the Danaw, when her barbarous sons
> Came like a deluge on the south.[56]

"nutation" at the close of Book II. Metaphors of circularity serve, in other words, to characterize physically both the centrifugal energy and centripetal attraction of Dulness' (pp. 37–8).
[53] Rumbold (ed.), *The Dunciad in Four Books*, I. 15.
[54] Ibid. I. 15, n.
[55] Ibid. III. 89–90.
[56] *John Milton: Paradise Lost*, ed. Alastair Fowler, 2nd edn. (Harlow, 1998), I. 351–4.

This pouring of offspring from the 'frozen loins' of the north offers an analogy not only for the ambivalent relation between stasis and movement articulated in Pope's vision of Maeotis and Tanais, but also for his characterisation of Dulness as both inert and destructively busy.

There is almost no end to the detailed reflections that might arise from a close reading of the poem's four books in terms of sleeping, flowing and freezing, and for the purposes of this lecture a few striking instances must suffice. The invocation at the beginning of Book I immediately invokes sleeping and flowing:

> Say how the Goddess bade Britannia sleep,
> And pour'd her Spirit o'er the land and deep.[57]

This torpid sleep reverses the Biblical figure in which spirit, like water, is 'pour'd' in creation and inspiration. Freezing is also associated with Dulness near the beginning of the poem, as she sponsors 'gay Description' that 'gives to Zembla fruits' in defiance of its freezing climate.[58]

Flowing and sleeping are again associated as the Thames is introduced by way of the Lord Mayor's procession by 'land and wave'; and later the city dignitaries doze after their feast, while poets attempt in vain to engage readers in their commemoration of the festivities:

> Now May'rs and Shrieves all hush'd and satiate lay,
> Yet eat, in dreams, the custard of the day;
> While pensive Poets painful vigils keep,
> Sleepless themselves, to give their readers sleep.[59]

Water is metaphorically invoked when the hero, Bays (based on the Poet Laureate, Colley Cibber), is introduced sinking, plunging and floundering in his own incompetence; and Pope focuses the traditional equation of coldness with lack of creativity by having Dulness extinguish the bonfire of his works with the sheets of Ambrose Philips's unfinished poem 'Thule', whose frozen subject and contemptible quality render it particularly fit for use as a literary fire blanket.[60]

Dulness then declares her ambition to fatten up favourites like Bays (recalling the proverbially overgrown fish of Maeotis?) and lull the nation

---

[57] Rumbold (ed.), *The Dunciad in Four Books*, I. 7–8.

[58] Ibid. I. 7–8.

[59] Ibid. I. 86; I. 94.

[60] Ibid. I. 118–20; I. 258, n. Philips had also associated himself with ice and snow in his 'Winter Piece' (see above, pp. 428–9).

into infantile sleep—sleep like that induced by listening to Bays's official Odes:

> O! when shall rise a Monarch all our own,
> And I, a Nursing-mother, rock the throne ...
> Fatten the Courtier, starve the learned band,
> And suckle Armies, and dry-nurse the land;
> 'Till Senates nod to Lullabies divine,
> And all be sleep, as at an Ode of thine.[61]

Finally, Book I invokes congested flow when it likens the newly chosen king Bays to the log that Zeus gave the frogs who, in Aesop's fable, asked for a king. The log plummets into their swamp with a gratifyingly loud splash; and it is evidently going to take a while for King Log's delighted subjects to realise that the rest of his reign will be characterised by absolute inactivity:

> Loud thunder to its bottom shook the bog,
> And the hoarse nation croak'd, God save King Log![62]

Book II of the *Dunciad* is full of the lakes and streams in which Dulness's supporters, summoned to celebrate her election of Bays, disport themselves in parodies of the heroic games of classical epic. Notably, fluids are constantly flowing over or out of the bookseller Edmund Curll. In the pillory he receives the 'Golden show'rs' that the 'Public pours' on him.[63] In the booksellers' sprint he slips in the contents of his alleged mistress's chamber-pot, the 'lake, | Which Curl's Corinna chanc'd that morn to make'.[64] Indeed, the reason he is running in the first place is his desire to recruit a phantom poet who has definite affinities to the fat fish of Maeotis: this prize plagiarist is 'plump, full-fed', and much more desirable to Curll than any 'meagre, muse-rid mope, adust and thin'.[65] When Curl prays it is to the goddess of the sewers, where he 'fish'd her nether realms for wit, | List'ning delighted to the jest unclean | Of link-boys vile, and watermen obscene'.[66] Finally, the bedspread he wins commemorates Pope's punishment of his sharp practice by tricking him into swallowing an emetic: in the tapestry, like the river of some perverted pastoral idyll, shall 'the fresh

---

[61] Rumbold (ed.), *The Dunciad in Four Books*, I. 311–12, 315–18.
[62] Ibid. I. 329–30.
[63] Ibid. II. 3–4.
[64] Ibid. II. 70–1.
[65] Ibid. II. 37.
[66] Ibid. II. 99–101.

vomit run for ever green'.[67] Characteristically, when it comes to the pissing competition, it is 'shameless Curll' who successfully emulates the River Po: 'impetuous spread | The stream, and smoking flourish'd o'er his head'.[68]

When Dulness suggests a diving competition in the Fleet Ditch, an open sewer, Pope's language recalls the great rivers of ancient epic:

> ... Fleet-ditch with desemboguing streams
> Rolls the large tribute of dead dogs to Thames,
> The King of dykes! than whom no sluice of mud
> With deeper sable blots the silver flood.[69]

By diving in, competitor after competitor illustrates the analogy between party writing and sewage; but a particular distinction is reserved for Blackmore, whose tub-thumping epics in the Whig cause have already won him the noise-making competition; and now he reduces the river to a stasis that anticipates Pope's couplet on Maeotis and the Tanais:

> No noise, no stir, no motion can'st thou make,
> Th'unconscious stream sleeps o'er thee like a lake.[70]

The last prize of Book II is for staying awake during the reading of boring authors; and sleeping and flowing are brought together as the image of excrement dumped into water enacts the inevitable onset of sleep:

> As what a Dutchman plumps into the lakes,
> One circle first, and then a second makes;
> What Dulness dropt among her sons imprest
> Like motion from one circle to the rest;
> So from the mid-most the nutation spreads
> Round and more round, o'er all the sea of heads.[71]

As night falls, competitors are found either dead drunk in the street ('inspir'd beside a sink' or sewer) or in the Fleet prison, here ironically called 'Haunt of the Muses': the polluted Fleet river, like the sinks or sewers that drain the refuse of the streets into it, is a wry reminder of the Muses' Helicon.[72]

---

[67] Ibid. II. 156.
[68] Ibid. II. 161–90, 179–80.
[69] Ibid. II. 271–4.
[70] Ibid. II. 303–4.
[71] Ibid. II. 405–10. For the complex and controverted history of the image, see authorial and editorial commentary, ibid., pp. 208–9.
[72] Ibid. II. 425–8.

If Book II is Pope's book of polluted waters, then Book III is the book of dubiously inspired sleep. At the opening Dulness lulls Bays on her lap and sprinkles him 'with Cimmerian dew' (the fabled Cimmerians supposedly lived north of Tanais in perpetual darkness); and the effect of this 'dew' is that 'raptures high the seat of Sense o'erflow', flooding Bays's brain with the dreams which constitute the substance of the book.[73] Another kind of narcotic is introduced when 'Shadwell nods the Poppy on his brows', an allusion that will be repeated when the poppy is identified as part of the heritage to be bestowed on Bays.[74] But already he can be hailed as 'born to see what none can see awake', from having been many times dipped into Lethe's 'oblivious Lake'.[75]

In this book Bays learns that Dulness has ruled most of the world for most of history, and this vision provides the context within which Pope places his couplet on Maoetis and Tanais.[76] Bays is invited to

> See Christians, Jews, one heavy Sabbath keep,
> And all the western world believe and sleep.[77]

Streams and springs no longer to be relied on for inspiration are invoked throughout this book: there are, for instance, the poets of the spa towns 'Whose tuneful whistling makes the waters pass', recalling the pissing competition of Book II; there is the memory of Denham's Thames, now cancelled in favour of Welstead's beer; and the book closes with the degeneration of the educational establishments on the banks of the rivers Thames and Isis.[78]

It is Book IV which, as the poem prepares to end in the world's return to Chaos and Night, engages most explicitly with the implications of 'hardly flows | The freezing Tanais', of motion barely faltering towards final stasis. The narrator begs 'Yet, yet a moment ...', knowing that the most that can be hoped for is a brief respite: 'Suspend a while your Force inertly strong, | Then take at once the Poet and the Song'.[79] Dulness ascends the throne, and 'Soft on her lap her Laureat son reclines', prompting an authorial note on the appropriateness to the poem of a hero who is asleep more often than not, and is entirely content to let Dulness act for

---

[73] Rumbold (ed.), *The Dunciad in Four Books*, III. 4–5.
[74] Ibid. III. 22, 317.
[75] Ibid. III. 43–6.
[76] Ibid. III. 87–8.
[77] Ibid. III. 99–100.
[78] Ibid. III. 155–6, 169–72, 335–8.
[79] Ibid. IV. 1–8.

him: 'he hath done little or nothing from the day of his Anointing', Pope remarks, noting provocatively that 'many *King-consorts* have done the like'.[80]

Rivers again feature in relation to the abandonment of intellectual activity: the university rivers Cam and Isis are called on to preach up divine right; and the gathering of academics in 'a sable shoal' suggests fish and sea; then we hear of 'the streams that murm'ring fall | To lull the sons of Marg'ret and Clare-hall'; and in them Richard Bentley—like the great fish of Maeotis mentioned by Juvenal—no longer sports 'tempestuous' but 'sleeps in Port'.[81] Even the young men who escape from English universities and embark on the Grand Tour are led by the great rivers of the Seine and Tiber only into the sleep of indulgence and absolutism:

> To where the Seine, obsequious as she runs,
> Pours at great Bourbon's feet her silken sons;
> Or Tyber, now no longer Roman, rolls,
> Vain of Italian Arts, Italian Souls:
> To happy Convents, bosom'd deep in vines,
> Where slumber Abbots, purple as their wines ...
> But chief her shrine where naked Venus keeps,
> And Cupids ride the Lyon of the Deeps;
> Where, eas'd of Fleets, the Adriatic main
> Wafts the smooth Eunuch and enamour'd swain.[82]

As the book moves towards its final sequence, the prophetic Silenus is found snoring, until woken for his speech.[83] The link with the wasteland of Maeotis and the Tanais is again recalled by Pope's play on 'Cibberian forehead, or Cimmerian gloom', offering as alternatives only the brazen face of Colley Cibber, Bays's real-life original, or the darkness beyond the Tanais inhabited by the fabled Cimmerians.[84]

When Dulness yawns ('More she had spoke, but yawn'd—All Nature nods: | What Mortal can resist the Yawn of Gods?'), the final sleep that comes upon the world recapitulates in earnest what was done in game in the staying-awake competition at the end of Book III; and the connection is marked by an echo, 'wide, and more wide', of the image of excrement being dumped into water.[85] The narrator asks the Muse—a notably infrequent

[80] Ibid. IV. 20 and notes.
[81] Ibid. IV. 187–8, 199–200.
[82] Ibid. IV. 297–310.
[83] Ibid. IV. 492.
[84] Ibid. IV. 532.
[85] Ibid. IV. 605–6, 613.

participant in this poem—to fill in as best she can in the brief moment before creation lapses; but even her song can at this juncture be only a lullaby: 'O sing, and hush the Nations with thy Song!'[86] 'The all-composing Hour' has indeed arrived, a universal lights-out when even 'The Muse obeys the Pow'r'.[87] The closing lines are introduced by mention of the northern murderess Medea, associated with the freezing landscape of Tanais by Ovid, and of the 'everlasting rest' imposed by magic on the watchful eyes of Argus.[88] Here are freezing and sleeping; but nothing 'flows', even 'hardly', as fires and lights are extinguished and Dulness 'lets the curtain fall' on the 'universal darkness' of Chaos and Night.[89] (Claude Rawson indeed suggests that Pope's 'culminating stroke … was to get rid of sleep altogether', by removing from the finale of the poem any lingering sense of sleep as renewal or refreshment, and emphasising instead the permanence of 'Universal Darkness'.[90]) For all the busyness of Dulness and her agents in maintaining what appears to be some kind of flow, Pope insists that such activity ends only in entropy.

VI

But, in 1743, when this final version was published, such a judgement could perhaps also have been turned against the author and his poem. After a decade and a half of working around the fixed points of George II and of Walpole, with Queen Caroline suggestively shadowed by Dulness herself, Pope does not radically rewrite when Caroline dies in 1737 or when Walpole resigns in 1742, before the first, separate publication of what in 1743 would appear as Book IV of the revised poem. Maynard Mack argued that Pope, freed from fear of Walpole, responded in that new book with satire of 'unparalleled specificity and boldness'; but it might also be argued that, in Pope's view, Walpole's system had effected damage that would persist long after he himself was gone (and Pope was, by the 1740s, markedly sceptical of Patriot promises of reform).[91] In the

---

[86] Rumbold (ed.), *The Dunciad in Four Books*, IV. 626.

[87] Ibid. IV. 627–8.

[88] Ibid. IV. 635, 637–8.

[89] Ibid. IV. 655.

[90] Rawson, 'The Sleep of the Dunces', pp. 280–1.

[91] Maynard Mack, *The Garden and the City: Retirement and Politics in the Later Poetry of Pope* (Toronto, 1969), pp. 150–62. Cp. Christine Gerrard, *The Patriot Opposition to Walpole: Politics, Poetry, and National Myth, 1725–1742* (Oxford, 1994), pp. 90–5.

poem itself, the novelty of Walpole's absence seems to be noted in a brief play on Edward Young's compliment to him as Palinurus: as the final sleep engulfs the centres of power, the narrator notes that 'Ev'n Palinurus nodded at the helm'.[92] This time, Walpole is set in no complimentary contrast with Aeneas's helmsman (who fell asleep at his post and fell into the sea).[93] Pope's Palinurus instead reverts to his Virgilian origins: he is nodding, and presumably about to fall; and, as Howard Erskine-Hill has suggested, this image could be read as doing 'a kind of honour to the great Prime Minister', if only in the sense that without Walpole 'the political world is left with neither direction nor life'.[94]

Yet if one had set out to imagine, from scratch, a myth of the national culture in 1742 or 1743, it seems unlikely that it would have been one so firmly posited on a trinity of king, queen and minister that harked back to the 1730s. In terms of the wider culture too, some of the issues not substantively engaged even in the final *Dunciad in Four Books* are striking: although in 1743 Colley Cibber, Laureate since 1730, is finally enthroned as hero of the poem, there are arguably deeper shifts in the world of literature that are not addressed. After long experiment in manuscript, Pope never included in any version of the *Dunciad* any substantive appraisal of the contribution of women to the published literature of his age: Aphra Behn, indeed, passes entirely unmentioned. Women writers, notably Eliza Haywood, are occasionally satirised, but not as part of any focused engagement with the issues their works might pose for a traditional conception of literature.[95] Indeed, by the early 1740s, the absence from *The Dunciad in Four Books* of prose fiction as a generic focus for change begins to be distinctly noticeable. In effect, the final lifetime *Dunciad* of 1743 still manifested origins that by this time lay rather a long way back, not only in the controversies of the 1720s and 1730s, but also in the late seventeenth-century Battle of the Ancients and the Moderns, whose lingering and constantly renewed reverberation in Pope's work keeps faith with much older friends like Atterbury and Swift for whom it had actually been a formative experience.[96] And it would be unrealistic to expect of a poet who had never

[92] Rumbold (ed.), *The Dunciad in Four Books*, IV. 614.

[93] Ibid., editorial notes on IV. 607, 614.

[94] Howard Erskine-Hill, *Poetry of Opposition and Revolution, Dryden to Wordsworth* (Oxford, 1996), p. 108.

[95] Valerie Rumbold, 'Women writers (not) in Pope's *Dunciads*', *Review of English Studies*, 52 (2001), 524–39.

[96] Rumbold (ed.), *The Dunciad in Four Books*, pp. 3–4, 7–9, 11–12.

been physically strong, and who had only a year to live when he published *The Dunciad in Four Books*, that he would so late in the day undertake a radical reimagining of what had become the major satiric project of his maturity. Indeed, at the opening of the fourth book, when the narrator invites Chaos and Night, as soon as this last book is completed, to 'take at once the Poet and the Song', we may sense that the author too entertains thoughts of the speedy extinction both of his own life, and of the poem over which he has laboured so long.[97]

<h1 style="text-align:center">VII</h1>

The anecdote that Johnson records may, of course, be misleading or mistaken; but even if it is, the layers of development that it invites us to explore are nonetheless suggestive. The record of Pope's revisions to this couplet shows how patiently and artfully he tuned even the tiniest unit for expression, and how integrally his adjustment of sound was related to development of sense. The way in which, as he shaped this couplet, he negotiated its verbal and thematic relation to the poetry he knew reminds us how productively imagined was his engagement with verse both ancient and modern. Johnson's anecdote, moreover, has the merit of fixing our attention on the detail of a passage that might otherwise be overlooked, perhaps dismissed as only a bit of background scenery, and very much a poor relation to some of the famously witty couplets so often cited as evidence of Pope's genius. Yet, if Johnson was correctly informed, 'the couplet by which he declared his own ear to be most gratified was *this*' (my italics), a couplet that makes its effects rather subtly, but makes them in a way that connects powerfully with the larger structures of the *Dunciad* and with the wider network of images and ideas brought to bear in that poem. None of us, in the absence of the poet's own testimony, can claim, any more than Johnson, to have discovered 'the reason of this preference'; but we can at least begin to suggest some reasons that would make it a comprehensible choice.

---

[97] Rumbold (ed.), *The Dunciad in Four Books*, IV. 8.

Note. I should like to thank my colleagues in the Restoration, Eighteenth-Century and Romantics research cluster in the English Department at the University of Birmingham for their tolerance and support during the preparation of this lecture. I should also like to express particular gratitude to Daniel Cooke, Howard Erskine-Hill, Tom Lockwood, Richard McCabe, James McLaverty, Pat Rogers, Adam Rounce, Kate Rumbold, David Vander Meulen, Margaret Small and David Womersley.

Donne, By Hand

TOM LOCKWOOD
The University of Birmingham

'WHY NOT DO DONNE—an edition and Life—for the Clarendon Press?'
With this letter of 1906 from W. A. Raleigh, newly installed in the new
chair in English Literature at the University of Oxford, to H. J. C. Grierson,
the first Professor of English at the University of Aberdeen, began a new
phase in the afterlife of John Donne's poetry.[1] The edition that Grierson
produced, *The Poems of John Donne*, published as a two-volume set by the
Clarendon Press in Oxford in 1912, decisively reshaped Donne for the
twentieth century as a manuscript poet and as a university poet.[2] Those
two claims—one about the material forms in which the texts of Donne's
verse circulated, and another about its institutional contexts—will be
explored in this lecture through an account of the making and the influence of Grierson's edition. What that exploration reveals, as I will argue,
is that his edition was made and conceived within what was, on the one
hand, a continuing manuscript culture and, on the other, the developing
institutional and intellectual culture of a new subject: university English.

This reshaping and relocation of Donne at the start of the twentieth
century is (of course) just one of the many through which his life and writings have passed; literary history is (among other things) the history of

---

Read at the Academy as part of British Academy Literature Week, 19–22 October 2009.

[1] W. A. Raleigh–H. J. C. Grierson, 11 Dec. 1906: Bodleian MS Eng. poet. e. 92, fol. 487r. Bodleian
MSS Eng. poet. e. 92–3 are together Grierson's own interleaved set of his 1912 edition; MS Eng.
lett. d. 363 contains correspondence and other items removed from this set and separately
bound.
[2] H. J. C. Grierson (ed.), *The Poems of John Donne*, 2 vols. (Oxford, 1912); unless otherwise noted,
quotations from Donne and other poets will follow this edition.

just so many equivalent reshapings and relocations, in different ways for, and of, different writers. But there are reasons to think that the privileged invitation extended to Chatterton lecturers—to talk 'on the life and works of a deceased English poet'—may make Donne, and *this* Donne in particular, appropriate as my subject. Raleigh's complementary pairing—'an edition' of the works and a 'Life' of the author—presupposes one kind of connection between writing and biography; here I would like to propose another, by addressing not the life *and* the work, but the life *of* Donne's works in later readings and writings, offering a study of some of their different afterlives. Donne has seemed to many readers to be a writer preoccupied with the problem and the possibility of posthumous existence, a preoccupation that extends to the continued life of his works, and more particularly still with their afterlives, a term whose varied meanings I will explore in the first section of my lecture.[3] I will turn then to the making and shaping of Grierson's *Donne*, before closing with some reflections on how this remaking and relocation of Donne in 1912 was itself remade and relocated over the later years of the century. Many early readers—like Ben Jonson—feared 'That Donne himself, for not being understood, would perish'; this lecture argues instead that subsequent understandings of Donne and his works, in manuscript and print, and by different audiences, are necessary elements of the poet we read today.[4]

Many factors bear on Donne's afterlife: here I would like to signal three, to be explored in more detail in what follows. The first is that his poems in many ways establish the terms in which subsequent readers and writers respond to them. The second is that although later responses very often remain within a poetic or a conceptual space established by Donne's writing, they may very well run counter to, or mis-recognise aspects of, the poems from which they depart, giving a new direction or a new emphasis to the older texts. The third is that debates about the kind of poet Donne is, or might be, have always formed the conditions within which readers first encounter his poems; and those debates have always partly at least been about whether Donne is a poet of manuscript or of print.

---

[3] See, for instance, Ramie Targoff, *John Donne, Body and Soul* (Chicago, 2008).
[4] Ben Jonson, 'Conversations with Drummond, 1.158', in Ian Donaldson (ed.), *Ben Jonson* (Oxford, 1985), p. 599; see further Ian Donaldson, 'Perishing and surviving: the poetry of Donne and Jonson', *Essays in Criticism*, 51 (2001), 68–85.

I

From the first printing of his poems in 1633, two years after his death, Donne's biography has been part of what a reader encounters in encountering his poems: 'POEMS, | *By* J.D. | WITH | ELEGIES | ON THE AUTHORS | DEATH', as the title-page of that first printed edition has it. That claim grows more specific with time, as the works collected as Donne's become more numerous, so that by the title-page of the last seventeenth-century edition in 1669 the simple initials of 1633 have given way to a full name, a profession and an institution: 'POEMS, &c. | BY | JOHN DONNE, | *late Dean of St.* Pauls. | WITH | ELEGIES | ON THE | AUTHORS DEATH. | To which is added | *Divers Copies under his own hand,* | **Never before Printed.**' This development across the century, however, was not only, or was not simply, a print phenomenon. It is clear that, following Donne's death in 1631, a manuscript debate about the kind of poet he had been took place; this debate was later transplanted into print, where it is most easily approached, and where its meanings changed as it expanded and developed.

The first elegies to Donne were printed in the last sheet of the posthumously published *Death's Duel* in 1632; by Henry King and Edward Hyde (not, most scholars think now, the future Lord Chancellor but a cousin sharing his name): the two poems were reprinted in the following year, together with ten other tributes in the *Poems* of 1633.[5] The placement of these elegies is important. Donne had preached upon the Penitential Psalms in 1623 that 'the whole frame of the Poem is a beating out of a piece of gold, but the last clause is as the impression of the stamp, and that is it that makes it currant'; we might say here, for a book as for a poem, that the elegies which close both books form a frame through which any new reader of Donne in print would encounter the preacher or the poet, and make that reading current.[6] These elegies were the last clause of a reader's experience of the book they held; to change metaphors, the Donne they read was always already placed and shaped by subsequent responses, his poems wrapped in the printed sheets of elegies as his body had been wrapped iconically in its winding sheet. Donne's death here is both an entry into the life of the poems, and an entry into their afterlife;

[5] John Donne, *Deaths Duell* (London: Richard Redmer and Benjamin Fisher, 1632), pp. 45–7; Donne, *Poems* (London: John Marriot, 1633), pp. 373–406.
[6] George R. Potter and Evelyn M. Simpson (eds.), *The Sermons of John Donne*, 10 vols. (Berkeley, 1953–62), 6.41.

and this frame, as we shall see, is one, vitally, preserved and extended in Grierson's edition.

Henry King's poem, 'To the Memorie of My Ever Desired Friend Dʳ. Donne', leads forth the tributes to the dead poet as the first of the two poems printed with *Death's Duel* in 1632, and as the first of a dozen poems printed with the *Poems* in 1633. But it is an odd poem with which to begin such a concluding sequence for it is itself already situated not so much at the start of a process as in its middle. The poem responds to a poem that King must have encountered earlier in manuscript: Thomas Carew's poem, 'An Elegie upon the death of the Deane of Pauls, Dʳ. Iohn Donne' (1.378).[7] Carew's 'Elegie' was printed in the pages following King's in the *Poems* of 1633, but had earlier circulated in manuscript among the circle of Donne's admirers;[8] and it is against Carew's poem, and in some ways against Carew's Donne, that King pushes at the close of the first section of his poem:

> Who ever writes of Thee, and in a stile
> Unworthy such a Theme, does but revile
> Thy precious Dust, and wakes a learned Spirit
> Which may revenge his Rapes upon thy Merit.   (1.371, lines 23–6)

These lines, as the best recent critics of the poem have argued, take up and then redirect phrases from Carew's earlier poem, in particular his claim that 'the flame' of Donne's 'brave Soule' 'Committed holy Rapes upon our Will' (1.378, lines 14–5, 17); King makes a claim for a fresh and accurate response to Donne partly at least by repositioning and correcting the errors and vocabulary of the earlier poet.[9] But the four lines of King's poem that I quoted, as well as looking back to Carew, also anticipate the epigrammatic close of his own poem, when the 'precious Dust' of these earlier lines becomes further refined:

---

[7] Three manuscript texts of the poem now survive, listed as CwT 195–7 in Peter Beal, *Index of English Literary Manuscripts, Volume II: 1625–1700*, 2 parts (London, 1987); the eight manuscript texts of King's poem listed by Beal as KiH 762–9 all seem to post-date print publication in 1632, though they may not derive from it.

[8] Though only three MSS now survive: CwT 195–7.

[9] Michael P. Parker, 'Diamond's dust: Carew, King, and the legacy of Donne', in Claude J. Summers and Ted-Larry Pebworth (eds.), *The Eagle and the Dove: Reassessing John Donne* (Columbia, MO, 1986), pp. 191–200; John Lyon, 'Jonson and Carew on Donne: censure into praise', *Studies in English Literature, 1500–1900*, 37 (1997), 97–118; Scott Nixon, 'Carew's response to Jonson and Donne', *Studies in English Literature, 1500–1900*, 39 (1999), 89–109; and Jonathan F. S. Post, 'Helpful contraries: Carew's "Donne" and Milton's *Lycidas*', *George Herbert Journal*, 29 (2005–6), 76–91.

Commit we then Thee to Thy selfe: Nor blame
Our drooping loves, which thus to thy own Fame
Leave Thee Executour. Since, but thine owne,
No pen could doe Thee Justice, nor Bayes Crowne
Thy vast desert; Save that, wee nothing can
Depute, to be thy Ashes Guardian.
    So Jewellers no art, or Metall trust
    To forme the Diamond, but the Diamonds dust.   (1.372, lines 51–8)

King's clerical experience shapes the communities through which these lines move, and which they create, just as much as his poetic memory; the lines are shaped not only by the allusion to Carew (and by self-allusion), but by an echo, and a complication, of 'The Order for the Burial of the Dead'. Ashes to dust is King's progression, and dust to dust in a new way his conclusion, even as the assonantal internal rhyming and thickened alliteration of the opening phrase, 'Committ we then Thee to Thy selfe', remembers the priest's intoned prayer at the graveside from the *Book of Common Prayer*: 'And his body we commit to the earth.'[10]

At the same time, King's line offers a very different and less fixed interment. As the poem's syntax extends out and across the following two line-breaks, different kinds of agency stir against one another as the grammatical structure concludes: the poem does not say 'Nor blame | Our drooping loves, which thus to thy own Fame | Leave Thee', which would commit the passive poet to the subsequent ministrations of a Virgilian or emblematic *fama*;[11] instead, it grants Donne a remarkable posthumous agency, the power to carry into effect the shaping and the organisation of his own afterlife, 'to thy own Fame | Leave Thee Executour'. King's lines are powerful not only because they reflect on, and from within, his own appointment as an executor to Donne's will,[12] and his predicament as one poet paying tribute to an earlier (and greater) poet; they are powerful, too, because they alert a reader to an impulse towards subsequent imaginings of future life with which Donne's poems are already shot through. For King's unbalancing phrase remembers, and enacts its own relationship to, earlier Donne: 'Though I be dead, which sent mee, I should be | Mine owne executor and Legacie', he had written in 'The Legacie' (1.20). Where

---

[10] John E. Booty (ed.), *The Book of Common Prayer, 1559: the Elizabethan Prayer Book* (Charlottesville, VA, 1976).

[11] I have benefited here, as throughout my lecture, from Keith Thomas, *The Ends of Life* (Oxford, 2009), esp. pp. 226–67 ('Fame and the afterlife').

[12] 'I make my welbeloved Frendes Henrye Kinge Doctor of Divinitie & John Montfort Doctor of Divinitie … Executors of this my Will': R. C. Bald, *John Donne: a Life* (Oxford, 1970), p. 563.

'The Will' had maintained, with a donor's wry sense of wrenched appro-
priateness, that 'I give my reputation to those | Which were my friends'
(1.57), only in the sure and certain hope that they would be false to it, King's
poem trusts only Donne finally to frame his own posthumous Fame.

The testamentary motives in Donne's poems, recalled and deployed
here by King, were a part of his mind formed by his legal training, and a
part, too, of his theological imagination; but the vagaries or reversals of
reputation may find their fullest exploration in his lyric verse. A poem
such as 'The Relique' captures this doubleness, and is given life by it:

> When my grave is broke up againe
>   Some second ghest to entertaine,
>   (For graves have learn'd that woman-head
>   To be to more then one a Bed)
>   And he that digs it, spies
> A bracelet of bright haire about the bone,
>   Will he not let'us alone,
> And thinke that there a loving couple lies,
> Who thought that this device might be some way
> To make their soules, at the last busie day,
> Meet at this grave, and make a little stay?
>
>   If this fall in a time, or land,
>   Where mis-devotion doth command,
>   Then, he that digges us up, will bring
>   Us, to the Bishop, and the King,
>   To make us Reliques; then
> Thou shalt be a Mary Magdalen, and I
>   A something else thereby;
> All women shall adore us, and some men;
> And since at such time, miracles are sought,
> I would have that age by this paper taught
> What miracles wee harmelesse lovers wrought.
>
>   First, we lov'd well and faithfully,
>   Yet knew not what wee lov'd, nor why,
>   Difference of sex no more wee knew,
>   Then our Guardian Angells doe;
>   Comming and going, wee
> Perchance might kisse, but not between those meales;
>   Our hands ne'r toucht the seales,
> Which nature, injur'd by late law, sets free:
> These miracles wee did; but now alas,
> All measure, and all language, I should passe,
> Should I tell what a miracle shee was.   (1.62–3)

A poem literally about what remains to survive from and of the past (its titular 'relic' deriving from the Latin *reliquiæ*), this is delightedly also a poem about the future. It is, though, a poem startlingly uncomfortable with the present, drawing only to the moment in its final two and a half lines with the darkening and self-undoing closure (for the poem, at least) initiated by the temporal pointing of 'but *now* alas' (line 31; emphasis added). There, rather than 'set free' from the formal restraint of the third stanza's closing triplet, the poem folds and holds itself within a triple rhyme beyond which, as its modal verbs acknowledge, it can not pass. Those different temporal layers in Donne's poem have their futures tensed by its religious daring, and are braced by the tact with which it imagines the future reception not only of the couple at its centre but of its own future material forms and audiences: all the women and, after an important concession, *some* men, 'by this paper taught' on the occasion of its projected and expected discovery.

'The Relique' is, as many of its best readers have reminded us, a poem about subsequent interpretation,[13] about (in Jonathan Miller's probing phrase) 'the peculiar transformation undergone by works of art that out-live the time in which they were made.'[14] Miller called this ongoing process of successive remaking and rediscovery the afterlife of an art object, and he drew attention to the changes that art objects may undergo in this process:

> If they are rediscovered after a long period of being lost or neglected, it is as if they are perceived and valued for reasons so different from those held originally that they virtually change their character and identity … As well as the physical effects that can be inflicted upon an object, comparable social and institutional influences change the life of a work of art. The work may be transferred to a place or setting that bears no resemblance to the one where it had a recognizable social, aesthetic or religious function.[15]

'The Relique' is not mentioned by Miller, but the poem seems both to know and to anticipate him, for Donne's poem resonates with his formu-lations: 'If this fall in a time, or land, | Where mis-devotion doth command,'

---

[13] Achsah Guibbory, 'A sense of the future: projected audiences of Donne and Jonson', *John Donne Journal*, 2 (1983), 11–21, an argument summarised by Dayton Haskin who makes the poem central to 'Donne's Afterlife': 'Donne's explicit inscription in "The Relique" and other works of an interest in what future audiences might make of his writing suggests a deep longing ultimately to be known and understood' [Achsah Guibbory (ed.), *The Cambridge Companion to John Donne* (Cambridge, 2006), pp. 233–46 (at p. 233)].

[14] Jonathan Miller, *Subsequent Performances* (London, 1986), pp. 23–8.

[15] Miller, *Subsequent Performances*, p. 28; Miller returned to these ideas later in *The Afterlife of Plays* (San Diego, CA, 1992).

the second stanza opens (lines 12–13), before moving through the confidence of doubled misapprehension, 'Then, ... | ... | ... then' (lines 14–16), to its centre:

> Then, he that digges us up, will bring
>   Us, to the Bishop, and the King,
>   To make us Reliques; then
> Thou shalt be a Mary Magdalen, and I
>   A something else thereby;
> All women shall adore us, and some men[.]   (lines 14–19)

Much of the poem's power comes, here and elsewhere, from its setting single striking verse lines against and within the three-part rhyme-scheme of its eleven-line compound stanza (each stanza expands from a couple of couplets through an arch-rhymed quatrain and into a closing triplet). The dazzling line from stanza one that was later to catch T. S. Eliot's eye and ear—'A bracelet of bright haire about the bone' (line 6)—gains that dazzle partly at least because its length, being the first pentameter line in the poem, is set off by the two framing trimeter lines before and after it; though companionably rhymed to the second of these short lines, this 'bone' does seem to enact that rhyme, standing 'alone' in the poem's structure.

In stanza two this structural effect is moved forward: it is not the long sixth that stands out, running on from the fifth as it does by the alliterating syntactical connection of 'then | Thou', but the seventh, 'A something else thereby'. This is a line whose meanings have occasioned much controversy. William Empson, writing in the late 1950s, owned himself 'glad to see that the recent edition by Mr Redpath of the *Songs and Sonets* (1956) is at last willing to envisage that "A Jesus Christ" is what the poet ostentatiously holds back from saying'.[16] Donne, or his critics, had been holding back for a long time, Empson maintained. In combative correspondence with Helen Gardner about a draft of his article he went further: 'By the way, I really did think years ago that this meaning was taken for granted; I certainly didn't learn it from Redpath's edition.'[17] Empson's sturdy heterodoxy may identify one source of the line's power to shock; but it may have a wider force, too. For every reader's encounter with the poem may (we might argue) make it 'A something else thereby' (Empson was clear about

---

[16] William Empson, 'Donne the spaceman' (first printed in 1957), quoted from his *Essays on Renaissance Literature, Volume I: Donne and the New Philosophy*, ed. John Haffenden (Cambridge, 1995), pp. 78–128 (at p. 87).
[17] William Empson–Helen Gardner, 26 Oct. 1956: John Haffenden (ed.), *Selected Letters of William Empson* (Oxford, 2006), p. 258.

the difference between 'something else' and '*a* something else'). This process—being made 'A something else thereby' by each new reader—is, we might maintain, the condition of a poem's afterlife, and a poet's after-life, in the minds of subsequent readers: poems become not just different, something else, but in subsequent readings may inhabit any one of the many possible different futures among the imagined and unimagined possibilities of a poet's afterlife.

This happened to 'The Relique' in 1912; the poem changed, and became, in Grierson's edition, a something else that it had not been before in quite that way. 'If this fall in a time, or land, | Where mis-devotion doth command,' the poem's second stanza begins in 1912, and its beginning in this way called from Grierson a sharp commentary note in the second volume of the edition:

> *Where mis-devotion doth command.* The unanimity of the earlier editions and the MSS. shows clearly that 'Mass-devotion' (which Chambers adopts) is merely an ingenious conjecture of the *1669* editor.   (2.49)

Grierson's collations, his record of the textual choices made by earlier editors of Donne, more starkly still show how the earlier history of the poem's vari-ant readings sides against those of the 1669 *Poems* and E. K. Chambers's popular Muses' Library edition of 1896. On the one hand stand the printed editions from 1633 to 1654 and, in unanimous agreement, all the manuscripts containing the poem that Grierson had seen; on the other stands the edition of 1669 and—the sole proper name in the note—'*Chambers*'. This massed agreement can be seen again in the note to the variant in line 15. Does the poem here read 'Us, to the Bishop, and the King' or 'Us, to the Bishop, or the King'? The note in its collational com-pression enacts its own deliberative decision: Grierson's edition, '*1633–54 and MSS.*' all unite in reading 'and'; while, isolated for a second time in a glum double act, '*1669, Chambers*' read 'or'. Read 'and' and you can be right, the note seems to say, or you can read 'or' and be wrong; it knows which side of the separative colon it wishes to stay.

In this, and in other innumerable editorial decisions, Grierson changed the Donne that readers read after 1912. I will return to Chambers's edi-tion—a more interesting and a more influential treatment of Donne than this skirmish might imply—later; now, though, I would like to pick up the implications of the first of the two variants I isolated, and to address the question of how 'mis-devotion' and 'mass-devotion' each have their place in the account of Donne that I am offering. For if Donne in the earliest phases of his reception history seldom seemed to be an author appealing to, and read by, a mass audience, it has often been a feature of supposedly new readings that they correct the mis-devotion of earlier readers. The ways in which literary history maps Donne's reputation, and how we give our accounts of the subsequent placement and recreation of his work in and through successive phases of his afterlife, have both changed in recent years, so that what was once a simple (and heartening) narrative of loss and recovery has now become a more complicated (if more nuanced) history of the various reading and writing publics that have formed audiences for Donne's writings in the centuries following his death. A. J. Smith—so it is reported—wished to call the second volume of his *John Donne: Critical Heritage* anthology 'The Critical Rehabilitation of John Donne', intending his title to mark the extent to which the fifty years covered in the volume, 1873–1923, offered new and revitalising responses to a poet who had been marginal over the previous century and a half.[18] Following the work of Dayton Haskin, in a series of articles and the book they shaped, *John Donne in the Nineteenth Century*, Donne's 'Rehabilitation' (if Smith's is the right word) can be seen to have come about over a much longer duration, and to have been the product of many different forces more complicated than criticism alone.[19] How Donne has been read, and the forms in which he has been read, have emerged as twinned concerns over this period.

Today, following the work of Peter Beal, Arthur Marotti, Harold Love, Henry Woudhuysen and others, early modern manuscript circulation has been recovered as a central mode in and for the material understanding of the texts written in this period; and Donne—in Peter Beal's phrase—has been confirmed in his position as 'clearly the most striking instance of a major Tudor–Stuart poet who flourished in the context of a manuscript culture'.[20] This idea is not new, but its prominence may be. We can find earlier versions of this formulation circulating at least a century earlier: William Minto, with whom Grierson was to work at Aberdeen, had written in an article published in *The Nineteenth Century* in 1880 that Donne's 'genius', and therefore his poetry, was determined 'by the conditions under

---

[18] A. J. Smith and Catherine Phillips (eds.), *John Donne: the Critical Heritage*, 2 vols. (London, 1975–96), 2.xi.

[19] Dayton Haskin, *John Donne in the Nineteenth Century* (Oxford, 2007); Haskin generously allows that 'the years 1901–1912 … warrant further probing', though they fall outside the scope of his book (at p. 269).

[20] Peter Beal, 'John Donne and the circulation of manuscripts', in John Barnard, D. F. McKenzie and Maureen Bell (eds.), *The Cambridge History of the Book in Britain, Volume IV: 1557–1695* (Cambridge, 2002), pp. 122–6 (at p. 122).

which he wrote'. Donne's poems, Minto continued, 'were not intended for wide publicity; they were intended for the delight and amusement of a small circle among whom they were circulated in manuscript'.[21] And here, as the focus of my lecture turns towards the 'small circle' within which Grierson came to Donne, it is appropriate to raise some of the difficulties, and also the rewards, of approaching literary texts through an account of the bibliographical and social networks through which they circulate.

Stefan Collini has written recently on the tension between the life and works of the individual in literary history and the networks within which both existed. How, he asks, are we to separate, if indeed we can separate, achievements that 'are bound to appear tangibly individual, the expression of apparently autonomous creative energies' from the wider 'enabling effect of belonging to certain advantaged groups'? How, too, are we to map the 'overlapping categories' to which any individual may at any one time be said to belong, if those categories are determined, one against (or within) the others, by different discriminating factors of birth, class, education, public recognition, and social situation.[22] An awareness of this tension (as Collini proposes it) between the individual's biography and the elite within which he—typically he—worked has real purchase on Grierson's work with Donne. This is so, I think, because it chimes with what has been one of the most influential readings of Donne over the last twenty years or so, that offered by Arthur Marotti in *John Donne, Coterie Poet* (1986). There, by tracking Donne's texts through the small social networks of his late sixteenth- and early seventeenth-century readership, Marotti offered a way of understanding poems as (in effect) social events. Marotti argued that Donne's poems should be understood 'as coterie social transactions, rather than as literary icons'; aiming to recover the first meanings of, and audiences for, the poetry, Marotti situated Donne's mainly secular verse as the product and record of 'a series of social relationships spread over a number of years', and over the phases of Donne's career into which the book's structure divides: 'Donne as an Inns-of-Court Author', 'Donne as a Young Man of Fashion, Gentleman–Volunteer, and Courtly Servant', 'Donne as a Social Exile and Jacobean Courtier' (Donne as a churchman is a marked absence from Marotti's book).[23]

---

[21] William Minto, 'John Donne', *The Nineteenth Century*, 7 (1880), 845–63 (at p. 863).
[22] Stefan Collini, 'Well connected: biography and intellectual elites', in his *Common Reading: Critics, Historians, Publics* (Oxford, 2008), pp. 283–98.
[23] Arthur Marotti, *John Donne, Coterie Poet* (Madison, WI, 1986), pp. 19, 24.

Marotti claimed for his approach the virtue of recovering 'some of what has been lost through the literary institutionalization of Donne's verse', but stopped short of exploring the processes operating within that 'literary institutionalization'.[24] Such restraint recognises that historical understandings change; we might add that there is, for one thing, an anachronism, or at least a geographical relocation, built into Marotti's application of the term *coterie* to the metropolitan elites, and metropolitan institutions, within which Donne moved; Cotgrave's French–English dictionary of 1611 defined *coterie* as a 'companie, societie, assocation of countrey people' (as the *OED* notes), where for many—including Barbara Everett, when she made Donne the subject of her Chatterton lecture in 1972—Donne has seemed best 'a London poet'.[25] The greater strength of Marotti's formulation may instead be that his conception of the coterie poet is flexible enough to accommodate and illuminate that very process of 'literary institutionalization' with which my lecture is concerned. For Donne *had* seemed to scholars before Marotti a coterie poet: following on from Minto's discusion of Donne's 'small circle' of manuscript readers, George Saintsbury's 'Introduction' to Chambers's edition had recognised ruefully that 'Donne is eminently of that kind which lends itself to sham liking, to coterie worship, to a false enthusiasm'. Saintsbury's contrast between 'the infidels' and 'the true believers' who make up Donne's audiences is clearly a kind of belle-lettristic over-bidding;[26] but it is useful, nonetheless, to see in some ways how closely the contrast does identify the audiences for Donne over the last third of the nineteenth century, audiences very different from those engaged by Grierson's Donne in (and after) 1912.

To see this clearly we must see that Donne, over the last third of the nineteenth century, was a rare poet, and he had rare friends. The two-volumes containing *The Complete Poems of Dr. John Donne*, edited by the Rev. Alexander B. Grosart for The Fuller Worthies Library, were 'PRINTED FOR PRIVATE CIRCULATION' (as their title-pages stipulate) in 1872; the limitation statement, '106 *copies only*', is primly noted at the foot, as if to confirm and enforce the privacy of the privileged circulation which this subscription edition enjoyed. Grosart, born in Stirling in

---

[24] Marotti, *John Donne, Coterie Poet*, p. 24

[25] Barbara Everett, 'Donne: a London poet', *Proceedings of the British Academy*, 58 (1972), 245–73; collected in her *Poets in Their Time: Essays on English Poetry from Donne to Larkin* (London, 1986), pp. 1–31.

[26] E. K. Chambers (ed.), *Poems of John Donne*, intro. George Saintsbury, 2 vols. (London, 1896), 1.xi.

1827 and educated at the University of Edinburgh (though he did not take a degree), was at the time he published his edition of Donne a clergyman, minister of St George's, Blackburn.[27] He was, as an editor of Donne, very much in the line established by Henry Alford, whose six-volume edition of *The Works of John Donne, D.D., Dean of St. Paul's, 1621–31*, published in 1839, even more strongly emphasised Donne's divinity, not only in its title, but by its placement of his selected poems only at the back of volume six, to be reached only after a long (if spiritually edifying) pilgrimage through the sermons and the prose.[28] Grosart was an editor of huge energy; and he worked with that energy to create an audience for Donne. His edition was dedicated to Browning;[29] and through the study of individual sets of the edition we can see that Grosart presented them as gifts to other poets. One set was given by Grosart to A. C. Swinburne, and although there is no inscription to date that gift Swinburne's letter shows him having received the volumes as part of a 'splendid present' for which he wrote in thanks in September 1875; the books he received included editions of both Donne and Herbert. Swinburne enjoyed these gifts: 'I have just read through carefully for the first time Donne's "Anniversaries"', he told Theodore Watts in March 1876; he wrote to Grosart later in the same year to report that he was now 'cutting the leaves of your admirable edition of Herbert'.[30] Later, the Donne volumes formed a second present, to 'J.C. Collins | from his friend | A.C. Swinburne', recorded by the donor in the volumes themselves.[31] The books are now in the Special Collections at the University of Birmingham, where John Churton Collins held the first Chair in English Literature, founded in 1904.

A second gift inscription may localise for us the rarity of a second late nineteenth-century Donne, here a resolutely East Coast phenomenon. A different kind of limitation statement introduces Charles Eliot Norton's edition of *The Poems of John Donne*, printed by The Grolier Club of New

[27] Arthur Sherbo, 'Grosart, Alexander Balloch (1827–1899), *Oxford Dictionary of National Biography* <http://www.oxforddnb.com/view/article/11659>.

[28] Six vols. (London: John W. Parker, 1839)

[29] This dedication had been proposed by Grosart in acknowledgement of 'enjoyment and profit in the deepest parts of him from Mr Browning's magnificent-thoughted Poetry': A. B. Grosart–Robert Browning, 22 Feb. 1871: BL Add. MS 59794, fol. 16 (at fol. 16v).

[30] A. C. Swinburne–A. B. Grosart, 7 Sept. 1875; A. C. Swinburne–Theodore Watts, 15 March 1876; A. C. Swinburne–A. B. Grosart, 31 May 1876: Cecil Y. Lang (ed.), *The Swinburne Letters*, 6 vols. (New Haven, CT, 1959–62), 3.64–5, 3.152, 3.188–90.

[31] Alexander B. Grosart (ed.), *The Complete Poems of John Donne, D.D.*, 2 vols. ([n.p.]: Printed for Private Circulation, 1872); these books are now University of Birmingham, Special Collections, r PR 2245.A2-1872, set 1.

York, again in two volumes, in 1895. Here, before a reader meets even the half-title of the first volume, printed on a tipped-in leaf, is another invitation to recognise oneself as part of a coterie audience, bound and constituted by the particularities of place and time:

> The Publication Committee of the Grolier Club certifies that this copy of The Poems of John Donne, in two volumes, is one of an edition of three hundred and eighty copies on hand-made paper, and three copies on vellum, and that the printing was completed in the month of August, 1895.[32]

What kind of audience, or what succession of audiences, for Donne might be recalled if we were able to follow these copies, on hand-made German paper, or on vellum, through their owners', or their readers', hands? One copy with which I have worked tells us this: 'Given by | Charles Eliot Norton | to G. Burne-Jones | And by her | to J.W. Mackail | Jan: 16: 1913'.[33] Georgiana Burne-Jones (Georgie) was the wife of the artist Edward Burne-Jones, a regular correspondent of Norton's; J. W. Mackail, classicist and former Professor of Poetry at Oxford, was her son-in-law. From such details might again be mapped out precisely that movement of Donne within different artistic and educational coteries towards which I have been moving; something similar might be done with the British Library set of the Grolier Donne, which once belonged to Henry Spencer Ashbee, a prodigious collector both of books and pornography, substantial collections of which he left to the (then) British Museum Library.[34] What kind of gift to Mackail was this? Where would the promiscuous texts of Donne's erotic verse fit within Ashbee's tastes? That both the sets of books I have been discussing were left to an institution is part of the story I am exploring, and will come back to; Donne, over the life of these copies and their histories of reading, was moving away from the coterie and into the university, away from a readership of the few and towards a readership of the many.

To one early reviewer of Grierson's edition, however, this talk of limitation statements and the coterie readership of a High Victorian and *fin-de-siècle* Donne would have seemed contrary to the evidence around them, and contrary in particular to the evidence of one further late-century Donne. Indeed, to the young Rupert Brooke it seemed that at the start of

---

[32] Charles Eliot Norton, *The Poems of John Donne*, 2 vols. (New York, 1895), n.p.

[33] The books are now University of Birmingham, Special Collections, r PR 2245.A2-1895.

[34] The books are now British Library Ac.4714/15; Ashbee's collecting is described by David Chambers, 'Ashbee, Henry Spencer [*pseud.* Pisanus Fraxi] (1834–1900)', *Oxford Dictionary of National Biography* <http://www.oxforddnb.com/view/article/737>; and more colourfully in Ian Gibson, *The Erotomaniac: the Secret Life of Henry Spencer Ashbee* (London, 2002).

the twentieth century Donne was travelling further and faster than ever
before: 'If one has entered, any time these last years, a railway carriage,
and found some studious vagabond deep in a little blue book, it generally
turns out to be Mr. Chambers's invaluable edition in the Muses' Library.'[35]
E. K. Chambers was 30 when he published his Donne, and had behind
him a prize-winning undergraduate career in Oxford; but he was not, as
Grierson would be, an academic. Chambers was a civil servant, working
for the Education Department, which he had joined in 1892 having been
disappointed in his hopes of a college fellowship.[36] If Chambers, then, is
closer to the developing subject of university English (Oxford founded its
English school only in 1894), he still remains crucially outside it—though
if Samuel Schoenbaum's account of Chambers's usual working practices
is to be believed, he might seem only minimally to have been employed
within the Education Department: 'In his early days as a civil servant he
would check in at the office in the morning, read his mail, dictate a few
replies, and then adjourn to the British Library, returning to the office to
sign the letters before going home.'[37] Chambers's *Donne* exists, then, to
one side of his professional life, but right at the centre of Donne's reputation over the turn of the century. Brooke's 'little blue book' could in fact
have been one of many with Chambers's name on it: a revised edition followed in 1901, and a smaller-format reprint in 1905. As a reprint of a
reprint, this last *Donne* may tell us something about the relations between
book trade economics and a poet's readership at the start of the century;
it may tell us something, too, about the very late date at which Donne
finally gained admission into that thriving run of stereotyped poetry series
current from the 1870s onwards.[38] But this apparent availability of Donne
matters more (to backdate the phrase with which Eliot finally signalled his
growing distance from Donne at the close of the 1920s) as 'an affair of the
present and the recent past rather than of the future'.[39] One reason for
thinking this is because Brooke in his review moved to a connected and
forward-looking present: 'And now Professor Grierson and the Delegates

---

[35] Rupert Brooke, 'John Donne', in Christopher Hassall (ed.), *The Prose of Rupert Brooke* (London, 1956), p. 85, repr. from *The Nation*, 15 Feb. 1913.

[36] F. P. Wilson, rev. Nilanjana Banerji, 'Chambers, Sir Edmund Kerchever (1866–1954), *Oxford Dictionary of National Biography* <http://www.oxforddnb.com/view/article/32354>.

[37] S. Schoenbaum, *Shakespeare's Lives*, new edn. (Oxford, 1991), p. 513.

[38] I explore the ways in which such series shape responses to Milton over a similar period in 'Milton in the Twentieth Century', in Paul Hammond and Blair Worden (eds.), *John Milton: Life, Writing, Reputation* (Oxford, 2010), pp. 167–86.

[39] The phrase is quoted by Frank Kermode, *Forms of Attention* (Chicago, 1985), p. 72, as part of his valuable short account of Donne's later reception.

of the Clarendon Press have given us, clothed in the most attractive garb possible, a perfect text of the poems, and an immense body of elucidatory comment.'[40]

To see what made Grierson's Donne stand out we need to attend to the institutions within which it was shaped, and we need to take seriously the opening words of his Preface: 'The present edition of Donne's poems grew out of my work as a teacher.' It was the difficulties faced by his students when encountering Donne—a poet they found 'difficult alike to understand and to appreciate'—that caused Grierson to look again at the passages in the verse occasioning their difficulties; the students' want of understanding quickly gave way to Grierson's own; and on undertaking 'a more minute study of the text of his poems than I had yet attempted', he discovered 'that there were several passages in the poems, as printed in Mr. Chambers' edition, of which I could give no satisfactory explanation to my class' (1.i). This, for the first time, is a Donne that begins not in the church or outside the university, but in the lecture room and seminar.

If this Donne began there, then we can quickly see it expanding out into the new world of the twentieth-century university. The conditions under which Grierson gained access to the documents in manuscript and print on which his edition was based are revealing. Once he had signed his contract with Oxford University Press, Christ Church, Oxford, lent Grierson their set of the early printed editions of 1633, 1639, 1650 and 1654 (1.xi; 2.lxiv, lxx); Raleigh, at whose suggestion Grierson had embarked on the project, complemented this with the loan of his copy of the 1669 *Poems*. Among others, Grierson thanked the libraries of Trinity College, Dublin, and Trinity College, Cambridge, 'for permission to collate their manuscripts on the spot' and 'for kindly lending them to be examined and compared in the Library at King's College, Aberdeen' (1.xi–xii). We can see from Grierson's notebooks what work he did in comparing the manuscripts from the two Trinitys.[41] The very fact of the loan itself, moreover, may seem to contain within itself a whole social history of the edition and the profession within which it took shape. The letter that authorised the loan only really becomes interesting at its signature:

---

[40] Brooke, 'John Donne', p. 85.
[41] National Library of Scotland MSS 9324, 9325 and 9325A comprise together a body of Grierson's working notes towards the text of his edition; NLS MSS 9326 and 9327 contain a similar body of working notes towards its commentary.

Dear Prof. Grierson

The Council having approved your request for the loan of MS. R.3.12 I enclose a bond for £50 for your signature & seal & shall also require a note from the Librarian of King's College accepting custody. When I receive these the MS shall be sent.

I hope you may make interesting discoveries!

Yours sincerely

W. W. Greg

Greg's postscript suggests one area in which such discoveries might be pursued: 'It will be worth your while examining the watermark of the paper on which the MS is written, which I suspect fixes the date c.1620.'[42]

Greg's period of employment as the Wren Librarian at Trinity, his one 'salaried' university job as Henry Woudhuysen reminds us, focuses again the developments that were at this time shaping the careers of would-be English academics.[43] What is fascinating to see here is not only the interplay between the personal and the institutional responsibility—Grierson's 'signature & seal' complemented by the Librarian's agreement—but the developing interchange between Greg's research and his collegiate responsibilities. Greg's two papers 'On certain false dates in Shakespearian Quartos', published in *The Library* in 1908, had been among the first to deploy watermark evidence to the dating and analysis of printed books; in this letter, the quasi-scientific confidence of the coming New Bibliographers interacts with Grierson's in many ways more old-fashioned scholarship, formed as it had been (in a phrase of R. W. Chapman, revealingly his publisher in Oxford) 'upon the application of principles which in the field of Greek and Latin textual criticism have been elaborated in the course of centuries. It is thus no accident,' Chapman continued, 'that the work done in English editing in the last five-and-twenty years has been largely in the hands of scholars trained in the Oxford school of *Literae Humaniores*'.[44] Scientific means very different things in these two cases; Grierson's edition is the lens through which those differences can be focused.[45]

---

[42] W. W. Greg–H. J. C. Grierson, 27 Jan. 1911: NLS MS 9333, fols. 192A–B.

[43] H. R. Woudhuysen, 'Greg, Sir Walter Wilson (1875–1959)', *Oxford Dictionary of National Biography* <http://www.oxforddnb.com/view/article/33549>; the journal *Textual Cultures: Texts, Contexts, Interpretation*, 4 (2009), has recently devoted a special issue to the fiftieth anniversary of Greg's death.

[44] [R. W. Chapman], *Some Account of Oxford University Press, 1468–1921* (Oxford, 1922), p. 75.

[45] The New Bibliography is brilliantly contextualised in Laurie Maguire, *Shakespearean Suspect Texts: the 'Bad' Quartos and their Contexts* (Cambridge, 1996).

But perhaps more important than these institutional loans were the personal kindnesses that Grierson received from collectors and men of letters as he went about his work. His was a period in which the infrastructure of academic research looked very different, as the disciplines in which it was conducted were themselves coming into the curriculum. Edmund Gosse lent Grierson a good deal of material, including notes by Brinsley Nicholson that had earlier been lent to Chambers,[46] but more importantly he lent early editions of the poems, and unique manuscripts, including the Westmorland manuscript. Such loans were not always easy on both sides. 'Now, I don't want to hurry you in the least,' Gosse wrote in January 1912 with a list of the on-loan materials, 'but I think you have had all these many months, and some of them years. They seem ceasing to belong to me altogether.'[47] But manuscripts were ceasing to belong to individuals more widely in this period. When Grierson listed and gave sigla for the principal manuscripts on which his edition was founded, only nine of the thirty-seven were still in private rather than institutional ownership; four manuscripts, those bequeathed by Charles Eliot Norton to Harvard, had only very recently moved from private to institutional ownership, and in doing so gave a clear indication of the direction in which the pattern of collecting was moving, away from the amateur and towards the professional, away from the individual and towards the institution.

But what of books, in manuscript and print, that could not be lent, either by institutions or collectors? These books take us further into the textual culture within which Grierson's edition was produced, and which— at the same time—it confirmed.

Print and manuscript, and their changing relationships, shaped Grierson's edition. The *mise en page* of the *Poems* 1912 was very closely modelled on that of the *Poems* 1633; indeed when the design for Grierson's later anthology of metaphysical verse was discussed, it was explicitly in relation to early modern texts.[48] But it was manuscript that had a greater formative effect. Grierson, who even in old age did not use a typewriter, and persisted in manuscript correspondence (a fact for which he apologised more than once), was working in a period in which a good living could be made as a manuscript copyist at the British Museum or the

---

[46] The notes are now among the uncatalogued Gosse–Grierson correspondence, 2 Aug. 1905–26 Sept. 1927, in the University of Leeds, Brotherton Collection.

[47] Edmund Gosse–H. J. C. Grierson, 27 Jan. 1912: University of Leeds, Brotherton Collection, uncatalogued Gosse correspondence.

[48] See Oxford University Press Archives, PB/ED 004577 and PB/ED 018269, consulted with permission of the Secretary to the Delegates of Oxford University Press.

Public Records Office: Henry Plomer, now remembered as a historian of print, was one such copyist, working on the borders of what was becoming academic study of the early modern period.[49] Other examples support this: when Logan Pearsall Smith discovered the Burley manuscript, for example, his first action was to commission a full transcript of it; the transcript, only recently recovered, is part of the larger story of disappearance and recovery associated with that manuscript, and examination of the transcript confirms that it is to Grierson that we owe the identification of the two hands, D1 and P, that he thought responsible for the transcription of the original on which it was based.[50] W. W. Greg, too, as his memoir for the British Academy recalled, employed two different hands: one for correspondence and one for transcription.[51] The extent and availability of such scribal cultures gloss the thanks Grierson offered to 'Mr. Charles Forbes, of the Post Office, Aberdeen, who transcribed the greater portion of my manuscript' (1.x). Donne and the Post Office make an odd collocation; but a docketing note in Grierson's hand, written on the reverse of a transcription of a poem, not by Donne, offers a longer institutional history for Forbes: 'Charles Forbes first in the Post Office & then the Library Aberdeen.'[52] For though this anonymous poem survives in Forbes's hand, I have not been able to locate any of the Donne transcripts he produced for Grierson: like the manuscript that served as printer's copy for the *Poems* of 1633, these manuscripts—though their characteristics can be inferred from the evidence of print and of related documents—have disappeared. Forbes may differ from these early modern scribes, it is tempting to think, only inasmuch as we now recall his name.

Better documented is the assistance that Grierson received from other transcribers. Unable to gain direct access to much American material—even copies of Norton's edition arrived with him only very late in the project (though not as late, perhaps, as his statements may have suggested)—Grierson relied on transcripts and answers provided from Boston by Mary H. Buckingham, who consulted both manuscript and printed texts on his behalf.[53] Grierson's former student, Rachel Annand Taylor,

---

[49] H. R. Woudhuysen, 'Plomer, Henry Robert (1856–1928), *Oxford Dictionary of National Biography* <http://www.oxforddnb.com/view/article/51567>.

[50] The transcript is now Bodleian Library MS Eng. poet. c.80, transcribed in ink by an unidentified hand from what is now Leicester Record Office, MS Finch DG7/Lit.2; Grierson annotated the transcript with identifications of the hands in the original manuscript in ink and pencil.

[51] F. P. Wilson, 'Sir Walter Wilson Greg, 1875–1959', *Proceedings of the British Academy*, 45 (1959), 307–34 (at p. 332; see also p. 320).

[52] NLS MS 9349, fol. 82v.

[53] Bodleian MS Eng. lett. d. 363, fols. 7–8.

was crucial, too, to the edition. Rachel Annand (as she was then) had graduated from Aberdeen in the first year of Grierson's appointment; he remembered her, when writing of 'The development of English teaching at Aberdeen', with a phrase that registers not only the novelty of his subject but the novelty of its being studied by women, as the 'first prize-man in the class, 1894–5' and 'the most gifted and interesting student it has been my lot to encounter'.[54] After her marriage and a move to London, Annand Taylor worked for Grierson as a *de facto* research assistant, primarily in the (then) British Museum Library, writing regularly to him in Aberdeen with the results of her researches, and the news (and frustrations) of her developing career. The map of such encounters is invaluable for our sense of how to place Grierson's work at this period. Take this letter of April 1909, written as Annand Taylor worked her way through seventeenth-century printed verse miscellanies in search of fugitive items by Donne:

> 'Wit's Interpreter' seemed undiscoverable till I learned from an edition of the 'Westminster Drolleries' that it was edited by J. C. (John Cotgrave). And so with others. One day M[r] Laurence Binyon found me at the catalogue and offered his help. I tried him with 'Vinculum Societatis' and the 'Marrow of Complements'. Perceiving M[r] E. K. Chambers in the distance, he went and inflicted them on him. Oddly enough, M[r]. Chambers was just engaged on a list of these very anthologies. He presently discovered that the 'Marrow' was by Philomusus, and in the catalogue under that name; while the 'Vinculum' was by John Carre, but not in the Catalogue at all.[55]

'The harvest is rather scanty after all,' she concluded; but the literary sociology is fascinating. Partly it is that the resources on which scholars so regularly now depend simply did not exist: the first *Short-Title Catalogue* of early printed books was not planned until 1919 by the Bibliographical Society, and Pollard and Redgrave's first edition did not appear until 1926. This was also a period in which the kind of scholarship to which Grierson was professionally committed, and which his career represents, existed alongside (perhaps existed behind) the kind of after- or between-hours amateurism of men such as Binyon and Chambers. Location mattered then as it does not now in an age of digital scholarship: a scholar in Aberdeen simply had to work in different ways from a scholar in London;

---

[54] H. J. G. Grierson, 'The development of English teaching at Aberdeen', *The Aberdeen University Review*, 1 (1913–14), 49–53 (at p. 50).
[55] Rachel Annand Taylor–H. J. C. Grierson, 5 April 1909: NLS MS 9328, fol. 9r. A letter of Binyon's, acknowledging receipt of presentation copies of the 1912 Donne is Bodleian MS Eng. poet. e. 92–3, 2 286b.

and, more particularly, a scholar with a full-time university position in Aberdeen worked very differently from a part-time amateur scholar in London.[56]

The impact of these contexts on the textual culture within which Grierson worked has not been fully appreciated. When the collaborators in the largest current edition of Donne's verse, the *Donne Variorum* under the general editorship of Gary A. Stringer, wrote about their undertaking in the early 1980s they tended to criticise Grierson for treating (in Ted-Larry Pebworth's phrase) 'manuscript poems' with 'print assumptions', reserving particular comment for Grierson's not having seen personally all the manuscripts whose readings he reported.[57] This is not untrue, far from it; but it has seemed to me at the same time a small failure of the tact of historical scholarship on the later editors' part. For one way to measure Grierson's difference from the processor-powered discoveries of the *Donne Variorum* is to remember, as Grierson's youngest daughter did, that his house in Aberdeen was without electricity, and all that it might represent of the coming world: 'electricity had come to symbolize for us a whole way of life, a social status, an emancipation. Its absence humiliated us,' she wrote.[58] It is not, quite, that the new technology here calls all in doubt, but perhaps that later technological assumptions have obscured historical understanding. Instead, I would argue that attending to the compatibility of Grierson's edition with its subject matter here allow us a way back into what made it so distinctive in its own time and for ours.

If these were the coterie conditions under which Grierson gained access to the documents on which his edition was based, what did he do with them? One answer is that Grierson's edition benefits from the textual culture of one twentieth-century coterie so that it can record the textual cultures of Donne's seventeenth-century coteries. In this sense the appendixes to Grierson's edition close the frame that the manuscript making of his edition opens; for there, after Donne's Latin poems and translations, follow the evidence for the texts circulated among the coterie manuscript

---

[56] Articles published by Grierson as he drew together the edition make clear the conditions of access to material under which he worked: see particularly 'Bacon's Poem, "The World": Its Date and Relation to Certain Other Poems', *Modern Language Review*, 6 (1911), 145–56 (at p. 152, on the use of Saintsbury's library).

[57] See, both pieces without coincidence from the early volumes of *John Donne Journal*: Ernest W. Sullivan, II, 'Replicar editing of John Donne's texts', *John Donne Journal*, 2 (1983), 21–9; and Ted-Larry Pebworth, 'Manuscript poems and print assumptions: Donne and his modern editors', *John Donne Journal*, 3 (1984), 1–21.

[58] Janet Teissier Du Cros, *Cross Currents: a Childhood in Scotland* (East Linton, 1997), p. 35.

cultures within which Donne became such a singular manuscript author. There are the poems attributed to Donne, as Grierson's formal phrase has it, 'in the old editions and the principal manuscript collections', organised by the names of those taken by Grierson to be their probable authors, among them Sir John Roe, Francis Davison, Henry Constable, John Hoskins, the Earl of Pembroke and John Dowlands (Appendix B). More radical a collection yet is Grierson's third appendix, containing poems only a few of which could claim an attribution to Donne, but which instead 'frequently accompany poems by Donne in manuscript collections'. Here, though the full force of the move is not trumpeted by Grierson, is a real editorial departure: an edition not of an author's work, but of his textual culture, his contexts and his contacts (Appendix C).

Culture, contexts and contacts: the capacity of Donne's writing to produce and energise audiences and publics with a sense of their own particular specific gravity runs through the correspondence around Grierson's edition, and the edition itself. At a point in 1911 when Grierson still planned to include *Biathanatos*, and was thinking about a possible future edition of Donne's Sermons, his sponsor in the project, Raleigh, wrote remarkably of that coterie sense of ownership that the new kind of academic, and the new kind of university press, felt towards authors such as Donne:

> I don't think *any* modern divine should be allowed to touch Donne. They have lost the explicit worldliness that would be their only possible qualification. [...] An Evangelical Life of Donne would no doubt run 'Wild Jack, and how he came to Jesus.' No; no clergy need apply.
> Donne belongs to us, not to them.[59]

This letter forms a part of a correspondence in which the two men, writing from their private addresses rather than the addresses of their employers, exercise a freedom that comes from and reinforces their community. 'Us', here, might be (in the case of Raleigh and Grierson) a matter of the two men being of similar ages, both now in their forties, and of their sharing the geographies and effects of a Scottish upbringing and a university education in Oxford; but it is also a matter of their both being, and sharing a powerful awareness of being, secular professionals attending to Donne with the intention of making his texts available to a purchasing public through a professional publisher, R. W. Chapman, and a newly

---

[59] W. A. Raleigh–H. J. C. Grierson, 9 Sept. 1911: NLS MS 9332, fols. 77v–78r.

confident university press: of not being, like Grosart, clergymen editing the poems for a subscription library series; of not being, like Chambers, a civil servant with literary and scholarly leanings, editing the poems for Lawrence and Bullen; and of not being, like Norton, a Harvard polymath, completing an edition of the poems begun in mid-century by James Russell Lowell, and published in a luxury edition intended for a society of New York bibliophiles. This was an edition of, and for, the university.

It was also an edition both of manuscript and print. Peter Beal takes as the epigraph to the first volume of his *Index of English Literary Manuscripts* a line of Latin verse by Donne, written to a friend, Richard Andrews, who, shame-faced at his children having torn up a printed book that belonged to Donne, returned instead a manuscript copy of the same book: *Sed quae scripta manu, sunt veneranda magis*, Donne replied, a phrase that scholars are now accustomed to render via the verse translation of Edmund Blunden: 'What Printing-presses yield we think good store, | But what is writ by hand we reverence more.'[60] Grierson knew the poem, and offered his own prose translation in a letter to *The Spectator* of March 1943, correcting an error in Evelyn Hardy's *John Donne: a Spirit in Conflict*, which had been reviewed a fortnight earlier: 'We are glad to get a printed book, but a written one is *more revered.*'[61] Grierson's Donne, I have been arguing, is worthy of our reverence not because it is a printed book, nor because it is a written book, but because it is both: because the process of its making is the process of the interaction between manuscript and print; and because its final form, using the evidence of manuscript circulation even as it echoed the physical shape of the 1633 *Poems* whose text (in Grierson's word) it vindicated (1.vi). At the same time, Grierson's scholarship inaugurated a way of reading Donne and his contemporaries that transformed scholarship in the twentieth century and continues that transformation today: Grierson's edition brings the afterlife of Donne's poems back to full life, because it returns them to the conditions in which they were composed and first circulated during Donne's lifetime. If the *Poems* of 1633 represent the beginning of Donne's afterlife in print, the *Poems* of 1912 open up the possibility of future life for Donne in manuscript—which is where, because of work done by hand, by Grierson and by others, they have stayed.

---

[60] I follow the connection made by Hilton Kellier, 'Donne, Jonson, Richard Andrews and the Newcastle Manuscript', *English Manuscript Studies, 100–1700*, 4 (1993), 134–73.
[61] Grierson's own press-clipping of this letter is now Bodleian MS Eng. poet. e. 92–3, 1.407v.

II

I began with a question that was an invitation; I want to close with the reply it received, and the consequences of that reply. 'Why not do Donne', Raleigh had asked. 'I should have answered your letter sooner', Grierson replied, 'but I have had some exams in & also a good deal of university business. Also I have wished to think it over.'[62] This will not have been the first time that an academic apologised to a publisher for slowness, or found that 'university business' has a way of making thought seem sometimes like an afterthought; but it may have been the first time that an editor of Donne apologised for his project in this way. We should read, I think, Grierson's edition as the product (and record) of a particular kind of university coterie, but with one exception: its later readers, in their number and in their diversity, do not constitute an equivalent university coterie.

Grierson chafed at the slowness with which Oxford University Press were prepared to make revisions to his first edition, or to countenance a selected edition, on one occasion in 1916 calling forth the firmly worded reminder from Charles Cannan that 'An O[xford]. P[oets]. Donne will be a task for the compositors when they return from the trenches.'[63] But the absence of revisions did not preclude frequent reprintings; and in a single-volume recension of the *Poetical Works* in 1933 Grierson was able to incorporate corrections to his first edition. In this single-volume format, Donne, now accepted as an Oxford Standard Author, was reprinted regularly through the mid-century, only falling out of print in this form remarkably late in 1985, long after Grierson's death in 1960. Between these dates, of course, came if anything an even more influential contribution to early modern studies: Grierson's 1921 anthology, *Metaphysical Lyrics & Poems of the Seventeenth Century, Donne to Butler.* The story of the making of this anthology remains to be told, but its canonical impact has been rehearsed many times before, beginning as it does with T. S. Eliot's (then anonymous) leader in the *Times Literary Supplement* (20 October 1921), a review that later became part of his essay on 'The Metaphysical Poets'.[64] What also remains to be told is the impact of Grierson's different Donnes on readers who scarcely could have encountered his verse in the

[62] H. J. C. Grierson–W. A. Raleigh, 29 Dec. 1906: OUP Archives, OP 669/4714.

[63] Charles Cannan–H. J. C. Grierson, 4 Sept. 1916: OUP Archives, OP 669/4714/2.

[64] [T. S. Eliot], 'The metaphysical poets', *Times Literary Supplement*, 20 Oct. 1921; T. S. Eliot, 'The metaphysical poets', *Selected Essays*, 3rd edn. (London, 1951), pp. 281–91; Cairns Craig, 'The last Romantics', *Times Literary Supplement*, 15 Jan. 2010, shows how this enquiry might now be taken forward.

tightly controlled circulation of earlier editions before 1912. Many of these readers may have had no family history of secondary education, still less a family history of university education; but in copy after copy, in mine and other families, there is testament to the opportunities and possibilities, the Americas and the new-found lands, opened up by Grierson's work with Donne's verse. A Donne made within, and designed for, the universities became a Donne beyond them, with a reach and a readership spread out over the twentieth century, and reaching now into the twenty-first.

Note.   I would like to thank the many friends and colleagues who helped me in the writing of, and research for, this lecture: Hugh Adlington, Peter Beal, Martin Butler, Ian Donaldson, Juliet Dusinberre, Arthur Freeman, Janet Ing Freeman, Achsah Guibbory, Paul Hammond, John Jowett, Martin Killeen, Sebastian Mitchell, Marcus Nevitt, Peter Redford, Valerie Rumbold, Cathy Shrank and Gillian Wright.

T. S. Eliot's Daughter[1]

ROBERT CRAWFORD
University of St Andrews

'IDEALLY HE SHOULD LIKE to have had about ten children,' Valerie Eliot once said of her late husband. 'He was,' she added, 'suited in every way.'[2] I first heard these words roughly a quarter of a century ago, and they have stayed with me. They struck me as moving, and lie behind this lecture. Mrs Eliot's remarks presented someone very different from that image of an 'unpleasant to meet Mr Eliot' which the poet himself was well aware of, and which has too often calcified into gaunt caricature.[3]

Eliot is one of the twentieth century's great poets, perhaps its greatest. He is so especially because of the music of his words. In his verse there is an insistent, insidious and magnificent sense of poetry as language which, as C. K. Williams says poetry must, 'achieves a forcefulness far beyond that of direct prose'. Eliot's work demonstrates Williams's assertion that 'By incorporating some of the elements of music, artificial rhythms, tonal organization, repetition, harmony and dissonance, poetry touches more deeply into the ground of our mental life than other kinds of language.'[4] Eliot is also the greatest immigrant poet in the English language; to

Read at the Royal Society as part of British Academy Literature Week, 19–22 October 2009, and at the University of St Andrews on 28 October 2009.

[1] This British Academy Warton Lecture on English Poetry has gained from points made by its auditors, especially suggestions from Danny Karlin, Phillip Mallett, and Josh Richards. Grateful acknowledgement is made to Faber and Faber and to the Estate of T. S. Eliot for permission to quote copyright materials in the text of this lecture.

[2] Valerie Eliot on BBC TV's 'Arena: T. S. Eliot', broadcast on 6 June 2009 (this remark was first made in a 1971 interview).

[3] T. S. Eliot, *The Complete Poems and Plays* (London, 1969), p. 136.

[4] C. K. Williams, 'The music of poetry and the music of the mind', *Poetry Review*, 99:3 (Autumn 2009), 121.

describe him as such may sound patronising and peculiar, yet an awareness of cultural displacement accompanying a sense of anxious fidelity is
fundamental to much of his best poetry and is part of what gives that
writing a distinctive, sometimes percussive modernity. More locally, this
immigrant author is the finest poet of London. He is that city's Baudelaire.
Moreover, as a result of artistic shrewdness, historical accident, and personal bravery, he is a remarkable poet of the Blitz. This creator of 'hollow men', a contemporary both of J. M. Barrie and of D. H. Lawrence, is
also a major poet of gender, a feeling anatomist of masculinity—and not
only in 'The Love Song of J. Alfred Prufrock'. That this same writer, like
England's magnificent republican author, Milton, should be the most
compelling religious poet of his age, and among the most hypnotic religious voices of his language makes Eliot all the harder to comprehend.
Repeatedly readers have had to set aside that he was too the poet of *Old
Possum's Book of Practical Cats*; to ignore that he was renowned as a
popular playwright; to forget he was one of his century's best known
publishers. In various ways he has been defaced or boxed in—because it
is just too difficult to allow him his multiplicity, his complexity, his life.

It is an irony that T. S. Eliot, whose very name became a byword for
'difficulty' in poetry, is now so often denied his right to a sustaining complexity as a poet and as a human being. Eliot came to be regarded as an
iconic poet, and he met his iconoclasts. However different from each
other they may be, iconic poets commonly undergo a kind of critical
mugging. Where Robert Burns has become for some a womanising, popu-
list, sentimental 'Scotch' drunk, Eliot has been reduced on occasion to a
marmoreal elitist, a poet only of the brain, a woman-hating anti-semite.
The problem with these caricatures is not just that they reduce the
humanity of the poet caricatured; they also come between the reader and
the poem. One-note criticism and caricature masquerading as biography
are reductive and damaging: they hurt our sense of the life and, through
that, of the work. Techniques of literary biography and attentive criticism
should work together to restore nuance both to our sense of the life that
nourished the work and to the poems themselves.

Purists may think this a soiling, a violation. For some the poem must
be kept uncontaminated, unsullied by the dirt of biography. A contemporary of the I. A. Richards who famously suppressed even the authors'
names when he gave poems to his student guinea-pigs for the purpose of
'practical criticism', T. S. Eliot was very, very wary of biography. In
Keepers of the Flame, his study of literary estates and the rise of bilogra-
phical writing, Ian Hamilton records that 'Eliot added a memorandum to

his will: "I do not wish my executors to facilitate or countenance the writing of a biography of me." [5] Arguably the best time for a new, full biography might be when all Eliot's poems, prose and letters are published, and when the work of his executors is over. Yet if we wish to assert or reassert the sometimes troubled, troubling humanity of this poet in a way that will win new readers, then the time for new biographical studies, and for allowing them to quote much more generously from his established and newly published works, is sooner rather than later.

In some cases—Chaucer and Shakespeare are examples—it can be easy to set aside the scanty biographical information we have. Readers may choose to accept 'the death of the author'. They can see the text, the poem, as produced through the confluence of social and linguistic networks, and only accidentally emanating from a specific individual who may at the time of writing have been feeling ill, in love, or amused. Eliot's most celebrated poem seems tailor-made for the sort of reading encouraged by Roland Barthes in *S/Z*. Surely *The Waste Land* is a work originating from a *réseau*, a network; its author is not, as Michel Foucault's famous essay has it, a 'who', but productively an impersonal 'what'. [6] If the technologies of Eliot's day—from typewriting to telephony—encouraged a viewing of poems as part of an age of mechanical reproduction, then our own digital technologies—computers, databases, electronically searchable e-books—might seem to have separated further 'the man who suffers' from 'the mind which creates' as Eliot put it so memorably in his 1919 essay, 'Tradition and the individual talent'. That essay was just one of his early and in part defensive attempts to snip apart the printed poem from the digits that first held the pen.

Yet the same Eliot urged we should preserve even Shakespeare's laundry bills in case eventually they might reveal something worth knowing about the making of the writer's work. Today the very ease with which crude caricatures too often pass for T. S. Eliot, for Robert Burns or for other authors shows how futile are efforts to keep poems sealed off from biographical information or misinformation about the poet. If it is still possible to read poems in blissful ignorance, it is impossible to do so for long. Our systems of knowledge soon intrude; and if they did not, reading would be rendered null. There is no such thing, Wittgenstein pointed

---

[5] Ian Hamilton, *Keepers of the Flame: Literary Estates and the Rise of Biography* (London, 1992), p. 292.
[6] Michel Foucault, 'What is an author?', in Josue V. Harari (ed.), *Textual Strategies* (London, 1980), pp. 141–60.

out, as a wholly private language. If words were denuded of all associations, all gestures towards context, knowledge, emotions, and history,
then poetry would cease. To accept the possibilities of poetry, it is necessary to take on board that, whatever the enabling fictions of poets, poetry
does not operate in a hermetically sealed realm, cut off from the world
and the life of the author as if locked away in a fridge.

Caricature supplies that dangerous thing: a little knowledge. Literary
biography risks supplying too much. But it is for readers to filter out the
irrelevant, not to pretend that knowledge about a poet is automatically
useless. Biographical study fights caricature by contributing to a rich
interpretative context. Indeed a biographical study of a poet must not be
'biography' as the *OED* so nakedly defines the term: 'a written record of
the life of an individual'. Instead, it will draw on life-writing as well as on
critical and interpretative skills to suggest how the life conditioned the
poetry and why the poetry matters. This is what I want to do in this
lecture on Eliot when it comes to reading 'Marina', but I am arguing also
that it should be done on a larger scale.

For all that in October 2009 Eliot was voted Britain's most popular
poet in a BBC online poll, it *is* now necessary to point out afresh why his
poetry matters—why it might count for all readers, not just afficionados
of online poetry polls or professors or graduate-school elites. Eliot has
suffered much from glib assumptions, from rumours of suppressed secrets,
from a kind of dismemberment—part happenstance, part anxious
guardianship—which has kept his writings scattered without any sort of
collected edition. It is precisely because of these things that, as his letters
begin to appear in their full form, as his voluminous prose is gathered,
and as for the first time his collected poetry is to be afforded a full scholarly edition, we are nearing the moment for a new biographical study of
Eliot. Such a book should be allowed to let readers—not least readers
unlikely to work their way through all of this poet's letters and published
prose—hear Eliot's own nuanced words as part of a twenty-first-century
crafted narrative, rather than having to rely almost exclusively on para-
phrasing and hearsay. A good biographical study needs a fine and shifting
balance between intimacy and critical distance. So far this has been very
difficult for Eliot's biographers to achieve, and it may be that sometimes
the result has been to make him seem all the more removed, reinforcing a
lingering suspicion of rebarbative inhumanity.

Eliot should not be presented as a saint. The more some of his defenders treat him as such, as if he were a man without worrying prejudices,
blind-spots, or issues, the more they play into the hands of caricaturists.

It is simply misguided to argue, for instance, that the poet of the privately circulated 'King Bolo' poems was untouched by sexism or racism:

> King Bolo's big black bassturd kween
>   Was awf'ly sweet and pure
> She interrupted prayers one day
>   With a shout of Pig's Manure.
> K. B. b. b. b. k.
>   Was aw'fly sweet and pure
> She said "I don't know what you mean!"
>   When the chaplain whistled to her[7]

Whether in the Bolo poems or 'The Hippopotamus', in his criticism of *Hamlet* or of Scottish literature, or in *After Strange Gods*, Eliot scandalised. And sometimes he got things wrong. His letters, such as those to Bonamy Dobrée, now in the Brotherton Library at Leeds University, can be disturbing and offensive as well as revealing and funny. It is right to acknowledge that troubling references to Jews, black people and others could be part of Eliot's private scurrility and, on occasion, of his public discourse. Rather than trying to argue with teetering sophistication that Eliot was everywhere pure as the driven snow, it may be more effective to make clear that the man who wrote the 'King Bolo' poems was also the publisher whose support for Amos Tutuola marked him out as a pioneering London publisher of black African writing; while the man who in 1934 published (then soon suppressed) *After Strange Gods* was also the dramatist who wrote for George Bell—a churchman notable for his outspoken criticism of the Nazi treatment of Jews in the 1930s—that 1935 play which invites a critique of state-sponsored 'necessary' killing, *Murder in the Cathedral*. The Bolo poems should be quoted. So should the letters to Dobrée and the references to Jews in *After Strange Gods* and elsewhere. Yet to see them as the focal point of Eliot's work is misguidedly reductive, and it would be foolish to insist that Eliot's writing would have been improved by perpetual moderation. Poetry depends on measure. However, no human being is always a creature of measure. To avoid either crucifying or beatifying the Pope of Russell Square is the best way to restore to the man and his poetry their deep, troubled and so acoustically insistent music of humanity.

---

[7] Eliot to Conrad Aiken, 10 Jan. 1916, in *The Letters of T. S. Eliot, Volume I, 1898–1922*, rev. edn., ed. Valerie Eliot and Hugh Haughton (London, 2009), p. 138. Eliot adds an asterisk after the word 'chaplain' and explains this refers to 'Charles, the Chaplain'.

If we stand back and see Eliot and his work in the round, we might realise that he was not just the most internationally influential poet of his age, impacting alike on George Seferis (who translated 'Marina') and the young Hugh MacDiarmid. Eliot was also—and this has sometimes bred resentment—England's greatest ever immigrant poet. It may be easier for readers who do not feel themselves to be English to appreciate this, because they—we—do not take an assumed Englishness for granted, and because we may be particularly alert to tensions in Englishness. Cultural dislocation is hardly a new subject in literature: it is part of the *Aeneid* and *Othello*. In Scott, Byron and others it becomes an important constituent element of Romanticism, and it is a pronounced topic in American writers as different as Fenimore Cooper and Henry James. Eliot is probably the master poet of cultural displacement. As an immigrant he wrote so many poems of dislocation. 'Marina' is one of these, and so is *The Waste Land*. If his early masterpiece, 'The Love Song of J. Alfred Prufrock', is an acute, astute presentation of male sexual anxiety—every bit as telling as *Peter Pan*—then so many of Eliot's poems also speak anxiously of displacement, *mélange*, hybridity and mix-up because this was a condition Eliot did not simply observe—it was not just the predicament of 'Hakagawa, bowing among the Titians'—it was the ground of Eliot's existence.[8]

He was a poet brought up with the most insistent familial ideals, yet at a crucial time in his life he was separated from his biological family by an ocean. From 'Chicago Semite Viennese' to 'Bin gar keine Russin, stamm' aus Litauen, echt deutsch', his poems repeatedly worry about a sense of existential homelessness: 'En Amérique, professeur; | En Angleterre, journaliste [. . .] En Yorkshire, conférencier; A Londres, un peu banquier . . . En Allemagne, philosophe [. . .] On montrera mon cénotaphe | Aux côtes brûlantes de Mozambique.'[9] Eliot's work is full of displaced wanderers, 'Spawned in some estaminet of Antwerp, | Blistered in Brussels, patched and peeled in London.' This immigrant poet displaced from Germany by war and who had not intended to come and live long-term in England, this Southern scion of Boston Brahmins who had in part reacted rebelliously against his own spiritual and intellectual heritage was both uneasily fascinated with and disturbed by those figures so long associated with wandering—displaced Jews. They epitomised what worried him about aspects of his own condition. His worry and disturbance

[8] Eliot, *Complete Poems and Plays*, p. 37.
[9] Ibid., pp. 40, 61, 47.

are bound up with his background and are hardly admirable: they are, though, unsettlingly understandable, awkwardly fused with what makes Eliot so powerful an immigrant poet.

Eliot went on being seen as an immigrant poet for years after he became a British subject and joined the Church of England. In 1931, the year after the publication of 'Marina', Chatto and Windus brought out Thomas McGreevy's *Thomas Stearns Eliot*. This book makes no mention of 'Marina', but does insist that most of Eliot's writings 'cannot be considered as the work of an English poet'. Instead, 'it is essential that his American origin should be kept in mind'. McGreevy, who had never been to the America he called 'the most vulgar plutocracy that the modern world has seen', related Eliot's work in particular to the 'rather priggish' mind of New England, that 'well-bred maiden aunt of the United States'.[10] Sometimes Eliot could use—and sometimes he could seek to counter—stereotypes, but he was also, as he has continued to be, viewed through them. What is remarkable about Eliot is not so much his immigrant status as how in *The Waste Land*, 'Marina' and elsewhere he manoeuvred within and beyond it.

If you stand outside the old Faber offices in London, at the corner of Russell Square, just opposite is a restored cabmen's shelter, erected by Sir Squire Bancroft in 1901. The cabmen then would have been riding horse-drawn vehicles, just like the ones in Sydney Paget's illustrations to Sherlock Holmes which had impressed Eliot as a boy in Missouri, long before he ever saw London. For all that *The Waste Land* has a taxi with a throbbing engine, not a horse-drawn cab, waiting for its passenger, Eliot's fog-bound London was closer than we might think to the London of Charles Dickens. Dickens's house still stands as a museum not so far from Russell Square. Only eighteen years separate the death of Dickens from the birth of the poet of 'He Do the Police in Different Voices', and if Dickens is the greatest novelist of London, T. S. Eliot, not Samuel Johnson of Lichfield or James Thomson of Port Glasgow, is London's greatest poet. Eliot's city is traceable on the map 'along the Strand, up Queen Victoria Street' or 'up the hill and down King William Street'.[11] Yet it is also forever compacted in that 'Unreal City' all the more eerie and hallucinatory because it is not a city of dreadful night but a persistent

---

[10] Thomas McGreevy, *Thomas Stearns Eliot, a Study* (London, 1931), pp. 3, 4. McGreevy's publisher seems to have been unsure what to call his book: on the front cover '*Thomas Stearns*' is replaced by the more familiar 'T. S.'

[11] Eliot, *Complete Poems and Plays*, pp. 69, 62.

daytime phantom. It is present, but disconcertingly absent, as the seen
and unseen oscillate. Again, Eliot felt this urban unreality from the inside,
perhaps all the more intensely because he was an immigrant from another
continent. Quoting Baudelaire's 'Fourmillante Cité, cité pleine de rêves, |
Où le spectre, en plein jour, raccroche le passant!', he wrote of how he
knew that phenomenon because he had 'lived it'.[12] His life, nourished by
his reading and in turn nourishing his writing, made Eliot London's most
haunting poetic voice.

    More than that, his life in London made Eliot probably the greatest
English-language poet of the Second World War. Like such notable war
writers as Naomi Mitchison and Elizabeth Bowen, he was a non-
combatant. Randall Jarrell's 'The Death of the Ball Turret Gunner' or
Sorley Maclean's 'Ruweisat Ridge' catch the shock of combat. Alun Lewis
catches the boredom, and Keith Douglas the regret. Yet it is Eliot who
most convincingly and defiantly sounds the note of mustered struggle and
spiritual fightback summed up in popular memory in the simplifying
phrase 'the spirit of the Blitz'. He catches that spirit profoundly and
enhances it with a courageously conflicted complexity in 'East Coker',
'The Dry Salvages', and 'Little Gidding'. For such a bookish person,
Eliot's life and work are surprisingly dramatic. The drama is insistent in
the deeply lacerating emotional fragmentation of *The Waste Land,* but it
extends as well to the rooftop firewatching and Blitz conditions of *Four
Quartets* where the most insistent pressure of being immured in history
provides also windows beyond.

    Still, rereading Eliot's poetry or re-examining his life should not levi-
tate him into heroic remoteness. It must refuse him the chill of a plinth.
The subtlest and most important work in recuperating this great poet is
to restore to our sense of him and his writings their full, moving, flawed
humanity. From that humanity Eliot's finest religious poetry springs; in
that humanity the music of his verse was so subtly formed. To understand
this, consider what Eliot withstood. Think of him in Glasgow at the height
of the Second World War, just along the road from blitzed Clydebank,
delivering a lecture at Glasgow University on—of all things—'The Music
of Poetry'. The pressures to pontificate, to propagandise, to preach, must
have been intense. Eliot, though, withstands all those wartime pressures
to focus instead on the acoustics of articulation in verse. Similarly in the
Quartets the apparently isolated struggle of the poet to make poetry is not

---

[12] T. S. Eliot, 'What Dante means to me', in *To Criticize the Critic and Other Writings* (1965; repr. London, 1978), p. 127.

directly compared to, but is fused with the struggles of fishing communities, fighters, and others. The *Quartets* turn on themselves, sometimes with striking self-laceration, even as they move towards attunement and resolution. These are poems that do partake of the marmoreal, but have also learned to voice vulnerability.

Vulnerability was part of Eliot's articulation from the start. It is there in Prufrock's love-song. Yet Eliot's articulation was also spikily self-protective. To realise the hypnotic power of vulnerable desperation that is in his greatest work you only have to read to primary-school-age children and see them react to the obsessive, intense longing in the section of 'What the Thunder Said' which begins with 'Here there is no water but only rock' and ends,

> If there were water
> And no rock
> If there were rock
> And also water
> And water
> A spring
> A pool among the rock
> If there were the sound of water only
> Not the cicada
> And dry grass singing
> But sound of water over a rock
> Where the hermit-thrush sings in the pine trees
> Drip drop drip drop drop drop drop
> But there is no water[13]

Eliot's poetry runs the gamut from difficulty to directness. Sometimes, as here, the acoustic complexity, the clear yet magnificently clogged music of the lines, is bound up with a directness felt before fully explicable. Nowhere is this more true than in 'Marina'.

Whether writing of 'No water', of 'Nothing again nothing' or of the 'Unreal', Eliot's work is suffused with negatives, vacancies, absences. His life, too, had its profound Macavities. He had no daughter, and once said so straightforwardly to a correspondent who asked him about 'Marina'.[14] T. S. Eliot might seem an unlikely candidate if one were thinking of parental poems. To some the suggestion might sound a joke, but that is where Valerie Eliot's remark that 'Ideally he should have had about ten children' might give us pause. Just as ideas of home, rootedness, and

---

[13] Eliot, *Complete Poems and Plays*, pp. 72–3.
[14] I am grateful to Professor Ronald Schuchard for telling me about this as yet unpublished letter.

rootlessness obsessed Eliot, if only because he felt himself a *metoikos*, a resident alien, a displaced person, so there came a time in his life when thoughts of paternity and children meant much to him. Out of that came both 'Marina' and the poems now best known through the musical *Cats*, and originally read to children, sometimes over tea, by the Edward Lear-loving author of *Old Possum's Book of Practical Cats*. Valerie Eliot has spoken of how 'deep in [Eliot] there was a need for family life . . . there was a little boy in him that had never been released'.[15] In *Old Possum's Book of Practical Cats* Eliot in the 1930s attempted such a release. This took him back to his own childhood when his father had drawn pictures of cats, but it also allowed him as a childless man to connect with the children of friends.

We can tell that lines which haunted Eliot many years earlier were Sappho's marvellous fragment of attunement and maternal regard,

> Hesperus, ferrying home all bright dawn scattered,
> You ferry home the sheep, you ferry home the goat, you ferry the child
> home to mother.[16]

If Eliot may incline towards Sappho's fragment in the verse of *The Waste Land*, he does so with irony:

> the evening hour that strives
> Homeward, and brings the sailor home from sea,
> The typist home at teatime . . .

Yet Eliot's note on this passage is odd. He wrote that it 'may not appear as exact as Sappho's lines, but I had in mind the "longshore" or "dory" fisherman, who returns at nightfall'.[17] Eliot fuses Sappho with Stevenson's 'Requiem', that poem which begins 'Under the wide and starry sky' and ends '*Home is the sailor, home from sea,* | *And the hunter home from the hill.*'[18] This may be an act of poetic intuition which recognises Robert Louis Stevenson's poem of stars and homecoming as a version of Sappho's, albeit a darker interpretation of the theme, where evening brings the homecoming of death. In *The Waste Land* the fusion of Sappho with Stevenson is ironic; one more gesture towards the death-in-life that

---

[15] See above, n. 2.

[16] This translation of Sappho's fragment is from Robert Crawford, *Full Volume* (London, 2008), p. 33.

[17] Eliot, *Complete Poems and Plays*, pp. 68, 78.

[18] Robert Louis Stevenson, 'Requiem', in Robert Crawford and Mick Imlah (eds.), *The New Penguin Book of Scottish Verse* (London, 2000), p. 372.

obsesses the poem. However, in Eliot's note the apparently superfluous glance towards dory fishermen, like other passages to do with sailing or the sea in his writing, harks back to his teenage years in New England where his father and mother had their summer home in the fishing port of Gloucester, Massachusetts.

It is absolutely characteristic of Eliot as a poet to secrete personal associations under an apparently impersonal carapace, then hint at what he has done. While the linking of Sappho's homecoming lines on the evening star to experiences of his own childhood and youth is interred below irony in *The Waste Land*, the cluster of associations which Eliot here constellates around a glance at Sappho's fragment will exfoliate elsewhere in his work. That exfoliation occurs not least in *Ash-Wednesday* and in 'The Dry Salvages', but nowhere more compellingly than in 'Marina'.[19]

'Marina' is so striking a sound system because of the way its lines ebb and flow, flow and ebb. Most obviously this happens in the second verse paragraph when four different long lines up to fifteen syllables in length alternate with the repeated one-word monosyllabic line, 'Death'. Each line flows out only to be called back to the same place. The second verse paragraph of 'Marina' is just one example from a poem full of tidal movement. The opening lines also ebb and flow, alternating in length and letting their surprisingly unpunctuated elements float so that line breaks, guiding and guided by the syntax while themselves acting as punctuation, are crucial to the poem's acoustic. Aspects of Eliot's poem may well be ghosted by Kipling's short story of hidden children, 'They', and by Whitman's whispering sea in 'Out of the Cradle Endlessly Rocking' with its 'Death, death, death, death, death,' but 'Marina' has a soundscape of its own.

'Marina' is one of Eliot's greatest feats of what he called 'the auditory imagination'.[20] Its use of internal rhyme is astonishing. He rhymes not only within a line, 'By this grace dissolved in place', but also (as presently published) across the division of the verse paragraphs, so that, after the blank, across the gulf between the sections, the rhyme is picked up again, mid-line: 'What is this face, less clear and clearer.' A similar device is heard a little later:

[19] All quotations from 'Marina' are taken from Eliot, *The Complete Poems and Plays*, pp. 109–10.
[20] T. S. Eliot, *The Use of Poetry and the Use of Criticism*, 2nd edn. (London, 1964), p. 118.

> Whispers and small laughter between leaves and hurrying feet
> Under sleep, where all the waters meet.
>
> Bowsprit cracked with ice and paint cracked with heat.

Here the end-rhymes, which would normally be confined to one verse or verse paragraph in a poem (other than in, say, a villanelle), are continued across the verse paragraphs, bridging the separation, while the 'ee' sound of 'feet', 'meet' and 'heat' is also fleetingly present mid-line in 'between' and 'sleep'. As the divisions between verse paragraphs enact a separation, so the persistence of sound patterns articulates a joining. The acoustic of separation, apparent disjunction, that is overcome by a further act of join-ing—of rhyme—is parallelled by the way the separation, the loss, of forgetting is balanced against the bringing back of memory. As poetry often must, 'Marina' activates the links between recall in the sense of remembering and recall in the sense of uttering repeated sounds or calls.

> Bowsprit cracked with ice and paint cracked with heat.
> I made this, I have forgotten
> And remember.
> The rigging weak and the canvas rotten
> Between one June and another September.
> Made this unknowing, half conscious, unknown, my own.

The focusing and refocusing of sound in that line—from 'unknowing' through 'unknown' to 'my own'—is part of the acoustic shifting of this foggy poem whose elements keep slipping in and out of focus, just as its sounds keep slipping in and out of rhyme. Elements in 'Marina', both sounds and images, seem far off, only to emerge close up. They appear remote, then re-emerge as internal. They are islanded yet joined, scattered but netted in a pattern, lost but found. It is in his finest poetry rather than in many of his social or critical writings (which are at their finest when closest to the music and making of poetry) that T. S. Eliot best sets out his ideas of order, his sounding of a sound system.

For many first-time readers of the poem, the title 'Marina' functions principally to emphasise the marine, flotational currents of the verse, and to supply a name for the 'daughter'. Listeners aware of the allusion to Shakespeare's *Pericles* (quickened, it seems, by the early work of G. Wilson Knight) will find confirmation that the poem is indeed about recovery, about 'recall' in the sense of memory, calling back, calling again and again.[21] Readers ready to grasp the allusion to Seneca's *Hercules Furens*

---

[21] See G. Wilson Knight, 'My romantic tendencies', *Studies in Romanticism*, 21 (1982), pp. 556–7. I am grateful to Professor John Haffenden for directing me to this article.

(from which the poem's Latin epigraph comes) will find backing for the perception that the poem is about loss, death, sundering: *Hercules Furens* features a man who has murdered his children. But these things are embodied in the poem's own sights, sounds, words, emotions. The allusions, however helpful, are less essential to the poem than its word-music. That word-music, that sound system, most fundamentally carries the meaning.

'Marina' remains one of Eliot's least discussed poems. It is, too, his most beautiful. It begins by being suspended between a stunned sense of dislocation and a longing for relationship,

> What seas what shores what grey rocks and what islands
> What water lapping the bow
> And scent of pine and the woodthrush singing through the fog
> What images return
> O my daughter.

Part of the poem's beauty comes to lie in its achieved hope and sense of newness, 'the hope, the new ships'; also in its confirmatory acoustic, strengthened by the rondo, the echo-sounding relocation that is the concluding verse paragraph,

> What seas what shores what granite islands towards my timbers
> And woodthrush calling through the fog
> My daughter.

As in the opening of the poem, these lines have so little punctuation that their tone is hard to fathom. Yet their recovery at the end of 'Marina', and the way the poem's cumulative effect has built for the words a new context, one of new life, new hope, has a confirmatory effect. We have moved from a longing or marvelling invocation at the start of the poem, to a closer, more assured conclusion where the daughter is recalled. Though her presence may be only something called up by a thrush's song (a phenomenon associated in *The Waste Land* and 'Burnt Norton' with childhood and with hallucination or mirage), nevertheless there is also in the clear, present finality of that short, two-word last line a sense of parental closeness.

This is so strong that sometimes readers are surprised to learn T. S. Eliot had no daughter, and that the 'I' of the poem is not Eliot himself as a parent. One can feel superior in pointing this out, calling attention to theories of impersonality, the persona, allusion—but there are dangers in such superiority if it leads us too far away from the undeniable power of the word 'daughter' in the poem, and from that sense of intense, personal-sounding longing it embodies.

That sense of longing is a predominant emotion in the work of a
writer so obsessed with what the Victorian poet James Thomson called
'memory and desire'.[22] More specifially, biographically oriented critics in
recent decades have tended to wish to relate Eliot's sense of longing in
Ash-Wednesday and other poems of the 1930s or early 1940s to a sense
of sexual sublimation associated with his relationship with Emily Hale.
She was the woman Eliot seems to have been in love with before he left
America in 1914, and with whom from the late 1920s, when he sent her
his essay on 'Shakespeare and the Stoicism of Seneca', he enjoyed for
many years a new, companionable relationship. This ended as Hale came
to realise that, even after the death of Eliot's first wife, there would be no
possibility of marriage. Eliot's relationship with Hale was so long hidden
that its disclosure in print in the 1970s created a flurry of interest.
Commentators like Lyndall Gordon who detect Hale somewhere in the
background to 'Marina' may have a point, but also miss a point.[23] The
female figure in 'Marina' is not the 'Lady' of *Ash-Wednesday*; she is
specifically, as in Shakespeare's *Pericles*, a daughter.

Eliot wrote the poem in May 1930. Corresponding that July with his
American friend E. McKnight Kauffer (who would illustrate 'Marina' for
the Ariel Poems series), he explained that its 'theme is paternity'.[24] There
are good reasons for thinking very seriously about why such a theme
might have been important to Eliot at this time, and why the poem as a
paternal poem, as well as a poem of rhyme and attunement, may be
infused with such power.

'What every poet starts from is his own emotions', Eliot stated in
'Shakespeare and the Stoicism of Seneca' in 1927, when he also wrote of
how

> I am used . . . to having my personal biography reconstructed from passages
> which I got out of books, or which I invented out of nothing because they
> sounded well; and to having my biography invariably ignored in what I *did* write
> from personal experience . . .[25]

But it is striking how sheerly and surely Eliot used passages out of books
to channel, fuse with, and articulate personal experience. If the young

---

[22] See Robert Crawford, *The Savage and the City in the Work of T. S. Eliot* (Oxford, 1987), p. 37.

[23] Lyndall Gordon, *Eliot's New Life* (Oxford, 1988), gives by far the fullest account of Emily
Hale and Eliot's relationship with her.

[24] T. S. Eliot, letter to E. McKnight Kauffer, 24 July 1930, published in James Olney (ed.), *T. S. Eliot:
Essays from The Southern Review* (Oxford, 1988), p. 211.

[25] T. S. Eliot, *Selected Essays*, 3rd enlarged edn. (London, 1951), p. 127.

poet astutely stressed impersonality, the middle-aged poet, equally rightly, could complain of the personal pain which had led to *The Waste Land*. When Eliot creates a poem about a daughter in 'Marina' and states that the theme is paternity, we might just choose to take him seriously. There is every reason to believe that the theme preoccupied him.

Eliot wrote the poem when he was in his early forties. His father had died over a decade earlier; his artistic sister Charlotte (with whom as a boy Eliot had relished hunting for New England birds' nests) had died in 1926; his mother died in 1929, the year before the composition of 'Marina' and two years before the publication of 'Difficulties of a Statesman' with its 'What shall I cry? | Mother mother'.[26] In 1927, when he joined the Church of England, in conversation with Bertrand Russell Eliot had said that he would have no children; in 1928, while still living in a tormented marriage with his first wife, he had taken a vow of celibacy, putting an end to any prospect of biological fathering; though for years, as he later told John Hayward, he had felt with great acuteness the 'desire for progeny'.[27] Eliot never became a parent, but at the end of the 1920s he did become for the first time a godparent—a role he hugely relished, taking it both playfully and seriously; and in the 1930s, his experience as a godparent allowed his poetry to take a new direction: he devoted considerable poetic energy to writing for children, sending to his godchildren several of the poems that would become *Old Possum's Book of Practical Cats*.[28]

Eliot's ability to engage with children mattered to him as a man and as a poet. Written in mid-life, when he was confronting the loss of his own parents and the painful fact that he would remain childless, but also when he was beginning to find a role as a godparent, 'Marina' articulates both a longing for paternity, for a child, and a recognition that conventional biological paternity may not be possible. The poem is suspended, like the Christian story, between the arrival and the loss of a child. Again, as in the Christian story, loss is redeemed through a sense of continuing presence, one still haunted by the fear of loss. Yet to 'Christianise' the poem too tritely is to misread it; one of the great strengths of Eliot's poetry is its resistance to religious triteness, its acceptance of religious depth. This

[26] Eliot, *Complete Poems and Plays*, p. 129.
[27] See Carole Seymour-Jones, *Painted Shadow: the Life of Vivienne Eliot* (London, 2002), p. 449; Seymour-Jones quotes Eliot's letter to John Hayward, 29 Nov. 1939 (Hayward Bequest, King's College, Cambridge).
[28] See Valerie Eliot, 'Apropos of Practical Cats', in *Cats: the Book of the Musical* (London, 1981), pp. 8–9.

is not a poem about 'the Son' or 'Our Lady'; it is a poem addressed to 'My daughter'; it is a poem involving longing for a child.

In terms of conventional assumptions, the expression of such a theme may have been associated more with women than with men. 'Marina' may be the first fully achieved poem by a male poet in English to articulate such a longing. There is a sense in which the poem moves beyond (some might say 'sublimates') this desire. Certainly Eliot in 1929 wrote of the uneasy connection between 'higher love' and 'the coupling of animals', and related Dante's *Vita Nuova* to 'what is now called "sublimation"'.[29] Eliot had an interest in the way Dante (as he put it in 1927) 'attempts to fabricate something permanent and holy out of his personal animal feelings'.[30] 'Marina' may involve a repression of animal feelings

> Those who suffer the ecstasy of the animals, meaning
> Death

and the daughter of the poem may come to represent a more general, more spiritualised *vita nuova*, a new life in 'the hope, the new ships'. However, to deny the sheer insistent longing for a child in the poem, the importance of the phrase 'My daughter', is to deny a source of its emotional power, one supported by the point in Eliot's life at which it was composed. To ignore the longing for a child in 'Marina' is also to ignore that tidal music which is all water and boats, memory and voyaging, and which heads from the name of a daughter through the longing words 'O my daughter' to culminate in the words 'My daughter'. Simply to see the poem as a spiritual quest, or a sublimated love poem, misses the longing urgency of those specific last words. The theme is not just spiritual journeying, but something more focused than that. Like Sappho's Hesperus fragment, the poem is about an attunement with the rhythms of creation 'more distant than stars and nearer than the eye', but it is also about longing for a particular form of creation, one known as a parent knows, rhymes with, yet is different from, a child. To skim beyond that, or brush it aside, is to misread the 'Marina'. The theme is not some generalised spirituality. The theme, as Eliot said it was, is paternity.

Readers often sense this. Muriel Spark, who read Eliot's poetry with great attention, chooses a phrase from 'Marina'—'What images return'—as the title of the brilliant short piece she wrote about her home back-

[29] Eliot, *Selected Essays*, pp. 274, 275.
[30] Eliot, *Selected Essays*, p. 137.

ground and her sense of exile at the time of her father's death.[31] A feeling for Eliot's own family background, and for a vital geography from which he, like Spark, had moved away, also conditions 'Marina'. With its long and short lines and its irregularly islanded verse paragraphs, linked as an archipelago by end-rhyme, internal rhyme, enjambment and syntax, yet also distinct from each other, this poem's acoustic and its sometimes peninsular, sometimes bitten right-hand margin—its coastline if you like—is one of bays and islands. Its imagery is of grey rocks, islands, pine, woodthrush and fog, but there are no placenames. Eliot's editing of the poem, in cutting a placename, lets 'Marina' speak of the shorelines of the planet rather than of a specific site. In an earlier draft, now in the Bodleian Library, Eliot mentions Roque Island in Maine where he had sailed as a student in a small boat, risking death in the fog, but also relishing being at sea.[32] The speaker's sense of being 'at sea' in more than one sense of that expression is essential to the poem.

These voyages of Eliot's youth stayed with him all his life. As an old man, delighting in photographs and the log book of his sailing in Maine, he recalled (in letters now at Harvard) putting in at Jonesport and passing Roque Island.[33] He also recalled spending a night nearby aboard a small boat moored to a buoy during fog.[34] Roque Island with its mile-long white sands, old boatyard, sawmill, woods and associations with long-established New England families like the Peabodies was the kind of territory Eliot had relished from his youth. In a 1930 letter he describes 'Marina' as set round Casco Bay in Maine, which is in the same vicinity.[35] Yet the associations of this area were not bound up only with his student sailing exploits, but rather with a familial sense of north-eastern North America. It was most likely when camping with his family near Lake Memphromagog in Quebec that the teenage Eliot seems to have heard the 'water-dripping song' of the 'hermit-thrush' which so haunted his inner ear; at least as much as that of the Coleridgean owlet of 'Frost at Midnight', and more than the nightingale's, thrushes' songs spurred and

---

[31] Muriel Spark, 'What images return', in Karl Miller (ed.), *Memoirs of a Modern Scotland* (London, 1970), p. 151.
[32] See draft with Eliot's letter to Michael Sadler, 9 May 1930 (Bodleian Library, Oxford University).
[33] T. S. Eliot, letter to Leon Magaw Little, 11 Aug. 1956 (Houghton Library, Harvard University, bMSAm1691.4).
[34] T. S. Eliot, letter to Leon Magaw Little, 12 Oct. 1956 (Houghton Library, Harvard University, bMSAm1691.4).
[35] Eliot to Kauffer, 24 July 1930, in Olney (ed.), *T. S. Eliot*, p. 211.

schooled the twentieth century's greatest poet.[36] Eliot spent a lot of time at Eastern Point, Gloucester, Massachusetts, where his father had built a house in 1896, when Tom was eight. Shortly after the completion of 'Marina' in 1930, Eliot wrote to William Force Stead that he had felt a nomad even in America where, having spent his boyhood in Missouri, he was sufficiently a southerner to be something of an alien in Massachusetts, and how even when he was young the New England of his associations existed more in Maine than it did in Massachusetts.[37]

It is Maine as the paternal geography of Eliot's associations that undergirds this great poem of paternity. 'Marina' imagines its way longingly forwards towards the image of a daughter, but also harks way back to a lost but recalled and universalised Maine which stands for the landscape of Eliot's deepest familial associations, his paternity now his parents are dead. As this paternity of past and future comes in and out of focus, is lost and found, the poem achieves its balance. It locates and enacts an attunement and momentary resolution with far and near, past and future. This is expressed in personal and impersonal terms. The personal—the daughter—becomes impersonal through the poem's allusive title, but retains surely the power of a secreted longing for paternity. The impersonal, the coastline, becomes personal through the release of familial associations, though this operates in a way that is hidden by the universalising voice. This poem's sound system is at once broken and whole, fissured in layout and lineation, yet linked through rhyme, repetition, rondo, so that its wholeness predominates, pronouncing it a sound system in both senses of that expression. Completely unconfessional, 'Marina' is nonetheless a poem born from the deepest longing for paternity, the kind of paternity which will provide a sense of home in the universe. That sense of home and attunement in this poem by an ingrained *metoikos*, is both intimate and out of reach: those two aspects of it are come to terms with in the poem as a whole, and, in miniature, in that most haunting part-line, 'more distant than stars and nearer than the eye'.

We have been cursed to live in an age not of poems but of 'texts'. It is the job of the poet to defend and reincarnate the 'sound system' of the poem so that it may both sound and be sound beyond mere textuality. The poem should work not *only* aloud; but it needs a fine sense of acoustic as well as textual life, if it is to be fully realised as a near perfect

---

[36] Eliot, *Complete Poems and Plays*, p. 79; Eliot, *Letters, Volume 1, 1898–1922*, p. 4.
[37] Eliot, letter to William Force Stead, 20 June 1930 (Stead Boxes, Osborn Shelves, Beinecke Library, Yale University).

ordering of language. In seeking the sound system, the poet aims for attunement; this attunement may be with tribe or nation, but may also, and perhaps more pressingly, be with those most intimately linked to the poet—a lover, a friend, a child, a parent—and with the wider rhythms of the cosmos. Poems from lover to lover are as old as lyric poetry, but, though there are ancient precedents, the great concentration of poems from parent to child is relatively recent. Changes in attitudes to gender have meant that in our own day there is a large number of poems addressed by parents to children. There are poems by men as well as by women about childlessness, and about parenthood. These are written out of that need for attunement with the processes of creation which, however deconstructed or derided, remains fundamental to the making of poetry, to the articulation of its sound system. This impulse goes back beyond poetry, but is part of what poetry comes out of. It articulates an impulse older than Stonehenge or Maes Howe. But in the last two centuries, in their very different and pioneering ways, no two poets have written out of such impulses in the context of paternity more eloquently than S. T. Coleridge in 'Frost at Midnight' and T. S. Eliot in 'Marina'. We can criticise these poems—not least for their seeming absence of mothers—but not for their sound systems, their music, their sense of parental longing, their deep communication of a desire for hopeful attunement with the cosmos. Biographical study confirms that in offering these things, T. S. Eliot's daughter poem does the most that poems can do. 'Marina', a poem shaped by biographical circumstances but also a crafted work of art made to resonate far beyond that experience, reminds us in our inner ears why we need the sound systems of poetry. In its rhythms, its open longing, its arresting and intimate justness, it also reminds us not only of the astonishing skill but also of the profound humanity of the poet T. S. Eliot

Arthur Miller:
Realism, Language, Poetry

CHRISTOPHER BIGSBY
University of East Anglia

ARTHUR MILLER, you might have good reason to think, was not only celebrated around the world but also in his own country. Curiously, this was not the fact, and certainly not in the last thirty years of his life, though in truth the hostility was born much earlier. Writing in *Partisan Review*, Phillip Rahv headed his essay, 'The myth of Arthur Miller's profundity'. In the same magazine, Susan Sontag commented on his 'intellectual weak mindedness'.[1] In *Commentary*, Delmore Schwartz spoke of 'the retarded conscience of Arthur Miller, the ballplayer for whom Marilyn Monroe consented to be circumcised',[2] seemingly confusing Miller with Joe Dimaggio. *The New Republic* greeted his autobiography with a grotesque caricature on the front cover and described it as 'unwieldy and blockish', composed, as it was, of 'glutinous sentences' which failed even to show a proper respect for logical order since 'the reader of an artist's autobiography naturally expects chronological order'. He was the kind of writer, it added, admired by assistant professors of drama for whom the stupidity of his moral assertions 'will never go out of fashion in the classroom'.[3]

According to the American critic Stanley Kauffmann, who has taught at the Yale School of Drama, Arthur Miller's plays 'suffer from fuzzy

Read at the Academy as part of British Academy Literature Week, 19–22 October 2009.

[1] Susan Sontag, 'Going to the theater and the movies', *Partisan Review*, 33 (Spring, 1964), 285.
[2] James Atlas, *Delmore Schwartz: The Life of an American Poet* (New York, 1977), p. 361.
[3] David Denby, 'Arthur Miller, America's connoisseur of Guilt: All My Sins', *The New Republic*, 8 Feb. 1988, pp. 30–4.

Proceedings of the British Academy, **167**, 499–513. © The British Academy 2010.

concepts, transparent mechanics, superficial probes, and pedestrian diction'. *Death of a Salesman* he thought a 'flabby, occasionally false work'.[4] Writing in *The New Republic* in 1971 he described Miller as 'all munched out', and the following year said that going to a Miller play was like going to the funeral of a man you wish you could have liked more. Struggling to account for Miller's international success, he suggested that it might be because his language 'improves in translation', which, of course, puts the British in a strange position.

The American academic and director Robert Brustein, regular reviewer for the *New Republic*, saw Miller as evidence of 'consumer theatre'. When the Long Wharf Theatre in New Haven embraced his work, it was opting for 'domestic realism—plays in which people discuss their problems over hot meals', the kind of theatre likely to appeal to New Haven's middle class who wished to be 'lulled by the sight of familiar lives on stage'.[5] This came, incidentally, from an admirer of Chekhov, a writer who once remarked that, 'A play should be written in which people arrive, go away, have dinner . . . just eat their dinner, and all the time their happiness is being established or their lives being broken up.'[6] For Brustein, Miller's talent was 'minor'. *After the Fall* was scandalous, *Incident at Vichy* 'an old dray horse about to be melted down for glue'.[7] The two plays were 'moribund in their style, ideas, and language'.[8] In retrospect, even *Death of a Salesman* seemed no more than 'a realistic problem play'.[9] He described Miller's 1994 play, *Broken Glass*, as another spiral in a stumbling career. In Britain, it won the Olivier Award as Best Play of the Year.

For American critic Richard Gilman, drama reviewer for *Commonweal* and *Newsweek*, and, like Brustein, once a professor of drama at Yale, Miller was 'a narrow realist, with a hopeless aspiration to poetry, and a moralist with greatly inadequate equipment for the projection of moral complexity'.[10] Only once, in *Death of a Salesman*, did his powers prove commensurate with his theme, so that he was able to compose 'a flawed but representative image of an aspect of our experience. One other time,

---

[4] Stanley Kaufmann, *Persons of the Drama* (New York, 1976), p. 144.
[5] Robert Brustein, *Making Scenes* (New York, 1981), p. 220.
[6] Ronald Hingley, *Chekhov* (London, 1950), p. 233.
[7] Robert Brustein, *Seasons of Discontent* (London, 1966), p. 259.
[8] Ibid., p. 19.
[9] Ibid., p. 242.
[10] Richard Gilman, *Common and Uncommon Masks: Writings on Theatre 1961–1970* (New York, 1971), p. 152.

in *The Crucible*, his deficient language achieved a transcendence through its borrowing from history. And that is all, literally everything.'[11]

The distinguished American drama reviewer John Lahr, in speaking of Miller's *The Price*, referred to his 'turgid naturalism', a phrase also used by American critic Leslie Fiedler, who thought Miller 'an over-rated playwright whose dramas were as devious as his public life',[12] while Mary McCarthy referred to what she called his long practice as a realist. So, I suppose that is clear, then. Arthur Miller, apparently, at least from a certain American perspective, was a writer of irredeemably realist works, a minor talent who had a problem with language and a preference for plays with hot meals.

Miller was stung by such critics, to the point sometimes of depression. As he remarked, 'they kill you. They can really destroy you . . . I remember Chekhov writing somebody a letter saying that if he had listened to the critics he would have died drunk in the gutter . . . I was just reading a biography of Ibsen, in which he was inveighing against the critics in the same way . . . I don't think twelve people in this country could name the Norwegian critics at the time of Ibsen, and yet they were the real bane of his life.'[13]

I am going to leave aside just why so many American critics responded as they did. I have tried to deal with that elsewhere. I will leave aside, too, the difficulty of reconciling Miller's supposed realism with such plays as *After the Fall*, *The Creation of the World and Other Business*, *The American Clock*, *Elegy for a Lady*, *Clara*, *The Ride Down Mount Morgan*, *Mr. Peters' Connections*, and *Resurrection Blues*. Instead I am going to concentrate on his earlier work, especially on *Death of a Salesman* and the question of realism, of language, of poetry.

> Under thy shadow by the piers I waited;
> Only in darkness is thy shadow clear.
> The City's fiery parcels all undone,
> Already snow submerges an iron year
>
> O Sleepless as the river under thee,
> Vaulting the sea, the prairie's dreaming sod,
> Unto us lowliest sometimes sweep, descend
> And of the curveship lend a myth to God.[14]

---

[11] Ibid., p. 153.

[12] Nathan David Abrams, *Struggling For Freedom: Arthur Miller, the Commentary Community and the Cultural Cold War* (Birmingham, 1998).

[13] Matthew Roudané, *Conversations with Arthur Miller* (Jackson, 1987), p. 208.

[14] Hart Crane, *Complete Poems* (New York, 2000), p. 44.

Hart Crane on Brooklyn Bridge of which Arthur Miller once remarked, 'To walk the bridge . . . without thinking of Hart Crane's poem was an impiety, and it came to one's lips the way grace does to the devout at dinner. But unlike grace at dinner, it somehow defined the object being blessed more vividly than even one's own eyes could.'[15] There, it seems to me, apart from an unforgivable reference to dinner, he is celebrating the bridge, Hart Crane's poem and the ability of art and language to capture and elevate the real.

This was the bridge from which he looked out on the Red Hook district of Brooklyn that would become the location for his play *A View From the Bridge* which opens with a lawyer and a speech in which American prose embraces American poetry:

> This is the slum that faces the bay on the seaward side of New York swallowing the tonnage of the world . . . every few years . . . the flat air in my office suddenly washes in with the green scent of the sea, the dust in this air is blown away and the thought comes that in some Caesar's year, in Calabria perhaps or on the cliff at Syracuse, another lawyer, quite differently dressed, heard the same complaint and sat there as powerless as I, and watched it run its bloody course.'[16]

The original one-act version of that play was in fact a verse drama which he subsequently transcribed into prose and expanded for the two-act version, but the poetry is still there. And it is a poetry that is even to be heard in the inarticulate forays into language by Eddie Carbone.

Frequently and erroneously characterised as a social realist Miller was always drawn to the poetic, sometimes quite literally, drafting parts of *Death of a Salesman* and *The Crucible* in verse, but he also remarked of Willy Loman in *Death of a Salesman* that he was not a real person but a 'figure in a poem'. What is that poem? It is the play but in a sense, surely, it is also America, the America, at least, that Willy Loman imagines himself to inhabit as he sets out, like a pioneer, to conquer not the west, where his father had ventured on a wagon, but the buyers in Macys, Gimbels and Filene's department stores. This is not simply, though, a play about a family and a man's last day on earth. It reaches out beyond the walls of a small Brooklyn frame house and in doing so, Miller insisted, required something more than a realist's touch. Prose, he declared, is the language

[15] Arthur Miller, *Echoes Down the Corridor: Collected Essays, 1944–2000*, ed. Steven R. Centola (New York, 2000), p. 186.
[16] Arthur Miller, *A View from the Bridge and All My Sons* (Harmondsworth, 1961), p. 12.

of family relations; it is the inclusion of the larger world beyond that naturally opens a play to the poetic.

Death of a Salesman, which opens with a flute 'telling of grass and trees and the horizon', is the story of something more than a salesman whose dream of America is fading, as that horizon shrinks to a Brooklyn backyard. It is the story of the poem that is America the perfection of whose form is no longer easy to sustain, a poem fast turning into prose. As Miller once remarked, 'what we do privately has consequences. But since trying to trace that in concrete terms is almost impossible we are backed up into metaphor and analogy and poetry, which is the only way you handle it anyway.'[17]

Robert Lowell, in an essay on 'Poets and the Theatre', invoked, not altogether without sympathy, the poet and critic Yvor Winters's observation that, 'In general I think the world would be well enough off without actors. They appear capable of any of three feats—of making the grossly vulgar appear acceptably mediocre; of making the acceptably mediocre appear what it is; and of making the distinguished appear acceptably mediocre.'[18] For his part, Lowell confessed to unease in the presence of drama insisting, somewhat oddly, that 'No two arts are more opposed than poetry and our theatre.' Since in origin poetry and drama were joined at the hip perhaps the clue is in the word 'our'. He was talking primarily about the American theatre, acknowledging the greatness of two playwrights—O'Neill and Williams—but suggesting that they were 'more on the fringe of our high culture than part of it'.

And there the key phrase is 'high culture'. In other words, drama might be invited to the party but for preference should use the tradesman's entrance. Poetry, however, was undeniably literature even, he confessed, 'if it may not be considered American, or even involved with the human race',[19] that last remark, admittedly, being somewhat gnomic.

For his part, he admitted, he had 'always felt splenetic about the stage, known very little of it, and shivered at the suggestion that I write for it'. Many American plays struck him as 'fun' but not to be compared with the work of Faulkner or Eliot. Then, as he says, 'I found I had written a play of my own', clearly a piece of inadvertance that left him astonished and not a little embarrassed. Helpfully, he explained, 'I now feel double-faced,

---

[17] Ron Rifkin, 'Arthur Miller', *Bomb Magazine*, 49 (Fall 1994), <http://bomsite.com/issues/49/articles/1827> accessed 11 March 2010.
[18] Robert Lowell, *Collected Prose* (London, 1987), p. 176.
[19] Ibid., p. 177.

looking on plays as some barbarian Gaul or Goth might have first looked on Rome, his shaggy head full of moral disgust, plunder and adaptation.'[20]

In a way his position is understandable. Certainly poets have frequently made a pig's ear of writing for the theatre. The last great English play in verse, Lowell explained in 1963, was Milton's *Samson Agonistes*, published in 1671, not much of a hit rate for poets in the theatre as far as Lowell was concerned. It was also, though, he thought, the only great English play that cannot be acted, which, given his view of actors, might be thought to be a recommendation. In the twentieth century he thought *Sweeney Agonistes* and the last short plays of Yeats had something going for them and that Brecht was a poet even if he wrote in prose. But there things, as far as Lowell was concerned, rather stopped. Arthur Miller, you will note, did not even make it into the tradesman's entrance though he and Lowell would be partners when it came to protesting against the Vietnam war, at one meeting, called Poets for Peace, held in New York's Town Hall in 1967, Miller even reading out an extended poem. And Miller wrote poems throughout his life, though seldom published them.

The fact is that Miller, who is thought of as a writer of prose realism, in fact wrote verse dramas and resisted descriptions of himself as a realistic writer. As he remarked, 'when I came to writing *All My Sons*, which was, indeed, avowedly a very realistic play in its structure, using very realistic speech . . . that stuck for the rest of my work in some minds . . . [in fact] I've been writing a kind of poem all these years, but I tried not to let the audience in on it because, once they hear that word, they go to the exit'.[21] It was Richard Eyre, though, who remarked that 'no theatrical naturalism—if taken seriously, as opposed to being half-hearted convention—is without poetry'.[22] He also said that 'Theatre is intrinsically poetic, it thrives on metaphor',[23] and Miller once remarked that he did not write plays, he wrote metaphors. His problem with the critics was that they took his theatrical poems and reduced them to prose. They took his metaphors and reduced them to their component parts. Presented with a butterfly, they saw only an artfully concealed caterpillar.

For Miller, 'the word "poetry" wasn't enough if a play's underlying structure was a fractured one, a concept not fully realized. A real play was

[20] Robert Lowell, *Collected Prose* (London, 1987), p. 177.
[21] Arthur Miller, *Arthur Miller in Conversation with Murray Biggs* (New Haven, CT, 2000), p. 8.
[22] Richard Eyre, *National Service: Diary of a Decade at the National Theatre* (London, 2003), p. 77.
[23] Richard Eyre, *Talking Theatre: Interviews with Theatre People* (London, 2009), p. xiii.

the discovery of the unity of its contradictions, and the essential poetry, the first poetry, was the synthesis of even the least of its parts to form a symbolic meaning.'[24] What he learned from Sean O'Casey was that 'the significantly poetic sprang from the raw and real experience of ordinary people'. Noting that J. M. Synge had rebelled against what he had called 'the joyless and pallid words' of Ibsen's realism, in search of a heightened language he recalled that James Joyce, having learned Norwegian expressly to read Ibsen, had understood the poetic structure of the plays and their sense of 'the spiritual failure of the modern world'.[25] Of his own work he noted that the speeches 'sound like real, almost reported talk when in fact they are intensely composed, compressed into a sequential inevitability that seems nature but isn't'. There is, anyway, he insisted, 'no such thing as "reality" in any theatrical exhibition that can properly be called a play'.[26] The very act of condensing time means 'that the artificial enters even as the first of its lines is being written'.[27]

When he left university in 1938, Miller expected to conquer Broadway. He submitted a play which had won a prize at the University of Michigan. It was rejected by Jewish producers as 'too Jewish'. He then worked briefly for the Federal Theatre, established as part of Roosevelt's New Deal, writing a play called *The Golden Years* about Montezuma and Cortes, not a verse drama but stained with poetry. It was to be over half a century before Miller's play was performed, and then not in America but in the UK when the BBC produced it as a radio play. So, for much of his career it remained unknown. But he had a taste for verse. When he began to write he would copy out speeches from Shakespeare's plays, the act of writing, it seemed to him, teaching him concision, what he called 'that intense inner connection of sound and meaning'.[28] He now set himself to write a verse drama for radio, and radio drama would become his chief source of income for several years before he broke through into theatre.

You may have some difficulty imagining American radio broadcasting drama, let alone verse drama, but we are talking about the late 1930s and early 1940s when radio had a mass audience and, as Miller recalled, it was possible to walk down the street in summer and hear the same programme

[24] Arthur Miller, 'On Broadway: notes on the past and future of American theatre', *Harper's Magazine* (March, 1999), 43.
[25] Ibid. 45.
[26] Ibid. 47.
[27] Ibid. 38.
[28] *Talking Theatre*, p. 127.

coming from every house. Nor was Miller, of course, the only one to write verse plays for radio. Archibald McLeish's *The Fall of the City*, in 1937, had convinced Miller that, in his words, 'radio was made for poetry'.

For the most part Miller's radio plays were journeyman work. For a series called *Cavalcade of America*, sponsored by Du Pont, whose slogan was 'Making better things for better living through chemistry', he would adapt books for broadcast a few days later performed by major actors. In amongst them, though, were some impressive works, including verse dramas, one of them about Sacajewea, the Native American who led Lewis and Clarke across America and in doing so doomed her people to destruction:

> I was young then; I saw them between the trees;
> I saw them with the West at my back. Over my shoulder
> lay the West, and their blue eyes gazed at the hills
> When they questioned me. I am very old but the memory
> Is like a pickerel shining in a pool, and I reach under
> Holding it bright and living across my palm.[29]

Later he wrote a play about Juarez and the last Emperor of Mexico. It was presented by Orson Welles and members of the Mercury Theatre whom he credited with its success. Welles, he said, could 'wrap himself around that microphone . . . So if it was in verse or not you never knew. They understood language.'[30]

> . . . They came from Tehuantepec,
> Durango and the river there, from the bay of Banderas,
> The fishermen of Marblehead came
> In their boats to crash the heights of Washington!
> The sowers of corn and the makers of bread,
> The black-eyed and the fair, the forest men
> Whose backs were bent like the trees they cut—
> They came, they came, sweetening with blood
> The deserts of long-dead centuries,
> And they scrawled new names on Mexico's face!
> *Dios y Libertad*! For God and Liberty!
> And the stones rang like bells from Guadalajara
> To the Gulf.[31]

These verse dramas were important to him not only in themselves but for what they taught him about writing. As he explained, 'I made the discovery that in verse you are forced to be brief and to the point. Verse

---

[29] Quoted in Christopher Bigsby, *Arthur Miller* (London, 2008), p. 199.
[30] Ibid., p. 201.
[31] Ibid., p. 202.

squeezes out fat and you're left with the real meaning of the language. I wanted to use language so that people thought I was using regular language. What I was slipping over was a hidden pattern, which permitted me to say much more in fewer words than I could otherwise.'[32] It is that hidden pattern that is woven into so many of his plays.

When Miller speaks of *Death of a Salesman* as a poem, though, it is not primarily its language he has in mind, though here, and elsewhere in his work, he looked for something more than authenticity. Consider Charley's speech at Willy Loman's funeral, a speech originally written in verse.

> Nobody dast blame this man. You don't understand: Willy was a salesman. And for a salesman, there is no rock bottom to the life. He don't put a bolt to a nut, he don't tell you the law or give you medicine. He's a man way out there in the blue, riding on a smile and a shoeshine . . . Nobody dast blame this man. A salesman is got to dream, boy. It comes with the territory.

Another American critic, Morris Dickstein, complained that the sentence, 'Nobody dast blame this man' was 'risible . . . pseudo poetry' and that nobody would actually say, 'I'm a dime a dozen', as Biff does to his father. This, Dickstein suggests, is an unreality as if Miller were reaching for and failing to achieve a realistic language. But the same critic rejected the play's Requiem even as he had to account for the fact that audiences for sixty years had judged otherwise. His explanation is that Miller's plays 'are ultimately performance pieces that play better than they read'.[33] Precisely. They are what we call plays.

Mary McCarthy objected to Linda's cry of 'Attention, attention must be paid to such a man,' suggesting that it was inadvertent evidence that Willy Loman was a Jew and that Miller was intent to suppress the fact. Miller had something else in mind. The construction enforces the thought, as in John Donne's poem 'Satire 3' in which we are told 'On a huge hill | Cragged, and steep, Truth stands and he that will | Reach her, about must, and about must go.'[34] 'Even the Jews have their Jews', a character observes in Miller's *Incident at Vichy*, the very echo generating a sense of the ironic and the tragic, as in Shakespeare's iterations ('to be or not to be;' 'If it were done when 'tis done.').

It was T. S. Eliot who remarked that 'What we have to do is to bring poetry into the world in which the audience lives and to which it returns

---

[32] Interview with the author, May, 2002.
[33] Morris Dickstein, 'False to life', *Times Literary Supplement*, 24 July, 2009, p. 3.
[34] A. J. Smith (ed.), *John Donne: the Complete English Poems* (London, 1971), p. 163.

when it leaves the theatre; not to transport the audience into some imaginary world totally unlike its own.' [35] He wrote in the context of a discussion of his own poetic dramas though Peter Hall suggested that he was trying to put poetry back into theatre by scattering it into ordinary dialogue like sequins. Miller, though, suggested that 'in the theatre the poetic does not depend, at least not wholly, on poetic language'.[36]

Tennessee Williams set his face against 'the straight realist play with its genuine frigidaire and authentic ice cubes, its characters that speak exactly as the audience speaks'.[37] There is a frigidaire in *Death of a Salesman* but it is located in a house which has, we are told, 'an air of the dream' about it. As Miller says, it 'seems actual enough', but there are no other fixtures. The roofline is one dimensional, the set partially transparent.

Miller's first successful play, *All My Sons*, was realistic. An earlier play, a fable called *The Man Who Had All the Luck*, had failed spectacularly, so he turned to Ibsen as a model. So close was *All My Sons* to Ibsen's work, indeed, that in early drafts the characters are given Norwegian names. But it was not the kind of play he wanted to write. Things changed when he attended the New Haven try-out of Tennessee Williams's *A Streetcar Named Desire*. Listening to Williams's language, he now felt he had permission, as he said, to speak out with full voice.

In his own mind, Miller was a restless experimenter, for whom language was not to be the transcribed speech of the streets. He was interested in the unconscious poetry of those struggling to express their needs and hopes, the shifting rhythms of personal encounters. Indeed, for him the poetry of a play was constituted from all the aspects of theatre which lift words from the page onto the stage. As he remarked, 'I recall thinking that all the important things were between the lines, in the silences, the gestures, the stuff above or below the level of speech. For a while I even thought to study music, which is the art of silences hedged about by sound. Music begins *Salesman*, and not by accident; we are to hear Willy before we see him and before he speaks. He was there in the hollow of the flute, the wind, the air announcing his arrival and his doom.'[38]

The opening of *Death of a Salesman* offers a series of metaphors, from the flute music which sounds out before the curtain has even been raised, to the scene which greets the audience as the lights come up and

[35] T. S. Eliot, *On Poetry and Poets* (London, 1957), p. 82.
[36] Christopher Bigsby, 'The poet: chronicler of the age', *Humanities* (March/April, 2001), p. 13.
[37] Christopher Bigsby, *Modern American Drama* (Cambridge, 2000), p. 35.
[38] Christopher Bigsby, *Arthur Miller: a Critical Study* (Cambridge, 2005), p. 116.

they become aware of 'towering angular shapes' and 'an angry glow of orange'. The Loman house we see is described as 'fragile-seeming', enclosed as it is by apartment buildings. The flute plays on, even as its tonalities, its lyricism, are in discord with what we see. Something is happening to time as past and present are brought together, in the same way as a metaphor brings discrete experiences together to generate meaning. It was a play, he said, in which he wished to explode the watch and the calendar. The setting, Miller explains, 'is wholly or, in some places, partially transparent'. The house will fade in and out as Willy's mind roams back and forth, bending time.

And when Willy appears he carries two large suitcases. Mary McCarthy and Robert Brustein would both complain that the weakness of the play lay in the fact that we never know what is in them, precisely the kind of literalism that so dismayed Miller for whom the suitcases contained Willy's life, his dreams, for what he primarily sold, what all salesmen primarily sell, was himself and as the play unfolds we will discover that he no longer has any confidence in this product even as he remains loyal to the profession the suitcases symbolise. Today, it is a rare production whose poster does not, as did the original, feature a man, shoulders rounded, carrying two heavy suitcases, that image containing the essence of a dispirited man who still struggles to achieve a dream, locked in his own necessities, bearing the burden of a national myth of possibility as Vladimir and Estragon await the epiphany of Godot's arrival. Willy, we are told, hears the flute but is not aware of it. It is an expression of the past that is a part of him, that has shaped him, but which exists as an irony.

And still no one has delivered a line. We do not enter this play as we do a realist drama. We step in part into the world created by Willy Loman's mind, a blend of memory and hope, a golden dream lost somewhere in the journey from an invented past to an imagined future. There is a rhythm to Willy's contradictions which is that of a society always looking for the spiritual in the material. For Jay Gatsby, Daisy Buchanan became the embodiment of a romantic myth, of the happiness Americans are instructed to pursue but which they must never possess because there can be no end to their journey. For Willy Loman, the dream of possibility becomes no more than the sale he seeks to close. And yet there is something more. Beyond anything, he wishes to bring into alignment his sense of himself and the life he leads. He wants to be acknowledged, for people to notice that he has passed this way. But, as Miller remarked, he was signing his name on a block of ice on a summer's day.

But what else does the writer, the artist, do, hoping, though, that their names will be inscribed on something more permanent. Miller signed his name on his plays but also on the furniture he fashioned in the great barn where he transformed fallen trees into a table or a desk, cutting through time as he did in *Death of a Salesman*. What his characters mainly fear is death unmaking their lives, wiping out their significance.

In a sense a function of art is simultaneously to make a claim on immortality and admit to the impossibility of this in the face of what George Steiner calls 'the affront of death'. The religion that Miller eschewed offered to resolve this tension. Religion abandoned, art stands alone. The poem that is a human life has to be composed anew each time. In a poem read out at his memorial service Miller spoke of living on through his art, 'vanishing' as he said, 'into what I made'.

As George Steiner has said,

> The central conceit of the artist that the work shall outlast his own death, the existential truth that great literature, painting, architecture, music have survived their creators, are not accidental or self-regarding. It is the lucid intensity of its meeting with death that generates in aesthetic forms that statement of vitality, of life-presence, which distinguishes serious thought and feeling from the trivial and opportunistic.

It is, he says, 'within the compass of the arts that the metaphor of resurrection is given the edge of felt conjecture'.[39] It is through his death that Willy hopes to keep his name alive, in that that alone will give a perfect shape to his life which in its completion will become a poem whose rhythm and rhyme will be sustained by his sons.

At the end of the play the stage direction indicates that as Willy drives off to kill himself, leaving as his inheritance a tainted dream, 'the music crashes down in a frenzy of sound, which becomes the soft pulsation of a single cello string'.[40] The characters then break the convention established in the opening stage direction which indicates that only in the scenes set in the past do the characters breach the imaginary wall-lines. They do so now because past and present are one and they are stepping into myth. The flute now sounds out again as Willy Loman is buried and Linda cries out 'We're free', when freedom is what she and her husband have laid aside in order to take up the American burden of becoming. But the man with whom she has lived since they first settled in a once rural, now urban setting, the man whom she loves and whose illusions she has supported,

---

[39] George Steiner, *The Grammars of Creation* (London, 2001), p. 141.
[40] Arthur Miller, *Death of a Salesman* (New York, 1998), p. 109.

has gone, leaving behind a tainted dream for which he had laid down his life. She is now to be alone, in a world whose modernity has become a threat.

Perhaps there is an echo of another play in which a character is left alone, as nature gives way to houses. Just as in *Salesman* we hear the sound of a single cello string so in another play, 'A sound is heard in the distance, as if from the sky'. Chekhov, in *The Cherry Orchard*, calls for 'the sound of a breaking string, dying away, sad'. The only other sound is that of the cherry orchard being cut down. In *Death of a Salesman* 'Only the music of the flute is left on the darkening stage as over the house the hard towers of the apartment building rise into sharp focus.'[41] We tend to think of Tennessee Williams as America's Chekhov but I think there is a case for thinking it might be Miller. And was Chekhov not a poet as he wrote of a daily life beneath which a current was exerting its pull towards dissolution.

Death of a Salesman has been and continues to be produced around the world not because it is a realistic account of an American salesman. It is embraced in part because it is a play about fathers and sons, about brothers, about husbands and wives, but also because at its heart is a man who struggles to make sense of himself and his life, who knows on some level that he has failed himself and others, that time is running out, that his name will soon no longer be spoken aloud. The same stunned silence which followed the lowering of the curtain after its first performance sixty years ago was repeated in China, a country in which at the time the salesman was an alien figure and the insurance policy with which he hoped to redeem himself an unknown phenomenon.

The identifications that were to lead so many to claim Willy Loman as a relative were an acknowledgement that Miller had succeeded in bridging the gap between the real and its fictive representation. There is a will on the part of the audience to reverse the flow from fiction back to its origins, as if themselves to authenticate characters presented as mere fictions. As George Steiner elegantly puts it, 'The dramatist, the novelist instigates. He or she initiates the paradox of fertile innovative echo, resounding in every recipient and across time. This echo substantiates and reciprocates, enabling the work of art, of literature, of music to realize and multiply its intentions, enriching it (ideally) with significations, with a continuum of relevance and renewal of which the author, artist and

---

[41] Ibid., p. 112.

composer may not have been aware.'[42] The audience, in other words, extends the text, detects resonances, translates it, becomes confederate in transforming fact into metaphor, prose into poetry.

That active bargain had always been part of Miller's appeal. Steiner contemplates the mystery whereby fictive creations can 'make ghostly so many of the women and men and empirical facts we come across "out there".'[43] That was surely what Miller had detected in Hart Crane's poem. It is an uneasy truth. Perhaps it is not really a truth at all. After all, those characters may be as vivid as they are precisely because they are forever locked inside a single narrative, no matter how we extend and gloss that story with our own. We see Joe Keller and Willy Loman in the last days of their lives. Nonetheless, Willy Loman, John Proctor, and Eddie Carbone have that transcendent truth that makes them both themselves and exemplary. They patently exist in the world but have become part of the broader story that we choose to tell ourselves about the struggle to be in the world, and to leave it with what we choose to see as our integrity intact.

In *Resurrection Blues*, a character remarks that

> I am convinced now, apart from getting fed, most human activity—sports, opera, TV, movies, dressing up, dressing down—or just going for a walk—has no other purpose than to deliver us into the realm of the imagination. The imagination is a great hall where death, for example, turns into a painting, and a scream of pain becomes a song. The hall of the imagination is really where we usually live; and this is all right except for one thing—to enter that hall one must leave one's real sorrow at the door and in its stead surround oneself with images and words and music that mimic anguish but are really drained of it.[44]

It is a speech that is something more than a regret at a world in retreat from itself. It is also, surely, a confession of art's inadequacy, or rather of the gap which of necessity opens up between the truth of art and the truth of life, between the rhythm, rhyme, the ordered integrity of a poem and the sharp and sometimes incommunicable immediacy of lived experience.

Yet language is what we have. It has to bear the burden of expressing the inexpressible, felt equally by Eugene O'Neill, a man accused by Robert Brustein of being a charter member of the cult of inarticulacy:

---

[42] *The Grammars of Creation*, p. 141.
[43] Ibid., p. 142.
[44] Arthur Miller, *Plays Six* (London, 2009), p. 175.

. . . I have tried to scream!
Give pain a voice!
Make it a street singer
Acting a pantomime of tragic song . . .

But something was born wrong.
The voice strains toward a sob.
Begins and ends in silence . . .

All this,
As I have said before,
Happens where silence is;
Where I,
A quiet man,
In love with quiet,

Live quietly
Among the visions of my drowned,
Deep in my silent sea.[45]

It was Tennessee Williams who said that 'poetry doesn't have to be words
. . . In the theatre it can be situations, it can be silence.'[46] A play is a poem
which, in the words of the American director Harold Clurman, tells lies
like truth. The degree to which this is true depends in part on those who
body forth that play, inhabit its language, and in part on those who listen
and watch as a woman calls out for the man she has loved but never fully
understood. Willy Loman lived and died the life of a salesman. On some
level his was an un-inspected life and he a person of no significance. No
one came to his funeral except his family and a friendly neighbour. No
one, that is, except the audience who for sixty years have sat in the dark,
listening to the fading sound of a flute until, in silence, the word and the
pain become one.

[45] Ibid., p. 30.
[46] Ibid., p. 34.

Abstracts and Notes on Lecturers

The History of Romantic Love in Sub-Saharan Africa: between Interest and Emotion
MEGAN VAUGHAN

In the extensive comparative and historical literature on romantic love, African societies feature very little. This reflects a wider neglect of emotional regimes in the history of Africa and is in marked contrast to the large and ever-growing literature on African sexualities. Much comparative work, whilst recognising that western notions of romantic love are historically and culturally specific, then goes on to treat these as a norm against which to measure other societies. This paper attempts to explore some of the methodological and theoretical issues involved in an historical study of love in Africa and also to sketch, very broadly, the outlines of that history.

The evidence for the emotional regimes of precolonial African societies is scanty, though there is a great deal more work possible in this field. Unsurprisingly, such evidence as we have points to wide variations in African ideas and lexicons of love. In many societies intense and exclusive feelings of attraction and attachment to another were associated with youth and were explicitly set up against the socially embedded ideals of marriage. But discourses on romantic love certainly existed in some precolonial African societies. This lecture argues, against some current scholarship, that romantic love in Africa is not simply an extension of an imperialist cultural and political project, but it also argues that emotional regimes cannot be divorced from economic circumstances. Colonial rule certainly brought changes to African emotional regimes, through economic transformation, legal systems and the influence of Christianity. It also brought literacy, new expressions of love, and an association between romantic love and modernity. Romantic love is a central theme in twentieth-century African cultural productions, and the ideals associated with it have also surfaced in debates around women's rights, male sexualities and the HIV/AIDS epidemic. Though the configurations of 'interest and emotion' take specific forms in African societies, there is nothing peculiarly 'African' about the evident need of individuals to balance realism and idealism in their emotional lives.

Raleigh Lecture on History

Megan Vaughan is Smuts Professor of Commonwealth History at the University of Cambridge, a Fellow of King's College, and Director of the Centre of African Studies. She is also Vice-President of the African Studies Association (UK). She formerly taught at the University of Oxford and the University of Malawi. She has worked on a wide range of themes in the historical study of African societies, including food supply and famine, gender relations, the history of medicine and psychiatry and the history of slavery in the Indian Ocean. She is currently working on two projects: an interdisciplinary study of the history of death in East/Central Africa (funded by the AHRC) and a historical study of the emotions in Africa (funded by the Leverhulme Trust).

Leon Battista Alberti and the Redirection of Renaissance Humanism
MARTIN McLAUGHLIN

If Petrarch (1304–74) was the founder of Renaissance Humanism, Leon Battista Alberti (1404–72) was a successor who sought to redirect the movement. Petrarchan Humanism had been a blend of the medieval *trivium* (grammar, rhetoric, dialectic) with history and ethics, but Alberti reorientated Humanism towards a wider range of disciplines drawing on the more mathematical *quadrivium*, as well as underlining the importance of humour, and embracing the fine arts and architecture. In the light of recent scholarship, the lecture compares Petrarch's and Alberti's notions of Humanism, and traces Alberti's inflection of the movement in directions that would never have been thought of by his predecessor: though steeped in ancient texts as much as Petrarch, Alberti moves humanism towards the vernacular, towards humorous works, and towards technical and artistic treatises.

Italian Lecture

Martin McLaughlin is Fiat-Serena Professor of Italian Studies at the University of Oxford and Fellow of Magdalen College. He has researched and published primarily in two areas: the literature of the Italian Renaissance and the contemporary Italian novel, especially the work of Italo Calvino. He is the author of *Literary Imitation in* *the Italian Renaissance* (Oxford, 1995), a monograph on *Italo Calvino* (Edinburgh, 1998), and has co-edited a number of volumes, most recently *Biographies and Autobiographies in Modern Italy* (Oxford, 2007), *Image, Eye and Art in Calvino* (Oxford, 2007), and *Petrarch in Britain. Interpreters, Imitators and Translators over 700 Years* (Oxford, 2007). He has been Italian Editor and Senior Editor of *Modern Language Review*, was Chair of Legenda 2002–9, and from 2004 has been Chair of the Society for Italian Studies. He is also the translator of Italo Calvino's *Why Read the Classics?* (London, 1999) and *Hermit in Paris* (London, 2003), and Umberto Eco's *On Literature* (London, 2005). Currently he is working on a monograph on Leon Battista Alberti and translating a volume of Calvino's letters.

Shakespeare, Oaths and Vows
JOHN KERRIGAN

The language-world of early modern England was thick with oaths and vows, from casual profanity in taverns to the solemn undertakings of those marrying or accepting public office. Moralists urged the seriousness of oaths, casuists advised on how to undo them. There were religious and legal debates about what it meant to swear and how firmly one should keep a promise. The literature of the time reflects the prevalence of oaths and vows and the arguments about their status. But Shakespeare was exceptional in the density, depth and subtlety with which he explored these issues. His plays are full of oaths and vows doing structural, psychological and verbally minute, inventive work. Ranging across the output, but paying particular attention to *Troylus and Cressida* and *The Winters Tale*, this lecture aims to rectify scholarly neglect of the topic, using historical, philosophical and stage-related arguments to highlight Shakespeare's awareness of the paradoxes of oath-taking and vowing and their potency in performance.

Shakespeare Lecture

John Kerrigan is Professor of English 2000 at the University of Cambridge and Fellow of St John's College. He was brought up in Liverpool and educated at Oxford. Among his publications are a widely used edition of Shakespeare's *Sonnets and A Lover's Complaint* (Harmondsworth, 1986), a study in comparative literature, *Revenge Tragedy: Aeschylus to Armageddon* (Oxford, 1996), which won the Truman Capote Award for Literary Criticism, a selection of his essays, *On Shakespeare and Early Modern Literature* (Oxford, 2001), and *Archipelagic English: Literature, History, and Politics 1603–1707* (Oxford, 2008). He is currently completing a book on British and Irish poetry since the 1960s.

Our Unwritten Constitution
JOHN BAKER

Perhaps the most important legal question facing the country at the present time is the future of the British constitution. There has been much talk of constitutional 'renewal' in recent years, and there has been endless tinkering by the Government; but some of its proposals, and some of the changes which have occurred, have differed markedly from those which it has professed to espouse and threatened to destroy the foundations of the previous system without following any coherent overall plan. There have been repeated attempts over the last few years to increase the arbitrary power of the Government and to sideline Parliament, which is no longer providing adequate scrutiny of or restraint upon the unprecedented masses of legislation generated by ministers who equate passing statutes with solving problems. As Parliament loses all sense of purpose, the country is slipping towards absolute monarchy—the 'monarch' being the Prime Minister—with none of the checks and balances found in other presidential systems. The lecture criticises some of the recent developments, considers whether we any longer have a constitution at all, in the sense of a working system of checks and balances, emphasises the prime importance of the House of Lords and its future, and assesses some of the potential difficulties in adopting a written constitution with a power for the Supreme Court to review legislation. It ends with a recommendation for the establishment of some body independent of Government to plan constitutional reform in a coherent manner, and for the renewal of public interest in constitutional affairs.

Maccabaean Lecture in Jurisprudence

Sir John Baker, QC, FBA, is Downing Professor of the Laws of England at Cambridge and Literary Director of the Selden Society. His research interests lie principally in early modern English legal history.

Many Legal Orders, One Law
FRANCIS G. JACOBS

Until recently it has been widely believed that a single system of law operates within each sovereign territory, the State. But developments in European and International law make it increasingly hard to sustain this view. In Europe, different legal orders—State law, European Union law, the European Convention on Human Rights, International law—seem to coexist, in relation to the same issues, within the same legal space; and questions constantly arise about which law is to prevail. There seem to be no adequate theoretical answers to these questions, but practical solutions have to be found by the courts. We can learn much from considering how they reach these solutions. At the same time, we may be led to reconsider the concept of law itself.

2008 British Academy Law Lecture

The Rt Hon. Sir Francis Jacobs, KCMG, QC, is Professor of Law at King's College London, Jean Monnet Professor, and President of the Centre of European Law. He was Advocate General at the European Court of Justice from 1988 to 2006. He is a Bencher of the Middle Temple and Reader (2009). He is the author of several books on European law, including *The European Convention on Human Rights* (Oxford, fifth edition by Ovey and White published in 2010) and *The Sovereignty of Law: the European Way* (Cambridge, 2007). He is General Editor of the Oxford EU Law Library, and was founding Editor of the *Yearbook of European Law*. He is President of the UK Association for European Law; a Patron of the UK Environmental Law Association; and Chairman of the European Maritime Law Organisation. He is a member of the UNIDROIT Administrative Tribunal (1984–), and President of Missing Children Europe.

Buddhist Archaeology in Republican China: a New Relationship to the Past
SARAH E. FRASER

Chinese archaeologists transformed the notion of the nation and its artistic history with a series of dramatic discoveries during the Republican Period—China's post-imperial interregnum before the establishment of the People's Republic of China in 1949. Fuelled by interest in German archaeology, particularly the writings of Adolf Michaelis (1835–1910), whose *Die Archäologischen Entdeckungen* (Leipzig, 1906) was later translated into Chinese by Guo Moruo (1892–1978), new professional archaeologists and artists developed an archaeology of art history, or *meishu kaogu*, that was well suited for the complex installations of sculpture and painting imbedded in tomb and temple of the north-west Silk Road in wartime China (1935–47). This essay addresses the impact of archaeological copies painted by Zhang Daqian (1899–1983) and Wang Ziyun (1897–1990); they rediscovered and popularised the history of early figure painting and pottery for a Republican audience.

2008 Elsley Zeitlyn Lecture on Chinese Archaeology and Culture

Sarah E. Fraser (Ph.D. 1996, University of California, Berkeley) is an Associate Professor of Art History at Northwestern University, Chicago, IL. She teaches and researches primarily in the field of Chinese painting with an emphasis on questions of artistic enterprise in medieval Buddhist art and national identity formation through archaeological and ethnographic projects in the Republican period (1912–49). Her books include *Performing the Visual: Buddhist Wall Painting Practice in China and Central Asia, 618–960* (Stanford, CA, 2004), recognised as a *Choice* Outstanding Academic title in 2004 by the American Library Association, and an edited volume on Buddhist material culture, *Merit, Opulence and the Buddhist Network of Wealth* (Shanghai, 2003). She is currently a Frederick Burkhardt Fellow at the Institute for Advanced Study, Princeton, completing a book-length manuscript, *What is Chinese about Chinese Art? Archaeology, Identity, and Politics, 1928–1947*, on which she draws for this essay on the history of Chinese archaeology.

The British Industrial Revolution in Global Perspective
ROBERT C. ALLEN

The Industrial Revolution was Britain's response to the global economy that emerged after 1500. Britain's success in world trade resulted in one of the most urbanised economies in Europe with unusually high wages and cheap energy prices, as the coal industry was developed to supply London with fuel. British businesses found it profitable to adopt technologies that substituted cheap capital and energy for expensive labour. Famous examples included the steam engine and the cotton spinning machines. At the outset, these were profitable to use in Britain but not elsewhere, which is why the Industrial Revolution was invented in Britain. The high-wage economy further contributed to industrialisation by providing many people with the income to educate their children. Seventeenth-century scientific discoveries relating to atmospheric pressure were necessary for the invention of the steam engine, but the incentive to convert the science into technology depended on the high wages and cheap energy prices that prevailed in Britain.

Keynes Lecture in Economics

Robert Allen is Professor of Economic History at Oxford University and a Fellow of Nuffield College. He received his doctorate from Harvard University. He has written on English agricultural history, international competition in the steel industry, the extinction of whales, and contemporary policies on education. His articles have won the Cole Prize, the Redlich Prize, and the Explorations Prize. His books include *Enclosure and the Yeoman: the Agricultural Development of the South Midlands, 1450–1850* (Oxford, 2009), and *Farm to Factory: a Re-interpretation of the Soviet*

Industrial Revolution (Princeton, NJ, 2003), both of which won the Ranki Prize of the Economic History Association, and *The British Industrial Revolution in Global Perspective* (Cambridge, 2009). Currently, he is studying the global history of wages and prices and pre-industrial living standards around the world. Robert Allen is a Fellow of the British Academy and the Royal Society of Canada.

Anthropology in the Territory of Rights, Islamic, Human, and Otherwise ...
LILA ABU-LUGHOD

Does anthropology have something particular to contribute to the analysis of the growing hegemony of 'rights' as the means of addressing and redressing suffering and social injustice? Travelling between transnational initiatives for Muslim women's rights and the everyday lives of some village women in Egypt, this lecture argues that anthropologists can provide critical insight into the limits and politics of global discourses on rights. Through juxtaposing the social, political, and moral relations in one Egyptian village, as revealed in one case of 'domestic violence', to another set of relations that constitute some innovative new forms of rights activism by Muslim women who are working explicitly within an Islamic framework, as represented by two organisations called Musawah and WISE, I use ethnography, some 'thick' and some 'thin', to question the adequacy of rights frameworks to assess or judge the lives of those rights workers seek to redeem. There is always a certain incommensurability between everyday lives and the social imagination of rights. Given the current geopolitical distribution of power, moreover, it is important to examine the intersection of rights work with global and class inequalities and to be realistic about what rights work actually produces in the world. As an anthropologist, I want to use my scholarship to intervene into the worlds of power that authorise, shape, and naturalise rights work and the understandings of human social life to which it gives rise.

Radcliffe-Brown Lecture in Social Anthropology

Lila Abu-Lughod is the Joseph L. Buttenwieser Professor of Social Science in the Department of Anthropology and the Institute for Research on Women and Gender at Columbia University in New York where she also directs the Center for the Critical Analysis of Social Difference. She is the author of three award-winning ethnographies based on fieldwork in Egypt: *Veiled Sentiments: Honor and Poetry in a Bedouin Society* (Berkeley, CA, 1987); *Writing Women's Worlds: Bedouin Stories* (Berkeley, CA, 1993); and *Dramas of Nationhood: the Politics of Television in Egypt* (Chicago, 2005). She is also the editor or co-editor of *Remaking Women: Feminism and Modernity in the*

Middle East (Cairo, 1998), *Media Worlds* (Berkeley, CA, 2002), and *Nakba: Palestine, 1948 and the Claims of Memory* (New York, 2007). She is currently completing a book called *Saving Muslim Women* about the politics and ethics of the international circulation of discourses on Muslim women's rights.

Shitao (1642–1707) and the Traditional Chinese Conception of Ruins
WU HUNG

Taking paintings by the seventeenth-century Chinese master Shitao as main examples, this lecture investigates the conception of ruins in traditional Chinese pictorial art. It starts by tracking down indigenous definitions of ruins as well as a broad variety of images related to the idea of ruination. An exploration of the historical, cultural, artistic, and technological conditions of these definitions and images in turn raises a range of issues, including the relationship between the concept of ruins and timber architecture, the idea of the 'trace' and its visual manifestations, the metaphorical use of images in representing time, and indigenous methods for recording damage and decay. The subtly divergent meanings of two archaic characters for ruins, *qiu* and *xu*, provide this study with a semantic basis, revealing different ways of imagining and constructing 'memory sites' in literature and art. Images of 'withered trees' then offer visual testimonies to understand how various temporalities—past, present, and rebirth—are realised in pictorial forms. The final section studies several of Shitao's Yellow Mountain paintings, and links his depictions of architectural ruins with the idea of *qi*—strange or extraordinary phenomena.

Aspects of Art Lecture

Wu Hung is Harrie A. Vanderstappen Distinguished Service Professor in Chinese Art History and Director of the Center for the Art of East Asia at the University of Chicago. An elected member of the American Academy of Arts and Sciences, he has published widely on both traditional and contemporary Chinese art. His major works on traditional art include *The Wu Liang Shrine: the Ideology of Early Chinese Pictorial Art* (Stanford, CA, 1989), *Monumentality in Early Chinese Art and Architecture* (Stanford, CA, 1995), *The Double Screen: Medium and Representation in Chinese Painting* (London, 1996), and *The Art of the Yellow Springs: Understanding Chinese Tombs* (Hawaii, 2010).

Timely Images: Chinese Art and Festival Display
JAN STUART

Displayed in museums, and often for long periods, Chinese scrolls, painted porcelains, and other works of art either seem unrelated to the passage of time or to defy its natural course. For the artists and original viewers, however, time was an essential element of how these objects were experienced and often provided the motivation for their creation. *When* a scroll painting or decorative object was placed on view was a part of its meaning and informed the interpretation of the imagery on its surface. Attending to the seasonal functions of these objects, used by many levels of society from the court to commoners, helps us understand how the visual arts were folded into the abiding rhythms of nature and human culture in China. In particular, the festival calendar of China that by the end of the Qing dynasty listed approximately 150 events that required some form of intervention or acknowledgement by the emperor provides a platform for understanding how closely the production and display of art in China was linked to the annual cycle. The celebration of major festivals, such as the New Year and Double Fifth (also known as Dragon Boat Festival), and lesser festivals—those that did not allow for time off from work or large-scale family reunions—but were widely enjoyed, such as Flower Festival in the second lunar month, were occasions that engendered significant production of artworks meant for timely display.

The close connection between the festival calendar and art is well documented in Chinese records, including in archives from the Qing dynasty court that show commissions for paintings and porcelains for the major holidays, and by the late Ming Calendar for Scrolls by Wen Zhenheng that explicitly lists what types of paintings should be displayed at each festival. This study draws attention to the significant, yet often overlooked bond between Chinese visual culture and its temporal conventions in order to expand the interpretive framework for understanding Chinese pictorial art.

Elsley Zeitlyn Lecture on Chinese Archaeology and Culture.

Jan Stuart is Keeper of the Department of Asia at the British Museum. Prior to that she was a curator of Chinese art at the Freer Gallery of Art and Arthur M. Sackler Gallery, Smithsonian Institution, Washington, DC. She was project leader for the creation of a new permanent gallery at the British Museum to display the Sir Percival David Collection of Chinese art that opened in 2009. Academic interests focus on material culture and functional arts in China, with special interest in studying the original contexts for display; an example is work on ancestor portraits published in

Jan Stuart and Evelyn Rawski, *Worshipping the Ancestors: Chinese Commemorative Portraits* (Stanford, CA, 2001).

Gaelic in Medieval Scotland: Advent and Expansion
THOMAS OWEN CLANCY

When first there are detailed records for the linguistic and ethnic make-up of northern Britain, in the seventh century, the Gaelic language was confined to the region of Argyll; by the twelfth century, most parts of what is now Scotland (and indeed parts of northern England) either had, or at some point had had, communities of Gaelic speakers. This expansion of the language happened during one of the least well-evidenced times in Scotland's history, and the timing and mechanisms of this expansion has been much theorised and debated. The primary evidence capable of helping understand these processes is that of place-names, and as such toponyms form the bedrock of this lecture's investigation. The paper reviews the different ways in which toponymic data can usefully be interpreted to inform our notion of the process of expansion, and corrects some more optimistic assessments. It reviews the evidence for Gaelic's arrival and expansion in the various different regions of Scotland in the middle ages, examining in particular a number of different nodes of controversy, where paradigms have been shifting over recent years. What emerges is a much more complex, nuanced series of interlocking episodes in Scotland's linguistic history. The lecture proposes that, contrary to received views, the twelfth and thirteenth centuries remained ones of expansion for the Gaelic language.

Sir John Rhŷs Memorial Lecture

Professor Thomas Owen Clancy holds the Chair of Celtic at the University of Glasgow, where he has taught since 1995, having previously been a British Academy Postdoctoral Research Fellow at the University of Edinburgh from 1993 to 1995. He is currently Research Convenor of the School of Humanities in the University of Glasgow, and chair of the Board of Celtic Studies (Scotland).

Surrealism and its Legacies in Latin America
DAWN ADÈS

Surrealism has a long but fragmented history in connection with Latin America. This history is outlined here firstly through an overview of journals, some self-defined as surrealist, some affiliated to the movement, and others which included surrealism in a broader coverage of modern movements, and secondly through surrealist exhibitions. Issues emerging that are of particular interest in assessing the nature of the cultural, political and artistic encounters include the tensions between surrealist internationalism and local cultural nationalisms, the contested relationship between surrealism and Magic Realism, the problems of modernity vs. indigenism and the enduring surrealist fascination with Pre-Columbian art and architecture. The work of two Mexican artists, Frida Kahlo and Gunther Gerzso, with very different links to the movement, was selected to highlight some of these issues and also to demonstrate that there is no such thing as a 'surrealist style'. The lecture ended with a glimpse at the work of the contemporary Brazilian artist Cildo Meireles, with the purpose of stimulating debate about the continuing legacies of surrealism. It is my contention that art from Latin America has flourished in recent years and that, without claiming surrealism as an exclusive source, many of the practices, aesthetic strategies and political attitudes that have brought it to prominence need to be examined in relation to the ideas of this movement.

British Academy Lecture

Dawn Adès is Professor of Art History and Theory at the University of Essex (now semi-retired) and is a specialist in Surrealism and in Latin American Art. She has been responsible for many important exhibitions in London and overseas over the past thirty years, including *Art in Latin America* (London 1989), *Dali's Optical Illusions* (Hartford, CT, and Edinburgh, 2000), and *Undercover Surrealism* (London 2006), and she co-curated *Dada and Surrealism Reviewed* (London 1978), *Fetishism: Visualising Power and Desire* (Brighton 1995), *Art and Power: Europe under the Dictators* (London 1994), and *Close-Up* (Edinburgh 2008). She organised the highly successful exhibition to celebrate the centenary of Salvador Dalí shown at the Palazzo Grassi in Venice and in Philadelphia in 2004. Among her publications are standard works on photomontage, Dada, Surrealism, women artists and Mexican muralists: they include *Photomontage* (London, 1976 and 1986), *Salvador Dali* (London, 1982 and 1990), *Art in Latin America: the Modern Era 1820–1980* (New Haven, CT, 1989), *Dali's Optical Illusions* (New Haven, CT, 2000) and *Undercover Surrealism: Georgés Bataille and Documents* (Cambridge, MA, 2006). She is Co-Director of the University of Essex Collection of Latin American Art and Co-Director of the Centre for Studies of Surrealism and its Legacies, a partnership between the University of Essex, the University of Manchester and Tate. She is a Fellow of the British Academy and was awarded an OBE in 2002 for her services to art history

'The Reason of this Preference': Sleeping, Flowing and Freezing in Pope's *Dunciad*

VALERIE RUMBOLD

When Samuel Johnson was collecting material for his life of Pope, one of his informants claimed to be able to identify for him 'the couplet by which he [i.e. Pope] declared his own ear to be most gratified'. The couplet, from the *Dunciad*, depicts the Sea of Azov and the river that flows into it. Johnson quoted it, but concluded: 'the reason of this preference I cannot discover'. By focusing on the process through which Pope shaped this couplet we can not only sharpen our appreciation of this one small unit, but also develop insights into the wider significance of its structure and themes for Pope's work more generally.

2010 Warton Lecture on English Poetry

Valerie Rumbold is Reader in English Literature at the University of Birmingham. She is author of *Women's Place in Pope's World* (Cambridge, 1989), awarded a Rose Mary Crawshay Prize by the British Academy. She has edited *Alexander Pope: the Dunciad in Four Books* (Harlow, 1999; revised 1st edition, 2008), and volume 3, containing the *Dunciad*s of 1728 and 1729, of *The Poems of Alexander Pope* (Harlow, 2007). She is currently editing volume 2 of the Cambridge edition of the Works of Jonathan Swift, which will contain, among other works, the Bickerstaff papers, *Polite Conversation* and *Directions to Servants*.

Donne, By Hand

TOM LOCKWOOD

'Why not do Donne—an edition and Life—for the Clarendon Press?' With this letter of 1906 from W. A. Raleigh, newly installed in the new chair in English Literature at Oxford, to H. J. C. Grierson, the first Professor of English at Aberdeen, began a new phase in the afterlife of John Donne's poetry. The edition that Grierson produced, *The Poems of John Donne* (Oxford, 1912), decisively reshaped Donne as a manuscript poet for the twentieth century, and as a poet of, and for, the new university discipline of English. This lecture explores those two claims through a detailed examination of the making and the influence of Grierson's edition, which, it argues, was itself vitally part of an ongoing manuscript culture just as it was shaped by Grierson's collaboration with his publishers at the Clarendon Press in Oxford. Many early readers—like Ben Jonson—feared that 'Donne himself, for not being understood, would perish'; this lecture argues instead that subsequent understandings of Donne and his works, in manuscript and print, and by different audiences, are necessary elements of the poet we read today.

Chatterton Lecture on Poetry

Tom Lockwood is a Senior Lecturer in English Literature at the University of Birmingham; he held a British Academy Postdoctoral Fellowship at the University of Leeds from 2002 to 2005. He is the author of *Ben Jonson in the Romantic Age* (Oxford, 2005) and was the winner, in 2003, of *The Review of English Studies* Essay Prize. His articles, many of which share an interest in the relationships between manuscript, print, and their changing textual cultures, have appeared in *The Review of English Studies*, *English Literary Renaissance*, *English Manuscript Studies* and elsewhere.

T. S. Eliot's Daughter
ROBERT CRAWFORD

After discussing issues to do with biography and Eliot's posthumous reputation, the lecture centres on his poem 'Marina'. Paying particular attention to the poem's word-music and to the circumstances of its composition, the lecture argues that 'Marina' is one of the greatest parent–child poems in the English language. A deeply moving work, it was written at a significant point in Eliot's career when he was coming to terms with the loss of his parents, with his own childlessness, and with what it might mean to be a godparent.

Warton Lecture on English Poetry

Robert Crawford is Professor of Modern Scottish Literature at the University of St Andrews. His sixth collection of poems, *Full Volume* (London, 2008), was shortlisted for the T. S. Eliot Prize. His *Scotland's Books* (London, 2007; Oxford, 2009) won the Saltire Scottish Research Book of the Year Award, and his biography of Robert Burns, *The Bard* (London and Princeton, NJ, 2009,) won the Saltire Scottish Book of the Year Award.

Arthur Miller: Realism, Language, Poetry
CHRISTOPHER BIGSBY

Arthur Miller may be one of the most distinguished playwrights America has produced but he has also been one of the most traduced. Even his early canonical work was often treated with condescension or political disdain. Dismissed by a number of influential American critics as prosaic, a simple realist, for the last thirty years of his life his new work found few enthusiasts even as it was eagerly received abroad, most particularly in Britain. This lecture is an attempt to explore his supposed realism, his language, his thirst for the poetic.

Sarah Tryphena Phillips Lecture in American Literature

Christopher Bigsby is Professor of American Studies at the University of East Anglia and Director of the Arthur Miller Centre for American Studies there. He has published more than forty books and has won prizes for fiction, criticism, and biography. His most recent book is a biography of Arthur Miller, the second part of which is due in 2011. He is a Fellow of the Royal Society of Arts and the Royal Society of Literature. He has written for radio and television and is a regular broadcaster.